THE BEGINNINGS OF EUROPEAN THEORIZING: REFLEXIVITY IN THE ARCHAIC AGE

One is enthralled by the way in which a complex and powerful intellectual argument is unfolded with magisterial dignity. This must be one of the outstanding productions of British sociology in recent years.
David Chaney, *Professor of Sociology, University of Durham*

With equally brilliant scholarship Sandywell reconstructs the origins of 'European' reflection in Homer, Hesiod, Pindar and the Orphic texts with particular reference to the 'genesis of the self'.
John O'Neill, *Distinguished Research Professor of Sociology, York University, Canada*

How did the cultural practices of early Greek society construct the self? How does the self appear in the earliest forms of Greek poetry and literature? What are the relationships between the art of the Archaic age and the emergence of autonomous political and theoretical institutions? How did these practices of self-reflection shape the emergence of later forms of theorizing, science and philosophy?

In *Reflexivity and the Crisis of Western Reason*, Barry Sandywell outlined and defended a central place for reflexivity in the human sciences. In this second equally outstanding and challenging volume of Logological Investigations, he reconstructs the origins of European reflection.

The author's central claim is that the world does not exist independently of human practices, but that it is constituted through the terms of our discursive categories. Rather than research being a triumphant exploration, it is more fully understood as agonized self-reflection on the grounds of knowledge production. Sandywell argues that this approach has been inherent throughout Western philosophy and in so doing, he shows that the reflexive character of human experience in Western culture can be traced through the desire for intelligibility that animated Greek drama, poetry, philosophy, and science as explorations of the cosmos, body-politic, and the soul.

Barry Sandywell is Lecturer in Sociology at the University of York.

THE BEGINNINGS OF EUROPEAN THEORIZING: REFLEXIVITY IN THE ARCHAIC AGE

Logological Investigations
Volume 2

Barry Sandywell

LONDON AND NEW YORK

First published 1996
by Routledge
2 Park Square, Milton Park, Abingdon, Oxfordshire OX14 4RN

Simultaneously published in the USA and Canada
by Routledge
711 Third Avenue, New York, NY 10017

First issued in paperback 2014

Routledge is an imprint of the Taylor and Francis Group, an informa business

© 1996 Barry Sandywell

All rights reserved. No part of this book may be reprinted or reproduced or utilized in any form or by any electronic, mechanical, or other means, now known or hereafter invented, including photocopying and recording, or in any information storage or retrieval system, without permission in writing from the publishers.

British Library Cataloguing in Publication Data
A catalogue record for this book is available from the British Library.

Library of Congress Cataloguing in Publication Data
A catalogue record for this book has been requested

ISBN 13: 978-1-138-87995-9 (pbk)
ISBN 13: 978-0-415-10169-1 (hbk)

Typeset in Garamond by Michael Mepham, Frome, Somerset

And a man who is puzzled and wonders thinks himself ignorant (whence even the lover of myth is in a sense a lover of wisdom, for the myth is composed of wonders).

(Aristotle *Metaphysics* 982b11–22)

Wonder is a seed out of which knowledge grows.

(Francis Bacon, 1985)

For Miriam

CONTENTS

Acknowledgements	ix
Abbreviations	x
Introduction: towards a sociological poetics	xiii

1 MYTHOPOIESIS: THE PRAXIS OF MYTH — 1
 1 Introduction — 1
 2 Mythopoiesis in oral culture: obscure moons in the firmament of reason — 2
 3 Myth as the matrix of early Greek thought and philosophy — 27
 4 The public and political nature of Greek religion — 30
 5 The dialectic of myth and philosophy: early Greek institutions of reflection — 34
 6 Myth - the logos of the life-world — 35
 7 Narrative strategies in Greek myth — 38
 8 Conclusion - Myth as the matrix of logos — 43

2 HOMERIC EPIC REFLEXIVITY: SELF AND SELF-REFLEXIVITY IN THE *ILIAD* AND *ODYSSEY* — 47
 1 Introduction — 47
 2 The logological significance of the Homeric texts — 48
 3 Epic narrative form(s) — 58
 4 The world of the poem: the Homeric life-world as a videological universe — 77
 5 Self and self-reflexivity in the Homeric world — 94
 6 The civilizing powers of Homeric discourse — 136
 7 Conclusion: Thersites' revenge — 157

3 HESIOD AND THE BIRTH OF THE GODS — 160
 1 Introduction: mythos-logos — 160
 2 Theogonic myth as discourse and prototheorizing — 163
 3 The discovery of the 'I': self-reflexivity in Hesiod's writing — 169
 4 The poetic 'I' and divine authorization — 174

	5 Hesiodic symbolism and the 'mythological world-view'	180
	6 The violence of differentiation and the appearance of the gods	182
	7 Hesiodic ideology: the valorization of justice and work	202
	8 Hesiodic utopianism	204
4	LYRIC REFLEXIVITIES	206
	1 The genealogy of individual lyric voices	206
	2 Choral lyric: from collective to individual forms of self-reflection	217
	3 From choral lyric to monody: the social construction of the individual lyric voice	222
	4 Conclusion: the 'concept' of lyric reflexivity	247
5	PINDAR AND THE AGE OF LITERARY CONSCIOUSNESS	250
	1 The life-world as a theatre of reflexive praxis	250
	2 The heroic ethic in reflexive mimesis	257
	3 Gods and men	263
	4 Death and the Elysian fields	265
	5 Death and the poetic logos	268
	6 Conclusion: Pindar's world	274
6	ORPHISM: ORPHIC DISCOURSE DURING THE ARCHAIC PERIOD	278
	1 Introduction: the appearance of Orphism in Greek culture	278
	2 Orphic cosmogony as an allegory of cosmic alienation	287
	3 The Orphic body or the doctrine of cathartic reflexivity	289
	4 The tropes of Dionysus	298
	5 The Orphic background of the logos	299
	Notes	302
	Bibliography	386
	Name index	411
	Subject index	415

ACKNOWLEDGEMENTS

I am grateful for permission to publish extracts from the following books: *Sappho and the Greek Lyric Poets* by Willis Barnstone, copyright © 1962, 1967, 1988 by Willis Barnstone, reprinted by permission of Schocken Books, published by Pantheon Books, a division of Random House, Inc.; *Greek Lyrics*, translated by Richmond Lattimore, second edition, 1960, copyright © 1949, 1955, and 1960 by Richmond Lattimore, reprinted by permission of the University of Chicago Press.

NOTE ON END NOTES

Notes to the main text have a variety of functions, among these: to provide further and more specialized bibliographical information; to suggest more advanced sources and investigations of related points; to comment upon and occasionally question the text; and to open up other lines of thought for anyone wishing to engage in further research on these topics.

ABBREVIATIONS

Acad.   Cicero, *Academica* trans. H. Rackham (London: William Heinemann/Loeb Clasical Library, 1933).
ANET   J.B. Pritchard, ed., *Ancient Near Eastern Texts Relating to the Old Testament*, 3rd edn (Princeton, Princeton University Press, 1969).
AP   K. Freeman, *Ancilla to the Presocratic Philosophers*, a complete translation of the Fragments in Diels, *Die Fragmente der Vorsokratiker* (Oxford: Basil Blackwell, 1948).
AVN   M.M. Austin and P. Vidal-Naquet, *Economic and Social History of Ancient Greece: An Introduction* (London: Batsford Academic and Educational Ltd., 1977).
CHCL   *Cambridge History of Classical Literature* (Cambridge University Press, 1989).
DH   Dionysius of Halicarnassus, *The Critical Essays*, trans. Stephen Usher, 2 vols, (London: Heinemann/Loeb Classical Library, 1974).
DK   Herman Diels and Walter Kranz, *Die Fragmente der Vorsokratiker*, 3 vols, 10th edn (Berlin: Weidmann, 1960).
DL   Diogenes Laertius, *Lives of Eminent Philosophers*, ed., and trans. R.D. Hicks (London William Heinmann/Loeb Classical Library, 1925).
Dox. Gr. *Doxographi Graeci*, ed. Herman Diels, (Berlin, 1879).
Il.   Homer, *Iliad* (many editions).
KR   G.S. Kirk and J. E. Raven, eds, *The Presocratic Philosophers* (Cambridge: Cambridge University Press, 1971).
KRS   G.S. Kirk, J.E. Raven, and M. Schofield, *The Presocratic Philosophers: A Critical History with a Selection of Texts* (Cambridge: Cambridge University Press, 1983).
LS   H.G. Liddell and R. Scott, *An Intermediate Greek-English Lexicon* (1889) (Oxford: Clarendon Press, 1964).
LSJ   H.G. Liddell, R. Scott, and H.S. Jones, *A Greek-English Lexicon* (Oxford: Oxford University Press, 1925–40).

ABBREVIATIONS

Met.	Aristotle, *Metaphysics*, in R. McKeon, ed., *The Basic Works of Aristotle* (New York: Random House, 1941).
MM	Pseudo-Aristotle, *Magna Moralia*, trans. H. Tredennick, vol. 2 (London: William Heinemann/Loeb Classical Library, 1935).
NE	Aristotle, *Nicomachean Ethics*, in R. McKeon, *The Basic Works of Aristotle* (New York: Random House, 1941).
Od	Homer, *The Odyssey* (many editions).
OH	J. Boardman, J. Griffin, and O. Murray, eds, *The Oxford History of Greece and the Hellenistic World* (Oxford: Oxford University Press, 1991).
OSAP	*Oxford Studies in Ancient Philosophy*, edited Julia Annas, 1983 –
Paus.	Pausanias, *Guide to Greece (Description of Greece)*, trans. P. Levi, 2 vols (Harmondsworth: Penguin, 1971).
Rep.	Plato, *Republic* (many editions).
Tod	M.N. Tod, ed., *A Selection of Greek Historical Inscriptions to the end of the Fifth Century B.C.*, (Oxford: Clarendon Press, 1948).
WA	P.V. Jones, *The World of Athens: An introduction to Classical Athenian Culture* (Cambridge: Cambridge University Press, 1984).

INTRODUCTION
Towards a sociological poetics

> It is in periods of social and political crisis that men are more aware of the enigma of their presence in the world.
> (Lucien Goldmann, 1964: 49)

The following investigations can be approached as an introduction to the sociological poetics of archaic discourse in that they focus upon some of the earliest attempts to represent symbolically the configurations of human experience in Western culture. But they are also attempts to think sociologically about questions of origins, self-representation, and identity. In this respect they are particularly concerned with some of the earliest forms of self and self-reflection constructed at the dawn of Western rationalism. But 'reason' and 'rationalism' are extremely complex concepts which must be subject to careful deconstruction. The idea of an autonomous 'community' oriented by self-determining goals and governed by reason was constructed over many centuries and is itself grounded in the 'pretheoretical' cultural formations of ancient Greece. Understanding the nature and dimensions of this ambivalent genesis forms one of the major objectives of the following chapters. The theme of the contested nature of 'rational reflection' and the 'question of the subject' links these studies to social theory in a direct and fundamental way, for many of the debates and controversies in modern theory now revolve around questions of the limits of rational self-reflection, the role of horizons of subjectivity and alterity within rational institutions, and the legitimation of 'political' order and power in contemporary society. A curious symmetry links the origins and terminal phases of European intellectual culture, a symmetry which directly involves the fate of the self as a key figure in Western consciousness. The theme of *mimesis* explored schematically in Volume 1, for example, returns as one of the main threads of the chapters which follow. How did the cultural logics of early Greek culture construct the self? How does something like autonomous selfhood first appear in the earliest forms of Greek poetry and literature? What were the consequences of the particular modes of *poiesis* that inaugurated Western literature,? What are the links between Greek mimetic art and the emerging idea of autonomous political and theoretical institutions? These are some of the questions which are addressed in the following chapters.

On the issue of method I would also like to emphasize that although the chapters adopt a broadly historical narrative (and periodization), they are also displays of a particular way of theorizing cultural phenomena, raising issues and problems that are wider than the conventional history of ideas or a purely philosophical exploration of early Greek culture. Pre-eminent among these themes is the active role of language in processes of subjectivity and world construction. Since these ideas presuppose the framework and analytical orientations elaborated in Volume 1 I would like to take the opportunity to review some of the central themes of logological inquiry. The general claim of the earlier book can be condensed in the thesis that what we call 'reality' is not independent of our methods and discursive strategies, but is rather constituted through rhetorical and, more broadly, semiopraxical media. Where common sense posits a reflective relation to 'the real', logological research approaches reality in constitutive and dialogical terms. These studies can thus be read as contributions to contemporary social theory as well as explorations in the emergence of poetic and literary reflexivity in ancient Greece. Recourse to the 'archaeology' of ancient discursive practices is an indispensable pretext for rethinking the impact of cultural forms on the subsequent course of European identity. The essays which follow, then, belong to the growing interdisciplinary field of reflexive cultural studies.

In Volume 2 I intend to explore aspects of the genesis of self-reflection and reflexive practices in some of the earliest discourses of Western thought – pursuing what might be called a genealogy of the European eye and voice. In this sense these studies are contributions to the historical understanding of the genesis of the critical spirit. To speak of the world-view of 'European thought' and 'the idea of European civilization' is unavoidable even though these abstract and generic locutions precipitate innumerable questions and problems which cannot be resolved without a great deal of preparatory work. Before it is a geographical, historical, or sociological concept 'Europe' is an imaginary ideal, an invented tradition with a diverse history in European culture. For our purposes it is important to note that the Western idea of the self and world was first elaborated and symbolically defined in particular forms of literary *poiesis*. The chapters of Volume 2 will explore the social processes by which this 'literary mimesis' was first constructed by early Greek poetics. In examining the self-construction of 'the European' I will try to move into a position where the distinctive rhetorical character of Western theorizing can be delineated in a more radical form. One of the main themes will be the thought that the Greeks construed the activity of *poiesis* as both an autonomous form of life and as a foundation for the civilizing process – or to translate this into more contemporary terminology, the discourses of ancient Greece invented the idea of 'culture' as a self-forming project of human liberty. As in the earlier studies I will be guided by the idea that beneath the dynamism and violent impulses of this ancient civilization lies a matrix of axiological principles sustaining distinctive modes of experience, thought, and ethical praxis. In studying the beginnings of reflexive thought the intention is not to excavate 'the foundations of European civilization' or 'the cradle of the Western mind' in an abstract and decontextualised sense, but to explore the historically specific narrative techniques, social practices, and institutions of reflection forged in Greece between the eighth and fifth century BC. Indeed we might construct a Weberian description of the chapters of Volume 2 along the lines of *The Homeric Ethic and the Spirit of the Greek Polis*. And like Weber, we are interested in the long-term effects and unintended consequences of poetic, mythological, and religious practices upon the forms of identity, political systems, and social development of Greek society.

But there is a darker side to the civilizing process; by identifying with Greek ways of thinking European culture has tended to obscure its own heterogeneous beginnings, effacing its complex origins in forms of life and prereflective reflexivity which, as we shall see in the following chapters, were already being repressed in the earliest articulations of 'the European idea' (the Platonic war on poetry – and the mimetic form of art more generally – is one powerful manifestation of this ancient struggle between theoretical reflection and poetic reflexivity). In sociohistorical terms these processes of occlusion can be traced to the social contradictions of the Archaic age itself. The return of the repressed, however, also has a contemporary significance: the analysis of the vicissitudes of ancient culture presents an opportunity to explore how particular discursive systems shaped the terrain of Western thought in subsequent periods and how the effects of these depth logics can still be felt in modern and postmodern formations.

The vicissitudes of liberty in Western thought and society provide a good example of this ancient legacy. Fernand Braudel, for example, has suggested a 'thought experiment' designed to isolate the singular spirit of European civilization. It runs as follows:

> Imagine that it might be possible to assemble the sum total of our knowledge of European history from the fifth century to the present, or perhaps to the eighteenth century, and to record it . . . in an electronic memory. Imagine that the computer was then asked to indicate the one problem which recurred most frequently, in time and space, throughout this lengthy history. Without a doubt, that problem is liberty, or rather liberties. The word liberty is the operative word.
>
> (1994: 315)

Following Braudel's *Denkenexperiment* we will begin by pursuing the hypothesis that the cultural 'deep structure' and imaginary formation of 'the European Idea' is to be found in the discursive formations and dialectics of liberty. In the actual history of Greek society the ethic of liberty was embodied in the civic life of the *polis* and in the proliferation of discourses which the city-state fostered and institutionalized. It is thus true to claim that the background to a sociological poetics of early Greek reflexivity is framed by the development of the city-state and its ideology of civic autonomy and freedom.

But how can we reconstruct 'premodern' or 'archaic' European identity? It is not an insignificant fact that the word 'Europe' appeared during the same period that saw the emergence of the attribution 'Hellene' as a unifying political symbol in a protracted struggle against a regime perceived as destructive of 'civic liberties'. At the level of political organization, 'Hellene' came to symbolize the freedom of the urban *polis* or self-governing state by contrast with the 'despotism' and 'unfreedom' of the Eastern Empires. Historically, 'Hellenic identity' was forged in a period of instability and crisis. The interconnected problematics of political freedom, intellectual reflection, and security are all folded in the language of the *polis* which emerged to neutralize the 'threat' emanating from 'the East'. Historically, the westward expansion of the Persian empire was the proximate context for the emergence of the ethical ideal of liberty in the Greek city-states. In overcoming the waves of military expansion at the end of the sixth century, Greek society shaped itself in the language of civic autonomy and freedom. In fact it has been claimed that 'by 500 BC a distinctive European style of civilization had emerged in Greece' (McNeill, 1979: 4). Ignoring for the moment the question of the precise origins of 'European civilization', it is true to say that the emergence of the embattled *polis* is the historical context for Aristotle's famous definition of human beings as by nature political animals (*Politics* 1.1253a). To see the emergence of a strong version of Hellenic identity we might compare the uncertain self-construals of 'Achaean' identity in the *Iliad* and *Odyssey* with the acute sense of Hellenic civilization expressed in the art, literature, and politics of the Classical age following the Persian wars between 490 and 479 BC (see, for example, Aeschylus' *Persae* (472 BC); Herodotus's *Histories* I, *passim*; Sophocles' *Philoctetes* 219ff. ; Gorgias' *Olympic Oration*; Thucydides' Melian Dialogue and Funeral Speech; Xenophon's *Hellenica*; Isocrates' *Panegyricus* 17ff., 68–9, 82–3, 176, 187; *Plataicus* XIV. 58–9; *Letter to Philip*; and Lysias II.21, 47, 59–60, *To Philip* V 9ff., 86ff., 132ff.). But we should also point out that the city-state and its imaginary mythology also developed over a long historical period. The language-games of the political and the intense concern for questions of status and identity evolved over several centuries during the so-called Greek Dark Ages. In fact the beginnings of this collective self-construction dates back before the Archaic age. As early as the eighth century we find such important pan-Hellenic discursive formations and institutions as the sites of recognized oracles, the Games at Olympia (*c.* 776 BC), the festival of Apollo at Delos, and variants of an identifiably Greek alphabet (Finley, 1981: 84; Webster, 1959: 1–15; Burnet, 1921: 65; Murray, 1993: 26–7, also 62–8). It is well known that the expression *panhellenes*, 'the whole race of the Hellenes', can be found in Hesiod's *Works and Days* (528) in the seventh century, even though it only acquires its full resonance and existential intensity for the generation that fought at Marathon and Salamis ('You have guessed right, we are Greeks [Hellenes]', Sophocles, *Philoctetes* 232-3; 'Of all the Hellenic powers we [Athenians] ruled over the Hellenes... [and] stood firm in the greatest wars against their combined forces and against individual states' Thucydides 2.64.3; cf. Paus. 1.32.4). By the time we reach the histories of Herodotus the cultural identity of the Hellenes had become a symbol of intellectual and political liberty and was being disseminated as an established fact by the literate intelligentsia of Greece. The very idea of a collectivity *choosing* the project of freedom had even attained the status of a civil morality. What had begun as an ethic of survival in pre-Homeric times and through the Dark Ages, emerged in the eighth century as the very *ethos* of Hellenic self-reflection. It is understandable that Herodotus, writing at the end of this development, should ground 'the European idea' in a communality of ethnic origins, religious culture, and customs promoting the ideology of freedom and civic autonomy. But above all, Herodotus traces the roots of Hellenic identity to the soil of a common language and shared traditions of free speech.

Of course it is a truism that 'Europe', like the terms 'Hellenes' and 'Hellas', is a cultural category shaped over many centuries as part of a long and often disparate campaign against the 'alien' and the 'other' (the individualizing phrase 'Asia and Europe' was already formulaic in Herodotus' account of the struggle between Europe and Asia (4.36, 4.42) and was frequently troped into the expression 'barbarians and Greeks' by later writers (Herodotus, 1.1, 2.35, and Books 7-9; Thucydides 1.2-19, 1.23.1-3; Xenophon's *Hellenica*; Isocrates' *Panegyricus* and *Panathenaicus*; Aristotle's *Politics*, etc.). In the first half of the fifth century the archetypal 'other' in this dialectic was symbolized by the 'Asian' threat of the Persian Empire under Darius and Xerxes (invoking the 'spirit of Marathon' as the essence of 'Hellenic civilization' became a stock ploy of later orators, for example Lycurgus, *Against Leocrates* 79-83 and 104-5 – 'those who confronted the barbarians at Marathon, by defeating an army from the whole of Asia, won... security for every Greek alike... whereby they made themselves the champions of the Greeks and lords of the barbarians'; cf. Demosthenes' *On the Crown* 206-10; Plutarch, *Aristid.* 21; Thucydides 2.43.2). By the middle of the fourth century the expansionary Macedonian empire had replaced Persian hegemony as the most immediate threat to the values and institutions of Greek civic freedom and justice (a vision of autonomous citizenship expressed most emphatically in Demosthenes' *Philippics* and *Olynthiacs* and Hyperides' *Funeral Speech* 20-1). Early Greek culture, in other words, had self-consciously integrated the normative ideals of citizenship, political autonomy, and free critical thought as a realizable form of *urban* life. It was this imaginary fusion of truth and justice with the physical and social structure of the city-state that provided the utopian matrix and initial motivation of philosophical speculation. This is the source of the constellation which unites the pursuit of reflexivity, the dynamism of urban culture, and political

INTRODUCTION

existence for later Western thought. The European spirit of reflexivity, in other words, has – if we can extend the meaning of this term – both utopian and sociological origins.

The present work aims to throw some light on these early ideological and cultural formations. Since the history and sociology of Greek civilization is a vast field in its own right, the chapters of Volume 2 concentrate upon one small part of the complex story of the 'genesis of the Western self', tracing the emergence of a culture of self-reflection in some of the earliest literary formations of Hellenic myth and poetry. But as the earliest forms of Greek culture were interwoven into the dominant institutions of political authority and civic association, we must relate the genealogy of classical thought and 'general intellect' to wider patterns of religious, social, and political life in Greek society. Volume 3 takes the story further by examining the social constitution of the practices of philosophical reflection from the Archaic period down to the Greek enlightenment in the fifth century, while Volume 4 investigates the specific ideological formation of the intellectual culture of the Greek enlightenment. Even from this highly selective perspective we will see that 'the origin of Western thought' does not follow a cumulative curve or progressive evolution 'from Mythos to Logos'; on the contrary the actual historical development is one of discontinuities, polemical struggles, and dialectical reversals. In terms of the intellectual horizon outlined in Volume 1 these essays are presented as preliminary sketches toward a history of the early self-formations of European consciousness. I thus wish neither to deprecate nor defend 'Greek thought' in its foundational roles, but rather to understand and explain its powerful impact and continued ideological significance in the contemporary world. By exploring the 'darker side' of European self-conceptions I hope to make a small contribution to a reasoned critique of the will to universality which appears to have determined Western modes of thinking from the sixth century to the present day.

1

MYTHOPOIESIS
The praxis of myth

[T]he knowing union with the totality, already sought in the Greek mythologies.

(Wilhelm Szilasi[1])

The quest for the totality is the modern secularized descendant of antiquity's quest for Logos, the sacred whole which was the fusion of reason and the god, of goodness and power, embodied in the word.

(Alvin W. Gouldner[2])

1   Introduction
2   Mythopoiesis in oral culture: obscure moons in the firmament of reason
3   Myth as the matrix of early Greek thought and philosophy
4   The public and political nature of Greek religion
5   The dialectic of myth and philosophy: early Greek institutions of reflection
6   Myth – the logos of the life-world
7   Narrative Strategies in Greek myth
8   Conclusion – myth as the matrix of logos

1 INTRODUCTION

A whole mythology is deposited in our language.

(Ludwig Wittgenstein)

Coming to the end of the second European millennium and living in what some have described as a disenchanted postmodern age it is appropriate that we should reflect on the thesis that Western conceptual thought and philosophy originated in the symbolisms of myth. At the limit of forms of life and knowledge systems informed by the project of pure reflection and universal reason we should take the opportunity to reflect on the mythological sources of Western science and power. If science has acquired a mythical aura and is accepted as an indispensable instrument in exploring and analysing the natural world is this not, as Aristotle observed, because myth is already a kind of knowledge? Of course, the expression 'natural world' has a very different significance for Aristotle and the language of modern science; and these differ again from the order of *phusis* posited by pre-Classical mythology. We need to reflect upon the paradox that the secular aspiration to create a system of rational knowledge has its origins in the *sacred ethos* of Greek myth which imagined a world in which our distinctions between the 'natural' and the 'supranatural' have no relevance. And perhaps what is enfolded in this 'affinity' between *philomuthos* and *philosophos* are experiences, values, and institutions that are older and other than the language of both myth and philosophy – older even than the Homeric world as 'the matrix of everything Hellenic'.

When we research the beginnings of European reflection we find ourselves in the unsettling presence of pre-Homeric cult practices and mythologies. How can *reflexivity*, the very spirit of the examined life and intellectual responsibility, have its roots in the sacred world of myth? What are the connections between the activities we know as 'ancient philosophy' and the mythical experiences of the pre-Hellenic world? In what sense does myth create the symbolic frameworks of poetics and theory? To pursue these questions it is necessary to devote some thought to Greek *mythopoiesis* as the logological context of Western cultural formations. But before examining Greek myth and its associated poetic traditions we first need a provisional understanding of the social-ethical functions of mythic *mimesis per se*. To advance in this direction we need to bracket our categories of 'nature' and 'the natural world' and put to one side the rationalist image which the word 'myth' conjures up in our minds. This will form the theme of Section 2. Within this bracketing methodology I then turn to Hellenic myth and its role in ancient Greek society (in Sections 3 and 4), before exploring the 'dialogue' of mythic narrative and early Greek philosophy (Sections 5 to 7). Throughout I will adhere to the directives of Volume 1 and approach *mimesis* as a mode of *poiesis* that is actively implicated in the construction of sociocultural worlds. We will thus focus upon collective processes of 'world-constitution' prior to the later European conception of the natural world and its naturalistic categories of reflective theorizing.

2 MYTHOPOIESIS IN ORAL CULTURES: OBSCURE MOONS IN THE FIRMAMENT OF REASON

The passage from metaphor to myth is very simple, for one has only to expand a metaphor into a narrative and one has a myth.
(George Boas, 1961: 100)

We must first admit that the concepts of *myth* and *myth-making* are indeed 'obscure moons in the firmament of reason'. If we invert Boas' maxim, turning from myth to narrative logics and their metaphoric rules, we are returned to interpretive schema of intelligibility inherent in ordinary language and its particular vision of the world. The impulse that gives rise to heroic tales and myths may then be traced to the universal imaginative desire to weave human life into a timeless, coherent order. And this realm of prepredicative activity is continuous with the imaginative work invested in some of the most archaic concerns of everyday language. Language already 'projects' the world as an intelligible context of being and sociality prior to individual acts of speech and social behaviour. If day-to-day speech presupposes an immensely complex, if unconscious, sense-making apparatus then we might say that the 'mythic' impulse accompanies every attempt to *transform* discourse in the direction of systematic order and coherence. Myth continues the mimetic desire of *logos* to establish the invariant and permanent that is already at work in ordinary discourse. As a medium of pre-literate abstraction, myth and poetry spring from the same desire for the eternal and teach the same lesson of the finite, *human* character of all our knowledge and understanding.

In its most generic meaning *muthos* designates an act of *saying* which strives to name the world and convey its meaning to the community as a whole. This is the moment of societal reflexivity or metacommentary in mythic narration. In striving to name the world 'once and for all', such 'speeches' grant a meaningful structure to lived experience, but unintentionally institute a polemical relationship between the demands of new cultural forms and the claims of everyday discourse and its embedded 'ways of knowing'. Lived experience that has been objectified and formulated as 'whole and timeless' may be further qualified and contested. In aspiring to articulate the eternal, myth generates countermyths and subversive processes of self-reflection. The very aspiration to essence and univocity creates occasions for interpretation and polysemy. This is why the mythic-religious impulse is 'discourse-productive'. The 'founders of culture' were thus those anonymous speakers who discovered the power of (re)ordering experience by elaborating metaphoric language into realms of coherent stories and sacred song cycles. Once instituted the process of articulating experience and offering counterformulations may continue indefinitely. This polemic within prereflective discourses occasions the subterranean dialectic of tradition and innovation that animates many of the great premodern civilizations.

Of course it should be emphasized that the nascent sociologics of ritual and magic antedate literate techniques and self-conscious symbolic institutions. Indeed we may hypothesize that everyday narrative practices form the deepest stratum in every oral tradition and that the forms of narrativity available to a society have a powerful role in articulating and defining its forms of subjectivity and sense of moral order. Radical contestation in received interpretation systems occurs when novel 'frames of meaning' displace older forms of embodied knowledge. This quotidian contestation and self-questioning indicates the appearance of nascent reflexivity.

Let us approach myth, then, as a universal desire to narrate the 'powers' governing the world of men and gods. In the terminology of Volume 1, a developed mythology is an extraordinary form of reflexive communication, a semiotic means by which a society communicates its sense of truth to itself and establishes and generalizes its norms of identity and sociality, and thereby its sense of reality. In this sense mythology already secretes a 'politics', a vision of communality for individuals it reflexively gathers as 'members'. For cultures without the communicative instruments of reflexive distanciation and criticism, the terms and metaphors of mythic discourse are understandably taken for reality itself. Mythic icons which began life by imaginatively transcending the *pragmata* of everyday life congeal, so to speak, as the face of the real and in this reified form offer their services as an axiological grid for the community. So-called ordinary language is in fact a graveyard of naturalized myths. Echoes of this ethical theme are still at work in Aristotle's definition of tragic myth as a *mimesis*, a telling symbolic imitation of action and life. The art of tragic drama thus articulates worlds of *action* and social *relations* already preformed by *muthos* (*Poetics* 1450a15). As Aristotle informs his readers at the beginning of the *Poetics*, the objects of imitation and identification are persons acting, individuals exhorting, cajoling, plotting, persuading, converting, seeking vengeance, consoling, struggling, disagreeing, and so forth (cf. 1449a17ff.). But, of course, Aristotle was writing about myth and expounding a theory of mythic drama in the wake of the complete destruction of primary mythology. Originally myth provided a prepredicative language of reflexive commentary which rendered the world intelligible and describable for small-scale communities.

The impulse to codify the moral universe is particularly emphatic in the anthropomorphic narratives of early Greek mythology and art. In the main these consist of stories about the elemental powers, heroes, and gods constructed from a grid of moral relationships. As a dramatic tradition Greek mythology effectively created a fabric of anthropomorphic relations between the worlds of gods, heroes, and men (by virtue of the theocentric stress on god-god, god-mortal, and Demigod-mortal relationships it would be more appropriate to speak of the 'theomorphism' of Greek mythology). In fact by the Archaic period the mythologies of preliterate 'tribal' Greece had evolved into a complex language of vital powers and forces, weaving an elaborate 'theory of heroic action' around the totalizing principle *that every human action has been performed before, repeating heroic paradigms defined in illo tempore.* Myth 'represents the legendary past which contained all the models of all that could happen' (Fränkel, 1975: 488). And as the boundaries between folk-myths, nature myths, dramatic art, and social reality became blurred so the conduct of individuals could be interpreted in the graphic – and often ambivalent and contradictory – images and metaphors supplied by the familial, moral, sexual, and political vocabularies of myth. By visualizing and universalizing problematic relationships myth constituted 'a vision about a common experience', providing ethical paradigms for life in this world (Bettelheim, 1990: 124). These 'maps of the sacred' were also, as we shall see, auratic cartographies of the self and self-consciousness. Here we can legitimately speak of mythological *knowledge*: Greek mythic *poiesis*, in other words, was a *culture-forming* process which shaped and universalized the traditional icons of social order, justice, goodness, and beauty (one of the most powerful techniques for mapping the ideal self lay in the realms of visual art and sculpture as mimetic expressions of imaginary embodiment (Webster, 1959: ch. 1; esp. 7ff. and n.24)). In George Steiner's words, myths 'are among the subtlest and most direct languages of experience. They re-enact moments of signal truth or crisis in the human condition' (Steiner and Fagles, eds, 1962: 3). Myth, in sum, is a dramatic *organon* of the ideal, a tribal allegory of the real and not its passive reflection.

In Volume 1 we argued that the dialectical conversations available to a culture actively shape the institutional body of the *socius* by defining prescribed rhetorics of motivation and normative conduct. Moreover these 'conversations' are activated and organized in the context of definite social relations and structures. The interplay between discourse and structure follows from the central idea of logological theory that myth-making is one species of *logopoiesis*: *human beings have created themselves through world-forming acts of storytelling* (inversely, different forms of social order can be 'read against the grain' as allegories of subjectivity). Where quotidian storytelling is manifold and dispersed, mythic poetry moves in the direction of unity, coherence, and universality. Yet the very multiplicity and endlessness of 'storytelling' undermines the will to meaning. We might even say that the language-games of myth represent an unstable compromise between universality and particularity, establishing a fragile equilibrium between the prosaic demands of the Many and the totalizing desire of the One. In ancient Greece the predominance of the systemic impulse is evidenced in the simultaneous appearance of coherent, if often rambling genealogies, long epic narratives, and expansive myth cycles in the late seventh century. The outcome of this codification and rationalization of heterogeneous tribal traditions was the creation of a structure of ethical, aesthetic, and political 'world images' rooted in the anthropomorphic symbolism of mythology, a 'sociology of morals ... an ethic which is perhaps the best guide to the social reality of Greek morals that we possess' (Vickers, 1973: 261). Mythic rationalization discovered the powerful community-forming ideal of a shared language of experience. Mythic imagologies were thus quite literally *embedded* in the normative discourses of artistic, social, political, and intellectual institutions and their correlated experiential complexes. Functioning as an ethical cartography of selfhood, myth 'gave the archaic Greeks their sense of, and knowledge of, their past, their history ... it sanctioned cults, festivals, beliefs, the authority of individual noble families (with their divine genealogies), and so on through a range of practices and ideas' (Finley, 1981: 126). Despite its irreparable confusion the normative impulse of myth had the effect of reordering the whole spectrum of personal and social experience, dramatizing the violence and contradictions of 'human experience, human crimes, human justice' (Vickers, 1973: 630, 262). And the primary vehicle of this mythic dialectic would be the poetry of the epic: 'The consistent tendency to anthropomorphism and the organization of the world of the gods in terms of political and social relationships are characteristics which, if not epic in origin, derive their continuing impetus from epic' (Murray, 1993: 66). In the particular sphere of poetry, myths 'did for choral song what sculpture did for a temple. They illustrated the importance of a rite by depicting episodes in legend which concerned the gods and their relations to men' (Bowra, 1961: 12). As they were perfected, mythic poetry and narrative displaced the performativity of rites to give rise to a wholly new order of institutions – which we would now recognize as the forerunner of the sphere of artistic production. Along this evolution we find the emergence of the practice of autonomous poetry, sculpture, drama, and prose genres. The victory ode, for example, had the explicit purpose of elevating heroic action into the realm of communal values, 'bringing the victorious athlete to his due place among the noble company of famous men, heroes and gods' (Fränkel, 1975: 489). Here individuation and collectivization represent two different aspects of the same process of aesthetic identity formation (in the following chapters we will repeatedly return to the theme of the 'heroization' of the self in the cultural discourses of Archaic Greece).

2.1 The social form of myth

Clearly this 'textualization' and 'mythicization' of early Greek society indicates the importance of investigating the semiotic work implicit in the languages of myth-making. It also suggests the continuous interaction between mythic discourse and other modes of speech and action as these shape a society's sense of identity and wider axiological formations (the 'spheres' of political deliberation, family norms, law, commercial life, social organization, etc.).

The word 'myth' was introduced into English less than a century ago 'as a name for a form of story characteristic of primitive peoples' (Fowler, 1950: 369). From being a designation for the generic activity of storytelling, 'myth' subsequently evolved into a synonym for 'the primitive thought patterns of small-scale societies' or the memorial techniques of 'oral-aural tribal cultures'. From being a playful redoubling affirmation of the forces of life (a sense of mimesis still alive in the ancient semantic network associated with the words *mimeisthai* and *muthos*), 'myth' became the stock target of enlightened reason and rationalist criticism. Armed by this negative attitude, myths were grouped with a motley spectrum of human errors and superstitions as the antithesis of representational truth. As Fowler noted: 'the meaning popularly attached to the word is little more than a tale devoid of truth or a non-existent person or thing or event' (1950: 369). 'Myth' simply designates a false order of representations, having no deeper 'ontological' functions in constituting social experience.

MYTHOPOIESIS

In contemporary usage, then, 'mythology' serves as a rhetorical operator by means of which we establish status differences and rankings in the realms of verbal culture. This device was already a commonplace in the intellectual circles of the city-states of fifth-century Greece. According to a well-known developmental schema, *Logos* secured its claim to privileged universality by faulting the truth-value of its adversaries as 'fables' or 'fictions'; *Logos* not only claimed *not* to be *Mythos*, but more actively desired the liquidation of all purely mythical traditions – practices that were tainted with non-Hellenic, 'barbaric', or 'oriental' origins. The logographer Isocrates, for example, was already apologizing to his audience for introducing a 'mere myth' – today we would say 'fiction' – in the opening passages of his encomium to Athens: 'for even though the story has taken the form of a myth (*kai gar ei muthodes o logos gegonen*), yet it deserves to be told again. When Demeter came to our land ... ' (*Panegyricus* 4.28). The critique of myth – construed as a fanciful story without any experiential basis or rational ground – unites the otherwise disparate writings of a Xenophanes, Thucydides, Plato, Euripides, Aristotle, Protagoras, Isocrates, and Lysias. The Hellenic ideals of self-standing truth (*aletheia*) and universal communication, in other words, required an opposing term of 'mythical tradition' complete with exemplary verbal pathologies – 'barbarian *mythos*', 'crooked speech', 'dissembling words' (cf. Thucydides 1.22.4 – 'the absence of the mythic element in my work will make it rather unpleasant in recitation'; Pindar, *Olympian* 1.27–9; Lysias 6.51; *Phaedo* 114D). To this end the tradition of 'pre-Hellenic' myth with its indisciplined multiplicity and duplicities was projected as the antithesis of rational consciousness. Localized cycles of myth repeating the same essential message must give way in the transition to a more universal conceptual existence. We now understand of course that the project of universal reflection created its own myth of the Other, a protagonist role that has been subsequently filled by a diverse range of signifiers. Even today we reach for the word *myth* to undermine the credibility of particular beliefs and assertions, to categorize and deprecate forms of storytelling we find irrational and untrue or otherwise unwarranted. It would certainly disrupt the empire of Reason to admit the symbolisms of myth as a creative source and constitutive moment in every form of discourse (or, to speak more historically, to understand the 'oriental' as the generative moment within Greek civilization (cf. Bernal, 1987; Burkert, 1992; Murray, 1993: ch. 6; Said, 1978)).

Muthos as a discursive field

Even when we reject this usage we are still grammatically primed to view mythology as a specious form of *intellectual speculation* – not the medium of 'wisdom' but a failed gesture of reason. An example of this kind of intellectualism can be found in Durkheimian sociology, a programme which initially set out to investigate the collective, 'social-forming' powers of rites and religious festivals. Durkheim claimed that myths 'are not merely poetic forms' but groupings of representations aimed at explaining the world, systems of ideas whose function is essentially speculative. In sum the essence of mythology is tribal 'science': 'For a long time, myths were the means of expression of the intellectual life of human societies. If men found a speculative interest in them, it is because this need corresponded to a reality' (1983: 76).

> What lies at the root of myths is not a practical need: it is the intellectual need to understand. Basically, therefore, a *rationalist* mind is present there, perhaps in an unsophisticated form, but nevertheless enough to prove that the need to understand is universal and essentially human.
> (1983: 77)

This, of course, would make 'mythic representations' essentially replaceable as more adequate cognitive means were invented to mediate between human culture and extra-social nature. Collective festivals are sites of cognitive functions, ritualized forms of a nascent ontology. For Durkheim all

> the cosmologies immanent in mythological systems are different from each other, but can nevertheless be said to be equally true, because they have fulfilled the same function for all the peoples who have believed in them, and because they performed the same social role.
> (1983: 87–8)

The following discussion will proceed by deconstructing the terms of this cognitive paradigm (and its developmental schema, 'from mythos to logos'), pursuing the hypothesis that mythic discourse *constitutes* experience according to culturally specific *dramatic* norms. Myth, as we have noted, is a mode of theorizing, not a reflection of the real; it produces rather than mirrors social relationships. With this shift of framework we ask another kind of question about myth. And for this questioning it is important that we begin to think in functional and performative terms: what kind of dramatic *field* is created by the language-games of myth? What is the *formal* temporality of mythic narrativity? What were the social *functions* and ideological *uses* of myths in early Greek culture?

As a corrective to intellectualism it is useful to recall the memorial functions of myth for preliterate societies. Myth cycles codified the collective memory and helped transmit knowledge from one generation to the next. Myth is a 'metacommentary' on experience which actively shapes the existence it codifies and narrates. A *muthos*, in Jane Harrison's words, is simply a thing spoken, uttered by the mouth – hence 'the spoken correlative of the acted rite, the thing done' (Harrison, 1912: 328). In this conception, myth-making is primarily an *ethical* engagement, an act of dramatic sociation and symbolic appropriation of experiences deemed to be socially valuable. This is particularly evident in early Greek myth which evolved in explicitly *dramatic* and *anthropocentric* directions. By dramatizing polemical images and stories about the relationships of its heroic *actants* – Zeus, Hera, Apollo, Kronos, Heracles, Prometheus, Dionysos, Athena, Adonis, Achilles, Pandora, Theseus, Agamemnon, and so on – mythic discourse interpreted the world as a sacred field of moral relationships for a preliterate community. By rationalizing the community's ethical norms mythology functioned as an indispensable medium of *social membership*, providing a dramatic code which opened a 'space' for other forms of discourse and communality (Barthes, 1973: 109; Vernant and Vidal-Naquet, 1981; Vernant, 1990: ch. 9). In this sense mythopoeic dramaturgy precedes all purely cognitive attitudes toward objects. In the idiom of Volume 1, mythopoiesis is a constitutive ontology before it is a reflective medium.

As elements of a discursive field *muthoi* are specialized narrative acts communicated in a face-to-face ring-exchange structure whose dramatic form reproduces the cyclical order of social membership (the same structure informs the ring dances of Greek folk-culture and ritual celebrations). In the logic of performance myth encircles its human links in a transindividual 'voicing', elevating a local drama into the realm of meaningful universality (it is not that 'objects' become language if they 'mean something', rather objects acquire significance through auratic circulation). But the collective spirit flows through its audience only on the singular condition that the ritual chain is never broken. This is where the older Cambridge School highlighted an important feature of myth: myths are ritual *acts* of self-constitution actualized in the time and place of their dramatic performance. In Jane Harrison's terms 'What a people *does* in relation to its gods must always be one clue, and perhaps the safest to what it *thinks*. The first preliminary to any scientific understanding of Greek religion is a minute examination of its ritual' (1903: vii). To modify Malinowski's insight: mythic language in one of its primary functions is a *mode of action* rather than a countersign of thought. Myth *socializes* the Word by *sacralizing* the World. Once established these circuits of auratic talk can then be incorporated into wider institutional relations and systems of symbolic exchange. This sociologic of myth also explains why in Greek culture 'myth was open-ended' and 'the myth-making process went on throughout Greek history'. Myth-making cannot be exclusively confined to tribal art or the sphere of imaginative literature. It is simply that 'imaginative literature' is a recoverable archive or embodied tradition 'where we can watch, so to speak, while Aeschylus or Euripides shapes or re-shapes myths' (Finley, in Easterling and Muir, eds, 1985: xix; cf. Vickers, 1973: ch. 6). During the course of what Gregory Nagy has called 'the hellenization of Indo-European myth and ritual' (1990: Part 1), 'imaginative literature' and 'art' were crystallized as the privileged sites of secondary myth. And in the diachronic movement of self-creation, autonomous 'art' and 'literature' sought to preserve what their own highly individualized work necessarily destroyed. But fully to understand the emergence and ideological pre-eminence of 'literature' we need to return to the social and political life of Greek civilization prior to the existence of 'the sphere of art'. We are guided by the thought that the construction of 'art' and 'literate myths' was both an expression of a new freedom with regard to traditional institutions and a sign of oral ruination.

Myth as a reflexive archive

We already have an intimation of the fact that the continuum of storytelling called 'myth' belongs to the great collective rhetorics of imagined identity and memory in societies without the technology of generalized communication. Narrative, in Eric Havelock's words, is a 'necessary instrument of memorization' (1986: 42). And even the most explicit and 'literary' myths are belated products of earlier world-making activities. This comes close to Paul Feyerabend's observation that

> if science is praised because of its achievements, then myth must be praised a hundred times more fervently because *its* achievements were incomparably greater. The inventors of myths *started* culture while rationalists and scientists just *changed it*, and not always for the better.
> (1978: 104–5)

Storytellers from traditional societies do not, of course, describe their activities in these terms. Here we exercise the charity of the ethnographer by adopting a definition of myth as a tradition of discourse incarnating the values and beliefs of a people concerning their origins and destiny, the gods, semi-divine heroes and heroines, the origins of the world, and related themes. In *The Secular Scripture*, Northrop Frye incorporates this element of societal reflexivity in his concept of myth as concern:

> myths stick together to form a mythology, a large interconnected body of narrative that covers all the religious and historical revelation that its society is concerned with, or concerned about ... myths take root in a specific culture, and it is one of their functions to tell that culture what it is and how it came to be, in their own mythical terms. Thus they transmit a legacy of shared allusion to that culture.
> (1976: 9)

It is essential to think of myth as both content and communicative form – *form* in the sense that myth-making strategies function as a generatrix of modes of thought and verbal performances, and *content* in that the lexicon and grammar of myth crystallize around 'auratic symbols' expressing the existential concerns of a particular society and way of life (Northrop Frye speaks of a developed mythology as '*a myth of concern*', borrowing an expression from Paul Tillich's account of the existential role of 'ultimate concern' in human affairs). In functional terms 'the myth of concern exists to hold society together, so far as words can help to do this' (Frye, 1976). But if we approach myth as semiopraxis we must resist the idea that thoughts first exist and are subsequently translated into language. The actual relationship flows in the opposite direction. Storytelling is not a *vehicle* of significance; rather its communicative patterns *constitute* forms of existence, and these enter the fabric of culture as both facilitating and constraining norms. A body of religious thought, as Jean-Pierre Vernant reminds us, 'constitutes a system in which the various concepts are defined and are modified in relation to each other. It is a system of symbols the logic of which may not take exactly the same form as our own' (1990: 141). This we can refer to as a society's 'reflexive archive'.

To clarify the archival dynamics of verbal structuration a distinction can be drawn between manifest and depth mythopoiesis, in a manner analogous to Wittgenstein's concepts of 'surface grammar' and 'depth grammar' (cf. 1968: I §664). Manifest myth-making designates the performative side of storytelling, the actual occasions of individual acts of narration to specific audiences and reference groups. Depth mythology, on the other hand, refers to the generative semantic and pragmatic networks of cultural knowledge from which the patterns and plots of narration are woven. The unconscious structurations of mythological schemata are brought into play, articulated, and enriched in the social processes of transmission where the available rhetorics are reshaped under the impress of local contexts, audience expectations, performance conditions, and so forth. The relationship between depth codes and performative realization is itself reflexive: surface enactments are not possible without the 'knowledge' embodied in depth matrices; but infrastructures are only effective in individual acts of elaboration and retelling. Understanding a given myth, therefore, assumes tacit knowledge of the social attitudes and modes of thinking which inform a performance in a particular time and place. Moreover such cultural competences also implicate definite audience expectations and interpretive strategies. And the 'skills' in question are not primarily intellectual since they draw upon wider realms of practical knowledge and situationally embedded judgements.

All narrative performances presuppose an archive of folk-tales and verbal rhetorics, but have the effect of recoding these tacit symbolisms in improvised performances. In the fundamental stories a society tells about itself an audience not only participates in the collective archive but also reproduces the tacit knowledge and sensibilities which make a given culture visible to itself. This is one of the central theorems of the logological paradigm: collective narrativity is an *organon* rather than a reflection of social life (in its most generic sense 'culture' refers to the totality of 'conversations' a society conducts with itself). Whatever the surface 'content' of myths they are also universally 'about' the passions, fears, longings, obsessions, and dilemmas faced by individuals. There is a kind of natural selection which preserves the most resonant symbolisms from older cultures. If myths fail to touch a chord in human experience they atrophy and disappear. Or they are reduced to allegories and, in a terminal state, collected as specimens of irrationality – a process culminating in Euhemerism and the Casaubon-inspired compilations of mythographers like Diodorus Siculus and Apollodorus. This is also what separates a living mythology from the myths of the mythographers – the former is concretely *embodied* in the social practices and institutions of a community, the latter have become detached, analytical specimens.

Myth as habitus

Before myth is a science of the concrete, an archaic philosophy of nature, or an expression of the 'mythic conception of the world', it is a matrix of existential interpretations concerned with central moral and social dilemmas grasped *sub specie aeterni*. In this respect myth is continuous with the essentializing powers of language: 'Language is always enclosing us ... Since we use it to think, there is nothing in us that is not mixed with it, nothing that does not participate in our existence. Reason seems to us therefore a kind of discourse' (Parain, 1971: 58). Nothing is more alien to mythic storytelling than the modern categories of 'belief' and 'knowledge'. Myths articulate meaning in the same way that dispositions and praxical reflexivities incarnate 'knowledge' (see Volume 1, Part III, Chapters 6–9). They embody a culture's values and empower a society engaged in self-reflection. Where the work of myth-making is delegated to specialist intellectual groups we have already left the primary world of myth (another way of saying this is to observe that *mythos* cannot serve as a 'belief system' – every self-conscious search for a 'faith' appears in the wake of the disintegration of myth as 'the revelation of the sacred'). The disintegration of primary myth is frequently experienced as the collapse of the art of storytelling or, more fatefully, the loss of communicable experience (cf. Walter Benjamin, 'The storyteller', in Benjamin, 1992. Benjamin claimed that the art of storytelling was in a terminal state of decline 'because the epic side of truth, wisdom, is dying out', a phenomenon he linked to the alienation of narrative from 'the realm of living speech'). This also finds expression in the tension between the narrative heteroglossia of myth and the centripetal motive of religious systematization and liturgical correctness. The elimination of the carnivalesque from oral traditions isolates one strand of the process by which verbal *poiesis* evolves into mythology and, appropriately systematized and domesticated, enters the soteriologies and cosmologies of 'religious orthodoxy'. From being a provocative occasion and stimulus of reflexivity (as in the *ethical* content of riddles, parables, gnomic sayings, and fables) the lessons of myth are incorporated into the normalizing offices of religious codification. The appearance of organized religiosity is generally an important index of the erosion of traditions of oral wisdom. Once underway the transition from primary myth to mythology is often encouraged by a ruling class or *élite* as it displaces the carnivalesque practices of folk-traditions with its own worldview. Mythology may then be used as an instrument of religious domination and cultural legitimation. In sociological terms, we shift from a constitutive principle of ethical integration to a regulative principle of societal organization.

To summarize: myths are typically vivid, enacted stories a society extends to its members who reciprocate by repeating and modifying them as they are returned to the collective archive. *Mythopoiesis* only survives and flourishes in the dialogical process of retelling; once the oral circuit is broken the spirit of storytelling is lost. Societies that have moved away from primary oral-aural means of communication typically transform the traditional arts of storytelling – laying the foundations for more mediated forms of symbolic transmission and, given appropriate technical conditions, written mythologies and organized religious systems. Literary mythology then plays into the hands of institutionalized power.

Mythic aestheticization

If myth is collective narrative, a discourse formation, and a reflexive archive it is also above all else a *protoaesthetic* event. The ceremonial contexts and framing conventions of myth bestow upon these speech acts the qualities of aesthetic distance and separateness from prosaic concerns: speech in such stylized performances is definitionally out of the ordinary, mysterious, and numinous. Yet once separated from vernacular discourse, speech acts become available to the community as a resource of ethical reflection (the *gnomai* or 'wise saying' might be considered to be the germ form of all subsequent genres of edifying stories, including the late reflective grand narratives of philosophy). The bracketing effect of a parable or fable encourages an audience to initiate self-reflection about the ordinary and the taken-for-granted course of the world. Indeed the playfulness and stylization of so-called 'premodern' forms of discourse positively enhance their cultural role as specialized media of societal self-reflection.

Aesthetic 'defamiliarization' (Shklovsky, in Lemon and Reis, eds, 1965) is a common feature of many premodern forms of 'ethical talk' and is invariably accompanied by special phonetic, syntactical, rhythmic, and prosodic patterns that can be found in widely differing traditions of magical naming, ritual invocation, and myth-telling. The phonological and prosodic features of ritual performances, for example, act as boundary markers informing an audience that another kind of verbal event will appear within the space of these frames. At the very least a community enjoying parables and fables must practically distinguish between surface and manifest 'content', literal and ironic 'meaning'. While such boundary-marking operators do not precipitate anything like the distinction between 'this-worldly' and 'other-worldly' orientations, the prescribed intonational features of rites and rituals are functionally analogous to the frames around visual artworks. Once in circulation such differentiated spheres of 'aesthetic' activity may be codified into bounded discursive domains. Frequently the control of these liturgical frames becomes the exclusive domain of intellectual groups specializing in the production and control of cultural information. As we shall see in Chapter 2, the evolution of sanctionable *formulaic techniques* in Homeric epic is one of the most striking examples of this process of aesthetic differentiation: by virtue of its distinctive sound patterns and repetitive syntax Homeric poetry distances itself from everyday speech and thereby aestheticizes the narrative field. Epic continues in the aesthetic sphere what ritual syntagms had already secured in the religious and ethical field. Once 'inside' this dramatic frame, heroic poetry can develop to a 'higher' stage of 'defamiliarization' by stretching out the narrative into elaborate sequences, subplots, and stories. When this has been achieved the medium of song has been shaped into something like a technique of collective reflection. This is one of the ways in which the category of literature is born from ritual discourse. As Benjamin observed this 'slow piling one on top of the other of thin, transparent layers' constitutes a paradigm of the way 'in which the perfect narrative is revealed through the layers of a variety of retellings' (1992: 92).

Recall that many traditional myth cycles are sung – often collectively or in celebratory 'relays' with instrumental accompaniment – rather than being recited monologically. We should not forget that the Homeric bard was a *singer* of tales, not a narrator in the modern sense of the term. Primary myths and epic narratives are first and foremost *dramatic performances* and *dialogical transactions*. Indeed some traditions of storytelling elaborate complex 'question-and-answer' rhymed formats in which members of the audience are invited to participate. The melodic stylization of vernacular speech patterns 'marked' as extraordinary is one of the most important steps in the genesis of an 'aesthetic field' within the stream of everyday activities. The carnivalesque rituals of many folk-cultures instituted a living art which consciously frames itself as an enclave of fantasy. Symbolic inversion, parody, and the violation of moral boundaries creates the bounded institution of ritualized art – which, of course, may also become 'automatized' as the official myths of a social group or liturgical community. However such formations are appropriated, the very existence of these discursive practices suggests novel possibilities of reflexive self-expression. To borrow Benjamin's terms once more, the articulation of *aura* is one of the primary functions of ritual speech. But unlike Benjamin's generic analysis of *mimesis*, we trace mythic aurality to specific forms of rhythmic narrativity and preliterate institutions of ethical reflexivity. Choral hymns are, for example, a powerful way in which a whole community can articulate and incarnate its sense of identity and alterity. Collective song belongs among the earliest 'media' of identity formation. Here the sonorous qualities of formulaic sequencing and rhythmical repetition become inseparable from communal stylization and cultural production. As we have observed, the performance of such liturgical hymns *constitutes* rather than reflects communality. In more developed traditions of myth, the 'extraordinariness' of the form – marked phonologically and morphophonologically as well as socially and ritually – is matched by the extraordinariness of its content and sense of festive occasion; when these practices have been institutionalized a society has discovered the idea of 'aesthetic form' as both a technique and an institution of reflection. This axiom might form the starting point for a sociology of premodern dance, song, and related dramatic forms.

The discovery of dramatic art *as an instrument of reflexivity* also revolutionizes a society's collective memory. While many cultures have no differentiated domain of activity corresponding to what we call 'art', members of these societies still use complex 'aesthetic' skills to articulate and transmit their traditions. The incomparable medium of collective reflexivity is, of course, language and its recursive forms – humour, song, poetry, and myth. With each differentiated subgenre the community has effectively created a new organ of self-interpretation, a new way of reflecting upon and exploring its own expressive possibilities. And as we have argued theoretically in Volume 1 the invention of a new symbolic technique invariably involves a transformation of self-understanding and individual and collective identity. As with carnivalesque 'self-reflection by inversion and parody', aestheticized myth is reflexive in the sense of being both created by a social order while actively transforming the structure of social relations – leading to further patterns of social engagement and expression. This is reflected in Lévi-Strauss' distinction between ritual *paralanguage* and mythical *metalanguage*:

> Myth and ritual do not always correspond to each other ... they complete each other in domains already presenting a complementary character. The value of ritual as meaning seems to reside in instruments and gestures: it is a *paralanguage*. The myth, on the other hand, manifests itself as *metalanguage*; it makes full use of discourse, but does so by situating its own significant oppositions at a higher level of complexity than that required by language operating for profane ends.
> (1963: vol. 2, 66; cf. Barthes, 'Myth today', in Barthes, 1973)

It is certainly no accident that a taste for subversive metaphor, puns, word-play, paradoxes, and fantastic imagery is one of the preconditions of defamiliarization. Once institutionalized these metaverbal devices serve to mark off the domain of mythic discourse from prosaic narrative. It is often at this point that myths give rise to ritual performances. But metalinguistic elaboration also has the unintended effect of instituting other demands upon an audience – creating an audience 'tuned' to the transgressive word-play that is associated with poetry and fiction. The kind of listening produced by myth is akin to the fixated gaze demanded by a numinous object. This is the point in storytelling where the attention of the teller disappears into the events of the tale told; where an audience is absorbed into the enchanted space of the telling. Listening avidly to the telling of myth – like the child absorbed in a fairytale – is a genuine source of pleasure, not untouched by fear, anxiety, horror, and related pleasures. The vicarious savouring of ambivalence and the anxiety of semantic incoherence is the oral equivalent of the *jouissance* of modern reading. A child's attention melts into the time of the telling, just as the self is pleasurably extinguished in the act of reading.

The experience of *wonder* is one such occasion. When human beings express anxiety or wonder before the mystery of existence they invariably turn first to the musical intensities of poetry, dance, and myth. For 'archaic societies' these are the only media of ethical self-reflection. This linkage persists in the elective affinity between poetic intonation and sublime occasions – Pericles' Funeral Speech is not a transcript of fifth-century everyday speech, but a particular representation of language and to some extent a poetic transfiguration of everyday language. We should not, however, think of *wonder* (the *thaumazein* of the ancient philosophers) as a once-and-for-all event. Mundane experience is saturated by analogous experiences of intense perception and destabilizing consciousness. Enchantment is a function rather than a discrete event, a possibility of discourse rather than an aboriginal act of meaning. Its universal source is the unanswerable doubt about the Other. Sublimity – for instance in the linguistic registers evolved by Greek tragedy and the Greek theatre more generally – is also a prototypical modality of questioning through which the world is approached as terrifying, awesome, and wonder-filled. Wonder – along with the questions it spawns – may be among the original intentional acts through which reality first appears as an affective totality – an intimation that there is an order of meaning in the chaos of appearances. Myth's intention is to imagine the world as an ethical Whole; or, to anticipate the conclusions of this chapter, myth *envisions* human experience in the symbolisms of unity and totality. It does not so much hark back to an idealized past as deny the validity of such temporal predicates as 'pastness' and 'futurity'. It posits the world as eternally the same by subverting time, change, and death as contingent and inconsequential. Whatever the fateful lessons of our finite experience everything is explicable when grounded in the great narrative of order. Perhaps this is what Franz Rosenzweig had in mind in calling the spirit of myth 'the foundation of the realm of the beautiful' (1970: 38).

2.2 The 'content' of myth

> Philosophy is not an absolute beginning; before it, there is already a complete language, that of myth.
>
> (Paul Ricoeur)

In the prolegomenon above I have sketched a concept of myth as figurative discourse symbolically enacting, codifying, and articulating orders of cultural knowledge incorporating a community's sacred beliefs, practices, sensibilities, forms of spiritual consciousness, and self-awareness. Mythic narratives provide a collectivity with the imaginative means of *constructing* worlds by locating self and destiny in supratemporal categories. The voice of mythic narrative takes an event out of time and embeds it in a timeless world of the eternal present. Three aspects of the mythic matrix can be singled out: myth as sacred discourse, as ethical self-formation, and as a way of life. As Brian Vickers observed: 'The Greek myths are resolutely human, and they demand to be analyzed in terms of the social and religious values of the culture that produced them' (1973: 205).

Homo significans: myth as sacred narrative

And God said, Let us make man in our image, after our likeness ... So God created man in his own image.

(Genesis 1:26)

As a form of pretheoretical discourse myth embodies a way of perceiving and interpreting experience, but also a way of thinking, acting, and living (a 'pragmatic charter' implicating its members in a sacred order). Myth changes reality by endowing it with a numinous value, transforming mundane events into sacred occasions (see Malinowski, 1926). It 'expresses, enhances, and codifies belief; it safeguards and enforces morality; it vouches for the efficiency of ritual and contains practical rules for the guidance of man'. Like magic and dance, myth is a world-making practice and must be understood as an ethical agency. Indeed if we follow Marcel Mauss' related suggestion, magic is 'essentially the art of doing things' consisting of a set of techniques, procedures, dexterities: 'Magic is the domain of pure production, *ex nihilo*. With words and gestures it does what techniques achieve by labour' (1972: 141). It is not only a practical art, but also a symbolic locus of knowledge. Magic is the original intuition that knowledge is power, an insight which lingers in all subsequent developments of concepts and thought. In another context Mauss suggests that the 'Aristotelian categories are not indeed the only ones which exist in our minds, or have existed in the mind and have to be dealt with. Above all it is essential to draw up the largest possible catalogue of categories ... It will be clear that there have been and still are dead or pale or obscure moons in the firmament of reason' (1979: 32; the last sentence in the translation of Ben Brewster in the original text reads: 'on verra alors qu'il y a eu qu'il y a encore bien des lunes mortes, ou pâles, ou obscures, au firmament de la raison').

Viewed as narratives, myths have an indispensable referential content. In primary oral communities they are one of the most important means by which individuals give significant form and coherence to their social worlds. In premodern societies the life of 'telling and doing' is inseparable from material concerns and practical performances. It is possible that narrative (including stylized gesture, spectacle, dance, musical performance, and the like) is one of the primary symbolic media involved in the construction of social worlds. And inevitably the 'content' of the oldest myths reflects the concerns and interests of a particular language and way of life. This is perhaps why 'the group of themes relating to the family is the most important of all for Greek tragedy' (Vickers, 1973: 230). Like Palaeolithic art, narrative functions as a mode of ethical self-definition. Myth

> cannot be separated from the community to which it belongs and which ritually assumes its dominion ... Myth is perhaps fable, but this fable is placed in opposition to fiction if one looks at the people who dance it, who act it, and for whom it is living *truth*.
>
> (Bataille, 1985: 232; 1988: 22)

Archaic Greek culture, like all the ancient civilizations, was formed on the soil of much older cultural traditions dating back to the migrations of the Bronze Age and Neolithic civilizations. We may assume that the imaginary life of these earlier societies was even more saturated with folkloric symbolism. The linkages between folk-narrative, material power, and 'symbolic power' are equally ancient (cf. Frankfort, *et al.*, 1949; Cornford, 1957, 1965). If we take our cue from the Creation myth of Genesis, humanity is created with the power of naming and imagination; the latter capacity is the decisive gift: in creating mankind God graces the species with the divine power of representation and image-making. In this prephilosophical myth of origins human reality establishes its dominion by the force of imagination. Naming is simultaneously envisioning, creation, and persuasion. Bearing a likeness to God their maker, human beings share in the sacred world-work of divine construction – they partake in the time before all beginnings. And, characteristically, the aboriginal trace of this participation is found in the most routine discursive activities: naming and classifying. In the Biblical account whoever can name objects possesses a fundamental authority, a divine power to shape and even create the real. Or to invoke Aristotle's more theoretical idiom, mankind is by nature a mimetic and myth-making species – human beings have a natural instinct for representation which reaches deep into their kinaesthetic abilities and thinking capacities. Only mimetic creatures are capable of living together as needful beings in organized communities ('man is by nature a political animal' at *Politics* 1253a2–3); from the simplest acts of mimetic address arise the complex domains of imaginative praxis and communal life. Significantly, Aristotle's image of human nature as fundamentally 'political' derived from his identification of the primordial capacity of human beings to create and manipulate symbols as they learn and acquire knowledge (*Poetics* 1448b5–9).

Plato and Aristotle indirectly endowed the theme of symbolic creativity with the greatest importance by warning of the dire consequences once the controls of rational self-reflexion are relaxed. But even in the reduced role as the target of rational criticism, symbolism preserves its integrity as one of the founding dimensions of ethical life. Both theorists remind their audience that mimetic practices serve different functions in different social and institutional contexts. While mythology may be a force of contestation and critique in one situation, in another context it consolidates the forces of domination and subordination. Moreover both concur that the magical spell of myth can only be effectively dispelled by the cold rigour of conceptual thinking: auratic myth and tragic *mimesis* must be overthrown by the dispassionate insights of *theoria*.

By recycling the symbolisms of myth, communities simultaneously objectify their distinctive forms of collective experience and reproduce specific worlds of normative praxis. Here we touch upon one of the basic themes of the logological perspective: the technologies available to a society shape the social processes through which selves are transformed and circulated. In societies where communicative technologies are undeveloped or non-existent, only oral techniques – dance, music, poetry and myth – can serve as a means of self-transformation. Such signifying practices help to define the terms of identity for the community as a whole. And here signification is less a question of discovery than of inventing social distinctions, a collective construction of reality rather than an individual revelation. The worlds constituted through story grids are quite literally imaginative constructs: the tale with its plotting devices and narrative grammar defines the quality of mind of its teller as it implicates the audience in the processes of transmission.

The narration of myths in ceremonial contexts and their embedding in ritual performances are collective 'techniques' for the social organization of space and time. Consider, for example, the collective interpretation of *time* and temporalized modes of being in different linguistic communities. The performance of rituals serves to anchor the events of everyday life in the context of the sacred archetypes of 'the Great Time', tales of the Great Age, the Dreamtime, or the founding events of the Great Spirit before all beginnings (Eliade, 1989; cf. 1974: 395, symbolized in Hindu mythology by the goddess Kali: 'that time out of which all things come and into which all things return', Campbell, 1989: 64). This is to stress the *content* of mythic narratives as a method of temporalizing the world. But the dramaturgical *form* of the myth-telling is equally, if not more, significant for the constitution of temporality. It is not that experience is sacralized by being narrated at meaningful intervals in recurrent prescribed occasions and locations. The causality runs in the opposite direction: 'meaningful intervals' and 'recurring contexts' (the oral/aural calendar of symbolic events which punctuate the continuum of experience) are first established by ritualized sayings and doings which relive the primordial time. Concrete temporal distinctions as socially significant dimensions of human existence are established by mythic practices (Elias, 1992). Or, to preserve the emphasis we have placed on semiopraxis: the social organization of time is an effect of mythic categorization.

Similar considerations hold for the construction of social space. Ritualized performances eventually assume the status of a sacralized 'field' of cultural communication (for example, where special times and locations, idiolects, costumes, objects, etc. are set aside as the stage of narrative). Ritualization establishes the *numinous aura* of a society's reality-relations, mapping out different regions in its symbolic topography. The first binary distinction may have been the separation of profane from sacred time and space in the service of communal forms of synchronization. But what began as discourse ends up as a power of institutional signification – in Elias' language time synchronization is a human activity 'not merely a relationship but a capacity for establishing relationships' (1992: 46). Rituals and stories about the sacred *Urzeit* enter the substance of institutions – the formation of cults, symbologies, and doctrinal liturgies are frequently organized in cycles of festive celebration synchronized in time and place to commemorate specific gods and heroes (and specialists readily develop who are experts in the determination of the 'right time' and place for these rituals: 'Almost everywhere in the long development of human societies priests were the first specialists in active timing ... When the struggles for supremacy between priests and kings went in favour of the latter, the setting of time, like the coining of money, became one of the monopolies of the state' (Elias, 1992: 53)). The institutionalization of the theatre of Dionysus in Athens is one late example of these processes.

When institutionalized as collective ideologies, myths help reproduce the world-work orchestrated by groups with a vested interest in accumulating sacred power and authority. In sociological terms, myths of origin are incorporated into the legitimation systems of state-organized religions. The suasive telling of myths is traditionally reserved for specialized speakers and groups invested with numinous power and symbolic prestige. In many traditional societies such groups have been gerontocracies – augurs, shamans, priests, etc. – organically linked to other powerful groups and classes. In some societies these groups evolved into powerful political organizations in their own right. This is also another sense in which rhetoric is embedded in the *pragma* of daily life. From this perspective our initial definition of mythopoiesis now shifts from the abstract concern with 'the mythic' to the questions, *'whose myths have been historically effective? Whose 'definitions of reality' have been incorporated into the textures of 'the real'? Through whose eyes do we see the world?*

In the idiom of logological inquiry, Greek mythology contains the founding stories of its cultural historicity, idealized versions of social relations, and a tradition of ethical distinctions found in pre-Hellenistic culture. Myth stands as a mute witness to the idea that language's role may not be exhaustively understood as the representation of the world, that our enlightened story of language's power to represent and dominate the world is one of our own deepest and most strategic myths. More positively, myth suggests the idea that language bears a constitutive relation to the world: myth is the lie that tells the truth about language. This 'lie' has a number of different aspects which we may, for analytic purposes, call the *dramatic, epistemic,* and *aesthetic* moments of myth-making.

The dramatic moment

Why myth at all? Why should something like myth be found in all societies? Why this universal desire to tell the story of experience in mythical frames? What are the founding experiences which motivate mythic expression?

First we have to abandon the Eurocentric idea that there is one essence or unequivocal core to all mythic practices (the fiction of a non- or pre-Western primitive mentality, prelogical thought, or archaic consciousness dominated by magical thinking from which we can measure our own cognitive progress). By rejecting this prejudice we can see that myths are as diverse as the domains of experiences which they articulate and the social worlds which they constitute. For one cultural tradition 'myth' may be concerned with the enactment of a sacred order – a Golden Age, for instance – that has already 'happened' in some 'time before time', often a Time before the creation of gods and men, an *Urzeit* before time itself was disclosed (we can compare the family resemblance between myth's 'There was a time before time' and fairytale's 'Once upon a time'). This may not, however, hold, for another culture or historical period. Many myths certainly attempt to 'abolish' temporal change and contingency (a theme which tempted earlier authors like Lucien Lévy-Bruhl and Mircea Eliade to say that 'the primitive lives in a continual present' (Lévy-Bruhl, 1910, 1923; Eliade, 1989: 86)). To regulate uncertainty may be one of culture's interminable tasks. This is one of the reasons why myths are frequently reborn in situations of extreme danger. Its themes are drawn from the radical insecurities that accompany human life.

The epistemic moment

Returned to their dramatic contexts and viewed semiotically, myths are typically oral mappings of sacred experience codifying originative events, divine agents and agencies, and primordial, founding relationships answering to an existential need to order, propitiate, evaluate, manage, and explain the otherness of the world (writers like Martin Heidegger and Mircea Eliade speak of myth as an expression of the desire not to lose contact with Being, testifying to the terror of losing the self by being 'overwhelmed by the meaninglessness of profane existence'). But myth is not an *ersatz* ontology; the conceptual resources necessary for scientific and metaphysical discourses are not available to mythic experience. Yet the mythologies of many preliterate cultures certainly function to render experience intelligible – articulating, objectifying, and overcoming the threat of pain, fear, disease, death, and oblivion. By imitating the demonic forces of life and death, individuals control and shape their responses to death. This may explain why many ancient narratives draw their plots from thanatonic dramas (*Gilgamesh* and the *Mahabharata* for example). Myths remind their listeners of a time before death was unleashed, a paradisical age without fear or corruption. They codify some of the most ancient poetry of mortality.

Perhaps the primary role of archaic myth is not prediction or certainty before the world, but the mitigation of horror in the face of contingency, chaos, suffering and loss. A large number of myths are existential dramas or festivals inviting identification, transference, and strategic participation, rather than aesthetic spectacles to be observed, enjoyed, and aesthetically appraised. The tragic theatre of the Greeks may be seen as a parody of the thanatonic substance of ancient festivals (an aspect which is elided in the Cambridge interpretation of the origins of *drama* in the sacred *dromenon* of the dithyramb: 'in its sacred sense ... not merely a thing done, but a thing re-done, or pre-done with magical intent ... The Dithyramb, from which the drama arose, was also a *dromenon* of the New Birth' (Harrison, 1912. ix)). In a modern idiom, *muthos* constitutes a space of *actants* and dramaturgical *functions* by means of which a culture constructs accounts of suffering and death by commending exemplary models of appropriate death-defeating conduct (the term 'drama', from the Dorian word for 'doing', *dran* and the Athenian term *prattein*, derive from the semiotics of action and representations of action: 'Our whole state is an imitation of the best and noblest life ... You are poets and we are poets ... rivals and antagonists in the noblest of dramas', Plato, *Laws* 817B).

The aesthetic moment

It is the presence of these auratic, numinous, and often visionary and violent experiences which separate the nascent logos of myth from the more restricted mimetic functions of legends, folklore, fables, and proverbial language (while nevertheless recognizing that complex genealogical relationships and family resemblances connect these different forms of narrative mimesis). But myth transcends diversion and entertainment. Unlike the tales of Aesop or the Arabian Nights they implicate the self in a more serious order of problems. For example many myths have a close affinity with the rites of religious conversion in demanding a transformation of the quotidian *persona* with respect to the numinuous promise of the whole. Mythic narration seeks to change the *psyche* of its listeners; like the rite or choral dance it demands a complete change of 'mental set' (if only for the duration of the rite); but unlike the solemn prescriptions of regulated ritual, myths often include the more Dionysian moments of excess, parody, distraction, laughter, dissembling, and pleasure: many ritual performances thus blend the promise of release, escape, transfiguration, and transcendence with affective and sexual licence. Before myths satisfy the 'metaphysical need' in human nature, they are celebrations of the metaphorical imperative to anchor the anguish of daily living in a timeless, ritual order (hence the important role of symbols of paradisical communality in mythological discourse and their absence from legends and fairytales).

Death's salutary drama

Art is not an imitation of nature but its metaphysical supplement, raised up beside it in order to overcome it. Insofar as tragic myth belongs to art, it fully shares its transcendent intentions.

(Friedrich Nietzsche, 1967: §24)

MYTHOPOIESIS

We are now in a position to formulate a more analytic definition of mythic narrative. Primary mythologies are among the first systematic campaigns against phenomenal mutability. The incomprehensibility of death provides myth with its unique 'problem' and 'intention'. Mythic narrative sets to work to sublimate the ultimate negativity of death. 'Death' in this context can serve as a metaphor for all those eventful forces which alienate and destroy the conditions of lived experience – forces symbolized by images of darkness and decline. If myth is a machine rendering suffering intelligible and collectively experienceable, its deeper, if at first occluded, theme is the irreversibility of time (and with it the inescapable facts of temporal decay and dissolution). Wherever myth appears we find the same attempt to make a virtue out of a necessity by reversing the simple truth of mortality that we are born, suffer, and die. It is as though mankind in intuitively grasping its own insignificance stumbled upon narrativity as the source of meaning. As in the legend of Scheherazade, telling tales keeps death at bay.

This is not to claim with Claude Lévi-Strauss that myths are machines for suppressing death (or Mircea Eliade's theory of Archaic ontology as a machine of 'archetypes and repetition' for denying contingency (Eliade, 1989: ch. 1)). On the contrary, myth makes death thinkable. Max Weber's theory of the origins of theodicies in rationalizing the meaning-threatening incidence of suffering and death is closer to the mark ('Religious rejections of the world and their directions' in Gerth and Mills, eds, 1948). We might also compare Umberto Eco's complementary view of the modern novel as a machine for generating interpretations from situations of chronic uncertainty and disagreement (1985: 2).

An acute *consciousness of death* – a heightened awareness of death's remorseless universality – appears to be the *condition sine qua non* for shaping spontaneous metaphor into reflective myth. This is why different ways of troping death can function as powerful generative principles for the worlds of culture. 'Our entire existence ... is produced ... in a sort of swirling turbulence where death and the most explosive tension of life are simultaneously at play' (Bataille, 1988: 123–4). Suffering and death may well be the prototypical symbols of 'historical contingency' which a society pledged to order must confront and assimilate for its own ends (cf. Eliade's observation that 'from the point of view of ahistorical peoples or classes, "suffering" is equivalent to "history". This equivalence can be observed even today in the peasant civilizations of Europe', 1989: 97 n. 2). The analytic problem every culture must resolve is how to turn death into a life-enhancing ally rather than a fateful antagonist (how to 'laugh together at representations of death' in Bataille's words, in Hollier, 1988). If friendship with death is beyond the limits of credibility, then myth's task is to transform death from the status of enemy to that of a salutary stranger – to take the forces of an-archy inside its symbolic forms and deflect its counterfinalities in 'civilizing' intentionalities. This ancient subterfuge of culture constitutes 'the nuclear structuring force of the rites and, thereby, the society' (Campbell, 1973: 23).

The fatal syllogism of culture runs: *in a perfectly ordered Cosmos death would have no place; but death is inescapably present; therefore we have somehow disturbed the Original Order; and must, consequently, find our way back to the Whole.* Myths are semiotic machines producing simulations of life and order from chaos and disorder. The threatening 'not-to-be' of death must be subordinated to the order of the *Logos*. Every culture-founding mythology is at root a symbolic economy of death in the interests of life. Without the ultimate anxiety, no ritual, and without ritual no theodicies, religion, art, or systematic thought. Myth then is less a form of representation or cognitive explanation than a salvational dramaturgy animated by redemptive desire. Myths explain the presence of suffering by troping difference as an effect of an underlying economy (Weber and Eliade both cite the Hindu ideology of reincarnation or *Karma* as a perfect example of this device: 'In the light of the law of karma, sufferings not only find a meaning but also acquire a positive value. The sufferings of one's present life are not only deserved – since they are in fact the fatal effect of crimes and faults committed in previous lives – they are also welcome, for it is only in this way that it is possible to absorb and liquidate part of the karmic debt that burdens the individual and determines the cycle of his future existences', Eliade, 1989: 98–9; Weber: 'The most complete formal solution of the problem of theodicy is the special achievement of the Indian doctrine of *karma* ... The world is viewed as a completely connected and self-contained cosmos of ethical retribution', Weber, 1966: 145; also 155, 179, 266–8).

Beneath their myriad forms myth gravitates to the same function: to render the irreversible process of death reversible, and by this operation anchor identity in visible images of life's ordering energies. In this respect mythic discourse, shamanism, magic, orgiastic ritual, and artistic imagery pursue the same goal by different means: to transfigure being-toward-death into a cipher of immortality (for later generations of course the promise of a 'return from death' tends to fall away leaving the empty husk of necessity as its allegorical truth). A myth is powerful to the extent that it can transmute darkness into a vindication of light: the irreversibility of experience must be shown to mask a hidden reversible structure. To this extent Eliade's thesis is valid: 'the myths serve as models for ceremonies that periodically reactualize the tremendous events that occurred at the beginning of time. The myths preserve and transmit the paradigms, the exemplary models, for all the responsible activities in which men engage' (Eliade, 1989: xii).

The will to intelligibility

Myth, in its original form, provided answers without ever explicitly formulating the problems. When tragedy takes over the mythical traditions, it uses them to pose problems to which there are no solutions.

(Jean-Pierre Vernant, 1990: 214)

MYTHOPOIESIS

We have suggested that *mythos* is first *ceremonial praxis* and only then *text*. Mythic dramaturgy instructs human beings that 'suffering is never final; that death is always followed by resurrection; that every defeat is annulled and transcended by the final victory' (Eliade, 1989: 101; for the etymological roots of the 'return from death and darkness' in prehistoric Greece see Frame, 1978: ch. 2). This is perhaps why some of the fundamental Greek myths could function as a model for later ontological thought. However, by recalling that myth's medium is song and music we should avoid judging narrative in terms of later epistemic concepts of evidence, certainty, and truth. *Mythopoiesis* secures 'being' from the darkness of oblivion prior to all representation. But paradoxically it accomplishes this effect by granting death a central role in the symbolic economy of culture.

Mythos cannot reflect reality; but it can refigure the world as a simulacrum of a numinous reality. Mythologies work, in Kenneth Burke's apt phrase, as *equipments for living*. Just as the first instruments have little to do with propositional truth, mythic thought cannot be said to be either true or false; myth operates according to other criteria (such as the successful reduction of existential anxiety, the erosion or strengthening of the ego, the social production of collective hope, fiduciary anticipation, wonder and pleasure, humour and tact); its symbols are not concepts or categories, but collective icons of experience, means of empowering existence in the face of non-sense. It is even anachronistic to situate myth as the first step on the path which leads from preliterate 'wisdom' to pure reflection (in the sense that as societies gain greater control of nature the existential questions addressed by myth are thought to be best answered by metaphysics, religion, theology, art, science, or technology). The fundamental mistake here is to approach myth as a cognitive medium rather than as a primary mode of address. We avoid this error by viewing myths as the stories collectivities tell themselves about themselves, thereby creating the frameworks of symbolic self-interpretation and societal self-definition.

It may be the perennial desire to tell the tale of life's victory over thanatonic forces which preserves life. This may also be the reason why a human society without myth 'has never been known, and indeed it is doubtful whether such a society is at all possible' (Finley, 1964: 25; cf. Cornford, 1952). Archaic consciousness impels its participants to believe that everything has been done before, that 'life is the ceaseless repetition of gestures initiated by others' (Eliade, 1989: 5). This desire is certainly close to the existential roots of art and magic. It is as though the impress of magical exhortation, symbolic singing, sanctification, salutary incantation, and the celebration of life was indispensable to the existence of life itself: the mimetic impulse to reverse the irreversible is implanted in human beings from childhood, an instinct of our nature, to borrow Aristotle's words. By enacting life's victory over death a community secures its own future, a field of possibilities, and a sense of purpose. Myth's dream of order is in this sense the voice of hope. 'What is primordial and essential', in myth, as Eliade has observed, 'is the idea of regeneration, that is, of repetition of the Creation', a return to paradisical Origins (1989: 64).

We know that the earliest forms of communal song developed from mimetic media such as cyclical nature rites, ceremonial music, and graphic arts performed by and for the community as a whole. Where the incantation of mimetic magic and ritual *mythos* ends, there death's siege begins: myth promises resurrection from rather than identity with the absolute. The transition from mute mimesis to verbal imitation marks the allegorical birth of poetry (which in the Indo-European cultures often revolves around the poetry of birth in cosmogonic narratives). Culture begins in a masque of death. But once objectified myth follows its own internal logic of development – frequently giving rise to differentiated superstructures of symbolic praxis – ritual games, sacred codes, metaphysical reflections, moral, aesthetic, and ethical systems, and the like. In sociological terms the transformative powers of magic, myth, and art also have the unintended consequence of forming the Self as they reflexively articulate the world. Indeed myths often contain unanticipated possibilities which, when articulated, work against the original impulses of ritual formality (for example, in situations where ritual practices encourage the development of autonomous art forms, poetic institutions, and cultural specialists). In some civilizations the evolution of mythic praxis prefigures its own dissolution as the very practices and rituals it makes possible are taken up and used against its own 'primitivism' and 'naivety'. A well-known example of this phenomenon is the violent animus of patriarchal religious ethics – with their more rationalized concerns and ethical interests – toward the matriarchal practices of magic and ritual (and of course in many mythologies the Mother goddess symbolizes the power of life and death, creation and regeneration). In the light of this we might hypothesize that the source of culture was literally the cult of the Mother as origin and preserver of life (Neumann, 1962).

In conclusion: *mimesis* is not only at the root of magical and mythic praxis, but presides over the development of art and and symbolism *per se*. Echoes of language's first raids on the inarticulate still resonate in the rhythms of repetitive rites, choral poetry, and epic song. The original synergy of these early oral forms is reflected in Aristotle's attempt to decompose poetry into its constituent elements: *ethos* – actants, character, *dianoia* – thought, *lexis* – expression, *melopoiia* – music, *opsis* – spectacle, and *mythos* – plot or theme (cf. *Poetics* 1449a18 and *passim*). Whatever else a culture must do to survive, it must dispel death's silence through recurrent acts of saying and making. If culture provides answers to the question 'What is the meaning of death?', to persist in asking the question of the meaning of life and death in the face of these answers is to exercise the vital capacity to philosophize.[3]

MYTHOPOIESIS

3 MYTH AS THE MATRIX OF EARLY GREEK THOUGHT AND PHILOSOPHY

Philosophy was born and nourished by poetry in the infancy of knowledge, and with it all those sciences it has guided toward perfection; we may thus expect them, on completion, to flow back like so many individual streams into the universal ocean of poetry from which they took their source.

(F.W.J. von Schelling, 1978: 232)

The social construction of early Greek poetry, art, and philosophy provides rich evidence for these general theses. The earliest appearances of Greek literary forms and philosophical language – Homeric epic cycles, elegiac lyric, tragic drama, historical narrative, medical *istoria*, cosmology, and so forth – are decisively informed by preliterate symbolisms. As oral institutions of reflection, earlier social forms constituted what I have referred to as a logological matrix for subsequent discourses. *Mythopoiesis* created an action matrix out of which different *logoi* ('things said', systems of categories, language-games, beliefs) could be elaborated. But the emergence of these ideological superstructures were subject to definite socioeconomic and political conditions. The differentiation of Greek culture did not proceed by some immanent logic or automatic evolution (contrary to the formulation of Werner Jaeger who writes that 'the evolution of the Greek mind from the earliest time reveals, after an initial period of mythological thinking, a growing tendency toward rationalization of all forms of human activity and thought. As its supreme manifestation it produced philosophy, the most characteristic and unique form of the Greek genius and one of its foremost titles to historical greatness' (1965: 41); rather, as we shall see in the chapters which follow, the 'evolution' was the product of a complex interaction of social, intellectual, and cultural developments.

The eroticization of nature

We are standing, as it were, at the dawn of the first phases of the social constitution of the European Eye, the basic figure of Western videological culture. I will argue that mythic narrative, as it was shaped into the earliest forms of epic and lyric poetry, educated Greek modes of thought in the forms of a visual ordering of experience. Archaic ontology taught the idea that contingent events and practices become meaningful only by participating in or repeating the realm of sacred prototypes and visual paradigms (Zeus, Hera, Apollo, etc.). A similar point has been made by Mircea Eliade in his suggestion that archaic ontology already has a quasi-Platonic structure (and conversely that Plato 'could be regarded as the outstanding philosopher of 'primitive mentality', that is, as the thinker who succeeded in giving philosophic currency and validity to the modes of life and behaviour of archaic humanity', 1989: 34; cf. 'the Greek theory of eternal return is the final variant undergone by the myth of repetition of an archetypal gesture, just as the Platonic doctrine of Ideas was the final version of the archetype concept, and the most fully elaborated. And it is worth noting that these two doctrines found their most perfect expression at the height of Greek philosophical thought', 1989: 123).

The fundamental point is that the development of Greek literacy did not replace myth, as if they belonged to distinct spheres of meaning, but that mythical symbolism facilitated the crystallization of the basic frames of meaning for subsequent representational discourses (for example, the impact of the myth of universal conflagration or *ekpyrosis* on the work of Heraclitus, Stoic cosmology, and Neopythagoreanism in the Hellenistic world, see Eliade, 1989, ch. 3). Later modes of visual representation (in Platonic-Aristotelian metaphysics, Stoicism, Neoplatonism, Neopythagoreanism and Graeco-Latin Gnosticism) were productive misunderstandings of the axial problems and question-frames first formulated in the Greek oral tradition. One striking instance of this dialectical misprision – which I will analyze at greater length when we turn to Presocratic thought in Volume 3 – is the manner in which the movement known as Ionian Philosophy transmuted the mythic icons of natural order and origin into reflective symbols, thereby instituting the project of cosmology and ontology (indeed, that most visual of iconic signs – *Kosmos* – is itself derived from the Olympian *view* of the world as an envisioned Whole – a divine theophanic order ruled by all-seeing Zeus. Again, the argument is not that these specular forms and practices are identical with later reflection, but that as social narratives they trace out some of the unanticipated possibilities of an older linguistic matrix. We begin to see that early Greek myth and art represents the first phase of a long historical process which can be described as the eroticization of nature: the constitution of the world as a pleasurable visual spectacle.

Mythic symbolism as tradition-constituting discourse

Myth-making dramatizes felt, but inchoate, emotional experiences into memorable shapes; it makes a coherent social vision, a social ethos, possible. The central claim of this chapter is that *mythopoeic* language is one of the fundamental metainstitutions of society.[4] From this point of view the expression 'Greek myth' can be used as shorthand for the stylized techniques of visualization in early Greek culture, a dialogue of discourses involving, in Hans-Georg Gadamer's expression, a 'fusion of horizons'.[5] In the following studies we will see that ancient Greek forms of thought were precipitated from a rich corpus of mythic discourses that were already active in eighth- and seventh-century Greek society.[6]

Mythic agonism: the meaning of origins/the origin of meanings

If, as we have claimed, the origins of literary and philosophical reflection can be traced to mythic symbolism, we should immediately clarify the meaning of the term 'origins'. We have already discussed the first sense of origin which might be expressed as the oral-dialogical horizon of communication. If we attempt an archaeology of the discourse foundations of Western philosophy we continually uncover the mediating symbolisms of mythology and religious praxis. We have suggested that it was the profoundly *visual* content of these beliefs which exerted a decisive influence upon the first generation of European thinkers, among whose number we find the individuals who first named the reflexive life 'philosophy' (*philosophia*), the love of wisdom. The ancient tradition of oral dialogue formed the 'inner horizon' for all subsequent forms of Western theoretical discourse.

This leads to a second sense of origin. We should not think of origin as a dispensable background or condition presiding at the birth of the *logos*, but rather as a living experience – what I have spoken of as a *matrix* rich with further semantic possibilities. In this sense origin has an eschatological sense, remaining for later traditions as a dialogic incentive inviting further adventures of thought. To rethink origins is to return to the founding events of *meaning* at work in a tradition. In Western culture it was the stream of Greek mythology that created the idea of archaeological indebtedness and the seductive image of tradition as an inexhaustible past. This concept of origin is also close to the phenomenological, concept of a sustaining *Lebenswelt*, instituting the conditions of the possibility of particular social and cultural practices and to Hans-Georg Gadamer's concept of effective tradition (*wirkungsgeschichtliches Bewusstsein*).

But perhaps the most fruitful sense of origin is that of the dialectical interaction between text and context, formulation and interpretive reception itself: the idea that the relation between *mythos* and *logos* is a dialogical rather than a simply chronological or empirical-causal connection. The essential tension at work here is closer to the struggle of master and servant than to the structures of empirical dependency. As a dialectical trope, '*mythos-logos*' symbolizes the presence of conflict and struggle at work in ancient Greek culture. Given that 'origin' is a polysemic word it is useful to distinguish these three broad semantic references of the term, which can be termed the chronological, phenomenological, and logological senses. We speak of origin chronologically when we refer to the empirical history of an event; we can also speak of phenomenological origins, where the event is located in an ideal meaning – or intentional genesis; and finally, we can speak of the logological origin of an event, of its place in a discursive matrix or tradition. To summarize: every quest for origins presupposes myth. 'Beginning', 'position', 'place', 'origin', 'development', 'differentiation', 'proposition', 'theory', 'thinking', and so forth, are in essence symbolic tropes, drawn from antecedent layers of metaphoric praxis.

Origination in the context of the following studies refers primarily to logological genesis, the structural dependence of speech acts upon prior discourse formations and textual praxis.[7] If myth aspires to the absolute sovereignty of magic – effacing the difference between word and thing, all subsequent discourses are anxious to secure their own authority and founded character, an anxiety produced by the dialogue of *mythos* and *logos* itself, most typically displayed in the desire of philosophical reflection to remove every trace of its own dialogic ancestry in the 'polysemic' work of myth.[8]

If we find a 'hiatus' between early Greek myth and reflective discourses, we also discover a conversation at work in the construction of discursive origination: namely, that every later discourse is constituted through an adversarial critique of its predecessors and necessarily retains traces of its dialogic origins in the *agon* of self-differentiation. We meet one of the central insights of logological analysis: the field of discourse displays reflexive properties by virtue of the fact that its formation rules are governed by a polemical rather than a dialectical logic. This can be distilled into three interdependent polemical moments: the *agon* or adversarial struggle with a precursor discourse; the *pathos* or critical 'suffering', involving the defeat of the 'upstart' discourse; and the *anagnorizis*, the 're-cognition', rebirth, and vindication of the new with respect to the old. To understand the affinity between discursive traditions and the content of heroic epics it is important also to see the parallel between this structure and what Joseph Campbell has called the universal formula of the mythological hero journey, as (i) separation, (ii) initiation, and (iii) return (cf. Frame, 1978; Harrison, 1978: 4).

As we will demonstrate in more detail in Volume 3, the earliest discourses of philosophy drew upon ancient adversarial discourses (the moment of *agon*). As a cultural achievement, philosophy secured its own identity by speaking against the mythical tradition (the moment of *pathos*). And each strong form of theoretical speech occluded its own legacy to claim recognition as an independent formation (the moment of *anagnorizis*). Formulated more generally: every discourse is striated by the hermeneutic struggles of its historical differentiation from a field of antecedent discourses (in the case of early Greek reflection, the *topoi* of mythos were reworked as abstract figures and schemata within the different discursive contexts of cosmogonic, cosmological, medical, and physical speculation).

4 THE PUBLIC AND POLITICAL NATURE OF GREEK RELIGION

We are now in a position to turn to the religious institutions of Archaic Greece. Ancient Greek religiosity was indissociably tied to mythological symbolisms institutionalized in public cults and religious festivals. In striking contrast to the Judaic-Christian tradition with its central core of doctrinal belief and liturgical theology Greek religiosity was predominantly ritualistic, a matter of cult not of creed.[9] More significantly for the differentiation of different modalities of critical discourse, the worship of the gods was frequently part of a spectrum of public performances and practices supported and regulated by the state (at Athens the most famous of these was the Great Dionysia); some of the more important gods, demi-gods and hero figures became state cults during the Archaic period.[10] It is therefore quite appropriate to think of Greek religiosity as evolving from a competitive struggle between state religious cults and festivities and private forms of worship; but in later periods of Greek history it was the political power vested in state cults which shaped the structure and dynamics of social and political life. And more generally it was the growth and spread of the Greek *polis* which aggressively promoted the visible manifestations of Greek religiosity. But no matter how far state codification went, the demands of personal religiosity would periodically reassert themselves against the dominant religious traditions.

The privileged theatre of Greek religion was the public sacrificial ritual in which offerings were made to a god as a mark of respect and continued recognition. However, these acts were not attempts to atone for sins or to win beatification for the celebrants. The more rationalized rites kept the objects and instruments of 'worship' to a minimum, usually only involving a celebrant before a simple public altar or shrine.[11] The gods demanded due respect for their powers – observance rather than obeisance or ecstatic self-transformation. In this context 'religious observation' also included an essential component of emulation: by recognizing the sphere of a particular God, the celebrant also celebrates the power and excellence typified by that divinity and its *locus*. And the spheres of divinity were intrinsically plural and heterogeneous. It is also important to observe that Greek religion knew no anti-god as the embodiment of evil and consequently never developed a demonology centred on individual sin and punishment; even where a belief in the Underworld appears, Hell was not ruled by a punitive anti-God and its 'geography' was left largely unmapped in the myths and epic song cycles. In short, public acts of expiation and sacrificial rites informed by mythological discourse formed the core of classical Greek religiosity.[12]

For individuals, intention and interior belief were less important than the careful – and typically public – performance of the rite and the conscientious execution of ritual duties. The latter obligations define the content of piety (*eusebeia*). It is symptomatic that the rhetor Isocrates instructs Demonicus about the most important maxim of religiosity in the following manner:

> First ... show devotion to the gods, not merely by doing sacrifice, but also by keeping your vow; for the former is but evidence of a material prosperity, whereas the latter is proof of a noble character. Do honour to the divine power at all times, but especially on occasions of public worship; for thus you will have the reputation both of sacrificing to the gods and of abiding by the laws.
>
> (*To Demonicus* 1.13–4)

Ritual led the way in mapping the spiritual and physical landscape into a visible quilt of divine domains. Piety was not so much an inner state, as an observable, socially sanctionable performance of religious duties. The voice of tradition instructed the young as follows: 'Fear the gods, honour your parents, respect your friends, obey the laws' (Isocrates, *To Demonicus* 1.16). The orator Lycurgus also invokes the same duties of 'piety towards the gods, reverence for your ancestors and ambition for your country', 'the guidance of the gods presides over all human affairs and more especially, as is to be expected, over our duty towards our parents, towards the dead and towards the gods themselves' (*Against Leocrates* 15, and 94). And since these observances were sanctioned and reinforced by the laws of the *polis*, sacrilege was regarded as both a religious and a political crime.

Spatial rather than temporal metaphors of divinity tended to predominate. The model of visible divinity was the out-of-doors visible shrine and its environs. Its eventual terminus would be the free-standing Greek temple of the Classical age. In terms of both its functional priority and ubiquitious visibility, the altar rather than the monumental temple is the most characteristic symbolic object in the landscape of the ancient Greek world. For this reason the desecration of altars and burial grounds by invading armies was one of the most graphic symbols of the loss of civic autonomy, by breaking the temporal chain which binds the collective present to the past. We should also note that the symbolism of the altar as a re-membering of the gods (and derivatively of heroes and ancestors) was profoundly important as a focus of collective solidarity. In Finley's words,

> the sacrifice was not only a way of offering the gods food and drink, it was also a way of establishing a table fellowship in which human beings shared with the divine. The feast commonly followed the sacrifice, and the edible parts of the sacrificial animals were largely reserved for the feast. Many meanings can be read into the burnt offering, not all of them logically compatible. One is the idea of a continuum that held together all living parts of the universe; men shared in the feast with each other as they did with the gods.
>
> (in Easterling and Muir, eds, 1985, xvii-xviii)

The altar as the focus of the moral economy of Greek religion evolved into the archaic and classical temple, the public image of the city-state.

Important shrines would thus spring up around a hero-figure or local deity as they might around one of the great Olympian deities.[13] Like every other aspect of early Greek culture, religion, art, dance, music, and literature were inseparably linked to political life and as a consequence of this linkage the rationalization of the *polis* in the direction of democracy from the seventh century onward was accompanied by the development of an essentially this-worldly, non-magical, and non-ethical form of religiosity (typified by the organizations known as *thiasoi*). The growth of individual city cults with their local figures and emblems played a decisive role in this civilizing process:

MYTHOPOIESIS

The devotion to a city cult was a crucial factor in ensuing lasting unity in the Greek city-state, and this religious centralization must have taken a great deal of effort to achieve, given the multiplicity of local beliefs inherited from the Bronze Age ... the Athenians pointed the way forward'.[14]

In the terminology of the present work, rationalization and centralization were expressed by an intense secondary elaboration of earlier mythological symbolisms: among these, the growth of pan-Hellenic shrines (particularly those at Delphi, Delos, and Olympia), the differentiation of city-cults (connected with aristocratic families and clans such as the Peisistratids, Philaids, and Alcmeonids), the fusion of political power, religious organizations, and ideology, the individualizing impact of literacy upon mythology – giving rise to the poetry of Homer, the Homeric hymns, Hesiod's verse, the role of interpreters, poets, and professional rhapsodes, the growth of a homogeneous 'pan-Hellenic' style in the visual arts and public building works. Mythic discourse, far from being displaced by these processes of rationalization, differentiation, and individualization, actually gained in importance; the stories of heroic myth in particular were increasingly codified and celebrated in the most public sphere of the city-state. The political arenas of the *polis* literally became spaces of divine, phallocentric provenance. When Thales suggested that 'everything is full of gods' he may also have been making an everyday observation on the topographical ubiquity of divinity in the Hellenic world (cf. Cook, 1967).

The Greek cities of the sixth and fifth centuries quite literally imagined themselves in the terms of narrative texts; the classical *polis* and its architecture became a reflexive icon to its own heroic mythology.[15] It refigured itself as an institutional space of mythic-religious praxis (most especially taken from the Olympian family of gods and epic narratives). And the central models for these self-construals were not derived from a centralized priesthood monopolizing a sacred doctrinal text or a theology based on divine revelation; rather the imaginary charter of Greek natural theology derived from the Olympian religion and the plot structures of two great epic narratives. Greek religiosity thus flourished without a consistent monotheism, without an institutionalized priesthood, and without a doctrinal theology or liturgical literature. What took the place of these institutions appears to have been the religious sites and precincts of the city itself. The work of unification carried out by the prophets and scriptural exegesis in ancient Judaea was performed in Greece by the civic institutions of the city-state and its Olympian ideology.

Where in the earlier Archaic period religion had served as an order-engendering machine, now the *polis* itself incorporated these functions into its own civic apparatuses. The city, or more accurately, powerful civic *élites* and intelligentsia, interpreted urban existence as the natural site of heroic action. Civic life itself became a medium of symbolic order. This is a vivid illustration of how a 'discourse formation' integrates three fundamental functions: the material institutionalization of rhetorics of reflection (here illustrated by mythic figures and their actions, and more particularly by the role of Homeric narrative in education, athletics, art, and so forth), their generalization through the practices of literacy, public cults, architecture, and so on, and their artful dramatization in a community's moral, ethical, and political vocabularies.

5 THE DIALECTIC OF MYTH AND PHILOSOPHY: EARLY GREEK INSTITUTIONS OF REFLECTION

Aristotle struck the keynote in the well-known text from the first Book of the *Metaphysics*:

> For it is owing to their wonder that men both now begin and at first began to philosophize; they wondered originally at the obvious difficulties, then advanced little by little and stated difficulties about the greater matters, e.g. about the phenomena of the moon and those of the sun and of the stars, and about the genesis of the universe. And a man who is puzzled and wonders thinks himself ignorant (whence even the lover of myth is in a sense a lover of wisdom, for the myth is composed of wonders); therefore since they philosophized in order to escape from ignorance, evidently they were pursuing science in order to know, and not for any utilitarian end'.[16]

As an art, questioning can only be pursued systematically in the context of supportive sociocultural practices and institutions. While all men are intellectuals, in Gramsci's phrase, systematic inquiry as a form of life is a product of very specific civilizational configurations. And we know that many cultures have stifled or disciplined the energy of inquiry into authoritative grids working in the interests of existing power relationships. Frequently repression has been carried out in the name of a 'true and inviolate' revelation or absolute religious intuition. In such regimes the practice of questioning inherited traditions and authorities is proscribed as it is correctly intuited that free speech breeds a most corrosive attitude – an awareness of the irreparable non-coincidence of socially transmitted *doxa* and the transgressive claims of experience. Invariably this mismatch leads to conflict, typically between the opposing claims of intellectual curiosity and innovation and the authoritative claims of inherited religious traditions.

In certain exceptional situations we find groups and subcultures openly encouraged to question existing social arrangements and orthodoxies; occasionally institutions evolved with the necessary material resources, independence, and power to create forums specializing in interrogation and free speech. We have called such arrangements *institutions of reflexivity*. In ancient Greece these institutions were historically associated with the growth of the urban civilization of the *polis*. Here religious polytheism appears to have been a productive and energizing force.

Muthos is not an antecedent stage on the arduous path toward 'genuine' science or philosophical reflection, but now appears in its full sociological significance as a discursive site providing symbolic resources for the social construction of reflexive experience. The dialectic at work here is not that of a diachronic opposition but rather one of a dialogue between a matrix and its generative offspring. This is one possible reading of Aristotle's acount of the kinship of myth and early philosophical speculation. But we must go deeper than the Aristotelian equation. If we take this step we find that the relationship between mythic symbolism and early philosophical metaphor is itself reflexive. Greek mythological traditions – embodied in law, public institutions, and religious organizations – provided the grammar from which epic narrative and the first stories of philosophy were developed: without religious *muthos*, no philosophy; yet on the other side, the categories of myth would have remained speechless without the literate resources of reflection – incarnated, for example, in the anonymous works of thought and articulation which we know as the *Iliad* and *Odyssey*. Myth is by no means a subordinate partner in this dialogical relationship. As the Greek case attests, the opposite appears to be true, where, for example, the great iconic symbolisms of *Kosmos, Dike, Kronos, Ananke, Dinos, Moira, Psyche, Thumos, Philia, Arete, Eros, Zeus*, and the like actively defined the question-frames, discursive problematics and, more importantly, the desire for intelligibility animating the earliest projects of cosmological reflection. These auspicious symbolisms were not negated and abandoned with the rise of philosophy. *Theorein* did not destroy heteroglossial speech. In fact it would be more accurate to see theoretical reflection transcending myth only by turning its formative symbolisms and motivation to other ends. A culture of the reflective eye was instigated by disciplining and marginalizing the amorphous figurations of the voice. In a genealogical sense, the mythological interpretation of being and becoming lives on within the auspices of the theoretical project (the totalizing motive of myth is reincarnated under the sign of theory's videological dream of absolute reflection – the quest for an Olympian knowledge of the Whole).

6 MYTH – THE LOGOS OF THE LIFE-WORLD

In the dialectic of *muthos-logos* there is no concrete origin apart from the *logos* nascent in the life of discourse itself. Both myth and theory appear as moments of a deeper configuration, referring back to a more primordial world of origins which phenomenologists have called the *Lebenswelt*. From the logological perspective myth and early philosophy are parallel articulations of world experience, different modes of articulating the essence of manifestation. Both myth and theory are languages of the life-world.[17] Myth strives to capture the essence of manifestation in its poetic symbolisms. If the metaphoric word discloses the sacred world it also limits the essence of manifestation to theomorphic forms. This is why the earliest thinkers lived ambivalently toward their own mythological traditions. By denouncing the 'irrationality' of myth, the first philosophers made different claims upon language. But these claims still presupposed the universal impulse at work in the mythic tradition. Myth was not abandoned but colonized for different ends – whether this was the world of the gods and heroes disclosed in the *Iliad* and *Odyssey*, the *theophanic* interpretation of reality at the root of Hesiod's poetry, the liturgical speech forms of choral lyric, Ionian speculation on the nature of the *kosmos*, Attic tragedy, lyric poetry, or the dialectical reflexivity of a Socrates, Plato, or Aristotle. *Muthos* continued its subterranean life as the inner horizon of these later practices.

One of the primal images created by Greek myth was a conception of the life-world as a sacred *chora* of elemental action. As theophany, *muthos* tells of the appearance of the divine. Human activities and institutions gain their identity and place in this cosmos by participating in a sacred drama; moreover every aspect of social life derives its significance and authority from sacred paradigms of moral thought and action. Translated into practices and institutions, these models of belief and conduct weave forms of narrative symbolism through every part of collective existence: the sacred is not an autonomous sphere separate from legal, familial, political, and socioeconomic experience. To borrow a Durkheimian idiom, the elementary structures of religious life not only provide the substantial content of belief and knowledge, but also the crucial forms and representations through which this knowledge could be articulated.

One product of this world image is the polarization of experience into a field of sacred and profane experiences. Stories constructed around the figure of polarity or opposition were subsequently generalized to other forms of experience. Another way in which mythic theophany operates is as a semiotic archive. Like speech more generally, myth provides a community with a sense of the symbolic unity of its past, present, and future possibilities. The myths of archaic Greece – not unlike the myths of non-Western cultures – utilized human and sociomorphic predicates to constitute a sacred network of relations. These in turn provided an archive of ideological images that were used in sanctioning festivals, legitimating aristocratic belief systems, and constructing the genealogies of noble families and tribal lineages.[18] At the level of substantial content, myth instituted a tradition of culturally valued folk-paradigms and principles of communal orientation. Thus the patriarchal, tribal-familial, heroic, and agonistic patterns of Greek ideology are only fully explicable in the context of the historical development of conflicts specific to the social systems of Archaic Greece (a history which includes the hegemony of aristocratic land-owning groups, the expansionary drive of Greek colonization in the late eighth and seventh centuries, and the internal political struggles dominating the early history of the Greek *polis*).

As with many other ancient religions and mythologies, the Greek pantheon dramatized forms of power. Olympus – that most visible image of hierarchy and transcendent power – evolved from earlier tribal-familial power relations into something like an allegory of political order. In its own way the Homeric pantheon represented a secularization of the older cosmological models of self and identity. Consider the deeply patriarchal representations of authority underlying the Homeric pantheon and its real historical roots in Mycenaean institutions of patrimonial kinship. The construction of a centralized monarchy was explicitly developed in opposition to the more plural and polycentric power formations of 'tribal' society. By the seventh century Zeus had become 'King of the Gods', the recognized supreme ruler of Olympus (Hesiod, *Theogony* 886).

Max Weber provides a useful terminological clarification: patrimonialism draws its legitimacy from earlier systems of patriarchy; in both the 'system of inviolable norms is considered sacred'. Patriarchal power reproduces its principles in narrative schemata and symbolisms drawn from the model of hierarchical family domination (kinship-ordered cosmologies). Zeus is the patriarchal head of the gods, 'the father of men', supreme autocrat of Olympus and transcendent source of value. As such his hegemonic rule exemplifies the normative order of Justice (*Dike*), Law (*Nomos*), and Civil Order (*Themis*). And like the rule of the imaginary patriarch, Zeus' rule is absolute. The justice of Zeus became synonymous with the fundamental structure of the universe itself. And any breach of these norms 'would result in magical or religious evils'. Authority is vested in the 'free arbitrariness and favor of the lord who in principle judges only in terms of "personal", not "functional", relations'.[19] But in the Greek case, what was originally the 'arbitrariness and favor of the lord' evolved into the prototype of the supreme kingship of Zeus, which in turn provided a matrix of visual predicates from which later representational mythologemes could be constructed, frequently detached from their original religious source:

> Homer's divine monarchy of Zeus became the basis of theological speculation leading to a kind of pagan monotheism ... This idea will be seen to influence also the first Christian political thinkers who certainly did not imagine they were indebted to the Mycenaean Greeks'.[20]

From the chthonian high god of natural powers (symbolized by giganticism, thunder, lightning, and earthquakes), Zeus is gradually transformed into 'father Zeus', patrimonial leader of the light-loving, truth-establishing Olympians, and eventually depicted as the patriarchal embodiment of social justice, until in the eighth century he becomes the god of civil order and communality itself, 'the stranger's god' guaranteeing the rights of all men against injustice (cf. *Od.* 14.280–5; 14.389), the *pater familias* and omniscient symbol of patriarchal kingship – visual centre of the cosmos and personification of the Archaic social order. And, of course this ideological shift was not without a transformation of meaning in Zeus' symbolic connections with the other Olympians who derive their power and status from relations which radiated from Zeus' hegemonic control (the dialectical conflict between masculine and female deities, for example, can be traced in terms of the revaluation of signifiers precipitated by the increasingly centralized hegemony of Zeus). The Olympian grid developed into a generic model of value for later generations who saw their own interests and ideals coded and represented by this map of divinity. It became, as it were, an ideological charter of pagan self-reference.

But these semiotic relationships should not be understood reductively: the mythological foundations of Greek ritual and religious practices were not a mechanical reflection of social and economic exigencies – whether of 'tribal' or 'archaic' social formations; on the contrary, the institutionalization of narrative forms and their concomitant reflexivities played an active role in the evolution of Greek culture. Olympian mythology provided a flexible charter for the collective life and culture of early Greek society, just as Zeus became the *actant* at the centre of the moral order of the Cosmos. The terms of this videological conception were unashamedly masculine, universalist, and hegemonic. Early Greek videology evolved into a patriarchal vision of social experience: videological experience was constituted around an Olympian grid of patriarchal metaphors. Myth as the spiritual 'Mother of Logos' was repressed and replaced by the hegemony of Zeus – a suitable patriarchal icon for the universal vision promised by pure theory.

7 NARRATIVE STRATEGIES IN GREEK MYTH

To anticipate later chapters we can isolate a number of related narrative strategies created by mythic discourse.[21] By approaching myth as both *praxis* and *language* we immediately raise the problem of how categories and symbolisms originally embodied in ritual action can create systems of meaning with more general application to non-religious spheres. I have suggested that this problem was resolved in the Greek case at the level of narrative deep structure: mimetic symbolisms created networks of narrative predicates and relations by means of which individuals and collectivities could articulate otherwise inchoate and discontinuous experiences. On the level of social conduct, these narrative functions provided a shared map of normative orientations, judgements, and world interpretations. Individuals gained a sense of selfhood by internalizing these orientations which, as generative rhetorics, could also serve as modes of self-expression.

What kind of strategy would we expect to find at the level of such narrative deep structures? Myth I will suggest elaborates its basic operations from generic semantic and social dilemmas. These can be summarized as a set of very general ordering principles.

7.1 The principle of order

The mythopoeic universe displays an intelligible structure with its own principles of coherence and functional dynamics, deriving ultimately from a theophanic structure of experience; order is typically mapped in societal categories and exemplified by the overdetermining presence of the narrative functions of *Agency* (Gods, Heroes, Spirits, and so on), *Action* (Epiphany, Divine Creation, Destruction, Copulation, Vengeance, etc.), *Instrument* (Divine Action at a Distance, Thunderbolt, Mouth, Word, Scission, etc.), and *Event* (Birth, Death Marriage, War, etc.). Given these elements and relations a narrative universe can be imagined as a theatre of praxis. The archetypal narrative is the divine ordering of *Chaos* into an intelligible, visible *Kosmos*. In general, spatial rather than temporal paradigms of order are valorized and plots tend toward the dramatization of moral transgressions and their 'attendant consequences' (Vickers, 1973: ch. 5).

7.2 The principle of polarity

A pervasive principle of coherence in the Greek mythopoeic universe is the principle of polarity; under this description the cosmos is structured according to a dichotomic logic of qualities and forces, distributed around oppositional fields which create semantic structures from which further oppositions, tensions, and antithetical transformations can be produced. The principle of polarity generates literary frames in which experience is troped into image systems of opposing forces and antagonisms. The paradigmatic opposition in the Homeric poems is, of course, the differences between mortals and gods, life and death, male and female, sacred and profane realms. But it is generalizable into the relationships between gods (Zeus and Hera, Athena and Poseidon) and between gods and mortals (Odysseus and Poseidon), and between mortals (Menelaus and Paris, Patroclus and Hector, Achilles and Agamemnon). The generative ground-rule here can be expressed: K *(kosmos)* = *(either) Sacred/Profane*. Applying elementary transformational rules produces more complex plot themes and structures in which mythical incidents, events, and speeches of the following type can be plotted:

- The Kosmos contains Immortals (Sacred) and Mortals (Profane);
- Mortals exist 'in the world';
- The Kosmos is governed by Gods;
- Powerful Gods/Powerless Mortals;
- Mortals living on the Earth/Gods living above the Earth;
- Birth-Suffering-Death for Mortals/Birthless-Deathless-Life for Immortals (thanatos/athanatos);
- Gods oppose the actions of mortals;
- Gods contest the legitimate domain of other gods;

What is polarized into opposite extremes – sacred and profane events for example – may also be coded metaphorically as contradictory bipolar elements: we experience the presence of the sacred only if we simultaneously enunciate the absence of the profane (later Aristotle would formalize this bipolar structure as the Principle of (non-)contradiction: the negation must deny the same thing that the affirmation affirms). The principle of polarity not only admits the construction of narrative elements and plots by means of the linguistic operations of metonymy, synecdoche, simile, and irony, but also encourages the development of further 'paralogical' or chiastic transformations which are fundamental to the development of narrative structures: (i) *Reversal* (of sacred and profane, honour and dishonour, good and evil, mortals and immortals); (ii) *Inversion* (what was rejected is accepted; what was last becomes first; what was primary becomes secondary); (iii) *Mediation* ('theorizing' the 'middle term' between the sacred and the profane, mortals and immortals – for example producing 'mediating' and 'ambiguous' objects such as man-gods (in Homer, Achilles is born from a man, Peleus and the goddess Thetis), semi-human agents (*daimones*), hybrid creatures (fauns, centaurs, 'spirits', satyrs, androgynous beings, transitional objects 'frozen' between levels of reality (Plato, *Parmenides*, *Sophist*, *Phaedrus*, etc.); (iv) *Fusion and Reconciliation* (the identity of opposites in, say, Heraclitus' day-night, winter-summer, war-peace, satiety-hunger, etc.); (v) *Chiastic transformation* (in the imagery of Hesiod, Heraclitus, and Parmenides); (vi) *Irony* (the reversal of order or appearance of the opposite signifier); (vii) Tropes of *Paradox*, *Agon*, and *Conflict* – among the most immediate and pervasive of these operations in subsequent Greek poetry and literature (for example in the complex choral odes of Pindar and Bacchylides). Following the structuralist theory of myth as a 'mediation' of contradictions, Jean-Pierre Vernant underscores the importance of these logological operators as follows:

> Myth is not only characterized by its polysemy and by the interlocking of its many different codes. In the unfolding of its narrative and the selection of the semantic fields it uses, it brings into play shifts, slides, tensions, and oscillations between the very terms that are distinguished or opposed in its categorical framework; it is as if, while being mutually exclusive these terms at the same time in some way imply one another. Thus myth brings into operation a form of logic that we may describe, in contrast to the logic of non-contradiction of the philosophers, as a logic of the ambiguous, the equivocal, a logic of polarity.
>
> (1990: 260)

Opposing elements can be 'fused' to create a third category (the *coincidentia oppositorum* – for example, the androgynous symbol uniting male and female predicates: *Male-Female* in contrast to the polarized structure of *Male/Female* (Plato's *Symposium*; Aristophanes' *Frogs*, etc.)). But in these verbal systems the content shapes the form. And the 'reconciliation of conflicts' is certainly not the only structure in play in mythic discourse. More abstract symbolic networks can be developed from this simple structure – for example, the 'boundary' between Night and Day in Hesiod, the *Apeiron* as the matrix of all opposites in Anaximander, the mediation of *past* and *future* by the *now* (in Demosthenes' *On the Crown*), the creative release of *tradition* and *innovation* in *repetition* (Aristotle's *Poetics*), the reconciliation of *particularity* and *universality* in a *concrete universal* (in the personifications and agencies of the orators and sophists):

> Ultimately, the mythologist has to admit to a certain inadequacy as he is forced to turn to the linguist, logicians, and mathematicians in the hope that they may provide him with the tool that he lacks, namely the structural model of another kind of logic: not the binary logic of yes and no but a logic different from that of the *logos*.
> (Vernant, 1990: 260)

Consider, for example, the generative possibilities of dichotomic conflicts in dividing the 'realms' of the Olympians and the Chthonian gods, the compound ironic mediations developed by later Greek tragedy[22] and, in the realm of theoretical thoughts, the so-called law of the excluded middle. 'It is evident, therefore, that there is a negation opposed to every affirmation and an affirmation opposed to every negation' as Aristotle notes in his *On Interpretation* 17a26.

7.3 The principle of hierarchy

The principle of hierarchy ranks and valorizes the binary opposition produced by the polarity principle. Thus we produce a vertical ordering or stratification where the superior member of the superordinate set is marked positively and the inferior member of the subordinate set is marked negatively (immortals/mortals, sacred/profane, up/down, sky/earth, light/darkness, etc.). The asymmetry of the constructed couplet can then be troped as a consequence of the hierarchical relationship of 'natural' superordination- subordination (sacred *versus* profane). Further interpretive work may 'reify' the hierarchy as a reflection of the natural order of things. Once established in the repertoires of tropes and figures a range of other semantic asymmetries are possible. For example, the 'inferior' element can be displaced from the space created by the 'superior' element. 'Inferior' and 'superior' can be glossed as reflections of the real rather than tropological principles. Applications of this rule might create such logological objects as: *Gods/Mortals, Infinite/Finite, Life/Death, Justice/Injustice, One/Many, Olympians/Chthonians, Unity/Heterogeneity, Male/Female, Good/Evil, War/Peace, Philia/Neikos*.

It should be observed, however, that the phallocentric axiom of 'goodness/evil' runs through all these metaphorical rankings (and would, in later Greek culture, become a prominent device in the well-known Pythagorean Table of Opposites and, through the subterranean impact of Pythagorean ideology, enter the fabric of Western European philosophy). To understand the organization of the field of Greek mythology we thus require more than a simple reduction of discourse to a binary grammar, and this 'understanding' can only mean a detailed analysis of the historical contexts shaping the mythical tradition. Indeed this older axiological code continues to inform the European way of visual thinking which spontaneously projects problems into binary terms: *is the Cosmos a unity (One) or a multiplicity (Many)? Is the substance of all things material or ideal? Am I primarily body or soul?*

7.4 The principle of analogy

A further narrative principle enables the objects produced by hierarchical stratification to be extended by analogy to other relations, events, experiences, and object domains, forming structures such as *Becoming/Being, Permanence/Change, Birth/Death, Health/Illness, Blindness/Sight, Knowledge/Ignorance, Bound/Unbound, Aristocracy/Democracy*. But once more, the process of extending and elaborating these figures requires social and historical explanation. In this respect the linguistic displacements of metaphoric and metonymic extension become crucial to analogic thinking (works like the *Oresteia* and *Oedipus Tyrannus* provide a rich harvest of these symbolic permutations) and, in a later period, to forms of typological thinking in different social environments.

7.5 The principle of taxonomy

This principle extends Hierarchy and Analogy by means of a rule of recursivity producing further binary orders and subclassifications (classifications of opposed elements – as in the famous table of binary opposites found in Pythagorean cosmology, adversarial groups of classes, and so on). This, of course, is what Durkheim and Mauss refer to as 'systems of hierarchized notions' producing 'primitive classifications': 'Things are not simply arranged by them in the form of isolated groups, but these groups stand in fixed relationships to each other and together form a single whole' (1963: 81–8). Such classifications articulate and render intelligible 'the relations which exist between things' – in connecting ideas and unifying knowledge they represent 'a first philosophy of nature'.

7.6 The anthropomorphic principle

This principle facilitates the construction of higher-order narrative objects and configurations through analogy, symbolization, plot extension, narrative elaboration, personification, and taxonomy, typically by projecting symbolic structures on the model of the human body or human actions and functions (including schemata drawn from the social and political world). Animating abstractions through personification is common to myth, epic poetry, and tragic drama: Arete, Eris, Eros, Nike, Eirene, Sophia, Peitho, Tyche, Dike (Clytemnestra's 'Not my hand alone, but *Dike* slew him' (Sophocles, *Electra*

528) and '*Dike* will catch me' (Sophocles, *Eurypylus*, *Select Papyri*: vol. 3, 17), etc.). In semiotic terms this kind of hypostatization is one of the basic preconditions for generalizing symbolic classifications from concrete into abstract phenomenal domains. And while not native to allegory it will later form the principle structuring device of allegorical consciousness. Lévi-Strauss, in particular, has stressed the networking mechanisms of symbolic systems:

> This modelling of the appearance according to specific, elemental, or categorical schemes has psychological as well as physical consequences. A society which defines its segments in terms of high and low, sky and land, day and night, can incorporate social or moral attitudes, such as conciliation and aggression, peace and war, justice and policing, good and bad, order and disorder, etc., into the same structure of opposition. In consequence, it does not confine itself to abstract contemplation of a system of correspondence but rather furnishes the individual members of these segments with a pretext and sometimes even provocation to distinguish themselves by their behaviour.
>
> (1966: 170)

8 CONCLUSION – MYTH AS THE MATRIX OF LOGOS

This very brief sociology of narrative functions serves to highlight the role of polarity in Greek thought and cultural life more generally.[23] Myth during the Archaic period appears to have elaborated these narrative principles to create an order-centred, anthropomorphic, and agonistic world-view. Conversely, the obsession with principles of binary order expresses the tenacious hold which earlier modes of thinking held upon the Greeks at the end of the Dark Ages. The expression 'world-view' is emblematically suited to the visualized themes of Greek mythology. By the middle of the eighth century – the period which saw the construction of alphabetic writing and the first experiments in monumental statuary – the assumption that reality *was* a unitary world order or *kosmos*, hierarchically structured, governed by an agonistic pantheon of divine beings animated by conflictual, 'all-too-human' passions and motives, had become a basic axiom of Greek popular culture. These processes helped shape the Classical age of videological culture.

A literary fantasy premised on a rejection of the chthonian past had, as it were, crystallized into an ontological truth, a narrative had been reified into a real structure. While this ontological hypostatization never fully replaced the carnivalesque folk-ontologies of popular religion and matriarchal folklore, it operated as a fecund resource of adversarial images and metaphors for a whole range of cultural practices. Hence from this moment onward narrative concretizations of the mythological world-view and its underlying ontology can be found throughout Greek pottery and sculpture, in the field of figurative art, in philosophy and even in the practices of medicine and political experience. Significantly the agonistic paradigm which opposed finite heterogeneity to infinite unity began to spread beyond the limits of mythology, and the logocentric quest to name and identify one absolute totality – and thus the 'one Truth' – behind the manifold appearances and changeable shapes of phenomenal events drew its inspiration and cultural mandate from this new matrix. *Early Greek mythological discourse, in other words, provided a generative charter for a phallogocentric view of the world and its eidetic regions.*

More radically, we might also interpret the Polarity principle and its narrative effects as one of the decisive sources of linguistic reflexivity itself with its acute consciousness of the irremedial, agonistic polysemy of signification and the idea of human existence bound to the open textures and belligerent contexts of speech and textuality. The agonism of narrative polysemy even suggested itself as a figure for the life of signification and the irreducible interplay of identity and difference evidenced in all things.[24] We again underline the fact that this view of language and cultural life legitimates a phallocentric view of experience. The generic agonism would resurface in literary culture as the great theme of Hesiod's *Theogony* and in the philosophical poems of the Presocratic thinkers. Polarity is thus more than a clue to the sociologics of mythic praxis; it celebrates the endless diacritics of the *logos* itself.[25]

The Greek obsession with organizing experience into rigid visual polarities, the Apollonian desire for imposed order, symmetry, and proportion, and the anxious awareness of the threat of difference, semantic slippage, and polysemy are anxieties made increasingly urgent in the later part of the eighth century by a concatenation of socioeconomic and political changes. For the 'founding fathers' of city-state culture *mythos* was increasingly seen as a gathering place for the unsettling forces of *eros*. For the Greek aristocracy, myth came to symbolize everything that was inimical to an ordered society. And because of its intimate association with *eros*, myth had to be disciplined and brought within the *polis* as a civilizing force. The matrix of discourse needed to be regulated by the phallocentric word of Law, Reason, and Knowledge. In this way the dialectic of formless matrix and patriarchal discipline surfaces as one of the hermeneutical keys to ancient Greek ideology.

From a logological perspective we need to understand the ways in which such 'dangerous' semiotic experiences were symbolically regulated, how the polysemic mimesis of matriarchal myth and poetry were controlled to form more disciplined projects and practices, and how these created the field for later cultural systems. This perhaps is the original 'anxiety of influence' between myth and rational philosophy. In the following chapters I will be particularly concerned with the attempt of the new language of reflection to discipline what was felt to be chaotic plurisignificance and subversive affective experience. I will also explore the irony that the *eros* of myth was countered by the civilizing *eros* of *logos* – the dream of conceptually mastering the structure of factuality by constructing realms of objective knowledge. But in keeping with the logological perspective outlined in Volume 1 we must also investigate the genesis of practices by locating them in the social dynamics of specific, class- and gender-based formations – in this case, in the period of social crisis which occasioned the forms of life of early Greek philosophy. Before turning to the Homeric resolution of the dialectic of patriarchal control and matriarchal creativity, totality and infinity, stable signification and polysemy, it is useful to summarize some of these interrelated themes.

First I have suggested that myth institutes an oral tradition of effective histor(icit)y in which the varied rhetorics of later Greek reflexivity were developed. As a dialogical process this occurred through a complex, agonistic series of discursive struggles. A sociology of reflexive logics and thought patterns – in this specific case of practices linked to the earlier discourses of myth, poetry, and early philosophy – indicates the enormous difficulties and obstacles that had to be overcome prior to the emergence of anything like a theoretical problematic. What began as a search for origins has uncovered a dialectic of traditions, an agonistic fusion of interpretive praxis at work within the institutions of archaic Greek *mythopoiesis*. And it is this agonism which appears to have occasioned a crisis within the very discourse and language of myth.[26] Traces of this struggle pervade the language and thought worlds of Greek philosophy and, by implication, the discourse formations which derive their orientations from this grammar.

The age which historians characterize as the Greek Middle Ages or Archaic period (*c*. 850–500 BC) is certainly a 'dark period of transition and creation'[27] in almost every field of social, political, and cultural life. The generalized adversarial processes during this period of Greek history decisively influenced the intellectual struggles which formed the background of Homeric literature, Hesiodic poetry, and early Greek philosophy. We would expect something like a dialectic of transference and countertransference, interpretation and reinterpretation, assimilation and rejection, to be operative in the discursive field of Archaic Greek culture. And once we view the struggles of early Greek civilization in polemical terms we see the traces of these conflicts inscribed in the Homeric corpus, the poetry of Hesiod, and the textual fragments of the Presocratic thinkers. Of course 'countertransference' is a limited metaphor for logological processes. It is more useful to think in terms of a *dialogical agonism*. We will see that the texts of the Presocratic philosophers exemplify the kind of hermeneutic dependence of later writing practices upon earlier oral tradi- tions (the complex writing practices of Anaximander, Heraclitus, and Xenophanes are striking instances of this process of revisionary reading, as we shall show in detail in Volume 3, where the development of a new *style* of philosophical poem and prose depends on a critical *contestation* of the earlier forms of myth and poetry – an *adversarial* relationship which can only be fully understood in dialogic terms as part of the great transition from oral to literate communication).

Important methodological and theoretical principles follow from this way of posing the problem of the genealogy of discourses. If *mythopoiesis* provided the metaphorical schemata of later modalities of *poiesis* and if these later forms emerged in a dialogical struggle with inherited canons we require more specific genealogies of the emergent forms of polemical reflexivity – explaining how, for instance, the early cosmology of a Heraclitus or the ontological language in the school of Elea, philosophical dialectic from Zeno down to the Sophists, the univocal *episteme* sought by Plato and Aristotle, a purified form of tragic drama (in Euripides) were constructed as attempts to shore up or 'civilize' the transgressive impulses of myth; we need to ask what views of language were presupposed by the earliest philosophers, how *Logos* came to be seen as the exclusive medium of absolute truth – the site where things stand revealed without perspective or shadows; we need to research how the emergence of a new confidence in conceptual discourse emerged, how these changed attitudes authorized new language-games and how, subsequently, these language-games became historically effective in different social contexts; which social groups functioned as mediators in these processes; the decisive material, political, and sociocultural constraints on their operations of cultural transmission. Of course, such questions invite both sociological and logological responses; but their significance for the culture of later antiquity (and the founding discourses of European thought) resides in the fact that the reflexive rhetorics constructed during this period formed the spiritual horizon which would shape the basic orientations of all subsequent Western thought and praxis. This being the case we now need to go beneath the kind of summary gloss provided by historians of philosophy[28] and explore in detail the transformations of language and attitudes toward knowledge and beliefs incarnated in the intellectual changes and social contexts of this period.

We can make a beginning by exploring the generative features of Greek epic, particularly the powerful rhetorics of self and self-reflexivity articulated in the *Iliad* and *Odyssey*. Chapter 2 will pursue a political hermeneutics of the epic as the source work of early Western self-reflection. We will see that the 'mirror of European self-consciousness' begins with heroic selves at war with one another. Greek agonism, bequeathed by the *polemos* of its mythological past, is reinscribed in the struggle enacted outside the walls of Troy. War and the struggle for honour form one of the fundamental themes of the European tradition of reflection, as it was the medium and agency of the earliest Greek conception of politics. But this generic polemics, as I will argue in subsequent chapters, did not merely constitute the *content* of the Homeric epics – violence would become the *paradigmatic form* of Western discourse.

2
HOMERIC EPIC REFLEXIVITY
Self and self-reflexivity in the *Iliad* and the *Odyssey*

> Just as our literature began with the novel so the Greek began with the epic and dissolved in it.
>
> (Friedrich Schlegel, 1968: 101)
>
> Memory is the epic faculty *par excellence*.
>
> (Walter Benjamin, 1992: 96)

1 Introduction
2 *The logological significance of the Homeric texts*
3 *Epic narrative form(s)*
4 *The world of the poem: the Homeric life-world as a videological universe*
5 *Self and self-reflexivity in the Homeric world*
6 *The civilizing powers of Homeric discourse*
7 *Conclusion: Thersites' revenge*

1 INTRODUCTION

The following chapters are concerned with intellectual developments from a period of ancient Greek history stretching from the beginnings of the Archaic epoch to the beginnings of the Classical age. My main concern in this chapter will be with the emergence of ancient Greek rhetorics of vision and self articulated in the *Iliad* and *Odyssey*. I will trace some of the tangled threads of a complex texture of relationships into which the problematics of self, alterity, and reflexivity were woven in these late products of Greek oral culture. Sections 2 and 3 describe the emergence of epic literature and the generic characteristics of the Homeric texts. In Section 4, I analyze the videological universe created by epic literacy as a context for exploring the nature of Homeric selfhood in Section 5. Finally in Section 6, I situate epic poetry in its historical context as a constitutive medium of early Greek self-reflection. As my general approach follows the form of a reflexive sociological poetics this study is not intended as an exercise in the sociology *of* literature, but attempts to uncover the sociology implicit *in* the epic text.

2 THE LOGOLOGICAL SIGNIFICANCE OF THE HOMERIC TEXTS

What we call the beginning is often the end.

(T. S. Eliot, 'Little Gidding')

We have no direct evidence of the person or life of Homer. Indeed many scholars regard 'Homer' as an iconic name for the Greek epic tradition itself – thinking of *epos* quite literally as the 'word' or 'culture' of ancient Greece. Like the pre-Homeric tradition of mythology, Greek epic is a product of anonymous or 'non-authored' discourses transmitted for centuries by word of mouth. As a stream of oral discourse it has no use for the indexical device which opens the first chapter of Thucydides' *History of the Peloponnesian War* (Book 1.1):

> Thucydides the Athenian wrote the history of the war fought between Athens and Sparta, beginning the *logos* at the very outbreak of the war, in the belief that it was going to be a great war and more worth writing about than any of those which had taken place in the past.

The war of the *Iliad* has never taken place, yet will always take place. In comparison with later prose works the *Iliad* and *Odyssey* appear like a visible outcrop from a vast subterranean tradition of oral poetry.

The literary composition of the Homeric texts is usually dated to the decades between 750 and 700 BC. But the intricate text we have today is the work of many centuries of copying, compilation, and editing – a truly 'foundationless' matrix of intertextual work 'poised between enduring tradition and momentary improvisation' (Fränkel, 1975: 8). As the earliest graphic *texts* in the Western tradition, the *Iliad* and *Odyssey* provide evidence of the rapid transition from oral communication to scriptural techniques during the late Archaic period (*c.* 750–500 BC). Some historians have described this epochal change in the eighth century BC as *the Greek literate revolution* (Havelock, 1982, 1986) but its causes and social consequences are still the subject of controversy (Trypanis, 1977: 54–8). When the basic composition of the proto-*Odyssey* was transcribed – probably in the last two decades of the eighth century – mythology had taken up residence in the medium of alphabetic script. With this singular displacement the epic faculty of memory was slowly transformed by the technology of writing into the hermeneutic art of reading. The culture-forming power of oral *mythopoiesis* had been transposed into the *polis*-forming world of the text, with its distinctive techniques of production, reproduction, and transmission. What had been performed for generations as an oral *event* could now be materially transmitted as a mobile textual object.

Although the literate transformation of Greek culture was discontinuous and uneven in its effects on everyday life, in terms of the genealogy of Western consciousness the literary objectification of the oral epic would prove to be a historical event of the first magnitude. While ostensibly celebrating the values and ideals of a warrior society, epic poetry implicitly defined the textual space of visible action and moral thought for the earliest Greek experiments in thought and politics. While other comparable civilizations have produced epic poetry – the *Enuma Elish* and *Erra* in Mesopotamia for example – that has been subsequently used as guides for living and spiritual orientation, only the ancient Greeks literally shaped their social life in terms drawn from the syntax and narrative structures of these encyclopaedic poems (making Homer, in Werner Jaeger's words, the *paideia* of the Greek people). Moreover, as I will try to document below the 'depth grammar' of this *paideia* was structured around the visual thematics and polemical logics of violent praxis: the moral complications of war, the springs of communal conflict, the winning and losing of honour and its ramifications. The very existence of the written text of the *Iliad* is itself the product of layers of polemical literary work. We might relate this to George Steiner's observation that Homer was the first great poet in Western literature 'because he was the first to have understood the infinite resources of the written word' (Steiner and Fagles, eds, 1962: 6–7). The violence of aggressive *self-assertion* marks the beginnings of the inaugural texts of the European tradition. 'In the beginning of poetry is the word, but very near the beginning of poetry on the scale of the *Iliad* is writing' (Steiner and Fagles, eds, 1962: 7). Reduced to its simplest form, my general argument is that the graphic visual language of the *Iliad* and *Odyssey* shaped the fundamental videological themes and imagery of European self-consciousness. I will also suggest that forms of social behaviour and moral practices that entered the arena of this videological space were inflected by the terms of reference of the 'Homeric code'. In short, the Greeks came to look at the world through Homeric eyes.

In speaking of 'epic', then, we are not merely dealing with works of literature in the modern sense of the autonomous 'artwork', but are faced with a generative cultural system, an 'oral encyclopaedia' of moral standards and social conduct that would determine the social, political, and intellectual identity of Classical Greek and Hellenistic civilization (Havelock, 1963: 319). Homeric epic functioned as a matrix of stylized values informing and directing the Graeco-Latin cultural complex for centuries after the disappearance of Greece as an independent political power. In a more extended study we would need carefully to reconstruct the manifestations of Homeric selfhood as they were differentially embodied in changing patterns of orality and literacy in different geographical and social settings. The traditional explanation involving a radical 'scriptural revolution' would have to be expanded to include the whole range of cultural production and an awareness of the discontinuous nature of such long-term processes of ideological change throughout the Hellenic and Hellenistic ages. For our limited purposes we can simply note that Homeric narrative functioned as the generative source for a vast range of expressive cultural practices: tragic drama (Aeschylus' 'slices from the great banquet of Homer'), visual art, sculpture, choral art and music, lyric poetry, oratory, political strategy, educational praxis, architectural paradigms, archaic cosmology and philosophy, Socratic dialectic, Platonic metaphysics, and so forth.[1]

In our preferred terminology, Homeric discourse represents a powerful institution of self-reflection embodied in the central cultural practices and ideological milieu of a whole civilization. It is thus not merely an index of expanded literacy, but a trace of a radical change in the consciousness of the early Archaic period. When Greek society came to reflect on its own origins, identity, and core values it did so by means of verbal repertoires and interpretive schemas drawn from the Homeric canon; and for the Classical period onward it would be no exaggeration to speak of the ideological saturation of social life with imagery and self-representations drawn from the epic heroes of Homeric 'oral literature' (Havelock, 1986: chs 10, 11). In Bruno Bettelheim's words: 'Homer's epics informed those who lived centuries later what it meant to be Greek, and by what images and ideals they were to live their lives and organize their societies' (1990: 123; cf. Fränkel, 1975: 26–7; Webster, 1959; ch. 1). Homeric *paideia* became the dominant moral tradition, 'the last distillation of the Dark Ages' in Peter Levi's phrase (1985: 25; cf. 59–60), and a practical method of cultural reflection. It was through the Homeric logics of Attic tragedy and classical education (*paideusis*) that later Greek civilization mapped its axiological origins and reflected upon its own contradictory identity. If Greek art, architecture, and material culture evolved into public displays of three-dimensional, sculptured epics (culminating in the great public works of a Hegias, Myron, or Phidias), the most pervasive and long-lasting impact of the epic was exerted by the unconscious generalization of narrative logics which helped to disseminate Greek thought patterns throughout the Graeco-Roman world. Oral epic, in other words, became historically effective as a powerful set of discursive practices and collective self-representations (Levi describes fifth-century tragedy as 'an urban substitute for epic poetry' (1985: 150)). This, we suspect, is the materialist core of what historians of Greece have called the Hellenic spirit, the 'miracle of Greece'. To analyze these formations it is necessary to undertake an archaeology of the imaginary formations of early Greek literary communication and its cultural fields.

We have, then, the unique phenomenon of a civilization virtually self-constituted through patterns of symbolic images and narrative plots derived from the stylized language-games of an aesthetic genre: the 'discourse on discourse' which forms the dialogical medium and fabric of Homeric poetry. The central claim here is that Classical Greek civilization codified its sense of identity, its idealized vocabularies of moral conduct, and its conception of the natural world in the specific rhetorics of Homeric discourse: in other words, *epic is not a 'domain' or 'sphere' of Greek culture, but rather its generative matrix of reflexive self-consciousness.*

What follows is thus – in the language of Volume 1 – a logological investigation of the constitutive cultural work of reflexive representation.

HOMERIC EPIC REFLEXIVITY

The Homeric epic as the paideia of Greece

The Homeric poems present a singular fusion of oral mythic symbolism, stylized dialogue, and narrative poetry. Organized in the metre of dactylic hexameter the *Iliad* and *Odyssey* were transcribed into a scriptural dialect of Ionian Greek shortly after the middle of the eighth century BC.[2] They can, however, be traced to even older traditions of epic verse (and perhaps writing) in the city-states of the eastern Aegean, the *poleis* of Ionian Greece. The long heroic poem conventionally called the *Iliad* (15,693 lines of hexameter verse compared to the *Odyssey*'s 12,110 lines) emerged as a remarkable product of an intertextual collaboration between the exponents of a rich oral tradition (we might better speak of *orature* rather than *literature* here) and a group of early masters of writing; the product of this unique enterprise effectively inaugurated European literature as a self-defining project. This is why Victor Ehrenberg can refer with some justification to the earliest period of Greek social history as 'the Age of the Singers' (1964: 1–22).

As *written* works the *Iliad* and *Odyssey* are the earliest transcribed poems of Western literature; the availability of written versions of these stories in the late eighth century BC presupposes a community skilled in the arts of writing. The *Iliad* was probably transcribed around 750 BC, the *Odyssey* is a later work, committed to writing perhaps two generations after this date. If a single poet was responsible for both works, he would have been born around two decades before 750 BC, and probably came from the colonial city of Chios or Smyrna on the west coast of Asia Minor. If different authors are admitted (as the so-called Separatists in the Homeric Question maintain) the texts may be separated by as much as eighty years (i.e. *c.* 750–740 BC for the *Iliad* and *c.* 680–660 BC for the *Odyssey*). Because of their unique cultural status the Homeric epics can be viewed as both a terminal product of earlier oral-mythic traditions and as instituting a new literate tradition in their own right.[3] In many respects the *Iliad* – like the *Mahabharata* – can be understood as both an auspicious and a terminal text: it represents the moment of culmination and destruction of an ancient oral poetic tradition, and the beginning of a new type of communicative institution, 'literature'. As a product of the Greek 'Dark Age' the epic genre appears like a brilliant supernovum in a collapsing galaxy. M. L. West has called these works 'the supreme monument of ancient epic poetry' (in Dover, ed., 1980: 15). In logological terms, the Greek *epos* traces the tradition from the verbal techniques of *orature* to the reflexive stratagems of *literature*. The textual and social possibilities created by this new technology would determine the visual orientations of Greek consciousness and shape the basic intellectual forms of European culture for centuries to come. As Havelock notes, 'Greek literacy changed not only the means of communication, but also the shape of the Greek consciousness' (1986: 17).

Traditions of primary heroic epic or long narrative song cycles can be found in very different social formations and historical periods. A brief survey of the genre would include the Sumerian *Epic of Gilgamesh* (c. 2000 BC), perhaps the oldest written epic in any literature, large sections of the *Old Testament* – the books known as *Exodus* for example, the Hindu *Ramayana* and East Indian *Mahabharata* (Great War of the Bharatas, c. 400–200 BC), the *Sagas* of Iceland tracing the adventures of Njal, the Old Norse or Scandinavian *Eddas* (the Havamal for example), the Finnish *Kalevala*, the epic legends of the Mongol Warlords, the Anglo-Saxon *Chronicles*, *Beowulf*, and *Maldon* down to Geoffrey of Monmouth's saga of Brut, the 'Trojan' founder of the British people and even the work of Geoffrey Chaucer (*Canterbury Tales*), the anonymous *Sir Gawain and the Green Knight*, and Sir Thomas Malory's *Morte d'Arthur*. In the literature of the Middle Ages we have the German *Nibelungenlied*, the Norman *Chanson de Roland* (*The Song of Roland*, composed around 1100), the court poetry of the *jongleurs* including the Arthurian romances of Chrétien de Troyes (c. 1170–90), Hartmann von Aue, Wolfram von Eschenbach (*fl.* c. 1195–1225, author of the *Willehalm* and *Parzival*) and Gottfried von Strassburg, the medieval German *Spielmänner*, and the tales of *El Cid* in the Iberian peninsula (*El Cantar de Mio Cid* – *The Song of the Cid* in the twelfth century). Traditions of primary oral epic produced the Zulu epic of *Shaka*, a legendary leader of the Zulu peoples in the early part of the nineteenth century as well as the Serbo-Croatian folk-traditions compiled by Milman Parry in 1934 (in research that was continued by his student Albert Lord; Lord provides a concise summary of the field in Wace and Stubbings, eds, 1962: 179–214).

We should also distinguish between the primary epic genre and the tradition of secondary literary epic.[4] The latter category includes the *Argonautica* of Apollonius Rhodius[5] and Virgil's *Aeneid*, which was explicitly designed as a Romanized version of the *Iliad* (Aulus Gellius also refers to an *Odyssey* by the poet Lucius Livius (*Attic Nights*, VI.vii.10–12)). It also embraces the minor Latin epics of Claudian and Prudentius (the latter's *Psychomachia*). In the early modern period Dante (1265–1321) conceived and wrote the *Divina Commedia* (*Divine Comedy* 1307–21) as a work inspired by Virgil's epic, informed perhaps by secondary knowledge of Book XI of the *Odyssey* which takes Odysseus into the Underworld (Dante's *Inferno* and *Purgatorio* are essentially allegorical texts on the same basic theme). We should also mention the Italian poets Boccaccio (in his *Teseide*), Ariosto (*Orlando furioso*) and Tasso (*Gerusalemme liberata*). Chaucer's *Canterbury Tales* have often been canvassed for inclusion in a medieval epic canon and Milton used the epic events of the Old Testament, the blinding of Samson for example, for his *Paradise Lost* as would Thomas Mann in his 'Joseph' novels. In the eighteenth century we find the parodic genre of the mock epic (*The Rape of the Lock*, *The Dunciad*, *The Battle of the Books* are among the most famous of these), the 'bourgeois epic' of the long English novels such as Fielding's *Joseph Andrews* and *Tom Jones*, and the fabricated 'folk epic' of Macpherson's *Ossian* and Percy's *Reliques of Ancient English Poetry*. In the twentieth century James Joyce modelled his own *Ulysses* on Homer's mythical panorama while Hermann Broch's *Der Tod des Vergil* (1945) recapitulates the last hours of the life of the Roman poet in a monumental prose work. The Cretan writer Nikos Kazantzakis (1885–1957) went even further, attempting to rewrite Homer's epic in verse form as a modern *Odyssey* (its 33,333 lines surpassing the original in length).

The success of the novel form of Joyce and Broch and the failure of Kazantzakis' attempt to revive the epic poetic genre are germane to the thesis of the present chapter. From the perspective of a sociological poetics it is ultimately the differences of communal functions which separate the primary oral epic from its later literary simulacra. The former constitutes the art of a living culture, a collective archive through which a way of life objectifies its reality and expresses its identity. Primary epic codifies practical logics for a whole culture. This is the core of sociological truth in Plato's resentful praise of Homer as the educator of Hellas (*Rep.* 606E; cf. *Protagoras* 325E–326A; Isocrates, *Pangyricus* 159). After the path-breaking researches of scholars like Heinrich Schliemann (1822–90; his archaeology of Troy and Mycenaea in the 1870s displaying epic qualities in its own right), Michael Ventris (1922–56), Carl W. Blegen (1887–1971), Milman Parry (1902–35), and Albert Lord, Homeric research now regards the *Iliad* and *Odyssey* as the culmination of a long poetic tradition of prehistoric oral poetry stretching back to the Mycenaean age (1400–1200 BC) or even to the Late Helladic period (the Late Bronze Age and the Early Iron Age beginning around 1580 BC); epic stories were transmitted by professional rhapsodes (or bards, *aoidoi*) patronized by royal courts and aristocratic families, each learning his craft in an oral apprenticeship tradition. But as written epics, it is now usual to regard the city-states of Ionian Greece as the centre for their diffusion throughout Greece, reaching a high degree of articulation around the middle of the eighth century. Like the Semitic Old Testament, the texts of the *Iliad* and *Odyssey* are palimpsests created from the confluence of a number of different oral streams, compiled and 'stitched'[6] into writing over a period of five centuries or more (from the destruction of Mycenaean civilization around 1200 BC, through the Dorian invasions from the north over two centuries from 1200–950, and the ensuing migration to Asia Minor from 1000 BC, to the formation of Greek-speaking colonies and the rise of Greek alphabetic script around 800–750 BC). I will return to this historical background in Section 6.

The Homeric epic as a historical magma of discursive styles and texts authorizes our use of the metaphors 'matrix' and cultural 'sedimentation' for the genre. The logological perspective directs research to the interaction of metaphors, textual practices, and discourses in verbal culture. These concepts sensitize us to the fact that the epic was by no means a naive or purely literary structure; in fact ancient Greek epic evolved into a highly crafted song cycle performed with musical accompaniment, a complex intertextual fusion of very different cultural codes, dialectal linguistic patterns, diverse thematics and motifs; it is therefore an instructive exemplar of the stratified nature of many textual formations.⁷ What generations of literary scholars have described as the epic 'mirror' or 'mimesis' of the Greek mind will be approached as a complex intertextual formation. Instead of mirror imagery an archaeological metaphor is more appropriate: epic functions as an archive of sedimented traces and schemata, a tribal memory of moral paradigms and narratives. Without Homer, no Greek culture; without the epic, no tragic drama or philosophy. This is the kernel of truth in the endlessly repeated claim that European history begins with the Greeks and more particularly with the reflexive syntax of the epic form.⁸ But as we have seen in Chapter 1, 'begin' and 'origin' are complex cultural constructions in their own right. The epic is not a literal begining, but a sedimentation and fusion of oral and literate knowledge.

Another logological directive is the idea that changes in communication technologies and discursive forms should not be separated from the history of institutions. From our analysis of the social dynamics of reflexivity in Volume 1 we can anticipate that 'the education of Hellas' was not an unmediated or homogeneous process. Without the organized practices of reflexivity and specific material preconditions, innovations in the techniques of communication and self-reflection will have minimal long-term effects. The creation of Homeric culture (or what might be better described as 'the Homerization of Archaic culture') from the Archaic to the Classical period and into Hellenistic Greece and beyond, presupposed definite institutional conditions. The first indispensable condition was the existence of a professional guild of singers (*aoidoi*) specializing in the codification and transmission of traditions of epic song traditions. And related to this, the existence of material support for such groups – here provided by the ruling class of aristocratic patrons. Homeric literature survived as a repository of pre-classical knowledge because of the concentrations of material wealth, power, and status in the hands of the Greek aristocracy. And, as Ehrenberg has observed, the pervasive influence of Homeric ideology depended upon the remarkable staying power of the Greek aristocracy:

> the aristocratic class, through all the vicissitudes of its history, acted as a kind of guardian of epic poetry. When the performance of this poetry ... was taken over by the rhapsodes, and Homer, as it were, became the property of the whole people, this was only possible because the nobles had maintained a leadership and an influence which was just as much cultural as political. It was a legacy that made poetry the predecessor of philosophy and the guide for Greek society.
>
> (1964: 10)

Max Weber also emphasized the same constellation of circumstances:

> In the Hellenic polis and in Rome there was no state bureaucracy that might have created a clerical educational system. It was only in part a fateful historical accident that Homer, the literary product of a secular

aristocracy which was most irreverent towards the gods, remained the major vehicle of literary education – which explains Plato's deep hatred against him – and prevented any theological rationalization of the religious powers. The decisive fact was the complete absence of a clerical system of education.

(1968: vol. 3, 1145)

Another critical precondition lay in the field of education. While earlier Greek education was primarily concerned with the practical training of body and mind in those skills deemed essential for an active military and political life – with Sparta in the sixth century as the extreme case – toward the end of the sixth century we see the beginnings of a 'high cultural' literate tradition involving the recitation and rote learning of texts from the Homeric canon (which by then also included the Homeric Hymns and Epic Cycles). The material resources required to sustain these cultural regimes were increasingly controlled by the new aristocracy and rich middle classes of the emerging city-states. As an orally-based education system, knowledge of the mythological tradition formed the central framework for the general curriculum.

If the original transmission of epic was primarily the achievement of an agrarian ruling *élite* patronizing professional rhapsodes as they supported the games and other public festivals, the penetration of the 'tribal encyclopaedia' into the literary consciousness of Classical Greece was a product of the growth of enlightened tyranny and the long-term institutionalization of oral mythology and literacy during the sixth and fifth centuries – the introduction of reading, writing, grammar, and poetic composition into the curriculum (for example in Athens under the 'tyranny' of Peisistratus from 546 to 527 BC and the Peisistratidai) encouraged the development of a distinctive pan-Hellenic ideology. We have a perfect example of the fusion of politics and culture as Homeric texts were transcribed and copied and, even more importantly, performed in the civic domains of the *polis*. What was first sponsored by the aristocracy and Ionian merchant princes was continued first by the Greek tyrants, and later by the reformed aristocratic families of the fifth century. Homeric discourse, in short, became the possession of a ruling *élite* which effectively managed the economic and political life of the city-states down until the end of the fifth century.

Peisistratus (or, as some historians maintain, his son Hipparchus) prescribed complete readings from the works of Homer at the Panathenaic Festivals and authorized a body of Ionian scribes to codify the various texts of Homer into a unified, consistent text (cf. Plato or Pseudo-Plato, *Hipparchus* 228B–C). The availability of this so-called Peisistratean Recension further encouraged rote learning and, later, grammatical analysis and critical interpretation of the Homeric poems. We should note the emergence of a network of relations linking the written epic to institutions of reflexivity and systems of political authority (Peisistratus' commission, the Homeric prescription for rhapsodes and writers of tragic drama at the Panathenaia, the role of alphabetic script, the introduction of scroll manuscripts, and so on). This constellation of factors encouraged the production of further manuscript copies of the *Iliad* and *Odyssey* (originally these would have been owned by the very wealthy or by the city-state itself) which, in turn, created a market for all things Homeric (from pottery painted with scenes from Homeric narrative – appearing as early as 680–670 B.C., 'Homeric sculpture' in the works of Phidias, wall-painting (e.g. Polygnotus), designs on armour, to texts from Homer on the conduct of civic festivals, war, and foreign policy – recall that the young Alexander of Macedonia identified his own ambitions and attitudes with the figure of Achilles, his favourite hero from the *Iliad*, and is said to have taken a copy of the *Iliad* on his campaigns.

What began as a local political strategy of the Peisistratids in Athens took root and proliferated as the basic charter of the Classical world-view. We have, in sum, the basic elements of an ideological field. And the symbolic worlds of this field, as logological analysts would say, became real in their practical effects and consequences.

Peisistratus achieved a temporary hegemony by both rebuilding the material structure of Athens and establishing a common ideology for the Athenians. If we can accept the testimony of later commentators, it was the Peisistratids (c. 560–510 BC) who actively cultivated literacy as a way of ideologically consolidating their own authority and hegemony; later writers also suggest that it was Peisistratus himself who first established a public library at Athens stocked with 'books relating to the liberal arts':

> the Athenians themselves added to this collection with considerable diligence and care; but later Xerxes, when he got possession of Athens and burned the entire city except the citadel, removed the whole collection of books and carried them off to Persia. Finally, a long time afterwards, king Seleucus, who was surnamed Nicantor, had all those books taken back to Athens.
> (Aulus Gellius, *Attic Nights* VII, xvii, 1–2)

Philological and linguistic research also supports the hypothesis of a sixth-century Athenian compilation of the *Iliad* and *Odyssey* (cf. Lycurgus, *Against Leocrates* 102: 'he [Homer] was a poet of such worth that they passed a law that every four years at the Panathenaea he alone of all the poets should have his works recited'). As W. A. Camps has argued:

> The observed influence of Attic dialect on the text we have may indeed indicate that a version preserved at Athens was its parent; though this influence could also be due to the fact that the Attic dialect was the basis of the all-purpose brand of Greek that spread as a *lingua franca* over the Eastern Mediterranean from the fourth century BC, and must have had

its effects on the wording in reproduction of such universally popular but linguistically antiquated works as the Homeric poems.

(1980: 82–3, n. 22)

Every major fourth and third-century Greek library had as its centrepiece a 'complete' version of the Homeric epics. In the first part of the second century AD the Roman orator Aelius Aristides was still marvelling at the Athenian libraries ('the libraries (*biblion*) are such as clearly nowhere else on earth, and are a particularly proper ornament for Athens' *Panathenaic Oration* 354). But the great work of compilation and editing was only systematically undertaken in the second century BC by the Alexandrian scholar Aristarchus of Samothrace (*c*. 215–*c*. 145 BC). It was from the Museum and Library of Alexandria that copies of Homer were disseminated throughout the Greek-speaking world.

We have of course to 'bracket' the modern concept of the library as a scholarly resource or form of entertainment. In the ancient world libraries were primarily instruments of civic status and political power. As such they were vulnerable to the vicissitudes of war and changing political fortunes. Aulus Gellius continues his account of the Peisistratidean library with a parallel description of the fate of the Library at Alexandria:

> At a later time an enormous quantity of books, nearly seven hundred thousand volumes, was either acquired or written in Egypt under the kings known as Ptolemies; but these were all burned during the sack of the city in our first war with Alexandria [the Roman occupation of 48 BC], not intentionally or by anyone's order, but accidentally by the auxiliary soldiers.
>
> (*Attic Nights*, VII, xvii, 3)

Suetonius (b. *c*. AD 69/70) reports that the Emperor Claudius, a prolific historian in his own right who wrote historical works in Greek, 'twenty books of Etruscan history and eight of Carthaginian', added another library annex to the old Museum at Alexandria 'and it was provided that in the one his Etruscan History should be read each year from beginning to end, and in the other his Carthaginian, by various readers in turn, in the manner of public recitations' (Suetonius, *The Lives of the Caesars*, Book V, XLII). Plato may well have been sensitive to the 'politics of literacy' when, with a deprecating and ironic intent, he described Homer (perhaps a Homer mediated by the 'tyrant' Peisistratus) as the educator of Hellas.

The other great medium of transmission (and corresponding institution of reflexivity) after oral and pedagogic recitation, followed from the consolidation of the Panathenaic Games in the sixth century, where contests between Homeric singers (*aoidoi*) and reciters (*rhapsodes*) were almost as popular as the athletic contests themselves. But while the Games were periodic festivals, the education system functioned continuously. By the end of the sixth century literary education had assimilated the corpus of myths and Homeric texts for its own disciplinary purposes. Greek educational regimes began to move from the palaestra and the gymnasium to the locations of the 'grammar' school (and for a select *élite*, professional schools of oratory, philosophy, and medicine). Finally in the fourth century Homeric exegesis combined with the Isocratean programme of oratorical instruction triumphed over the traditional disciplines of Archaic Greece and the Platonic-Aristotelian curricula. In Hellenistic Greece down to the Roman period this Classical rhetorical and grammatical curriculum achieved such a dominant position that the 'Greek pattern' became synonymous with 'learning' down to the early modern period. Athens thus helped to turn Homeric poetry into a truly pan-hellenic ideology (Mackail, 1926: 20–1; Nagy, 1990). 'The Homeric rhapsodes turned into mere reciters who declaimed and interpreted the fixed text, and eventually into schoolmasters and grammarians' (Fränkel, 1975: 22). Without hyperbole we can say that the grammatical tradition in education and the grammatical form of life more generally (pedagogy as a careful disciplining and schematizing of the child's mind and behaviour) arose on the ruins of the Homeric institutional ideal, but in response to the continuing vitality of Homeric ideology.[9] In this way Graeco-Latin civilization became a 'hostage' to Homeric ideology (Lucian, *Vera Historia* II.20 makes the point by punning on the etymology of *homeros*, a theme that was already apparent to the authors of the Greek work, *The Contest of Homer and Hesiod* 314).

3 EPIC NARRATIVE FORM(S)

As a 'monument of oral education', classical epic preserved the repetitive impact of oral storytelling (Havelock, 1982: 14; Fränkel, 1975: 6–25). But by the sixth century the rhythms and dynamics of oral performance had been translated into a powerful literate technology. As Havelock observed, the Muse had learned to write (1986). We have already suggested that epic's overwhelming impact on non-literate forms of artistic praxis from the eighth century down to the Hellenistic period depended directly on its flexible plotting and, more particularly, its videological thematics. In this section I will begin to document this claim.

The *Iliad* is first and foremost a narrative *envisioning* of the heroic ethos of power and power struggles. By reinscribing epic's visual grammar Greek art became figurative, representational, and pictorially allegorical (Eric Auerbach in fact claimed that the epic genre overwhelmingly determined the norms for 'the representation of reality' in European literature, 1957: 1ff.). Art forms such as wall painting, painted pottery, relief sculpture, and public architecture evolved their distinctive 'realistic' style by transposing the visual concreteness of Homeric narrative into other media: in the terminology of semiotics, a dominant narrative code elaborating the logic of conflict was extended to non-literary practices to create a range of secondary signifying practices. The dramatic visual syntax of epic encouraged the rapid evolution of figural semiosis which in turn generalized the conventions of heroic visual representation across a wide range of ideological systems (cf. Robertson, 1975: chs. 1–3). In this way Homeric action narratives helped to disseminate the dichotomic logics of mythology (see Chapter 1 above) and create the paradigms of Classical Greek visual culture.

Originally the epic tales were composed for a specific audience of knowledgeable listeners rather than readers. This apparent obstacle to continuous appreciation actually served as a motive for the invention of a range of visualization techniques – to ensure that epic's thematics were repetitively embedded and anchored in the minds of listeners. An audience restricted to preliterate memorial techniques had to develop the intellectual equivalent of visual tableaux. As a response to these mnemonic needs, self-conscious 'embedding' and *media res* 'disembedding' of action episodes and events were evolved as a distinctive feature of epic narration. As Havelock has argued, a grammar of action rather than reflection 'appears to be a prerequisite for oral memorization' (1986: 75–6). Epic unfurls a story organized sequentially as a recursive set of embedded subplots. Given the constraints of aural attention its presentation of action and events requires immediate assent: dramatic narration moves swiftly and continuously from one heroic tableau to another, from one specular encounter to another, without breaking the diegetic thread. The primitive auditory requirements of episodic embedding and narrative sequencing thus made the technique of telling interlocking stories a stylistic necessity (Aristotle would later theorize the simultaneity of multiple plots as a constitutive feature of epic plotting).

As a panoramic 'suture' of relatively autonomous graphic scenes and events, however, artful *disembedding* techniques are also necessary. One such disembedding technique is to have agents – whether mortals or gods – comment upon the action and describe the theatre of praxis, or engage others in dialogue about the nature and limits of their activities, responsibilities, and obligations. The problem of orchestrating discrete, synchronic 'plots' gives the *Iliad* and *Odyssey* a cinematic structure of interlacing cause-effect series. Elaborately 'nested' plots provide an instructive contrast with the relatively simple plot devices of myth and the fabulations of folk-tale and customary wisdom. Epic, then, presupposes a rich narrative tradition of already-known videological themes and convoluted action problematics. This is also confirmed by the fact that poems dating from the same period were frequently part of a song 'cycle' of highly involved tales from well-known myths and hero tales (the 'Cypria' and 'Little Iliad' mentioned by Aristotle at *Poetics* 1459b1 and the 'Theban Cycle' are examples of this background tradition). This interplay of embedding and disembedding techniques had the effect of further enhancing the 'aesthetic' effect of mythic narration.[10] With these preliminary remarks we are now in a position to explore some of the specific devices of epic visualization.[11]

HOMERIC EPIC REFLEXIVITY

In medias res

He [Homer] never attempts to make the whole war of Troy the subject of his poem ... he selects a single portion, and admits many episodes from the general story of the war.

(Aristotle, *Poetics* 1459a30)

Homeric narrative is doubly praxial: as a praxis of narrative visualization and as positing conspicuous interaction as its central thematic. Homeric syntax projects a scenario of praxis for both its heroes and its audience.[12] As if reflecting this duality, the central agents of the epic – Achilles and Odysseus – are at once masters of heroic action and virtuosos of narrative expression.

The epic life-world defines a theatre of heroic praxis. Everything but the fateful life and death struggle of heroes is backgrounded into irrelevance in deference to the focal struggle for honour and power. Indeed we may even say that epic invented the strategic use of the primary disembedding device of figure and ground. As a *logos* of memorable heroic deeds epic fashions a dramaturgical logic of agonistic struggle. Nature is displaced as the dark ground of human action. The natural world is marginalized by the epic's thematization of action and the clash of opposing wills (in logological terms, a figure of grammar helped to frame a definite orientation toward the natural world). Jasper Griffin (1980a: 33) is thus correct to see the epic's foregrounding of action as strictly correlated with its backgrounding of scenic particulars and natural environment: 'the rest of the world is tacitly abolished' (Griffin compares this Homeric convention with the analogous technique of the confrontational climax of the traditional Western film). The depiction of exaggerated agonistic praxis abstracted from the natural environment further enhances the 'sculptural' quality of epic description. Again we emphasize that these structurations of action and landscape are the effects of Homeric linguistic forms, particularly the verbal structures developed to narrate *agency* (see Redfield, 1975: 99–103 and Fränkel's observation, 'The Trojan field is only an arena for the Trojan War, not a countryside', 1975: 36).

Everyone knows that the *Iliad* ('the song of Ilium') relates the tale of the Trojan War. In keeping with its dramatic logic, Book I of the *Iliad* opens *in medias res* with the anger of Peleus' son, Achilles, caused by King Agamemnon taking Achilles' slave girl Briseis as spoil, thus shaming the hero before the Achaean warriors. Achilles' extreme reaction is only comprehensible in the context of the heroic code of a culture where loss of face entailed a loss of honour (*time*) and consequently a loss of selfhood and social status: the taking of the girl Briseis marks the status mortification of Achilles as the first warrior of the Achaeans and son of the sea goddess Thetis. Books 1 and 2 immediately confront an audience with a hiatus caused by Achilles' damaged self-esteem. In the heroic code such public damage to the self could only be remedied by an exaction of vengeance in accordance with the Greek equivalent of the *lex talionis* principle. Achilles' loss of self cannot be healed by suasive means – it can only be undone through purposive violence (a causation which is effected by the instrument of the Trojan army in Books 8 and 9 and 11 to 15). The creation, loss, and recovery of honour may be said to be the fundamental motivational theme of the *Iliad*.

Book I thus begins with the reflexive topic of the *loss of honour and political status* – a generative 'problem' that would have been immediately intelligible to its original audience: Achilles' spoiled sense of identity occasioning his wilful withdrawal from the Achaean war effort (the same pattern is repeated later in the *Iliad* (Books 18–22) where a similar blow to his identity motivates Achilles to strive to avenge the death of Patroclus by slaughtering Patroclus' slayer, Hector). This loss of self-esteem links the theme of Achilles' selfhood with the collective integrity of the Achaean war effort – and indirectly with more abstract themes concerning the conditions of the (im)possibility of the warrior community, political order, and the existential paradoxes of warfare. The Wrath motif and the Vengeance motif function as *plot-generating mechanisms* on a number of different levels. On the most immediate semantic plane of the narration it generates subplots such as the hero's absence from the site of his heroism, the threat this poses for the Achaean war effort, the content of the important dialogues with Patroclus, Ajax, and others, the causation of the death of Patroclus, the return of Achilles to exact vengeance for the wrong committed by Hector, the slaying of Hector, and the conference with Hector's father, King Priam, and so on. On a more formal plane the mortification of self motivates the song cycle of the *Iliad* itself. Finally, at the level of political representation or political metanarrative, Achilles' identity crisis creates a semantic space in which the heroic form of life itself can be reflexively displayed and critically examined.

The motive of Achilles' anger allows the narrative to cut into the Achaean-Trojan saga around ten years into the campaign; it also 'cuts' into the presuppositions of its audience who are expected to understand the abduction of Helen as the initiating cause of the war, the proximate cause of the impasse which threaten the Achaeans with disaster, and the final tragic consequences of Achilles' return. The war is literally occasioned by the theft of a woman (Paris' seduction of Helen – 'the face that launched a thousand ships'). But the opening Books of the poem are primarily concerned with the adversarial relationships between the Achaean chieftans created by a further 'stolen woman': Achilles withdraws from the battle; he is aided by Zeus in granting the Trojans temporary success against Agamemnon's forces; Achilles loses his friend Patroclus who falls to Hector in his desperate struggle to resist the Trojan onslaught; at the eleventh hour Achilles returns to reap his vengeance; he kills Hector, dragging the corpse around the walls of Troy behind his chariot; finally he allows Hector's father, the aged King Priam, to recover the mutilitated body of his son. At a deeper level we might even claim that the interlacing Wrath and Vengeance motifs give the *Iliad* its self-displaying narrative unity (Trypanis, ed., 1971: xxviii; 1977, 17; Trypanis claims that the compact thematic plot of the *Iliad* is woven around only four basic themes: the 'Wrath of Achilles', 'Vengeance', 'Single Combat', and 'the Old Father'; with the Old Father motif forming perhaps a later addition to the epic structure; 1977: 22; also 1981: 34–40).

Of men and gods

We can appreciate the power of this simple generative structure by reducing the narrative to its skeletal form:

(i) Achilles and Agamemnon (with their allies Menelaus, Diomedes, Odysseus, etc.) attack Troy in order to recover Helen, the wife of Menelaus, taken and held by Paris (Alexandros);

(ii) Agamemnon appeases the god Apollo by surrendering the slave-girl Chryseis, reduced to the status of war booty;

(iii) Achilles quarrels with Agamemnon over Agamemnon's refusal to return Briseis, a Trojan girl given to Achilles as a war prize;

(iv) Agamemnon returns Briseis to Achilles, who rejoins the Achaeans and, killing Hector, is victorious in the struggle with the Trojans. The death of Hector, however, precedes Achilles' own destruction, foretold by his mother, Thetis.

These relations can then be plotted as the terms of a simple narrative matrix:

	Agent	Action	Object	Agent/Recipient
(i)	Paris	refuses to return	Helen	to Greeks
(ii)	Achilles	refuses to give	Briseis	to Agamemnon
(iii)	Achilles	refuses to fight		for Agamemnon
(iv)	Achilles	agrees to give	the body of Hector	to the Trojans

(We find the same generative plot structure in early Attic tragedy:

(i) Agamemnon sacrifices a woman (his daughter Iphigenia) to gain a woman (Helen);

(ii) Agamemnon captures a woman (Cassandra) who foresees his death at the hands of a woman (his wife, Clytemnestra);

(iii) Clytemnestra murders a woman (Cassandra);

(iv) Clytemnestra is murdered by her son Orestes (a son murders a woman, his own mother);

As a deep structure the patriarchal grid operates by orchestrating further causal, temporal, and spatial relationships for an oral audience:

(i)   narratively motivating the action of the *Iliad* by occasioning the key thematic of Achilles' conflict with Agamemnon over the daughter of Chryses, a priest of Apollo;
(ii) generating a narrative syntagm of further actions and events motivated by Achilles' visible absence (Patroclus' impersonation of Achilles; the struggle for Patroclus' body and armour; the vengeance of Achilles after the news of Patroclus' death, and so on);
(iii) pretextualizing the panoramic narrative of the battle, the outcome of which is rendered uncertain by Achilles' absence;
(iv) preparing Achilles' revenge in Book 9, his victorious struggle against Hector after the death of Achilles' host-friend Patroclus (in *Iliad* 16), and the narrative framing of the crucial scene in Book 24 with King Priam, Hector's father;
(v)   concluding by reversing or symmetrically negating the action of Book 1: Achilles gives an individual (Priam) the dead body of his son, Hector (Achilles the man-slayer of Book I is transfigured by this inversion into the ethical figure who encounters Priam on the level of a common humanity older and deeper than the limited universe of heroic values);
(vi) providing further themes and subplots by which the Trojan adventure might be continued (thus Aristotle was already glossing the plot of the *Odyssey* as a subplot of the Trojan story: 'The story of the *Odyssey* is not long; a man is away from home for many years; Poseidon is constantly on the watch to destroy him, and he is alone; at home his property is being wasted by suitors, and his son is the intended victim of a plot. He reaches home, tempest-tossed; he makes himself known, attacks his enemies and destroys them, and is himself saved. This is the heart of the matter: the rest is episodes' (*Poetics* 17.1455b15ff.; cf. 1459a30, 1462b10));
(vii) prefiguring the end of epic heroism: the figure of Odysseus in the *Odyssey* serves to 'relativize' the warrior culture of epic *arete* by returning to the bucolic life of his estates and faithful Penelope.

In both poems the antithetical plotting of temporal events is mediated by the figure of a woman (in the *Iliad*, the struggle is initiated by a woman – Helen – who relates both the warrior life beyond the gates of Troy and the inner world of Trojan society; and the successful termination of the war is jeopardized by the conflict between Agamemnon and Achilles over two women – Chryseis and Briseis; in the *Odyssey* the mediator between the world of Odysseus and the besieged palace of Ithaca is Penelope). The contrastive function of women in the narrative also serves to distinguish the plotting of both works: women in the *Iliad* motivate the events as property or booty, but once initiated the central actions of the poem are overwhelmingly patriarchal, while in the *Odyssey*, relations with women structure many of the central scenes (Odysseus' encounters with Calypso, Circe, Nausicaa, his own mother in Hades, and, of course, his ultimate return to Penelope are archetypal scenes which later appear in endless variations on pottery and wall paintings). The *Odyssey* is also closer in its plot structure to Aristotle's model of the perfect tragedy (*Poetics* Book 26, esp. 1462bff.): every tragedy has two parts, Complication and Unravelling (the *dénouement*); the *Odyssey* contains the four elemental types of tragedy: the Complex – depending on reversal of fortune and recognition (Odysseus' triumphant return to Ithaca, the Scar episode), Simple (where the change in the fortunes of the central hero takes place without reversal (peripety) or recognition (discovery)), Pathetic (where the motive is passion: the reunion with 'faithful Penelope'), and Ethical (where the motives are ethical: vengeance, destruction of Penelope's suitors, justice, etc.).

To summarize: the theme of themes of the *Iliad* is *agon* as a condition of personal and collective identity – the endemic process of difference, conflict, and struggle to secure *honour* which animates the worlds of men and gods. Even the lyrical description of the figures decorating the Shield of Achilles (*Il.* 18.478–608) centres on an adversarial scene of two men quarrelling over the blood-price for a dead friend, until the *agon* is settled by a mediator:

> the people were shouting in applause supporting both sides. And heralds kept order among the people, while the elders sat on polished stones in the sacred circle, holding in their hands the staffs of clear-voiced heralds. They then stood up before them and gave judgement each in turn. And in the middle lay two talents of gold, to be given to the one who should plead most justly among them.
>
> (18.584; cf. *Il.* 3.218)

As a narrative operator the conspicuous *agon* of Achilles and Agamemnon enables the text to weave the gods into the theatre of human praxis. The tenth year will bring the strands of mortal and divine temporality together. The opening words of Book I inform the audience that this moment is imminent. The emblematic struggle between Agamemnon and Achilles (a patriarchal microcosm which temporarily suspends the larger struggle between Achaeans and Trojans) prefigures the final act of the whole drama – the defeat of the Trojan heroes and the sacking of Troy. It is a synecdoche of the history of the war and a moral parable for the conflict-ridden life of mortals. This suggests a principled explanation as to why the tale would be reinscribed by later Greek culture and even rewritten as a coded allegory of religious and philosophical wisdom.

Formulaic logics, repetition and paratactic description

> The formula makes the Homeric style what it is and is fundamental to any understanding of it.
>
> (Sir Maurice Bowra, in Wace and Stubbings, eds, 1962: 28)

We know that epic narrative favours paratactic repetition and formulaic devices.[13] As a mnemonic technology[14] epic draws upon stock thematics, known heroic figures and action sequences, rigidly patterned descriptions (and descriptive elements), symmetrical plotting and realistic, paratactically organized stories governed by consistent rules, controlled and manipulated, within traditional limits, by the oral poet. Fidelity to the canon rather than original composition is the general rule of epic narrative. The composers of the Homeric corpus made one of the greatest of literary discoveries: in constructing narratives of power they revealed the power of narrative. The formular fictionality of Homeric verse – its aesthetizing of the universe of heroic praxis by means of the epic aorist, parataxis, and stylized dactylic hexameter – distinguishes Greek epic from the more didactic claims of, say, Biblical epic. Each genre elaborates a different view of community – for the Greek an idealized aesthetic form of life, for the Hebraic an equally idealized ethical community.[15]

The interweave of genres

One important feature of the long narrative poem is its ability to assimilate very different types of discourse within the flexible 'additive' structure of dactylic hexameter. Epic created a collage-like matrix of genres. The Alexandrian critics were thus not mistaken in viewing the Homeric corpus as a 'genre of genres', an archive of diverse oral and literary styles. To mention only the most prominent of these – the *genealogy*, the *catalogue, extended narrative description, monologue, reported speech, forensic debate, dialogue, lyric description of nature, extended simile and metaphor, folktale and adventure story*, and the subgenre of *moral reflection*. This tempts many commentators to see the epic genre as a synergy of 'knowledges'.[16] But it also suggested *topoi, schemata*, and narrative *syntaxes* which would later be developed as independent genres in their own right: the cosmogonic poem (first fully explored by Hesiod), the lyric description of nature (in Alcman, Alcaeus, and Sappho), cosmology (the Ionian philosophers), public oratory, philosophical discourse, tragic drama, the dialogue form, the prose epic, the Greek 'novel', among these. If we define these frames of meaning as knowledge forms it would not be inaccurate to define the Greek epic as an epistemic matrix. It is one small step from the universal claims of epic storytelling to the art of telling the story of the universe. Moreover the commitment to writing and literacy implicit in the written epic suggested the idea of cosmological and philosophical writing, inspiring the hitherto unimaginable project of narrating the birth of the *Kosmos*, the life of *Phusis*, and the story of human origins. It is no accident that the first appearance of cosmological speculation and written philosophy occurs in the same Ionian culture that produced epic narrative (see Volume 3, Chapters 1, 2).

Realist description

One important register in the epic matrix is the truth-telling 'realist' description or 'reality effect' of a vivid simile. Although descriptive fidelity is not the primary aim of the epic (Trypanis, 1977: 65–78), one profound effect of the epic narration is the creation of a panoramic scene prior to a particular act or event set in that scene. By means of this strategic scene-setting an auditor is invited to 'prefigure' and to 'complete' the details of the situation in imagination. An example of this anticipatory figure-ground technique of visualization occurs in Book 13 of the *Odyssey*. Odysseus has returned to Ithaca and anchors at a particular promontory on the island. The well-known text prefigures the scene as follows:

> There is in the land of Ithaca a certain harbour of Phorcys ... and at its mouth two projecting headlands sheer to seaward, but sloping down on the side toward the harbour... At the head of the harbour is a long-leafed olive tree, and near it a pleasant, shadowy cave sacred to the nymphs that are called Naiads ... Two doors open to the cave, one toward the North Wind, by which men go down, but that toward the South Wind is sacred, nor do men enter thereby; it is the way of the immortals.
> (13.95–114; cf. 13.344–50; cf. the description of the spring of Ithacus at *Od.* 17.205ff.)

Epic narration also utilizes language's descriptive power to depict both the singular, accidental qualities of immediate experience and the invariant features of the life-world of action. This often results in extended paratactic inventories. The best example of parataxis is the catalogue of ships and troops along with their geographical origins in the Second Book of the *Iliad* (*Il.* 2.483–2.877) – in this inventory we hear of Mycenae, Pylos, Argos, Knossos, Amnisos, Phaestos, Cydonia but also of Eutresis, Asine, Aigina, and Epidauros. Other examples include the listing of participants at the games of the Phaeacians in Book 8 of the *Odyssey* (*Od.* 8.110ff.), the genealogies of noble families, and the list of actions of the queens of the past in Book 11 of the *Odyssey* (*Od.* 11. 235–341).

Another more gruesome product of 'paratactic' depiction is the graphically detailed cataloguing of wounds inflicted during hand-to-hand combat (e.g. *Il.* 4.456–539, *Il.* 5.9ff., *Il.* 6.5ff., *Il.* 14.508–22). Their effect, as Peter Levi, has remarked 'is to draw the listening imagination into nothing less than a world' (1985: 28). A sample of these latter strategies can serve to illustrate the visual possibilities of this literary device.

Worlds of the dying

First, the perfection of the art of the 'telling', and often apparently inconsequential, detail (in describing the horses drawing the chariot carrying the wounded Agamemnon: 'With foam were their breasts flecked, and with dust their bellies stained beneath them as they bore the wounded king forth from the battle', *Il.* 11.280–3). Visual accuracy, impersonal description, and a lucid concern for anatomical detail are recurrent properties of the *Iliad*'s depiction of death in battle, creating formulaic *tableaux* of death.

The death of Pandarus

With that, Diomedes hurled. His spear, guided by Athene, struck Pandarus on the nose beside the eye and passed through his white teeth. His tongue was cut off at the root by the relentless bronze, and the point came out at the base of his chin. He crashed from the chariot ... This was the end of Pandarus.

(*Il.* 5.290–6)

The death of Damasus

the stalwart Polypoetes, cast his spear and hit Damasus on his bronze-sided helmet. The metal of the helmet failed to check the metal of the spear. The point went through it, pierced the bone and splattered the inside of the helmet with the man's brains.

(*Il.* 12.182ff.)

The death of Oenomaus

Then Idomeneus cast. He struck Oenomaus full in the belly, breaking the plate of his corslet, through which the spear-point let his bowels out. Oenomaus fell down in the dust and clutched at the ground. Idomeneus dragged his long-shadowed spear out of the body, but overwhelmed as he was by missiles, he was unable to strip the man's splendid arms and armour from his shoulders.

(*Il.* 13.506ff.)

The death of Patroclus

Phoibos Apollo now struck away from his head the helmet four-horned and hollow-eyed, and under the feet of the horses it rolled clattering, and the plumes above it were defiled by blood and dust.

(*Il.* 16.787–96, trans. Lattimore)

When Hector saw the great Patroclus creeping wounded from the field, he made his way towards him through the ranks, and coming up, he struck him with a spear in the lower part of his belly, driving the bronze clean through. Patroclus fell with a thud.

(*Il.* 16.158ff.)

The ethos of everyday life (Iliad 6.390–502)

Another descriptive innovation is the narrative's interpolation of apparently 'inconsequential' quotidian fragments between more monumental panoramic scenes. One of the most striking instances occurs in the domestic scene at *Iliad* 6.464. Hector, in full bronze armour, is about to leave his wife Andromache and their child Astyanax to face death in combat with the Greek champion Achilles; Andromache pleads with her husband to avoid direct combat with Achilles, a struggle that will make her a widow and his son an orphan; when Hector bends to embrace his child for the last time the terrified boy clings to his nurse; Hector and Andromache laugh; he removes his helmet, places it at his feet and takes his son in his arms, asking Zeus to bless the child:

> glorious Hector held out his arms to take his boy. But the child shrank back with a cry to the bosom of his girdled nurse, alarmed by his father's appearance. He was frightened by the bronze of the helmet and the horsehair plume that he saw nodding grimly down at him. His father and his lady mother had to laugh. But noble Hector quickly took his helmet off and put the dazzling thing on the ground. Then he kissed his son ... and prayed to Zeus: 'Zeus, and you other gods, grant that this boy of mine may be, like me pre-eminent in Troy; as strong and brave as I; a mighty king of Ilium.

(6.476–81, trans. Rieu)

Taken out of context these ephemeral details are of little consequence; but when interspersed between epic descriptions of war and death, they are transfigured into potent symbols of mortality.

The universe of everyday objects

A related 'reality effect' is produced by the precise descriptions of everyday objects, many of which have been actually found to date back to the Mycenaean period before 1300 BC. Given limited space we can only select a representative sample from a rich vein of descriptive passages.

Weapons

Descriptions of weapons and armour are particularly noteworthy (see A. M. Snodgrass, *Early Greek Armour and Weapons*, 1964, *Arms and Armour of the Greeks*, 1967, P.A.L. Greenhalgh, *Early Greek Warfare*, 1973: chs 1–3, and J. V. Luce, *Homer and the Heroic Age*, 1975: ch. 5). One of the most cited cases is the portrait of the Mycenaean boar's tusk helmet at *Iliad* 10.261–5. Odysseus reconnoitres the enemy camp wearing a felt cap protected by ox-skin into which boars' teeth have been stitched:

> He set on his head a helmet made of ox-hide; inside, it was made of thongs tightly stretched and on the outside the tusks of a white-toothed boar, thick-set, ran in contrary directions, well and skillfully set, and in between a cap of felt was fitted.

At *Iliad* 10.260ff. the narrative details the history of ownership of this precious object:

> This cap Autolycus on a time stole out of Eleon when he had broken into the stout-built house of Amyntor, son of Ormenus; and he gave it to Amphidamas of Cythera to take to Scandeia, and Amphidamas gave it to Molus as a guest-gift, but he gave it to his own son Meriones to wear; and now, being set thereon, it covered the head of Odysseus.
> (*Il.* 10. 265–71)

The same concern for detailing an object in the context of its social history and ownership recurs throughout the *Iliad* (the sceptre of Kings, Nestor's cup, armour, and so on). In general these objects derive their meaning from being embedded in patterns of past or present heroic action.

A comparable description features a hide skull-cap: 'about his head he set a helm of bull's hide without horn and without crest, a helm that is called a skull-cap, and that guards the heads of lusty youths' (*Il.* 10.256–9). Here again, this piece of descriptive information appears in the context of a raid or foray behind the enemy's lines.

We might compare these vivid images with the historically accurate account of the full-length Mycenaean body-shield (probably of the 'Dipylon' or tower-shaped type) carried on his back by the Trojan hero, Hector: 'As he walked, the dark leather rim of his bossed shield tapped him above and below, on the ankles and on the back of his neck' (*Il.* 6.116–8; cf. the shield of the Mycenaean warrior Periphetes at *Il.* 15.646 and Achilles' shield at *Il.* 18.474–82; Idomeneus is also completely hidden behind his tower shield at *Il.* 13.405–8; and Ajax carries 'a shield like a tower' or 'city wall' (*Il.* 7.219, 7.244–8, 11.485, 17.128, cited by Luce, 1975: 105–6)).

As the 'tower' shield and boars' tusk helmet were no longer found amongst the arms of eighth-century Greek warriors the description of such objects has been used as evidence for the accuracy of the poet's knowledge of the Mycenaean world (see also Nilsson, *Homer and Mycenae*, 1933)).

Dress and equipment

Luce observes that this eye for detail also extends to the precise sequence in which the Homeric warrior donned his armour:

The equipment is always donned in the same order: greaves, corslet, sword, shield, helmet; finally, the warrior picks up his spear(s), and is ready for combat. Greaves are put on first while the warrior can still bend down to fasten them unencumbered by other items. Sword and shield are suspended by belts over the shoulders, and so are put on before the helmet.

(Luce, 1975: 107)

Another instance of this sequence occurs in *Iliad* 3 where Alexander is dressing himself for the coming battle: first greaves, then silver ankle pieces, bronze corselet, silver-studded sword, helmet, and finally, spear ('and in the self-same manner warlike Menelaus did on his battle-gear', in Murray's translation, *Il.* 3.339; see also *Il.* 11.15–46); the formula is repeated in *Iliad* Book 16 where we see Patroclus being armed: first with greaves, fitted with silver ankle pieces; then the bronze corselet; after this the sword is placed around the shoulder; the shield is taken up next; this is followed by the donning of the bronze helmet plumed with a horse-hair crest. Patroclus finally completes the process by taking up two spears (*Il.* 16.130–40).

The human body

The same realism is evident in the vivid description of Odysseus' swollen body caked with salt after several days in the sea:

he flexed both knees and his ponderous hands; his very heart was sick with salt water, and all his flesh was swollen, and the sea water crusted stiffly in his mouth and nostrils, and with a terrible weakness fallen upon him he lay unable to breathe or speak in his weakness.

(*Od.* 5.453–7)

Interiors

A similar respect for detail is evident from accounts of the design and furnishings of royal palaces: the bronze-floored palace of Alcinous (*Od.* 13.4), the gleaming interior of Hephaestus' hall (*Iliad* 18.369–427), the great hall of Menelaus' palace at *Odyssey* 4.37–75 with its 'high-roofed' structure, walls lined with bronze, polished baths, golden and amber goblets, silver wash basins and bowls (*Il.* 23.741–5; *Od.* 4.615–9), inner rooms teaming with precious objects inlaid with ivory and silver; the precise description of Nestor's two-handled cup of gold decorated with images of doves at *Il.* 11.632–37 (cf. *Od.* 4.96, 13.55, 15.115ff.); the riches contained in Apollo's shrine at Delphi; Odysseus' golden brooch at *Od.* 19.225–31; Hephaestus' silver tool-chest (*Il.* 18.420ff.).

The fact that this phenomenological eye for pictorial detail is not confined to 'noble' or 'picturesque' objects and scenes is illustrated by the care in visualizing Eumaeus' pig pen at the beginning of Book 14 of the *Odyssey* (*Od.* 14.5–25); or the equally cinematic description of Telemachus' ship as it prepares to leave harbour for Pylos:

> Telemachus went aboard the ship, but Athene went first and took her place in the stern of the ship ... The men cast off the stern cables and themselves also went aboard and sat to the oarlocks ... Telemachus then gave the sign and urged his companions to lay hold of the tackle, and they listened to his urging and, raising the mast pole made of fir, they made it fast with forestays, and with halyards strongly twisted of leather pulled up the white sails ... When they had made fast the running gear all along the black ship, then they set up mixing bowls, filling them brimful with wine, and poured to the gods immortal and everlasting but beyond all other gods they poured to Zeus' gray-eyed daughter. All night long and into the dawn she ran on her journey.
> (*Od.* 2.416–34)

Phenomenological events

The careful choice of a powerful sensuous image or simile is frequently used to corroborate the 'reality effect' of a descriptive passage. A well-known instance is the simile of the red-hot shaft (*mochlos*) hissing as it is thrust into Polyphemus' single eye 'as when a smith dips a great axe in cold water'(*Od.* 9.391–3); or the flight of retreating soldiers 'like deer', the battlefield 'running' with blood, among numerous analogous images of war and its consequencee (see below).

The natural world

A paradigm case here is the description of the night sky inscribed – or rather inlayed – upon Achilles' Shield: the Pleiades and the Hyades (which are permanently visible in the northern sky), 'mighty Orion', 'the wain' or Great Bear constellation (Ursa Major, also known as the Great Bear or Dipper) 'which revolves in her place and watches Orion and is the only one of the stars which does not dip in the Ocean' (Ursa Major is, of course, only permanently visible for observers in the northern hemisphere). Formular epithets for natural events pervade the texture of the epic form; through these epithets

> we are called to awareness of the wide expanse of sky, bright sun, shining moon; black earth, bearing grain, giving life; landscapes with shadow-traversed hills, edying rivers, hollow caves, windswept headlands, deep harbours; the boundless sea, heaving and murmuring, misty, grey or violet-blue; of windswept Troy, fertile Phthia, sandy Pylos, rocky Ithaca, Mycenae rich in gold.
> (Camps, 1980: 45–6; cf. Redfield, 1975)

The topography of war

Finally, when applied to the topography of war itself, the panoramic eye creates an effect of 'sublime' realism. To use a cinematic analogy, the high-altitude panning of the Trojan camp fires produces one of the most memorable descriptions in the whole of the *Iliad*:

> Thus all night long they sat, across the corridors of battle, thinking great thoughts (*mega phronestes*) and keeping their many fires alight. There are nights when the upper air is windless and the stars in heaven stand out in their full splendour round the bright moon; when every mountain-top and headland and ravine starts into sight, as the infinite depths of the sky are torn open to the very firmament; when every star is seen, and the shepherd rejoices. Such and so many were the Trojans' fires, twinkling in front of Ilium midway between the ships and the streams of Xanthus. There were a thousand fires burning on the plain, and round each one sat fifty men in the light of its blaze, while the horses stood beside their chariots, munching white barley and rye, and waiting for Dawn to take her golden throne.
>
> (*Il.* 8. 553–65, trans. Rieu)

(Murray translates the same passage in a more archaic but perhaps more evocative style: 'Even as in heaven (*ouranos*) about the gleaming moon the stars shine clear, when the air is windless, and forth to view appear all mountain peaks and high headlands and glades, and from heaven breaketh open the infinite air (*aither*), and all stars (*astra*) are seen, and the shepherd joyeth in his heart; even in such multitudes between the ships and the streams of Xanthus shone the fires that the Trojans kindled before the face of Ilios. A thousand fires were burning in the plain and by each sat fifty men in the glow of the blazing fire. And their horses, eating of white barley and spelt, stood beside the cars and waited for fair-throned Dawn' (*Il.* 8.553–65).)

Other examples of this 'Olympian' perspective include Helen's description in *Iliad* Book 3 of the different Achaean nobles from her high vantage-point on the walls of Troy and Poseidon's panoramic vision of Troy from a mountain top in Samothrace (Samos, the island facing Thrace): 'from thence all Ida was visible, and visible too was the city of Priam and the ships of the Achaeans' (*Iliad* 13; cited in Luce, 1975: 121).

The Rashomon effect of Odyssean perspective

Given the prevalence of poetic visualization and the valorization of objects known through visual perception we should not be surprised to find the image of specular 'viewing' as one of the most pervasive rhetorical figures of Homeric narration. The composers of the *Iliad* discovered the strategy of multiple perspective or what might be more accurately called the Rashomon effect of mobile narrative (after Akira Kurosawa's famous film *Rashomon*). Following the pluralism of narrative forms and styles, the perspectives constituted by these idioms also 'wander' across the fictional *mise-en-scène*. Each technique we have sampled above embodies a different narratorial perspective: the precise ambulatory eye 'touring' a singular object (Nestor's four-handled cup 'set with golden nails, the eared handles upon it were four, and on either side there were fashioned two doves of gold feeding, and there were double bases beneath it', *Il.* 11.632–7); the inconsequentially glimpsed domestic fragment or scene from daily life – Odysseus walking past his aged and infirm dog Argos at *Odyssey* 17.260–334; the insistent analytic eye celebrating the phenomenological particularity of weapons and armour; the high-altitude, lyrical vision of the Trojan camp-fires; the 'intimate close-up' of the last conversation between Hector and Andromache (*Il.* 6.404ff.).

The Rashomon effect adumbrates an 'Odyssean' hermeneutics of visual possibilities. We can let one example suggest a whole programme of further research. This might be called the 'Odyssean eye'. Normally the epic follows an objective, anonymous, impersonal, and omniscient optic, moving resolutely from scene to scene like a camera eye, portraying heroic events and actions as though they were unfurling in a timeless present. But the discrepant perspectives of characters, dialogue, and reported speech allow the 'eye' of the narrative to wander, so to speak, both vertically and horizontally – just as it wanders with Odysseus in his meandering journey back to Ithaca. The stability of the 'omniscient' narrator serves as a foil for the errant perspectives introduced by the Rashomon effect. Book 13 of the *Iliad* opens with an account of two perspectives; Zeus has turned away from the events of the War to observe the horseman of Thrace, the Mysians, competing with other warrior people, while Poseidon looks down with wonder on the plain of Ilium from a mountain in Samothrace. The narrative then tracks Poseidon from his elevated perspective down to the struggle being waged around the ships of the Achaeans – where he appears in the shape of the prophet Calchas to urge the Greeks to counterattack. Here, once more, a contrastive structure is presupposed: the 'elevated', superior knowledge of the gods (exemplified by their absolute knowledge) and the 'inferior' and 'sectarian' partial perspectives of the heroic agents as protagonists of the action. The device of double perception would subsequently become one of the central techniques of tragic irony in Attic drama. The knowledgeable listener, of course, 'sees' the action from both standpoints.

Dialogue

The ambulatory voice of the *Iliad* not only aspires to an Olympian vision of the struggles of Heroes, but seems to possess a God's-ear access to the inner conversations of epic agents, whether these be mortals or gods. Heroic speech is a present memorializing of immemorial praxis.[17] One of the most striking manifestations of this ear for language spoken in the present is the prominence given to narrated dialogue and reported speech. The pre-eminent role played by the speeches of heroes and Gods is often considered to be the most innovative product of the whole genre – the beginnings of an authentically heteroglossial art form. But of more immediate significance is the construction of highly crafted dialogues and controlled dialogic interaction between the main characters. As Rhys Carpenter once remarked, the discovery of the reality effect of epic poetry leads to a paradoxical theorem: 'since it is fiction which imparts verizimilitude to his scenes, we may say without fear of paradox that the more real they seem the more fictional they are' (Carpenter, 1962: 26–32).

We have already observed that speech in Homer belongs to the field of praxis. Hence the central characters of the epic are great speakers as well as great agents: an Achilles or an Odysseus can, when required, step onto the stage as a master of rhetoric, persuasion, and 'honeyed' flattery. They readily slip from public dialogue to public monologue (thinking aloud) and forms of interior dialogue (with a God, for example) and silent monologue. Like a mirror image of the craft of the rhapsode, the central hero of the *Iliad* is proud of his command of words. We can even plot a determinate shift within the text's development from the austere, if rather limited, rhetoric of Achilles to the subtle rhetoric of Odysseus, pictured by the formulaic predicates 'cunning', 'resourceful', 'intelligent', 'wily', 'strategic', and the like. Where Achilles' mode of speech is firmly tied to the counsels of war, Odysseus' language is already responding to the different rhetorical demands of the *agora* and law court. Remarkably, the contrastive structure symbolized by Achilles/Odysseus prefigured the actual historical development of the arts of speech in Greek culture.

Reported speech

Almost half of the *Iliad* and more than two thirds of the *Odyssey* are devoted to speeches by the characters, often quite long speeches. One may search the *Chanson de Roland* and the *Nibelungenlied* in vain for anything of the kind'.[18]

While the narrative voice of the poem frequently presents actions and events independent of the speeches of characters, Homeric verse introduced the important device of the reported speech, where an account is put into the mouth of one or other of the characters. In fact the most frequent appearance of speech in Homer is the reported speech of a God – introduced by a formula of the type 'And gray-eyed Athena stood close by him and addressed him: "... "' or 'Telemachus, the dear son of godlike Odysseus, came up to Menelaus, and addressed him, saying: "... "' (for example, at the opening of *Odyssey* Book 15).

Extended reported dialogue also functions as a powerful technique of heroic characterization. We know the 'judicious' nature of Nestor from the 'measured' nature of his speech with others; he is 'the clear-voiced orator of the Pylians', berating both Achilles and Agamemnon for their needless quarrel; we know of his long career as a warrior – he has fought beside men of greater strength and nobility than either Achilles or Agamemnon; that he bears his old age with dignity and forebearance by replacing his earlier prowess in hand-to-hand combat with his wisdom in counsel; we learn that he served for many years as an advisor to these warlords; and that, by implication, the quarrelling Greeks should listen to his wise words: 'I beg you to put aside your anger with Achilles. He is for all the Achaeans a great bulwark against evil war.' Nestor is, in short, a living memory bank for the Achaeans (see *Il.* 1.260ff., 2.360ff, 7.123ff, 23.625ff., 23.306ff., etc.).

As a narrative framework studded with long sections of monologue and dialogue, Homeric fiction positively encourages second-order reflexion and metacommentary. I have already suggested that its use of dramatic irony anticipates the complex role of this technique in Sophoclean tragedy. Like a scenario for a stage play, the interweaving of monologue and dialogue implicates the audience as active participants in the play of events (another fundamental discovery of epic dialectic that would be put to profound effect in the philosophical dialogues of Plato). Unlike other comparable forms of ancient literature – the Hebraic Old Testament or Hindu epics for instance – the *Iliad* and the *Odyssey* were not readily assimilated to theological interests; nor did they encourage the crystallization of a sacerdotal profession of commentators and exegetes (although something akin to a secular aesthetic profession of Homeric devotees had evolved by the early sixth century). The *Iliad* does not present itself as an unimpeachable record of the word of God; it is structured as a heteroglossial tale of epic conflicts, and its humanism unintentionally promoted the secularization of archaic myths and religious thematics, preparing the way for more self-conscious patterns of secular moral experience that we find in later Greek religion, art, and intellectual speculation. Its self-referential fictionality is most evident in the figural pleasure displayed by the narrative and by the text's concern for its own status as text (and here, as we will see shortly, the *Odyssey* provides an even richer source of self-reflexive stratagems).

Visual figuration

But the greatest thing by far is to have a genius for metaphor.
(Aristotle, *Poetics* 22)

Metaphor is the application of an alien name by transference either from genus to species, or from species to genus, or from species to species, or by analogy, that is, proportion.

(Aristotle, *Poetics* 21)

Epic exploits many of the ordinary semantic properties of linguistic figuration in its pursuit of visual concreteness; the poetry is rich in metonymy, synecdoche, and irony. One of the most insistent devices of the Homeric epic is the *personification* of non-human events and agents: experiences, emotions, events, dreams, and so on take a concrete human form just as natural powers are visualized in human predicates:

> the Dawn rose from her couch from beside lordly Tithonus, to bring light to immortals and to mortal men; and Zeus sent forth Strife unto the swift ships of the Achaeans, dread Strife, bearing in her hands a portent of war.
>
> (*Il.* 11.1–4)

Metaphor, however, tends to be given second place to metonymy and simile. When metaphors do appear they are characteristically visual and concrete – even where there is a margin of doubt as to whether we should speak of simile or metaphor. One graphic instance is the *sperma puros* figure of the slowly burning log applied to the exhausted Odysseus:

> Odysseus ... lay down in the middle, and made a pile of leaves over him. As when a man buries a burning log in a black ash heap in a remote place in the country, where none live near as neighbours, and saves the seed of fire (*sperma puros*), having no other place to get a light from, so Odysseus buried himself in the leaves, and Athena shed a sleep on his eyes.
>
> (*Od.* 5.488–92)

A savage instance occurs in the tableau where Odysseus hangs his unfaithful serving-women from a ship's cable 'like thrushes or doves' – 'each had her neck caught fast in a noose, so that their death would be most pitiful. They struggled with their feet for a little, not for very long' (*Od.* 22.465–72).

Other well-known examples occur in descriptions of the assembled Greek army:

> As they fell in, the dazzling glitter of their splendid bronze flashed through the upper air and reached the sky. It was as bright as the glint of flames, caught in some distant spot, when a great forest on a mountain height is ravaged by fire.
>
> (*Il.* 2.455)

Or compare the analogy between the army and a swarm of flies: 'Thus these long-haired soldiers of Achaea were drawn up on the plain, facing the Trojans with slaughter in their hearts, as many and as restless as the unnumbered flies that swarm round the cowsheds in the spring, when pails are full of milk' (*Il.*

2.469ff.; the same figure reoccurs at *Il.* 16.635ff.); swarming bees and wasps are also used to create the same effect: 'Even as the tribes of thronging bees go forth from some hollow rock' (*Il.* 2. 87ff.); 'they poured forth like wasps of the wayside, that boys stir up ... having a heart and spirit like theirs the Myrmidons then poured forth from the ships' (*Il.* 16.260ff.). Warfare is troped with the image of crashing surf:

> And now battalions of Danaans swept relentlessly into battle, like the great waves that come hurtling onto an echoing beach, one on top of the other, under a western gale. Far out at sea their crests begin to rise, then in they come and crash down on the shingle with a mighty roar, or arch themselves to break on a cliff and send the sea foam flying. Each of the captains shouted his orders to his own command, but the men moved quietly. They obeyed their officers without a sound, and came on behind them like an army of the dumb. The metalled armour that they marched in glittered on every man.
>
> (*Il.* 4.422ff.)

Warriors are cut down like blades of corn: 'And as reapers over against each other drive their swathes in a rich man's field of wheat or barley, and the handfuls fall thick and fast; even so the Trojans and Achaeans leapt upon one another and made havoc' (*Il.* 11.67–70). Finally, war's inevitable aftermath produces some striking images: 'and many horses with high-arched necks rattled empty chariots along the dykes of battle, lacking their peerless charioteers, who were lying upon the ground dearer far to the vultures than to their wives' (*Il.* 11.169ff.); 'So there he fell, and slept a sleep of bronze' (*Il.* 11.241); the 'earth laughs with the gleam of bronze'; 'and the earth ran with blood' (*Il.* 8.66).

We might also record the singularly unheroic description of Nireus, the son of Aglaia and King Charops who brought three ships to fight on the side of Agamemnon: 'Nireus the handsomest Danaan that came to Ilium, excepting the flawless son of Peleus. And yet he was a weakling and his following was small' (*Il.* 2.670–5). With an eye to symmetry the text balances this with an instance from the forces of the Trojans; one of the tribes supporting Priam came from the non-Greek Carian people ('men of uncouth speech', *barbarophone*) led by Nastes and Amphimachus; the latter 'like a fool' came to the battlefield dressed in gold 'like a girl': 'Not that it saved him from a dreadful end. He fell to Achilles the great runner, there in the river-bed; and the provident Achilles made off with the gold' (*Il.* 2.867–75).

4 THE WORLD OF THE POEM: THE HOMERIC LIFE-WORLD AS A VIDEOLOGICAL UNIVERSE

In constructing the plot and working it out with the help of language, the poet should place the scene, as far as possible, before his eyes. In this way, seeing everything with the utmost vividness, as if he were a spectator of the action, he will discover what is in keeping with it, and be most unlikely to overlook inconsistencies.

(Aristotle, *Poetics* 17.1455a20ff.)

We will not pursue the question 'How does Homeric poetry represent ancient Greek society and culture?' – legitimate and fruitful though this question may be (e.g. Luce, 1975), but instead follow a different order of question, the logological question 'How does Homeric discourse rhetorically construct its world?' In posing this question we are primarily interested in the social-semantic correlates of poetic syntax.

The world as a theatre of praxis

There remains to be mentioned one peculiarity of the Homeric language – the tendency of verbs expressing perception to take on the middle form ... Such a usage underlines the interest of the subject in the action, and it may be related with a still more widespread phenomenon of the Greek verbal system – the tendency for future tenses to appear in the middle voice. This is doubtless due to the fact that future formations have developed from expressions of will and wish, where it was natural for the interest of the subject to be stressed.

(L. R. Palmer, in Wace and Stubbings, eds, 1962: 145–6)

We have seen that the world of the epic is a theatre of heroic praxis, a highly visual panorama of violent encounters, actions, and events. And the most characteristic outcome of violence is the conspicuous death of one of the antagonists, the enslavement of a city's population, or the destruction of a whole community (*Od.* 9.40ff.). Agamemnon's affront to Achilles' honour reveals the limits of the warrior code. Through the difficult *moral* education of Achilles we become conscious of the limitations of the heroic world and its military class structure – we are allowed to see the warrior ethos as *one* possible social code. Of all the Homeric *actants*, it is Achilles – in his nascent self-consciousness – who comes closest to the hero of tragedy. But the code of martial valour ensures that Achilles' growing insight into the nature of his own form of life will not be allowed to destabilize the aristocratic order as a whole.

The world projected by the Greek epic is a visible pyramid of power based ultimately on military conquest, raiding, and piracy. The social order is a rigid and unchanging status system: at the top of the hierarchy stands a male *élite* of heavily armed warrior kings trained for man-to-man combat. Each side is led by a great king (Agamemnon, the imposing though often injudicious warlord of the Achaeans, and Priam King on the Trojan side). The honorific status of kings is sustained by other warlords, each controlling a definite pyramid of personal power and patronage. In battle great kings are marked by their command of a chariot, reinforced by the swirling masses of infantry; the subjects of this class system are the foot soldiers and ancillaries to the infantry, the mass of citizens, and – by far the majority – the non-citizen classes of artisans, skilled workers, peasants, slaves, metics, and servants – the undifferentiated *demos*. As dependent subjects the latter groups form the nameless masses drawn in the wake of the violent action of the military *élite*.

For this power structure the exemplary synactical structure is the tense form of the *aorist*, the active and middle verbal 'voice'; the latter 'indicating the especial interest of the subject in the event referred to by the verb, or that the action takes place in the person of the subject' (Palmer, in Wace and Stubbings, eds, 1962: 145). Palmer distinguishes three types of verbal aspect: (i) the present, depicting the action as a process in being – the 'durative aspect' as in '*he is in flight*'; (ii) the aorist, representing the action as a total event, a discrete unit of history, the 'momentary or punctilinear aspect' as in '*his death took place*'; and (iii) the perfect, expressing the completion or result of an action as in '*he is dead*', '*he is in his grave*', '*I have made my choice*'. While all three syntactical frames foreground praxis, only the aorist captures the 'timeless', visual-spatial totality of the Homeric *theatre* of action. The aorist verbal form is thus ideal for expressing a spectacle of belligerent violent encounters spread out in a series of discrete encapsulated episodes. In the syntactical frame of the aorist decisions emanating from agents are translated into actions by others working upon recalcitrant materials, culminating in a totalized course of action or climactic bounded event. One of a myriad of such grammatical complexes occurs at *Odyssey* 15.220–2 in the following sequence of completed actions: '*So he spoke*'; '*they listened well to him*'; '*they obeyed him*'; '*they quickly went on board the ship*'; '*they sat down to the oarlocks*'.

We should also recall that the plot frame of the *Iliad* as a whole is governed by a conception of divine control working to bring about the total destruction of Troy and its terrrible consequences for both Achaeans and Trojans; I refer, of course, to the motif of the 'will of Zeus'. Zeus is the supreme diety, source of all power and 'lord of all'. It is through Zeus' 'all-seeing' ordaining mind that the events of the Trojan war are brought to completion. Zeus's will literally flows from the Olympian peak of divine authority to determine the fate of gods and mortals. Zeus is 'father' of all (*Od.* 13.51). The divine actant thus controls and predetermines every act in the Trojan drama. In Murray's translation from the opening verse of *Iliad* 1: 'thus the will of Zeus was being brought to fulfilment; sing thereof from the time when at the first there parted in strife Atreus' son, king of men [Agamemnon], and divine Achilles' (*Il.* 1.5–7).

Of course the aorist is the panoramic tense *par excellence*. Its use accentuates the spatial visibility of events, the decisiveness of choice, and the momentary manifestation of objects and activities as outcomes of a predetermined sequence of praxis. The aorist voice is thus perfectly suited to express the anticipated effects of a planned action, the real fulfilment of a project, the defeat of an antagonist, or decisive 'unfurling' of a necessary sequence of acts; hence the curious tense structure in Book I of the *Iliad: the will of Zeus was-being-brought-to-fulfillment* (Zeus' thought 'moving toward its end' in Fagles' recent translation). The aorist articulates the grammar of envisioned necessity ('the will of Zeus was accomplished' in Lattimore's version). The ordering will of the Lord of Olympus weaves the webwork of heroic struggles into a structure of manifest events.

We can see the timeless aorist in action in the syntagmatic sequence at *Odyssey* 15. 282–300:

(i)   Telemachus spoke;
(ii)   Telemachus took the bronze spear from him;
(iii) Telemachus laid the bronze spear on the deck;
(iv)   Telemachus went on board the ship;
(v)   Telemachus made Theoclymenus sit down beside him;
(vi)   His men loosed the stern cables;
(vii) Telemachus ordered his men to hold the tackle;
(viii) His men obeyed;
(ix)   His men raised the fir mast pole;
(x)   They set the pole in its socket;
(xi)   They secure it with forestays;
(xii) They haul up the white sail;
(xiii) They sail past Chrouni and Chalcis.

This in turn is a repetition of analogous paradigms of a completed action being broken into 'unit acts' (for example, the preparation for Telemachus' voyage to Pylos at the end of *Odyssey* Book 2 and Odysseus' departure from the Phaeacians at *Odyssey* 13.70– 90). Here the verb form of completed or 'fulfilled' action (*teleutesai*) punctuates the event into its visible elements: 'they spread a linen sheet for Odysseus', 'he went aboard', 'laid down in silence', 'they sat at the benches', 'she sped on her way', 'he slept in peace', and so on.

Homeric politics

The rule of many is not good; let there be one ruler.

(*Iliad* 2.204)

In times of peace Homer's universe is a world of noble palaces, rich in fine-worked artifacts, magnificent buildings, artworks, and the luxurious trappings of an advanced palace-civilization (for example, Priam's palace with its marble porches and colonnades in *Iliad* 6, the palace of King Alcinous in Scheria, *Od.* 7.81ff. and 13.1ff., or Menelaus' palace in Sparta, *Od.* Book 4, memories of which date back centuries to the palaces of the Mycenaean kings – 'the high roofed house of glorious Menelaus' at *Od.* 4.45–6).

The social cosmos is governed by a strict code of customary morality, a set of understood rules which regulate the hierarchical power structure by sanctioning definite rights and duties. These are not typically expressed as explicit precepts or laws, but are accepted as the taken-for-granted moral fabric of an aristocratic society. Yet the customary order of hospitality, politeness, reciprocity, status, and ceremonial sacrifice is a fragile achievement. Valuable gifts, for example, must be recurrently given and received. If Odysseus is given a giant tripod and cauldron as a symbolic token, King Alcinous will have it replaced by taxing the *demos* (*Od.* 13.14). Typically such rare gifts are only passed from equal to equal among the strata of 'nobles' (the *aristeia* or *kaloi kagathoi*); only occasionally is the principle extended to exchanges with social inferiors. The rules of the social game of reciprocity are held in place by tensile, antagonistic forces which might at any moment escape the bounds of civility.

As a circle of relatively equal warriors, Homer's warlords or *basileis* adhere strictly to the honorific norms of heroic struggle, reconciled to the ever-present threat of suffering and sudden death. The 'aoristic present' is the 'now-time' when death may appear (but equally so, in times of peace it is the timeless moments of joy, kindness, pleasure, song, and love). At the head of the class structure of hereditary nobles stands the Great King, a virtuoso among thanatonic warriors. Achilles, Hector, Nestor, Ajax, and so on, are lords (*basileis*) in their own right holding dominion over their own lands, households, and slaves (the institution of the Great King may even have been a temporary institution evolved to hold together an imperialist confederacy of 'kings' while campaigning). While Achilles is lord of the Myrmidons, Agamemnon is the great King of Mycenae and its island dominions, and, temporarily at least, overlord or 'high king' of the confederation of the other great *basileis* assembled before Troy. At *Iliad* 1.282–3 Agamemnon's hegemony is depicted in quantitative terms: the son of Atreus is king over more men than Achilles. His *arete* (or excellence) extends as far as his patrimony and military authority. Among the *aristeia* he is temporarily *primus inter pares*. We can also presume that material wealth – in terms of both the ownership of land and mobile wealth (objects, slaves, and animals) – reflects Agamemnon's authority over the other Achaean warlords. The ability to amass, control, and use wealth to augment political prestige was a major source of social status and political legitimacy. But accumulating wealth is not an end in itself; exemplary possessions are merely a necessary instrument of honorific status – symbolized by the sceptre of office or the right to perform sacrifices to the gods.

'Politics' is confined to the eminently visible war councils and aristocratic assemblies which punctuate the events of the war. For the ruling *élite*, existence is consummated in public theatres of conspicuous belligerence (measured in the increase or loss of mobile treasure and symbolic loot – tripod cauldrons, slaves from the royal household of the vanquished, bars of iron, body armour, chariots, war booty, and so forth). As all the symbols of communality are keyed to displays of physical prowess in battle, so the decisive events of political communality occur within the arena of public visibility. Honour (*time*) and glory (*kleos*) are the supreme values of human action.

The public *chora* is a *site* in which heroic acts (*erga*) and speeches (*logoi*) are witnessed, acknowledged by the community, and narrated (the aorist tense also serves as a technique in the construction of descriptions and narratives by the heroic agents themselves). Even death is accepted as a necessary event: to live and die honourably is the highest ideal; to die heroically at the hands of another warrior of equal prowess is the *telos* of existence, its fulfilling *arete*. Hence the vein of paradox which runs through the Homeric code: warlords exist for the illiterate iron of war and killing, yet honour and heroism require art and symbolic recognition. As Oliver Taplin observed, the *Iliad* 'is not so much concerned with what people do, as with the way they do it, above all the way they face suffering and death' (in *OH*: 57). What saves action from oblivion is the sculptural medium *par excellence* – the poetic *logos* – which is therefore accorded a high status in the Homeric ethic. Every warrior aspires to become a phrase on the tongues of a singer, a hero for some future audience assembled in the great hall or *megaron* (this is the ultimate goal of 'eternal reknown' (*kleos aphthiton*) sought by the warrior). *Aretai* – the excellences which exemplify and sustain the heroic life – must be named and remembered in song; in the absence of a strong belief in life after death the immortality of honour is the service poets render to power (the poets Phemius and Demodocus are thus essential elements of the palace complexes of Odysseus and King Alcinous (*Od*. 1.325, 8.336; 8.477ff., 22.342ff.)). Pindar in the fifth century would still invoke the same heroic complex in celebrating the role of the poet:

> Great valour dwells in deep darkness for need of song. In one way only we know a mirror for noble deeds – if thanks to bright clad Memory reward is found for labour in the famous song of poetry ... I fancy Odysseus' story has become greater than his sufferings because of the sweet poetry of Homer.
>
> (*Nemean* 7.11ff.)

Here again we find a rigorous homology between heroic values and Archaic grammar – in this instance embodied in the cultural code of the perfect tense in Homeric action descriptions. As an example Palmer gives the link between the process of *seeing* and its 'product', *knowledge*:

> given the basic meaning of the perfect, it is easy to see how the *active* perfect, for instance, of a perception-verb *derkomai* may be used, because it is in the subject of *dedorke* that the experience and knowledge which result from the action of seeing persist. Thus it is that the perfect of the IE root *weid*, 'to see', is used to express the notion 'I know': *(F)oida*.
>
> (in Wace and Stubbings, eds, 1962: 149)

To see is the first phase of power, to look, observe, and seize. Seeing is consummated in a state of knowledge. And, of course, the notion of 'knowledge' here is primarily *visual* (the Homeric root of our expression 'videology' (*vida/video/logos*): to witness, to see, to remember, to record and relate the exemplary actions and glorious deeds (*erga*) of aristocratic men (*agathoi*)). The power of vision is enhanced by the aorist's vision of power.

Where there are centralized sources of power there must also be passive subjects. The implicit economy of Homeric authority is fundamentally that of a zero-sum game. Domination flows to and from the citadel of the *élite*. The rest of the population are more or less subjected to the dominion of this subject. It follows that the field of political causality excluded all but those agents drawn from the aristocracy ('on the field of battle, as in the power struggle which is the Ithacan theme, only the aristocrats had roles', Finley, 1964: 55–6). The world the poems depict is pre-eminently a patriarchal, warrior society of kings and warlords in search of status in the form of victories bestowing publically recognized authority (enabling the *élite* to remain within the visible circle of the *agathoi* and avoid a life of shame (*aischron, aidos*) and oblivion). In this sense the Homeric life-world stands at the polar extreme to the later Epicurean ideal of private anonymity.

The natural world is also perceived from the hegemonic perspective of aristocratic action – nature is an instrument, threat, or background for aggressive, masculine interventions on behalf of particular reference communities (*oikos*) and cities. Nature's significance is tied to the agonistic culture of competition, combat, and war, projected as a background field of theatricalized encounters. Competition with others is both the means and the end of human flourishing. War is not an exceptional situation, but, rather, the fundamental setting of virtue, the bitter crucible where *eudaimonia* can be won or lost (the competitive ethos of Classical culture has Homeric roots: 'supposing you and I, escaping this battle, would be able to live on forever, ageless, immortal so neither would I myself go on fighting where men win glory. But now, seeing that the spirits of death stand close about us in their thousands, no man can turn aside nor escape them, let us go on and win glory for ourselves, or yield it to others', *Il.* 12.322–8). Yet the *Iliad* does not glorify or celebrate war as an end in itself. War is 'hateful' and 'bitter', an unavoidable means to publically valued goals. Life is the greatest good; but honour demands that the warrior risk his life to win glory (*kleos*) or fall at the hands of an antagonist.

Political action flows from decisions taken by kings – the 'greatest among the great'. In Aristotle's observation: 'This is clear from the ancient political systems described by Homer; there the kings first decide and then announce their decision to the people' (NE 1113a5–10). Freely-chosen decisions are taken by those who possess – and are seen to possess – virtue (*arete*) – defined in terms of the excellences most conducive to the effective conduct of war. As even kings must comply to the Will of Zeus, so those subject to the king's edicts are obliged to obey (we thus hear nothing of disloyalty or desertion on the part of the rank-and-file soldiery). The ordinary soldiers grumble and occasionally question the wisdom of a given strategy or local tactics, but mass desertion is unthinkable. The justness of decisions is retrospectively rationalized in terms of the outcome of the ensuing events. Justice emanates from the free will of the king or hero. And the king leads his fighting men in the same way that he is the 'shepherd of his people' (*laos*) in times of peace. His hegemony is secure only as long as his authority inspires actions which bear fruit or realize their objectives (an expression of what Adkins calls a 'results-culture').

The ideal king would embody the capacities of judgement, wisdom (*sophia*), and power. To decide on the right course of conduct requires practical judgement (*phronesis*) and such judgement is possible only in the light of knowledge (*episteme*) and wisdom (*sophia*), but the wisdom of the decision is only ultimately known in terms of the outcome of action which either reinforces or cancels its initiating conditions (for example, both Agamemnon and Achilles are found wanting in their understanding and foresight, as their judgements are clouded by personal ambition or momentary emotions). The cultural consequence of this idealized unity of *sophia*, *phronesis*, and *praxis* would prove decisive for the later rationalist turn taken by Greek ethical and political thought. The ideal carrier of *arete* should not only possess the necessary physical strength, bravery, and leadership qualities required of a Homeric hero – these are possessed in full by heroes like Ajax, Achilles, Hector, and Agamemnon – but they must also possess the virtues of generosity, foresight, wisdom, and strategic intelligence (the skills embodied respectively by Nestor, Odysseus, Priam, and Patroclus). The ideal warrior would be a man uniting these different virtues. It is inevitable that agents will appear who only possess one or, perhaps, several of these qualities – often in exaggerated and self-conscious forms – but who rarely embody the full range of the heroic virtues. One capacity in particular is singled out as indispensable for the effective functioning of the warrior ideal – the faculty of self-knowledge or wisdom (*noos* at Il. 13.726–35). Without a deep knowledge of the self – a mindfulness which demands a fundamental awareness of the motivation and conduct of others – no amount of strength, military prowess, or courage will transform a warrior into a wise leader. For example, neither Achilles nor Agamemnon fulfils this ideal (cf. *Il.* 18.105–6). The basic ingredient of practical judgement – the phronetic reflexivity and flexibility necessary for cool decision and self-comprehension – is lacking. Thus Agamemnon is presented as a deeply unreflective agent whose failure to understand and placate Achilles risks both the loss of his own leadership and the destruction of the Achaean army. The partial, flawed, or one-sided development of the heroic virtues serves as a powerful plot device. In fact Agamemnon's unreflective nature provides the setting for the *Iliad*'s psychopathology of actions carried out without self-understanding. In this sense the *Iliad* could be described as a dramaturgy of the consequences of a failure of self-reflection in its most important agents. In a phrase: without wisdom power strays from the *telos* of excellence. And in the disorderly and violent world of Bronze age warlords, this 'straying' from considered judgement may mean death for the individual and his family and slavery for his *polis*. But conversely, knowledge and wisdom *on their own* are manifestly incapable of creating the *thumos* of a great leader or noble spirit. Hector on the Trojan side and Nestor on the Achaean – both exemplars of wisdom, insight, and judicious counsel – come closest to melding the qualities of understanding and practical experience required by the ideal leader.

At *Iliad* 2.204 the hegemony of one king over a hierarchy of subordinate kings is justified by an appeal to the divine kingship of Zeus. Zeus personally symbolizes the hierarchy of governmental excellences in his overlordship of the Olympian divinities. As such he is the paragon of Homeric virtues, the phallocentric symbol of archaic values: power, knowledge, wisdom, strength, justice, decisiveness, judgement, and so on. In the narrative elaboration of the justice of Zeus, listeners (and later readers) could, so to speak, witness these qualities personified and see them at work in anthropomorphic terms (cf. 1.279, 2.24–5).

The *polis* of the Achaeans is another eminently visible stockade against the dangerous forces of nature and death, a temporary *chora* or protective space (a *temenos*, in Mycenaean Greek) cut out of an otherwise life-threatening environment. It represents the campaign equivalent of the heavily fortified citadel cities of Mycenae. The portion of land in which discussion and debate takes place is also an aristocratic *temenos* in the later Archaic sense of this word, a term which would later become saturated with religious and ceremonial significance (analogous to the 'auspices' in Roman religion). In the *Iliad* this is variously symbolized by the Greek siege-camp circling the walls of Troy, by the hastily constructed wooden wall encircling the ships of the Achaeans, and by the counsel circle – the *agora* – which plays such an important role in the narrative dynamics of the epic plot.

In Greek society during this period only members of the patriarchal, land-owning warrior caste were full citizens of the *polis*; the citadel evolved from the warrior camp of the king (just as in Mycenaean political topography the citadel-acropolis was self-stratified from an agricultural periphery which it taxed and exploited and from which it conducted its belligerent political and cultural transactions). The environing landscape is defined as a source of materials and resources for the city – a sustaining countryside for the essentially male world of the city. The acropolis provides a vivid analogue of the male eye which plans the violation and exploitation of the surrounding hinterland. Even as late as the fifth century, the ideal *polis* was a self-governing city-state secured by military strength as a consumption centre sustaining the good life of an *élite*, sustained by a surrounding envelope of agricultural and artisanate production. As an agent in its own right, the central acropolis formed the cyclopean hub of praxis from which radiated aggressive rays of phallocentric action. The fundamental purpose of these ancient citadels was, of course, security, rule, and domination. Those who stood outside the walls of the city and its gods have no political or social existence; they formed the invisible providers of the warrior class but could never become agents in the full Homeric sense: they could not become the subject of the imperfect, aorist, or perfect syntax of the Homeric verb form just as they could not enter the ethical space defined by the paradigms of virtuous conduct. They are therefore absolutely excluded from the making of history just as they are absent from the active doings of the Homeric grammatical system. This is how the symbolism of the *polis* created an imaginary cartography of the active self which helped to define the Classical ideal of an optimum political order.

With one or two notable exceptions (the mythical Amazonian queenship for example) only masculine *élites* are named agents in the epic world. Those beyond the videological horizon of the *polis* are destined to remain the passive objects of verbal systems, never becoming the agents of action. Women, peasants, bonded farmers, and the slaves who sustained the life of the city are thus excluded from its political space and therefore meet the *polis* only at the point of taxation and the extraction of surplus. Similarly, craftsmen and traders do not belong to the inner citadel which they serve. By inhabiting the margins of the *polis* they are absent from its history. They do not make events but form the raw materials, instruments (recall that Aristotle still speaks of the slave as an 'instrument' of the Athenian landowning class), and anonymous mass for those who command the subject positions of this authoritarian syntax.

In conclusion, the Homeric *polis* is essentially a fortified military space (the aristocratic landowners outside the destroyed citadels of Mycenean civilization may have been the group that first preserved the Homeric stories – their nostalgic obsession with recreating an age of heroic struggle providing the context for the survival of epic narrative which, as a living art form, decayed when these same aristocratic patrons lost their social and economic functions). The 'causality' uniting the worlds of war and peace derived from the ostentatious displays of noble (and occasionally ignoble) action and counteraction, the causality of agonistic struggle and its inevitable *pathos*. This is reinforced by the preference granted to the grammar of conspicuous action by Homeric syntax (on the future-directed voluntative subjunctive of the will and the optative mood see Palmer, in Wace and Stubbings, eds, 1962: 149–53). This is the aspect singled out by Hans Kelsen where he argues that divine retribution 'is the chief motive of both epic poems' (Kelsen, 1946: 190). Causality is coded into anthropomorphic metaphors and metonymies of action, force, suffering, punishment, revenge, and retribution: the causal texture of things manifests itself in an internecine network of events, a visible spectacle of contests overlooked by the Gods (who are also subject to similar experiences, joys, setbacks, pain, and suffering at the waxing and waning of the fortunes of their favoured heroes). If the domain of human actions is heroically motivated, this is ultimately grounded in a more primordial figure of language for which the whole *kosmos* – and not only the human world – is troped as a theatre of agonistic forces.

Epic humanism

We should underline once again the fact that the idea of the universe as a praxial system of retributive exchanges and balances governed by remorseless fate was a major *aesthetic* innovation of the epic genre. Death – as the ultimate consequence of this legality – is not simply another theme in Homer; the possibility of sudden death pervades the text not only as its central existential concern, but as the text's organizing schema and *telos*. The *Iliad* articulates the world of a militant, thanatonic society (Simone Weil rightly called the *Iliad* 'the Poem of Might' (*le poème de la force*)). Its images of self and society are thus troped in the symbols of Thanatos, not Libido. But Homeric fatalism does not linger obsessively on death and the meaning of violent death. In fact the 'theological' question concerning the ultimate significance of death is never raised in either of the epics. The question 'What is the meaning of death?' has no place despite death's omnipresence. Human existence has its necessary *telos* in death (where *telos* bears the triple sense of limit, necessary end, and horizon as at *Iliad* 16.502: 'Even as he spoke the *telos* of death enfolded him' (cf. *Il.* 16.855)). The delimitation of boundaries and *telos* are consequences of the Justice of Zeus (and through Zeus, the workings of Moira and Themis – the word *moira* derived from 'share' or 'portion': hence, the 'differentiating apportioning of things'). *Telos* derives its rule from *Themis* which orders and distributes the 'share of life' to creatures with her 'strong destiny'. Human activities are undertaken under the ancient sign of *Themis*, governed by Fate and subject to the will of Zeus (the *thémistes* or ordinances of Zeus at *Od.* 16.403). Zeus is also given a new role: he is not only the God of thunder and master of the thunderbolt, 'the dark-clouded son of Kronos', but also the all-seeing 'lord of men' (*Od.* 13.25). By his mind Zeus oversees the beginnings and ends of all things; he is the God of measures and just proportions possessing the wisdom which grasps that the life of everything mortal is completed by death. As a God of order and justice, Zeus grants and destroys life according to measure. Fate plays a central role in this cosmology, and is frequently imagined as a thread spun and woven into a fabric by one of the Olympian gods. Kronos and Lapetus, the two most influential Titans, spin the thread of good and bad fortune for men and are associated with the realm of the underworld (*Od.* 4.207; cf. Hesiod *Theogony* 736ff.).

For mortals, Lethe's Plain is the darkling scene of life:

> Yes, my friend, you too must die ... Even Patroclus died, who was a better man that you by far. And look at me. Am I not big and beautiful, the son of a great man, with a goddess for my Mother? Yet Death and sovereign Destiny are waiting for me too. A morning is coming, or maybe an evening or a noon, when somebody is going to kill me too in battle with a cast of his spear or an arrow from his bow.
>
> (*Il.* 21.100ff.)

Each existence that enters the choric space is ruled by its essential measure, its share of life, and appropriate time of growth, maturity, and decline. Thus Odysseus bids farewell to Arete, the wife of King Alcinous, with the toast

'Farewell, O Queen, and throughout all the years, until old age and death come to you, which are the lot of all human creatures' (*Od.* 13. 59–60). Every being is bound to the ineluctable laws of a *kosmos* divided into a world of mortal creatures separated from the spectatorial realm of the immortals: the Gods are literally the deathless ones ('deathless' from *athanatos, a* – not, *thanatos* – death); mortals are creatures of a day whereas the radiant gods live forever. Yet even the gods are not free from the pathos of finitude: some gods suffer, fall from grace, experience passions, needs, and wants, and are occasionally threatened by death (*Il.* 5.388). The text of the *Iliad* does not hesitate in depicting the goddess Cypris pursued and wounded by the warrior Diomedes ('[Diomedes] had gone in pursuit of Cypris with his pitiless bronze (*nelei chalko*), discerning that she was a weakling goddess, and not one of those that lord it in the battle of warriors – no Athena she, nor Enyo, sacker of cities ... the spear pierced the flesh upon the wrist above the palm and forth flowed the immortal blood of the goddess, the ichor' *Il.* 5. 320ff.; cf. Heracles' wounding of the god Hades at *Il.* 5.395–404).

Gods appear in visible forms; they walk and converse with mortals, possess a spatial identity, a particular style of being, speech, and comportment and a typical causal effectivity (consider Poseidon's intervention on the side of the Achaeans in Book 13 of the *Iliad*). In the *Odyssey* gods take the form of animals and birds. Moreover like Cypris they experience joy and suffer pain (5.330–431). Indeed the epic's generous anthropomorphism includes the full range of human attributes: for example, the Olympians treat the lame smith god Hephaestus as a butt for their cruel humour: 'uncontrollable laughter seized the blessed gods as they observed Hephaestus limping up and down the hall' (*Il.* 1.599–600, 18.410ff, ; 18.368ff.; cf. 21.389). Like physical deformity, life and death are depicted in untragic terms; the narrative literally has no place for individualized tragedy or emotionality when confronted with the force of Necessity:

> the tragic plot of the *Iliad* unfolds against the backdrop of this Olympian comedy, and the more that human woes multiply and oppress the atmosphere, the more extravagant and comic the scenes of the Gods become. It is indeed because of these scenes that the *Iliad* can not be exclusively described as a 'great tragedy'. It is at the same time a comedy, and perhaps the only serious poetical work of the Western world that harmoniously interweaves tragic and comic emotions.
> (Trypanis, 1977: 96)

Whether or not Trypanis' observation can be sustained it remains the case that in the epic death is simply one of the facts written into the nature of mortal existence. This view of the human condition as a mode of life-in-the-world embracing the ever-present fact and pervasiveness of death is expressed by the Trojan hero Sarpedon, speaking to Glaucus:

Ah, my friend, if after living through this war we could be sure of ageless immortality, I should neither take my place in the front nor send you out to win honour in the field. But things are not like that. Death has a thousand pitfalls for our feet; and nobody can save himself and cheat him. So in we go ['Let us go on', trans. Lattimore], whether we yield the glory to some other man or win it for ourselves.

(*Il.* 12.322–8)

'Let us go on'. This is the elemental principle of epic humanism. Not bravado, stoical resignation, or resentment, but recognition and acceptance of the law of necessity. Unlike later Greek drama, heroic sacrifice is necessary not because men aspire to be Gods or commit the mortal evil of *hubris*; rather death's empire is an absolute *horizon*: the hero is sacrificed in the full light of the world-play, death being part of the warrior code which all agents live by. The honorific code has no place for obsessive fear or morbid celebration of death (an Egyptian cult of the dead or modernity's morbid 'sickness unto death' are inconceivable in this culture). And as if to reinforce this will-to-life, the Mycenaean custom of royal burial with its elaborate inhumation funeral rituals is replaced by efficient cremation. As M. P. Nilsson, among others, has observed: while there is a cult of ancestors there is no cult of the dead or hero cult in Homer (Nilsson, in Thomas, ed., 1970: 68). Human beings live, suffer, die, and return to the heavens like smoke. Life is not a rehearsal for an afterlife; mortals essentially *are* their actions and when the life of praxis ends, life itself disintegrates.

Perhaps the most inconspicuous hero of the Homeric world is the rhythmical movements of the *kosmos* itself, the deathless presence of the Earth and Heaven, the timeless horizon of heroic action and divine existence *generated by the discursive functions of the heroic code*. Death may even be welcomed as a friend to mortals, a harbour from life's misfortunes in the words of 'Longinus', reconciling enemies in a shared recognition of a common fate. One of the most poignant instances of the epic view of life and death occurs in the fifth book of the *Odyssey* (5.201–27). The deathless nymph, Calypso – the nearest the *Iliad* comes to personifying *Eros* – has promised Odysseus immortality if he will stay and live with her, joining the company of the immortals; the alternative is to put to sea on a raft, facing further years of wandering and uncertainty – to accept human finitude bounded by the necessity of death. Odysseus chooses the human path, the way of mortals, articulating his decision with the first literary celebration of love and nostalgia – both, of course, reflexive emotions: nostalgia for his own city and community and love for his faithful wife, Penelope. Calypso – with her offer of libidinous immortality – is rejected for the finite joys of human existence, all of which are edged by the inevitability of death. He responds to Calypso's speech by embracing the unheroic demands of human existence:

Goddess and queen, do not be angry with me. I myself know that all you

> say is true and that circumspect Penelope can never match the impression you make for beauty and stature. She is mortal after all, and you are immortal and ageless. But even so, what I want and all my days pine for is to go back to my house and see my day of homecoming. And if some god batters me far out on the wine-blue water, I will endure it, keeping a stubborn spirit (*thumos*) inside me, for already I have suffered much and done much hard work on the waves and in the fighting. So let this adventure follow.
>
> (*Od.* 5.215–24; cf. *Rep.* 620C3–D2)

Another important instance is the final reconciliation of Achilles and Priam, the father of Hector. In begging Achilles to surrender the desecrated body of his son, Priam reminds the warlord of the Achaeans of their rooted condition, their common destiny and humanity. Both scenes – Odysseus remembering his love for Penelope and Achilles' recognition of his own humanity in the tears of Priam – are transgressions of the heroic code as well as breaches in the stereotypical epic formulae. In these anomalous moments the epic structure questions its own basic principles. And each hiatus in the Homeric way of life opens up new possibilities of the self that strike out beyond the warrior code. As deconstructive moments which temporarily 'undo' the dominant movement of the text, they reveal ethical possibilities unrecognized by epic grammar. Eros breaks through the interstices of the epic's thanatonic universe. Like another instance we will return to toward the end of the chapter – the violent confrontation between Thersites and the Assembly of warlords – these anomalies actively disturb the text's own values. We are reminded that other modes of being, other selves, other ways of experiencing and speaking are possible: the force of everyday reality asserts itself in the places where epic narrative breaks down – for example, in the gentler claims of family life, in friendship, and the ethic of a shared humanity. This is the conclusion reached by James Boyd White: 'The poem's fundamental value is the recognition of the equal humanity of those who must die', 'the center of the achievement is a kind of friendship ... even across the lines of enmity' (Boyd White, 1984: 53). The mutual recognition and compassion experienced by Priam and Achilles is the paradigm case of this immanent deconstruction: in glimpsing a form of justice older than and other than the contractual duties of the warrior code, we transcend the terms of the Homeric world; in their mutual recognition we glimpse a deeper form of self-knowledge beyond phallocentric domination:

> When, on Achilles' urging, Priam has eaten food, he is able to say, 'I had not eaten since you killed my son'. The calmness with which this is said enacts an acceptance that puts the events of the war, even the death of Hector, as far into the distance as if they were woven into the tapestry of Helen. Priam and Achilles come to see and express what Homer has led us as readers to see, to forget, and to learn again. They have moved to a new understanding of life, fully expressed, an understanding that

seems to make the heroic civilization impossible for them. The world of Book One is left wholly behind.

(1984: 53–4)

To frame these insights in logological terms: the this-worldly, humane ethic of reflection produced by epic narrative creates culturally specific possibilities of discourse and being-in-the-world which transgress and deconstruct the traditional terms of reference of the heroic ideal. I agree with Boyd White that the reflexivity of Homer's text 'teaches us a method of cultural analysis and criticism', and that this instruction is not informational or cognitive, but *affective* and *ethical*:

> the poem teaches us by the way it constitutes us. The ideal reader of this poem will be newly aware of the contingency of a language and culture, of his responsibility for how he speaks and what he is, and of his own need for a life of continual self-education.
>
> (1984: 58)

Conclusion: videological objectivity

> Homer, admirable as he is in every other respect, is especially so in this, that he alone among epic poets is not unaware of the part to be played by the poet himself in the poem. The poet should say very little in propria persona, as he is no imitator when doing that.
>
> (Aristotle, *Poetics* 24.1460a5–9)

The videological impulse of Homeric narrative relates to what Eric Auerbach (1892–1957) and others have defined as the basic impulse of Homeric style, its ability to represent phenomena in a fully externalized form, visible and palpable in all their aspects and completely fixed in their spatial and temporal relations.[19] This mode of representation required the rigorous exclusion of the voice of the poet *in propria persona*, as Aristotle says. Epic narrative is unique not only in its motivational understanding of causality and its phenomenological fidelity to the three-dimensional appearance of things, but in the narrative's obsession with the utopian principle which delineates the videological form of life: nothing must remain hidden and unexpressed. Under the auspices of this principle, the syntax and rhythm of the poety are organized to let the panorama of narrated events and phenomena manifest themselves in 'a uniformly illuminated, uniformly objective present'.[20]

But Auerbach's analysis tends to ignore a significant detail which Aristotle had grasped – the use of verbal rhetoric and 'paralogism' to 'bring off' the reality effect in often quite unpromising and improbable circumstances: 'Even in the *Odyssey* the improbabilities in the setting-ashore of Odysseus would be clearly intolerable in the hands of an inferior poet. As it is, the poet conceals them, his other excellences veiling their absurdity' (*Poetics* 24.1460a30–5).

Epic's descriptive emphasis creates a vivid illusion of truth – as though its readers might independently check its depiction of objects and events. Auerbach's thesis is that Homeric narrative displays a phenomenological obsession with the localized nature, concrete shape, form, causal workings, and relations of events and objects which enter its space. The Greek *epos*, as Auerbach expresses this, knows no background. In contrast with Biblical narrative epic strives to picture 'externalized, uniformly illuminated phenomena, at a definite time and in a definite place, connected together without lacunae in a perpetual foreground'. We may compare this technique with that of the Aesopian fable. The latter form openly advertises its fictionality and allegorical nature. It demands interpretation for its completion, whereas the epic only requires witnesses. 'Homer can be analyzed, but he cannot be interpreted.'[21] Biblical narrative on the other hand is saturated with proverbial, doctrinal, theological, and allegorical 'truths'; and here depth rather than videological surface, background rather than foreground is thematized. Homeric epic is the poetry of manifestation and visualization; biblical narrative invites interpretation and allegory. According to Auerbach, the canon of mimetic foregrounding[22] 'remained effective and determinant down into late antiquity', functioning as an ideal paradigm for 'the representation of reality in European literature'.[23]

I have argued that the visuality of epic description privileges spatial over temporal relations, topographical and topological description over temporal rhythms. Space is understood as a circular plane, a place enveloped by the stream of Okeanos (*Il.* 21.196–7). The shield Hephaestus makes for Achilles is also a perfect synecdoche of the Homeric conception of the natural order. The universe is a vast bowl, like an upturned shield; the shield represents the Earth (*Gaia*), supporting a realm of shining Ether (the upper Air) above and a dull, misty realm below. The rim of the Earth is bordered by Okeanos in the same way that Achilles' shield is ringed by the river Okeanos (*Il.* 18.607). And the light of the sun is extinguished each day by falling into the waters of Okeanos. The God Atlas supports the pillars which separate and conjoin Earth and Heaven (*Od.* 1.52). Beneath the bowl of the Earth lies dark Tartarus reaching downward without cease (the epithetic 'boundless' or 'infinite' (*apeiron*) is a common adjective accompanying the name '*Gaia*' (the boundless or endless Earth at *Od.* 15.79), just as Heaven is always 'broad Heaven'). Tartarus is the deepest stratum of the world order, as far beneath Hades as heaven is above the earth (*Il.* 8.14). Mortals struggle in an endless quest for mastery and nobility upon the aboriginal Earth. Significantly the totality of existing things is encompassed not by an indeterminate Chaos but by a dynamic, circulating river. Like the actions of mortals and immortals the plain of action is resolutely finite – the river circling back upon itself also serves as a seminal metaphor for reflexivity itself.

Homeric space, then, is not a three-dimensional Euclidean field of rectilinear forms and relations; it is a planar continuum distributed into definite fields; and these regions are not homogeneous or isotropic, but 'zoned' by the waxing and waning of heroic praxis: it is a *chora* analogous to the sculptural space of the so-called Egyptian period in early Greek sculpture. To borrow Auerbach's words, this space is filled with a plenum of present events 'so that a continuous rhythmic procession of phenomena passes by, and never is there a form left fragmentary or half-illuminated, never a lacuna, never a gap, never a glimpse of unplumbed depths'. We might call this the *ur-arche* or primordially immobile Earth.

The immobile Earth provides the ground for epic struggle, the sustaining horizon and gathering in which all things find their measure. For example, the circle of action around the Walls of Illium, the Trojan fortress – as an envisioned space of heroic encounter, a site of life and death struggle (cf. the city portrayed on the shield of Achilles, surrounded by warriors debating whether they should accept a ransom or sack and plunder the city). And as befits the perspicacity of heroic deeds decided by self-advertising acts of single combat, magical intervention plays little or no role in the central events.[24] Magic only intrudes at the margins of the Homeric world and, most typically, at the points of slippage and deconstruction.

To summarize: the *kosmos* presupposed by epic is essentially non-Euclidean, and certainly non-Copernican in the sense of positing a world in which things, mortals, and Gods interact upon the dark, immobile Earth fixed once-and-for-all in a universal present (Auerbach's uniformly illuminated, uniformly objective present). It makes no sense in the Homeric universe to speak of the Earth evolving or changing; the concept of an evolutionary earth (or evolutionary cosmos) has no place in the terms of the epic, precisely because *Gaia* is the universal frame in which all change and transformation takes place – and is necessarily beyond the reach of change (it is of course precisely this choric stability which later thinkers will question and reject). Thus the sun and stars (apart from the Great Bear) climb from and sink back into the encircling stream of Okeanos (*Il.* 18.489; *Od.* 5.270ff.). Earth in its majestic immobility is the eternal fundament of all other changes and transformations. The Homeric *chora* cannot be mapped by the coordinates of Euclidean geometry and we are not in the presence of mathematical 'nature as an impersonal order' (Frye, 1957: 319): its parameters are symbolic and its logic is dramaturgical. Yet as a videological container of three-dimensional objects and events, it prefigures all subsequent attempts to refigure the universe in the impersonal and abstract terms of purely visual logics.[25] If we could interpret the immobile *chora* in temporal terms and strip it of its praxial deformations we would come close to the Newtonian idea of the absolute frame of homogeneous time in which all events and phenomena have their being. There are no hidden depths as there are no undisclosed secrets; the Homeric godhead is the extreme antithesis of the hidden God. The later philosophical universe of the physical plenum and the mathematical manifold – forerunners of the rectilinear space of the Renaissance and the Cartesian grids of modernity – are recognizable variants of the Homeric *chora*.

5 SELF AND SELF-REFLEXIVITY IN THE HOMERIC WORLD

Many Homerists view the humanism of the heroic world and its anthropomorphic depiction of the Gods as the greatest contributions of epic narrative to Western consciousness.[26] In this section I will invert the traditional emphasis, viewing the humanization of the Homeric self as a consequence of its basic narrative strategies.

5.1 Grammar and Odysseus' scar

I have suggested that Homeric narrative crystallizes a grammar of wilful social action, exemplified by conspicuous displays of violence. An Achilles, Hector, Patroclus, or Agamemnon must be 'individuated' as the embodiment of epic virtue, individual bravery, military prowess and other beligerent *aretai*,[27] just as the first fictional hero of European literature must incarnate forethought (*nous*), cunning, and duplicity to survive the adventures of his return to Ithaca. But neither the demigod Achilles nor the cunning and wily Odysseus are yet masters of their own fate. They still have no way of fully dissociating themselves from the normative predicates of the heroic code. Odysseus may be the resourceful agent of his own homecoming, an embodiment of calculative rationality – the Reality Principle overcoming the Pleasure Principle of the Sirens – but he is not yet a self-conscious 'character' in the style of modern fictional narrative; his escape from the seductive web of Circe the temptress is not an absolute victory, but a temporary reprise from a universal temptation; as with the Agents who populate the *chora* of Old Tragedy, it makes no sense to ask after the interior life of these *actants*. Homeric narrative is not primarily interested in reflection in the sense of introspection, but focuses resolutely upon the grammatical requirements of heroic praxis.[28]

Yet we should not to reduce the reflexivity of epic agency to a static typology of fixed predicates. There are striking differences between the accounts of intelligence and selfhood given in the *Odyssey* and the earlier descriptions of mind in the *Iliad*: while the magical and more self-consciously literate and fictional elements of the *Odyssey* do not necessarily imply a later period of composition, they do support the idea that the *Odyssey* is the product of a more 'literary' craft. Odysseus is scarred by literature in more than one sense. By contrast the *Iliad* appears almost flat in its discursive homogeneity and formal treatment of character. The thematic contrast extends to the different semantic logics of space and time in each work. The plot of the *Iliad* unfurls and is laid out visually like the very ground-plan of Ilium; in the *Odyssey* it resembles a labyrinth in which the identity of the hero is repeatedly questioned. The plot of the *Odyssey* is designed to 'question' its central *actant* by setting Odysseus existential problems which he must resolve by using his many-sided powers of *noos*. In this way the tension of the plotting reinforces the earlier characterization of Odysseus as a reflective, problem-resolving agent. Beneath the armour, weapons, and heraldry of war we are left in no doubt that Achilles is a stable identity, convinced of his heroic role and social status – indeed the strength of these beliefs is what occasions the conflict with Agamemnon; Odysseus, on the other hand, has lost the insignia of social position, is cast up on alien beaches, nameless (*Outis* at *Odyssey* 9.500ff.) and disoriented. He has become a homeless wanderer – a sherd of an identity trying to relocate his place in the social order (Douglas Frame has reconstructed Odysseus' *noos* by relating it to the verb *neomai*, 'return home' (1978: chs 1–3)). The *Odyssey* is a tale of exile, an 'epic of the displaced person' (Steiner, in Steiner and Fagles, eds, 1962: 4).

On another level, the *Iliad*'s plot is silent about the personal and familial ties of Achilles; but Odysseus' identity is bound up with a complex web of domestic and societal relationships. Where Achilles is wholly inscribed in the text of war, Odysseus writes himself into the wider dramas of family, place, home, and origins. Odysseus, so to speak, has a life beyond the fixed scenarios of war and martial encounters. He has been liberated from the choratic syntax of the *Iliad* and launched upon the uncharted seas of fiction. Where Achilles' predetermined fate is to die and never return to his homeland, Odyssey's destiny is to evade death and return to Ithaca.

We *survey* the events of the *Iliad*, but we have to acquire the stratagems of the trickster to survive the journey through the magical topography of the *Odyssey*. The *Iliad* is constructed around visual panoramas of decisive confrontations (Achilles/Agamemnon, Patroclus/Sarpedon, Hector/Ajax, Hector/Patroclus, Menelaus/Paris, Achilles/Hector, Achilles/Priam) whereas the *Odyssey* weaves its story around a mobile, reflexive figure wandering through space and time. The *Iliad* models its plot on the cinematic, masculine space of Troy while the *Odyssey* follows an erratic, discontinuous, ungrounded, feminine signifier.

> The people of the *Odyssey* no longer live in an almost empty space; they take pleasure in the abundant variety of things to be seen and heard and experienced. The world is wide and full of wonders, which a man may visit to try his powers against them. The joy of discovery and the love of adventure form the background for a large part of the epic.
>
> (Fränkel, 1975: 86)

But even more important for our purposes, for the first time we hear the *voice* of Odysseus as the *narrator of his own story*. The *Odyssey* is the first explicitly reflexive and, at several notable points, self-reflexive work of literature in calling attention to its own construction, language, and belated derivation from the events depicted in the earlier work. If the *Iliad* is closer to the older genre of heroic stories (the *Epic of Gilgamesh* for example) and prefigures epic tragedy, the *Odyssey* resembles the later European novel (George Steiner writes: 'there is in the tale a flavor which has little in common with the classic

Greek sensibility. It foreshadows the romances of Alexandrine Hellenism', Steiner, in Steiner and Fagles, eds, 1962: 11). The mixing of short episodes with longer, self-contained narratives is less obvious here, while the narration of a large part of the epic by the hero himself marks a major innovation in epic technique. In the *Odyssey* both the flashback and first-person narration (*Ich-Roman*) make their first appearance in Western literature, opening up the well-known 'Chinese box' effects of literary reflexivity (cf. Trypanis, 1977: 37).

We have already noted the decisive role of women and the voices of women – particularly dangerous femininity (Circe the enchantress), libidinous sexuality (the 'dark' and mysterious Calypso), and seductive femininity (Nausicaa) – in Odysseus' struggle to gain self-knowledge. Odysseus navigates in space and time to avoid the temptations of women and the seductive language-games they weave. And these women – even the radiantly beautiful Nausicaa – are all directly connected with death or the threat of death. Odysseus can only avoid destruction by acquiring 'feminine' knowledge from the various seducers he meets on his journey. Matriarchal wisdom is superior to the patriarchal crafts of war (his comrades who fail to understand this difference typically end up dead – and to this extent the *Odyssey* can be read as a metacritique of the values of the *Iliad*). Odysseus' guardian goddess, Athena, also appears as a more protean force of transfiguration – a *magical* power controlling life and death who can, by the touch of a wand, metamorphose Odysseus into an old man:

> So spoke Athena, and with her wand she tapped Odysseus, and withered the handsome flesh that was upon his flexible limbs, and ruined the brown hair on his head, and about him, to cover all his body, she put the skin of an ancient old man, and then she dimmed those eyes that had been so handsome. Then she put another vile rag on him, and a tunic, tattered, squalid, blackened with the foul smoke, and over it gave him the big hide of a fast-running deer, with the hairs rubbed off, to wear, and she gave him a staff, and an ugly wallet that was full of holes, with a twist of rope attached, to dangle it.
>
> (*Od.* 13.429–38)

Women in the *Odyssey* have supernatural powers that are hardly mentioned in the *Iliad*. They threaten temptation, sudden metamorphoses, danger and death – their beauty intoxicates men, leading them far away from the vocations of war or fidelity to home and city. Women possess a sacred knowledge of demonic transfiguration and use this magic both for good (Athena's transformative spells) and evil (Circe's porcine magic which transforms Odysseus' companions into swine and leads Odysseus into the underworld). But women are also important as 'signifiers' in the network of marital exchanges and kinship arrangements (marriage contracts within the *élite* were historically based on the exchange of a dowry or bride-price). Above all, women are thought to possess the secret of life and death. Where the duels of the *Iliad* are patriarchal and terminate in death, the conflicts of the *Odyssey* include women and not infrequently involve a transformation of men – Circe's salutary magic, Calypso's release of Odysseus, and Nausicaa's courageous rescue of the shipwrecked Odysseus.

We hear Odysseus *narrating his own fortunes* – telling of his earlier career while fighting against the Trojans; we also hear him versifying stories from the *Iliad* at the request of his host and some of these stories contain, in Chinese box fashion, embedded accounts of his own activities at Troy (for example, the performance before Aiolos in Book 10); Odysseus – the 'man of many turns' – even engages in self-conscious pastiche and florid elaboration 'in the epic style' (at *Od.* 4. 271–89, 8.492–520 and 11. 523–32 telling the tale of the Wooden Horse and the fall of Troy, episodes not included in the *Iliad* itself). Thus strictly speaking the story of the Wooden Horse is a creation of the fictional Odysseus – the first work of metafiction in the European canon. The *Odyssey*, then, contains *the first explicit examples of reflexive narration and explicit intertextual plotting in European literature* (the qualification 'explicit' is important since we know of the existence of earlier narratives taking the form of multiple stories within stories, and these might be claimed as the first documents of reflexive plotting – for example the tale literary historians refer to as the 'The shipwrecked sailor', from the early Middle Kingdom testifies to the existence of the technique in ancient Egypt – see William Kelly Simpson, ed., 1973: 50–6). However, only the Homeric poem in the ancient world makes the *mise-en-abyme* technique an integral element of its art, even placing this technical insight about its own textuality into the mouth of one of Odysseus' listeners, King Alcinous, who remarks:

> We do not think you are a deceiver or a liar, Odysseus, as the black earth bears many men who tell many lies. Your tale has form, and your mind is noble, and you have told your story skilfully, like a regular singer.
> (*Od.* 11.362–8)

While Odysseus paints the world of the *Iliad* in nostalgic colours, the fall of Troy is presented as the result of Odysseus' intelligence – symbolized by the episode of the Trojan horse (8.494). In these moments of metacommentary and self-parody Odysseus becomes a singer of tales (*aoidos*), a figure on the verge of a philosophy of the epic. Like Don Quixote in a later mock epic, Odysseus steps in and out of the fictional space created by the craft of epic writing: he begins to explore the vertiginous paradoxes of fictional language. But unlike the Knight of the Mournful Countenance, Odysseus did not have the benefit of more than two millennia of fictional artiface and narrative reflexivity to guide his ambivalent ontological status. The *Odyssey* was in fact the first exploration of the multiple worlds of narrative self-reflection. We are faced with the existence of a premodern work which utilizes postmodern narrative strategies.

Significantly, the only figure who unambiguously engages in such metacommentary in the *Iliad* is Helen, the abducted 'cause' and wilful initiator of the ten-year war against Troy. From her elevated viewpoint on the walls of Troy she reflects on the events unfolding below. She appears in the house of Paris weaving herself into a tapestry depicting the course of the War (*Il.* 3.125; cf. 130–8, 156–60, 164–5). Like the self-fictionalizing Odysseus, Helen has acquired a tragic insight into her guilt in deserting king Menelaus for Paris – or, to maintain the spirit of Book 3 of the *Iliad*, a more perspicuous perspective toward her role in the causal texture of the unfolding events (3.139ff.). The cruel longevity of the war around Troy has forced her to accept her own guilt (3.172ff.). In self-consciously theorizing about her own moral responsibility she invokes the language of agent causation, presenting the suffering of the Achaeans and Trojans as a product of both contingent and necessary causes. Her soliloquies reveal the mind of a reflexive agent (for instance at *Iliad* 6.344ff.).

The presence of metanarrative indicates the appearance of literariness within the structure of the epic. At the level of character it also indicates the emergence of figures like Hector, Helen, and Odysseus as palpable living and breathing *individuals* rather than as the semiotic vehicles for stereotypical qualities. Paradoxically the emergence of 'Odysseus' and 'Helen' as rounded characters is an effect of highly complex literary devices: intertextual reference, metacommentary, first-person narration, autobiographical reflection, disguise-and-recognition scenes, and so on. The first 'characters' of the European tradition are the creatures of highly crafted rhetorics of reflection. In the *Iliad* Odysseus is narratively destined to be simply 'the cunning Odysseus', whereas in the *Odyssey* he is not only cunning, intelligent, thoughtful, and discursive, but also given to sudden fits of sorrow and melancholy; he is nostalgic, perhaps even romantic (for example in his carefully crafted speech in response to Calypso's offer of immortality), familial (the plot's basic thematic motive is that of the homecoming hero overcoming all obstacles to return to his faithful wife and family), dangerous, and even brutal when necessary (the vivid scene of the blinding of Polyphemus). In the act of questioning the limits of Archaic characterization, the metanarrative experiments of the *Odyssey* generate the possibility, if not indeed the necessity, of a more complex, many-sided literary *persona*, creating the first individualized hero of Western literature. In this respect the *Odyssey* represents a major turning point in the history of European consciousness. Odysseus is no longer contained by the Archaic universe. His self-reflexive narratives mark the birth of literature and the spirit of freedom. The scar which leads Eurycleia to recognize Odysseus at *Odyssey* 23.73 is also the first sign of recognition in the European novel. Odysseus literally becomes a sign (*sema*) to be 'tested' and deciphered in the dialogues of *Odyssey* 23 and 24. Unlike an Agamemnon or Achilles he can move with ease through several universes of meaning (the worlds of his travels which he narrates to Penelope at *Odyssey* 23.310–44). His 'wilyness' is graphically displayed in his 'manysidedness' (*polymetis* meaning both 'of many counsels' and 'of many tricks'): he is as strong in war as the other warlords, but he is also subtle of speech and can even turn his hands to agriculture and artisanate crafts ('Odysseus of many devices').

Of equal significance for the development of secular reflexivity, we begin to hear less of the gods in the *Odyssey*. Unlike the *Iliad* where the gods' continual intervention is a grammatical norm, the plot of the *Odyssey* follows the wandering signifier without the overbearing presence of the divine. Causation shifts from the Olympian gods with Zeus at their head to the wilful designs and actions of men – symbolized by the reflective speech and actions of the 'wise Odysseus' (*Od.* 1.32–54). Where the gods do appear they are less predictable and stereotyped. The gods have not yet become allegorical symbols, but we have intimations of their displacement from the centre-stage of this society. This, of course, is one of the central theses of Theodor Adorno and Max Horkheimer in their *Dialectic of Enlightenment*:

> The venerable cosmos of the meaningful Homeric world is shown to be the achievement of regulative reason, which destroys myth by virtue of the same rational order in which it reflects it ... The myths have been transformed in the various layers of the Homer narrative. But the account given of them there, the unity wrested from the diffuse sagas, is also a description of the retreat of the individual from the mythic powers ... the opposition of the surviving individual ego to multifarious fate ... The prehistoric world is secularized as the space whose measure the self must take ... the *Odyssey* is already a Robinsonade.
> (1979: 43–80, esp. 57, 58–9, 61)

With these clarifications in mind we can now turn to analyze the epic's rhetorics of selfhood and its related images of speech and language.

5.2 Rhetorics of self and self-reflection

Archaic Greek has no equivalent term for the word 'self' (consciousness, self-consciousness, or self-reflection) and we have little explicit evidence in the earliest works of literature of anything like a residential core of personal identity in the modern, Cartesian sense. If the notions of an introspective ego and self-consciousness were unavailable to the epic, how did Homeric discourse handle questions of identity and selfhood?

The Homeric psyche or 'soul'

Unlike Bruno Snell (1953: ch.1) and others who have argued that the Greeks had no conception of a unitary self or personalized will, I have suggested that the dramatic conflict which occasions the narrative movement of the *Iliad* forms the paradigmatic instance of an *agon* of individuated wills and that in the later work, Odysseus introduces himself as a self-centred agent: 'I am Odysseus, Laertes' son, known all over the world for my cunning' (9.19). In the light of this claim we should also revise the conclusions reached by Michel Foucault ('What was missing in classical antiquity was the problematization of the constitution of the self as subject', 1988a: 253) and Jan Bremmer (it is 'only in fifth-century Athens that we start to find the idea that the citizen can determine his own, independent course of action. By the end of that century *psyche* became the centre of consciousness, a development not yet fully explained but upon which, most likely, a strong influence was exerted by the rise of literacy and the growth of political consciousness. And it seems likely that the systematic reflection on the soul started precisely at the end of that century because the *psyche* had become the centre of consciousness and for that reason would have provoked a much stronger interest than before' (Bremmer, 1983: 68). Foucault's assumption of an homogeneous 'Classical antiquity' and Bremmer's view of the sudden emergence of the self as citizen-subject in the fifth-century *polis* distorts the textual and historical evidence we have analyzed but illustrates the need for a more accurate account of the emergence of self-reflexive experience and representations during the Archaic period. These theories also, more fundamentally, ignore the intertextual relationship between the conceptions of self in the *Iliad* and the *Odyssey*. If the *Odyssey* is a critique of the Archaic values of the *Iliad* (Steiner, in Steiner and Fagles, eds, 1962, 13), it is also, more profoundly, a critique of Archaic selfhood.

We have already seen that the *Odyssey* is explicitly designed as an adventure of a singular agent and that Odysseus' *'polymetic'* self is already reflectively reading and interpreting his fate in the imagery and narrative codes of the *Iliad* (he presents himself to the Phaeaceans, in the text cited above, as a 'literary' hero, a stylized, if not stereotyped, figure 'famous all over the world' for his intelligence and trickery). It is surely appropriate that the first reflexive classic of European literature should have as its central theme the Return to the Source (Ithaca) and the hero's recovery of his lost Patrimony (an identity tied to the social order of the Name, Memory, and Matrix (Penelope). We are again reminded of the wisdom contained in Walter Benjamin's description of the *Odyssey* as an epic of the human spirit, whose figure is called No-one and Everyman (Aristotle – at *Poetics* 24.1459b14 – had already contrasted the *Iliad* and the *Odyssey* as a story of suffering as against a story of character (*ethos*)). But we should amend Benjamin's Aristotelian insight by observing that the spirit in question here is the reflexive spirit of disguise, multiplicity, artifice, deceptive appearances, and trickery. Odysseus survives as a self (even perhaps as a parody of the epic Self) by perfecting the amoral arts of pretence and fictionality, by existing as a virtuoso of subterfuge and deceit, a man of many ways (*polutropos* at *Od.* 13.291–2). He constructs his own singular personality by manipulating the 'force-field' embodied in the grammar of the Homeric soul (cf. Adkins, 1970: 13–48). It is this linguistic and dialectical achievement that has been overlooked by many commentators on the Greek epic tradition. Certainly this is not the reflective *psyche* theorized by Socrates, Plato, or Aristotle, but it is nonetheless a complex vision of selfhood which antedates the concerns of the fifth-century sophists and philosophers. We will pursue two theses in what follows: first, that the exploration of the *persona* does not have to wait until the linguistic experiments of the lyric-poets, and second, that something like a 'typology of personality' is already implicit in the epic's characterology.

We have to proceed with some care at this point; we agree that Homer's heroes do not experience the world in terms of a subjective vocabulary of inner 'cognition', 'affectivity', and 'volition' ('Human beings, in Homer, simply do not have the unity needed for conscious choices and creative acts', Feyerabend, 1987: 139). We also accept that *psyche* is not equivalent to self or soul in its post-Classical senses (Adkins, 1970: 13–14; Claus, 1981). And, further, that Homeric Greek has no concept of the will as an autonomous 'faculty' of a personal Ego or self-monitoring soul (these latter notions are indeed the product of a later historical period and fundamentally different form of life). But this should not lead us to ignore important contexts where knowledge, foresight, and strategic wilfulness are formulated as experiential orders of the first importance. Returning to the Homeric texts suggests a more nuanced position on the question of Homeric psychology – a position favoured by Adkins: 'The unitary self may not be important, but the unity represented by the personal pronoun exists: it can check the *thumos* and the other "parts" [of the Homeric personality]' (1970: 46–8). This becomes even more manifest if we read the *Odyssey* as an epic of identity (foregrounding its recurrent themes of 'mind' (*noos*), self-recognition, misrecognition, reflexive adventure, and the like). Odysseus could in fact be said to be the paradigm of practical intelligence as practical reason began to extricate itself from earlier forms of consciousness in the Archaic period. He is a paragon of tactics and stratagems, the trickster who can turn an adverse situation to his own advantage – someone who thinks on his feet, a cunning individual (*polumetis* may be translated as 'many tricks') who manipulates the arts of persuasion and deception to further his own ends.

Where modern thought speaks of 'consciousness' and 'self-consciousness', Homeric Greek uses idioms involving words such as *thumos*, *phrenos*, *nous* (or *noos*), and *psyche*. These terms designate 'aspects' of a loosely articulated personal order, a confederation of parts interrelated into a constellation of agonistic forces and energies:

> Humans, as they appear in late geometric art, in Homer, and in archaic popular thought, are systems of loosely connected parts; they function as transit stations for equally loosely connected events such as dreams, thoughts, emotions, divine interventions.
> (Feyerabend, 1987: 139)

More significantly this motivational vocabulary indicates *actions*, visible physical displays of character and qualities often proceeding from exogeneous 'causes'. As Murray observes, 'the whole language of psychic phenomena is reified and externalized: mental states are identical with their physical symptoms, and head, lungs, belly and knees are thought of as the seats of the emotions' (1993: 53). As decentred capacities of action the powers of physical force, emotion, reason, intellect, judgement, and will have their own economic demands within a vortex of forces centring upon the life experiences of agents. We have, then, a paradigm not of the 'non-self', but of a dramatic decentred selfhood. It is more accurate to see the self of the epic as a plural network of demands, a shifting configuration of conflicting functions which play across the heroic body rather than a self-present identity in the manner of our own favourite Platonic and Cartesian metaphors. But, as Feyerabend has stressed,

> this lack of integration *of the individual* is more than compensated by the way in which the individual is embedded into its surroundings. While the modern conception separates the human being from the world in a manner that turns interaction into an unsolvable problem ... a Homeric warrior or poet is no stranger in the world but shares many elements with it.
>
> (1987: 139)

The point is also made by Hermann Fränkel in his observation that Homer understood man essentially in dynamic terms: 'Man is seen as what he does rather than as what he is' (1975: 77).

As we have noted, for the *Odyssey* this vortex of motives forms the topic of the narrative itself as the protean self of its central hero is thrown into a labyrinthine world of complex deceptions, false appearances, and trickery. This is the primary reason why the *Odyssey* can be read as an odyssey of the will-to-reflexivity beset by all the powers obstructing self-understanding. Natural and supernatural forces thwart Odysseus' goal of returning to his place of origination (what Frame calls 'the return to life and light', 1978: 28). In contast to the poem of force, the *Odyssey* is a poem of selfhood. We now turn to the task of documenting these claims.

The complex and the multiple self in Homer: *thumos, phrenos, noos,* and *psyche*

Thumos as 'life'

The complex word *thumos* introduces our major theme. *Thumos* (or more accurately, the manifold rhetorics in which the word functions in the surviving literature) was used widely as a term for 'animation' or 'life' in general; it frequently appears in the context of an animating principle or functional source of movement (where later and more technical usage might resort to *dunamis*). In Ionic and early Attic Greek *thumos* is used generically as an expression for life, soul, or spirit. Like the English word 'life' it is metaphorically extended to cover a very wide range of 'life-full' and 'life-less' experiences: 'nor is there any life (*thumos*) in your festivity, because of so much suffering', *Od.* 10.464

(a situation which has its modern parallels in the multiple rhetorical uses of the words 'life' and 'spirit'; and we should not need reminding that the referents of *'the Holy Spirit'*, *'wood Spirit'*, *'high spirits'*, and *'a spirited horse'* share no essential core of meaning).

Some of the functions of *thumos* in ancient Greek overlapped with the semantic range of the word *psyche*. At *Works and Days* 686, for example, Hesiod uses the word *psyche* (*psuche*) with the meaning of 'life' or 'source of life' in the foreground, claiming that 'wealth means life (*psyche*) to poor mortals'.

Thumos as 'aggressive spirit'

Thumos often appears in contexts where we would transliterate the term as 'temper' or 'aggressive, military spirit'. An instance of this appears at *Il.* 6.72 where Nestor urges the Greeks to take no prisoners and by 'so saying he aroused the strength and spirit of every man'. Appropriately, *thumos* has its physical locus in those parts of the anatomy associated with volitional, passionate, or affective action – the heart, diaphragm, and limbs (cf. Jaeger, 1947: 74). Like a causal, physical force *thumos* prompts the body to move and take decisive action. The 'body' is 'stung' into action by the directive, corporeal causality of *thumos*. Thus *thumos* sows uncontrollable panic in the ranks of a fleeing army. It is especially applied to emotions and moods: vexation, rage, courage, desire, satisfaction, hope, pain, astonishment, timidity, pride, and cruelty (Fränkel, 1975: 78). This summarizes one of the central motivational folk psychologies in Homeric culture – actions are frequently under the controlling 'powers' of non-reflective, non-individual forces.

If *thumos* is like an overpowering causal agency, it is also the life force which opens the receptive soul to the words and gifts of the gods; and as a vectorial power within a complex field of forces it is subject to counteractive influences, particularly countervailing powers with a divine provenance: the gods literally take up residence in the soul, and direct an agent from within. Consider, for example, the visitation of Pallas Athena and her galvanizing effects on Telemachus: 'So spoke the goddess gray-eyed Athena... she left in his spirit (*thumos*) determination and courage' (*Od.* 1.320–1). Again we might think of analogies with the grammatical functions of 'courage', 'inspiration', 'enthusiasm', and analogous expressions in English usage ('to be filled with enthusiasm', 'to be eager', 'to feel inspired', etc.). As *thumos* works at a visible corporeal level, the spectatorial eye of the narrative frequently depicts the visible impact of the goddesses' intervention: 'and he guessed the meaning, and his heart was full of wonder, for he thought it was a divinity. At once he went over, a godlike man, to sit with the suitors' (*Od.* 1.322–4).

Thumos as the location of the emotions

Thumos is typically invoked as a material locus of the emotions and affective life. We can briefly outline some of the most typical contexts in which this sense is dominant.

Suffering

Thumos is the site of suffering, a place of emotion and *pathos*. The opening words of the *Odyssey* begin the narrative of Odysseus' wandering with an account of his pain and suffering ('... *algea ... thumos*' at *Odyssey* 1.4), experienced in the years spent struggling to return to Ithaca. Like many Indo-European languages, ancient Greek possessed an idiomatic equivalent to the English paradigm 'pain in my heart'. And just as our everyday speech acts resort to such locutions without any ontological commitment to the existence or location of their referents, so pain and suffering are described as 'filling', 'possessing', 'shaking', 'threatening', 'moving', etc. the *thumos* of the heroic agent: *thumos* was neither 'in' the heart nor existentially identical with this particular organ (the Ionic dialect uses the word *kardia* for heart, as when Athena 'puts courage into the heart (*kardia*)' of the princess Nausicaa confronting Odysseus on the beach at Scheria).

Compassion

Calypso's reflective confession that she has no evil plans in allowing Odysseus to build a raft to escape from her island provides another good example of *thumos* as the decentred *locus* of compassion:

> this is no other painful trial I am planning against you, but I am thinking and planning for you just as I would do it for my own self, if such needs as yours were to come upon me; for the mind (*noos/nous*) in me is reasonable, and I have no spirit of iron inside my heart (*thumos*). Rather, it is compassionate.
>
> (*Od.* 5.187–91; cf. *Il.* 22.357, 24.205)

Love

A similar paradigm occurs after Calypso's failure to win Odysseus' love at *Odyssey* 7.258, or the analogous synecdochic description of Penelope's constant love as her 'enduring heart' (*thumos*) at *Odyssey* 11.181.

Heart and soul

As we have noted above, *thumos* often appears in contexts where the translation would best be served by the term 'heart', especially in contexts relating to the emotions, volition, and affectivity. For example, the Homeric formula *'phrenos and thumos'* indexes a special form of knowledge of the emotions beyond the reach of intellectual cognition, where an appropriate English paraphrase would be: 'I knew in my heart that ... p' (a formulaic sequence based on the phrase *oida kata phrena kai kata thumos*). The expression with its implication of a prereflective 'moral knowledge' would later become a stock-phrase of tragic drama. The expression with its implication of a prereflective, 'moral knowledge' would later became a stock phrase of tragic drama. Thus the prophetess Cassandra is said to possess the 'divine gift' in her soul (*phrena*) even though a slave and unskilled in formal learning (Aeschylus, *Agamemnon* 1080ff.).

Pride

'She spoke, and the proud heart in us was persuaded' (*Od.* 12.28).

Courage

'Only the daughter of Alcinous stood fast, for Athena put courage into her heart, and took the fear from her body... ' (*Od.* 6.139–40); or consider *Iliad* 13.135 where the 'minds' (*phrena* here has the predominant meaning of will or passion) of the counterattacking Achaeans can not be diverted from the struggle; or Hector arousing 'the strength and spirit (*thumos*)' of the Trojans (*Il.* 13.155).

Anger

Thumos appears to be most active in the passions aroused by extreme anger or similar uncontrollable emotions: 'Now you have stirred up anger deep in the breast within me by this disorderly speaking' (*Od.* 8.178). We have seen that the great-souled Achilles was poetically characterized by the uncontrollable and hyperbolic nature of his anger (*Il.* 18.107ff.). Achilles is, so to speak, anger incarnate (cf. 'hard-hearted Strife' (*Eris*) in Hesiod, *Theogony* 225 and the bitter anger of Zeus at *Theogony* 868). The dishonouring of the 'best of the Achaeans' is also physically displayed in the definite physiognomic language of anger that Achilles assumes throughout the narrative of the *Iliad*. Here the expression 'Achilles' anger' is an indexical consequence of a collective transgression of the heroic code. Achilles assumes the behavioural mantle of anger on behalf of the Achaean warriors. Anger is, so to speak, a collectively coded emotion recognizable to all who subscribe to the same value system.

HOMERIC EPIC REFLEXIVITY

Thumos and the 'thinking heart'

Reflection

If *thumos* is closely related to the 'affective soul' or the sources of 'inner emotion', anger and aggression, *phrenos* – the 'heart' – is also the intellectual site of doubt, uncertainty, and 'reflection', exemplified, for example, in the kind of self-questioning to which both mortals and Gods are subject: 'there was no easy sleep for Zeus. He was pondering in his heart how he might vindicate Achilles and slaughter the Achaeans beside their ships' (*Il.* 2.3).[29] We might contrast this Homeric psychology with the later folk-psychology summarized in the formula 'heart and *head*' (where the locus of reflection has, so to speak, migrated upwards). It is very important to note the dual location of 'thought' in the couplet *'phrenos and thumos'* as a formula rhetoric called upon to dramatize situations where decisions – particularly those involving different, equally weighted, courses of action – are at issue; if we can speak of 'will' in epic narrative, it often makes its appearance in an agent's decisive act of overcoming the paralyzing effect of a dichotomic choice. Thus at the beginning of Book 20, Odysseus debates with himself 'in heart and mind' whether to kill his unfaithful servants immediately or defer their punishment (*Od.* 20.5–15). And not unexpectedly, such situations most frequently prompt elaborate rhetorical activities. This also illustrates the semantic principle of polarity in the evolving language of Homeric reflection.

Consider the 'heart and soul' paradigm in: 'he pondered then in heart and soul whether he should pursue further ... ' (*Il.* 5.671; and cf. *Il.* 8.169, *Il.* 11.411, and *Il.* 17.106); also: 'consider well in your heart and spirit' (*Od.* 1.294); 'and now he pondered two ways within, in mind and in spirit, whether he would leave it to him to name his father, or whether he should speak first and ask and inquire about everything. While he was pondering these things in his heart and his spirit ... ' (*Od.* 4.117–20; cf. *Od.* 5.365, *Od.* 5.424, *Od.* 6.118); and an example which includes a reference to thought in embedded speech: 'So she spoke, but I, pondering it in my heart, yet wished to take the soul of my dead mother in my arms' (*Od.* 11.204). Nestor's son, Peisistratus is pictured 'wondering/admiring in his heart' before the rich gifts his father has given to Odysseus' son, Telemachus (*Od.* 15.132), and later 'pondering' or 'taking counsel with his heart (*thumos*)' (*Od.* 15.202). The same figures of speech would become canonical for later Greek poets. Thus in the *Works and Days*, the errant Perses is urged to 'take these things to your heart' (*Works and Days* 25).

Thoughtful speech

Since speech – particularly the kind of persuasive speech which we know as *rhetoric* – is a mode of praxis, the dilemmatic logic of choice applies most forcefully to active interventions of speech and language; indeed *thumos* often appears to be the motivating occasion, stimulus, or source of consequential speech. The voice of *thumos* functions as a relatively independent 'agency' within the mind of the Homeric hero. It is characteristically presented in 'act predicates': *thumos* 'bids', 'does', 'intervenes', 'restrains', 'encourages', 'blocks', 'uplifts', and so forth. An interesting example of the dramatization of *thumos* as the soul in dialogue with itself occurs at *Odyssey* 4.140–1: 'Shall I disguise my thought, or speak the truth? My heart (*thumos*) tells me to speak.' The same formula of *thumos* conversing with itself appears in *Iliad* 22.122, and once more at *Iliad* 22.385: 'why does my soul speak with me?' (we might think of modern vernacular equivalents: 'I listened to my heart', 'My head said no, but my heart said yes', etc.).

Understanding

If *thumos* is typically the voice of impulse, it can also be the place of 'understanding' or 'insight' after a difficult decision has been made, a plan hatched, or a project agreed upon: 'Helenus, the dear son of Priam, understood in *thumos* this plan, that had found pleasure with the gods in council' (*Il.* 7.46ff.). The *thumos* can also plant a thought or plan in the mind of a man. Frequently the thought (*noema*) is presented as emerging from the soul unannounced ('Why has such a thought come into your mind?' *Od.* 15.326). In later Greek culture we know that the faculty of the understanding was itself understood both cognitively and rhetorically; it is the place that Aristotle has in mind when locating the speaking mind as 'the faculty of discovering all the available means of persuasion in any given situation' (*Rhetoric* 1355b 26). Here, of course, rhetoric (and along with its judicious reflection, *phronesis*) takes command of the wilful passions and surging powers of *thumos*. *Phronesis* disciplines and organizes the different claims of the soul in the interests of reason. This is why Odysseus seems to possess a power of judgement resembling divine wisdom as well as a spirit (*thumos*) which had suffered and survived many hardships (*Od.* 13.89–91). In Hesiod, we hear of 'misguided *thumos*' as the text depicts the story of Hesiod's errant brother, Perses (*Works and Days* 646).

Sorrow and melancholy

The paralysis of thought by sorrow and melancholic reflection is presented as a morbid condition of the *thumos*. Like passion in general, 'sorrow' comes from outside the Homeric self like a dark wave or miasmic vapour. Take for example the scene where the Phaecean youths urge Odysseus to snap out of his dark mood:

> It seems that you know the games, for there is no greater glory than can befall a man living than what he achieves by speed of his feet or strength

of his hands. So come then and try it, and scatter those cares that are on your spirit (*thumos*).

(*Od.* 8.145–9)

Penelope makes promises to her suitors, 'sending them messages' (at *Od.* 13.380–1) but her heart mourns for the return of Odysseus, her mind (*noos*) is set on other things – 'has other intentions' (trans. Lattimore). Powerful emotions like sorrow and melancholy – as with joy and happiness – are self-reflexive possibilities of the soul (great sadness cuts one to the heart, joy elevates the spirit to 'great deeds', hatred turns heroes into bestial killers); the Homeric hero thus consciously experiences the whole range of human emotions from raw grief to ecstatic joy (both extremes are presented in well-established formula: emotions as heart-rending, heart-breaking, heart-touching, and so on – 'glad at heart' (*Od.* 14.113), 'touched my heart' (*Od.* 14.360–1), 'he spoke and stirred the heart in her breast' (*Od.* 17.150), 'a heart that is slow to believe' (*Od.* 14.391), a 'heart like stone' (*Od.* 23.100–4), 'an understanding heart' (*Od.* 14.420–1), *hubris* as an immoderate or insolent heart (*Od.* 17.169)).

Inspiration

The *thumos* is also that part of the soul which animates the speaking and singing self. Consider the power of the Muses to 'move' the singer to utter fine speech and memorable words: 'summon also the inspired singer Demodokos, for to him the god gave song unsurpassing in power to please, whenever the spirit (*thumos*) moves him to singing' (*Od.* 8.43–5).

Fitting the traditional image of Homer, Demodocus is a blind bard; his *thumos* is tuned to the oral-aural world of preliterate song (cf. *Homeric Hymns*. 3.172); the metacommentary of *Odysseus* 8.62–5 even suggests a logic of compensation for the singer's disability: 'The herald came near, bringing with him the excellent singer whom the Muse had loved greatly, and gave him both good and evil. She deprived him of sight, but she gave him the gift of sweet singing.'

The blind poet accompanies himself on the lyre and in another remarkable instance of textual reflexivity sings the poem of the Trojan War before Odysseus – one of the main protagonists of the narrated events. Odysseus' response is one of the purest examples of epic melancholy:

Odysseus, taking in his ponderous hands the great mantle dyed in sea-purple, drew it over his head and veiled his fine features, shamed for tears running down his face before the Phaeaceans; and every time the divine singer would pause in his singing, he would take the mantle away from his head, and wipe the tears off, and taking up a two-handled goblet would pour a libation to the gods, but every time he began again, and the greatest of the Phaeaceans would urge him to sing, since they joyed in his stories, Odysseus would cover his head again, and make lamentation.

(*Od.* 8.83–93)

Odysseus' *thumos* is powerless before his own uncontrollable emotions; his only response is to hide his tears: he covers his face, the visible mirror of what he feels in his *thumos*.

The psyche as an inner dialogue of voices: Achilles as a rhetorical virtuoso

Achilles' uncontrollably violent response to Agamemnon's demand that he should surrender the slave girl Briseis, one of his war prizes – the event which instigates the main plot structure of the first books of the *Iliad* – is presented as an inner struggle of voices: one voice flows from his enraged *thumos* and speaks with the violent emotion of a warrior being publically disgraced; Achilles should draw his sword and kill Agamemnon on the spot; the other, the voice of self-control and calming discipline, tries to quell the violence of his angry *thumos*:

> grief came upon Achilles son of Peleus, and inside his shaggy chest his heart debated two separate courses; whether to draw the sharp sword from his thigh and stir up the others and kill the son of Atreus, or to put a stop to his rage and restrain his anger. While he pondered this in his heart and mind, and was drawing the great sword from its scabbard, Athena came from the sky; for white-elbowed goddess Hera despatched her, because she loved and cared for both men alike in her heart. And Athena stood behind Peleus' son and seized him by his brown hair, appearing to him alone. None of the others saw her, but Achilles was amazed, and turning round he instantly recognized Pallas Athena, and her eyes looked terrible to him.
>
> (*Il.* 1.163–200)

Will and reflexivity in the *Iliad*

The fact that the goddess Athena must restrain and 'persuade' Achilles marks a departure in epic characterization. Only the violent restraint of Athena can prevent Achilles from beginning a course of action that will have consequences which only the goddess can foresee. Achilles' rage must be checked.

Achilles' complex self

The dialectic of the Homeric soul can be represented as a struggle between different types of *thumos*, where, for example, one powerful emotional force is overridden by another force (dramatized by the conflict of irrational *thumos* and the calming deliberation of the goddess at the beginning of the *Iliad*).

Achilles' multiple self is described in agonistic language. Book 1 sees Achilles momentarily suspended between two alternative courses of action before resolving the conflict on the side of control and sublimation – represented by the civilizing appearance of Pallas Athena restraining Achilles by bodily dragging him by the hair back from the brink of regicide. The king and overlord of the Achaeans is thus saved by an invisible agency, a civilized goddess speaking to the *psyche* of Achilles and, as such, visible only to him (*Il.* 1.195–200). Persuasion by the goddess reins in the dangerous forces of extreme *thumos* and, equally significantly, the advice given by the constraining goddess is to encourage Achilles to resort to the sublimated violence of verbal aggression: pierce Agamemnon with words; ensnare the king in the net of culture and the fruits of this for you will be multiplied threefold; control and sublimate your violence – '*Know yourself*': listen to the rational part of your *psyche* and you will reap unanticipated gifts (*Il.* 1.205ff.; cf. *Od.* 9.302). The goddess of War and Reason reminds Achilles of his own self-image as not only a 'doer of heroic deeds', but as a rhetorical virtuoso[30]; he should ignore his momentarily imbalanced *psyche* – with aggressive *thumos* pulling the strings of his soul – and withdraw from violence into responsible speech. His 'bitter' anger and shame (*aidos*) remain unabated, but in complying with the request of the goddess he displays the soul of a more complex, self-differentiated, and thoughtful being.

Achilles' multiple self

Achilles' withdrawal from the struggle against the Trojans is thus a powerful metaphor for the moment of disengagement that accompanies all self-reflective thought. A space of individual responsibility has opened in the collective fabric of the Homeric world. 'Thinking' can be both an agent as well as an instrument of the will (in Achilles' particular case, the will represented by the voice of his 'heart' to exact immediate vengeance on King Agamemnon). By attending to the voice of his other self Achilles shows himself to be larger than his own epic archetype; he asks to be read as an icon of civilized culture and not merely a slave of the Homeric code. It is inner discourse which saves Achilles' *psyche* from the precipitate action of his own *thumos*; and it is the power of disengaged self-reflection which foreshadows the classical spirit of later Greek civilization. In the last Books of the *Iliad* Achilles' *persona* develops a more complex balance of reason and passion – of *thumos* and *phronesis* – which would form a major logological theme for Greek culture (Plato's image of the *psyche* bridling its powerful stallions belongs to the same tradition as Achilles' unconsolable anger reformed by wisdom and compassion).

We have seen that Book I ends with Achilles venting his violence upon Agamemnon through words: a screed of deprecation and personal insult culminates in his fateful oath to withdraw from the war until his honour and moral standing have been restored. Agamemnon remains alive because Achilles' thoughtful will has constrained the lethal will of anger. Yet Achilles' anger remains irreversible and unconsolable. Pride and inflexible self-esteem overrule loyalty to the war effort, self-interest, and his better judgement (his wounded *thumos* makes him forget the war against the Trojans – replacing the original objective with a bitter personal hatred of Agamemnon). No treasure on earth will persuade him to return to fight on the side of the Achaeans (an intransigence which no compensatory gifts or strategic persuasion, not even when mediated by the combined rhetorical virtuosity of Odysseus, Phoenix, or Ajax (in Book 9; cf. *Il.* 9.442–3), can soften). Even Agamemnon's consolatory gesture to return the slave-girl Briseis leaves Achilles unmoved:

> Not if he offered me ten times or twenty times as much as he possesses or could raise elsewhere, all the revenues of Orchomenus or of Thebes, Egyptian Thebes, where the houses are stuffed with treasure, and through every one of a hundred gates two hundred warriors sally out with their chariots and horses; not if his gifts were as many as the grains of sand or particles of dust, would Agamemnon win me over. First he must pay me in kind for the bitter humiliation I endured.
> (Homer, 1950: 171)

His lost *time* cannot even be restored by an equivalent exaction of honour from Agamemnon. It seems that Achilles' humiliation can only be rectified by the destruction of the King and the army he leads.

In the figure of Achilles, then, we find the first embodiment of the western idea of the singular will consumed by its own self-importance: 'I do not choose to fight with my lord Hector.' Achilles has taken the measure of his own role in the war; he understands his strategic place as the Greeks' champion, and actively wills that his own inactivity will bring disaster to the Achaeans. His personal sense of grievance over his lost honour is more important than the fate of the vast army of Greeks fighting around the walls of Troy. In his disengaged musing he even questions the purpose of the Trojan campaign and expresses a desire to return to his homeland and a peaceful existence. In these scenes of self-objectification and, it must be said, self-expression, Achilles contemplates an alternative to the Homeric form of life (cf. *Il.* 9.378).

Epic psychology

What account is given of the *psyche* or 'soul' in Homer? The *Iliad* can be understood as a story structured around the unintended consequences of the dialogue between *psyche* and *thumos*, between Achilles as a one-dimensional oral sign and Achilles as a more complex, dialogic existence. This is the dialectic which surfaces when Achilles reflects upon how the 'son of Atreus' has stolen his honour and turned the greatest of warriors into a laughing-stock (9.646–53). The epic revolves around a psychopathology of lost honour and humiliated selfhood.

Psyche as life-source or animating principle

Like the *thumos* of man, *psyche* is also a principle of movement and life experience (hence the aptness of our own term 'animation', from the Latin term for 'breath' or 'wind', *anima*; cf. the Hebrew *nishmat hayyim* ('breath of life' – hence 'soul', *nefesh* and *ruach*, 'wind', 'spirit')). Even animals give up their *psyche* at the point of death (the swineherd Eumaeus strikes the boar and its *psyche* – here synonymous with 'life' or perhaps more concretely with 'breath-life' – leaves the body (*Od.* 14. 425–6; cf. *Od.* 11.221, 15.354; *Il.* 13.671); cf. the Hebraic account of the origin of the human soul from God's animating breath: God shapes man 'out of the dust of the ground, and breathed into his nostrils the breath of life; and man became a living soul' *Genesis* 2:7; cf. *Ezekiel* 37:1–10). The *psyche* is first animation and only then 'thought' or 'intellect'. A rough definition of the Homeric *psyche* would be the principle of individuation which articulated the body and *thumos* of a creature (an integration which dissolves at death).

Thumos at the point of death

The *psyche* of the dying person leaves the body (or as this is frequently expressed in Homer, 'the limbs') like air or a vapour at the point when 'hateful darkness' envelops the corpse (*Il.* 16.605ff.). Unconsciousness is presented as a loss of life spirit, a state of existence similar to death (cf. *Il.* 5.696, 9.409, 14.518, 16.505, 16.856, 22.362, 22.467). The living body loses its principle of animation as the 'ghost' of the living individual flies away to Hades. In the oldest artistic representations of this process the *psyche* is pictured leaving the mouth of the dying individual. Patroclus' death, for example, is described in the following terms: 'Even as he spoke the end (*telos*) of death enfolded him; and his disembodied soul (*psyche*) took wing from his limbs for the house of Hades, bewailing its fate and the youth and manhood left behind' (*Il.* 16.855ff.).[31]

Psyche as breath or the breath-soul

The *psyche* leaves the body as a creature dies, exhaling its life and individual existence. Like air with which it is closely associated, *psyche* is exhaled at death (*Il.* 9.409, 16.856; *Od.* 14.425–6). The phenomenon is usually presented as an irreversible process, 'loosening the limbs' of the body, dissipating the unified structure of the life form (cf. Adkins, 1970: 13–14; Fränkel, 1975: 84). The corpse or *soma* remains as a lifeless shell. In this respect the multiple functions of the Homeric *'psyche'* follows similar grammatical patterns to the English word 'life'. Sleep, unconscious states, madness and, ultimately, death are stages in the disintegration of a living personality.

Psyche as diaphanous 'material' or vapour

While not being made of the same stuff as the flesh, the *psyche* is consubstantial with the materiality of the living body – a rather evanescent, and insubstantial substance (*Il.* 23.104; *Od.* 11.51, 11.83). At the moment of death *psyche* flies like an immaterial image from the body, a ghost or phantom (*eidola*) of the corporeal individual, flapping like a bat or bird.[32] By the fifth century this metaphor had become a standard image for the soul as the ghostly source of individuation and the active will (cf. Plato, *Rep.* 469D and *Phaedo* 69E–70A; Aristotle, *De Anima*, Book 1). We also find the same family of metaphors for death as a loss of the breath-soul: an exhaling of the individual's *psyche* which flies wraith-like to Hades, the realm of the dead. English usage retains the same locution in describing the dying person as 'giving up the ghost' (cf. *Od.* 14.134).

Psyche as a person's double

The paradigm case of this representation is the way in which Patroclus appears in Achilles' dream at *Iliad* 23.65ff. (see below). In another example the goddess Athena fashions a phantom (*eidolon*) as an imaginary double of Iphthime, the daughter of Icarius, to help calm the sorrow of Penelope (*Od.* 4.795–800). In many important texts of the *Iliad* and the *Odyssey* the *psyche* is likened to an *eidolon* or passionless 'phantasm' ('dim phantom' at *Od.* 4.824, 835).

Psyche after death: Aticleia's Lesson

Homeric psychology has relatively little to say about the postmortem *psyche*. After death the exhaled *psyche* in its vaporous state becomes a shadow-soul. The mediator and ambassador of the gods, Hermes, is responsible for conducting the *psyche* of the dead person to Hades (*Il.* 23.71–6; *Od.* 11.51–4, 216–22; *Od.* 24.1ff.). In the underworld the *psyche* leads a disembodied quasi-existence (which frequently appears in Homer as a symbol of the greatest evil that can befall mortal beings: 'hateful in my eyes as the gates of Hades' *Od.* 14.156). Book 24 of the *Odyssey* opens with a description of Hades where the ghosts of mortal men are depicted as chattering bats in a cavernous underground cave:

> Cyllenian Hermes called forth the spirits of the wooers ... and they followed gibbering. And as in the innermost recess of a wondrous cave bats flit about gibbering, when one has fallen off the rock from the chain in which they cling to one another, so these went with him gibbering, and Hermes, the Helper, led them down the dank ways. Past the streams of Okeanos they went, past the rock of Leukas, past the gates of the sun and the land of dreams, and quickly came to the meadows of asophodel, where the spirits dwell, phantoms of men who have done with toils.
> (*Od.* 24.1ff.)

A similar description of the spineless, disembodied *psyche* occurs in the account of Patroclus' enfeebled *psyche* after death; his *psyche* returns like a vaporous, chattering ghost to speak with Achilles (*Iliad* 23.65ff.) Patroclus' ghost is a phantasm completely disengaged from the passionate contexts of praxis and active intentionality. Yet it is important to note that Patroclus' *psyche* includes all the items that individualized his way of life – including his clothes and armour. It is also significant that his disembodied *psyche* retains the power of speech:

> the *psyche* of poor Patroclus, in all things like his very self, the same stature, the same lovely eyes, and the same clothes he used to wear... and said to him... 'You neglect me now that I am dead; you never did so when I was alive. Bury me instantly and let me pass the Gates of Hades. I am kept out by the disembodied spirits of the dead, who have not let me cross the River and join them, but have left me to pace up and down forlorn on this side of the Gaping Gates ... for once you have passed me through the flames I shall never come back again from Hades ... Achilles held out his arms to clasp the spirit, but in vain. It vanished like a wisp of smoke and went gibbering underground ... Achilles leapt up in amazement ... 'Ah then, it is true that something of us does survive even in the Halls of Hades (*Aïdes*), but with no intellect *(phrenes)* at all, only the ghost *(psyche)* and semblance *(eidolon)* of a man' [cf. *Od.* 24.6].

Patroclus' *psyche* is a simulacrum of life, but being disembodied has no 'place' for reason or mind *(phrenes)* (23.66).

This very important text contains a number of significant features. First, the *psyche* floats free from the corpse of Patroclus like a ghost (without embodiment it has no way of gearing into the customary world of epic action); second, its ultimate destiny is to 'pass through the Gates of Hades' and never to return; third, total escape from the body after death must be secured by ritually burning the mortal remains (the *soma*) in an act, so to speak, of conspicuous destruction; fourth, the unquiet *psyche* may linger, haunting mortals; fifth, the *psyche* is a simulacrum or double of the living person – groaning as it flies off to Hades (cf. 22.356–6); finally, as a shadow or *eidolon*, the *psyche* cannot possess the faculty of intellect *(phrenos)* – *phrenes* is thought of as a real organ, associated with the liver and diaphragm – and this disintegrates at the point of death.

Significantly, only the *psyche* of the blind prophet, Teiresias ('the soul of Teiresias the Theban', *Od.* 10.565) retains its sensory consciousness, memory, and active intelligence in Hades – the 'rest of the souls are flittering shadows' (*Od.* 10.494–5). Like the traditional bard, Teiresias sees beyond the visible world to the realm of the invisible – the assumption being that absolute truth can only be found beyond the realms of corporeal things.

These descriptions of the *psyche* should be compared with the text of

Odyssey 11.204ff., where Odysseus vainly tries to embrace the *psyche* of his dead mother, Anticleia:

> Three times I started toward her, and my heart was urgent to meet her, and three times she fluttered out of my hands like a shadow or a dream, and the sorrow sharpened at the heart within me ... 'Are you nothing but an image [*eidolon*; Murray translates this as 'phantom', Loeb Classical Edition, II.400] that proud Persephone sent my way, to make me grieve all the more for sorrow?'

The ghost of his mother responds by describing the state of the soul after death:

> this is not Persephone, daughter of Zeus, beguiling you, but it is only what happens, when you die, to all mortals. The sinews no longer hold the flesh and the bones together, and once the spirit [*psyche*] has left the white bones, all the rest of the body is made subject to the fire's strong fury, but the soul flutters out like a dream and flies away.
>
> (*Od.* 11.218–22)

Psyche is not only the unique force that individuates mortals, it effects the corporeal work of 'binding' or 'uniting' body and spirit – being 'liberated' when this unity is destroyed. Anticleia's spirit instructs Achilles about the irreversible transition that death extorts from the active living body. When the body loses its *psyche* nothing can reform the integral structure of the living body. The only element missing from Anticleia's description is that of the vampiric quasi-existence of the psychic *eidolon*; at *Odyssey.* 11.25 and 24.1 the disembodied *psyches* of the dead (including Odysseus' own mother, Anticleia) swarm about a pit brimming with the fresh blood of slaughtered sheep, like nightmarish spirits thirsting to taste the dark, life-creating liquid.

When Plato later campaigned for the censorship of *mimesis* it was precisely these accounts of the *psyche* after death and the gloomy descriptions of the House of the Dead which caught his attention (see *The Republic*, Book III, especially 386A–387B on the Homeric vision of death and Hades, where Plato cites a sequence of unacceptable descriptions from *Od.* 11.489–491; *Il.* 20.64; *Il.* 23.103; *Od.* 10.495; *Il.* 26.856; *Il.* 23.100; *Od.* 24.6–10). Plato was also offended by the untoward descriptions of the hero's *thumos* when alive – given to violent emotions, tearful outbursts (when Achilles openly expresses his grief at the death of Patroclus in *Iliad* 24.10–12), and conspicuous displays of mourning (Priam rolling in the dung after the death of his son and Achilles' mutilation of the corpse in *Iliad* Books 23 and 24; Plato inventories the precise texts to be censored at *Rep.* 387E–388C).

The whole of Book III of the *Republic* can be read as important evidence of the change in moral values and cultural sensibilities between the Archaic and Classical age regarding the emotions, the necessary self-control before extreme experiences such as death and the loss of self – as we noted in Volume 1, how a culture manages the mortification of self provides valuable evidence for what that society assumes as the normal and culturally warranted definition of identity. With Plato we see the language of *thumos* which predominates in the Homeric epic being displaced by the language of *psyche* understood in cognitive terms. *Thumos* is no longer a generic term for the animate life of consciousness, but is used as a special term for the violent and spirited emotions, especially for human passions which disturb the necessary self-possession and composure which Plato and other Classical writers deemed appropriate for their ideal of the rational soul. From the perspective of the well-ordered *polis*, the Homeric values typify all that is uncivilized, excessive, and even antithetical to the establishment of the virtuous City. The Homeric emotions of violence, open manifestations of aggression, public grief, delight in poetry and song, and even laughter (cf. *Rep.* 388E) are to be ruthlessly excised from the pedagogies of the rational state (*Laws* 10.886).

Psyche as the soul weighed in the balance after death

We have seen that the Homeric texts pay relatively little attention to the fate of the soul after death. The house of Hades and its deepest region, Tartarus, have no concrete dramatic topography or major epic functions; for instance, the breath-soul does not assume another life or live out another existence in Hades; there is no real afterlife beyond the Gates of Hades or after crossing the river Acheron – certainly nothing comparable to the eternal suffering or expiation that we find in the Judaic-Christian Hell (although we do hear of the punishment of Tantalus, Sisyphus, and Tityus for their sins). The souls of the dead are simply abandoned by the text to an insubstantial, shadowy, wraith-like non-existence, stripped of every quality and relationship that made life rich and colourful prior to death. This is the setting for Odysseus' conversation with the shade of Achilles, who describes hateful Hades in the following terms: 'Try not to console me for death, shining Odysseus. Rather would I be the hired workman of another man on earth, a landless man who has but little livelihood, than be king over all the dead and departed' (*Od.* 11. 488; cf. 11.568–72).

It is as if speculation about the actual physical existence of the embodied soul after death had been severely proscribed (an attitude that may have still been in force when Heraclitus wrote that 'corpses are more fit to be thrown out than dung', DK 96).[33]

Yet subsequent speculation about the postmortem *psyche* has its roots in the world-view of epic narrative. From here it migrated to the thinkers of the sixth and fifth century – most notably to Thales and Heraclitus and then to Orphic and Mystery traditions. Attic tragedy construed the soul's destiny as being weighed in the balance after death, and by the middle of the fifth century the 'question of the soul' was moved into the centre of speculative thought by Socrates and the Socratic circles. The fifth-century dramatists would also extend the word *psyche* to collective entities such as the community and city-state (as far as I am aware the linkage between *psyche* and *polis* is not made in the epic tradition). Sophocles has Oedipus take upon himself the grief and suffering of the city of Thebes, conjoining the idea of the soul with the political community as a whole (*psyche polis* at *Oedipus Tyrannos*, 64).

Homeric melancholy

Sicklied o'er with the pale cast of thought.

(Shakespeare, *Hamlet*)

Something close to a sense of *anomie* or, if we can pry the term from its modern introspective meaning, *melancholy* appears to be the reason Paris gives to Hector in explaining his withdrawal from the fighting: 'Not so much by reason of wrath and indignation against the Trojans sat I in my chamber, but I was minded to yield myself to sorrow' (*Il.* 6.333ff., trans. Murray). Helen excuses her husband by suggesting that his failure to experience heartfelt indignation at the suffering of his fellow Trojans arizes from his unbalanced mental state; his mind (*phrena*) is unbalanced by melancholy – the same unstable condition will lead him to his ultimate fate (*Il.* 6.349ff.).

Melancholy is a condition of normlessness which Paris experiences in falling short of the warrior code exemplified by the figures of Hector and Menelaus. But Hector is also no stranger to melancholia – he is depicted in one of the first domestic scenes of intimate familial understanding as he stands before his wife, Andromache, and their child (*Il.* 6.404ff.). His speech against withdrawing from the battle represents the victory of the warrior code over the domestic values she invokes (6.441ff.):

> if I hid myself like a coward and refused to fight, I could never face the Trojans and the Trojan ladies in their trailing gowns. Besides, it would go against the grain, for I have trained myself always like a good solider, to take my place in the front line and win glory for my father and myself. Deep in my heart and soul (*phrena/thumos*) I know the day is coming when holy Ilium will be destroyed ... I see you there in Argos, toiling for some other woman at the loom, or carrying water from an alien well ... may the earth lie deep on my dead body before I hear the screams you utter as they drag you off.

We might even see Achilles as the first melancholic hero in Western literature – withdrawing from the battle in the shadow of public shame, sulking – skulking even – in his tent while the Trojans seize the advantage, finally killing Achilles' guest-friend, Patroclus. Achilles is plunged into even deeper despair by the news of Patroclus' death and the shameful squabble over his armour-stripped body (in *Il.* 18.5ff.; 'grief' translates the verb *akhnuai* at 18.59ff.). Yet Homeric grief (*akhnutai*) is not the modern experience of *accedia*; it is the ritualized grief appropriate to a shame culture: the Homeric rhetoric of melancholic reflection is a culturally sanctioned behavioural disposition demanded of the humiliated hero, a mode of being-in-the-world rather than a psychological or mental state. The public display of shame (*aidos*) is, in fact, a good example of what we have called a cultural rhetoric of reflexivity; and Achilles is a prototypical melancholic in the sense that he lives and dies by the Homeric code.

The cultural differences between the rhetorics of modern *anomie* and Archaic-Homeric melancholia can be illustrated by Achilles' emotional reaction on learning of the fate of Patroclus. Where modern *anomie* plunges the self into silent introspection, the warrior code demands an excessive display of public grief:

> When Achilles heard this he sank into the black depths of despair. He picked up the dark dust in both hands and poured it on his head. He soiled his comely face with it, and filthy ashes settled on his scented tunic. He cast himself down on the earth and lay there like a fallen giant, fouling his hair and tearing it out with his own hands. The maidservants whom he and Patroclus had captured caught the alarm and all ran screaming out of doors. They beat their breasts with their hands and sank to the ground beside their royal master. On the other side, Antilochus shedding tears of misery held the hands of Achilles as he sobbed out his noble heart, for fear that he might take a knife and cut his throat.
>
> (*Il*. 18. 22ff.; cf. Laertes' grief at *Od*. 24.315)

Achilles' grief even resounds throughout nature and the depths of the sea, awakening the very Gods themselves to his plight, who sympathetically fall into the same escalating cycle of grief and lamentation (*Il*. 18. 35ff.).

The code requires warriors to display grief in a public ritual of cutting off the customary long hair ('long-haired Achaeans' being a standard formula in Homer) and placing it on the corpse. Achilles cuts from his head 'a golden lock he had allowed to grow ever since its dedication to the River Spercheus' (*Il*. 23.143ff.), placing it reverently in the dead hands of Patroclus, a gesture whose humanity 'moved the whole gathering to further tears'. Before Patroclus' corpse is consumed by the flames it is covered by the hair of Achaean nobles 'like a garment' (*Il*. 23.134ff.). We should also observe that sheep and cattle were routinely slaughtered for their fat which is spread over the corpse to speed up the process of cremation, along with jars of honey and oil. Patroclus' four horses and his nine hunting dogs are placed with him on the pyre and, the text informs us, Achilles completed the ritual with an evil act, killing twelve Trojan captives, 'twelve noble sons of the great-hearted Trojans', and throwing their bodies onto the same burning pyre: 'Achilles wept as he burned his comrade's bones, moving round the pyre on leaden feet with many a deep groan. After the funeral he orders chariot races and games to be instituted before the ashes of his friend' (*Il*. 23.170–7, 23. 260ff.).

Other examples of the overcoded expression of sorrow and melancholy can be readily cited: the unearthly moaning of Hector's father and the people of Troy at the death of their hero (*Il.* 22.405–11); Penelope's grief on hearing that her son, Telemachus, has left Ithaca in search of Odysseus (*Od.* 4.715; cf. 2.373ff.); Odysseus' periodic bouts of despair at his peripatetic fate (*Od.* 13.219–20); Odysseus before the cave of Calypso where we find the hero sitting on the beach:

> Hermes did not find great-hearted Odysseus indoors, but he was sitting out on the beach, crying, as before now he had done, breaking his heart in tears, lamentation, and sorrow, as weeping tears he looked out over the barren water.
> (*Od.* 5.81–4; cf. *Od.* 5.118ff., 150–8)

We should also mention the complex collective emotion, an amalgam of fear, disorientation, and panic experienced by the Greeks at the beginning of the ninth book of the *Iliad*, resembling a melancholic contagion flowing from the recognition that the fortunes of war had turned against the Achaeans (*Il.* 9.1ff.): the silence which greets Agamemnon's speech to his troops is the melancholic silence of war-weariness ('For a long time they sat in speechless dejection', *Il.* 9.30).

Collective *anomie* functions as a perfect pretext and discursive strategy for reintroducing Achilles to the dramatic action of the text (recall that Achilles has been both a real and textual absence for the first nine books of the *Iliad*); E. V. Rieu, the translator of the Penguin prose version of the *Iliad*, quite reasonably titles Book 9, 'Overtures to Achilles' (Homer, 1950: 161–80), followed by Book 10, 'Night interlude' (181–96), and Book 11, in which Achilles begins his triumphant return, 'Achilles takes notice' (197–220). Only the gleaming bronze of heroic action can dispel the darkness of despondency and black melancholy.[34]

Homeric friendship

In keeping with the sociological premises of logological analysis we should always view the construction of the self in the context of the dynamic interaction and social dialogue within and between persons; if melancholy represents a coded response to the collapse of social value, then Homeric friendship is the concrete social medium of valued reflexivities.

It would not be inaccurate to see the Archaic culture of friendship as a structure of social bonding rather than a vehicle of personal relationship. Friendship functioned primarily as a contractual arrangement between fighting men (the roots of the institution of male companions or *hetairoi*); it would be marked by a solemn friendship oath accompanying the warrior oath of fealty taken by soldiers as they allied themselves to an individual warlord (cf. the friendship swearing and oaths of service accompanied by sacrifices in *Iliad* 3.245ff. which confirms the truth of Mauss' claim that it is the collectivity that imposes contractual obligations upon its members (Mauss 1954: Introduction). The breach of a sacred oath may be one class of transgressions which led the soul to eternal punishment (*Il.* 3.278-9, 23.452, 23.582-6; the river Styx being associated with the protection and enforcement of oaths). Like other important values in an oral shame culture (as acts of exchange Mauss lists banquets, rituals, military services, women, children, dances, festivals, and fairs), the pact of friendship (*philotes*) represents a symbolic exchange that had to be collectively performed if it was to maintain its reality and social effectiveness. Friendship (*philia*) was inextricably linked with the reciprocal giving of tokens and gifts, and served to reinforce such heroic values as clan honour, loyalty, self-sacrifice, magnanimity, and reciprocity amongst equals. Thus custom requires that King Menelaus give Telemachus valuable gifts before his return to Ithaca – among these the two-handed silver mixing bowl finished in gold that Menelaus had originally received from the Phoenician hero Phaidimus, 'king of the Sidonians', *Od.* 15.115-19). The silver bowl then circulated as a public token of friendship and hospitality (cf. *Il.* 3.351ff., 13.620ff.).

Civil and military *philia* (*hetairoi*) provided the basic metaphors of social order and, as focal rituals, required conspicuous displays of reciprocity; here it is impossible to separate the political, social and ethical, and even aesthetic aspects of the friendship code (in Marcel Mauss' terminology, epic friendship is an example of a total social phenomenon). No doubt the experience of shame and indignation in its full impact was experienced personally (as in the scenes between Helen and her war-shy, 'effeminate' husband, Paris), but it is more appropriately viewed as a loss of public face and social standing in the networks of hierarchical friendship. The fact that powerful individual friendships (always of social equals in the military pecking order) transcend this status structure – the friendship between Patroclus and Achilles or even, across sex lines, the friendship and mutual respect of Andromache and Hector – is an exception which proves the general norm.

Martial friendship has its play forms in a range of competitive struggles. Spending their time in enforced relaxation, the troops of Achilles entertain themselves by various forms of friendly competition: archery, throwing the discus, and javelin practice (*Il.* 2. 774-5; cf. *Od.* 17.166ff.). The *polemos* of competition and the *agon* is never forgotton. Thus we hear nothing of the affective or sexual relationships within these warrior groups or in the class of chieftans; homosexuality – even as a military code of behaviour – is notably absent from Homer. Of course the epic idealizes the friendship code of the Bronze Age warrior, just as it fictionalizes the code of hospitality, and resorts to hyperbole in describing the wealth and material splendour of the royal palaces. But even these caricatures contain significant cultural information. The author of the *Odyssey*, for example, is both literally and metaphorically larding the plot with an eye to his oral audience when the swineherd Eumaeus promptly slaughters two of his best pigs to honour a stranger who, unknown at this point to Eumaeus, turns out to be his old master, Odysseus ('I cannot bring myself to name him stranger, though he is not here: he loved me greatly and cared for me', *Od.* 14.145–6). This hyperbolic act of hospitality – an exaggerated requirement of the code of friendship, but in Eumaeus' reduced circumstances, almost a self-destroying *potlatch* – serves as a contrastive device to prepare the later scenes of Odysseus' violent retribution:

> stranger, it were not right for me, even though one meaner than thou were to come, to slight a stranger: for from Zeus are all strangers and beggars, and a gift, though small, is welcome from such as we ... So saying, he quickly bound up his tunic with his belt, and went to the sties, where the tribes of swine were penned. Choosing two ... he brought them in and slew them both, and singed, and cut them up, and spitted them. Then, when he had roasted all, he brought and set it before Odysseus, hot upon the spits, and sprinkled over it white barley meal [the *oulochytai*]. Then in a bowl of ivy wood he mixed honey-sweet wine, and himself sat down over against Odysseus, and bade him to his food, and said: 'Eat now stranger, such food as slaves have to offer'.
>
> (*Od.* 14.55ff.)

Here the subcodes of hospitality, contractual friendship, feasting, oath-taking and 'respecting the word' coalesce into an insistent moral idea: ritualized, conspicuous friendship – symbolized by the participation in a communal meal – functions as a paradigm of social order (cf. *Od.* 11.185ff.). As a normative configuration the *ethos* produced by these norms preserved a communal sense of truth, order, intelligibility by concretely dramatizing the consequences of their transgression – in images of status-blurring, duplicity, disorder, and social chaos. This is the unspoken premise of Menelaus' friendship for Odysseus:

> I would have settled a city in Argos for him, and made him a home, bringing him from Ithaca with all his possessions, his son, all his people. I would have emptied one city for him out of those that are settled round about and under my lordship. And, both here, we would have seen much of each other; nothing would then have separated us two in friendship and pleasure, until the darkening cloud of death has shrouded us over.
> (*Od.* 4.174–80; cf. Odysseus' conversation with Eumaeus at *Od.* 17.264ff.)

That the making and honouring of friendship and fealty oaths was of great importance is also reflected in the fact that breaking rank or desertion are capital offences; those who flee from the battlefield, deserting their comrades, also transgress the sacrificial community, destroying the primary bond of social order. Troops found deserting are often executed on the battlefield without judicial procedure. Severe punishment even extends to the family of the guilty: the wives and children of such transgressors might be legitimately taken or sold into slavery (cf. *Il.* 4.234ff.). Deviations from the exchange system of martial friendship quite literally threaten the existence of the community.

The customary code of Homeric warfare applied analogous sanctions to the breach of truces and other military agreements. At *Iliad* 4.265, Idomeneus, King of Crete, addresses Agamemnon in the following terms:

> Son of Atreus, you can rely on my loyal support and the solemn assurance I gave you when this business began. Rouse the rest of the long-haired Achaeans, so that we may join battle at once, now that the Trojans have broken their oath. As for them, they have nothing to expect but death and disaster, since they went back on their word and broke the truce.

As if to underline the importance of such agreements the terrifying 'spirits', the *Erinyes*, are said to seek out those who break their oaths (*Il.* 19.259)

The ethos of gift-giving hospitality operated as a powerful normative framework for the social order as a whole. Male friendship networks provided the social organization, normative training ground, and background 'culture' for the reproduction of the ideology of honorific behaviour; and these forms of solidarity were naturally extended to other spheres of social life and relationships (forming the sociological substance of the expression 'heroic culture'). The whole system depended upon 'giving' and 'keeping' promises, adhering to the terms of oaths, respecting the truth-claims of others. Agamemnon is speaking to the converted in galvanizing his troops in the following terms:

> my friends (*philoi*), be men. Have a stout heart, and in the field fear nothing but dishonour in each other's eyes. When soldiers fear disgrace, then more are saved than killed. Neither honour nor salvation is to be found in flight.
>
> (*Il.* 5. 529ff.)

Agamemnon's speech already anticipates the survival ethic of the hoplite phalanx. In the *Iliad* we have a vivid contrast between the individual obligations and responsibilities of martial friendship and the growing corporate ideal of friendship evolving with the increasing strategic importance of the phalanx (which, as it were, generalized and collectivized the code of military friendship). We might also compare the Homeric paradigm of friendship exemplified by Achilles and Patroclus with the interlocking collective friendship celebrated in the martial elegies of the seventh-century Spartan poet, Tyrtaeus (see Chapter 4 below).

Even though the highly individualized bonds linking Achilles and Patroclus serve primarily as a plot device motivating Achilles to rejoin the Greeks to avenge the death of Patroclus at the hands of Hector (Books 17–19, 21, 22), the author of the *Iliad* broke new ground in personalizing the collective friendship code of the Bronze Age warrior class; and what was initially motivated as a textual imperative was later implemented as a new ethical value, giving a powerful stimulus to the development of more individualistic modes of social life. In this way the martial contractuality of Archaic friendship norms were generalized to other, non-aristocratic social strata and groups, helping to create a more open culture. Once institutionalized these new formations strongly influenced the development of public systems of rights and obligations across very different spheres of social discourse (law, economic relations, artistic competition, philosophy, science, and so forth). We have a pure form of what Emile Durkheim called the precontractual origins of contract (1964).

5.3 Rhetorics of speech and language

I stand upon the dangerous edge of speech.
                    (Sophocles, *Oedipus Tyrannos* 1169)

Discourse as praxis

We have seen that the *Iliad* as a literary work is as much an epic of speech as an epic of deeds, given that the central events of the narrative are framed by the specialized forms of heroic language. What, then, can we learn about epic sociology from exploring the text's own rhetorics of speech and language? In what ways does the epic celebrate the constitutive powers of the *Logos*?

The Greek word for speech and discourse is *muthos* – the root term of our words 'myth' and 'mythos', and concern for the active powers of *muthos* runs through both texts like a continuous thread[35]: speech, usually in the form of highly crafted, stylized oratory, introduces and accompanies all the decisive actions of the *Iliad* – the violent exchange of utterances between Achilles and Agamemnon which frame the whole story; the military and political debates which open the text after Achilles' withdrawal from the campaign (*Il.*, Books 1, 2); the discourses on strategy in the Achaeans' Assemblies before attacking Troy (*Il.*, Book 9); the attempt by Odysseus, Ajax and Phoenix in Book 9 to persuade Achilles to rejoin the Achaeans (9.630ff.); discourse in the form of monologues (Priam's supplicant monologue in *Il.* 24.349–447) and the ubiquitious interior monologues of reflective thought; and reflexive discourse such as Odysseus' own narrative of his adventures (and implicitly of the *Iliad*'s narratives) before the Phaeacian community in *Odyssey* Books 9–12. In these contexts the juxtaposition of action *and* speech breaks down; in the Homeric universe all significant human intervention has a performative logic.

Discourse as power and bewitchment

In Chapter 1 I have argued that primary oral cultures privilege the formative powers of oral expression in articulating issues and problems relevant to a particular form of life; epic poetry displays the same respect for the poetic word. *Logos* first manifests its world-forming powers in naming, in persuasion, and in the magic of rhetorical ritual acts. All of these verbal performances are different modalities of constitutive social action.

A man's name

Names possess their own magic. To command the 'correct names' of things is to have power over those things. Names and the act of naming are among the first acts of power. Thus something like a primitive name magic clings to the evolution of personal names; these express the central attributes of their bearers (Oedipus, Odysseus, Polynices, Apollo, Agathon, Prometheus, etc.). Thus the name *Prometheus*, from *pro* and *metheus*, 'fore' 'thought/thinking', allows the figure of Power (*Kratos*) in Aeschylus' *Prometheus Bound* to suggest that the chained God punished by Zeus had been badly named ('spuriously named' (*pseudonomos*), given that he manifestly lacked forethought about his own fate or how he might escape his punishment, *Prometheus Bound* 82–7). The basic plot device of *Oedipus Tyrannos* also relies on Oedipus' stubborn inquiry into his own paternity, a quest for his own origins and lineage that leads to a destructive self-knowledge (cf. Jocasta's plea to Oedipus to abandon his search (1060–1) and Oedipus' wilful response: 'Let the storm burst, my fixed resolve still holds, To learn my lineage, be it ne'er so low... why should I fear to trace my birth? Nothing can make me other than I am' (1076–85)). Finally, of course, for both Archaic and Classical Greek culture, the loss of name is a synecdoche for the loss of face or social death. An instance occurs in *Oedipus Tyrannos* after Oedipus has accused Creon and Teiresias of murdering Laius; Creon's speech (522ff., 555ff.) links the accusation with the fate of being shamed before his friends and the City itself, a calumny which undermines his name and status. By 'losing' one's good name an individual falls from the orbit of political power. Such a loss of face threatens social disgrace and, in extreme cases, social death.

Status and self-knowledge are inextricably connected in the Homeric social order; indeed a person's full name contains an implicit genealogy of clan lineage, region, city-state, and even neighbourhood. Words, as we have repeatedly observed, have a constitutive and communal function. They index and articulate the dramatic occasions of collective identity. Hence the formulaic question addressed to strangers: 'Where is your city? Where are your parents?' (*Od.* 1.170, 15.264).

> Tell me the name by which your mother and father called you in that place, and how the rest who live in the city about you call you. No one among all the peoples, neither base man nor noble, is altogether nameless, once he has been born, but always his parents as soon as they bring him forth put upon him a name. Tell me your land, your neighbourhood and

your city, so that our ships, straining with their own purpose, can carry
you there.

(*Od.* 8.550–6)

Pallas Athena, disguised as Mentes, leader of the Taphians, questions Telemachus about his paternity, to which Telemachus responds with a reflection on the ambiguity of origination: 'I will accurately answer all that you ask me. My mother says indeed I am his. I for my part do not know. Nobody really knows his own father' (*Od.* 1.214–6).

Persuasion

Almost every social and linguistic context in which the word *muthos* appears is linked to language's role in persuading or practically affecting the person of the listener. In many of these contexts speech is regarded as a form of magic, possessing the power to 'bewitch' and 'transfigure' its audience. Odysseus, for example, is a prisoner on the island of Calypso not only in a physical sense, but more importantly in being beguiled by the soft and bewitching *words* of Calypso, the siren voice of persuasion making Odysseus forget Ithaca, his homeland, and his wife Penelope (*Od.* 1.55–7). We recall that it is Agamemnon's *lack* of persuasive speech and tact which precipitates Achilles' violent behaviour in Book 1 of the *Iliad*; and Priam's persuasive pathos which results in Achilles' surrendering the body of Hector. Persuasion is a fundamental function of language in Homeric epic (cf. Penelope's bewitching of her suitors at *Od.* 18.282–3; Aegisthus' beguiling of Clytemnestra with deceptive words at *Od.* 3.264). And again we should primarily think of 'persuasion' as a term for a whole range of social activities in establishing collective agreement and order within the life of a community.

Bewitchment – the charismatic singer

The virtuoso of persuasion is the singer of epic tales, the master of winged words. In general the singer is a master of the 'bewitching' power of song.[36] Even the Olympian Gods are rendered silent in amazement at the power of Zeus' words (' they all became hushed in silence, marvelling at his words; for full masterfully did he address their gathering', *Il.* 8.28–9). Commanding a similar godlike power with words, Odysseus holds the court of Alcinous spellbound with the force of his storytelling (*Od.* 13.1ff.; cf. 14. 387, 17.514–21).

The Homeric text is quite explicit about the psychological and even physiological effects of the lyre-accompanied voice, and rhapsodes such as Phemius of Ithaca – forced to sing by Penelope's suitors (*Od.* 1.154), and Demodocus of Scheria (*Od.* 8.43ff, 471ff.) are regarded as more than simply suasive experts. Such singers are touched by the divine, and are, consequently, vehicles of

HOMERIC EPIC REFLEXIVITY

charisma. A pathetic instance of the powerful social role of the singer-player in an oral culture occurs in the exchange between Penelope and Phemius:

> Phemius, since you know many other actions of mortals and Gods, which can charm men's hearts and which singers celebrate, sit beside them and sing one of these, and let them in silence go on drinking their wine, but leave off singing this sad song, which always afflicts the dear heart deep inside me, since the unforgettable sorrow comes to me, beyond others, so dear a husband do I long for whenever I am reminded of my husband.
> (*Od.* 1.337–43)

In Homeric oral culture the *aoidos* is highly valued as the personal embodiment of a society's memory and cultural values (the noble Phemius who knows 'many other actions of mortals and gods'). The singer is the messenger of the gods – in the shape of the Muses, who 'know all things' – while mortals hear only rumours and 'know nothing at all' (*Il.* 2.485); they are graced with divine gifts and as such form a central reference point for the charismatic economy of the Homeric polity. It is thus appropriate that Odysseus should describe the blind singer Demodocus in words of the utmost respect – respect not only for the person of the singer, but for his unique social function as the personification of divine values, the very medium of the *logos*:

> Here, herald, take this piece of meat to Demodokus so that he may eat, and I, though a sorry man, embrace him. For with all peoples upon the earth singers are entitled to be cherished and to their share of respect, since the Muse has taught them her own way, and since she loves all the company of singers ... Demodokus, above all mortals beside I prize you. Surely the Muse, Zeus' daughter or else Apollo has taught you, for all too right following the tale you sing the Achaeans' venture, all they did and had done to them, all the sufferings of these Achaeans, as if you had been there yourself or heard it from one who was. Come to another part of the story, sing us the wooden horse ... the strategem great Odysseus filled once with men and brought it to the upper city, and it was these men who sacked Ilion. If you can tell me the course of all these things as they happened, I will speak of you before all mankind, and tell them how freely the goddess gave you the magical gift of singing.
> (*Od.* 8.477–98; cf. *Od.* 17.518, 17. 383, 8.44ff.)

Homo Loquens – Odysseus Rhetor

Demodocus is invariably introduced with the adjective 'divine' – Demodocus, the divine singer ('... *theios aoidos...* ', *Od.* 13.27–8), and also the singer 'held in honour by the people' (*Od.* 13.28; cf. 17.381–5), a worker for the community (*demioergoi*). The singer of tales is a functionary of the whole community (*demos*). Thus it is a singer who Agamemnon appoints to guard his wife, Clytemnestra, during his absence at Troy (*Od.* 2.267). As Homeric man is a speaking being, the more perfect a man's powers of persuasion, the more perfect – the more godlike – the man. Such an individual must be rendered due respect and the material goods commensurate with his social function. To command the powers of speech is not merely to show one's civility and cultivation (schooled by the poet and rhapsode), but also to be wise of heart (*thumos*), to possess intelligence (*phrena*), and good judgement (*noos*) in councils and assemblies. Skill in persuasion is ultimately a gift of the gods, endowing its possessor with sacred qualities. In fact some of the most decisive modalities of reflexivity in the epic are profoundly verbal and practical – an insight which makes Homeric verse a logological manifesto.

It is natural, therefore, that Odysseus' precocious reflexivity should not only take shape in the skills of a warrior, in native cunning, in tactical deception, cunning diplomacy, invention, and strategy (put to exemplary use in the physical and linguistic disguises which release Odysseus and his companions from Polyphemus' cave), but more strikingly in his divine command of the rhetorical resources of language (cf. Odysseus' dissembling speech to Athena at *Odyssey* 13.255ff.). He is both Bowman and Wordman, uniting the different arts of the Bow and the Lyre. Odysseus, then, is 'Odysseus rhetor', master of words, a skilled speaker in the counsel of kings, a virtuoso rhetor long before the concept of 'rhetoric' was understood as a teachable 'art'. Perhaps it is Odysseus and not Corax, Empedocles, Gorgias, or the fifth-century rhetoricians who is the true founder of European Rhetoric. And for Odysseus, rhetoric remains essentially a strategic art or, to modify Clausewitz's phrase, politics carried out by verbal means (*Il.* 2.273).

We can illustrate with the important text of *Odyssey* 13.291ff. (esp. 294–5) where, after listening to Odysseus' invented tale of his fortunes, the Goddess Athena describes Odysseus as a lover of fictions and narrative invention:

> Bold man, crafty in counsel, insatiate in deceit, not even in thine own land, it seems, wast thou to cease from guile and deceitful tales, which thou lovest from the bottom of thine heart. But come, let us no longer talk of this, being both well versed in craft, since thou art far the best of all men in counsel and in speech, and I among all the gods am famed for wisdom and craft.'

In *Iliad* 3, Odysseus' discourse is contrasted with the speech style of Menelaus who addresses the assembly in a fluent, concise, and semantically precise manner ('Menelaus spoke fluently, not at great length, but very clearly, being a man of few words who kept to the point', *Il.* 3.210–24 and his soliloquy at *Iliad* 17.92 – what later Classical Greek rhetorical theory would call the Attic style of declamation); Odysseus, on the other hand, speaks with a deep, sonorous voice; his words pour from his lips 'like flakes of winter snow'; and he commands a power of discourse which no other speaker can match for its intelligence and persuasive power.[37]

The authorial voice at *Odyssey* 19.203ff. depicts Odysseus' prowess with words; the disguised Odysseus has secretly returned to Ithaca where, still in disguise, he tells Penelope of his encounter with her lost husband: 'He spoke, and made the many falsehoods of his tale seem like the truth, and as she listened her tears flowed and her face melted as the snow melts on the lofty mountain.' This text should be compared with similar formulae describing Odysseus' son, Telemachus, who being graced by the same divine gifts as his father describes himself in the opening lines of *Odyssey* Book 17 as a lover of true speech – 'I truly love to speak the truth (*aletheia muthesasthai*)', which has the literal sense, 'I love to tell true stories'; earlier Telemachus confesses his youthful embarrassment at the prospect of addressing 'wise' Nestor: 'how shall I go up to him, how close with him? I have no experience in close discourse. There is embarrassment for a young man who must question his elder' (*Od*. 3.22–4).

It is also important to note that Nestor, another rhetorical virtuoso,[38] recognizes the kinship of Telemachus and Odysseus not by any physical resemblances but by Telemachus' innate discursive facility:

> For surely your words are like his words, nor would anyone have thought that a younger man could speak so like him. For while I and the great Odysseus were there together, we never spoke against one another, neither in council nor assembly, but forever one in mind and in thoughtful planning, we worked out how things would go best for the Argives.
> (*Od*. 3. 124–9)

Odysseus – self-reflexive hero

Nestor's portrait of Odysseus can be understood logologically as a fundamental discovery concerning this paragon of persuasive mortals. Odysseus, unlike many of his warrior comrades – certainly unlike the 'unthinking' souls who accompany him back to Ithaca – has the capacity to withdraw from immediacy, to entertain alternative strategies, and thoughtfully plan courses of action. Odysseus stands above his peers in cunning and the planning of tricks of all kinds (*Od*. 3.120ff.).

The poem reinforces this by granting Odysseus proportionally more reported inner monologues or thoughtful soliloquies than any other Homeric hero. A paradigm case occurs as he awakes after his soujourn with the Phaeaceans, not realizing that he has been returned to his native Ithaca:

> Ah me, what are the people whose land I have come to this time, and are they savage and violent, and without justice, or hospitable to strangers and with minds that are godly? And where shall I take all these many goods? Where shall I myself be driven? I wish I had stayed among the Phaeaceans ... Now I do not know where to put all this, and I cannot

leave it here, for fear it may become spoil for others. Shame on the leaders of the Phaeaceans and their men of counsel, for they were not altogether thoughtful, nor were they righteous, when they took me away here to another land; but they told me they would bring me to sunny Ithaca, and they did not do it. May Zeus of the suppliants punish them, for he oversees other men besides, and punishes anyone who transgresses.

(*Od.* 13. 200–14)

In Odysseus' inner dialogues we have one of the first displays of self-reflexive praxis. He routinely engages in self-depiction, producing accounts of his own scheming nature which frequently contradict the skill and civilization required in their formulation. In his own eyes he is a warrior. His profession is not words or work, but killing and stealing the booty of the dead; yet his rhetoric belies his own account:

Such was I in the fighting; but labour was never dear to me, nor care for my house, though that is what raises glorious children; but ships that are driven on by oars were dear to me always, and the wars, and throwing spears with polished shafts, and the arrows, gloomy things, which to other men are terrible, and yet those things were dear to me which surely some god had put there in my heart, for different men take joy in different actions. Before the sons of the Achaeans embarked for Troy, I was nine times a leader of men and went in fast-faring vessels against outland men, and much substance came my way, and from this I took out an abundance of things, but much I allotted again.

(*Od.* 14.222–32)

Dialogic self-reflection

To return to the text at *Odyssey* 13.200–16: Odysseus externalizes his own doubts and reflections, turning his situation into an episode in a narrative – as though by this means he could better understand and control his situation. He is, as we say, thinking out loud. The omniscient narratorial voice re-emerges, continuing the text from a point of view outside the mind of Odysseus:

So he spoke, and set him to count the beautiful tripods, and the cauldrons, and the gold, and the fair woven raiment, and of these he missed nothing. Then, mournfully longing for his native land, he paced by the shore of the loud-sound sea, uttering many a moan.

(*Od.* 13. 217–21)

Thought as interior discourse

We have seen that Homeric representations of thought typically involve a conflict or struggle within the soul. The most obvious model for this *agon* is inner conversation (for example Hector at *Iliad* 22.122), for example, the inner dialogue of Achilles after Agamemnon has disgraced him over the slave girl Briseis (*Il.* 1.163–200), or at the beginning of Book 10, where doubt and concern about the conduct of the war is presented as an internal debate preventing Agamemnon from sleeping; inner reflection is powerful enough to disturb and shake his whole being: 'Groan after groan came up from the depths of his being, and his heart was shot through by fear' (*Il.* 10.5ff.). The turmoil induced by this divided state of mind results in Agamemnon pulling out his hair by the roots, before relieving his condition by seeking out the rhetor Nestor – 'wise of counsel' – to externalize his anxiety. Agamemnon discovers the talking cure for melancholia.

Prayer as inner conversation

A related dialogical rhetoric appears with prayer. Achilles' withdrawal into self-reflective dialogue after Agamemnon takes Briseis from him provides an instance of suppliant prayer (*Iliad* 350–6).

The priest Chryses adopts a 'cajoling' liturgical style in calling upon the god to assist him against Agamemnon. Apollo is remined of the past services of Chryses in sacrificing at the alter of the 'Lord of the silver bow' and asked to repay the priest by destroying Agamemnon (*Il.* 1.36–42). Here the relationship between priest and Godhead is expressed in contractual terms (cf. *Od.* 13.356–60). And, of course, the prayer to Apollo is a public speech act.

We first hear of *silent* prayer when Aias before his confrontation with Hector urges the Greeks to pray to King Zeus, son of Cronos 'in silence, so that the Trojans may not overhear you' (*Il.* 7.195). But most typically prayer occurs as a public invocation, a performative rite calling upon the god to fulfil an obligation, to correct a misdemeanour, or to rectify a situation that affronts divinity. Like many liturgical rites this type of direct person-to-god invocation is common in Homer, and offers many opportunities for interior speech and self-reflection about the circumstances that require divine intervention. The set formula is a paradigm of symbolic exchange: having honoured the God/Goddess in the past, I now ask for assistance, reminding him/her of my piety, sacrificial benevolence, and so on.

To return to Chryses' liturgical invocation: Book 1 of the *Iliad* begins with Chryses, priest of Troy, unsuccessfully appealing to Agamemnon for the return of his captured daughter; after being rudely rebuked by Agamemnon, Chryses speaks directly in prayer to the God Apollo. The older translation of A. T. Murray reads:

> Hear me, thou of the silver bow, standing over Chrese and holy Cilla, ruling mightily over Tenedos ... if ever I roofed a shrine to thy pleasure,

or if ever I burned fat thigh pieces of bulls or goats in your honour, fulfill
my prayer: let the Danaans pay for my tears with your arrows.

(*Il.* 1.35–42)

The God, in other words, is reminded of an obligation – a symbolic covenant to which he is tied (recall the etymology of the word *religio*). Apollo's divine intervention falls under the generic rubric of Homeric interaction – that is, the fundamental norm of reciprocity. Dutifully, Apollo responds by visiting the Achaeans with nine days of destruction and plague, a setback that leads to the calling of the first Assembly of the Achaeans, the immediate scene for the conflict between Achilles and Agamemnon which forms the pretext of the epic as a whole (see *Il.* 1, 2, 9; cf. the similar liturgical form in Clytemnestra's prayer to Apollo in Sophocles' *Electra* 634–59).

The Odyssean spirit of enquiry: Odysseus' reflexivity as curiosity

One of Odysseus' dominant traits might be described as his obstinate curiosity, a characteristic which plays a more central role in the adventures he himself narrates in the *Odyssey* than in the more peremptory acts of counsel and strategic intelligence that are called for by the war-centred action of the *Iliad*. The cunning figure of the *Iliad* now turns his earlier peripatetic intelligence toward 'inquiries' which a more prudent mind would avoid (the figure of Nestor, for example, could not be represented as curious). It is insatiable curiosity that lies behind the episode on Circe's island which results in half of Odysseus' crew being transformed into swine (Book 10); curiosity – inspired by the possibility of booty – leads to imprisonment in the cave of Polyphemus (Book 9); and curiosity eventually results in the loss of his ships and men in Book 12. What else but 'the spirit of inquiry' motivates the tale of the Sirens in Book 12 which sees Odysseus strapped to the mast to experience for himself the bewitching tones of the Sirens' song and thus satisfy his own gnawing curiosity? Odysseus is prepared to risk total loss by embracing the siren song of inquisitiveness.

We might say that Odysseus acts as the 'feminine' mediator between the epic of Nature and the epic of the Spirit. But it is misleading to cast Odyssean reflexivity as an incipient conquest or domination of Nature. Odysseus' goal is to return to his point of origin by surmounting divine and natural forces. He cultivates his own reflexivity by tricking rather than dominating Nature (in this he resembles the traditional figure of the Trickster who appears in many oral cultures). If his protagonist Poseidon, God of Sea and Earthquakes, symbolizes the unpredictable powers and 'unharvested' wildness of nature then Odysseus essentially deceives the powers of nature in order to use them for his own ends. He outwits Poseidon and, with the help of other Olympians, returns after ten years to his patrimony on Ithaca. In this sense human wisdom could be said to triumph over the powers of Poseidon. Odysseus outwits

Poseidon in the sphere of knowledge. He is the archetypal Searcher who must know Nature (and Self) in order to accomplish his chosen goal. And one of his most powerful instruments of trickery is embodied in his command of words and the metaphoricity of language: the 'No-man' episode in the Cave of the Cyclops (he kills the son of Poseidon, Polyphemus, by word and deed); the way he avoids being turned into a swine along with his crew; they ignorantly – or perhaps 'wantonly' (1.4–9) – slaughtered and ate the oxen of Hyperion the Sun; his 'feminine' mastery of disguise and dissembling after his return to Ithaca, etc. The root cause of the fate of his comrades is their failure to connect practice and theory, *ergon* and *logos*; being 'unmindful' they die by failing to integrate the Bow and the Lyre. And this 'feminine knowledge' is not purely speculative or 'theoretical', it is 'crafty' in knowing the ways of things, a form of knowledge that incorporates self-knowledge (what later Greek culture would call *phronesis* with its Odyssean root of 'ruseful judgement'). To modify a phrase of Ernst Bloch: curiosity constitutes the specific and distinctive quality of his being.

Odysseus is not only the earliest literary prototype of *homo loquens* ('pre-eminent in speech') and *egocentric homo sapiens* ('beyond all mortals in wisdom'), but more precisely of *homo curioso*, prefiguring another allegorical hero of insatiable reflexivity, Sophocles' King Oedipus; Oedipus, intoxicated by the will to truth, is drawn into a quest to 'know thyself' which ends in disaster. Odyssean curiosity is transformed into an insatiable desire to inquire whatever the cost, to reveal the secret of Thebes' misfortunes – a 'cause' which, of course, he eventually recognizes to be his own self.

Both characters are prototypes of the dream of intellectual omniscience (which, because of its intrinsic connection with vision or the 'light' of the mind, we have described earlier as the will to absolute reflection).[39] The egocentric predicament common to both figures is striking; and either might have spoken the following lines, and made the same commitment to follow the light of evidence wherever it may lead:

> I will start afresh [go back to the ground, search
> out the beginning of things] and once again make
> dark things clear...
> Not for some far-off kinsman, but myself,
> Shall I expel this poison in the blood;
> For whoso slew that king might have a mind
> To strike me too with his assassin hand.
> Therefore in righting him I serve myself.
> *Oedipus Tyrannos* 132ff.)

Light, illumination, disclosure, and clarity are, of course, metaphors for the type of unrelenting inquiry that will be characteristic of the Greek spirit in later science and philosophy – the commitment to follow rational argument and evidence wherever they may lead; to abandon everything rather than relinquish the will of knowledge. With these early European texts we already move in the orbit of the idea that the unexamined life is not worth living.

The hermeneutics of dream interpretation – language and the gate of horn

Then wise Penelope answered him again, 'Stranger, dreams verily are baffling and unclear of meaning, and in no wise do they find fulfilment in all things for men. For two are the gates of shadowy dreams, and one is fashioned of horn and one of ivory. Those dreams that pass through the gate of sawn ivory deceive men, bringing words that find no fulfilment. But those that come forth through the gate of polished horn bring true issues to pass, when any mortal sees them.

(*Od.* 19.559ff.)

Discourse also comes into prominence in acts of reading oracles and interpreting dreams. The interpreter is skilled in the art of distinguishing the ways of ivory and horn. In the Homeric world, while their functions overlap, there is a clear division of labour between the crafts of the singer accompanying himself on the lyre (Demodocus, for example), the prophet (or 'seer'), the priest, and the 'interpreter of dreams' (*oneiropolos*, *Il.* 1.63). The aged seer Eurydamas appears in the *Iliad* as a specialist 'reader of dreams' (*Il.* 5.149). Homeric warriors bring their intellectual hermeneuts on their campaigns just as they bring along other useful craftworkers (the *tekton*), physicians,[40] diviners (the *mantis*), heralds (the *kerux*, e.g. Peisenor at *Od.* 2.38, Medon at *Od.* 4.706ff.; cf. *Il.* 7.277), and 'singers of songs' (the *aoidos*). Often, however, these different roles and functions are combined in a single person. Accepting the assumption that dreams are planted by Zeus or some other divinity, their interpretation necessarily acquires a quasi-religious aura. Such an interpreter and 'public worker' is Calchas, Agamemnon's seer, who accompanies the Achaeans to Troy and is presented as a person without equal in his knowledge of things that have been, things that are, and things that will be (*Il.* 1.63ff.; cf. Theoclymenus at *Od.* 15.223–56, 525–34, 17.151–61, 20. 350–72; cf. *Il.* 24.221; *Od.* 21.145, 22.318–23).

Dreams require interpretation as they convey coded messages and ambivalent signs (*sema*) from the gods. But the dream is even more significant for understanding Homeric attitudes toward cognition and understanding. Frequently a god will appear suitably disguised in the imagery of dreams. The god might take the form of a known individual or even an animal (cf. Nestor's amazement – *thaumazein* – at the departure of Athena in the shape of a vulture at *Od.* 3.371-3). In Agamemnon's dream, Zeus' messenger assumes the shape of Nestor, urging Agememnon to throw all his forces against the Trojans (*Il.* 2.15ff.). Athena appears before Penelope in the dream image (*eidolon*) of her sister, Iphthime (*Od.* 4.795–841), and to Telemachus in the form of Odysseus' friend Mentor:

So he [Telemachus] spoke in prayer, and from nearby Athena came to him likening herself to Mentor in voice and appearance. Now she spoke aloud to him and addressed him in winged words: 'Telemachus, you are to be no thoughtless man, no coward, if truly the strong force of your father is instilled in you; such a man he was for accomplishing word and action. Your journey then will be no vain thing nor go unaccomplished.
(*Od.* 2.267–73)

Oracles and natural signs

Other seers and healers specialize in reading the discourse of nature – for example, divination by reading the flight of birds or interpreting other natural appearances (*phainomenai*). The aged warrior, Halitherses the son of Mastor, appears in the second book of the *Odyssey* as an expert in deciphering the meaning of bird flight ('He was far beyond the men of his generation in understanding the meaning of birds and reading their portents', *Od.* 2.157–9).[41] He foretells the return of Odysseus and his violent destruction of Penelope's suitors to a disbelieving audience. The reply of Eurymachos to the 'bird diviner' is indicative of the practical scepticism already at work in Archaic culture:

Old sir, better go home and prophesy to your children, for fear they may suffer some evil to come. In these things I can give a much better interpretation than you can. Many are the birds who under the sun's rays wander the sky; not all of them mean anything; Odysseus is dead, far away, and how I wish that you had died with him also. Then you would not be announcing all these predictions, nor would you stir up Telemachos, who is now angry.
(*Od.* 2.178–85; cf. Hector's rejection of Polydamas' interpretation at *Il.* 12.243)

The outcome of both individual and collective dream interpretation would typically involve some specific action to correct a wrong, remedy a ritual breach or profanation, or, more usually, the performance of a sacrificial act to propotiate an offended god. Thus Calchas interprets the meaning of Apollo's anger to the assembled Achaeans:

The god is angry because Agamemnon insulted his priest, refusing to take the ransom and free his daughter. That is the reason for our present suffering and for those to come. The Archer-King will not release us from this loathesome scourge till we give the bright-eyed lady back to her father, without recompense or ransom, and send holy offerings to Chryses.
(*Il.* 1.92–102; cf. *Il.* 2.320–2)

Occasionally a prophecy or interpretation of an unusual natural event will be offered by an 'amateur hermeneut', such as Menelaus' wife Helen who proposes a reading of the flight of an eagle carrying a goose:

> Even as this eagle came from the mountain, where are his kin, and where he was born, and snatched up the goose that was bred in the house, even so shall Odysseus return to his home after many toils and many wanderings, and shall take vengeance.
>
> (*Od.* 15.172-7)

It is also usual for signs and portents to be tragically misinterpreted (as in the famous case reported by Herodotus 1.46-53); and the theme of misrecognition provides a rich source of dramatic irony in the Homeric corpus, even more so in Greek tragedy (the dialectic of misrecognition is central to the dramatic ironies of Sophoclean tragedy and the 'plotting' of later historiography (cf. Herodotus 4.131-2; Thucydides 2.54.3)).

Unlike the theocratic pronouncements of liturgical speech, the interpretation of oracles, dreams, and natural phenomena offered by Greek seers and 'prophets' was fundamentally defeasible and as such subject to criticism and counterinterpretation. Oracular 'wisdom', even though formulated in the same dactylic hexameter as the epic, produced a conflict of interpretations as different expositions would be favoured by different parties. Agamemnon's response to Calchas' interpretive diagnosis is a good example of the emergence of contestation and critical debate in Archaic Greece. From Agamemnon's standpoint, Calchas is a false prophet, a 'prophet of evil' (*manti kakon*, *Il.* 1.106):

> Prophet of evil ... never have you said a word to my advantage. It is always trouble that you revel in foretelling. Not once have you fulfilled a prophecy of something good ... And now you hold forth as the army's seer, telling the men that the Archer-God is persecuting them because I refused the ransom for the daughter of Chryses.
>
> (*Il.* 1.131ff.)

In a similar vein Hector rejects Polydamas' reading of an omen requiring the Trojans to cease fighting outside the Acheaean stockade, countering his interpretation with the message of Zeus ('let us be obedient to the counsel of great Zeus, that is king over all mortals and immortals. One omen is best, to fight for one's country', *Il.* 12. 241-4). Telemachus also has his reasons for rejecting the readings of prophets and diviners – the presuppositional context to lines 412-19 of *Odyssey* Book 1 can be noted, in that it assumes that an extraordinary phenomenon might require the collective advice of several different hermeneuts. Upon assuming control of his father's household he asserts his authority by rejecting their help: 'I believe no messages any more... nor paying attention to any prophecy, those times my mother calls some diviner into the house and asks him questions' (for later instances of this phenomenon see Herodotus 4.131-2; 6.139-40).

6 THE CIVILIZING POWERS OF HOMERIC DISCOURSE

Our analysis of the epic self continually returns to a single question: what form of life does Homeric discourse empower? What version of community is implicit in the grammar of Homeric language? I have been guided by a point made by A. W. H. Adkins (1972: ch. 1): that it is as true to say that the psychological vocabulary a society uses moulds the manner in which it experiences as to say that its experiences mould its psychological vocabulary. Having concentrated upon grammar we should now explore the same question from the perspective of the world which inspired the epic. I refer, of course, to the culture of the Mycenaean monarchies c. 1480–1100 BC.

Mycenaean civilization

For our purposes, 'Mycenaean civilization' designates a social formation which spread from mainland Greece to Crete during the Bronze Age from around 1480 to 1100 BC. After the Ventris-Chadwick decipherment of the Linear B syllabary tablets we know that Greek-speaking feudal monarchies dominated this part of the Mediterranean from the sixteenth century BC down to the destruction of the palace system in the twelfth century. The empire of the Mycenaeans in central and southern Greece probably reached its height during the half century between 1300 and 1250 BC.[42]

The panopticon empire

The Mycenaean world formed a unique fusion of military-feudal power centres located around fortified palace complexes with a highly organized bureaucratic apparatus. Economic and political power in Crete and the Peloponnese was organized around a network of powerful cities such as Pylos, Mycenae, Argos, Knossos, and Tiryns, each headed by an absolute king controlling a centralized administration (in the epic these are symbolized by Agamemnon, king of Mycenae and Menelaus his brother, king of Sparta). The Mycenaeans may have also taken control of Orchomenus, Thebes, and Thisbe in Boeotia, and the fortress citadel of Athens in Attica (but cf. Finley, 1981: 52). The main economic rationale of these bureaucratically organized monarchies lay in the economic control and monitoring of agrarian property (Blegen and Rawson, 1966). Agricultural production and the coordinated division of labour on which it depended were rationalized under the direction of the military and civil apparatus, the whole economic infrastructure being controlled, monitored, and administered by the Mycenaean civil serivce from the offices of a central palace.[43] Evidence of the existence of bureaucracies appointed by the holder of a royal demesne (or *temenos*) emerges from the written remains of records inscribed on clay tablets from the ruins of these commercial centres. A complex division of manual and intellectual labour developed, giving the role of royal scribe and civil servant tremendous prestige. The state carried out routine, detailed, even meticulous inventories of every economically relevant manifestation of trade and wealth – property inventories of commodities, registers of personnel, valuable objects, and the like forming the greater bulk of the surviving tablets and ostraca. The script in which these entries were recorded was a hybrid language, an alphabetic syllabary with around eighty-seven symbols for vowels or vowel-consonant combinations together with concrete ideograms depicting objects.

We can characterize the state formation of the Mycenaean period as a panoptical civilization. From the archaeological remains and the Linear B tablets its mode of production seems to have been equally unique and impressive – a type of centralized distribution economy organized by an actuarial civil service around a feudal land tenure system. The state owned the lion's share of land and mobile property, and power and authority flowed from the control that could be exerted over goods, productive land, and slaves.

The Mycenaean actuarial-distribution polity

The functional heart of the bureaucratic system was the palace of the Mycenaean monarch who, while not being an absolute dictator, nevertheless dominated the social system through the instrument of his actuarial civil service. The urban palace formed the gathering point for tithes of agricultural and artisan surplus produce, which were meticulously inventoried and stored in royal granaries and warehouses, to be distributed by the bureaucracy (a distributional empire requiring complex physical structures like the so-called Treasury of Atreus at Mycenae). By using their literate officials in this way, the palace kings effectively feudalized local manufacturing classes and peasant strata.[44]

The configuration of monarchical and bureaucratic power seems to have been crucial to the actuarial economies of a Pylos or Knossos. The ideal-type of the Mycenaean palace political economy included the following elements:

- a centralized monarchy controlling a complex system of feudal land tenure;
- a centralized bureaucratic government operating from the king's palace;
- an omniscient division of governmental functions, 'pervasive and penetrating, assessing and collecting and distributing, measuring and counting and recording' (Page, 1959);
- the specialization of labour, particularly in manufactured products, which were traded 'internationally' throughout the Aegean and beyond from the network of urban power centres;
- literate systems controlled by scribal guilds and used primarily for transferring property through trade, efficiently recording transactions and inventorying 'profit margins';
- an advanced and probably clearly differentiated social system of human

property, particularly slavery ('slavery was an integral institution in social and religious life', Page, 1959).⁴⁵

The royal bureaucracies of the Minoan and Mycenaean worlds supervised a complex system of land tenure which 'differentiated between royal, private, and common holdings'; at the head of the power structure was the king or *wanax*, who also possessed a *temenos* or 'portion' of land measured as thirty units of seed corn; below the *wanax* were many aristocratic 'lords' (the word that would be later used for king – *basileus* – here 'meant little more than a minor princeling under a superior *wanax*', Page, 1959). The leader of this feudal *élite* was another landowning figure, the *Lawagetas* or 'Leader-of-the-War-Host', the military commander. Each of these minor warlords controlled a 'commune' of bound peasants who worked on their estates – the anonymous mass of 'folk' who have dropped out of the historical record.⁴⁶ In addition to the personnel of the army and 'service men' we know of the existence of artisans, metal-workers and small manufacturers, and traders. We may assume that the social relations between these different classes were well defined and controlled by systems of customary rules and traditional codes of behaviour.

Scribal power: the bureaucratic monopoly of writing as a reflexive technology

The recording and collation of written records formed an indispensable precondition for the successful operation of this distributional economy. And not surprisingly, writing was monopolized by the state bureaucracy (or that specialist sector of the bureaucracy skilled in the scripts we now call the Linear A and Linear B syllabaries). What is striking here is the extent to which written information relating to economic transactions formed an integral part of the armature of domination; yet the Homeric texts fail to mention this singular feature of Bronze Age culture.⁴⁷ Wealth in this world was drawn from two main sources: the exploitative extraction of surplus product from a dependent peasantry, and goods acquired from intercity trade, exchange, and war. The leading *wanax* supported by a feudal circle of dependent warlords and lesser nobility, each holding land and functioning as a lord in their own demesnes, formed the basic structure of the whole political system. The fragments from Pylos and Knossos portray a hierarchical society culminating in the office of a patriarchal figurehead; below the king, a network of feudalized lords and a governing class administrating the production, exchange, and circulation necessary to a precapitalist economy; below these classes a tribal peasantry, small-scale manufacturers and artisans, and mercantile traders; and at the bottom of the pile, an undifferentiated stratum of workers and slaves. There is no mention of autonomous judicial offices and no references to the administration of justice or legal discourse; while the absence of written expression does not necessarily mean the absence of legal institutions, it suggests that litigation was either carried out at the local level by the bureaucracy itself or, in a more patrimonial and dictatorial style, was the prerogative of the *basileus*.

From the evidence of recent archaeology we can say that the Homeric texts constructed an idealized and one-sided image of the Bronze Age world; the Homeric scribes' knowledge of this period was already filtered and to some extent distorted by legends and stories popularized in Ionia. The conclusion is inescapable that the imaginary representation of Bronze Age Greece frequently confirms, but often contradicts, the archaeological record (see Luce, 1975 for a judicious summary of the scholarly debate and research). The oral prototypes of the *Iliad* and *Odyssey* were composed in and for a very different social world. Compared with the eighth-century city-state and its tribal-familial mode of agricultural production, the social structure of Mycenaean civilization resembles the urban, bureaucratic cities of ancient Sumeria or Minoan Crete; and like the 'lords of Ur and Lagash', Mycenaean civilization also 'began the practice of having their scribes make up inventories of their holdings and record lease agreements and grain deposits and countless other operations' (Finley, 1978: 161). 'Literacy' in this world was dominated by the institution of reflexivity we can call 'scribal literacy' (following Harris, 1989: 7–8). Scripts were functionally specific, overwhelmingly oriented toward the needs and purposes of palace economies, and organized to facilitate the workings of a large tax-gathering state apparatus. A vast social revolution separates the Bronze Age from the Archaic world, and Mycenae's eventual destruction took with it not merely an urban way of life, but the institutional superstructure of a civic and literate (if not a 'literary') culture. Odysseus' Ithaca 'has no need for records or for scribes, in fact, on the evidence we have at present, they had no need for the art of writing and they lost it altogether' (Finley, 1978: 162).[48]

The destruction of Mycenaean civilization

The apogee of the Mycenaean world appears to have been reached in the fourteenth century. Here the great kings of Mycenae were at the hub of a large empire that stretched from the Peloponnese to Knossos in Crete. Extensive networks of trading relationships with Egypt and other great kingdoms (such as the Hittites and Syrians) is suggested by the kind of wealth recovered from the graves at Mycenae and the appearance of references to these early Greek kingdoms in the royal archives of Sumer and Assyria. It was probably during this period that the social system was systematically 'feudalized' and politically centralized. But the Mycenaean Empire was to be short-lived. The empire of the Mycenaean monarchies collapsed around 1250 BC and was gradually replaced by an aristocratic system organized around hereditary warlords and noble dynastic families. With the collapse of the Mycenaean economy the urban palace complexes were left deserted and completely vanished from Greek history. In what is often called the Greek Dark Age (c. 1100 to 800 BC) we see emerging a tribal peasant society founded upon subsistence agriculture and the *oikos* institution. This is the society that would eventually give rise to the *polis* during the Archaic period (from the eighth to the sixth centuries). These small-scale agrarian communities had no use for writing and so the traces of the Mycenaean scripts vanished along with the physical evidence of the palace economies.

While historians and archaeologists still disagree about the causes of the Mycenaean collapse – some suggesting internal explanations in terms of economic crisis[49] or political and social conflicts, whereas others emphasize external factors such as natural disasters[50] or the impact of changing patterns of trade and commerce, one of the major proximate factors was the effects of a century-long mass migration of tribes from the north of Greece; this is often referred to as the Dorian invasion, itself part of a global shift in tribal organization and migration patterns which effectively terminated the Bronze Age in Greece.

As the economic infrastructure of the palace system decayed, central power and suzerainty over minor feudal lords was eroded, the administrative system collapsed, and Mycenaean ideology, religion, and ritual practices disappeared, taking with them one of the great technologies of reflexivity used by this society: actuarial writing as an instrument of codification and social control. After about 1100 BC writing disappeared for almost four centuries. What remained of the great Mycenaean culture was transmitted through oral techniques of reflection by waves of emigrants forced to move eastwards and found communities and cities along the coast of Asia Minor.[51] It was in these new societies of aristocratic exiles that the heroic legends and myths of Bronze Age life were preserved. In this respect Homer may be considered to be one of the last links in a chain of recollective oral discourse reaching back to the Mycenaean monarchies.

One feature of great sociological importance for subsequent Greek history in the decline of monarchy and the rise of feudal aristocracy is the fact that the tribal organization of peasant production and subsistence agriculture retained its invariant form throughout the long period of the Dark Ages; it is even possible that masses of exploited small farmers, peasants, and slaves in cities such as Pylos and Mycenae actively participated in overthrowing the bureaucratic monarchy and establishing various types of transitional military dictatorship or 'tyranny', which over many generations crystallized into tribal aristocracies claiming descent from heroes and Gods.[52] It is also probable that the disappearance of centralized urban administration temporally emancipated the masses of working people, leading to village and community-based systems of land tenure and property ownership. Thus the dissolution of monarchical state property accumulated by the kings of Mycenae may have unintentionally encouraged experiments in more collectivist uses of land and also more local, individualist, and self-sufficient forms of political and economic life (creating in the process the germ form of the Homeric *oikos* system).

Homer's world: the oikos economy

The collapse of Mycenaean Greece left an economic and political vacuum that was only slowly recolonized by an agrarian system based on the self-sufficient patriarchal household or *oikos*. The tenure system of the Mycenaean monarchy was broken up and land was either feudalized or returned to the community as communal property. By the eighth century property was once more in the hands of rich landowners claiming aristocratic lineage; but power was now more localized and segmented, symbolized by success in herding rather than by the accumulation of treasure and the conspicuous consumption of artifacts and services. Productive and social activities centre around an estate economy. The oldest written texts still speak of local 'kings', but these are a shadow of the Mycenaean monarchs; typically we are dealing with a subsistence, barter economy in the hands of local landlords with no use for money.[53] The social relations of the patriarchal *oikos* economy framed the normative order of Homeric culture; its dominant values are 'excellences' which help reproduce the self-sufficiency and economic expansion of the *oikos*.[54] While martial values still rank higher than those of the *oikos*, there is no systematically negative attitude towards agrarian labour and little institutionalized mysogyny; the landowning stratum is not adverse to working the land themselves; Homer's society in the *Odyssey*, for example, expresses a way of life based on an interlocking network of kinship groups and interdependent households, an economy closer to the farming communities described in Hesiod's *Works and Days* than the kingdoms of the Mycenaean world. Odysseus' Ithaca is a familial, tribal society with little evidence of technological innovation, urban culture, or centralized political authority separated from patrimonial authority; women play an important and active role in organizing the household economy; we even learn that Odysseus sleeps with Penelope in a bed he has made himself (*Od.* 23.178ff., esp. 192–200), we hear of his skill with a sickle (*Od.* 18.366ff.), see him reaping corn (28.366–75), and constructing a raft to escape from the island of Calypso (*Od.* 5.243ff.).[55] The world of the Ithacan rulers is far from the imperial splendour of the palace economies. Thus Odysseus' faithful dog, Argos, lies sick and lice-ridden on a mound of dung piled up before the 'palace' doors ('in the deep dung from the mules and cattle, which lay in heaps before the doors, until the slaves of Odysseus should take it away to manure his great estate', *Od* 17. 296–300).

The preliterate morality of kinship and familial networks formed the axis of the *oikos* system. According to Moses Finley, the Archaic *oikos* was not only the consumption and production unit of early Greek society, but also the *locus* of moral and legal regulation. The ubiquitous fabric of kinship and marriage ties also preserved the moral code and governed the allocation of punishment. In the absence of a recognized and separate public authority responsible for the rectification of transgressions, powerful families functioned as the basic institutional location for the workings of *dike*. Justice, in its Homeric sense, was thus inseparable from the authority vested in the hierarchical order of the household.[56] As a corollary, the decline of the absolute power of aristocratic families and households is also correlated with the growth in authority of the public sphere and of publically sanctioned offices and apparatuses of justice (the King's daughter, Nausicaa, is seen helping the palace slaves with the laundry, and in her encounter with Odysseus, is acutely aware of the normative power of public opinion (*Od.* 6.1–120)). Needless to say, the disengagement of an articulate and self-reflectively 'independent' sphere of political legality from earlier familial, moral, and ethical notions of transgression is the work of several centuries. But as a rough simplification we can say that the weakening of tribal '*oikos* justice' formed one of the historical preconditions for the rise of civil law and the gradual institutionalization of a concept of political authority and public judicial procedure. The construction of this type of public sphere and its associated institutions of political reflexivity would be one of the fundamental achievements of the democratic revolution in the fifth century.

From oral to written epic

The contrast between the unrecorded, oral verdicts of *oikos* justice (the vendetta, *lex talionis*, and so forth) and the recorded, literate technologies of civil jurisprudence runs parallel with the development from oral to written epic.

The writing system that disappeared with the great cataclysm of the twelfth-century Dorian invasion was ill-suited for prose or poetic purposes. As an administrative tool utilized by the palace bureaucracies it was 'an unusually inefficient system even by the standards of its time'.[57] Unlike the later Phoenician-Greek script, Linear B was not alphabetic. It used a syllabary of some eighty-seven signs for vowels and consonants followed by vowels. Its main use was as an instrument for recording commercial transactions and inventories. And the disappearance of writing appears to have been so complete that Homer fails to mention such scribal offices and functions, and only once refers to a written message (*Il.* 6.168–9; cf. *Il.* 7.175ff.).[58] It is not until the middle of the eighth century that a form of consonantal system begins to emerge, appearing in crude form in inscriptions on pottery, epitaphs on tombs, and dedications. It is also significant that the 'incomparable gift' of a phonetic alphabet was constructed in the context of Phoenician trade and commerce and not as a state-monitoring, bureaucratic instrument (cf. Trump, 1980: 249–50).

Prior to the middle of the eighth century the Homeric poems were transmitted orally. Between 750 BC and 600 BC, however, alphabetic writing appears, the *Iliad* and *Odyssey* are transcribed more or less in their contemporary form, heroic hymns and lyric verse are circulating through the city-states, and toward the end of this first great period of reflexivity, we find the prose and poem texts of the Presocratic philosophers.[59] Ironically as Homeric epic began to be transcribed the society which made this poetry possible had already begun to disintegrate. In the seventh century the patronage of the epic shifted to the new mercantile and commercial classes and other rich landowners who were actively contesting the traditional powers of the aristocracy. It was men from these strata who would support the Peisistratids in their struggle for hegemony in Athens, and under whose tyranny the Homeric poems were first codified and transcribed. The death and transfiguration of Greek oral epic has its counterpart in the social revolution marking the transition from the Archaic to the Classical age.

Who speaks? The discovery of the 'true Homer'

In literary history the question of the status of the *Iliad* and *Odyssey*, their source, date of composition, and transmission has a venerable past. Even at the time of the Alexandrian critics the debate about Homer's authorship was already an overworked topic (Aristarchus of Samothrace (*c*.217–*c*.145 BC) for example attacked the joint authorship thesis in his *Answers to the Paradox of Xenon*). But the modern formulation of the 'Homeric problem' derives from the work of the German philologist, Friedrich August Wolf (1759–1824) who defined the essentially oral origins of the epic and its later transcription in his Latin tract, *Prolegomena ad Homerum* (*Prolegomena to Homer*, 1795); see also his influential *Vorlesungen über die Geschichte der griechischen Literatur* (Leipzig, 1831). Wolf's theory was itself indebted to the German translation in 1773 of Robert Wood's (1717–71) speculative study *An Essay on the Original Genius and Writings of Homer* (1769). Like Rousseau in his *Essay on the Origin of Languages*, Wood theorized that Homer was an illiterate, mnemonic oral poet operating within a preliterate tradition of oral transmission; he dated the oral composition to around 950 BC and the written facsimile to the time of Peisistratus; the sketch of a similar thesis can also be found in Francois Hédelin d'Aubignac's *Conjectures Académiques ou Dissertation sur l'Iliade* (1625). However, the Italian scholar Giambattista Vico (1668–1744) in his *Principi di Scienza Nuova* had already established the crucial link between 'Homer' and the oral tradition of Archaic Greek folk-culture. The received idea of an individual author of the epic poems is first replaced by the idea of dual or multiple authorship (especially in the eighteenth century) and then by the concept of a collective tradition of composition and oral transmission, a concept of the 'creative *Volk*' celebrated by the Romantic movement through the work of Johann Gottfried von Herder, Johan Joachim Winckelmann, Gotthold Ephraim Lessing, Hermann Gottfried, and Goethe, but later discredited (in 1916) and eventually rejected by Ulrich von Wilamowitz-Möllendorff's revaluation of the *Iliad* as a disconnected patchwork of heterogeneous compilations and agglutinative constructions ('*ein übles Flickwerk*', 'a poor patchwork').[60]

The Neapolitan jurist and philosopher Giambattista Vico was the first fully to understand the *epos* as a community's celebration of its own conditions of existence, an oral tradition's way of concretizing, recollecting, and transmitting its own 'consciousness of self'. Vico's history of the 'gentile nations' is divided into three great epochs: the age of the Gods, the age of heroes, and the age of men. Homeric poetry belongs to the epoch of heroes which follows the age of myth and ritual and precedes the epoch of philosophy, law, and history. The Greek people, Vico informs his reader, were themselves Homer (1970: 875); the epics are the folk-voice or epic story of the 'entire gentile world', but our traditional concerns for the single author 'Homer', a rare and consummate poet, 'have hitherto concealed from us the history of the natural law of the gentes of Greece' (1970: 902). 'Homer' is in fact a collective noun for a folk tradition: he 'was in no sense a philosopher' (1970: 892):

> the poverty of Homer were characteristics of the rhapsodes, who, being blind, whence each of them was called *homeros*, had exceptionally retentive memories, and, being poor, sustained life by singing the poems of Homer throughout the cities of Greece; and they were the authors of these poems inasmuch as they were a part of these peoples who had composed their histories: the poems.
>
> (1970: 875)

Indeed to make his point Vico asserts that 'the Homer who was the author of the *Iliad* preceded by many centuries the Homer who was the author of the *Odyssey*' (1970: 880).[61]

Vico, in other words, anticipates the oral-formulaic composition theory of Greek epic poetry (and by implication, of oral epic in general). We might also call this approach the Parry-Lord theory, after the work of the American scholars, Milman Parry and Albert Lord. Parry echoed the central thesis of Vico, that Homer represents 'all singers of tales from time immemorial and unrecorded to the present. Our book is about these others singers as well.'

The rules of oral poetry

Albert Lord was a student of Milman Parry (he would eventually use the Chair of Slavic and Comparative Literature at Harvard to popularize Parry's theory of the formulaic structure of epic verse). In essence Lord expanded upon Parry's original ideas based upon recordings made of Yugoslavian guslars or epic oral singers. Parry's original research on the Serbocroatian material dates back to the 1920s (see Parry, 1928, 1971). The generalized theory of the oral epic was published in their work *Serbocroation Heroic Songs* (1954). Lord, in his book *The Singer of Tales* (1971) formulated Parry's central thesis of oral composition as follows:

> the question of originality of style means nothing to the oral poet, because he has at his command ready-made phrases which have been built up by generations of poets to express all the ideas needed in the

poetry. In order for the tradition to have come into being and to have continued to exist, one must suppose that singers made changes from time to time, but these changes would have been slight and new formulas would have been modelled on the old ones'.[62]

By identifying the formulaic patterns and mnemonic devices of Serbocroatian heroic poetry – the repetitive structuring of scenes and situations in fixed syntactical-semantic sequences – Parry contended that a similar formulaic organization was at work in the Homeric epics (in *L'Epithète Traditionelle dans Homère* (1928)). The formulae and syntax (or better, syntaxes, given that different grammatical rules govern these different elements) of oral epic poetry included:

Repetitive formulae

The repetition of formulaic verse structures organized in regular, quantitative 'phrases' and metrical patterns: standardized formulaic opening and closing sequences; repetitive alliteration; prevalence of direct speech and dialogue; and so on (see Lord, 1962: 186–8; Parry, ed., 1971).

Adjective-noun/noun-adjective constructions as in the stock Homeric epithets such as 'honey-sweet wine' (*meliedea oinon*), 'boundless earth', 'wine-dark Sea', 'rose-fingered Dawn', 'golden-throned Dawn', 'well-greaved Achaeans' (*euknemides Achaioi*), 'the long-haired Achaeans', 'much-enduring Odysseus', 'pale-eyed Athene', 'godlike Odysseus', 'wily Odysseus', 'white-armed Hera', 'swift-footed Achilles', 'flashing-eyed Athena', 'Zeus cloud-gatherer', 'winged words', 'the wide and boundless Earth'; as elements of more complex syntagms these combinations are evolved in order to fit the strict quantitative and syntactic frames of the dactylic hexameter (Bowra: 'the rules are determined by the demands of the hexameter and the inflected nature of Greek syntax', in Wace and Stubbings, eds, 1962: 29; Trypanis, 1977: 43–5).

Descriptive epithets; the prevalence of standardized, ornamental epithets: 'child of aegis bearing Zeus', Apollo 'who shoots from afar', Hera, the 'white-armed goddess', Zeus as 'the gatherer of the clouds', 'father Zeus', Nestor 'master of the chariots', 'Odysseus of many sufferings', Agamemnon 'king of men', 'Agamemnon, son of Atreus, shepherd of the host' (*Od.* 3.155–6), 'swift-footed Achilles', (or 'Achilles, swift of foot'), 'Agamemnon, king of men' ((*w*)*anax andron Agamemnon*), 'Zeus-born Patroclus' (Parry, 1928); Hector's 'flashing helmet'.

Standardized phrases; the repetition of standardized expressions, from stock-phrases such as 'death and black fate', 'the sun set and all the ways grew dark' (*Od.* 3.487, 497), and 'of the bronze-armoured Achaeans' (*Achaion* *chalkochitonon*) to longer formulaic syntagms as in the regular narrative sequences describing heroes donning their armour, the death of heroes, the course of a sacrifice (*Od.* 3.336–46, 430–96), ships departing, and so on.

Preference for antithesis and oppositional structures (contrastive structures dictated by the phonological patterns and 'dialogical' syntax of direct speech in oral myth).

Thematic blocks, what Maurice Bowra once described as 'blocks of lines, or themes, which describe conventional actions' such as the standard sequence of arming a warrior, and 'Homer operates far less with single words than with phrases, and these phrases may often be of some length' (in Wace and Stubbings, eds, 1962: 28, 29), or what Lord describes as 'the thematic technique of oral story making in verse' (Wace and Stubbings, eds, 1962: 188; cf. Camps, 1980: 46–9, 101–2 n. 53 and Hainsworth, 1968).

Agglutinative or compound words, compound words (phrase-like or holophrastic structures) of the type 'silver-studded' (*arguroelos*), 'Triton-born' (*tritogeneia*), or 'horse-pasturing Argos' (*Argeos ippobotoio*), many of which are dictated by the prosodic requirements of the hexameter line in early Greek epic poetry (e.g. at *Od.* 3.378).

Fixed thematic conventions of plot, character, and scenario

The repetition of stereotypical themes and thematic stories; hence the characteristic narrative techniques of 'framed' action into beginning-middle-end; 'blocks' of action composed from unit acts; improvised variations upon and transformation of a central theme (the return of the hero, vengeance, the set speeches at assemblies, single-combat, etc.).[63]

Obligatory formulaic performance conventions emphasizing rhyme and rigorously patterned rhythms

As with the thematic rules of epic structures, performance conventions introduce definite constraints in phonology, pronunciation, and delivery.

Restricted frames for poetic innovation

Creativity is limited to the fixed stock of stylistic canons, thematic motifs, and thematic syntagms such as the paratactic list or catalogue.[64]

Oral performance on the epic scale might be compared to a complex formulaic game based on a menu of finite phrasal elements and transformation rules which provide an indeterminate set of combinations and permutations of elements; the prescribed or canonical permutations are enhanced by countenanced deviations within the rules of the game by individual singers whose creativity, however, is constrained by means of combinatorial logics within the traditional hexameter paradigms. The singer may add or delete phrasal sequences at will, while preserving the formulaic pattern set by the metre; according to personal taste and skill whole sections may be stretched or compressed; traditional formulae may be elaborated into unusual verbal patterns, rhythmic resonances, and novel materials inserted under the changing stimulation of audience requirements in the concrete situation of oral performance. Different interpretive communities encourage or constrain different types of improvisation and permutation. Like naturally occurring narrative in everyday discourse the oral poet does not mechanically repeat traditional formulae, but provides versions and variations of traditional structures and thematic syntagms. While the social contexts and audiences at a given performance determine the particular act of verbal recomposition, the 'choice of the epithet is dictated by the meter' (Knox, 1990: 16). And we should have no doubts that even Archaic poets experienced their own participation in the great tradition of orally transmitted verse with something akin to the anxiety of influence theorized by Harold Bloom (1973). As we know from the dialectic of everyday language and literary genres, traditions are often transmitted with highly untraditional forms and with distinctive and atypical innovations. This is the importance of Lord's argument that the oral poem is not composed *for* but *in* performance (1971: 13).

Thus when we ask the modern question of authorship we are literally asking the wrong question: *who speaks?* in this context, is like asking: who controls the rules of chess? The conventions of oral poetry, like the rules of chess, are a collective legacy. Epic poetry has no concrete author and its creative potential is rooted in the generative capacities of a collective tradition. More precisely, its form is dictated by the interpretive requirements of an oral audience faced with the cognitive problems of following a long poetic narrative. An individual's creativity is not ignored, but is made subservient to the traditional game moves of the canon. Individual speech is more of an intervention within and a concretization of generic conventions, than an expression of individual genius.[65] The creative poet is one who has a complete working knowledge of the inherited corpus of formulaic themes and can, as it were, swim in the traditional ocean of formulae by revising and reanimating the tradition in the act of transmission; here – in the 'premeditated spontaneity' of performative improvisation – lies the creative intertextuality of oral culture, the fusion of traditions implicit in epic art.[66] The anxiety of the oral poet is thus not the dread of his voice being simply a repetition of what went before, but anguish at the possibility of not being poetically strong enough to inflect the inherited tradition in the act of performance. Once more to borrow Bloom's terminology (1973), in comparing modern and ancient poetry we are dealing with different modalities of verbal inventiveness and poetic strength. As Knox observes, 'every time he sings the poem, he does it differently. The outline remains the same but the text, the oral text, is flexible. The poem is new every time it is performed' (1990: 17).

The written transcription of the Homeric epics preserved the traditional formulas – 'the building of metrical lines and half lines by means of formulas and formulaic expressions and of the building of songs by the use of themes' – which were 'evolved over many generations by singers of tales who did not know how to write' (Lord, 1971: 4). The Homeric poet, like the Yugoslav guslar, is at once an embodiment of the tradition and an individual talent, demonstrating 'not so much in learning through repetition of the time-worn formulas as in the ability to compose and recompose the phrases for the idea of the moment on the pattern established by the basic formulas' (Lord, 1971: 5; 'the resulting performance is the singer's own. He is not the mouthpiece of tradition; he *is* the tradition', 1962: 192). We are asked to distinguish between mechanical reproduction or copying of generic narratives and the creative appropriation through which an oral culture reflexively improvises, transforms, enlarges, and reactivates its own collective traditions. The 'tradition of improvisation' explains the profusion of non-synchronous texts and the juxtaposition of old and new elements as a consequence of verbal reinvention.

Lord also suggests that the 'impetus to write down the *Iliad* and the *Odyssey*' would not have come from Homer himself, but from an exterior source; perhaps the precipitating event was a crisis of confidence in the oral tradition itself and the 'saving grace' presented to the oral tradition by the novel ideal of stability and objectivity implicit in alphabetic writing. But why this 'impetus' should have manifested itself in such monumental works is left unexplained. The primary oral singer knows nothing of writing or songs fixed in signs; the concept of a 'fixed text' is not available to him; there is no audience for the written text. Lord evades any resolution of this difficult issue by handing over the transcription of the *Iliad* and *Odyssey* to an anonymous scribe (or scribes). In Lord's reconstruction, the masters of epic orality dictated their performances to an amanuensis. In this way Lord sidesteps the analytical and the sociological issues involved in establishing the contexts and dating of these transcriptions: 'It was probably the age of transition from oral to written technique in literature' (in Kirk, ed., 1964: 73; cf. Havelock: 'the epics as we now know them are the result of some interlock between the oral and the literate ... the acoustic flow of language ... has been reshuffled into visual patterns created by the thoughtful attention of the eye' (1986: 13));

> I cannot conceive of the author of the *Iliad* as semi-literate. The poem is too great, is done with far too much assurance, to be the first hesitating steps in a new technique. It seems to me rather that it is the product of a great oral poet in a rich oral tradition. The poems of a semi-literate oral poet are awkward in construction because they mix two techniques, one

of which has not yet had time to develop, and the other of which the poet already disdains.

(Lord, in Kirk, ed., 1964: 73–4)

Why in the first place should an oral poet go to the immense trouble of writing out his repertoire of songs. Perhaps this effort began quite humbly with poets using alphabetic script as 'a mnemonic device'? But this too must be rejected as 'unrealistic': 'that the singer wishes to preserve his song for posterity'? But his 'song will be handed down to younger generations, even as he received it and other songs from his elders'.

For Lord only one conclusion is left: the idea of transcribing oral song came from an 'outside source' and not from the singer himself. This interpretation is, of course, perfectly in keeping with the traditional image of Homer as a *blind* singer of songs, someone who could not possibly have mastered the technologies of reflexivity that alphabetic script introduces; Homer is still a poet of the earth, not a scribal artisan. Perhaps all we can say with any empirical justification is that Homer dictated his poetry to a corporate body of writers in the first decades of the sixth century. The perfect control and intricate complexity of these early compositions strongly suggest a high level of literacy (or 'protoliteracy') for both poet and transcribers.

Despite the interdictions of Parry and Lord, an explanation for the 'literate revolution' might be sought more productively in the larger pattern of social and political changes during the late Archaic age. This axial period in European history seems to have extended the revolutionary idea of the *polis* to the equally radical idea of constructing a city guarded and expressed in written laws. Perhaps the new mental technology of writing and the obsession with inscriptive permanence reflected both the impermanence of the vast changes of the eighth and seventh centuries and the desire for order and stability. Lord suggests that the explanation might be found in the 'external' diffusion of 'oriental' influences from Palestine and Assyria. These great empires had produced complex archival civilizations; writing may have been appropriated by semi-literate Greeks and turned to political and aesthetic ends:

> The Greeks and the Hebrews were reliving in their own terms the cultural experiences of older civilizations. The scribe who wrote down the Homeric poems was doing for the Greeks what the scribes of Sumer had done for their people many centuries before.

Contemporary research has provided more evidence of the coexistence and continuous interaction of scribal and oral traditions of heroic and epic verse, and we see no difficulties in accepting the Homeric poems as complex transitional forms (Parry's son, Adam Parry in his work, *The Language of Achilles* (1989) offers a more satisfactory account of the breakthrough to literate epic).

Homer's worlds: What form of life does Homeric discourse empower?

> What after all, is an education system, other than a ritualization of speech, a qualification and a fixing of the roles for speaking subjects, the constitution of a doctrinal group, however diffuse, a distribution and an appropriation of discourse with its powers and knowledge?
>
> (Foucault, 1981: 64)

After this Odyssean digression we can now return to the question posed at the beginning of this section. The economic life of Homer's world is that of the *oikos*, yet this sits uneasily with Homer's idealized world of Bronze Age warlords. We have an example of a deep fissure within the Homeric imagination; and perhaps the most obvious conclusion is to accept that these texts are themselves schizogenic, suspended between the actual world the Homeric poets knew and the imaginary community of narrative desire, a divided mind which is itself indicative of a major transitional experience during the period of their literary transcription. This is essentially J. V. Luce's point in situating Homer on the cusp of a radical shift in Greek history:

> Homer stands on the borderline between the pre-literate and literate stages of Greek culture. His comprehensive grasp of the oral tradition gave him an historian's insight into the past, while his feeling for the deeper realities of human experience saved him from any tendency to pedantic antiquarianism. He felt free to include significant elements from his own world in his poetic evocation of the Heroic Age. Hence the depth and richness of the presentation, which this chapter has attempted to explore under the concept of overlapping worlds.
>
> (Luce, 1975: 68)

Epic as a logological matrix

The questions 'Who and what does Homeric discourse *empower?*' can be best answered by uncovering its matrix presuppositions.

Who speaks?

From our brief review of the grammar of oral poetry we are tempted to answer the analytic question 'Who speaks?' by citing a collective subject, perhaps even an unconscious Subject: the voice of community here is the anonymous traditionality of oral civilization itself. Whatever the virtues of such a response, however, we are still left with an explanation in which the specifics of Greek epic are dissolved into a mythical object, 'primary oral poetry'. To avoid taking this step we might rephrase the question and provide a more historical and sociological response.

As a specialized technique of cultural reflection the task of memorizing, performing, and transmitting epic tales was placed in the hands of a specialist group; and these specialists in reflexivity frequently gained great prestige and status from their role as the collective memory of a family, tribe, or whole community. In the words of Albert Lord:

> The ancient Greeks looked upon the *aoidos* as divinely inspired, and in some of the central Asiatic tribes the singer is actually a shaman or seer and priest. He is the intermediary between the world of spirits and the ordinary every-day world of man. Frequently the singer is professional or semi-profesisonal, and this professionalism may be of great moment in maintaining a tradition. But professionalism is not a *sine qua non* for oral epic ... It is not uncommon to find that epic poetry is sung by two men together. Such seems to have been the practice in Finland, and one can still hear this kind of performance in Albania and Yugoslav Macedonia today.
>
> (Lord, in Wace and Stubbings, ed., 1962: 181–2)

Homeric epic was the work of nameless traditional *rhapsodoi* weaving together song cycles and trained in an oral apprenticeship; from contemporary parallels we know that this system did not involve mechanical memory learning and repetition training; it is probable that epic discourse was formulaically recreated on each occasion of transmission. Epic poetry is thus inseparable from the social institution of narrative singers; the singer of tales stood at the end of a long evolutionary development from more ancient traditions of folk-poetry, choral song, and ritual music. The reference to the social conditions of patronage leads us to the logological question '*For whom?*'

For whom?

Originally heroic poetry was sung before a circle of kings, warrior nobles, and princes. Almost without exception the excellences or *aretai* embodied in the central heroes and plots of the *Iliad* reflect the martial world of patriarchal warriors. In the later context of Archaic Greek aristocratic society, however, only the wealthier patrons possessed the necessary surplus wealth and leisure to cultivate epic as a domestic art form – given that some of these performances would be spread over a period of many weeks or even months. Where the Mycenaean bard had been a full-time functionary of a palace, the Archaic singer may well have been a semi-professional performer or occasional court poet employed by the richest stratum of aristocratic households. Along with semi-divine lineage and an hereditary aristocratic family name, the emblematic form of life for this stratum was one based on secure landholdings and mobile wealth. This is the social world celebrated by the Homeric poets.

By 700 BC the aristocratic order was in retreat but its heroic values continued to inform the evolving social and political system of the seventh and sixth centuries. The way of life celebrated by the Homeric poems is that of an idealized patriarchal, status-organized, aristocratic warrior society. As J. V. Luce observes, the Homeric epic served as a powerful nostalgic ideology for Greek communities on the Ionian coast, leading them to 'cherish and idealize memory of the palace-kingdoms of the thirteenth century BC', a process

> reinforced by a second cause, the nostalgia of exiles displaced from the Greek mainland at the time of the early migrations ... The conjunction of these two causes goes far to explain the strength and persistence of the Greek heroic tradition. The art of song survived the dissolution of the Mycenaean world, and the lore of the past was transmitted by a succession of singers to comfort and inspire the dispossessed survivors.
> (Luce, 1975: 47)

Homeric culture derived its imaginary representations of patriarchal power relations, ritualized honour, and social norms from this underlying ideology. Telemachus' unexpectedly sharp rebuke of his mother, Penelope at *Odyssey*. 1.353–9 exemplifies the patriarchal ethos, condensing the spheres of power, language, and labour in one sharp exchange:

> Go therefore back in the house, and take up your own work, the loom and the distaff, and see to it that your handmaidens ply their work also; but the men must see to discussion, all men, but I most of all. For mine is the power in this household (*to gar kratos est eni oikos*).[67]

While epic poetry waned with the passing of the great aristocracies, tragic drama provided a powerful aesthetic vehicle for the transmission of phallocentric values and patriarchal ideologies. The tragedies of Aeschylus and Sophocles, for example, are invariably set in the type of royal households which patronized the recitation of the *Iliad* and *Odyssey*.

Compare the conflict between Antigone, daughter of Oedipus, and Creon the ruler of Thebes, a living symbol of phallocentric power and 'tyrannical' monarchy (bearing in mind the different connotations the term 'tyrant' had for the Archaic and Classical Greeks). Her sister, Ismene tries to convince her that the right path for women is to follow the dictates of patriarchal rule:

> weak women, think of that,
> Not framed by nature to contend with men.
> Remember this too that the stronger rules;
> We must obey his orders.
> (Sophocles, *Antigone*, 60ff.)

Antigone, of course, ignores the voice of common sense as the counsel of female subordination and strikes out on her own wilful path to bury her brother Polynices against the express command of Creon. She authorizes her actions by citing an older principle of right against the 'new order' of the *polis* (represented by Creon as the voice of the City (cf. 182–3)). Her stand is an act of defiance to male domination, a solitary transgression against the collective power of the Law:

> I will go alone
> To lay my dearest brother in the grave.
> (*Antigone* 80–1)

In her defence, Antigone invokes the primordial unwritten law of Justice (*Dike*), contrasting this with the civic interdiction imposed by Creon:

> For these laws did not come from Zeus.
> Justice (*Dike*) who sits enthroned with the gods
> below, knows no such law.
> I do not think your edicts strong enough
> To overrule the unwritten, immutable laws
> of God and Heaven, you being only a man.
> They are not of yesterday or to-day, but everlasting,
> Though where they came from, none of us
> can tell.
> (Antigone 450ff., esp., 450–7; trans. Watling, 1983)

From Creon's standpoint Antigone represents a direct threat to civic order based on the rule of law and the universality of Right; but more fundamentally, she has wilfully violated the underlying 'law of the Father', the patriarchal separation of masculine and feminine principles which, in the eyes of male domination, is the founding moment of society and social order. As a manifest threat to the *polis* she must suffer and be destroyed:

> this proud girl... First overstepped the established
> order, and then –
> A second and worse act of insolence –
> She boasts and glories in her wickedness.
> Now if she thus can flout authority
> Unpunished, I am woman, she the man.
> (*Antigone* 480ff.)

Antigone adheres to the older, matriarchal ethos of mutual love transcending the will of individuals ('My nature is for mutual love, not hate', 523); Creon embodies the belligerent powers of the phallic City; and as such he can only respond with disbelief and cynicism – to deride the value of compassion (*sumphilein*):

> Die then, and love the dead if love you must,
> No woman shall be master while I live.
> (524–5)

We are back with the sentiments of Telemachus:

> we must maintain authority
> And yield no quarter to a woman's will.
> Better, if needs be, men should cast us out
> Than hear it said, a woman proved his match.
> (676–80)

Antigone, the child of an act of incestuous transgression, born from a confusion of fixed sexual boundaries and marital rules, is thus an appropriate symbol for even more radical acts of social and political transgression. In Creon's eyes Antigone is transgression personfied – the fruit of an unholy union between Oedipus and his own mother, Jocasta; the last of the heirs (along with Ismene) of the cursed Theban king; the sister of the rebels, Polynices and Eteocles. Antigone even seems to transgress natural and metaphysical categories ('I go to the fresh-made prison-tomb. Alive to the place of corpses, an alien still, never at home with the living nor with the dead' (849–51); a woman out of place geographically – wandering far away from Thebes with her disconsolate father; a woman out of place in the symbolic order – articulately speaking against the male *Logos*, a strong-minded, wilful *individual* in a world where women are closeted and locked away behind the doors of phallocentric power (echoed at 929–30 by the Chorus: 'The same ungovernable will drives like a gale the maiden still'); a deviant in disobeying the Law of the Father she introduces the seeds of anarchy and change into the structure of the City (cf. Creon's speech, 640–80); and finally, in daring to 'teach' Creon the essential difference between *Dike* and *Nomos*, between the great unwritten law of Nature and the man-made conventions of the City-state (at 454–5), she introduces a principle of difference and dispersal into the phallic universe (only what comes from *Dike*, the female personification of natural justice, is truly just).

In psychoanalytic terminology, Antigone is an overdetermined signifier of excess, transgression, transitionality. But in her extreme marginality she is also gifted with the power of wisdom, seeing to the heart of the workings of Greek patriarchy. She is the archetypal disturber of the principles of patriarchal power, law, governance, and foundations in general (the *arche/anarche* play at 640–80). And Creon – whose identity is grounded in the universality of legal order – must have Antigone destroyed as a reminder of an alien form of life.

To whom?

The answer to the question 'To whom?' is as open as the actual audiences of Homer. Given its uniquely oral, formulaic structure, Homeric epic would have been typically performed before a non-literate audience; its first addressees were the communities of Archaic Greece, including the same classes that formed the taste communities of Greek mythology, hero legends, and folk-tales, and more sophisticated groups who read their own fate in the stories of an Achilles, Agamemnon or Hector.

Through whom?

As oral performances presupposing a shared knowledge of traditional mythology, story pattern, and schematic paradigms, the epic demands strong bonds of audience identification; the diverse satisfactions it offers are rooted in the social psychology of heroic projection, mythic recognition, and traditional Greek value systems.

As poetic artisans who produced and performed their own work, traditional rhapsodes did not require a separate agency to communicate these songs; the ideal singer is simultaneously a teller of tales, actor, and musician accompanying his own performance (a composite role that is still recognizable in the troubadour figure of mediaeval Provence composing love poetry and chivalric tales in the *langue d'oc*, and in oral poets who still practice the art of traditional, epic poetry today); the question 'Through Whom?' only becomes relevant when a mediating school of Homeric reciters comes into existence in the sixth century. By then Homer has been assimilated to the events of the great religious festivals, a social setting and communicative situation which further led to the formalization and rationalization of epic verse forms. But even more importantly, the festivalization of Homer led to performances heard by thousands of Greek-speaking listeners, drawn from across the class structure of the ancient *polis*.

How?

We have already answered this question: heroic epic was primarily oral performance; its rules of production were similar to those of all epic poetry: composition-in-performance; elaboration of traditional motifs and schemata; stereotypical thematics (of events, characters, actions); elaboration of elements to embellish and extend the traditional mythological stories; creative use of formulae and formulaic syntagms by the individual singer or reciter; the importance of strong plotting to ensure syntagmatic continuity in a situation where the events of the main story required an extensive period of time; a preference for realistic detail, concreteness, objectivity, dignity of style, and the intertextual openness of dactylic hexameter; the interweaving of song, music, and stylized performance – which may have taken original epic closer to choral dance than 'narrative' in its modern sense. The unique medium placed a premium on the face-to-face impact of the telling/singing, especially on the impact of sonority of voice, melody, temporal rhythm maintained by the lyre, continuous structures, repetitive patterns, and so forth.

What?

We have also explored some central thematic elements of the epic. The most important *motifs* were embodied in formulae relating to the life of heroism, combat, heroic action, and the 'excellences' of war and its prizes. Many of its stock of themes were derived from earlier mythologies. Because of these connections, the epic form tends not to be primarily a medium of characterization or the psychological exploration of heroes, but of character types.

In ideological terms, epic celebrates aristocratic values, military success, and patriarchal hegemony. It concretizes the core of Greek mythology: the rule of Zeus, the Gods of Olympus, the different regional authority of the Gods, and so on; but it also questions these values and interjects quasi-philosophical ideas of the governance of life by omniscient Fate and Justice (*Dike*). In a similar manner, Homeric 'ethics' follow the contours of a virile humanism in which the public display of heroism and courage are supreme values. Shame and public opprobrium act as powerful mechanisms of social control. After finding Odysseus shipwrecked Nausicaa fears the recriminations of the city if he accompanies her to the city:

> since there are insolent men in our community, and see how one of the worse sort might say when he met us, 'Who is this large and handsome stranger whom Nausikaa has with her, and where did she find him? Surely, he is to be her husband, but is he a stray from some ship of alien men she found for herself, since there are no such hereabouts? Or did some god after much entreaty come down in answer to her prayers ... Better so, if she goes out herself and finds her a husband from elsewhere, since she pays no heed to her own Phaeacean neighbours, although many of these and the best ones court her'. So they will speak, and that would be a scandal against me, and I myself would disapprove of a girl who acted so, that is, without the good will of her dear father and mother making friends with a man, before being formally married.
>
> (*Od.* 6.273–89)

In this world human beings are defined by the customary sanctions of tradition (*dike* originally had the sense of 'traditional ways') and customary moral codes. We establish a recognizable Self only through our community with Others – here exemplified in our moral relations with others as mediated through tradition's sanctioning work (in face-to-face situations such as gossip, loss of face, status damage for family, friends and acquaintances following a transgression, ostracism, and so forth). By aestheticizing such responses Homer creates a heightened awareness that the excellences by which his characters live are incarnate values. *Arete* is a matter of customary forms of conduct, public performance, and conspicuous social display. Values are concretely realized as verbalized motives, as a community's practical techniques of world-making.[68]

We have seen in Volume 1 that the articulation of a culture's thematic concerns, its imaginary formations, and motives depends upon the availability of societal language-games through which communities come to objectify, interpret, and reflect upon their own projects. These form the rhetorics and instruments of collective self-reflection for a society. It also follows that one way of tracing the changing psychological and social-psychological imperatives of a culture is to explore the dynamic interaction between existing rhetorics of reflection and novel motivational discourses. In this chapter we have approached Homeric epic as texts from a culture experiencing the transition from the motivational structure appropriate to a traditional, tribal shame culture to the motivational structure required by a more rationalized, urban, and political guilt culture. The Homeric *epos* is a transitional text in creatively straddling both these ideological worlds and their associated conceptions of self and community.[69]

7 CONCLUSION: THERSITES' REVENGE (*ILIAD* 2. 200–277)

> All utopian thinking has an element of fantasy, of dreaming, or at least yearning, for a better life and a better world. And all men dream in this way, about themselves and their families if not about society in general or the world at large.
>
> (Finley, 1967: 3)

Reflexivity should have the last word in this study of Homeric discourse. I have argued that the manifest aim of epic to preserve an aristocratic world in heroic speech produced discursive forces that undermined and vitiated this ideal; to recall one important instance, the narrative grammar of epic created a polycentric intertextuality of speech genres and discursive registers. But the text also has many other deconstructive and even utopian moments. One of the most famous of these erupts in the destructive speech of Thersites.

The place in the *Iliad* (*Il*. 2.200–5, 212–19, 219ff.) where the 'foul-mouthed' soldier Thersites denounces the pretences and posturing of the aristocracy – in particular Agamemnon's conduct of the war – is the first Greek text that alludes to the darker side of the heroic ideal. Thersites' discontent emerges from the nameless and voiceless masses who toiled to maintain aristocratic *arete*. As we might expect, Thersites is depicted as the very antithesis of the noble ideal, both in word and appearance. Accordingly, his dissonant, transgressive voice is not countered by argument and persuasion but by physical force. His complaints against the wasteful Agamemnon and his mutinous appeal to the nameless community of nobodies is violently silenced by Odysseus – blows not words teach Thersites the meaning of Homeric *Dike*.

Thersites is not only presented as ugly and physically deformed, but – by contrast to the measured speech of Achilles and Odysseus – as a source of uncontrolled, disordered, and vicious talk. He is the archetypal Other of the heroic ideal, the carnivalesque transgressor who 'when he felt inclined to bait his royal masters, was never at a loss for some vulgar quip, empty and scurrilous indeed, but well calculated to amuse the troops' (*Il.* 2.211ff., trans. Rieu). Odysseus 'answers' Thersites' verbal protest with a physical beating (*Il.*244–78). The vernacular voice of the fighting masses is violently silenced – Thersites is literally beaten and laughed to the margins of the Assembly (and thus symbolically effaced from Greek culture and history). Thersites would not only make the campaign against the Trojans impossible – as all soldiers know, once enemies begin talking to one another imaginary antagonisms are dissolved by the insistent call of a common humanity – his humour reveals the heroic world as a tissue of illusions. Thersites' bid to speak freely, like the poetic cynicism of Archilochus, saps the imaginary foundations of the epic order.

The text completes this graphic scene with an untypical authorial intervention placed in the mouth of one of Thersites' own companions:

> Good work! cried one man, catching his neighbour's eye and saying what they were all feeling. 'There's many a fine thing to Odysseus' credit ... But he has never done us a better turn than when he stopped the mouth of this windy ranter. I do not think Thersites will be in a hurry to come here and sling insults at the kings.
>
> (*Il.*265–77, esp. 272–7)

The public degradation and silencing of Thersites ends on a note of putative universal accord: 'Such was the verdict of the gathering' (*Il.*278).

We can now appreciate why the Thersitean moment was more than an amusing interlude in the course of the epic; the violent repression of Thersites reveals the axiomatic principle of the epic universe. Epic logocentrism is bought at the price of assimilating particularity to the realm of universal rules. Epic projects a world of universal values – a transcendent authority incarnated in the figure of the King. But Thersites speaks for the voice of repressed particularity; indeed it is this very idea of epic universality that Thersites' humour disturbs. Logocentrism is interrogated not by its own instruments – the techniques of reflexivity we have described as persuasion and universal *logos*, but by crude humour and the vernacular idioms of everyday life. Against the voice of the Other, the *Logos* must be centred and controlled by the aristocratic warlords of Greece (cf. *Il.*2.286, 339–41). The epic world of noble deeds and timeless values has no place for the wrangling and political questioning of Thersites (the dramatist Sophocles in the fifth century was still denigrating Thersites as a symbol of evil – see *Philoctetes* 445–52). It cannot admit the viability of dialogue or the possibility of reasoned dissent, let alone the idea of *institutionalized* dialogue which characterizes the political experience of the fifth-century *polis*. Yet against its own monologic intentions, epic language produces a plurality of Thersitean voices. Its logocentrism encourages a multiplicity of dialogical genres, idiolects, and speech forms. It is as though Homer was aware of the insight implicit in his narrative blindness, and not only parodies the voice of transgressive speech but understands its force even as he sets out to repress it. Thersites' punishment is lenient compared to the punishment meted out to Melanthius:

> They took Melanthios along the porch and the courtyard. They cut off, with the pitiless bronze, his nose and his ears, tore off his private parts and gave them to the dogs to feed on raw, and lopped off his hands and feet, in fury of anger. Then, after they had washed their own hands and feet clean, they went into the house of Odysseus. Their work was ended.
> (*Od.* 22.473–8)

The world of the *epos* must be made safe for hereditary monarchy; yet the voice of the *demos* is only temporarily stilled.[70]

The Thersitean moment would not go away; it might be repressed but it would return in a number of different guises during the subsequent course of Greek history to undermine and destroy the aristocratic order. Thersites' revenge is the key to the master-slave dialectic of Greek history. The lyric voices of an Archilochus or Hipponax, the sixth-century Tyrants, Aristophanic comedy, Socrates, the Sophists, Diogenes, the Cynics, and their ilk are spiritual inheritors of the Thersitean moment. Thersites' revenge marks the failure of Greek civilization to accommodate otherness, difference, and heteroglossia as social and ethical values in an institutional cosmos founded on Homeric sameness, order, and perfect speech. We shall see in Volume 3 that the earliest philosophical thinkers also confront a similar contradiction in struggling to reconcile the Many in the One at the expense of dialogical reflexivity.

3
HESIOD AND THE BIRTH OF THE GODS

> The origins of things, which were the same for gods as for mortals.
> (Hesiod, *Theogony* 109)

> For Homer and Hesiod were the first to compose Theogonies (*theogonien*), and give the gods their epithets, to allot them their several offices and occupations, and describe their forms.
> (Herodotus, *History* 2.53.2)

> They [the Spartans] delight in the genealogies of heroes and of men and in stories of the foundations of cities in olden times, and, to put it briefly, in all forms of *antiquarian lore [archaeologia]*.
> (Hippias, in Plato, *Greater Hippias* 285D)

1 Introduction: *mythos-logos*
2 Theogonic myth as discourse and prototheorizing
3 The discovery of the '*I*': self-reflexivity in Hesiod's writing
4 The poetic '*I*' and divine authorization
5 Hesiodic symbolism and the 'mythological world-view'
6 The violence of differentiation and the appearance of the gods
7 Hesiodic ideology: the valorization of justice and work
8 Hesiodic utopianism

1 INTRODUCTION: *MYTHOS-LOGOS*

> He also who loves myths is in some sense a philosopher.
> (Aristotle, *Metaphysics* 982b18)

Following the analyses in Chapters 1 and 2 the 'movement' of discourse from *Muthos* to *Logos* will be approached as an imaginary structure with numerous hermeneutic applications, a metaphor for the endemic 'strife of principles' characterizing all beginnings, most particularly the beginning of 'theoretical reason' projected by early Greek theorizing and philosophy. We have seen that the polemical 'coupling' of *Myth* and *Logos* was already a rhetorical device used by many ancient Greek thinkers; and as we proceed, the figure will turn out – rather like Aristophanes' androgynous creature in the *Symposium* – to contain a more complex constellation of themes and questions. The apparent stability and coherence of *Logos* predisposed Greek thought to represent truth as a fixed and eternal order opposed to the vagaries and contextuality of myth-making (forgetting that even the most abstract philosophical investigation is also an act of communication and as a 'saying about' and 'saying for others' presupposes the oral techniques of narrative praxis). This ambivalence is already prefigured in Herodotus where we read that it was the *language* of poetry that was of seminal importance in articulating the names and determining the nature of the gods (2.53.2). Poetic *muthos* first allowed the world of the gods to take shape and appear as an intelligible totality (cf. Xenophanes, *fr.* 10). Poetic naming fixed 'once and for all' the true order of the sacred. In this respect the craft of poetry founds and sustains the possibility of community. Yet as a man of the Greek enlightenment Herodotus was satisfied that 'Archaic' myth had performed its formative work and could be safely set aside in deference to the sober language of empirical evidence and reason. Indeed Herodotus is one of the leading demythologizers of the earlier mythic tradition, grounding his critique in an idealized conception of stable truth (for Herodotus' criticism of Homer's poetic licence see 2.116). The Herodotean pursuit of the path of true 'existence' (1.95) occasioned the fundamental desire of the whole European tradition to separate a self-sustaining rationality from the darker horizons of prereflective tradition and mythological culture. Where myth entertains with its grotesque tales, 'cold reason' illuminates with the sharpness of its evidence and rigour of its concepts. Where Myth appears as an *anarchy* of heterogeneous fables, Truth stands autonomous and unchanging. Where stories – and storytellers – come and go, the truth, once grasped, can be possessed in perpetuity (Thucydides 1.22–3).

In what follows we will proceed by bracketing the philosopheme of 'Myth-or-Logos', and investigating the rhetorical genesis of this progress narrative which helped to create the Greek self-understanding of an autonomous reflective form of life. To anticipate the conclusion of this chapter, what the Archaic Greeks designated with the polysemic term *muthos* was the 'fecundity of storytelling' itself, the matrix of plurisignificance and discursive transgression with its dense interweave of *symbols*, *metaphor*, and *diegesis* without which any tradition would be literally unthinkable. In Chapters 1 and 2 we have identified this with the mythological and Homeric culture of ancient Greece. From the logological perspective we should think of 'poetry' as a collective act of self-representation, a work of articulation that was valued both for its social and 'spiritual' effects. In this respect the project of Western self-reflection was always-already mediated by figural structures and pretheoretical symbolisms. We have also seen that Greek myth appears to have broken free from its magical and ritual origins prior to the texts of Homer and Hesiod. We can begin to examine this complex of problems by recalling the metaphoric richness of the Greek word *Mimesis*.

HESIOD AND THE BIRTH OF THE GODS

The symbolic work of *Mimesis* was already in place before it became the adversarial counterpoint of *theoria* in the fifth century. The mode of mimesis the Greeks called 'myth' was sufficiently powerful to act as an adversary for the first intellectual attempts to constitute an autonomous theoretical language in the sixth century (we will explore the detailed phenomenology and history of this process in the chapters of Volume 3). In fact the outlines of this critical struggle were already implicit in the first *written* theogonies of the Greek tradition dating back to the seventh century. As John Burnet observed, Hesiod's *Theogony* 'is an attempt to reduce all the stories about the gods into a single system, and system is fatal to so wayward a thing as mythology' (1930: 6). The will-to-system, of course, does not belong to the same semantic space as *hieroi logoi*, sacred discourses. The stories of the sacred are anything but systematic and orderly judged by the measure of theoretical reason. Burnet's claim is reversible: 'mythology is fatal to so monologic a thing as system.' This reversibility helps to avoid the simple evolutionary idea of the demise of myth clearing a space for the construction of philosophical science.

In Chapters 1 and 2 we have seen that *muthos* is the ordinary Greek word for 'story' and the products of storytelling. The speeches and discourses in which Themistocles and Jason appear may look superficially similar in their referential orientation, but they are governed by fundamentally different objectives, organizing intentionalities, and principles. Themistocles 'really was' a famous Greek general who rebuilt the Athenian navy, whereas the Jason who sailed with his fellow Argonauts in search of the Golden Fleece belongs to the world of legend. One discourse pursues the intentionality of referential truth, the other implicates an audience in a magical tale with no existential basis: Themistocles 'really existed'; Jason is a 'product of fabulation'. Yet both genres claim to articulate truths for their respective communities. What are we to make of a culture that divined the truth in the stories of Zeus and Hera, Heracles and Apollo?

The clue lies in the functional nexus between a society's means of communication, imagination, and symbolic expression. A society which projected its desires and fears in the imagery and patterns of *muthos* is, quite simply, a culture of storytelling praxis. *Muthos* in its most generic sense, then, names one of the most insistent and universal features of human experience – its 'story-shaped' character. In historical terms, myth belongs to societies without literate technologies. Diegetic form is in this sense the medium of re-collection, or, said more sociologically, it institutes a community's diverse ways of recalling, inscribing, and commemorating all that is deemed to be of value for that community. Stories constitute a community's primary mode of calling-to-mind, collectively repealing, and remembering its past, and the singer or *aoidos* is a most valued role in reproducing a shared culture. To make sense of experience is tacitly to invoke narrative schemata lying sedimented in the layers of pretheoretical oral culture. Such sense-making enterprises are, as we have argued at length in Volume 1, primary reflexive processes in societies without writing. *Muthos*, in other words, belongs with a constellation whose other terms are *value* ('that which is worthy of being remembered'), *memory* (understood as a culture's oral 'techniques of (re)presentation'), *identity* and *difference* (what *we* remember provides our collective sense of being-in-the-world), and *authority* (both in terms of who is empowered with the *right* to speak and also in terms of the social uses of narration as *authoritative* media of shared values and communality).

Myth-making creates a society's basic memorial systems which in turn define the terms of reference of social action – memory being 'the chain of tradition which passes a happening on from generation to generation' (Benjamin, 'The storyteller' Section XIII, in Benjamin, 1992). From the perspective of logological analysis, terms like 'value', 'identity', and 'difference' are themselves indices of ancient knowledge systems acquired with the enculturation practices of a community. *Muthos*, then, combines both narrative *remembrance* and communal *desire*: the social desire to say what is memorable and in the act of so-saying to be remembered ('recollection' should be understood in both the personal and collective sense of communal identification: by participating in the logosphere 'individuals' become persons worth remembering; we are literally 're-membered' as participants in a wider social cosmos). And we can only remain 'members' of a community by participating in the speech and action of ongoing social praxis. This is why the earliest literature from the Archaic period invariably makes *Mnemosune* – Memory – first among the Gods and mother of the Muses (*Homeric Hymns, To Hermes* 429–30). Culture – the domain of Apollo and the Muses – is the matrix of identity and community. The role of shared values, symbols, and practices is thus to transform heterogeneous communities into a unitary community. The theme of the 'One and the Many' as this emerged in Presocratic thought was already prefigured in the Archaic opposition of unitary Reason and polysemic Myth.

Myth is thus not a secondary elaboration of pregiven experience; it is a constitutive form in which disparate experiences are given coherent expression. A shared comitment to language-games of myth, so to speak, creates the underlying narrative framework of possible experience for the community. And in transmitting these stories, individuals function as the medium of tradition. In *muthos*, then, we have an exemplary instance of a generative *matrix*, a tensile intersection of different orders of desire: to speak of beginnings and endings, to celebrate the presence of things, to name the gods or, as the poets of the Archaic age had already grasped, 'to sing of the divine' (*to theion*).

2 THEOGONIC MYTH AS DISCOURSE AND PROTOTHEORIZING

Greek Myth is an expression of the desire for mimetic coherence. As a will-to-articulation, myth adumbrates themes which later become the characteristic topics of more reflexive cultures. In Chapter 1 we have seen that the symbolic formations of the oldest Greek myths coded the structure of experience in anthropomorphic categories. Because talk of the transition from mythopoeic narrative to philosophical discourse *(theoria)* is itself a logological product of a literate culture we can anticipate that the actual transitions were blurred, historically uneven and ambivalent. To study the margins on either side of this 'transition' requires a bracketing of the anachronistic scheme itself in order to return to older, prephilosophical contexts. The dialectic of beginnings is most evident in the emergence of the first explicit theogonies or theophanies to pose the *question* of the origins of the gods. We are invited by the logic of our own concern with origins to approach this new kind of questioning as a crucial phase in the history of reflexivity, given that the theogonic puzzle – *where did the gods come from?* – the childlike question that follows in the wake of every anthropomorphic formulation of the sacred – opens up a further discursive space for theological speculation – *what, then, is the being and nature of the gods?* Which in turn occasions other questions: *what comes before the gods? Why are there gods?* And perhaps even: *what if there are no gods?* Myth, so to speak, precipitated a whole nexus of 'ontological questions' – but more importantly, it releases the full imaginative force of what we have earlier called the *reflexive imagination.*

It is no doubt wrong to collapse this sequence of analytic questions into the historical genesis of every known theogony or to ascribe the theophantic desire as a human universal. To avoid this kind of a priorism we will proceed from the perspective of a sociological poetics, arguing that the particular *symbolic form* of theophany constituted by Hesiod's *Birth of the Gods (Theogony)* occasioned critical reflection by virtue of its textual structure and grammatical conventions. The discursive field presupposed by the appearance of an explicit theology is subject to numerous material and cultural contingencies and like other cultural phenomena may be blocked by the operation of particular institutional circumstances. Many highly developed cultures do not appear to have elaborated such discourses or their sustaining institutions. So-called hydraulic civilizations for example, from ancient China and India to Meso-America, constrained by the exigencies of an extensive state machinery supervised by theocratic priests, state officials, and scribes would not present an optimum social environment for speculative theology or cosmogonic theorizing. In these civilizations anthropocentric diegesis was rigidly controlled by a mediating priesthood. No 'transition' from primary myth and traditional religion to autonomous poetic traditions and dialectical discourse could take root in such a culture. In parenthesis, we should also note that civilizations that have not explicitly verbalized such experiences should not be regarded as 'unreflexive'.

It appears to be the case, then, that the impulse to speculative thought presupposes a definite constellation of social practices, material preconditions, institutional conditions, and historical circumstances. Among the most important of these factors in the context of Greek history were the absence of a dominant institution of sacred kingship, the rapid expansion of the Ionian mercantile economy, the development of the city-state, the long-term social and political consequences of the 'crisis of the aristocracy', the spread of literacy, the emergence of Homeric poetry and pan-Hellenic cultural formations such as the cult of heroes, trans-Hellenic oracles (the oak-oracle at Dodona, the Delphic Oracle), and the Olympic Games (Nagy, 1990: 10).

Religious pluralism, social dynamism, and the heteroglossia of Ionian culture in particular can be singled out as critical preconditions encouraging experimentation in new reflexive forms and media. The mercantile city-states of Asia Minor provided a propitious environment for both speculation and cultural rationalization. Here relatively autonomous political institutions and volatile economic markets created a fertile setting for speculative poets, dissident aristocrats, merchant adventurers, and oracular 'prophets' of the 'new learning'. The polycentric 'agonism' of the Near Eastern world provided a seminal environment for experiments in critical self-reflection. And this was further enhanced by continuous exchanges with other cultures and civilizations. Greek religion from the earliest period elaborated an ever-expanding – perhaps even inchoate and sprawling – pantheon of divinities which principally resisted 'unification' under the auspices of a state priesthood of the kind that dominated the civil life of ancient Egypt and the Near Eastern empires of Lydia, Babylonia, and Persia. More directly, the new mercantile groups inhabited a dynamic commercial world that looked favourably upon innovation, criticism, and individual expression, a culture of 'free thinking' which encouraged speculation about the nature and form of things.[1] At the very least such a culture did not proscribe speculative inquiry as an affront to the godhead or its earthly representatives. The absence of a sacred monopoly over matters of faith guarded by a hereditary priesthood proved to be one of the decisive factors facilitating the development of Greek speculative reflexivity – one particular manifestation of which is the emergence of explicit theogonies and rational theologies.

Together with the absence of institutionalized priesthood in the Ionian city-states of the seventh century there existed another facilitating institution unique to this culture: the tradition of non-religious poetry which may have already been organized around something like a guild of professional practioners. I refer, of course, to the institution of public reflexivity associated with the epic hexameter and civic poetry (what today we would designate with the expression 'Homeric poetry'). A tradition of professionally trained reciters and singers specializing in codifying traditional stories and myths into extended symbolic-dramatic performances is a cultural innovation that is unique to Hellenic civilization. Many other civilizations have developed reflective monitoring practices (the ancient archives of Mesopotamia and Egypt and the cultural technologies of Meso-America provide other instances of self-representing media), but only the Greek rhapsodes elaborated their narratives in *dramatic* form within public arenas subject to public scrutiny and rigorous criterial appraisal. The institution of the *agon* in particular encouraged *competitive* norms and *individual* experimentation separated from centralized state control and priestly adjudication. This unique Ionian institution appears to have been one of the fundamental conditions of the earliest manifestations of pan-Hellenic thought: the public tradition of critical articulation and self-criticism, and connected with these protoforms of self-reflection, an infrastructure of educational, ritual, and political institutions that gave these practices a material presence in the cultural life of Ionian civilization. Only here did the poetic tradition evolve into a form of collective education and cultural self-reflection.

These are some of the decisive contexts of early Greek reflexivity. Henceforth when we speak of Greek myth and poetry we should understand the term 'myth' in its full institutional and ideological significance – as the performative practices, techniques, and institutions of poetic reflexivity. The earliest form of rationalization of the mythic tradition – removing untoward tales, refining alternative versions, emphasizing more aesthetic and anthropomorphic cycles, humanizing oral traditions, moving toward recitative praxis, and so forth – took place in the urbane palace economies and *poleis* of the Ionian coast during the eighth century. Rationalizing the mythic corpus was well advanced before the composition of the Homeric and Theban song cycles. This was the period when the more magical and 'bestial' folklore of the earliest inhabitants of Ionia were filtered out of the canon, or at least regarded as below the dignity of the aristocratic clients of the new poetic guilds. In broad outline this corroborates the logological theory of the evolution of genres: every new technique of reflexivity involves a measure of repression and exclusionary practices toward existing discourses.

The process of oral stylization and the refinement of critical judgement went hand in hand with the discovery and perfection of more formalized and, to some extent, 'artificial' poetic metres. Both processes are more or less complete by the middle of the seventh century. For the limited purposes of this argument the striking *absence* of mythic motifs, story forms, and supernatural plots – for example, those involving magical transformations, talking animals, and the like – are symptomatic traces of underlying shifts in modes of thought and intellectual attitudes. We know that the kind of tales that were later popularized under the name 'Aesop' existed in ancient Greece by this time, but were effectively displaced by the more mature forms of mythic narrative and are absent from the epic. In Chapter 2 I have suggested that the 'magical' and 'fabular' elements of the *Odyssey* represent a 'return of the repressed' when compared to the magisterial style and humanistic content of the *Iliad*.

Another example is the invention of the literary metre we know as dactylic hexameter – the most reflective and aesthetically stylized form of the *epos*. Here the sociology of the epic's audience and its transformation is as important as an immanent analysis of the dactylic form itself. It is reasonable to assume that the 'author' (or 'authors') of the works we know as the *Iliad* and *Odyssey* as well as the more individualized author of the *Theogony* and *Works and Days* (*Erga kai hemerai*) received their training and drew upon the critical traditions of the same performative culture. These 'works' were written – or at least, orally recited – for a relatively sophisticated audience. Moreover, the transmitters of the Homeric epics and hymns explicitly identified their role as self-interpreters of a unique civilization, becoming, as it were, self-appointed propagandists of the Hellenic way of life. Another important dramatic form that evolved during the same period was the public genre of choral poetry – particularly the choral works associated with seventh-century Spartan culture. Together with epic, choral song and dance became powerful vehicles for the pan-Hellenic ideal of the ruling aristocratic *élites*. Both epic and choral poetry – in the experiential context of their sustaining dialogic institutions and political contexts – also encouraged the growth of cosmogonic and theogonic speculation. With this innovation a new intellectual field had come into existence.[2]

We know that the period from around 750 to 700 BC was characterized by rapid economic and social changes in the Mediterranean world; the 'Dark ages' following the Dorian invasions were brought to a close, the first great period of colonization of the Ionian mainland – stretching over several centuries – had been consolidated, and new social and political forms were brought into existence – the basic elements of the classical civilization of the *polis* were adumbrated, interdependent markets began to link diverse cities and nations, money economies increasingly invaded and displaced the traditional social structures of the Bronze Age economy and, of course, great waves of colonization after 750 BC spread this civilization and its culture beyond the limits of the Ionic states and Asia to mainland Greece – one such merchant from the Aeolian city of Cyme being the father of the future poet Hesiod (for the mercantile occupation of Hesiod's father see *Works and Days* 630–5).

At the outset we should record the accepted facts concerning the poet/singer Hesiod. The name *Hesiodos* is itself indicative of the privileged cultural role of song, having the sense 'he who speaks or sings' to and for the community. The poet bearing the name Hesiod ('one who voices') is the first identifiable, named singer and *writer* in the narrative tradition. Hesiod was first and foremost a creative master of a novel invention – the 'spiritual' technology of alphabetic writing; more precisely, he displays a perfect command of the new literary culture, a competence comparable to the scriptural skills of the anonymous transcribers of the *Iliad* and *Odyssey*. The *Theogony* is said to be an earlier work than *Works and Days*. From the logological perspective, alphabetic writing appears as an exemplary reflexive technology, a system of cultural practices which when actively applied to traditional spheres of life activated a qualitative transformation in the possibilities of human self-experience and literary consciousness. Here we also meet one of the first paradoxes of early

HESIOD AND THE BIRTH OF THE GODS

Greek poetry: what was originally designed to be sung was preserved and disseminated as a text to be read, a work of writing.

This puzzle holds a graphic clue to the nature of Hesiodic reflection, a clue revealed in a certain ambivalence in the traditional biography of Hesiod: inheritor of the cultural – but not the material – capital of an old Ionian mercantile family, yet stranded on a wind-blasted farm in Boeotia. That Hesiod was one of many epic poets competing against one another in a public, poetic *agon*-system is suggested by the biographical information he provides about himself – claiming that he was awarded a golden tripod for reciting his own verse at the funeral games of Amphidamas at Chalcis (Chalkis) on the island of Euboea (657–8). The short voyage to Euboea may have been his only journey away from Ascra (*Works and Days* 633–8, 646–51, 661). We may also presume that the genre of the 'genesis of the Gods' was also a popular theme at such gatherings and that Hesiod acquired his repertoire of basic themes from listening to other travelling rhapsodes. In Hesiod's case the prize was dedicated at the sanctuary of the Muses of Helicon, the place where Hesiod was granted the gift of 'clear song' (*Works and Days* 651–9).[3]

The first explicit *written* theogony and cosmogony known to Western culture is found in the poetry of Hesiod. Two major works are linked to his name, the *Works and Days* and *Theogony*. While the former text is largely devoted to didactic, practical instruction in the communal arts of agriculture, housekeeping, navigation, folkloric astronomy, and divination, the latter work – written in epic prose – presents a 'systematic' genealogy of the cosmos and the gods. As *written* texts the existence of these works is itself important documentary evidence of a remarkable expansion in alphabetic technology and scriptural competence during the later part of the eighth century; and as texts produced by and directed to a primary oral/aural audience of 'middle-strata' farmers and cultivators, they trace a significant change in social attitudes and consciousnesss when compared with the audience of the earlier epic.[4]

Hesiod's dark poetry contains one of the first social critiques of the rapacious life of the Boeotian aristocracy as well as numerous coded references to the bitter class struggles and social crisis during this period of ancient Greek history. He is also the first Western 'author' to provide biographical information about his own personal and social circumstances. For example, we know that he and his brother, Perses, had inherited a smallholding under Mount Helicon, near Ascra in Boeotia; his father had emigrated to this part of Greece after failing as a maritime merchant in Aeolian Cyme (in Asia Minor):

> Your father and mine, foolish Perses, used to go to sea in search of a good livelihood. One day he came here over a great expanse of sea, leaving Aeolian Cyme in a black ship. What he fled was not riches, wealth and prosperity, but evil penury, which Zeus gives to men. And he settled near

Helicon in a miserable village, Ascra, which is bad in winter and unpleasant in summer, and no good at any time.
(*Works and Days* 633–40, esp. 633–4, 637, 639–40; cf. 646–62)

The death of the father marked the beginning of a family feud between Hesiod and Perses over the legal title to the land and inheritance (*kleros*); evidently Perses had canvassed the help of powerful local magnates and magistrates – possibly by bribes – to outwit his brother in this archetypal property conflict. It is no doubt significant that one of the first didactic texts of the tradition documents the course of a familial struggle over landed property. The poem *Works and Days* thus opens with a struggle over a disputed inheritance. While nothing like 'autobiography' is at issue here we should, nevertheless, regard Hesiod's text as a significant indicator of new forms of expression and personal sensibilities, prefiguring the rise of identifiable individual voices in later Greek lyric poetry. Standard histories of Greek literature which depict Hesiod as the father of didactic epic tend to underestimate his crucial role in the evolution of the personalized language of 'lyric' subjectivity. I will return to this theme in Chapter 4.

Hesiod can be read more productively as an epic *writer* attempting to move away from the 'heroic' style and themes of Homeric epic. His work reflects a major turning point in the epic tradition. The ensuing conflict between desire and form produced two antithetical generic forms: the prosaic narrative of everyday agrarian life and the theophantic drama of the Birth of the Gods. The textual conflict of desire and inherited literary structures occasioned the earliest known attempt to write reflexively, creating a text in which the author, like a prophetic mediator, is himself embedded.

3 THE DISCOVERY OF THE '*I*': SELF-REFLEXIVITY IN HESIOD'S WRITING

One striking innovation in Hesiod's hieratic style is the appearance of an insistent first-person narrative form within the structure of the poem. Hesiod foregrounds his poetic Self against the anonymity of the poetic tradition. He comes forth as a unique speaking agent, a man with a salutary message. By this strong poetic act Hesiod differentiates his singular 'prophetic' voice from the anonymous, collective voice of epic tradition and sings/writes from the standpoint of his own concrete situation. Again we should understand this act of individuation as an expression of a unique change in values and normative orientations in the world of the early *polis*. We thus find no comparable examples of personal authorship in the literature of the ancient Middle East. Furthermore, this apparently innocuous textual invention opened up a number of vital cultural possibilities which bear comparison with the consequences of adding a second and third actor in tragic drama. Behind both discoveries we should recognize the impress of a whole new structure of lived experience. The 'insistent I' of Hesiodian theogony is one expression of this experiential transformation.

Historians and literary critics have frequently drawn attention to this creative departure from the inherited epic tradition. Two examples can be cited. The first is from I. M. Finley's *The Ancient Greeks* (1963: 31):

> Hesiod was both bard and farmer, and the main theme of the *Works and Days*, written, it seems, late in the eighth century or early in the seventh , is the life of the farmer, his toil and routines, his slaves and hired hands and oxen, his dislike of the nobles and their injustice on the one hand and of the sea and its small merchant craft on the other, his minute technical knowledge of farming and of the many ritual acts and taboos which went with it, and his perpetual fear of disaster and poverty. Nothing could be more unlike the Homeric poems in subject or outlook.

The second comes from C. A. Trypanis' *Greek Poetry: From Homer to Seferis* (1981: 61):

> Hesiod abandoned the self-suppresssion of the Ionic bards and came forward in his own person ... naming himself in what constitutes the first *sphragis* [the inclusion of the poet's name in his work] in Greek poetry. This new personal element opened the way which Archilochus and, after him, other iambic, elegiac and lyric poets were to follow.

The 'discovery' of the poetic use of the first-person perspective, the appearance of the *sphragis*, and the self-referential nature of Hesiod's writing are connected with a more profound reflexive discovery – that the poetic word can and perhaps must articulate the truth – that the poet's unique vocation is to speak the truth as a concrete, situated individual existent. The authorial 'I' forms one element of a more portentous innovation – the idea that personal poetry is a truth-aspiring *institution* – that poetic 'art' is a medium not only of sacred traditional myths and legends, but of the highest truth possible for human beings. What is at issue here is less an internal semantic innovation of poetic form than the development of a new attitude toward experience as a whole, a new form of self-consciousness. The attitude suggests that Hesiod was ideally situated on the wave of a major change in cultural experience at the end of the Archaic period, and perhaps was the first to register the 'orientalizing' beliefs and religious culture of the Near East (cf. Murray, 1993: ch. 6). Experience is no longer an unknowable horizon to be manipulated by magical interventions or arcane rites, but an articulate order of divine succession to be delimited by the poetic word. The *kosmos* is so structured that only a rare kind of utterance can preserve its intrinsic order – and this exalted role is to be filled by the language of poetry. It may even have been the case that the truth-telling vocation of poetry led Hesiod self-consciously to break with the tradition of Homeric epic which, by the beginning of the sixth century, had been transformed into something like a form of popular entertainment. Existence as a 'divine' order can receive appropriate articulation only in the medium of sacred poetry.

Although exaggerating the rupture within the Homeric *epos*, Eduard Zeller preserves an important truth about Hesiod's innovation, namely, that this new reflective writing anticipated the kind of radical discursive innovation necessary to imagine and institute the project of universal truth-claiming. The critical reflexivity of the poet's voice bears an elective affinity with the critical reflexivity of theoretical discourse and philosophy. Zeller suggests that

> Hesiod is the first definite individual in Greek literature, and it is in his writings that we meet the first effort at systematization which is completely lacking in Homer. He is consciously opposed to the Homeric poetry and will tell no 'lies' but 'reveal' the truth.[5]

We can briefly follow some of the secondary literature treating of Hesiod's unique place within the Greek poetic tradition. This literature has not hesitated in drawing wide-ranging contextual and cultural inferences from the self-referential and reflexive properties of these texts. First, as an index of cultural changes in reflective experience Hesiod's creative writing is second only to the complex diegesis of the Homeric corpus: 'What they did, both in the action itself and in its substance, implies a human self-consciousness and self-confidence without precedent, and pregnant with limitless possibilities'. Second, Hesiod's text is treated as an exemplary metonym for the cultural vitality of the social totality itself: only a society accomplished in literate techniques 'is capable of systematic inquiry into its religious beliefs (or any other kind)', and, third, Hesiod's careful unravelling and genealogical organization of the differential space of the gods was the first step toward a critical rationalism – the first step was a theogony and the first proper theogony must be assigned to Hesiod.[6] For other interpreters Hesiod's writing techniques and choice of perspective represent a transitional phase between Homeric objectivity and the self-conscious subjectivity of sixth-century lyric poetry, a transitional experience exemplified in Hesiod's 'lyric' evocation of 'the long silent struggle of the farmer with the "black earth" and with the elements'. Yet the 'sober and practical character of Hesiod's poetry remained one of the basic factors in Greek civilization, and his literary progeny was prolific'.[7] A related feature of this 'discovery of Self' and 'individual perspective' accompanies Hesiod's unique 'pastoral' awareness, flowing from his celebration of the life style of agrarian work. Hesiod's discovery of the truth-telling Self was equally an invention of the theme of 'nature' in its modern sense:

> The slow, changeless wisdom of the countryman and his relentless, daily toil are here presented for the first time as *arete*. In the process – and this, too, is a landmark in European literature – Hesiod becomes the first Western poet to write of nature for its own sake'.[8]

Other commentators not only register the presence of an incipient pastoral phenomenology in Hesiod's *Works and Days*, a rhetoric of nature and natural struggle which prefigures later pastoral forms, but see in the dark colours of his personal vision the shadow-play of a whole mode of production and social structure in crisis. Hesiod's form of life within the social drama of Archaic Greece is traced in his uniquely reflexive text:

> the *Works and Days* presupposes yeomen rather than peasants. The farmer does not work alone but can employ a friend (370), as well as servants (502, 573, 597, 608, 766), has a lively forty-year-old free labourer to follow the plough and a slave-boy to turn in the seed (441–6, cf. 469–71), together with a female servant at home (405, 602). Of draught animals he has plough oxen and mules (405, 607ff.). On the other hand he cannot afford merely to oversee the work of others: he must take his share too (458–61). For all Hesiod's harping on poverty (638; cf. 376ff.), life at Ascra cannot have been too uncomfortable'.[9]

Socially Hesiod was neither an itinerant *rhapsode* (or professional singer) nor a 'peasant poet'. He was firmly rooted in the stratum of landowning producers for whom slavery was taken for granted as an essential condition of life.[10] He is often pictured as a 'surly conservative countryman, given to reflection, no lover of women or of life, who felt the gods' presence heavy about him'.[11] Occasionally his reflexive attitude is presented as the voice of social criticism, perhaps the first social critic speaking for those excluded from history:

> Hesiod has a great significance as the first spokesman of the common folk. In the history of Greek society, his is the first voice raised from among the toiling classes and claiming the interest of mankind in their lot. It is a voice indeed of acquiescence, counselling fellow-toilers to make the best of an evil case; the stage of revolt has not yet been reached. But the grievances are aired, and the lords who wield the power are exhorted to deal just judgements, that the land may prosper'.[12]

Perhaps all these aspects are condensed in what has been described as the 'prophetic vein' of his writing:

> The figure of Hesiod is in fact more at home in the thought world of the near east; it is not surprising that he describes his call to poetry in terms very similar to those used by the Hebrew prophet Amos about a century earlier.
>
> (Murray, 1993: 90)

As a self-confessed spokesman of the Boeotian peasant class or small agricultural proprietors, the first Western voice to celebrate the hard calling of agrarian labour and the strict morality of a disciplined, ascetic way of life, Hesiod certainly bears comparison with the writers of the Old Testament. His denunciation of the corrupt, wealth-devouring, landed aristocracy and uninhibited demand that they should cleave by justice and return to a 'righteous' and simpler form of life also parallels the activities of an Isaiah, Amos, or Job. Unlike Homer who celebrates the militant virtues of heroic struggle and an imaginary aristocratic existence, Hesiod's poetry is premised on a critique of the present world (the Age of Iron) informed by an indictment of rapacious feudal lords and petty kings – the 'gift-devouring lords' (*basileis dorophagoi* as he calls them at *Works and Days* 39, 221, 264). Moreover, Hesiod's 'social criticism' represented the first literary voice to advocate a salutary transformation of the political and social order. In choosing a sacred, admonitory idiom, Hesiod joins the Hebrew prophets in decrying the present social arrangements and arguing for radical social and ethical change.

While it would be otiose to depict Hesiod as part of a class struggle between an oppressed peasant class and feudal landlords in the modern sense of these terms, it is not unrealistic to view the critical stance taken in his poetry as a literary trace of a larger movement of social discontent marking the transition from the seventh-century Archaic economy to the social and political world of the *polis* system. Undoubtedly Hesiod lived through a period of severe economic distress and agrarian change. We know that increased rural exploitation and repression periodically exploded into social and political conflict as once independent peasant farmers were forced to alienate their land and even to sell themselves into debt slavery to pay off accumulated debts.[13] While Hesiod shared many of the traditional values and attitudes of the ruling class he criticized – its élitism, paternalism, phallocentric subjection of women, and so on – he was also aware of other ways of life and ethical possibilities. Hesiod may have been an archetypical marginal intellectual. The economic and political forces that disenfranchised independent peasants, transforming them into dependent serfs and day-labourers on the large farms of the local aristocracies provided the necessary context and spur to his critical perspective. We might reasonably speculate that what remains of his writing activities forms the merest fragment of a richer tradition of radical disquiet as the property and social conditions of Archaic Greece rapidly gave way to another, initially more repressive, economic and political configuration. The metaphorics of struggle and violence which serve to structure his poetry parallel the widespread presence of force and terror accompanying the spread of serfdom and debt slavery during this period. Hesiod's dislike of the nobles and his call for change is one instance of a more general disenchantment and alienation from the emerging social order, a poetic indictment of the same inequalities that later motivated the legal and political reforms of Draco (*c.* 620–610 BC) and Solon (*c.* 580–570 BC).

In other words, Hesiod's appeal for justice is a forerunner of a wider movement of social criticism that gave rise to the creation of written law codes designed to mitigate the worst excesses of class exploitation, a code which historians now interpret as one of the crucial preconditions for the 'democratization' of the ancient Greek world. Solon's 'crisis legislation' around 594 BC, for example, would have been perfectly intelligible to Hesiod a century earlier:

the cancellation of the institution of debt slavery, the abolition of the excesses of serfdom, the restoration of traditional land to peasant farmers, partial redistribution of land, reform of the coinage, import and export legislation, radical reform of the aristocratic constitution, and so forth. The comparison with the great Athenian legislator can be taken further. As chief archon of Athens in 594–3 Solon used traditional poetical forms to advance his programme of reform, writing verses with an explicit political content. The 'message' in much of Solon's verse needs little explicit interpretation or decoding. Consider his aggressive first-person diagnosis of the chaotic political situation of class struggle in Athens and its ultimate economic origins:

> the citizens themselves in their wildness are bent on destruction of their great city, and money is the compulsive cause. The leaders of the people are evil-minded. The next stage will be great suffering, recompense for their violent acts, for they do not know enough to restrain their greed and apportion orderly shares for all as if at a decorous feast ... they are tempted into unrighteous acts and grow rich ... and quickly it happens that foul slavery is the result, and slavery awakens internal strife, and sleeping warfare ... of the impoverished, many have made their way abroad on to alien soil, sold away, and shamefully going in chains of slavery.

Where Hesiod resorted to ethical admonition to realize *eunomia*, Solon advocated the transformation of the legal and political structure; his own assessment of his legislation and constitutional reforms should also be treated as a primary document of cultural reflexivity from the sixth century:

> I gave the people as much privilege as they have a right to: I neither degraded them from rank nor gave them free hand; and for those who already held the power and were envied of money, I worked it out that they also should have no cause for complaint. I stood there holding my sturdy shield over both the parties; I would not let either side win a victory that was wrong ... I took away the mortgage stones ... Into this sacred land, our Athens, I brought back a throng of those who had been sold, some by due law, others wrongly; some by hardship pressed to escape the debts they owed; and some of these no longer spoke Attic, since they had drifted wide around the world, while those in the country had the shame of slavery upon them, and they served their masters' moods in fear. These I set free; and I did this by strength of hand, welding right law with violence to a single whole'.[14]

4 THE POETIC 'I' AND DIVINE AUTHORIZATION

While stepping forth as an individualized literary 'persona', a self-designating poet, Hesiod does not presume to speak without divine authorization. In fact he cleaves to Homeric formular precedent,[15] invoking the gods of song, the Muses – daughters of *'aigis*-bearing Zeus' and Memory – as the source and motivation of his poetic calling: 'with the Muses of Helicon – the great and holy mountain – let us begin our song' (cf. *Il.* 2.484; Pindar, *Olympian* VI). Following the traditional literary conceit, the goddesses *command* Hesiod to remember the community of immortal, blessed gods 'and always to sing of them, first and last' (*Theogony* 33–4; in Richmond Lattimore's translation: 'always to put themselves at the beginning and end of my singing'). They also claim to possess the measure of truth and falsity governing all things: 'We know how to speak full many things that wear the appearance of truth, and know also how to tell the truth when we will' (*Theogony* 26–7). The whole text of the opening lines of the *Theogony* should be cited as the symbolic frame for this new epistemic motif:

> Begin and sing with the Muses, daughters of Helikon, who preserve the great and holy mountain of Helikon, and dance soft-footed round the water-spring of the violets and the altar of the mighty son of Kronos. They have washed their soft bodies in Permessos or the Horse's spring (*Hippokrene*) of holy Olmeios and set up their dances on the summit of Helikon, dances of beauty and attraction. From there they went, hidden in deep air, moving at night, offering their lovely cry, praising Zeus in song ... It was they who once ['of old' in A. W. Mair's translation, (Hesiod, 1908: 31); cf. Lattimore's *Hesiod* (1959a)] taught Hesiod his beautiful song, as he grazed his sheep, under holy Helikon. These are the words the goddess Muses of Olympos, daughters of Zeus the Lord of the Aegis said to me first of all: 'Shepherds of the fields, base shameful creatures, nothing but bellies, we know how to say many false things like real things, and we know when we wish how to tell the truth' [Mair's 'We know to speak full many things that wear the guise of truth, and know also when we will to utter truth'; Lattimore's 'but we know also how to speak the truth when we wish to']; So they spoke, the clear-voiced daughters of Zeus, and they have made me a staff, a branch of flourishing laurel, a fine one they cut, and breathed into me a divine voice, to utter aloud what shall be and what was. And they commanded me to sing of the birth of the blessed ones which are for ever, but always to sing their own selves first and last.
> (*Theogony* 1–35; esp. 27–8, 30–4; cf. *Theogony* 94; *Il.* 2.485ff.)

The divine vocation of truth

Theogony 27ff. contains a theme of great originality and importance. The Muses' reference to their skill in uttering falsehoods (*pseudea*) which can be given the appearance and aura of truth and also in speaking the truth (*alethea gerusasthai*) when necessary might be regarded as one of the seminal appearances of the epistemic (and with it the hermeneutical) motif in early Greek thought, linking the problem of knowing and knowledge to the dissembling powers of language (as true, prophetic *logos* – 'as they speak of what is, and what is to be, and what was before now' – and as the deceptive power of *peithos* or persuasion – creating simulacra of things which deceive mortals and lead them to their fate); the chronic human failure to understand the 'true nature of things' would become a stock motif of lyric poetry and tragic drama. Error and the pain and suffering which flow from error are inseparable from human life; for a tragic poet like Aeschylus, misrecognition leading the mind away from the truth is the primary source of human suffering. Men conduct their lives without recognizing the consequences of their acts – symbolized, for example, by the fateful decision of King Agamemnon to sacrifice his own daughter Iphigenia to save the Greek fleet on the way to Troy (*Agamemnon* 220–6). The tragic consequences of misrecognition and ignorance would later become the central theme of Sophoclean tragedy – most famously in the consequences which turn upon the difference between appearances and reality in *Oedipus Rex* and *Oedipus Tyrannos*.

If the order of being is divine, it appeared quite natural to think of its poetic articulation as also participating in the sacred experience of existence; concealing and revealing the truth in human affairs has a provenance in divine disclosure and deception. This epistemic *motif* prefigures the central dialectical image of knowledge in the work of a later explorer of apperances where another goddess promises to teach the truth. The 'youth' of Parmenides' *Proëm* must also distinguish between the unshakable heart of persuasive truth and the deceptive, shifting opinions of mortals in which there is no true belief (Parmenides, B 1.1–30, esp. lines 11–12 see Coxon, 1986 and Gallop, 1984): 'You will learn everything: both the immoveable heart of a well-rounded truth, and the opinions of mortals, in which there is no truly convincing force – nevertheless, you will learn how these opinions, which pervade all things, had to be acceptable' (B 1.28–32; compare *Theogony* 27, 30–2, 38; *Od.* 19.203 which contains the line: 'He knew how to say many false things that were like true sayings', trans. R. Lattimore).

Like Parmenides' guiding goddess of truth, the Heliconian Muses, living beyond appearance and truth, preserving the 'great and holy mountain of Helicon', function as the sacred matrix of persuasive opinion (*doxai*, of things that seem to be or 'be in truth', of 'things that will be and things that have been') and of an absolute truth behind the deceptive appearances mortals have of things. The theme had already appeared at *Iliad* 2.484. The Muses have become witnesses and exemplars of a universal necessity. Following the pattern of the Homeric poems, the goddesses of 'divine utterance' – 'knowing all things' – are now the true measure of human culture. The nine Muses – Cleio, Euterpe, Thaleia, Melpomene, Terpsichore, Erato, Polyhymnia, Urania and Calliope (*Theogony* 76–9) – are revisioned as a yardstick of the chronic problem of error and deception in human affairs and a reminder of the fundamental *telos* of

HESIOD AND THE BIRTH OF THE GODS

divine *logos* as opposed to the erroneous wanderings and distorted perceptions of mortals. In the desire to uncover the truth, the poetic vocation and the linguistic vocation of humanity are at root one: to sing of the gods, of the 'coming-to-be' of their truth and in that singing to celebrate and preserve their holy dominion over the human and natural order. To be human, Hesiod seems to be saying, is to desire to bring the fallible, suffering mind into the vicinity of truth (*aletheia*). To be human is to strive to gain knowledge of reality (cf. *Odyssey* 1.1–10; Herodotus 1.95.1). It is only because of the guardian Muses that there are 'singers (*aoidoi*) and harpers (*kitharistai*) upon the earth' (*Theogony* 95). The 'singers' and the 'harpists' preserve the 'truth' of an oral culture, acting as literal embodiments of the poetic tradition.

The problem of how 'doxa' can be said to 'seem to be true' as contrasted with what is 'known to be true' will subsequently form one of the central themes of Greek philosophy. What claims to be true or to state what truly 'is' may always turn out to be a deception. Like the early tragedians Hesiod operates with a notion of 'truth' which could be readily transposed into ontological terms: 'truth' appears when appearances coincide with what 'is' (*einai*), or, more speculatively, where appearances are 'evidence' for what exists (making the opposition 'appearance/truth' homologous with the opposition 'appearance/being'). Time is frequently presented as the process which 'tests' whether the apparent unity of 'appearance/being' turns out to be a true unity – where 'in due time' Agamemnon will 'learn' of his deception at the hands of his apparently faithful and truthful wife Clytemnestra or Oedipus will recognize 'in time' the true nature of his patricide.

As epistemic claimancy is intrinsically subject to error, all candidate 'truths' are subject to further test and temporal clarification. And this process of 'clearing' putative truths is animated by existential rather than epistemological motives. Human beings live by the light of partial truths, but what appears to be true in the present needs time to be established. The 'things of the present' must await the verdict of 'things to come'. Reports and signs which are 'taken for truths' out of the emotional and affective needs of human beings need to be carefully sifted and examined in the light of past and future experience. Mortals persistently deceive themselves and others about the true nature of the universe (cf. *Theogony* 1–103).

Texts like Hesiod's *Theogony* or, later, Aeschylus' and Sophocles' dramatic works strongly suggest that the demand for 'marks' of proof, for criterial evidence concerning the 'true reality' of things had become one of the insistent motifs of early Greek consciousness. The beacon lights which 'shine' throughout the dramatic space of *Agamemnon* may turn out to be a false sign and prophecy, not the 'disclosure' of Agamemnon's triumphal return, but his own imminent demise. And the 'bright light' of truth may itself be drowned in forgetfulness (*lethe*) and darkness. The search for the 'grounds' of belief (*pistis*), the evidential warrants of assertions, and the reasons for epistemic claims (for example, the question-answer exchange between Clytemnestra and the Chorus in *Agamemnon* 270ff.) helped institutionalize a distinctly ethical orientation to questions of deception and knowledge. Hesiod's poetic discourse thus prefigures a more complex configuration from which philosophy would eventually shape its questions concerning the nature of truthful discourse. Hesiod, in sum, anticipates the Classical logological theme of the foundational interweaving of language (*logos, dianoia*), knowledge (*gnosis, episteme, phronesis, sophia*), opinion (*doxa*), persuasion, truth (*aletheia*), and being (*to on, ousia, eidos*). I will return to the important topic of the 'universalization of truth' in Volume 3.

The poet as teacher

To return to Hesiod's text: several important features of the *proema* to the *Theogony* should be noted. First, the gift of poetic – which is to say 'truthful' or 'truth-disclosing' – language belongs to female deities, the Muses – daughters of Zeus and Memory (*Mnemosune*) – as tutelary protectors of expressive culture. Second, poetic speech and its incarnated 'intelligence' (*phronesis*) is regarded as an ambivalent *power*, touched by divinity (the knowledge of 'true things' is a sacred gift symbolized by the gift of a *skeptron*). Third, the female protectors of the poetic vocation (in the widest sense of *poiesis*) hold the keys of both error and knowledge. Of the manifold forms of 'not knowing', the deception woven around human beings by the gods has the most pernicious and consequential effects. Falsity is often credited to the malign influence of a god – the errors planted for divine purposes unknown to mortals (cf. Aeschylus, *Agamemnon* 272–4). We have seen that in the *Iliad* and *Odyssey* deception leads mortals to error, rash action and, ultimately, death. Blindness – in all its forms, physical, moral, and intellectual – is inflicted by the immortals who guard the true ways of *seeing*. As the gods cover up the truth of things, so they have the power to reveal the truth (*aletheia*). The Muses choose to hide or to reveal, to cloud human sensibilities or to draw them toward the light. Fourth, 'truth-saying', like the guardians of truth and self-reflection themselves, is inherently dangerous; no mortal can know the 'whole truth' and each must live content with partial knowledge, with glimpses of the Whole (we will meet this theme again in the analysis of Pindar's visionary poetry in Chapter 5). The gods disclose the nature of things through the 'dark glass' of intermediaries – mantic speakers, prophets, oracles, symbolic portents, omens; they visit human beings in disguise (the association of Hermes with beggars was already a Homeric cliché), or code their instructions in the enigmatic language of dreams. Or, to return to Hesiod's world, they bestow the gift of 'truth-telling' upon singers and prophets. The extreme dangers attending the disclosure of things is the *raison d'être* for the 'interpretive' arts which, it might be suggested, begin as the attempt to decipher the signs and symbols of divine speech.

Hesiod is to some extent following the tradition of Homeric seers (like Calchas and Theoclymenus) in claiming not only to be able to interpret the command of the Muses, but to accurately differentiate the actual genealogy which brought the gods into being and allocated them to their offices within the Olympian economy. The same idea introduces Hesiod's *Works and Days* where the text is addressed to Hesiod's brother Perses, promising to disclose the 'true path of existence' (*Works and Days* 10).

The craft of memory

The poetic calling separates itself from other modes of speech as the self-interpretation of divine truth. In Hesiod, as in many ancient texts of the Near East – the Gilgamesh Epic, for example – *knowledge* (awareness, consciousness, reflexivity) is a dangerous possession, bringing with it life-threatening temptations. Among the most seductive is the transgression the Greeks called *hubris*, one cause of which stems from the human proclivity to forget the difference between divine and human knowledge, to regard a glimpse of existence as though it were the whole truth, and thereby forget the dissembling aspect of truth. What could place mortals in greater danger than the claim to possess certain knowledge of the beginnings of all things, particularly a knowledge of the birth of the gods and the origins of the *kosmos* itself? To guard against the immoderation of theophantic knowledge the poet's reflexivity as a singer and seer (*aoidos* includes both aspects of the poetic calling) must be justified. Danger is implicit in both the excess that leads the poet to sing of the race of blessed ones and in the nature of its product, mimetic texts which replicate the order of existence in the realm of language.

The dangers of excess and unauthorized supplementarity require divine mitigation. Or, as we might now say, Hesiod must provide a satisfying answer to the founding problem of all strong expression: *why speak?* His response was already dictated by immemorial tradition: to ground poetic utterance in an imperative coming from the gods themselves. Ultimate responsibility lies with the gift of the daughters of great Zeus who 'plucked and gave a staff, a shoot of sturdy laurel, wonderful to see' (Hesiod, *Theogony* 27–8; Wender, trans., 1985). The female Other is responsible for the unanticipated excesses of poetic speech. It is this Other who 'breathed a divine voice' into the poet, authorizing him to 'celebrate things to come and things which were before'. The auspices of a new mode of speech lie in the authority of the gods: 'They ordered me to sing the race of blessed ones who live forever, and to hymn the Muses first and last.' It is the supreme goddess of articulation, Calliope – the 'fair speaking' attendant of the high god Zeus – who pours sweet dew upon the tongues of certain men, granting them the flow of words, of persuasive speech in general and political judgement in particular. Language, at once an expression and an instance of divine order, achieves its highest form in articulating the ordering work of the Olympians, of the gods who established order from disorder, protecting things from primordial Chaos. Insight, speech, language, and the noble arts of persuasion and good judgement are the Muses' holy gifts to mortals. But what is truly unique about this divine authorization is that the continuous 'presence' of the gods, their gathering within language, needs to pass through the mediating circuitry of poetic speech: the Olympian deities are themselves beholden to the 'gathering', 'memorializing' work of the spoken word, and more especially, to the poetic symbol. Language and vision are intimately related in the primary revelation of pre-philosophical Greek thought. This intimacy is most evident in the gifts of the prophetic self and what lies implicit in this act – the perennial question of the authorization of human speech.

The prophetic self

We have suggested that for Hesiod poetic speech is the reflexive celebration of divine remembrance.[16] Human speech exists, Hesiod seems to say, so that we will not forget the gods as the radical source of articulation, the 'ur-praxis' which secured 'presence' in the face of nothingness. Speech which preserves meaning thus possesses enormous authority over the hearts and minds of individuals. Poetry is thus quite literally the sacred space of articulation. In lines that prefigure the teaching of the Sophists, we learn that

> when a man has sorrow fresh in the troublement of his spirit and is struck to wonder over the grief in his heart, the singer, the servant of the Muses singing the glories of ancient men, and the blessed gods who have their homes on Olympos, makes him presently forget his cares, he no longer remembers sorrow, for the gift of the goddesses soon turn his thoughts elsewhere.
>
> (*Theogony* 95–103, trans. Lattimore)

Without the authority of divine *logos* every practice that depends upon speech and language risks falling into oblivion: the poetic logos is, as it were, the living point of articulation – if not the foundation which remains beyond speech – of all the arts that make civil existence possible: speech is at issue in the celebration of the laws and 'gracious customs' (*Theogony* 66), the rigours of good judgement and justice (*Theogony* 80–94), the arts of civil persuasion (*Theogony* 90ff.), religious interpretation, music, and poetry (*Theogony* 95).

We are tempted to phrase the central Hesiodic insight in contemporary terms and claim that for Hesiod – as later for Vico – culture has its grounds and medium in the power of the poetic word. It is in perfect accord with this valorizing of poetic speech that Hesiod's text should literally unfurl as an epic of self-differentiation.

5 HESIODIC SYMBOLISM AND THE 'MYTHOLOGICAL WORLD-VIEW'

> Hesiod's basic postulate is that even the gods have come into being.
>
> (Werner Jaeger, 1947: 11)

On the plane of metaphor and allegory we immediately meet two insistent motifs: the idea of the differential *genesis* of the gods and their powers and the equally pervasive figure of the Olympian *family* of divine beings – 'procreation' and 'creation' stories naturally complete and complement the '*ur*-narrative' figures of familial discourse. What better general framework for thinking of 'the divine' (*to theion*) than the predicates of familial relations and kinship ties? What better images for a differentiated whole of articulated parts than the divisions of desire, sexuality, and familial conflict?

By following these narrative threads we find ourselves in a patriarchal universe; both 'agonic' theogony (the violence of manifestation as birth) and familial agonism (the internicine war of the gods) display and exemplify the violent struggle between phallocentric and matriarchal principles, a 'metaagon' of forces straining to be the dominant powers over the worlds of human and divine experience.

In Chapter 1 we have seen that Greek mythology was structured and striated by phallocentric principles, by an anthropomorphic grid upon which are inscribed the formative narratives of the early Greek religious tradition. In this sense, *agonism* – the mythical adumbration of the structure of tragedy and its sublimated form, dialectic – is already at work as a narrative principle in the earliest Archaic symbolisms: most evidently in the principled struggle of the chthonian divinities in Hesiod's narrative of violent differentiation and the struggle for hegemony within the family of the gods.

But Hesiod's text also foreshadows the great dichotomic *agon* of the One and the Many. Differentiation, as both a metaphor of order and principle of intelligibility, assumes its aggressive role as a male imposition upon the inchoate matrix of primal chaos and undifferentiated desire – constituting the germ of reasoning at work in the differential *logos*. Intelligibility is achieved by repressing the forces of difference, and by periodically celebrating the tamed powers of dedifferentiation in the 'social imaginary' formation of Greek civilization. Hesiod's *muthos* rearticulates a primal differentiation prior to the visible universe, the emergence of difference which provided the very matrix for all subsequent unities and differences. It is an invitation to think differently about a difference which antedates everyday experience, to enter voluntarily into a 'poetic' experience of the involuntary abyss in all 'making'.

Considered as a work of writing Hesiod's textual cosmogony generalizes the formular device of sexual differentiation. The poem itself proceeds by means of a dehiscent, dichotomic mechanism: splitting, dividing, differentiating into components, regathering and recoiling upon itself. In this way the *Theogony* syntactically exemplifies – and thus 'doubles' – the emergent itinerary of the gods which it sets out to recollect and celebrate. The Hesiodic text is like a hologram of the erotic phenomenology that forms its 'topic' and 'content'. The style and movement of the text incorporates a phenomenological rhetoric on both its rhetorical and material planes. We find a *logos* of the 'things themselves' as *phainomenai*: the genesis of the gods and other elemental forces; but we also have a promise of truth and an implicit sense of the distinction between discourses which have the appearance of being true and discourses which are true. This dual phenomenology is sustained by truth's legitimation which, in the opening lines of the text, is elaborated in the symbol of the goddesses' truth-preserving language. These aspects of the poem have led interpreters to view Hesiod's cosmogony as 'no longer a myth', but a discourse that has 'advanced so far along the road of rationalization that only a very thin partition divides it from those early Greek systems which historians still innocently treat as purely rational constructions'.[17] Others interpret the central mythic dramas in Hesiod (for example between Zeus and the Titans) as social and cosmological allegories.

We should not overlook the fact that Hesiod's mythical 'phenomenology', at both the thematic and stylistic levels, incorporates violence in the ambivalent figure of 'strife'. Hesiod fabricates a 'phenomenology of violence' in both senses of the genetive: an ambivalent structure of violence coded in violent oppositions. To rephrase this point in terms of the semiotic codes woven into Hesiod's text: in assuming the reader role created by the poem we are presented with a violent *logos* of the birth of violence. The new style of writing unfurls in a sequence of ambivalent dialectical images. Its 'codes' are, as I will show, permutation rules for a stock of interrelated dialectical *terms* (*Chaos, Eros, Eris*, etc.) and agonistic *relations* (*Strife, Dispute, Error, Falsehood*, etc.). And the paradigmatic 'thread' of the whole poem lies in the polemical figure of violent scission itself, the work of 'splitting' and 'repetition' as the ground of manifestation, the *violence of differentiation* which produces the origins of the gods and the world. Rhetorically, then, Hesiod's text appears as a meditation on violence – violence forms both its theme and its symbolic medium. When subsequent Greek traditions raise the theme of the *logos*, they would proceed on the terrain of Hesiodic problematics. Bearing these observations in mind we can now explore the image systems organizing the Hesiodic text.

6 THE VIOLENCE OF DIFFERENTIATION AND THE APPEARANCE OF THE GODS

We have already observed that the English word 'story' is a secularized translation of the multilayered word *muthos*. The term 'story', however, distorts the polysemic field of significance associated with the ancient Greek word *muthos*. Originally the term is associated with power (later translated into philosophical terms as *dunamis, genesis, entelecheia*, and so forth); the *logos* of myth is a power to bring the sacred 'into the open', to preserve what 'appears' or manifests itself as worthy of recollection. The modern concept of 'story' is also detached from ritual contexts, from the performative enactment that is fundamental to preliterate narrativization. In pre-Classical Greece *muthos* was still organically connected with the 'things done' of cultic praxis and ritual behaviour (indeed the earliest *muthoi* are accounts of 'things done' by the gods, heroes, and legendary agents). The gods of the mythological *ethos* are primarily vectors in a space of action, and the 'telling' function of the bard or rhapsode was inseparable from the role of dramatic re-enactment. 'Personal' poetry was yet to be 'discovered' – that is, constructed as an expressive possibility of civic life. Poetry in the ancient world begins as a radically *public* discourse.

As a sacred act and in keeping with the logological insight that language is symbolic praxis, *muthos* should be regarded as a form of creation, in this case a 'making' which allows what appears to be articulated, conserved, and thus 'known' for a community. Language – the discourse of myth – is immediately invoked as part of the essence of manifestation and here, 'what is manifest' is to be understood as whatever is disclosed for a collectivity of shared speakers and auditors. In the case of Hesiod's texts, their acknowledged 'poeic' purpose is to preserve the essence of 'manifestation', the formation of that which is most noble and highest, the society of the gods; this is the *'phainomenon'* which must be spoken and thought; and it is not only a matter of how the gods 'appear' or 'show themselves' to mortals which informs Hesiod's poetry, but more significantly the aboriginal process by which the gods themselves 'came to be', disclosing their individual natures to become part of an articulate order:

Hesiod, as he explicitly announces at the beginning of his work, will tell the truth about the origins and manifestation (*a-letheia*) of the gods; and the most concrete image of 'unhiddenness', of bringing something into the light, of letting something show forth is given in the sequence of procreation: coitus-birth-natural development. The poetry of the *Theogony* – as a work of disclosure and preservation – participates in the 'birth' which it celebrates. The 'Birth of the Gods' is itself a celebration of the birth of poetic narrative and the creation of an audience for poetic truth.

6.1 Functions of the dialectical image: difference and differentiation in Hesiod's *Theogony*

I have suggested that the narrative structure of Hesiod's *Theogony* revolves around the allegorical image of cosmogonic differentiation whereby a violent 'event' of scission or 'rupture' of the hitherto undifferentiated void of *Chaos* produces an aboriginal difference separating Earth and Heaven. This 'spacing' forms the primordial site where gods and beings appear and act. For Hesiod no single god created the universe; the gods are themselves parts of the process of universal differentiation; they are, as we might say today, moments of the cosmic Whole.

HESIOD AND THE BIRTH OF THE GODS

One of the remarkable achievements of Hesiod's language is its artful use of *the dialectical image*, a device by means of which complex 'contradictory' ideas and polysemic themes can be fused into a powerful symbolic focus. Here 'dialectical' refers to the unresolved dissonance of opposed meanings temporarily unified in a single image. The semantics of personification and abstraction (Strife, Toil, Eros, Forgetfulness, etc.) is one of the most striking expressions of this tendency toward allegory. These figures were clearly a more abstract development of themes popularized by earlier fables and myths. Many examples of the dialectical image can be found in Hesiod's text: the inexplicable 'origin' of Chaos, the ambivalent operations of *Dike*, the 'gifts' of Pandora,[18] the contradictory workings of *Eros*, the antithetical nature of *logos* itself and, in the deep structure of the text, the narrative machinery of Difference or Differentiation by which both the text of the *cosmos* and the *cosmos* of the text are organized. In these respects Hesiod's poem can be approached as an experiment in creative abstraction.

Differentiation

Tell me these things, Olympian Muses, tell
From the beginning, which first came to be?
Chaos was first of all, but next appeared
Broad-bosomed Earth, sure standing-place for all
The Gods who live on snowy Olympus' peak,
And mysty Tartarus, in a recess
Of broad-pathed earth, and Love, most beautiful
Of all the deathless gods.
    (*Theogony* 114–20, trans. D. Wender)

Consider the first 'concrete abstraction' of the work – the dialectical image of *Chaos*: 'First of all there came Chaos' (*Theogony* 116ff.). Difference is the process in which all modes of being and forms of life are violently torn from the void of Chaos. Chaos marks the unintelligible 'source' of intelligibility, the 'point' from which all the gods emerge into being. Every subsequent mode of existence is indebted to this violent 'scission': both mortals and immortals stand within the polarized horizon of Earth and Heaven. Two gods in particular serve to personify the contrary predicates of unity and dispersion central to the dialectical allegory: Zeus and Eros. Cosmogenesis is but the 'conceptual splitting' of an unnameable primary unity, a separation within the One unspeakable 'no-thing', and as all things are thought as having been 'born' from this fission, they all bear the signs of 'injustice' (*adikia*).

As a 'fissile' text, Hesiod's story re-enacts the violent birth of reality, commemorating the reality-event by symbolically repeating the fissured processes through which a *kosmos* or world order was brought into being. In later attempts to 'save' Homeric and Hesiodic literature, the central devices of Hesiod's poetry would be used as allegorical techniques to extract an arcane wisdom from the text. Allegory became a way of appropriating cosmogonic poetry by a more rationalist audience. This hermeneutic strategy would retain its authority down to the modern period.

> The so-called epics of Hesiod, the *Theogony* and the *Works and Days*, represent the earliest surviving attempt to rationalize the mythical elements of the epic tradition and to bring them into closer correspondence with the data of actual existence. Poetry and philosophy had not yet become in practice, as they were not in Plato's thought to become even in theory, separate arts.
> (Scholes and Kellogg, 1966: 118)

Homer's and Hesiod's schizogenic images were read as anticipations and prefigurations of later Presocratic accounts of the cosmic origin of things:

> Theagenes of Rhegium (c. 525 BC) is generally credited with having been the first to resort to an allegorical interpretation of a supposed under-meaning (*hyponoia*) in explaining such offensive passages in Homer as the battle of the gods. Beneath the literal meaning (*logos*), the battles of the gods were held by Theagenes to be descriptions either of the conflicting elements – Hephaestus, Hera, and Poseidon representing fire, air, and water – or of moral conflicts. Anaximander, Heraclitus, Anaxagoras, and lesser pre-Socratic philosophers likewise recognized a *hyponoia* in the Homeric texts. Metrodorus of Lampsacus, the disciple of Anaxagoras, was the most thoroughgoing of the early allegorical interpreters. He assigned 'physical' meanings to both the human and the divine personages: Agamemnon was ether, Achilles the sun, Helen the earth, Paris the air, Demeter the liver, Dionysus the spleen, and Apollo the gall. This tradition of Homeric allegoresis was well established at the time of Plato's birth, an important element in Greek philosophical speculation.
> (Scholes and Kellogg, 1966: 117–18)

Whatever the merits of such allegorizing, evidence of Hesiod's imagery and language can be detected in the text of Anaximander in which all finite beings are described as committing an 'injustice' against the Infinite or *Apeiron* and are thus required to recompense by returning to their 'unbounded' source. Hesiod's meontology also adumbrates the figure of Non-being in Parmenides and Plato (particularly the author who speculated on the mutual belonging of Being and Non-being in the *Sophist* and *Timaeus*), the logic of the One's emanations in the Plotinus' *Enneads*, Meister Eckhart's 'nothing in nothing', the bottomless *Ungrund* in Jakob Böhme's (1575–1624) mystical speculations, the *Urgrund* in Schelling's *Identitätsphilosophie* and *Abgrund* in Hölderlin's poetry (*Hyperion* for example) and, more recently, the *No-thing* (or *Abgrund*) in the philosophy of Martin Heidegger, and, perhaps in the meditation upon *différence* that has lately exercised Jacques Derrida and those influenced by his strategies of deconstructive reading. In Schelling's words:

HESIOD AND THE BIRTH OF THE GODS

> We can think of nothing better fitted to drive man to strive towards the light with all energy, than the consciousness of the deep night out of which he was raised into existence ... We must imagine the primal longing in this way – turning towards reason, indeed, though not yet recognizing it, just as we longingly desire unknown, nameless excellence.
>
> (Schelling, 1936: 35)

For all these variations, the process of coming-to-be of Being is troped as an emergence from aboriginal difference, negation, and contradiction: the Many are torn from the indeterminate One in order to *be*; conflict is given an ontological role in the origination of phenomena (as 'manifestation', *phainesthai* or 'appearing', *erscheinung*). In the idiom of Christian mysticism, God discloses His essence through the objectifications of nature (*natura naturata*) and thus returns to self-awareness and perfect self-identity through natural cognition. Schelling even preserves the Hesiodic moment of *eros* in his theogony:

> This Spirit, moved by that Love which it itself is, utters the Word which then becomes creative and omnipotent Will combining reason and longing, and which informs nature, at first unruly, as its own element or instrument.
>
> (1936: 36)

A distant echo of Hesiod's dialectical image resonates in the work of our contemporary explorers of the heterological interplay of Being and Nothingness, Identity and Difference, the Same and the Other.

Primordial chaos

Hesiod posits the origins of manifestation in an unspeakable primordial Chaos: 'Chaos' itself has no intelligible structure, no determinate origin or 'nature' (other than to be a nameless source of what strives to be named), though it is the cosmological eruption of Difference from within Chaos that symbolically accounts for the grounding of all things, the emergence of 'broad-bosomed Earth' (*Gaia*) and Heaven (*Ouranos*), the 'habitation unshaken for ever of all the deathless gods who keep the top of snowy Olympos'(*Theogony* 106ff., trans. Mair). Like Derrida's *archi-écriture* or trace-structure, Chaos is not a unitary point of origin or a rational foundation; in fact Chaos is itself contingently produced from a nameless 'ground' (as H. J. Rose notes, the text at *Theogony* 115 uses the word *geneto*, 'came into being', rather than 'was', 1989: 19). Chaos has an unnamed (and perhaps unnameable) origin. We have, as it were, to cite and simultaneously erase the term 'origin' in defining Hesiod's theogony.

Chaos is not – despite Aristotle's gloss at *Physics* 208b31 – a vacuous space (*topos*), let alone an aboriginal *chora* (as Plato taught in the *Timaeus*); the concept of 'empty space' – associated with the verb *chaskein* – is a later intellectual construction – and was certainly not available in the ideological world of the Boeotian poet. Chaos is a zone of unnameable difference, a variant of the more Homeric 'chora' which separates while uniting Earth and Heaven (Jaeger, 1947: 13; Cornford, 1965: 194–5). Chaos is the very movement of 'zoning' without which no concrete place, space, differentiation, and genesis can proceed. The Greek word 'zone' with its girdle-like connotations expresses this strange concept very well. The zone of difference (if we can so call it, for it has as yet no articulate structure that would make it appear as a 'domain' or 'region') separating Earth and Heaven is functionally a 'hyphen', an invisible gap conjoining while separating two possible regions of existence. As a 'zone' it has neither Being nor Non-being; it is not to be identified with the later Platonic *chora*, nor the Aristotelian *topos* and most resolutely not with the metaphysical concept of *Being*. This non-substantial phenomenon may explain why Aristotle proved unreceptive to the cosmological implications of Hesiod's idea (Aristotle mentions Hesiod simply as one of the ancient sources of the idea that Earth was generated as the first of corporeal things (*Metaphysics* I.8.989a11–13)). Aristotle's silence on the Hesiodic *Chaos* marks it down as a prephilosophical notion, which can be safely left to the poets and mythographers. Chaos has literally nothing to say to the categorial philosopher (there being no 'place' for this notion in the categorial predicates of Being).

Cornford has observed that the opening of this hiatus between Earth and Heaven, as a figure for the birth of light from darkness, is the key to Hesiod's vision, connecting the motif to a similar theme in the Orphic tradition:

> In the Orphic system Eros has another name, Phanes, the Bright One; and it is even suggested that the word Eros is primarily to be connected with a root meaning 'light'. In physical terms the lifting up of the sky from the earth lets in the light of day where before there was darkness. We note that this appearance of light precedes the formation of the heavenly bodies. For the next event is that Earth gives birth to the *starry Heaven*.
>
> (1965: 197)

Chaos gives birth to Tartarus, Erebus, and Darkness ('black Night'): 'From Chaos came forth Erebus and black Night; in turn from Night came forth both Day and Aether' (*Theogony* 123–34); and in the same phase of differentiation and coequal with these chthonic powers arises Eros – Desire or Love, 'fairest among the deathless gods' which 'unties the limbs and overpowers within the breasts of all gods and all men their mind and wise counsel'. Night and Erebos in turn generate Sky (*Ether* or *Aither*) and Day (*Hemera*, 'whom Night conceived and produced after loving union with Erebos'). From the primordial Earth (*Gaia*) springs Ouranos, Pontos (the Sea), and the Mountains of the Earth. And so the process of Differentiation continues giving birth to *Oceanos, Koios, Krios, Hyperion, Iapetus, Theia, Rheia, Kronos, Kyklopes*, and other minor deities, among these Mnemosune, 'golden-crowned' Phoebe, and the 'lovely' Tethys (*Theogony* 136).

One singular aspect of this process of narrative differentiation should be carefully noted. The 'dehiscence' cannot be described as an emanation of Being from Chaos since Chaos itself 'comes to be' ('first Chaos came into being ... '); the logic of Hesiod's theophany presupposes an originating unnameable Nothingness, a paradoxical 'origin before origins', a source prior to the differentiation process itself, an *Abgrund* which, as we know, all subsequent Greek thought found resistant to thought or even an affront to reason and intellect. Origin is this unspeakable limit. In the *Theogony* its pre-sense motivates the whole structure of articulation; yet it remains covered over and unthinkable as 'that' which occasions differentiation. The idea of Chaos marks, in other words, the border between theogonic and philosophical thinking. And in Hesiod's text it is explicitly dramatized as a margin of articulation, intelligibility, and civility. It is in keeping with archaic thought that the text explicitly proscribes the idea of creation *ex nihilo* – just as it neglects the possibility of creation as a consequence of the Will of a God (Zeus is a late arrival in the process of cosmic differentiation). One of the decisive contexts of Parmenides' thought, for example, derives from the paradox of trying to *say* what such an aboriginal matrix of 'non-being' *is*, and tacitly admitting a 'non-being' as the unnameable ground of Being (this 'origins game' was well known in antiquity, see for instance, Sextus Empiricus, *Against the Mathematicians* 10.18–19; 10.342).[19]

'Nature' and the chthonian powers

In order of both poetic precedence and ontological emergence, Hesiod grants priority to the powers of Nature: Earth, Tartaros, Night, Light, Sky, Mountains. *Eros* is also, significantly, given equal status with these elemental forces (116–22). Gaia (Earth) 'produces' Sky, Ocean and Mountains 'without the passion of love' whereas encircling Okeanos and the pantheon of gods are the offspring of Earth's coition with Sky (Ouranos or Uranus). Gaia lay with Ouranos and

> gave birth to Okeanos with its deep current, Kios and Krios and Hyperion and Iapetus; Theia and Rheia and Themis and Mnemosune; also golden-crowned Phoebe and lovely Tethys. After these came cunning Kronos, the youngest and boldest of her children; and he grew to fate the father who had begotten him.
> (*Theogony* II.104–38; cf. Plato, *Cratylus* 396B)

The world, sprung from Okeanos, is a continuous flux of eddying streams of change. Primordial violence and strife rage in the world of the gods until one of the minor gods ('the youngest and boldest'), Zeus, son of Kronos and Rheia, takes power by ousting his own father Kronos, just as Kronos had castrated and dismembered his father Ouranos before him with 'a sickle, edged like teeth.' Zeus' hegemony in Olympus is presented as a victory of order over aboriginal natural forces (here Hesiod prefigures the mature theology of Aeschylus in which Zeus has become an absolute patriarchal ruler of the gods and to all intents and purposes has assimilated the older powers of nature: *'Zeus is Air; Zeus is Earth; Zeus is Heaven; Zeus is all things and whatsoever is higher than all things'* (*Heliades*, Fr. 70, cf. *Supplices* 524–6; cf. the playful etymology on the name *'Zeus'* as *'zena'* and *'dia'* in Plato's *Cratylus* 395E–396C and Socrates irony: 'If I remembered the genealogy of Hesiod and the still earlier ancestors of the gods he mentions, I would have gone on examining the correctness of their names until I had made a complete trial whether this wisdom which has suddenly come to me, I know not whence, will fail or not', Plato, *Cratylus* 396C).

In Hesiod's account, the phallus of Ouranos falls into the sea to form the flesh of Aphrodite (and after her Eros and Desire); the blood from the dismembered organ falls like rain upon the bosom of Gaia, the primal Earth – from which arise the 'powerful Furies' (Erinyes), 'the Nymphs of the Ash Trees' (called Meliai) and the titantic forces of nature (the hundred-armed Giants). Other goddesses are named as 'products of the phallus': 'garlanded Kythereia' because 'from the sea foam she grew', Kyprogeneia, 'because she was born from wave-washed Cyprus', and Philommedea because – with etymological playfulness – she appeared from the *'medea'* (or 'members', *Theogony* 200). Eros is the attendant of these gods of dismemberment. Eros, the guardian and preserver of the works of Love, is also the offspring of primordial violence.

Mnemosune and Eros

Memory is one of the primordial deities, first daughter of the marriage between Heaven and Earth and matrix of the Muses (*Theogony* 135, cf. 53–4, 915). In order of genesis, the personified forces of Law (*Themis*) and Memory (*Mnemosune*) antedate individual gods; and throughout Hesiod's account, Eros is continuously present as the procreative matrix of Themis, Mnemosune, Theia, Rheia, Hyperion, and the rest. Eros is one of the first of the gods (cf. Sophocles, *Trachiniae* 441–3: 'love rules at will the gods'; cf. *Trachiniae* 488–9: Heracles, who has never yielded to any enemy, is conquered by love; Parmenides, Fr. 13; Phaedrus' speech to the god *Eros* in Plato's *Symposium* 178A–180B, cf. 195C; Aristotle, *Metaphysics* 1.984b23–985a6) binding and separating opposites, instilling passion, overruling reason. Eros is the cosmic source of the most pervasive oppositions in human life – pleasure and pain, union and separation, birth and death and, as such, is a power present from the beginning of the world (Parmenides, *Fragments* 13, 18). Mnemosune and Eros are thus gods that are primordially linked – both concerned with the 'binding' and 'gathering' of dispersion and opposition. Wherever there is difference (differentiation) there you also find Eros.

Hesiod might be described as the first philosopher of agonistic Love and Hate, anticipating Empedocles' cosmic cycle of Love and Strife and Plato's dialectical exploration of Eros in his dialogues *Phaedrus, Lysis*, and the *Symposium* (in the *Symposium* the first speech on Love – given by Phaedrus – speaks in Hesiodic terms of Love as one of the first great gods 'revered among men and gods for many reasons, and not least on account of his birth' – citing Hesiod, Acusilaus, and Parmenides as witnesses, *Symposium* 178). Plato also elaborates a Hesiodic genealogy in the *Timaeus*, in which

> Okeanus and Tethys were the children of Earth and Heaven, and from these sprang Phorcys and Kronos and Rheia, and all that generation; and from Kronos and Rheia sprang Zeus and Hera, and all those who are said to be their bretheren, and others who were the children of these.
> (40D; cf. *Theogony* 120ff., 133–6)

The common patrimony of Zeus and Hera would make their future marital union incestuous. As we have observed, one way subsequent commentators could 'rationalize' this violation of the incest taboo was by interpreting the traditional theogony allegorically. Aristotle characteristically naturalizes Hesiod's god Eros (which he also speaks of 'Love (*eros*) or Desire (*epithumia*)', misquoting *Theogony* 116–20: 'First of all things was Chaos made, and then Broad-bosomed Earth... And Love (*Eros*), the foremost of immortal beings'): Hesiod has discovered Eros as a first principle (*arche*) 'thus implying that there must be in the world some cause to move things and combine them' (*Metaphysics* 984b30). Rather than entering into a poetic interaction with Hesiod's text on *Eros*, Aristotle pursues the strategy of the librarian, reducing the metaphoric play of the text to the filing system of the practising teacher and historian of philosophy: 'The question of arranging these thinkers in order of priority may be decided later' (*Metaphysics* 984b30–5; Alexander in his commentary on this passage expands the text:

> Aristotle means those who spoke about love as a principle inasmuch as they showed good sense [in doing so]; for they made love a principle because they realized that there must exist, among the things that are, some moving and efficient cause. There will be occasion later on, he says, to investigate who first touched on this sort of cause, whether it was Anaxagoras (as seems likely), or Hermotimus before him, or even before Hermotimus the associates of Hesiod.
> (*Commentary on Metaphysics* I, 33.5–11; see also Simplicius, *Commentary on Physics* and Plutarch, *Amatorius* 756ff.)

HESIOD AND THE BIRTH OF THE GODS

Familial Eris

As we have seen, Hesiod's *kosmos* originates in and is pervaded by violence, or in Hesiod's image, by the ineradicable presence of *Eris*. Indeed the appearance of the domain of Light between Heaven and Earth arises from the violent castration of Ouranos by his own child, Kronos. In fact the *Theogony*'s poetic principle is woven around a phenomenology of familial violence:

- the 'realms' of Heaven (light) and Earth (darkness) are produced by the scission of Chaos;
- the gods are born in the differentiating Chaos of coition and the violent 'labour' of birth;
- Gaia mates with her son Ouranos and bears his children (the nature powers or Titans, Koios, Krios, etc.);
- the chthonian Titan Kronos, with the connivance of his mother Gaia, overthrows and castrates his own father, Ouranos;
- from the flesh and blood of Ouranos arise the Fates (or Furies), Giants and, eventually, the most beautiful of all the gods, the goddess of love, Aphrodite;
- Kronos devours the offspring of his mate, the Titan Rheia (his child Zeus is saved by Rheia's successful substitution of a stone for the child);
- Kronos disgorges his other children (Demeter, Hades, Hera, Poseidon, etc.);
- Zeus wages war on Kronos (and the dragon, Typhoeus) in order to achieve familial domination, struggling in particular against the chthonian Titans who are eventually defeated, blinded, and imprisoned in Tartarus or the Underworld;
- as an omnipotent patriarch, survivor of the 'Oedipal' volence which mark his origins, he fathers other divinities and reigns as the uncontested king of the Olympians, apportioning their limited domains of power and authority as the absolute autocrat of Olympus.

From this selection of narrative scenes it becomes evident that *Eris* is more than another deity in the unfurling structure of Hesiod's narrative; Eris codifies the structuration principle of the text itself: the 'plot' of the *Theogony* crystallizes and evolves around variations of familial struggle and violence (incest, life and death struggles between son and father, alliances between mother and son against the father, sexual mutilation, cannibalism, Zeus' will-to-power, and so on). These conflicts are not described; they appear spontaneously as if produced by the discontinuous working of the principle of differentiation itself. Indeed they assume the appearance of 'everydayness' – a 'leaden' sequence of violent acts designed to move the plot along to its denouement with the ultimate victory of Zeus and his patriarchal hegemony over the Olympian gods. Justice and civilization are the fragile achievement of a protracted period of conflict and bitter war.

HESIOD AND THE BIRTH OF THE GODS

The essential point is that at the level of poetic narrative the symbolism of Familial Eris is struck and put into circulation for subsequent generations of mythographers, cosmogonists, and – eventually – philosophers.

Kronos (Cronus)

The Titan Kronos – still allied with the matriarchal forces of the Earth (*Gaia*) – also plays a pivotal role in Hesiod's narrative: it is Kronos' action of destroying the ubiquity of Sky (*Ouranos*) that allows the 'breathing space' of a world order to appear and remain open (*Theogony* 154–210). Kronos' ordering and apportioning of the world is the primary cosmic event and, as Cornford has observed,

> to that extent Kronos fills the role of creator. Also he was the king, who originally distributed among the Titans their privileges and provinces in the order of the world (*Theogony* 392ff.). But his reign has receded into the dim past. In the hymn the foreground is occupied by his son, the young king, Zeus. Zeus is the hero whose exploits established the world as it now is'.[20]

The struggle between Zeus and Kronos provides one of the most graphic examples of Hesiod's chaos-theorizing, depicting cosmogenesis as a process of catastrophic violence. This is perfectly captured in the slightly archaic translation of A. W. Mair (*Theogony* 678–721):

> The boundless sea roared terribly around them, and the earth crashed aloud, and the wide heaven groaned as it was shaken, and high Olympos was shaken from its foundations at the onset of the immortals, and a grievous convulsion came on misty Tartaros, and the sheer din of their feet in onset unspeakable and noise of mighty blows: so they hurled against one another their grievous shafts ... Nor did Zeus any longer restrain his soul, but straightway his mind was filled with fury and he showed forth all his might. And from heaven and from Olympos he came to join them, lightening as he came. And his bolts flew near at hand with thunder and with lightning, thick bolts from his strong hand rolling a holy flame; and around the life-giving earth crashed as it burned, and the infinite wood cried aloud with fire. And the whole earth boiled, and the streams of Okeanus, and the unharvested sea; and the hot breath beset the Titans under the earth, and infinite flame came unto the holy ether, and the flashing glare of thunderbolt and lighting robbed their eyes of sight, albeit they were strong. And a wondrous heat beset Chaos. And it seemed, to see with the eyes and to hear the din with the ears, as if Earth and the wide Heaven above drew night to one another. For such a mighty din would have arisen if Earth were ruining and Heaven above hurling it to ruin. Such was the din when the gods met in strife.

HESIOD AND THE BIRTH OF THE GODS

The hegemony of Zeus

As is well known, Zeus ousts Kronos, usurps his place as the chief deity, has the other Titans – now blinded and restrained – fettered, and thus secures his hegemony on the basis of unrestrained terror. Zeus' dominion is presented as the outcome of an unstable balance of forces. For Hesiod, even the highest of the gods is caught in a network of darker, ambivalent conflicts. From being one god among gods, Zeus' violent path to supreme kingship is marked with familial violence. Zeus' will to power is a repetition of a more primordial chthonian struggle with the forces of 'nature', personified by the Titans, Gorgons, and Moirai. These struggles antedate the final victory of Zeus, enabling Hesiod to construct the work of Zeus as the victory of Order, Law, and Justice.[21] Strife (*eris*) is a precondition for the ultimate hegemony of Zeus. It is as though Hesiod wished to underline the point that even the supremacy of Justice and Order is marked by irreparable forces of discord and difference: no secure power or authority is possible as a stable unity; all power is configurational and subject to adversarial forces – including the power which leads men from barbarism and founds the moral order of the *polis*. Even the high god Zeus is not immune from the 'madness' of passion and desire (indeed this would be one of Plato's main indictments against the imagery of the Homeric and Hesiodic poems).

The ambivalence of Dike and Eris

Dike – typically identified with the 'judgement' of Zeus – serves Hesiod as another source of dialectical images. Justice in Hesiod's text is at once both a protagonist and an antagonist of human happiness, anticipating the reflections of the great fifth-century dramatists on the vagaries of human destiny. In this respect Aeschylus inhabits the same mental world as Hesiod. Justice invariably appears in the context of violence and conflict.

Hesiod introduces *Works and Days* by appealing to the Muses to convey his words to his brother Perses (1–10); the text is occasioned by an overriding personalized 'intention': to persuade Perses to turn from his dissolute ways and return to the path of justice and diligent work. We should also note, in keeping with the theme of textual reflexivity in Hesiod's writing, that the text makes reference to his earlier account of Eris in the *Theogony* (*Works and Days* 11ff. and *Theogony* 226; see Jaeger, 1947: 12, n. 41). Perses' wandering from right conduct is, paradoxically, dramatized in the opening lines by another powerful dialectical figure – that of the 'double-Eris', Strife or Discord as an ambivalent power in the affairs of gods and mortals, as a force of good and evil (*Works and Days* 11–24):

> Strife is no only child. Upon the earth Two Strifes exist; the one is praised by those who come to know her, and the other is blamed. Their natures differ: for the cruel one makes battles thrive, and war; she wins no love

but men are forced, by the immortals' will, to pay the grievous goddess due respect. The other, first-born child of blackest Night, was set by Zeus, who lives in air, on high, set in the roots of earth, an aid to men. She urges even lazy men to work: a man grows eager, seeing another rich from ploughing, planting, ordering his house; so neighbour vies with neighbour in the rush for wealth: this Strife is good for mortal men – potter hates potter, carpenters compete, and beggar strives with beggar, bard with bard'.[22]

The complex duality or 'strife of Strife' also creates a literary frame and imaginary motivation for *Works and Days*, namely, as a conceit to persuade its addressee, Perses, to return to the original division of their father's property, to abandon the world of the lords 'who love to try a case like that, eaters of bribes' (*dorophagoi* at *Works and Days* 38–40, 221, 264), and to return to the way marked out by Good Strife, the path or way Hesiod exemplifies with his advice on good husbandry, navigation, ethical, magical, and religious lore. As a symbolic structure, Strife enables Hesiod to construct a tale of two ways – one, the way of injustice and *hubris*, the other the way of justice and order:

> come, let us finally settle our quarrel with straight decisions (*dike*), which are from Zeus, and are the fairest. Now once before we divided our inheritance, but you seized the greater part and made off with it, gratifying those barons who eat bribes, who are willing to give out such a decision.
>
> (*Works and Days* 35–40)

We should also note the misogyny in Hesiod's personification of evil Strife, a misogyny which extends to his account of the feminine origins of evil and misfortune: Hesiod follows earlier folk tales in ascribing the origins of evil to the wilful act of Pandora in releasing misfortune upon the world as punishment for the crimes of Prometheus in violating Zeus' will (*Theogony* 501–616, esp. 535–6, 561–4, 570–613; *Works and Days* 42ff., 90ff., 238–47, 695ff.; cf. *Il.* 5.385–91; 24.527ff.); only hope (*Elpis*) is left to console and inspire mankind (*Works and Days* 42–105, esp. 96–7, 102). Evil which now pervades both the earth and sea is the responsibility of Pandora (*Works and Days* 100–5). Hope belongs to the realm of 'good Strife', inciting and motivating mortals to activity and benign struggle. In this way Hesiod provides an early codification of the competitive value system of ancient Greece.

6.2 The birth of the world in Egyptian and Near Eastern creation myths

Chaos gives choum, then cavum ('hollow', 'cave') and from this caelum, 'sky', that which holds in its embrace the earth, the *cavum caelum*, hollow sky.

(Varro's spurious etymology of *caelum* ('sky') from *chaos*,
Marcus Tullius Varro, *De Lingua Latina*)

Hesiod's conception of *Chaos*, as we have seen, is not 'a formless mixture', but rather, as its etymology indicates, a 'yawning gulf or gap where nothing is as yet' (Burnet, 1930: 7; cf. Cornford, 1950: 95–116 on *Chaos* as the 'gap' or 'void space' between Sky and Earth; also Jaeger, 1947: 13–14). Hesiod's theogony shares a common meontic metaphor (from *me on*, non-being) with other creation stories:

> Somehow even earlier than the first gods there was a state which we now like to call by its Hesiodic name Chaos. But Chaos does not just mean disorder, because then there would at least exist something. Literally Chaos means yawning. The same word appears in the *Edda*: *Ginungagap* is yawning of the deeps. This state can only be described by negations. None of the things that make our world were there: neither heaven nor earth, neither grass nor sea, neither name nor fate. If you want to describe an absolute beginning you cannot do it otherwise... The beginning must be a kind of nothingness; but since it is the beginning of something it must have some part in being. Let us call it nothingness pregnant with being.
>
> (von Weizsäcker, 1964: 36)

F. M. Cornford provides a lucid formulation of the protodialectical character of Hesiod's mythical image as a 'primal Unity, a state of indistinction or fusion in which factors that will later become distinct are merged together ... Out of this Unity there emerge, by separation, parts of opposite things ... This separating-out finally leads to the disposition of the great elemental masses constituting the world-order, and the formation of the heavenly bodies ... The Opposites interact or reunite, in meteoric phenomena, or in the production of individual living beings' (Cornford, 1965: ch. 11; cf. also Cornford 1950: 103–4: 'all these cosmogonies begin with a primal unity, which is separated apart, when the sky is lifted up from the earth, leaving the yawning gap of void or air between' (1950: 98)). 'To Hesiod', as Jaeger has observed,

> who thinks in terms of genealogies, even Chaos came into being. He does not say, 'In the beginning was Chaos', but 'First Chaos came to be, and then the Earth', etc. Here the question arises whether there must not have been a beginning (*arche*) of becoming – something that has not itself become. Hesiod leaves this question unanswered; indeed he never goes so far as to raise it.
>
> (1947: 14)

A more recent theorist, interpreting the contemporary relevance of Hesiod's dialectical image, writes:

> In Hesiod, who preserved earlier stages of thought, laws *came* into existence (the rule of Zeus) and are the result of a *balance of opposing forces* (Titans in fetters). They are the result of a dynamic equilibrium. In the nineteenth century laws were regarded as eternal and absolute, i.e., not due to a balance of mutually restricting entities. Hesiod's cosmology is far ahead of nineteenth-century science.
>
> (Feyerabend, 1978: 105 n. 37)

It is now generally recognized that Hesiodic theogony has its roots in much older systems of thought, and that without these traditions – from Sumer, Mesopotamia, Phoenicia, and Egypt – it is unlikely that a work such as the *Theogony* could have been written. Here again, we note the role of early Greek literature as a conduit for the cultures of the ancient Middle East. Cornford makes ancient Crete the point of dissemination of the myths and legends of Mesopotamia, Egypt, and Syria (1965: 250–6). In Egyptian cosmology (dating back to the Old Kingdom *c.* 2850–2000 BC), the formless Ocean was considered to be the aboriginal source of the world, a dark, primeval, limitless depth personified by the god *Nun*, 'father of the god's', *Geb* (Earth), *Nut* (Sky), *Oriris*, *Horis*, *Isis*, and so on (Erman, 1966; Frankfort *et al.*, 1949: 18; Simpson, ed., 1973). The god Re-Atum creates himself from a mound of mud arizing from this watery chaos; all the other natural deities and forces were derived from the body of this god (air, water, earth, sky). Analogously, in the 'Creation Poem' of ancient Mesopotamia – the *Enuma Elish c.* 1500 BC – Chaos assumes the formless character of a wild Ocean, *Tiamat* (in the original Akkadian, *Ti-amat* or *Mummu-Tiamat* personified as the mother goddess of the sea – 'She who gave birth to all things') and the life-giving waters of *Apsu*; every form of being is created from the copulation of Apsu and Tiamat (cf. Cornford, 1965: 239–49, where he argues that Hesiod's *Theogony* is directly linked to the Babylonian cycle of creation myths, esp. 248–9 and note 1 appended by E. R. Dodds).

In many of these ancient cosmogonies, creation emerges from the 'mixing' of the divine elements, forming a matrix or womb from which the gods and the natural elements are born. In the Book of *Genesis*, itself closely modelled around the cosmogony contained in the Mesopotamia texts (for example Tablet XI of the Gilgamesh epic; see *ANET*), creation begins as the primordial Waters – the *Tehom* – are separated by the moving spirit of God:

> In the beginning God created the heaven and the earth. And the Earth was without form, and void; and darkness was upon the face of the deep. And the Spirit of God moved upon the face of the waters. And God said, Let there be light: and there was light. And God saw the light, that it was

good: and God divided the light from darkness. And God called the light Day, and the darkness he called Night

(*Genesis* 1:1–5)

However, the Biblical account differs significantly from the Babylonian Flood narratives, the Egyptian creation myths, and Hesiod's poetic cosmogony:

> Some details of the Biblical report seem to indicate a conscious polemic against the Babylonian myth. Thus the Chaos of the beginning is still remembered: 'the Earth was without form and void'; *tehom*, the deep waters of the same verse, is the same word as *Tiamat*. But it is not Chaos which has borne the God; no: 'In the beginning God created heaven and earth'. God was there first and you cannot ask whence he came.
>
> (von Weizsäcker, 1964: 46)[23]

Jaeger is even more emphatic about the philosophical implications of these two different cosmogonies:

> if ... we compare this Greek hypostasis of the world-creative Eros with that of the *Logos* [in the Mosaic account of Creation], we may observe a deep-lying difference in the outlook of the two peoples. The *Logos* is a substantialization of an intellectual property or power of God the creator, who is stationed *outside* the world and brings that world into existence by his own personal fiat. The Greek gods are stationed *inside* the world; they are descended from Heaven and Earth, the two greatest and most exalted parts of the universe; and they are generated by the mighty power of Eros, who likewise belongs within the world as an all-engendering primitive force.
>
> (1947: 16)

The Genesis narrators have universalized and personalized the Mesopotamian myths. Yahweh is depicted as a solitary creative *person*, unlike the ancient Babylonian gods of Chaos, a being who will methodically shape mankind in His own image; the work of Creation is imagined and executed from an unnameable site beyond Being – Creation is designed, it has a purpose; and the creator God is transcendent to His own created order (Tiamat, recall, is identified with only one element of creation – the sea). And even more importantly, the Being that calls himself Being ('I am that I am'), a *personal* Being that is wholly *other*, creates the whole universe from nothing, by exercising the divine will to create. In the Egyptian and Babylonian narratives, creation occurs as a war between the old and new gods, a struggle over an existing distribution of matter. The Hebraic Creation story is a narrative of Creation '*fiat ex nihilo*'. And, even more striking, the *instrument* and *medium* of this Creative *fiat* is the voice of the one absolute God: it is the Word, God's divine language, which contains the secret of Creation (*Genesis* 1:1–6). The 'cause' of creation is the divine Voice ('the word of the Lord'), the 'effect' is

Creation itself (*Genesis* 1-2; 15:1; *Numbers* 3:14-6). '*And on the seventh day God ended his work which he had made*' (*Genesis* 2:2). Here we have the beginnings of the idea of a *designed* cosmos. A universe informed by intentionality – literally articulated by the instrumental force of breath – is already at work in the ancient Hebrew account of creation: '*And the Lord God formed man of the dust of the ground, and breathed into his nostrils the breath of life; and man became a living soul*' (*Genesis* 2:7; cf. *Isaiah* 44:24; 45:7, 18; *Job* 38-9; *Psalms* 104). With these observations in mind let us return to Hesiod's creation narrative.

6.3 *Eros/Eris: the world as a theatre of desire*

It is now possible to reconstruct Hesiod's world-view. The text assumes the physical world to be a dish-shaped Earth bounded by the encircling river Okeanus; every river in the world streams into this vast circular flow; above stretches the bright dome of the Sky; below lies the murky pit of Tartarus into which the souls of the dead descend; bounding the sky is a fiery auratic layer (the *aither*) through which the Sun, Moon, and Planets wander (the word 'planet' derives from the Greek word for 'wanderer'); the whole *kosmos* is ordered and held together as an articulated Whole. This symbolic frame sets the stage upon which the actions, passions, and sufferings of gods and mortals are enacted. In sum, like the Homeric epic, Hesiod pictures the Earth and Heavens as a theatre of action (cf. *Il.* 15.187-93). But before the world-frame is a scenario of epic praxis, it is a site of desire.

By the time the Homeric texts were transcribed we know that Greek culture represented *Okeanos* less as a formless void than as a limit or mobile boundary encircling Earth; *Okeanos* is the articulated ('cyclical') and ordered ('flowing') trace of the primordial Chaos. The formular expression in Hesiod is 'the holy stream of Okeanos' (*Works and Days* 566). For Hera, the consort of Zeus, Okeanos is the 'source of the gods'. In Hesiod's symbology *Okeanos* begins to assume the functions of a mythpoeic reflexivity: it is a symbol of primeval order. Unlike the Near Eastern cosmogonies where order has to be imposed upon the primal Waters, *Okeanos* bounds and delimits the Earth. In this structured opposition 'dark Earth' – the unknowable depths of the Earth – functions as an icon of opacity, disorder, and disarticulation. Finally, *Okeanos* is dynamic and mobile (*Theogony* 133-6): it flows eternally in a circular movement, the very image of self-reflexivity, turning back upon itself as though it was 'filled with life' or 'animated' (*anima*). These Hesiodic images would be later refashioned in the earliest texts of the Presocratic thinkers (Thales, Anaximander, and Anaximenes in particular) as they reworked the symbolisms of reflexive movement into their own discourses. In other words this unique construction of Homeric and Hesiodic ideology – the reflexive *Okeanos* – provided metaphorical terms and predicates for an active genealogy of the world, creating a framework for a dynamic world-view (the absence of this perspective is noticeable in the cosmologies of Mesopotamia, Egypt, and Semitic myths which tend to resort instead to anthropomorphic *actants* and plot structures: the struggle between Marduk and Tiamat, the binding of Kingu, the voice of Yahweh, and so forth).

For both gods and mortals, desire – personified in the figure of Eros – is a potent and dangerous force. The very framework of the world order, the balance of unity and difference, are effects of Desire. Desire in the most concrete form of sexual attraction draws human beings together, but it also separates and divides individuals and families; in this it shares the work of *logos* (*legein* having the sense of collecting or gathering into a whole) and of strife (*eris*). Like other ancient mythologies Greek myth fuses these opposites into a single image, usually personified as a goddess (for example the beautiful 'gray-eyed' Pallas Athena is also the goddess of war and destruction, or the fusion of both roles in the ancient Sumerian religion, where Ishtar is goddess of love and war). In the *Iliad*, *eros* provided the basic motivation for the siege of Troy. *Eros*, however, is also the key to the opening scene of the epic which follows the consequences of Achilles' anger after Agamemnon seizes Briseis.

Hesiod is thus following ancient mythical and folkloric traditions in presenting *Eros* as one of the oldest of gods (with Earth and Tartarus). Eros 'loosens the limbs' and unhinges the mind; it is an unpredictable and, perhaps, magical force which overrides sense and reason, consubstantial with the beginning of the world. It is the force controlled by women in giving birth to other living beings – and in the earliest patriarchal societies is hedged with dark and ambivalent emotions. Yet in the Greek world eros is also associated with the 'light-footed', 'modest, lovely goddess' Aphrodite, the Muses, and civilized life. But dissonance is never far away, as eros is at work in 'the whispering together of girls, the smiles and deceptions, the delight, and the sweetness of love, and flattery' (*Theogony* 205). Eros mediates between nature and culture just as it relates the primordial partners, Earth and Tartarus. It is both an invariant horizon and an ambivalent power governing human experience. *Eros* also mediates between the realms of animate and inanimate nature – it even has the power to move inanimate nature – the beginnings of an 'affectivity' flowing through natural phenomena was already a stock theme in early Greek poetry.

In conclusion: Eros gathers life into a unity; but it is also at work as one of the primary order-disturbing forces leading to strife and war. Eros is the daughter of Night, the goddess of violence, disputes, envy, lawlessness, struggle, and transgression. Both gods preside over an ambivalent life force, simultaneously creating and destroying human arrangements. Eros, in more modern terminology, is a dual-aspect force working for both good and evil. It is thus the central dialectical image in Hesiod's poetic universe.

A similar motif can be found in the Gilgamesh Epic where a harlot (or temple prostitute) is sent to break the strength of Enkidu, a wild 'natural' man. Eros destroys Enkidu's powers and yet also 'civilizes' him, transforming him into a thoughtful, reflexive being; his transition to civility is marked by the fact that wild animals now fly from his presence. By seeing his own being as one among a myriad of finite creatures he gains the power of self-reflection. The 'fall' from nature is the price that must be paid for the gift of reflection shaped by thoughtful desire: 'the thoughts of a man were in his heart'.[24] Hesiod appears to have developed a strikingly similar social vision of the fall of man.

6.4 The fall of mankind: the five epochs

Hesiodic cosmology identifies the fundamental process of becoming as *differentiation*: all things are generated from the differentiation of primal 'indifferent' Chaos and are held in being by a tensile system of conflicts. The *kosmos* itself emerges from the background of an elemental breach of the abyss; whole worlds are born in a similar manner, marked by the experience of violence, strife, and suffering.

In the discourse made available by Hesiod's text, we have no rational way of inquiring reflexively into the 'origins of Chaos'; Chaos' origin is simply posited as an unnameable indifference. Paradoxically, divinity like every other phenomena of the natural world has its roots in a 'non-rational', unspeakable source of difference. This might be regarded as Hesiod's way of marking the fundamental limit of human knowledge and inquiry – poetically we can turn our thought to the origin of the gods, but asking of the origin of origins produces silence.

For a comparable poetics of becoming we have to turn to the Hindu *Rigveda*, specifically to the *Brihadaranyaka Upanishad* where the 'time' before creation cannot be described as a state of existence or non-existence, being or nothingness: 'There was no air, nor sky that is beyond it. What was concealed? Wherein? In whose protection? And was there deep unfathomable water?' In contrast with the *Theogony*, however, for the Hindu myth 'None knoweth whence creation has arisen; And whether he has or has not produced it; He who surveys it in the highest heaven, He only knows, or even, he may not know.'

The matrix of existence and becoming, the primal 'unity' (if it be such) out of which all things have emerged is prior to time; for both traditions, Chaos is a non-temporal matrix, a 'timeless' site of possible worlds; and in this undifferentiated state there can be no 'subject' or 'object'. The cosmological difference antedates even the actions of the gods – for they too are differentiated as parts of the world order and not its creator-source.

Another contrast will bring out the originality of Hesiod's account. We can compare Hesiodic Chaos theorizing with the benevolent God or Demiurge in Plato's *Timaeus* who,

> finding the whole visible sphere not at rest, but moving in an irregular and disorderly fashion, out of disorder he brought order, considering that this was in every way better than disorder ... we may say that the

world came into being – a living creature truly endowed with soul and intelligence by the providence of God.

(*Timaeus.* 30A–B)

Hesiod's *kosmos*, however, is governed by endemic conflict, and both man and god stand within the polemical space of order and chaos, sharing the same condition of coming-to-be and passing-away. In this vision mankind is suspended between the gleaming realm of the gods and the dark Earth; and with birth comes pain, old age, temporal dissolution, and the reflexive self-consciousness of death (Hesiod concretizes this in making Kronos – Time – devour his own progeny as they are created from the womb of Earth). There is nothing comparable to this existential drama in the symbolisms of later Greek thought.

The Golden Age

Hesiod's vision culminates in a myth of human degeneration. The 'universe' of mortals has become estranged from the Whole – the paradisical state of bliss known as the Age of Gold (forerunner of Ovid's *aetas aurea*). The alienation of mankind is presented in a sequence of deteriorations, a progressive falling away from the original Golden Race ('guardians of justice' who lived in Kronos' age, when he was the monarch of heaven', *Works and Days* 109–26; *Laws* 713B–714A), through an Age of Silver (*Works and Days* 140–2), a Bronze Age with its semi-divine Heroes (161–73), to the violent Age of Iron. A similar chronology also informs Hindu mythology with the decline represented in the *Mahabharata* as a falling away from a Golden Age (*Krita* or *Sattya Yuga*) to a Silver (*Treta Yuga*), Bronze (*Dvarpa Yuga*) and eventually an Iron Age (*Kali Yuga*):

> The Krita Yuga [Perfect Age, from *kr*, 'to make, accomplish'] was so named because there was but one religion, and all men were saintly: therefore they were not required to perform religious ceremonies. Holiness never grew less, and the people did not decrease. There were no gods in the Krita Yuga, and there were no demons ... Men neither bought nor sold; there were no poor and no rich; there was no need to labour, because all that men required was obtained by the power of will; the chief virtue was the abandonment of all worldly desires. The Krita Yuga was without disease; there was no lessening with the years; no sorrow, no fear. All mankind could obtain to supreme blessedness.
>
> (in Heinberg, 1982: 50)

The Age of Iron

Hesiod contrasts the 'reign of Kronos' with the Age of Iron in the following dark images of degeneration:

I wish that I had never belonged to the fifth race, but had either died earlier or been born later. For truly it is a race of iron. Neither by day will men cease from toil and woe nor from suffering by night. And the gods will give them troubles hard to bear. None the less, even they will have some good mixed with their woes. But Zeus will destroy this race of mortal men too, when they come to have grey hair at birth. A father will not be in harmony with his children, nor the children with their father, nor guest with host, nor comrade with comrade, and a brother will not be able to be dear to his brother as they were in the past. Men will dishonour their quickly ageing parents and will reproach them with hard words of abuse, wicked men who do not understand the vengeance of the gods. They will not repay their aged parents the cost of their nurture, for might is their right, and one man will sack another's city. There will be no respect for the man who keeps his oath or for the just or the good; instead they will praise the man who does evil, insolence incarnate. And right and reverence shall depend on might. The bad man will harm the better, telling lies about him and confirming them with an oath. And ugly Envy, that causes uproar and delights in evil, will keep company with the whole of miserable mankind. Then Aidos and Nemesis will wrap their fair bodies in white robes, and go from the earth with its broad paths to Olympos to join the race of the immortals, forsaking men, and bitter sorrows will be left for mortal men, and there will be no help against evil.

(*Works and Days* 174–201; cf. *Statesman* 269A–273E)

7 HESIODIC IDEOLOGY: THE VALORIZATION OF JUSTICE AND WORK

The only hope Hesiod holds out for those who live in the Age of Iron is that suffering will be tempered by Justice – identified as we have seen with the patriarchal rule of Zeus. *Dike* – the virgin daughter of Zeus – is mankind's sole protection and defence against conflict and strife – or more locally against the injustices perpetrated by the seventh-century landowning stratum of Boeotia. The guardians of 'mortal men', ancestors of the original Golden Age exist as spirits (*daimones*) under the earth. These guardian spirits, servants of Zeus, preserve the law and avert evil (*Works and Days* 121ff., 200–1; *Theogony* 603–10; Plato, *Cratylus* 397E–398A). Socrates explicates the 'moral' behind the allegory: 'I think he means that the golden race was not made of gold, but was good and beautiful. And I regard it as a proof of this that he further says we are the iron race' (Plato, *Cratylus.*, 398A). Here the Hesiodic text is shifting the older meaning of *dike* away from 'customary morality' and 'the normal course of nature' (see '*dike*', *LSJ*) to embrace wider normative concerns and thematics, especially ideas associated with 'divine justice'.

If the gods honour justice and 'right conduct' (*Od.* 14.84–5), then the poetry of divinity must become an instrument on the side of 'just dealings' and 'fair judgements'. By revealing injustice – 'crooked judgements' – the poetic word expresses the voice of the nightingale caught in the clutches of the Hawk. In Hesiod's innovative text Justice is transfigured into a universal salutary force which, as Trypanis notes, was later to become one of the fundamental themes of Greek thought and literature: 'by connecting Zeus with *Dike*, Hesiod takes a great step forward in the history of religion'.[25] In this respect Hesiod's phenomenology of the gods is situated in the same ideological space as Aeschylus' articulation of Zeus as a Just divinity, punishing those who transgress what is *themis*. In the Aeschylean vision every act of injustice (*adikia*) and immoderation (*hubris*) is countered by divine punishment (cf. Aeschylus, *Agamemnon* 366–400). Retribution is particularly directed at those who step out of line in moral and ethical matters – those who commit evil actions are compared to the high mountain that is the first to be struck by lightning (*Agamemnon* 469–70). This is also the world of Sophocles' *Antigone*, where the eponymous hero of the tragedy grounds her defiance of Creon the king of Thebes by citing a source of justice that is higher and more fundamental than the legislation (*nomoi*) of men. For Antigone, *Dike* relates to a legality with an authority older and higher than the laws of man. In the words of *Antigone* 450–60:

> for these laws were not ordained of Zeus, And she who sits enthroned with gods below, Justice [*Dike*], enacted not these human laws. Nor did I deem that thou, a mortal man, Could'st by a breath annul and override the immutable unwritten laws of Heaven. They were not born to-day nor yesterday. They die not; and none knoweth whence they sprang.

The Sophoclean chorus might be understood as the literary realization of Hesiod's voice of Justice. The 'civilizing' ethics of *Dike* ('justice'), *Eunomia* ('good order'), and *Eirene* ('peace') still resonate in Socrates' intepretation of the Hesiodic word for 'spirit' (*daimone*) – an ironically apt exegesis given his own guidance by such a spirit:

> This, then, I think, is what he certainly means to say of the spirits: because they were wise and knowing (*daemones*) he called them spirits (*daimones*); and in the old form of our language the two words are the same. Now he and all the other poets are right, who say that when a good man dies he has a great portion and honour among the dead, and becomes a spirit, a name which is in accordance with the other name of wisdom. And so I assert that every good man, whether living or dead, is of spiritual nature, and is rightly called a spirit.
>
> (Plato, *Cratylus* 398B–C)

Works and Days is also unique in early Greek literature as one of the rare texts from the Archaic period to positively valorize physical work *as a creative medium of self-definition and self-formation*. Hesiod's errant brother Perses is urged to abandon his dissolute ways and to return to productive agricultural labour: 'foolish Perses, go to work! The gods have given work to men.' Work is the natural state of human existence, the fate of all mortals, bequeathed by the gods and not a shameful or unnatural punishment (*Works and Days* 280–1). Those who refuse honest toil are like the 'stingless drones' who waste the honey gathered by the productive hive (*Works and Days* 303–6):

> From working, men grow rich in flocks and gold and dearer to the deathless gods. In work there is no shame; shame is in idleness. And if you work, the lazy man will soon envy your wealth: a rich man can become famous and good. No matter what your luck, to work is better'.[26]

In this important fragment we can again detect themes that resonate with the Aeschylean ideal of civic legality and the peaceful pursuits of work and everyday life – values associated with the finite horizons of the self-ruling *polis*: 'Glory in excess is fraught with peril ... Prosperity unassailed by envy is my choice. Let me not be a destroyer of cities; no, nor let me be despoiled and live to see my own life in another's power' (*Agamemnon* 470–4).

8 HESIODIC UTOPIANISM

To conclude these reflections: where Homeric poetry had been an integral part of the aristocratic world, Hesiod turns his poetic craft against the corruption and injustice of the Boeotian nobility. And in the *Erga* we even have the intimations of a critical utopian sensibility. Hesiod's life-world is woven from images embodying the values of diligent work, family, agrarian life, justice, right dealing, nature's sustaining cycles, and respectful acts of sacrifice to the gods. Despite the social chaos of the last decades of the eighth century there is still an underlying order in the universe and those who transgress either natural or moral legality will be punished. Conversely, the righteous who recognize and sacrifice to the gods will flourish (*Works and Days* 336–41). As the supreme protector of Justice, Zeus now actively monitors and judges the ethical qualities of human conduct (*Works and Days* 238–40).

Hesiod's 'utopianism' is the vision of a late eighth-century Boeotian farmer striving to maintain a threatened and precarious way of life. Like Aeschylus' voice of *Dike*, the Hesiodic figure of Zeus articulates the civilizing values of domestic peace and agrarian labour against the violent Homeric ideals of war and 'booty capitalism' ('hateful war'). Not surprisingly he warns his auditors about the immoral ways of the Sea. Only an existence securely planted in agricultural values and practices befits a community of honest working men. This conservative ethic prefigures the pragmatic idiom of the ordinary working man, forerunner of the figure who would enter the ranks of the *Demos* in sixth-century Greek politics. The new demotic attitude is not untouched by the spirit of righteous indignation and vengeance: 'You princes, mark well this punishment; for the deathless gods are near among men and mark all those who oppress their fellows with crooked judgements, and reck not the anger of the gods' (*Works and Days* 248–50).

Zeus' all-seeing eye searches the hearts and minds of those who deviate from the moral law (Hesiod personifies this divine concern by means of the figure of 'virgin Justice (*Dike parthenos*) who sits at the right side of Zeus' (*Works and Days* 256–60)). Justice will protect those who labour as well as those who fight if Zeus is the high king and lord of all reality (396–7).

At this point we have completely left the world of the Homeric epic. This is perhaps the exemplary value of the story which has Hesiod competing with Homer and winning a golden tripod: 'The king gave the crown to Hesiod, declaring that it was right that he who called upon men to follow peace and husbandry should have the prize rather than one who dwelt on war and slaughter' (*Contest of Homer and Hesiod* 322, in Hesiod, 1914).

Hesiod's didactic realism in matters relating to work and his utopianism in his image of the Golden Age would exert a profound and complex influence on subsequent Greek and Roman literature and social thought. Hesiodic themes can be found transformed and refigured in the writings of Plato, Aristotle, Callimachus, Plotinus, Porphyry, Ovid, Pausanias, Virgil, Seneca, and in the works of many lesser figures. In terms of the subsequent course of European culture it was through Ovid's revisionary *Metamorphoses* that Hesiod's utopian image of the Golden entered into the fabric of later European art and thought. The promise of an idealized world of peace, industrious work, and prosperity became the *sperma puros* that would fire the imagination of modern utopianism with its dream of justice and peace:

> The first age was golden. In it faith and righteousness were cherished by men of their own free will without judges or laws. Penalties and fears there were none, nor were threatening words incribed on unchanging bronze; nor did the suppliant crowd fear the words of its judge, but they were safe without protectors. Not yet did the pine cut from its mountain tops descend into the flowing waters to visit foreign lands, nor did deep trenches gird the town, nor were there straight trumpets, nor horns of twisted brass, nor helmets, nor swords. Without the use of soldiers the peoples in safety enjoyed their sweet repose. Earth herself, unburdened and untouched by the hoe and unwounded by the ploughshare, gave all things freely... Spring was eternal... untilled the earth bore its fruits and the unploughed field grew hoary with heavy ears of wheat'.[27]

In articulating the divine images of *Eros*, the *Horae* (hours), *Eunomia* (Order), *Harmonia*, *Dike* (Justice), and *Eirene* (Peace) Hesiod provided a voice and symbolism for the utopian aspirations of the Hellenic tradition. All subsequent attempts to imagine a radical alternative to the present social order would in essence be variations of these mythical themes. The underlying tableau of the 'City of *Dike*' corrupted by the 'City of *Hubris*' would itself undergo many metamorphoses in the imagination of later European utopian thinkers.

4
LYRIC REFLEXIVITIES

> The *polis* is the teacher of the man.
> (Simonides, Fr. 95)

1. *The Genealogy of Individual Lyric Voices*
2. *Choral Lyric: From Collective to Individual Forms of Self-Reflection*
3. *From Choral Lyric to Monody: the Social Construction of the Individual Lyric Voice*
4. *Conclusion: the 'concept' of Lyric Reflexivity*

1 THE GENEALOGY OF INDIVIDUAL LYRIC VOICES

> The lyric work hopes to attain universality through unrestrained individuation.
> (Theodor W. Adorno, 1991: 38)

A Boeotian winter

In certain respects Hesiod can be regarded as one of the first great lyrical poets in the Greek canon; not in terms of his chosen poetic form – in this he stood firmly within the *epos* tradition – but in the singularity of his personal vision of the nature of everyday events, objects and, above all, for the descriptive power and concreteness of some of the lyric passages scattered through the otherwise didactic *Works and Days*. From the perspective of a sociological poetics of Greek literary genres, the lyric form originated as a critical self-reflection on the Homeric art of the oral bards and the dominant choral traditions of Archaic Greece. As a reflexive product of a definite discursive field the emergence of the autonomous lyric voice already displays definite 'metacritical' characteristics; the lyric evocation of the first-person perspective, for example, implicitly negates the ritualism of primary myth and the collective 'authorship' of the epic to articulate a personalized vision of life. The lyric genre considered as a sociological form – indeed, as I will argue in this chapter, as a form of reflexive theorizing – discloses the discursive possibility of affective, self-centred expression. But it also creates the possibility of a non-Homeric conception of the nature of reality – what we might call an ontology of the particular.

Two pre-eminent effects of this lyricism of the particular can be cited – the 'photographic' description of a harsh Boeotian winter and the equally memorable imagery of the oppressive 'fullness' of high summer. The following text may well be the first recorded *personal* description of nature in European literature:

> Avoid the month of Lenaeon [i.e. Winter], wretched days, all of them fit to flay an ox, and the frosts, which are severe when Boreas blows over the earth. He blows across horse-breeding Thrace and on the wide sea and stirs it up, and the earth and the woodlands roar. Often he falls upon oaks with their lofty foliage and thick pines in the mountain glens and brings them down to the bountiful earth, and then all the immense wood groans. And the beasts shiver and put their tails between their legs, even the ones whose hide is covered with fur. But his cold blasts blow through them despite their shaggy breasts. And he goes even through oxhide and it cannot resist him, and through the thin-haired goat. But the strength of Boreas does not penetrate the sheep, because their wool is abundant; yet it makes the old man bent like a wheel.
>
> (*Works and Days* 504–18)

Of course we are not dealing with a work of 'literary naturalism' or 'realism' in the modern senses of these terms. But the celebration of the concrete particularity of experience suggests something like a different sensibility or 'world-view'. The poem is constructed like a *tableau vivant* of sensuous images rooted in a recognizable world of everyday objects and experiences: the savage aspects of the month of Lenaion (in the Ionian calendar Lenaion includes the latter part of January and first weeks of February), the stretched corpse of the flayed ox, the pinched skin under the bite of early frosts, the wind in the trees on the mountain, the snapped pine tumbling into the valley, the man bent double with age – 'like a wheel'. All these inconsequential tokens are indicative of the genre of 'lyric realism'. Moreover, as a display of mind or cultural attitude, the *intentio operis* ('intention of the text' in Umberto Eco's phrase) displays a resolutely personal response to the natural world – an experience liberated from the limited patterns of earlier mythical symbols and the formular designs of Homeric verse (or its allegorical variations in the late seventh century). With the discovery of the syntax of personal expression we see the emergence of the possibility of literary mutation: the legacy of poetic genres is not eternal; they can be modified and changed, under the impress of personal experience. Hesiod's poetic vision thus outlines a sense of nature that is still open for exploration and poetic naming. For lyric expression as a form of signification, truth lies in the detail and the particular. Lyric is the act that names the salt of our tears, the texture of skin, the unconsolable pain of personal loss. The simple discovery made by these poems is that the 'naming of the world' has not been exhausted by the work of *mythos*. Other *acts of signification*, other genres of speech, are possible.

A Boeotian summer

Hesiod's poem on the dangerous presence of Summer is also unique in Archaic Greek literature, anticipating the auratic invocation of a 'symposium' attributed to Empedocles a century or so later. If lyric celebrates the poetry of phenomenal singularity, the following lines deserves to be called the first lyric – and perhaps, erotic – verse in European literature:

> When the golden thistle is in flower, and the chirping cicada sits in a tree and incessantly pours out its shrill song from under its wings in the time of exhausting summer heat, then goats are fattest and wine sweetest and women most wanton and men at their feeblest, for Sirius burns their heads and their knees and their skin is parched in the heat. Then is the right time for the shade of a rock and Bibline wine and milk-bread and late-season goat's milk, and the meat of a heifer that has been put out to graze and has not calved, and of firstling kids. Drink the bright wine sitting in the shade when you have had your fill of food, turning your face towards the fresh Zephyr, and pour in three parts of water from a perpetually running, unmuddied spring, and the fourth part of wine.
>
> (*Works and Days* 582–96)

The lyric poets

> – Sind wir vielleicht hier, um zu sagen: Haus, Brücke, Brunnen, Tor, Krug, Obstbaum, Fenster, – höchstens: Säule, Turm...? (– *Are we, perhaps, here in order to say: House, Bridge, Fountain, Gate, Jug, Peartree, Window, – at most, Pillar, Tower...?*)
>
> (R. M. Rilke, 1978: 85)

In what follows I will argue that the 'lyric' moment within Hesiodic verse (and, it should be said, the lyric ontology plotted within the interstices of the epic genre) opened a creative vein of poetic reflection that was first thoroughly mined by the great lyric poets of the sixth century. Furthermore, it is only in the wake of this radical departure from tradition that anything like literary history and 'literary self-consciousness' becomese possible in European culture. I will suggest that the moment of lyrical criticism contains the reflexive possibility of metacritical thought – that it already prefigures an 'aesthetic' mentality. But we have seen already that in the work of Hesiod and the epic genre, there is both change and continuity in the Greek literary tradition. Our knowledge of the evolution of poetic and literary experiment during the later part of the Archaic age (c. 800–500 BC) is severely limited by the lack of surviving texts reflecting the verbal culture of this period. But we know that Hesiod's cosmogonic verse already prefigured some of the major *topoi* of the great exponents of lyric poetry: the foregrounding of the poet's own voice, the detailed evocation of natural phenomena – particularly the sonorousness of nature ('the chirping cicadas' oblivious to audience or motive), the use of sensuous images anticipating the genre of pastoral verse, the idyllic promise of festivals and sacrifice – the fattening goats that will sacrificially mediate between Mortals and Gods, Earth and Heaven, the Dionysian fullness of life, the ripe grape and pleasures of Bacchus, drunkenness and sexual licence, the symbolism of the languorous dog-days and their mystical significance, the 'lascivious heat of summer' (I borrow the phrase from Vernant, in Detienne, 1977: xvii), 'the period when spices are collected, when women experience sensual abandonment, when earth and sun are in the closest proximity and when erotic seduction in all its aspects is at its height' (1977: xvi), the impotence of men – or the low ebb of the patriarchal powers of law and order – and the return to a more ancient, matriarchal world, the elemental pleasures of shade and food ('the shade of a rock and Bibline wine and milk-bread and late season goat's milk ' *Works and Days* 589), the auratic promise of a renewed communality in the sustaining circle of a symposium, symbolized by the mixing bowl which sweetens wine with spring water. This truly irreplaceable text integrates Demeter (wheat, bread, the fruitfulness of the Earth), Aphrodite and Eros (the erotic desires of women), Dionysus (the flowing wine), the gods of the Heavens who guide Sirius, the Dog Star to bring these elements into a living constellation, and the gods of place who spread the cooling Zephyr, preserve the purity of water and other natural gifts.

In entering this regime of signification an audience is positioned in the role of witness before elemental images of pleasure and happiness shaped from words stolen from the margins of the masculine world of heroic power and military virtue. Lyric enters the world through the spirit of concreteness – of the feminine – in language. And perhaps the seed of lyric desire itself was born under the bright sign of Sirius, the flaming star of the harvest ('The fact is that, in Greek thought, the brightness of Sirius is simply a metaphorical reference to the sun's fire', Detienne, 1977: 9). The pitiless heat of mid-summer evokes the world of Kronos before the onset of the Age of Iron.

We need to explore the different ways in which the discursive forms of lyric poetry 'constituted' the self and self-reflection. Unlike conventional literary history, sociological poetics examines the ways in which the lyric genre as a practice of signification makes new forms of subjectivity possible. We should begin by reflecting on the self of lyric reflexivity. What, then, is meant by the lyric genre?

After Hesiod we meet a dazzling spectrum of lyric voices, already known in antiquity as a constellation of *individual authors*: Tyrtaeus, Alcman, Archilochus, Callinus of Ephesus, Alcaeus, Sappho, Praxilla, Mimnermus, Semonides, Stesichorus, Hipponax, Theognis, Ibycus, Anacreon, Simonides,

Bacchylides and the last and greatest artist of the lyric form, Pindar.[1] The Alexandrian editors had already condensed this list to a canon of nine lyric poets: Alcaeus, Alcman, Ibycus, Simonides, Stesichorus, Anacreon, Sappho, Bacchylides, and Pindar (Bowra, 1961: 2; Levi, 1985: 67).

Each of these names marks the appearance not only of a distinctive individual voice, but of the idea that the universe unfolds in a play of different 'perspectives' – that the worlds of human experience are manifold in form and heterogeneous in their modes of manifestation. As members of a highly individualized civilization it is hard for contemporaries to appreciate the importance of the discovery of the principle of difference – the Rashomon effect of perspectival experience. It is even more difficult to understand the impact of the thought that only the voice of the poetic vocation – and in this case the voice of lyric expression – can articulate the singular truth of things. Even to formulate this idea *as a truth* implied an intellectual leap beyond the thought patterns and values of the dominant tradition. In fact it presupposes something like a cultural revolution in the received ways of imagining the self and tradition. The lyric epoch is thus an age of great light and great danger. The older generic constellations of myth and epic narrative are being eclipsed by the 'dessicating' light of new poetic principles and practices. The lyric voice rises like the Phoenix from the eclipsed body of the collective folk-tale and rigidly structured martial epic.

On a superficial level we know that the lyric form is the archetypal genre of the personal, the particular and the ephemeral – even, as with Sappho's verse, to the extent of speaking solely of the sufferings of the erotic soul. As a genre, lyric is said to reflect changes in social life and political experience during the Archaic age, changes which encouraged the growth of 'Greek individualism'. 'Lyric poetry presents a complex and varied picture of the world of early Greece' (Murray, 1993: 21). At a deeper level, however, it would be more accurate to see the idea of lyric expression as a polemical exploration of the principle of *difference*, represented most emphatically by the discovery of the 'voice-in-the-text' (of the text as the vehicle of the poet's *personae*, the self-reflexive *énonciation* placed into the fictional ego of the poetic text). Even when the 'voice' of the first choral lyrics are public and collective agents, the principle of lyric subjectivity introduces historicity and polyvocality into the traditional collective legacy of Greek poetry. As such the lyric ontology anticipates the actual dissolution of Archaic culture, foreshadowing the beginnings of the Classical age (to borrow one of Nietzsche's conceits we could say that the radical exponents of the lyric are invariably 'untimely'). But it is misleading to think of lyric reflection as the ideology of individualism in either its classical or modern senses. Lyric's power lies in negating all ideologies, with the exception of the ideology of authentic selfhood. Furthermore, choral lyric is an explicitly *collective* genre concerned with the possibilities of *social* expression. As Bowra emphasizes, the choral poet 'composed for others to sing, and these represented not an individual but a society' (1961: 13). In the earliest appearances of the lyric form we may have left the world of myth and folk-culture, but we are, nonetheless, still within the expressive *habitus* of an Archaic society. It would be more appropriate to say that with the literary discovery of the Rashomon effect in epic dialogue (see Chapter 2 for the centrality of this 'lyric' moment within the epic genre) lyric verse extended the fruitful interplay between the *intentio operis* and the *intentio auctoris*:

> So when the poet speaks of himself or praises his hosts or patrons, he speaks as one who interprets the meaning of the occasion and has behind him the authority of the gods. It is more his public than his private self which speaks.
> (Bowra, 1961: 13)

The *intentio operis* might thus be the will of a god or hero conveyed in the poet's *intentio auctoris*: 'when he spoke in the first person, he was in some sense the god's spokesman, who stated what had to be stated and fulfilled the requirements of the ceremony' (1961: 13). To borrow an expression from the Russian literary theorist, Mikhail Bakhtin, lyric discovered, without necessarily exploiting, the heteroglossial principle of expressive language.

The personalized ethos of early lyric poetry

> The fact that man can have the idea 'I' raises him infinitely above all other beings living on earth. By this he is a *person* and by virtue of his unity of consciousness through all the changes he may undergo, he is one and the same person ... This holds even if he cannot yet say 'I'.
> (Immanuel Kant, 1978)

It is often claimed that the social origins of 'individual expression', the personal sense of being a singular voice with a unique biography, emotional life, and world-view can be traced to the rapid overseas expansion of Greek colonies, trade and warfare in the seventh and sixth centuries. An obsessive concern for the 'I' of personal expression reflected the breakdown of the ancient body-politic, the crisis of the aristocratic order of the late eighth-century, and the first hesitant steps toward a reconstituted political society in the democratic constitutions of the first city-states (Snell, 1953, chapter 3; Bowra, 1961, 9; Murray, 1993, ch. 2).

From this perspective the origins of lyric individualism lie in the disruptive socioeconomic and sociocultural transformations accompanying colonization and the spread of the *polis*-system around the Aegean and Asia Minor. The 'organic' solidarities of myth and folk-culture disintegrated with the appearance of the circuits of exchange value and societal mobility. The advanced form of this 'cultural deconstruction' occurred with the crisis of the late Archaic period. The revolution that destroyed the historical social structure which sustained the Homeric bards and rhapsodes also sapped the possibility of the long narrative poem. When the age of the epic 'passed into another more civically minded' age, 'another means of expression was needed and was found in choral song' (Bowra, 1961: 9). Choral was, so to speak, a half-way house between the collective self of the epic and the individuality of lyric. The reflexive lyricism of the early poets was released by the disruptive impact of a series of wide-ranging social and cultural changes upon traditional forms of life throughout the seventh century ('the epic no longer satisfied all the spiritual needs of men' Bowra, 1961: 9; cf. Fränkel, 1975: 136).

It is unquestionably true that these major institutional changes stimulated the emergence of new forms of aesthetic reflection, encouraging experimentation with unorthodox modes of thought – developments which, when allied to the spread of literacy, led to important literary innovations, one of which we know today as Greek lyric poetry. In this sense the social chaos out of which the *polis* emerged was certainly the *principium individuationis* of early modalities of self-reflection. However, as we have seen in Chapter 2, concern with the self, self-reflection, and self-transformation were already insistent themes in the *Odyssey* and Homeric Hymns. And similar epochal changes were occurring elsewhere in the ancient world without producing anything like a literary revolution. It appears then, that the seed-bed for the new sensibility antedated the rise of the lyric self. We certainly have strong evidence of the interdependence between the new literate instruments of expression and traditional forms of coded experience: the sayable (the *énonciation*) and the experienceable (the *énoncé*) pursuing each other in a resonant interaction. But without prior changes of thought and intellectual culture the energies released by the diffusion of literacy in the late Archaic age would have remained directionless.

In Chapter 3 we have suggested that the ideological attitude of poetic and textual criticism is prior to the existence of the object 'literature' (in the sense that the Hesiodic critique of the Archaic canon placed the question of 'literariness' on the poetic agenda). We are once more confronted by a dialectic of innovation and tradition. The first great exponents of the lyric form not only created new modes of expression and articulation from within the traditional melic genres, but spread the inherited competitive *ethos* of Archaic Greece into the expanding world of textual praxis – contributing to the idea that 'making poetry' is a powerful medium of self-definition. Unlike the collectivist legacy of folk-verse and the anonymous *langue* of ritualized magic, folk-tales, and nature wisdom – forms arizing from the oldest melic institutions of antiquity – lyricism is associated with the primary narcissism of the Greek poetic institution and its obsession with transcending the evanescent moment to remain eternally on the lips of anonymous successors. The lyric poets became, so to speak, the first self-conscious propagandists of verbal reflexivity, creating the practice of 'writing poetry' in something like its modern sense. The lyric genre is thus inseparable from the concept of 'original composition': by means of crafted compositions poets can claim to be literate 'authors', conscious of their role in competing with and, not infrequently, contesting the work of their predecessors.[2] Within the agonistic spirit of preliterate Greece any poet with ambition had self-consciously to innovate – or as we might say, 'dramatize' – their break with the received tradition. The demands of the poetic *agon* created the idea of autonomous poetic *expression* flowing from a uniquely individualized writing *subject*. Somewhat paradoxically, the social radicalism of lyric verse lies in its own rule that it be received as an autonomous poetic *event* separated from the act of enunciation. The production and reproduction of lyric texts began to be crafted as the work of autonomous selves. This further reminds us of the important logological principle of approaching all textual praxis in the context of wider cultural attitudes and social institutions.

The Age of Lyric (*c.* 680 – *c.* 480 BC) traces a crisis of personal experience and institutional life. Lyric's elaboration of a new idea of cultural creativity is premised upon the dissolution of the austere collective forms of social life embodied in the existing genres. By tearing the fabric of Homeric *poiesis* lyric transformed the sensuous life of poetry into the singular vocation of creative language. The sonorous resonances and rhythms of language now became signifying media for further thought and exploration. Inspired by this newfound faith in language, the lyric poets could even return to the declining epic tradition to salvage some of its own experiments with sound and rhythm, retrieving earlier traditions as a repository of lyrical thought (for example by ransacking such 'lyric' passages as the pastoral scenes on the shield of Achilles at *Iliad* 18.692ff., the cave on Calypso's island at *Odyssey* 5.63–72, *Iliad* 14.345ff., *Odyssey* 9.105–43, etc.). We find evidence of this practice in many of the early lyric poets, most emphatically in the work of Archilochus, Semonides, and Stesichorus (see below). By objectifying and transcribing the musical phrases of an earlier poetry, the new idioms of lyric accentuated their singularity as both sonorous pleasure and replicable structure. The act of poetic speech could now be 'frozen' in a permanent verse form and circulated to anonymous audiences. In other words, the experiment in lyric *writing* then appears as a dialectical compromise between the immediate demands of oral attention and the promise of aesthetic objectivity. By grasping lyric's active role in the decline of oral composition we can modify Aristotle's well-known claim by saying that poetry strives to know the universal *through* the particular (*Poetics* 1451b6) – in Adorno's words, to attain universality through unrestrained individuation.

No doubt the original polemic that created the praxis of lyric expression continues *within* the institution of poetry to the present day. Once poetry can be *transcribed*, the treasury of myths and 'divine knowledge' can be plundered for poetic *topoi* and metaphorical figures; once verse is available as a text to be read, the poet can combine, amalgamate, permutate and, it should be said, *alter* and *ironize* the mythological tradition in response to needs that are uniquely generated by written communication and its new audiences. The poet in effect becomes a writing subject within an intertextual circuit of literate producers, readers, and critics. With the erosion of primary orality, the beginnings of a cumulative tradition of 'literary criticism' becomes possible. The technology of alphabetic writing is thus dialectically implicated in the differentiation of poetic genres which literary historians bracket under the general category of 'lyric'. In the historical invention of literature the 'trial of Homer' by writers like Archilochus and Hipponax should be understood as a constitutive condition of the logic of lyric expression. A similar point has been made by Vernant:

> When works are written down, even when they continue to be sung or recited at appointed times, the specifically literary features of the text gain emphasis while at the same time the genres of expression become diversified, each with its own public and its own formal rules and aesthetic aims. Elegiac, lyric, and tragic poets all draw on the common stock of mythology; but while creating literature out of mythical themes, they treat these themes with great freedom, adapting them to fit their needs and sometimes even attacking them in the name of some new ethical or religious ideal.
>
> (1990: 212)

The subject – whether composer or reader – does not use the lyric form for expressive purposes; rather lyric form creates new kinds of subjectivity (lyric textuality prefigures a society of 'authors', a reading public, an industry of transcribers, a circle of critics, and so on). In the terminology of Volume 1, the technopoeic possibilities of writing create new modes of literary intersubjectivity. In the case of early Greek poetry a well-developed analytic attitude toward the received forms of speech and song was a necessary precondition for the construction of the object 'literature' as a mobile signifier and form of cultural capital (we should emphasize the importance of the development of a market for 'texts' that followed the institutionalization of literary production in the Greek world at this period). We can see this process at work in the appearance of textual self-reference which accompanies lyric expression from about 650 BC onwards. It is already fully developed in such works as the *Hymn to Apollo* ('farewell, son of Zeus and Leto; but I will remember you again in another song'), the *Hymn to Demeter* ('I begin to sing of rich-haired Demeter...') and the *Hymn to Pan* ('Muse, tell me about Pan, the dear son of Hermes, with his goat's feet and two horns'). And here the decisive intellectual changes occurred prior to the rise of the *polis*.

It is important to underline the fact that 'poetry' – the different forms and modes of verbal *mimesis* in the European canon – evolved to become one of the first important vehicles of *collective* reflection. And that lyric in particular was perhaps the first influential practice to fuse the collective ethos of early Greek cultural life with the individualism of affective self-reflection. The seminal importance of hybridization can be appreciated if we compare the barren inventories of the Mycenaean bureaucrats or the monumental signs of contemporaneous legal statutes with the sensuous tone poems of Sappho or the bitter literary ironies of Archilochus. Each of these 'orders of semiopraxis' expresses a radically different vision of social life and cultural expression.

Where the Mycenaean tablets 'index' the power of the palace monarchies and the Law tablets intone the virtues of civic legality, the verses of Sappho celebrate the conflicting affective demands of the everyday. Perhaps the earliest Greeks, as with the earliest phases of many cultures, first expressed their 'sense of self' in song and only later pursued more prosaic cultural forms. Whatever the ultimate origins of expressive art, it is undoubtedly the complex culture of lyric discourse which created one of the more enduring forms of self-consciousness – precursor of later Greek experiments in verbal self-reflection and *katharsis*. What were the decisive motives for the emergence of lyric *mimesis* in ancient Greece?

The triumph of the lyric: choral and monodic forms

The formative period of lyric poetry spans the period from the middle of the seventh century to the end of the fifth century. Histories of early Greek literature distinguish between the essentially religious tradition of *choral* lyric and *monody* (or monodic lyric). While both forms of *mimesis* were originally accompanied by choral dance and the lyre (hence the adjective 'lyric'), choral song was usually restricted to more liturgical and religious occasions, where they were performed in a collective, celebratory style (what might be called *liturgical discourse*), while lyric verse liberated itself from ritual festivals to experiment with a diverse range of individual emotions, moods, rhythmic forms, and themes, not exclusively 'religious' or 'liturgical' in character. In these respects the *Kunstsprache* of the *Iliad* and *Odyssey* paved the way. The 'middle ground' between these two types of *mimesis* would later be colonized by Greek tragic drama which initially tried to synthesize the choral and lyric elements of early Greek verbal culture.

The elegiac lyric of Archilochus, Alcaeus, Sappho, and Mimnermus, for example, self-consciously departed from the older traditions of liturgical song to produce new forms of *personal* expression, performance by *recitation*, a foregrounding of self-related experiences, the exploration of such extreme emotions and mental states as love, happiness, madness, jealousy, loss, nostalgia, bitterness, and melancholy. In stark contrast to choral epic the elegiac form displays a preference for shorter stanzas and condensed 'concrete' symbolism and metaphor – lyric being in many ways the paradigmatic fragmentary genre of inchoate moods and sensibilities; the lyric voice embraced the value-axis of particularism – the singular ethos of the *factum* – as against the grave 'objectivity' and serious 'universality' of the epic genre. This is marked in its stylistic preference for episodic and occasional verse forms; and as lyric evolves throughout the sixth century, an increasing focus on landscape and natural phenomena, concrete everyday objects, and mundane events. Ironically, lyric's 'particularism' is precisely the feature which allowed it to spread throughout the Greek-speaking world. As it moved further and further away from its roots in folk-verse, elegiac poetry would finally dispense with the lyre and musical accompaniment to become one of the first 'transportable' aesthetic objects.

The disjunctive features of the elegy had the effect of 'bracketing' the traditional understanding of sacred verse (and implicitly its social and institutional *chora*) and helped to expand the field of musical *mimesis*. The space opened by this new medium created a site for something like 'biographical reflection' as the expressive medium of selfhood. The traditional image of the oral performer was now split into that of the composing 'author' and the poetic *persona* internal to the poetic text. Above all, the lyric poets were the first great explorers of the logic of mimetic space itself – imagining and inventing different modalities of 'imitation' in an adversarial struggle with the inherited canons and traditions of choral verse. In its first appearances lyric may well have been the 'play form' of epic verse. But this is not to say that lyric 'corrects' or 'remedies' the austerity of the *epos*; lyric evokes another form of life that is hardly imaginable within the monumental discourse of the epic. The new *chora* is the open domain of personal consciousness, a site of multiple 'voices' (as many in principle as the imagined *personae* granted expression). This is the coded message of the ancient *Contest of Homer and Hesiod* (see Hesiod, 1914: 567–97). While the thirty-three extant Homeric hymns (dating from between 650 and 400 BC) still represent the collective voice of tradition, with lyric we have a plural ontology of different sites of self-experience. As C. M. Bowra observed, the genre of the single short lyric poem was for the Greeks an 'incomparable medium for getting to know their own emotions'.[3] Lyric, in short, is an organon rather than a reflection of experience.

It is important that the reflexive 'turn' toward the personal self should not be construed in a psychological or mentalistic manner. Instead, the generic innovation should be understood in logological terms as defining new technical possibilities for the (re)presentation of self and language. Lyric's 'immanent critique' of the Homeric epic is displayed immediately in its deviation from the stylistic and musical demands of the hexameter verse form. It represented an immanent criticism of a generic possibility already implicit in the older language-games of epic: in logological terms, lyric began as a parasitic discourse within the body of the Homeric epic. The corollary of this, of course, is that the epic survived in the lyric as a 'negated resource' of archival symbols – for example, in the inverted form of the Sapphic epic of everyday existence or the mock epic qualities in the Pindaric ode. The polemic in question should be traced to the expressive codes and symbolic matrices of lyric heteroglossia, rather than ascribed to a change in the 'personality' of individual poets. Paradoxically, the construction of forms of personal experience presupposed new modes of public expression for feelings and attitudes that were systematically excluded from the earlier choral canon. And for traditionalists the very idea of lyric was perceived as a fatally flawed *aufhebung* of the great stream of epic verse.

To see these discursive struggles at work we must explore in more detail some of the dialectical tensions that lyric expression created within the received Hellenic canon.

2 CHORAL LYRIC: FROM COLLECTIVE TO INDIVIDUAL FORMS OF SELF-REFLECTION

The experience of self-reflection was not wholly absent from choral poetry and liturgical language; but it tended to take a predominantly collective and impersonal form, as we might expect given that the cultural functions of chorodic poetry were defined initially by the requirements of ceremonial praxis and, in the latter part of the Archaic period, by the mimetic needs of the *polis*. The continuum of choradic *mimesis* included a range of relatively well-defined subgenres:

- the funeral or commemorative dirge (*threnody*, or the Homeric *linos*);
- the maiden-songs or *parthenia*;
- the *Paian* (*paean*) or hymns honouring the god Apollo;
- the wedding or nuptial song (*hymenaios*);
- the mimetic-narrative dance (*hyporchema*);
- the processional song (*prosodion*);
- the carnivalesque song or *dithyramb* (honouring Dionysus);
- the song of praise or *enkomion*.[4]

As a public religious institution the fate of the choral lyric is inextricably tied to the cultural viability of specific forms of life – among the most important being the aristocratic kin system and the 'tyrant' patronage institutions of the early *polis*. And as the traditional aristocratic power structures were eroded so the choral lyric tended to give way to other musical forms – a process accelerated by the differentiation and dissemination of the Homeric *hymnos* – most notably to the elegy and personal lyric and, later, to the genres we know as 'tragic drama', 'comedy', and the sceptical *logos* of the first philosophers and sophists. The decades from the beginning to the middle of the fifth century appear to have been the decisive turning point in this process of poetic delegitimation; the change did not occur as a sudden collapse or disappearance of traditional genres, but rather appears as a discontinuous evolution of different elements and formations already at work within the older culture (for instance these changes proceeded most rapidly at Athens, but were effectively resisted in the more traditional centres of Sparta, Argos, and Thebes – city-states which also blocked innovations in musical techniques that had been accepted elsewhere in the sixth century). However, even the most conservative city-states were subject to the slow attrition of the new culture of reflexivity: among the most important forces involved in this erosion of 'choral culture' being the secularization and politicization of the pan-Hellenic festivals, the dissociation of the various elements of choral culture (dance, music, and poetry) and their development into 'professional' concerns, and the displacement of the traditional 'Dorian' chorus with its stately balanced rhymic structures ('the golden mean') by new forms of expression:

> More than almost any other literary form, choral lyric is bound up with the values of city and clan in a world where things changed slowly. By 450 the tyrants and aristocratic families which had commissioned the odes of Pindar and Bacchylides were gone or endangered, their values threatened by the fast-rising power of Athenian democracy. By the last quarter of the century the festivals which provided the occasion for choral song were losing their religious basis. The power politics of the latter half of the fifth century, the scepticism and rationalism brought by the sophistic enlightenment, the disruption of the Peloponnesian War, and the rapid social and cultural changes which these movements precipitated were all inimical to the old poetry... Choral lyric implied a stable community founded on universally shared religious and moral beliefs, well established rituals and firm traditions. By the midpoint of the century these old values were no longer unquestioned. Tragic drama rather than the genre of lyric poetry *per se* expressed the forces and tensions of greatest concern to the thinking and feeling men of the day'.[5]

Elegiac lyrical reflexivity

We have seen that one important index of generic change was the shift of emphasis away from the austere values embodied in the liturgical forms of aristocratic choral culture. Where the older patronage system had commissioned poets to 'imitate' and celebrate their own power and authority, monodic experimentation openly embraced local concerns, individual desires, and heteronomous themes.

The change in metrical form was also reflected in a change in musical structure – with all the social implications this entailed for a culture saturated with a sense of the importance of musical form (see note 5 above). Where choral poetry celebrated stable systems of symbols and myths threaded like pearls across its harmonious rhythms and balanced clauses, the lyric poets manipulated the texts of antiquity and introduced new and idiosyncratic rhythmic patterns. They advanced the cause of a new music, a non-Dorian sense of language's sonorous rhythms, and a more innovative relationship to the traditional canon. The demands of lyric performance could no longer be contained within the choral frames of the sixth century. In terms of the structure of the traditional genres the 'messages' the lyric poets tried to articulate were definitionally transgressive – where is the affective self within the rules of the threnody or paian?

Where chorodic poetry was strictly tied to its ceremonial occasions, lyric poetry was 'mobilized' by the promiscuous medium of alphabetic script (stimulated by an increase in travel and contact with non-Hellenic cultures).

The 'monologic' voice of the *threnody, paian, hymenaios*, and *enkomium* gave way to the playful, dialogic *voices* of the dithyramb, autobiographical reflection, the dissembling mime and erotic satyr play, the lampoon and even, as in Archilochus' and Theognis' bitter texts, satire and social criticism. The discovery made by these poets was that writing could be used not only to record political life, but also to question political arrangements. Writing could *subvert* as well as *subserve* power. Even the sound patterns of language and semantic unities were not safe from the spirit of verbal deconstruction (in this sense lyric verse was the precursor of all subsequent language play from Heraclitus to the *Cratylus* and beyond). As later Greek critics bewailed, the Doric order and rhythmical proportion of the lyre was increasingly displaced by the temptations and anarchy of the flute (*aulos*). Lyric can thus be understood as the codification of new social forms of desire, political experimentation, and 'heteroglossial' forms of subjectivity. In Northrop Frye's terminology, the epic hero of the high *mimetic* mode gave way to the quotidian 'anti-hero' of the *ironic* mode. In more sociological terms, lyric was one of the long-term products of the 'pan-Hellenization' of poetry and song:

> The local community's public self-esteem, in order to live up to the proper degree of admiration both from outside and consequently from within, must seek the least occasional and most catholic aspects of its seasonally recomposed choral self-presentation. The impulse of pan-Hellenism in Archaic Greece begins at home.
> (Nagy, 1989: 51)

Certainly, as far as the genesis of reflexivity is concerned, this shift marks a decisive phase in the history of subjectivity, an epochal revolution which still echoes in the poetry of Villon, Rimbaud, Verlaine, and Mallarmé.

> An important factor may have been the evolution of the aulos, which increased the available range of melody and facilitated modulation. String-players, too, envious of the freedom of their fellows, added strings to the cithara. Furthermore, the balance of importance between choir and instrumentalist began to change. The chief factor, however, was mental rather than technical. Individualism was in the air and convention suspect; and the interpreter of tradition intimately associated with religion became a virtuoso bent upon giving pleasure to an audience. Thus variety took the place of simplicity: the melodic range was extended, modulation (and perhaps vocal and instrumental embellishments) cultivated; rhythmical structure became freer; the poetry mattered less in comparison with the melody.
> (*Oxford Classical Dictionary*: 711)

In short, the parasitic music of lyrical form displaced the epic content of traditional poetry.

Symptomatically we find the name of the poet appearing as a phrase within the lyric form (for example with Hesiod, Hipponax, Theognis (19–24), and Phocylides of Miletus (c. 544/41) (*'kai tode Phokilides'* – 'Phocylides said this also...' or 'And this is by Phocylides')). Where the strict rhythms of traditional genres were anonymous, ritualistic, and collectivist, the rules of lyric reflection are personal, prosaic, and individualistic. We are confronted by the first signed literary compositions. The opening of this discursive front in Archaic Greek popular culture is, I wish to claim, the material site for a radically individualist tradition of reflexive praxis – exemplified in a new spirit of free expression and linguistic experiment. Not accidentally this 'opening' is associated with the region that formed the bridgehead between East and West – the city-states of Asia Minor and the islands off the Anatolian coast. The lyric poet's invitation – 'I wish to speak to you of ...' – inaugurates a new space for authored discourse – the language of personal confrontation, biographical immediacy, confession, and ironic experience; a new 'music' appropriate to a change of technique and cultural sensibility. In short, lyric articulates the first phenomenology of the local spatial and temporal settings of affectivity.

By colonizing these new poetic spaces the lyric poets were responsible to a new commitment: 'In the compression of images and signs I will tell you of *my* experiences.' We can imagine an Archilochus or a Sappho uttering the words of another great lyricist: *'Hear me! For I am such and such a person. Above all, do not mistake me for someone else!'* On the side of literary reception, lyric individualizes its audience as it articulates and universalizes personal experience. These shifts in cultural sensibility are particularly emphatic in the form known as the *elegiac lyric*:

> Elegiac poetry in Greek means not poetry of a particular mood or subject, but poetry composed in elegiac couplets: a line of six feet followed by a line of five feet, both lines consisting of feet that are either dactyls or spondees or part of a spondee. Originally elegiac couplets were written for the flute (*elegos*) and so got their name. But soon elegiac couplets were used for other kinds of poem, and from being sung at banquets came to be engraved on tombs. They continued to be written in Greek for many centuries and were to be the form of some of the finest Latin love poetry by Catullus, Propertius, and Tibullus'.[6]

In what follows we will view the evolution of this hybrid genre of alternating dactylic hexameter with pentameter verse (the elegiac distich in Archilochus, Callinus, Mimnermus, Tyrtaeus, Solon, Xenophanes, and others) as a 'technique of reflection', made possible by the expansion of an even more powerful technology of reflection – the alphabetic objectification of meaning and information placed in the hands of ever-widening circles of individuals. The scriptural form, as it were, becomes a material embodiment of new possibilities of affective self-reflection. We will follow this sociological argument inside the metric organization and text of the elegiac lyric itself: the *structural form* of the elegiac couplet – either by design or unintentionally –

encouraged the cultivation of *personal* self-reflection, providing a more flexible and 'democratic' medium than either the traditional epic hexameter (of the *Iliad, Odyssey*, and *Theogony*) or the liturgical discourse of popular choral praxis. The elegiac couplet precipitated two related experiential modalities: a new precision and phenomenological sense of the concreteness of articulated experience, opening up new descriptive, narrative possibilities, and a symbolic site in which the Homeric epic stream was temporarily stilled, making personal 'thought' and 'dialogue' with the terms and grammar of that 'stream' possible. In this latter respect elegiac lyric facilitated another unique 'institution of reflexivity' – the sociosymbolic 'space' of personal meditation and critical thought – the inner dialogue of the self with itself that is a precondition for any critical appraisal of tradition: 'A continuous flow of hexameter verse sweeps the mind onward with it; in the elegiac couplet, the effect of the pentameter is to give a meditative pause, a moment of reflection – inviting our thought to return upon itself'.[7]

As Trypanis observes:

The unit of composition was no longer the paragraph but the couplet, a change which allowed the poet to express himself on a scale smaller than that of the unrestricted periods of the old epic style ... the elegiac couplet lies half-way between the free epic style and lyric monody.

(1981: 87)

This sociological, aesthetic, and logological innovation opens up a suggestive hypothesis for those trying to 'excavate' the sociocultural genealogy of discursive reflexivity: the elegiac couplet provided a suitable vehicle for poetic experiments in critical thought and expression marking the transitional age of Archaic culture, 'an age of gradual transition from monarchy to democracy, an age of enterprise and discovery, of colonization and commerce, when fresh interests and widening experience stimulated individual thought and feeling'.[8] It created a more complex differentiation of discursive *roles* and *practices* which laid the symbolic foundations for the late sixth and fifth-century development of 'critical discourse': writing elegiac poetry schooled an audience to more critical attitudes toward traditional practices. Lyric is one important voice created by the expansion of 'democratic' speech which loosened the stranglehold of aristocratic tradition. And here it is primarily a matter of verbal codes and vocabularies rather than 'mental' experience: the elegiac form became an indispensable medium of the personal self. It was not so much that new *individuals* searched and found the elegiac couplet, rather the semantic grammar of the elegiac verse form created the possibilities of new forms of individuality. To put the matter simply, the lyric form offered itself as a constitutive means for more differentiated literary roles. Here the conclusions of Gregory Nagy are relevant. Speaking of the evolution of different patterns of composition and performance he writes:

These different patterns reveal different models for the distinction or potential distinction of performer and poet. By now we may note not only the model of the *rhapsoidoi* in the realm of poetry but also the various different models of *kitharoidoi, auloidoi, tragoidoi,* and *komoidoi* in the realm of song. In all these models, the common point of departure is that the *persona* of the composer can be re-enacted by the performer or performers ... the performer may impersonate the composer as well as the characters represented as speaking within the composition. The word for such re-enactment or impersonation, to repeat, is *mimesis*.

(1989: 62–3)

3 FROM CHORAL LYRIC TO MONODY: THE SOCIAL CONSTRUCTION OF THE INDIVIDUAL LYRIC VOICE

The 'democratizing' logic of individual reflexivity provides a clue to the long-term shift from choral lyric in the seventh century to monody and individualized poetry in the sixth century. As one historian has remarked, an important feature of the rise of seventh-century lyric is

the fact that its practitioners were often drawn from other walks of life, notably the political and the military professions: Terpander of Lesbos, a pioneer of the lyre, had been summoned to Sparta, traditionally as early as 676 BC to play a statesman's role in settling political disputes there ... Tyrtaios and Kallinos were particularly concerned with the citizen as a soldier; Tyrtaios might have been equally well fitted by the description which Archilochos gave of himself, as first a servant of the war-god and then a poet'.[9]

Tyrtaeus of Sparta

It is appropriate to begin with one of the most important transitional figures of this period, the elegiac poet Tyrtaeus (Tyrtaios), whose poetic activity coincided with the twenty-year struggle for hegemony launched by the Spartans which history records as the Second Messenian War (c. 650 BC). An early tradition made him an Athenian called to Sparta sometime in the middle of the seventh century (the Suda lexicon for example). According to later writers he played a central role in reforming the educational system of the Spartans (Lycurgus, *Against Leocrates* 106–8; Paus. 4.15.3). He also served the Spartans as one of their generals in the campaigns to forcibly impose Spartan authority upon Messene (Strabo 8.4.10).

Tyrtaeus appears to have been at his most productive in the latter half of the seventh century. Ironically the very success of these protracted campaigns transformed Sparta from a relatively open and intellectually creative civilization in the seventh century into the inward-looking, collectivist, militarized society that was to play such a decisive role in the development of ancient Greek culture in the sixth and fifth centuries: the civilization Tyrtaeus celebrated and preserved in his poetry would eventually destroy the material and intellectual preconditions of the poetic culture he exemplified; and perhaps the seeds of this inversion are already implicit in the overriding militaristic purposes of Tyrtaeus' poetic vocation.

Tyrtaeus can be understood as the lyrical voice of the hoplite phalanx. Many historians have seen his poetry as the most important literary source of both the workings of the hoplite phalanx in Sparta and the progressive conquest of Messenia using these new 'shock-troops' in the seventh century (e.g. Andrewes, 1956: 18–19; Huxley, 1962: 34, 36; Oliva, 1981: 172; Murray, 1993: ch. 8, esp. 132–6). He is also said to have written a *Politeia* ('Politics') and *Eunomia* ('Good Order') extolling the Spartan virtues of the self-governing city-state (Aristotle, *Politics* 1306b40). His martial poems praise the Lacedaimonian virtues (*aretai*) of the Spartan military spirit – valour, order, discipline, obedience – and they were reputedly sung at banquets during campaigns or performed when marshalling for an armed assault against an opposed hoplite square ('For Tyrtaeus left them elegiac poems by his own hand, and through listening to these they are trained to be brave' Lycurgus, *Against Leocrates* 106–7; also Plato, *Laws* 629B and Suda lexicon):

> no man ever proves himself a good man (*aner agathos*) in war unless he can endure to face the blood and the slaughter, go close against the enemy and fight with his hands. Here is 'goodness' (*arete*, courage), mankind's finest possession, here is the noblest prize that a young man can endeavour to win, and it is a good thing his city and all the people share with him when a man plants his feet and stands in the foremost spears relentlessly, all thought of foul flight completely forgotten, and has well trained his heart to be steadfast and to endure, and with words encourages the man who is stationed beside him ... And he who so falls among the champions and loses his sweet life, so blessing with honor his city, his father, and all his people, with wounds in his chest, where the spear that he was facing has transfixed.
>
> (Lattimore, trans., 1960: 14)

In Tyrtaeus' order of values, military valour and courage within the collective phalanx hold pride of place. The *polis* must first and foremost be a justly proportioned *cosmos*. *Arete* – the skills and capacities required to become *agathos* – are rooted in the cooperative virtues of organized warfare – but these are no longer the individual military skills of the Homeric warrior but the martial skills required by the collective operations of the self-moving phalanx: self-discipline, bravery, steadiness under attack and defence, resilience, and so on. But while composing elegies to courage and the military values of the *polis*, Tyrtaeus' voice still belongs to the 'choral' ideal of the public virtues of a noble society: second only to a victorious struggle against the city's enemies, the noble ideal is to die in a life-and-death struggle ('You should reach the limits of virtue before you cross the border of death', trans. Barnstone, 1972: 40; cf. Heraclitus DK B 24). And nobility in death is not an individual achievement exemplified by the single combat struggles of the *Iliad*, but a collectively sanctioned *role*, an ideal public and thus 'political' death:

> Our man should be disciplined in the work of the heavy fighter, and not stand out from the missiles when he carries a shield, but go right up and fight at close quarters and, with his long spear or short sword, thrust home and strike his enemy down. Let him fight toe to toe and shield against shield hard driven, crest against crest and helmet on helmet, chest against chest; let him close hard and fight it out with his opposite foeman, holding tight to the hilt of his sword, or to his long spear. And you, O light-armed fighters, from shield to shield of your fellows dodge for protection and keep steadily throwing great stones, and keep on pelting the enemy with your javelins, only remember always to stand near your own heavy-armed men.
> (Lattimore, trans., 1960: 16)

It is also important to observe that this 'choral' element in the transitional genre developed by Tyrtaeus (the martial elegy) persisted in Spartan culture down into the fifth century; after a relatively short-lived but brilliant experiment in lyric art and music, Spartan civilization returned to the collectivist semiotics of the choral ode.[10]

Alcman of Sparta

Counterbalanced against the iron is the sweet lyre-playing.
(Lattimore, trans., 1960: 36)

Where Tyrtaeus' lyrics and Terpander's musical innovations were attuned to the disciplined rhythms and values of military life and no doubt provided direct ideological self-interpretations for the Spartan state and its ruling class, the later Spartan poet, Alcman (*c.* mid-seventh century) turned away from the martial elegy and patriotic discourse to explore the flexible possibilities of the new elegiac form. Tyrtaeus' hymns to the hoplite phalanx and Spartan patriotism are replaced by songs of the joys of life, love, music, and the fragile presence of beauty – the so-called Virgin-songs or *Parthenia*. A radically personal tone enters the choral form or the *Partheneion* as Alcman leads his audience away from the public arena of noble life and death to the 'inconsequentialities' of personal experience, pleasure, and desire. The particular setting of the poem places the reader before the concrete situation of Alcman's *mimesis*: 'Look, beside me sings my friend, my cousin, of the ankles small: Agido and she commend alike our ceremonial. Immortals, who possess the end of every action, hear their call with favour, as their voices blend' (trans. Bowra).

> I must praise the
> light of Agido. I see
> her like the sun, whose shining
> on us is witnessed through Agido.

The grave accents of the Dorian liturgy and solemn choral ode are mitigated by the consciously crafted 'lightness' of the *aperçu*. 'Here we are, you and I, on this summer morning, observing, experiencing, desiring the youth of these playing girls.' Alcman's poetic *persona* appears in the role of an ageing Self separated from the radiant sphere of youth, beauty, and pleasure. Alcman's poetic message is *carpe diem*, live for today; savour the moment before it vanishes forever. The beauty of Hagesichora – the leader of the chorus – and Agido are more important than life itself: 'O girls of honey-sweet voices, my limbs are weak. They will not bear me. I wish, ah, I wish I were a carefree kingfisher flying over flowering foam with the halcyons – sea-blue holy birds of spring' (trans. Barnstone, 1972: 52).

Alcman's delicacy of touch and playfulness were no doubt appreciated by his circle of Spartan patrons in an age before the more serious demands of Spartan expansion and military hegemony.[11] He is not above celebrating the most humble objects of everyday life, producing condensed images of striking simplicity and power:

> Often at night along the mountain tops, when gods are revelling by torch light, you came carrying a great jar (like one shepherds use) but of heavy gold. You filled the jar with milk drawn from a lioness, and made a great cheese unbroken and gleaming white.
>
> (trans. Barnstone, 1972: 47)

But in the history of lyric consciousness Alcman's intense focus on natural phenomena and symbols proved to be his most important contribution to poetic reflexivity. Of the earliest Greek poets (*c.* 650–630) he is one of the first to use nature as both a topic and resource of poetic description – influencing later poets such as Theocritus (the *Idylls* written *c.* 275–260 BC) and Virgil (the *Eclogues* and *Georgics*). In this respect Alcman can be said to have inaugurated the pastoral tradition of 'lyricizing' nature as an auratic, salutary landscape – 'the mountain of Rhipae, blossoming with forests, the breast of black night':

> And the mountain-peaks are asleep and the ravines, the headlands and the torrent-beds, all the creeping tribes that the black earth nourishes, the wild animals of the mountains, the race of bees and the monsters of the depths of the surging sea; and the tribes of long-winged birds are asleep.
>
> (trans. Campbell, 1982: vol. 2, 455, 457)

Archilochus

With Archilochus, a contemporary of Tyrtaeus, we meet the first fully reflexive, *personal* poet in the Western canon.[12]

Archilochus was the son of a Thracian slave-woman named Enipo; his father, Telesicles, appears to have been a leading figure – perhaps an aristocrat – in the city-state of Paros in the Aegean and an individual of some importance in founding the Parian colony of Thasos in the 680s; but by being born outside the strict marital framework of his society, Archilochus was juridically destined to be displaced to the margins of the aristocratic circles of his native city (cf. Burn, 1960: 161–2); this may also explain why he was forced to earn his living as a mercenary soldier – becoming one of the earliest examples of the nomadic poet-soldier in Western literature. Traditionally Archilochus is supposed to have died fighting as a mercenary. After his death a sanctuary or cult to his memory was established at Paros.

Given that he was born at the beginning of the seventh century we may date his iambic and elegiac poetry to the middle of the seventh century, perhaps forty years before the work of Alcaeus and Sappho (born *c.* 630 BC). It is thus Archilochus rather than the Mytilene poets who first explored the 'individual voice' or *persona* as a poetic device; in this respect he extended some of the reflexive practices institutionalized by the writers of the Homeric epics, the choral tradition, and Hesiod's self-publicizing literary activities. How much – or how little – these poets knew of one another's work remains a controversial topic in ancient Greek literary history.

Not the least of Archilochus' revolutionary experiments in personal reflexivity were his considerable innovations in the art of *writing* personal poetry, his commitment to sublimate his thwarted inheritance by creating his own *literary* celebrity; reading the remains of his corpus we have little doubt that he set his face firmly against the 'dominant' cultural forms, experimenting with the new iambic metre of lyric expression. He also began to write poetry as a way of attacking and scandalizing known individuals (Lycambes and his daughters, Glaucus son of Leptines, etc.). The effectiveness of such attacks, of course, depended upon an effective medium of literary dissemination. In this way Archilochus became one of the first great *writers* of the lyric form.[13]

Unlike the author of the *Iliad* or the martial poet Tyrtaeus, Archilochus' attitude to war and its martial values is highly pragmatic and anti-Homeric: war is simply one way of surviving and making a living in the volatile world of the warring Archaic city-states; he either ignores altogether or openly flaunts the idealized heroic code of the epic – best exemplified in his poem occasioned by the loss of a shield while campaigning with the Thasians against a Thracian tribe in the far north of the Greek world: 'Some Saian glories in a shield – which I abandoned under a bush; but I saved myself from death, so what does it matter? Let that shield go; I can get another one equally good' (Fr. 5).

Archilochus' use of the personal voice is frequently and not without reason taken as documentary evidence for a new individualism spreading with Parian colonization in the latter half of the seventh century; some have read his vernacular poetry as a vehicle of anti-traditional forces within Archaic Greek civilization itself – the 'I' in the poem becomes, as it were, a heroic expression of individual experience, the authority of concrete individuality and everyday speech consciously pitted against epic values and their artificial literary and ideological codes. To articulate his idiosyncratic experience of the world he could no longer write in the traditional dactylic hexameter. Thus he chose to write in iambic metre rather than the traditional hexameter of the Homeric epic.[14] Choosing iambic metre *in this context* constituted a social and political as well as a poetic act: 'They wrote for themselves and their friends, and they used a language which was closely related to their ordinary talk' (Bowra, 1961: 14).

While such generalizations must remain speculative, we can justifiably infer the emergence of more individual modes of reflection and reflexivity from the texts attributed to this unique poet. If we can make allowances for the distinction between Archilochus the poet and 'Archilochus' the '*I-persona*' of many of his poems, it is evident that the self-reflexive literary 'speaking Self' begins its long history with couplets such as:

> I am two things: a fighter who follows the God of Battles, and one who understands the gift of the Muse's love.

> By spear is kneaded the bread I eat, by spear my Ismaric wine is won, which I drink, leaning upon my spear'.[15]

Archilochus is undoubtedly the poet of the opening 'I am', and we may take his foregrounding of Self in Fragment 1 as one of his fundamental inventions ('I am the servant of the God of Battles [the lord Ares]; and I know well the lovely gift of the Muses'). The Archilochean Self also steps forward as the source of the first 'complaint' in Western literature (cf. Aristotle, *Poetics* 1449a and 1448b23):

> I don't like the towering captain with the spraddly length of leg, one who swaggers in his lovelocks and clean shaves beneath the chin. Give me a man short and sparse set upon his legs, a man full of heart, not to be shaken from the place he plants his feet.
>
> (Fr. 114)

His individualized, realistic perception of events and places is equally impressive in some of the surviving fragments of his work which often have the freshness and directness of the Japanese *haiku*:

LYRIC REFLEXIVITIES

On boredom

> What breaks me,
> Young friend,
> Is tasteless desire,
> Dead iambics,
> Boring dinners.
>> (Archilochus, Fr. 249, in
>> Davenport, trans., 1964)

On the City of Thasos

All the griefs of all the Hellenes came together in this place.
(Lattimore, trans., 1960: 4)

On the landscape of Thasos

This place sticks up like a donkey's back, crowned with wild woods. There is no good land here, nor lovely nor desirable, as around the streams of Siris.

Desire

Significantly the poet's 'object of Desire' is a named, historical person, the daughter of Lycambes, Neoboule:

> As with a leafy myrtle-spray she played
> And a sweet rose, and her long tresses made
> Over her shoulders and her back a shade ...
> her scented breast and hair above;
> Even an old man would have fallen in love!

> O that I might touch Neoboule's hand.

> Say goodbye to Paros, and the figs, and the seafaring life.

> For Gyges' gold I do not care;
> I do not envy him, nor dare
> High heaven, nor lust for power of kings (*tyrannis*);
> Far from my eyes are all such things.

The poetic representation of a named individual corroborates the claim that Archilochus' text was moving toward a more self-conscious ideological individualism ('Thus in Archilochus we see the first shift of Greek poetry from Hesiod's comprehensive attack on womankind to the satire of individual women, an important further move towards the new individualism', Trypanis, 1981: 84).

LYRIC REFLEXIVITIES

On war

The War-God is the same for all.

Of seven who fell, whom we overtook by running, a thousand were we the slayers!

On death

Thick was the foam about his lips.

On fate

[R]ejoice in times of joy, and in reverses, sorrow then, Not Too Much; but understand the tide that rules the lives of men.

On lice

Tickled by lice.

The 'haiku-like' couplet also extended to aphoristic verse, the most famous and most-quoted example from Archilochus is the epigram:

The fox knows many things, the hedgehog one big one.

The use of iambic verse as an instrument of personalized invective allied with the direct, earthy and critical orientation of its message made Archilochus the natural choice for later historians tracing the sources of satirical and comedic verse (even the staunch Herodotus has a word for 'Archilochus of Paros', 1.12). The fundamental rule of satire, a heightened sense of aggrieved selfhood incarnated in an explicit semiotic 'self-conception' or critical poetic voice, is part of Archilochus' legacy. The influence of his satirical attack on the pomposity of the high-and-mighty, the conduct of war, and idealized military virtues can still be felt in the comic theatre of Aristophanes. Indeed in the second act of Aristophanes' comedy *Peace*, the motifs of the Chorus and Chorus leader (1129–84) are taken directly from Archilochus's writings (also cf. 1291ff. where Archilochus' lines on the abandoned shield are recycled; cf. *Birds* 967–88).

The popularism of his shorter poems is also in tune with the new sensibilities of the early sixth-century world. Without the insistent and often 'aggrieved' edge of the 'I am', the development of later satirical verse and comedy is unthinkable. For instance, the idiom of ignominious failure and complaint has no place in the discursive formation of epic poetry. No epic hero ever seriously complains about his lot – or doubts the absolute claims of honour and military solidarity. Like the demotic authority-pricking figures of Aristophanic comedy or the wily slaves of Menander's domestic theatre, Archilochus' hero is the Good Soldier Schweik of the ancient world – the eternal survivor and pragmatist who will gladly lose his shield to save his life. Where Archilochus was parodying the warrior code, Aristophanes' anti-heroes literally shit upon the 'noble' armour of war and, by implication, the values and institutions of warfare (*Peace* 1239ff.). Horace quite justifiably highlights Archilochus' satiric inventions in his work *On the Art of Poetry*:

> Archilochus invented the iambic measure as the weapon for furious satire; it was adopted both for comedy and for high tragedy, since it is appropriate for dialogue, is capable of drowning the noises of the audience, and is by its nature well suited to accompany action'.[16]

Perhaps Horace had in mind such urbane confessions of human weakness as Archilochus' poem on the shipboard watch:

> Along the rowers' bench bring your cup,
> And lift the lids of the big wine-jars up
> And drain the good, red wine; we can't 'tis clear,
> Be sober all the time we're watching here.
> (Fr. 4, in Burn, 1960: 163)

or the epigrammatic advice contained in the lines:

> That man, my friend, who cares what people say
> Will not find many pleasures come his way.

or his 'all-too-human' reaction to a personal affront:

> One great thing I know: how to repay with bitter wrong wrongs done to me.

If iambic trimeter provided one of the formal preconditions for 'satirical reflexivity', it also, perhaps more significantly, encouraged the development of dialogic forms which – as the Roman poet Horace suggested – readily incorporate the polemical and praxical orientation of *discursive* action. Archilochus was adept at using verse as a social and political instrument. The semiotic linkages between Archilochus' prosaic manipulation of the new iambic metre and the emergence of 'dialogical reflexivity' are direct and powerful. If these subterranean relationships between lyrical expression and the reflexive possibilities of later Greek forms can be substantiated, it would certainly not be hyperbolic to claim the epithet 'revolutionary' for Archilochus' poetic experiments.[17] And like all revolutionary innovators, the consequences of Archilochus' break with traditional forms and ideologies were neither total nor culturally homogeneous in their impact upon the next generation of poets. The most receptive environment for these innovations lay in the cosmopolitan city-states of Ionia in the early sixth century (Archilochus was accorded a shrine and was venerated as a hero in his native Paros); the role of Milesian culture in spreading the critical 'individualism' of the iambic lyric is especially important for the subsequent history of reflexivity.[18] Before turning to the two greatest poets of Asia Minor, Alcaeus and Sappho, we might highlight Archilochus' originality by contrasting him with his contemporary Callinus of Ephesus.

Callinus of Ephesus

Unlike Archilochus, Callinus (c. 670 BC) remained a traditionalist with respect to the thematic content of his poetry and his strict devotion to the ethos of the *polis* and the ideals of the *kalos kagathos*; he used the new generic forms to elaborate verses on epic themes, particularly on his two favourite subjects, martial virtue and the vicissitudes of fate. The contrast with Archilochus' pragmatism is most extreme in the traditional sentiments of the following lines from Fragment 1:

> and let each man as he dies make one final javelin-cast. For it is honourable and glorious for a man to fight against the enemy for his land and children and wedded wife. Death will come whenever the Fates spin their decree. But each man must go forward with spear upraised and stout heart covered by his shield, the moment war begins. There is no way a man can escape the destiny of death, not even if he were a child of immortal ancestors. Often a man avoids the fighting and the thud of spears, and comes home to meet the death that is his fate. But the people do not regard him as their special friend or grieve over him. But the whole people feels grief when a brave man dies, and while he lives he is reckoned the equal of heroes. For they see him as a tower before their eyes, since all alone he does the work of many.

Alcaeus

With Alcaeus, however, we have an innovator in both poetic form and lyrical content. Alcaeus, like Sappho, came from the Ionian island of Lesbos and was also forced into exile during the rule of the 'tyrant', Pittacus. As an influential member of the besieged aristocracy of Lesbos c. 620–600 BC – perhaps even a member of the ruling faction that secured Pittacus' rise to power – he wrote openly polemical and political lyrics, but in the tradition of other Mytilene poets also celebrated the life of wine, love, and friendship in works designed to be read at the *symposia* of rich patrons and friends.[19] As Victor Ehrenberg once remarked, with Alcaeus the lyric Muse became political (1964: 31). In portraying the turbulent political situation of his day he was the first to draw upon the figure of a storm-tossed vessel, the 'Ship of State':

> I cannot understand how the winds are set against each other. Now from this side and now from that the waves roll. We between them run with the wind in our black ship driven, hard pressed and labouring under the

giant storm. All round the mast-step washes the sea we shipped. You can see through the sail already where there are opening rents within it. The forestays slacken ...

(Lattimore, trans., 1960: 42–3)

The same Alcaic conceit would become a staple image of later poets, particularly in the descriptive speeches of Attic tragedy. The ship of state metaphor occurs in the opening speech of Eteocles in Aeschylus' *Seven Against Thebes*: 'Citizens of Cadmus, to say what the hour demands, is the duty of him who guards the fortunes of the state, guiding the helm upon the stern, his eyes not closed in slumber'; and, later in the same tragedy: 'Our city has escaped the yoke of servitude ... the ship of state is in smooth waters.' Consider also the opening speech of the Priest of Zeus on the desperate situation of the Theban *polis* which frames Sophocles' *Oedipus Tyrannos*:

our ship of state, sore buffeted, can no more lift her head, foundered beneath a weltering surge of blood ... the God of Plague has swooped upon our city emptying the house of Cadmus, and the murky realm of Hades is full fed with groans and tears.[20]

The same image reappears in Creon's message from the Delphic oracle that the city needs to be 'purged' (*katharsis*): 'Banishment, or the shedding of blood for blood. This stain of blood makes shipwreck of our state'.[21]

Alcaeus may have placed his lyrical gifts in the service of a reformed aristocracy working to consolidate the new world of the *polis* against the threat of either mass rule or 'tyranny'; certainly many of his poems read like propaganda, patriotic defenses of the independent and autonomous city-state freed from the iron grip of tyrants:

> Not homes with beautiful roofs,
> nor walls of permanent stone,
> nor canals and piers for ships
> make the city – but men of strength.
> Not stone and timber, nor skill
> of carpenters – but men brave
> who will handle sword and spear.
> With these you have: City and Walls.[22]

Suffering as an exile from his native Mytilene, he expresses a nostalgic desire to hear the herald 'summon the Assembly and the Council'. His repertoire also included descriptive poems of great power; like Alcman and Hesiod he seems to have turned a cold eye on nature with its seasonal changes and transformations beyond human control or understanding. His poem on winter rivals Hesiod's description of a Boeotian winter in its refusal to glorify or tame the forces of nature:

Zeus rains upon us, and from the sky comes down enormous winter.

Rivers have turned to ice. Dash down the winter. Throw a log on the fire and mix the flattering wine (do not water it too much) and bind on round our foreheads soft ceremonial wreaths of spun fleece ... We must not let our spirits give way to grief ... Best of all defenses is to mix plenty of wine, and drink it.

This 'turn' to quotidian realities as the subject of lyric poetry is perfectly displayed in his famous portrait of an armourer's workshop:

The great hall is aglare with bronze armament and the whole inside made fit for war with helms glittering and hung high, crested over with white horsemanes that nod and wave and make splendid the heads of men who wear them. Here are shining greaves made out of bronze, hung on hooks, and they cover all the house's side. They are strong to stop arrows and spears. Here are war-jackets quilted close of new linen, with hollow shields stacked on the floor, with broad swords of the Chalkis make, many tunics and many belts heaped close beside. These shall not lie neglected, now we have stood to our task and have this work to do'.[23]

Sappho of Mytilene

But I claim there will be some who remember us when we are gone.

This is the dust of Timas, who died before she was married and whom Persephone's dark chamber accepted instead. After her death the maidens who were her friends, with sharp iron cutting their lovely hair, laid it upon her tomb.[24]

(Sappho)

When we come to the intensely personal verse of Sappho we are well within the new world of lyrical consciousness of the Mytilene poetic enlightenment. Alcaeus' poetic celebration of the affective life is now identified as the sole theme and highest aspiration of the poetic craft. The short lyric verse has been refined as the unique vehicle of articulate love – anticipating the basic premise of all European love poetry that the poetic word is the medium of codified emotion.

Sappho lived from about 630 to 580 BC and wrote short lyrics in her native Aeolic dialect, using the colloquial language of Lesbos. Like other Lesbian poets, her background is aristocratic. But the aristocracy of the period had learned to appreciate the new world of the erotic elegy and lyric meditation. Sappho takes the next logical step, creating an *ars erotica* by turning the confessional themata of personal love and the immediacy of erotic life into the substance of her verse. Lyric in her hands becomes an exploration of the grammar of quotidian *eros*. Sappho is the first explorer of the 'logic of the passions': the mortal fragility of love; desire and obsessional infatuation with the beloved; portraits of the self-in-love; eros' transgression of reason; the fragile nature of personal beauty; identity and difference in the loving relationship; the dialectic of absence and presence, pleasure and pain; the conventions of marriage; explorations of the subtle dimensions of affectivity and emotion, nostalgia, melancholy; and so on.

Many of these 'themes' are often fused in a single line or couplet. Consider the condensed, 'spectral' image of love, the 'self-in-love', absence, reflection, and nostalgia evoked by the following line – perhaps the most perfect example of the precision and subjective power of Sappho's koan-like verse: 'The moon has set, and the Pleiades; it is midnight, and time goes by, and I lie alone'.[25]

Or the equally lucid expression of the imaginary presence of the beloved in the following lines on *eros*:

> Now in my
> heart I
> see clearly
> a beautiful
> face
> shining,
> etched
> by love.[26]

Sappho all but defined the terms and rules of the lyrical logic of passion in such bitter-sweet reflections as:

> You came, and I was longing for you; you cooled my heart which was burning with desire.[27]

> I loved you, Atthis, long ago,
> when my girlhood was in full flower
> and you were like a graceless child.[28]

> For I am
> a slave of the Kypros-born,
> who lays a net of trickery.[29]

> From all the offspring
> of the earth and heaven
> love is the most precious.[30]

From the perspective of the development of cultural reflexivity the theme of lesbian attachment, while central to the literary and ideological appreciation of Sappho's place in the development of Greek literature, is more fundamentally important as an implicit critique of pre-lyrical patriarchal thought. The lyrical foregrounding of erotic desire and individualized beauty gains its true critical weight against the 'martial' values of Archaic culture (celebrated to excess in the poetry of Callinus and Tyrtaeus). Implicitly the poetics of affective self-experience rejects the phallocentric culture of epic art. We thus hear nothing of the exclusively male spheres of work, politics, and war. And wherever the *topoi* of city life and war appear in the Sapphic corpus it is in contexts of devaluation and negative comparisons. From the lyric perspective, the phallocentric world of war and politics is inimical to the concrete truths of human feeling. One of the most striking examples of this immanent critique occurs in a poem which makes the clash of lyric and martial culture thematic:

> Some there are who say that the fairest thing seen
> on the black earth is an array of horsemen;
> some, men marching; some would say ships; but I say
> she whom one loves best is the loveliest.[31]

Equally striking is the self-conscious rejection of Homeric universalism for an ethic of the concrete and the personal:

> Like the very gods in my sight is he who
> sits where he can look in your eyes, who listens
> close to you, to hear the soft voice, its sweetness
> murmur in love and
> laughter, all for him. But it breaks my spirit;
> underneath my breast all the heart is shaken.
> Let me only glance where you are, the voice dies,
> I can say nothing.
> but my lips are stricken to silence, underneath
> my skin the tenuous flame suffuses;
> nothing shows in front of my eyes, my ears are
> muted in thunder.
> And the sweat breaks running upon me, fever
> shakes my body, paler I turn than grass is;
> I can feel that I have been changed, I feel that
> death has come near me.[32]

The routine demands of physical work – for women of Sappho's class, the repetitive monotony of the loom – are deflected by the intrusion of affectivity. Compare the voice of the love-sick girl confessing: 'I cannot mind my loom, mother, subdued by Love's desire.'

If the masculine world of the *polis* has its allegorical equivalent in the public realm of the Agora and the city temples, the world of Sapphic desire is preserved under the canopy of the stars and reserved for the solitude of sacred groves and female intimacy. Its utopian ideal is not the civic community of the city-state, but the affective communality of lovers guided by the cult of Aphrodite. The logic of the heart displays a 'spatial' as well as a temporal structure. The natural 'site' of eros is not abstract, homogeneous 'space' – the space of phallocentric power – but the feminine enclosure, the place of a shrine, an altar or sacred *temenos*: 'the holy temple ... a pleasant grove of apple trees, and altars fragrant with frankincense' (Page, trans., 1941: III, p. 377). Its temporal correlate is the interiority of personal self-consciousness, suspended in a nostalgic meditation on the loss of a lover or the memory of mutual friendship.

The new sensibility extends to themes wider than love and personal existence. Or, to preserve the resonance of Sapphic verse, the poetry of poignancy incorporates a changed attitude toward the world beyond the closed circle of lovers. Sappho seems to have been one of the first European thinkers to have envisaged the idea of the whole natural world as an 'objective equivalent' and sustaining horizon of human passion. The oscillation between nature symbolism and concrete human emotions creates a poetic universe of allegorical images; consider the 'imagism' of the following poem which effortlessly slides from 'planetary' to 'flower' symbolism to concretize the emotion of personal grief and erotic melancholy:

> Now she shines among Lydian women as
> into the dark when the sun has set
> the moon, pale-handed, at last appeareth
> making dim all the rest of the stars, and light
> spreads afar on the deep, salt sea,
> spreading likewise across the flowering cornfields;
> and the dew rinses glittering from the sky;
> roses spread, and the delicate antherisk, and the lotus
> spreads her petals
> So she goes to and fro there, remembering
> Atthis and her compassion, sick
> the tender mind, and the heart with grief is eaten.[33]

The singular physical beauty of the beloved outshines every natural light. Even the wasted embers and sad traces of desire appear more valuable than the holy light of heaven.

Praxilla

The allegorical imagism of Sappho's poem above can be compared with the experimental poetry of Praxilla of Sicyon (c. 450 BC) especially the 'bathos' of the fragment which juxtaposes the 'sublimity' of planetary symbolism with the prosaic 'vegetable' world; again the literary merits of the following lines are less important than their documentary value as evidence of the increasing acceptance of linguistic innovation:

> Loveliest of what I leave behind is the sunlight,
> and loveliest after that the shining stars, and the
> moon's face,
> but also cucumbers that are ripe, and pears, and apples.[34]

Mimnermus of Colophon

> What then is life, what is pleasure without golden Aphrodite?
> (Fr. ff1.1)

Colophon (Kolophon) was one of the great mercantile city-states of Ionia whose most famous son in the seventh century (*c.* 630 BC) was the love poet Mimnermus (the same lyric tradition also sustained the speculations of one of the great sixth-century thinkers from Colophon – Xenophanes, *fl.* 540–530). Like Sappho and Alcaeus, Mimnermus' central poetic themes crystallized in a series of vivid personal descriptions of human experience, particularly the sweetness and fragility of love and the inevitable decline into old age and death (e.g. in Frs 5, 6, 9; cf. Solon, fr. 22):

> But we, like the blooms that blossom in the season of many flowers,
> Spring, when they suddenly shoot, caught by the sun's bright rays –
> like these, for a cubit's length of time the flowers of youth
> we enjoy, at the hands of the gods knowing not evil days
> nor good. But beside us there stand the black spirits of Death,
> one of them holding an end in age with its dreadful pain
> and the other in death: but of youth only a short time lives
> the fruit – for as long as the sun spreads itself over the plain.
> (Fr. 2.1–8)

He also appears to have written heroic lyrics in elegiac metre, and may also have been a musician (Strabo, 633, 643). In living from the middle of the seventh to the early part of the sixth century he would have witnessed the decline of Colophon as a cosmopolitan centre encircled and eventually overun by the expanding Lydian empire. Like many of his contemporaries he wrote elegiac verse on the nobility of the warrior and the glory of virtuous death in battle (Frs 12–13).

His most famous poem (Frs. 1–3) has been frequently interpreted as a pessimistic allegory of his city's old age and decline:

What good is life when golden Aphrodite is gone?
Frankly, I would rather be dead than ignore
a girl's warm surrender, her soft arms in bed
at night: lovely flower of youth that all women
and men desire!
When old age comes
a man feels feeble and ugly and crawls under
a crushing sorrow.
He loses the simple joy
of looking at the sun.
Children despise him.
He is repulsive to young women – in this sad
blind alley which God has made of old age.[35]

Semonides of Amorgos

By contrast, Semonides (a late seventh-century poet originally from the island of Samos, but associated with the small Greek colony on the island of Amorgos) represents one of the first satirical voices in early Greek poetry (probably following the revolutionary lyrical innovations popularized by Archilochus, who was universally regarded later as the father of iambic satire). Semonides wrote iambic and elegiac verse in the Ionic Greek dialect (Suda IV 360.7); his poetry returns compulsively to two themes that would become *clichés* of later European literature – the illusions and vanity of human desire (e.g. Fr. 1) and the pernicious character of women (Fr. 7 – the *Iambus on Women*). With lines like 'Woman is the worst of all evils', Semonides might well be described as the first literary misogynist.[36] The Gods created various types of women to deform and poison the lives of men. The bitter 'typology' of women is unique in its vitriolic imagery, images that were most certainly derived from ancient Greek folkloric literature. The folklore device of human-animal parallels is used to identify the 'race' of women with negative animal stereotypes (the pig-woman, the yelping bitch, the lazy donkey, the weasel, and so on). Denouncing the 'ways and wiles' of women would form a distinct genre in ancient literature from Semonides and Hesiod down to the Roman satires of Varro and Juvenal. Juvenal's sixth satire, for example, continues a tradition which dates back to before the Archaic age.[37]

Semonides, with his native Ionic Greek, seems to have been a careful *reader* of both Homer and Hesiod, given the intertextual evidence of his borrowings from their texts, an influence which encouraged him to rework whole passages from Hesiod in his own chosen metric form.[38] Explicit references to Homer and cross-referential substitution are also in evidence. One famous example incorporates the embedded text from the *Iliad* 6.146: 'The finest thing the man of Chios [i.e. Homer] said was this:

Like the generation of leaves, so is that of men'. Few mortals taking this in with their ears have stored it in their hearts; for each man is attended by hope, which grows in young people's breasts. And while he has the lovely bloom of youth a mortal man is light-hearted and full of impossible ideas: he doesn't expect to grow old or die, and while he is healthy he has no thought of being ill. They are fools who think this way and don't understand that for mortals the time of youth – and life – is short. So be aware and bear up as you near life's end, indulging yourself with good things.[39]

Stesichorus of Himera

Like Semonides' works, Stesichorus' poems also 'translate' Homeric and other mythic and epic themes into lyric structures. The name 'Stesichorus' is a title for a professional function, translated literally it means 'arranger of choruses'. His birth place is traditionally given as either Himera in Sicily (Plato, *Phaedrus* 244A) or Metauros, in Italy (c. 630–560 BC) and he is often judged to be the first important literary figure in the western fringes of the Greek world – the direct precursor of Pindar and Simonides (Trypanis, 1981: 104; Bowra, 1961: 74–129; Fränkel, 1975: 281–3).

Unlike Pindar's works, however, only a fragment of Stesichorus' poetic output survives: 'Of the considerable body of the works of Stesichorus (some twenty-six books) only about fifty lines survive' (Harvey, 1984: 407; Bowra, 1961: 126–7). Many of his poems set out to 'naturalize' epic figures as a way of exploring human emotions and conflicts. These efforts were, in effect, hybrid experiments in fusing epic narrative themes with lyric metres. He may also have been one of the first to experiment with the longer prose-poem genre as a possible vehicle of love poetry (for example, the dactylic narrative epic on Heracles and the cattle of Geryon (the *Geryoneis*) running to 1,500 lines, a poem on the murder of Agamemnon, Helen of Troy, the vengeance of Orestes, among others). These linguistic 'hybrids' represent a transitional phase in the deconstruction of the *epos* and the elaboration of more flexible forms, prefiguring the later heroic hymn, love poetry, and even the didactic novel form.[40] His *Oresteia* anticipated fifth-century tragic drama and the Greek novel of the Hellenistic period ('His lyric treatment of popular love stories, as in his *Calyca* and his *Rhadina*, carried the germ of the romance, later to be developed in prose by the Greek novel writers; and his lyric pastoral, *Daphnis*, was the earliest example of bucolic poetry' (Trypanis, 1981: 104–5)). Pastisches of Stesichorus' style and themes can be found in Aristophanic comedy (e.g. *Peace* 762ff.).

Hipponax of Ephesus

After Archilochus, it is the relatively unknown poet with the non-Greek name of Hipponax who advanced the deconstruction of the epic ideology on both formal and substantive planes. His dates and biography are controversial, but the most likely period is the mid-sixth century (*fl.* 540–537 BC). From the sherds of poetry ascribed to Hipponax of Ephesus his unheroic presence, like Homer's Autolycus, stands out as a thief of the everyday. If Hesiod and Homer pray to the high God Zeus, Hipponax's guardian 'daemon' is Hermes, the protector of thieves and wanderers. Hipponax is the François Villon of the Archaic age; for him the epic world-view is illusory; disrespecting the influence of the *epos* and with little or no apparent 'anxiety', he systematically ignores both the metre and the thematics of the *Iliad* to turn forthrightly to the prosaic world of daily life. Hipponax is the patron poet of the mundane which, in a literary environment disciplined in the values of 'high culture' – the heroic and liturgical culture of a waning aristocracy – must have been savoured and enjoyed by receptive circles and audiences beyond the patrons of the rhapsodes and choral liturgy. Emblematically and wholly appropriately he is said to have invented the *choliambic* or 'lame' iambic metre occasionally termed the 'limping' (*skazon*) iambic (produced by having the iambic trimeter terminate with a spondee, leaving his listener literally on the wrong foot). This atonal form – and the lyric medium of iambic trimeter, trochaic tetrameters and short dactylic forms – seems to have been perfectly suited to Hipponax's debunking and carnivalesque message. He turns a caustic, satirical eye upon the 'trivia' of ordinary life and its immediate concerns. Thus we find him confessing his desperate pecuniary situation in a poem where 'Hipponax' appears as both the authorial and narrative *persona* (the sign 'Hipponax' also disrupts the iambic trimetre by protruding at the end of the second line):

> The God of Wealth [Plutus], who's altogether blind, never
> came walking in my door and told me: 'Hipponax,
> I'm giving you thirty silver minae pieces,
> and much beside'. Not he. He's far too mean-hearted.
>
> (Fr. 36)

Or the fragmentary glimpse into the working life and everyday world of triremes:

> Mimnes, you lousy pervert, when you paint the serpent on the trireme's
> full-oared side, quit making it run back from the prow-ram to the pilot.
> What a disaster it will be and what a sensation – you low-born slave, you
> scum – if the snake should bite the pilot on the shin.
>
> (Fr. 28)

Another fragment describes the marginalized social status of an exile (perhaps reflecting his own estranged position in the political circles of Clazomenae):

> Keep travelling, you swine, the whole way toward Smyrna. Go through

the Lydian land, past the tomb of Alyattes, the grave of Gyges and the pillar of Megastrys, the monument of Atys, son of Alyattes, big chief, and point your paunch against the sun's setting.

And finally, the self-parody of Fragment 32:

> Hermes, dear Hermes, Maia's son from Kyllene, I pray to you, I'm suffering from extreme shivers, so give an overcoat to Hipponax, give him a cape, and sandals, and felt overshoes, sixty pieces of gold to bury in his strong chamber.

Hipponax also ventured without inhibition into the 'unlyrical' world of human sexual relations and bodily functions. If Aristophanes is the closest Classical antiquity comes to the scatological Hipponactean world (with the 'fecal' word-play in a comedy such as *Peace*), his true successors – in terms of the concrete detail of his phenomenology of the body and its workings – are Petronius (*c.* 138 AD) and Rabelais. B. M. W. Knox provides an illuminating analysis of some recently discovered papyrus fragments attributed to Hipponax which display an almost Rabelaisian approach to sexuality:

> Hipponax is a grand master of obscene fiction. One damaged papyrus gives us a tantalizing but lacunose portrayal of what seems to be a love encounter rudely interrupted: '... on the floor ... undressing ... we were biting and kissing ... looking out through the door ... so they wouldn't catch us ... naked ... she was hurrying things up ... and I was doing my part ...'. An obscure (and certainly obscene) passage about a sausage is followed by 'telling Bupalus to go to hell ...' and two lines later 'and just when we were on the job ...'... Another fragment manages to combine two of Hipponax' themes, sex and evacuation, in one wild orgiastic scene which may well have been the model for the Oenothea episode in Petronius' *Satyricon* (138) ... a woman, who is introduced as 'speaking Lydian'... carries out some magical and obscene rite on the narrator (it includes, besides some obscure anal operation, beating his genitals with a fig branch); the object, presumably, is, as in the *Satyricon*, to restore his lost virility. In Hipponax, however, all this takes place in a privy (its smell is specially singled out for mention); the protagonist gets spattered with excrement and this provokes an invasion of dung-beetles – they come 'whirring more than fifty of them' – to provide a Rabelaisian finale.[41]

Restricting any commentary to the immediate subject matter of this chapter – the germ forms of reflexivity in Archaic lyric poetry – we can read the fragments of Hipponax as symptomatic of his fundamental rejection of Homeric 'aristocratic' culture, a 'mytholiterary' discourse which essentially allegorized everyday life by seeing it as a codification of symbolic and mythical values. In the Hipponactean order of things, everyday life is the 'all-too-human' scenario of profane actions and events, a realm of sexual encounters, absurd comedy, and futile struggles. We know of his quarrels with specific individuals – for example, the sculptors Bupalus and Athenis ('Hold my jacket, somebody, while I hit Bupalus in the eye. I can hit with both hands, and I never miss punches'). His colloquial imagery suggests the 'anti-allegoresis' of a Villon, Rabelais, or Baudelaire. Like Villon he tells us of his passionate desire for Arete (Frs 15–22). He was also not adverse to introducing non-Greek expressions in his poetry. His eye (and ear) for the quotidian – indeed obscene and 'fecal' – detail and his prolific use of satirical inversion and parody suggests Attic comedy or the theatre of abuse and cruelty. We have a perfect instance of a 'dialectical' criticism which, in its very extremity, carries a partial truth about the object of its contempt: Hipponax could only 'leave' the world of the *epos* by imagining a counterworld of carnal, quotidian values; he deposits his poems like fecal matter outside the gold and ivory gates of Homeric high culture.[42]

Theognis of Megara

We have repeatedly encountered the political content of lyric reflection and suggested that the elegiac form could be readily turned to a variety of ideological uses. One of the most striking instances of this can be found in the elegiac verse of Theognis (*c.* 540 BC). In antiquity Theognis of Megara was viewed as the archetypal spokesman of a beleaguered aristocracy faced with the rapid decline of the Archaic form of life and its traditions of landed wealth and nobility sustained by traditions of martial *aretai* – honour, military power, sacred law (*themis*), and so on. In defending the old social order, Theognis poured scorn on three related groups who had been active in the revolution that had violently overthrown the aristocratic party in his native Megara: the sheep-like *demos* manipulated by the tyrant Theagenes (who is portrayed in a rich and varied symbolism of evil: vulgarity, unlimited appetite, encouraging rule by the wrangling, contentious mob, pandering to the corrupt *hoi polloi* given to bribes and the pursuit of private gain before the interests of the state, ignorance, factionalism, and so on); the upstart *nouveaux riches* created by the economic revolution in trade and commerce which accompanied the 'Greek tyrants' (Theognis in fact mounted one of the first systematic critiques of the divisive consequences of generalized monetary exchange upon the status system of traditional society); and finally, a more amorphous stratum whose activities had helped to sap and undermine the hegemonic rule of the Megarean *élite*, most probably a disenfranchised intellectual stratum (the kind of marginal social groups which may have formed the audience for the cynical poetry of an Archilochus or Hipponax), the 'bad men' who, Theognis believed, had corrupted the masses and paved the way for the hated 'democracy'. In combination, these social forces have, in Theognis' opinion, turned the order of the good and the noble upon its head: the *polis* has become a universe of permanent strife and *stasis*: 'this city is big with child and I fear it may give birth to a man who will chastize our wicked pride' (39–40).

The Theognidean ideological standpoint is that of the dispossessed landowning stratum owning property around the inland city-state of Megara. The social landscape has become a world bereft of justice and honour (Theognis 345). The pursuit of wealth has replaced the quest for *arete*. Aristocratic powers and property have passed into the hands of the 'new men'. The rigid social stratification of Megara has been thrown into chaos and disorder. His poetic mood is pessimistic and occasionally vengeful towards these three subversive forces ('May it be mine to drink their dark blood', 349). The *persona* of many of Theognis' poems is bitter at the loss of wealth and status of this class of *agathoi*; it is the voice of downward social mobility, of the dispossessed aristocracy railing against the disorder and instability of the times (Theognis 346–7). The fabric of the traditional social order (*cosmos*) has been destroyed by party factionalism, violence, and force. We can certainly read these poems as documentary evidence of the 'revolutionary' impact of trade and the rise of a mercantile *élite* in the city-states around Megara – the most important of these being Corinth on the Isthmus, the trade link between the Peloponnese and Attica, Nisaea, Aegina and of course the vast increase in commercial activities passing through the Piraeus, the port of Athens, and neighbouring city of Megara.

The *leitmotifs* of the *Theognidea* are, not surprisingly, *injustice*, *nostalgia* for the stable hierarchical world of noble values that has been overthrown, and an unremitting *misanthropy* – a vision of mankind as an endless parade of deceivers, a spectacle of immoral individuals who have learned to survive in this Iron Age by learning the arts of guile, deceit, distrust, and cynicism: 'For man the best thing is never to be born, never to look upon the hot sun's rays. Next best, to speed at once through Hade's gates, and lie beneath a piled-up heap of earth:[43] 'The sense of shame has disappeared from men, and shamelessness roams over all the earth'.[44]

Unlike the remains of the lyric poets of the seventh century, a large part – around 1400 elegiac verses – of Theognis' work survives, written in elegiac metre, most typically in the generic form of 'wisdom' literature, prescriptive advice written directly to similar-minded aristocratic friends (Cyrnus, son of Polypaus, Simonides, Onomacritus, and others). Like his contemporaries, Theognis made good use of the *sphragis* in 'authoring' his compositions and advocating a form of stoic resistance to the 'new times' (Theognis 19–24, 543–6). Theognis' texts give us an irreplaceable insight into the social dynamics of the ancient class structure during the transition to more democratic forms of state in the fifth century. In denouncing the political corruption of his day, he became the first authentic polemicist in Western literary history.

In keeping with aristocratic Greek mores, he also wrote poetry celebrating male companionship and homosexual relations as praiseworthy and honourable institutions: 'The love of boys is sweet'; 'That man is never happy who does not love dogs and smooth-hooved horses and young men'; 'Blessed the lover who exercises, then goes home to sleep all day with a handsome boy'.[45]

Ibycus of Rhegium

Ibycus was born at Rhegium (Reggio di Calabria) on the tip of southern Italy. As a lyric poet of the mid-sixth century BC he wrote most of his poems on the Ionian island of Samos at the court of the 'tyrant', Polycrates (c. 537–c. 523/2). The most cited poem from his seven books of poetry contains a reflection on the dark side of *eros*:

> In Spring the quince trees
> ripened in the girls' holy orchard
> with river waters;
> and grapes turn violet
> under the shade of luxuriant leafage
> and newborn shoots
> But for me, Eros
> knows no winter sleep, and as north winds
> burn down from Thrace
> with searing lightning
> Kypris [i.e., Aphrodite] mutilates my heart with black
> and baleful love.[46]

Anacreon of Teos

Anacreon was most productive around the period 560–490 BC. He appears to have been driven into exile by the Persian armies of Cyrus c. 545 (the citizens of Teos formed the colony of Abdera in Thrace, c. 540). He was sufficiently well-known to have become the court poet of Samos under the powerful tyrant Polycrates (sometime during the years 533–522) and, after Polycrates' murder by the Persians in 522, he finished his eventful life being lionized by the Athenian intelligentsia of post-Peisistratid Athens (pseudo-Plato, *Hipparchus* 228B–C).

Antiquity unanimously named Anacreon the father of the love song and the symposium lyric – his name entered popular Greek usage and as an adjective 'anacreonic' became a byword for erotic writing in general (collections known as the *Anacreotea* were popular down to the Byzantine period and 'had a huge influence on the poets of the seventeenth and eighteenth centuries in France, England and Germany' (Trypanis, 1981: 100)). We may take his influential position in the Athenian ruling circles of the Peisistratids from around 525 to 510 as evidence for the increasing importance of symposia as channels of information exchange and political influence. He is suposed to have been brought to Athens by Hipparchus in one of the fifty-oared state triremes

(Pseudo-Plato, *Hipparchus* 228C). Popular verses like the following undoubtedly helped Anacreon extend his audience from the traditional tyrant-patron class of the Samian aristocracy to other strata of society, and there is evidence that his writings circulated in 'published' form throughout the city-states dominated by Athens:

> The love god (*Eros*) with his golden curls
> puts a bright ball into my hand,
> shows a girl in her fancy shoes,
> and suggests that I take her.
> Not that girl – she's the other kind,
> one from Lesbos. Disdainfully,
> nose turned up at my silver hair,
> she makes eyes at the ladies.
>
> Like a blacksmith Eros has hammered me and
> crushed me on his anvil, and has plunged me
> in a winter torrent.
>
> Boy with the virgin glance, I pursue you, but
> you pay no attention, not realizing that you hold
> the reins of my soul.
>   (Lattimore, trans., 1960: 42–3)

Anacreon was also gifted with a sharp eye for the telling detail and most probably wrote ironic and satirical portrait-poems of the new social types thrown up by the structural changes in the Greek world during his lifetime. Hermann Fränkel thus speaks of Anacreon as one of the first Greek writers to have perfected the urbane art of subtle irony ('the calm maturity of a master artist, who can unbend without loss to himself, and detachment from the subject matter and from oneself' (1975: 293)). Compare the vivid portrait of the social climber, Artemon, with its cinematic concern with the unique and the specific (the wooden dice ear-rings, the oxhide from a derelict shield, customary torture, the ivory parasols, etc.):

> Once he went out huddled in dirty clothes with his hair skimped up, buttons of wood hung in his ears for rings, and the hide of a thread-bare ox scrubbed from a cast-off shield to wrap his bones to keep him warm. He was the lousy Artemon. He lived the life of a useless bum. He got his neck framed in the pillory, he got whipped till his back was raw, he had hairs pulled out of his head.
> Look at him now, Kyke's boy; he rides in a coach and four, and wears gold on his arms, gold on his neck, shaded by ivory parasols, like some dame in society.

In other writings he turned away from the sympotic love lyric to the desired *eromenos* and 'occasional poetry' (Fränkel, 1975, 294) to darker, though still personal, themes. The following poem on the poet's old age evokes his own imminent death:

> I have gone gray at the temples,
> yes, my head is white, there's nothing
> of the grace of youth that's left me,
> and my teeth are like an old man's.
> Life is lovely. But the lifetime
> that remains for me is little.
> For this cause I mourn. The terrors
> of the Dark Pit [Tartarus] never leave me.
> For the house of Death [Hades] is deep down
> underneath; the downward journey
> to be feared, for once I go there
> I know well, there's no returning.
>
> (Lattimore, trans., 1960: 46–7)

Or from a related poem written in the feminine gender, probably from a portrait of a prostitute:

> Already I am becoming a wrinkled old thing.
> over-ripe fruit, thanks to your lust.[47]

Finally, we should briefly mention two poets who carried the lyric traditions of archaic Greece into the world of the fifth-century Enlightenment: Simonides and his nephew, Bacchylides.

Simonides of Ceos

The poet Simonides came from Iulis on the island of Ceos, in the Aegean; he lived from about 557/6 to 468 BC writing elegiac poetry on war, fate, valour, the games – his most famous verse on the Spartan king, Leonidas and the fallen of Marathon and Thermopylae appears to have been commissioned by the Athenian *polis* under the Peisistratid tyrant Hipparchus (*c.* 527 BC). He anticipates Pindar in glorifying the *arete* of athletic power in the national games as a symbol of the human condition. Toward the end of his life he gained fame as the court poet of Hieron, the 'tyrant' of Syracuse and was also connected to the Aleuad and Scopad dynasties of Thessaly. For Socrates' generation he was renowned as the first poet to amass a fortune from his art by publishing popular choral laments (*threnoi*), paeans to the gods, encomia, and Olympic victory songs (*epinikia*) to order. As Peter Levi observed, for a fee he 'could transform a team of mules into "daughters of storm-footed horses"' (1985: 134; cf. Fränkel, 1975: 303–4, 323–4; Fränkel gives the line of Simonides 515 as 'All hail to you, daughters of wind-swift steeds' (1975: 435)).

Simonides was also an innovator in poetic delivery and techniques of memory involving refined mnemnonic *topoi*. His 'many-sided genius' (Guthrie, 1977: 131) brought him close to bring the most popular pan-Hellenic poet of the fifth century and forerunner of the sophistic enlightenment (Segal, in *CHCL*: 226; Fränkel, 1975: 303–24, esp. 311–12, 315–16, 321).

Bacchylides

The 'nightingale from Ceos' (Bacchylides 3.96). Born on the island of Ceos (Keos) about 510 BC, a nephew of Simonides; Bacchylides was one of the most influential fifth-century lyric poets, reaching something equivalent to a 'popular audience' throughout the Athenian-dominanted Greek world. He is known to have competed for rich and powerful patrons with the Boeotian poet Pindar, and like Pindar, is well known for his odes on war, for dithyrambs, paeans, hymns, dirges, *hyporchemata*, epigrams, encomia, and epinician odes (the genre of the *epinikion* celebrating military victories received a new impulse during the Persian wars). His taste for innovation is best illustrated by his novel use of lyric poetry as a *narrative* form in his transcription of key episodes of the Trojan War into verse form.[48]

4 CONCLUSION: THE 'CONCEPT' OF LYRIC REFLEXIVITY

Experiment is the beginning of learning.

(Alcman)

In gathering together some of the threads of this chapter it is important to underline the fact that 'lyric reflexivity' is neither a 'conceptual' attitude nor a homogeneous content present in the work of all the poets of the Greek lyrical tradition. This brief tour of a selection of lyrical fragments is not intended to force these diverse verbal practices into a single mould or to read them as expressions of a shared 'mentality'. The extant texts and fragments are too manifestly heterogeneous to be treated as expressions of a single world-view or to be marshalled as documentary evidence of an evolving ideology. The main point I have tried to establish is simply that by virtue of mounting a critical assault on the inherited generic forms of liturgical discourse, choral poetry, and Homeric culture, the poets of the Archaic age were obliged to accentuate the singularity of their own language and personal vision, creating a poetry which is less a *mimesis* of universal and eternal values (following the precedent of the Homeric table of 'virtues' (*aretai*), than an adventure of personalized self-reflection, an intervention and even – as in the cases of Archilochus and Hipponax – a radical critique of the performative canons of early Greek culture.

We have seen that much of this poetry is related to the spread of new social practices and institutions following the breakdown of the aristocratic system of privilege and the emergence of local courts, the patronage of tyrants, the spread of the pan-Hellenic festivals, the increasing popularity of male phratries, and the crystallization of the *symposium* as a political-cum-cultural forum for the activities of political groups and aristocratic clubs.[49] Yet it is still organically rooted in the resilient rhythms and motifs of folk-culture.

We have also linked this explosion of individualized poetry to one of the most important changes during the sixth century – the spread of literacy and the associated shift toward scriptural and written forms of communication. But we must not exaggerate the impact of this innovation taken in isolation from wider patterns of social and political changes. Even well into the fifth century

> literature was known chiefly through performance: epic poetry from the performance of rhapsodes; lyric from choral performances, for which young people were given training by teachers; tragedy and comedy were primarily known from the dramatic festivals; even early prose was given performance ... The change from oral to written publication of literature has been compared to the revolution brought about by the introduction of printing in the fifteenth century and to the introduction of the computer in the twentieth.
> (Kennedy, in Kennedy, ed., 1989: 87–8)

As Peter Levi also cautions, the

> progression of poetry is not a question of a succession of ages, but of what is thrown up from many different levels into the constantly changing formal structures which history and social history determine, and of what is thrown up from many levels into the work of an individual genius.
> (1985: 149)

The same social conditions that favoured the development of lyric also contributed to its decline:

> the most important poetic activity had taken place mainly in the Greek world beyond the Aegean Sea – that is, in the Ionian and Aeolic areas – though Boeotia, represented by Hesiod and Pindar, and the western Greeks, with figures like Stesichorus and Ibycus, had their part to play as well. Nonetheless, by the end of this period the centre of interest had moved to Attica, and thereafter Athens dominated the cultural and political picture until the rise of the Macedonians and the conquest of the East by Alexander.
> (Trypanis, 1981: 114)

We conclude, then, not with a homogeneous 'concept' of lyric reflexivity, but with diverse experiments in hitherto unexplored worlds of expressive self-reflection – the dawning realization of the unanticipated semiotic possibilities of reflexivity and self-knowledge created by the poetic *logos*. Yet poetry, like all cultural forms, is a child of its time; and the aristocratic world which sustained lyric and choral poetry had all but disappeared by the time of the Persian Wars. The last and most powerful inheritor of the tradition of lyrical reflexivity was the Theban poet, Pindar (518–438 BC).

5
PINDAR AND THE AGE OF LITERARY CONSCIOUSNESS

Prophesy (*manteueo*), Muse, and I will be your interpreter (*prophateuso*).

(Pindar, Fr. 150)

And I touch nothing with falsehood.

(Pindar, *Nemean* I.1)

1 The life-world as a theatre of reflexive praxis
2 The heroic ethic in reflexive mimesis
3 Gods and Men
4 Death and the Elysian Fields
5 Death and the poetic Logos
6 Conclusion: Pindar's world

1 THE LIFE-WORLD AS A THEATRE OF REFLEXIVE PRAXIS

For we are but of yesterday, and know nothing, because our days upon earth are a shadow.

(Job 8:9)

The work of the Theban poet Pindar presents us with something like a case study of the transition from the oral poetry of the latter part of the Archaic period to the crafted, complex compositions of the age of literary consciousness. Pindar's life coincided with the decline of the traditional aristocracy and the spread of the democratic *polis* (c. 518–438 BC). He died at the very moment when the Greek enlightenment was in full flood and can be said to mark the end of the great experiment in lyrical expression. What follows is an exploration of the rhetorical preconditions for the Pindaric self and its role in defining some of the contours of Greek intellectual culture. I will try to show that the self-conscious ornamentation and aesthetic reflectiveness of his poetry trace some of the fundamental tensions and contradictions at work in the social and cultural changes experienced during the middle decades of the fifth century.

PINDAR AND THE AGE OF LITERARY CONSCIOUSNESS

To appreciate the quality of Pindaric lyric we have to return the language of the Victory ode to the social and cultural system of which it is an integral part.

The lines from the author of the Book of Job could have been enunciated by the writers of the Homeric epic, by Hesiod, or by any one of the lyric poets. Homer's universe, as we have seen in Chapter 2, was essentially a theatre of heroic action, a configuration of praxis predelineated for mortals by the Gods. Hesiod's verse frames a darker vision of struggling mortals thrown upon the black earth observed by an imperious, often indifferent, and not infrequently malevolent pantheon of divinities. With the Theban poet, Mortals, Gods, and *Kosmos* are gathered in an articulate universe of light and darkness encompassed by the horizon of earth, creating a field of action heavy with a sense of its finite limits.

Pindar begins by reworking some of the great themes of the Homeric and the choral traditions. But subtle changes in emphasis and style are already noticeable. In comparison with the Master of Olympus, lord of death-dealing lightning strokes (now increasingly intellectualized as 'the great mind of Zeus' (*Pythian* V.4)), mankind is powerless and human life is salted with a bitter self-consciousness of temporal passage, rounded by inescapable death. We have already seen the punitive 'will of Zeus' gradually shaped into the guardian of Justice in Homer and Hesiod. For Hesiod, Zeus was troped as the 'all-seeing eye' who judges and punishes the actions of mortals ('The eye of Zeus, seeing all and understanding all', *Works and Days* 267). In Pindar's world Zeus is also omniscient, a guardian of aristocratic values, and 'lord of all' (*Isthmian* V.25).

The Pindaric ethic also shares Hesiod's vision of the social world as a place of injustice and violence. Yet Pindar's poetry is not cut from the deep vein of Greek pessimism. The gleaming universe of the Pindaric Self transcends the brooding world of the Boeotian farmer. Hesiod's dark vision of the human condition is redeemed by one salutary fact: mortals have been granted gifts touched by the presence of divinity, among the most precious being the gift of reflexivity itself – mind, thought, speech, poetry, action: 'If men are brave, or wise, it is by divinity' (*Olympia* IX). Insight, courage, and wisdom are gifts from the 'all-wise Zeus' (cf. *Works and Days* 273). For the aristocratic Pindar the *psyche* of human beings is displayed most perfectly in understanding and knowledge, and these are gifts of the immortal gods. Only mortals among nature's creatures can be said to 'envision' the radiant presence of divinity in the world order.

The mediating link between mortals and the holy Gods is the poet – the *prophet* of the 'sweet-voiced' Muses, selected by the Gods to utter the truth of existence. The holy Muses bestow the powers of speech and song to chosen mortals. Appropriately the Goddesses of art and beauty are pictured in the act of giving ('gift of the Muses' in *Olympian* VII; in *Olympian* IX the poet is carried on the chariot of the Muses (cf. *Olympian* X.64 and *Isthmian* VIII)). If for Hesiod the supreme gift of Zeus is Justice, for Pindar it is Beauty embodied in the grace and heroism of the human body. Again, Pindar adheres more or less consistently to the traditional ethos of athleticism and physical prowess that remained unchanged from the Homeric period to the age of the Greek tyrants. Yet, following the precedent of the Homeridae, the traditional heroic paradigms have been self-consciously aestheticized (cf. *Nemean* 2.1ff.). Indeed it might be said that the Pindaric moment is already prefigured in the self-conscious artistry of the Homeric Hymns. The poem *To Pythian Apollo*, for example, contains the lines:

> the deathless gods think only of the lyre and song (*kitharis kai aoide*), and all the Muses together, voice sweetly answering voice, hymn the unending gifts the gods enjoy and the sufferings of men, all that they endure at the hands of the immortal gods, and how they live thoughtless and helpless and cannot find healing for death or defence against old age.
> (188–93)

We should recall that Pindar's highly crafted art is addressed to an audience that has only recently witnessed the earliest works of tragic drama, an audience still ignorant of the theorizing of the first thinkers and philosophers, but fully versed in the symbolic actions of mythology, Homeric epic, and choral poetry. And Pindar draws upon the whole range of mythic motifs in crafting his literary works (stories of the god-like Achilles, Perseus slaying the many-headed Gorgon (*Pythian* XII), Aphrodite and the Graces (*Pythian* VI, *Pythian* XII), Apollo in *Pythian* IX, Orion's pursuit of the doves in *Nemean* II, Kronos and Zeus in *Nemean* V, Heracles in *Olympian* II, III, VI, X; *Pythian* X; *Isthmian* IV, Poseidon in *Olympian* I, VI and *Nemean* VI, Jason's winning of the Golden Fleece in *Pythian* IV, the judge of the Underworld, Rhadamanthus in *Olympian* II, Bellerophon in *Olympian* XIII and *Isthmian* VII, Hector in *Nemean* IX.39–42, the marriage of the Goddess Thetis and the mortal Peleus in *Isthmian* VIII, Pelops in *Olympian* I, the Nymphs dancing by the hot springs at Himera (*Olympia* XII), the stirrings of Orphic and other forms of popular culture (the Horae at *Olympia* XIII), etc.). In retelling these ancient stories the poet assumes the task of preserving the traditions of the Hellenes, and hence is appropriately called a *sophos* (*sophia* at *Pythian* III.113; IX.78; cf. *Olympian* I.9; *Isthmian* II.12–3). By reinscribing the ancient hero myths Pindar followed the lead of Alcman, Stesichorus, Sappho, and Simonides as virtuoso practioners of a highly self-conscious literary art.

Yet Pindar's 'mythological poetry' (his *sophia* as he describes his own poetic vocation) is firmly rooted in the social, political, and ethical concerns of Archaic Greece (to such an extent that a poem like *Pythian* IV, woven around the tale of Jason and the Argonauts' quest for the Golden Fleece, would not be misdescribed as a 'lyrical epic' celebrating the quasi-mythical founding of Cyrene). The element of conscious orchestration – what Aristotle would call 'emplotting' in the *Poetics* – gives the Pindaric line a conspicuous 'literary' quality. Where Hesiod inventoried the narrative traditions of the old Gods and allocated them to their individual functional offices, Pindar reworks the old stories to produce perfectly calculated and intricate aesthetic effects ('intellectualism' and 'contrived complexity' are terms that have been frequently and not unjustly used of Pindar's later works). Where for Hesiod the primary focus is on the content of the narrative, for Pindar, the narrative has become an occasion for weaving intricate patterns of symbolic allusion. Unlike Hesiodic verse, the social form of the audience is already a potent force in dictating the nature and content of Pindar's work.

Pindar's stylized verse is thus less a 'reflection' or 'representation' of the Gods and Heroes than their *musical invocation* for a definite social stratum. The Gods are not contemplated, but presented within the concentrated dynamics of the choral victory ode. With Pindar, as with the tragic dramatists, *mimesis* is redefined as a complex performance following the instructions of a literary script. 'Poetry' does not re-present images of the gods in the manner of a privately read stanza but strives to articulate their gleaming presence ('the splendour of the immortals') before an audience steeped in mythological narratives. To mark this performative function, we should technically speak of Pindar's symbolism of Light (*phaos*), Gold (*chrusos*), the sacred (*to theia*), Victory (*nike*), Ordeals (*kamatoi*), the field of the Game, and so forth not as 'signs' of a pre-existent order of existence or 'symbols' of an already formed 'reality', but as literary *icons* (in the ancient Greek sense of *eikones* which participate in the disclosure of what they reveal). A victory ode to a successful athlete is thus designed to reactivate the glory of his triumph before the victor's home city. As this iconic 'logic' plays a fundamental part in premodern reflexivity we will come across its operations again when dealing with the language of the Presocratic thinkers and philosophers in Volume 3.

Pindar's poetic vision of the fragile dignity of human beings acting in an intractable universe is distilled in the opening lines of *Olympian* I: *ariston men hudor, ho de chrusos aithomenon pur* ('Best of all things is water; but gold is a gleaming fire'(1.1– 2)). Where the sustaining gift of nature is 'water', the completion and perfection of existence is the divine element symbolized by 'gold'. A related Pindaric icon is the symbolism of the dual body, the human body under its description as a corporeal medium of action and the *agon*-body as the iconic 'vehicle' of disembodied *aretai* – the 'deathless excellences' which may be momentarily 'exemplified' in heroic achievements of the lived body. Pehaps the relation of the natural to the divine body could be mapped in the parallel of water and gold? The mortal body 'participates' in the golden light of 'things divine' as Gods manifest their powers in human form, both sharing a common origin (compare the Hesiodic conceit in *Works and Days* 107–8 that the race of gods and mortals originated from a common source). And it was not unusual to think of this 'common source' in terms of the chthonian elements – with Earth and Water at their head. The symbolism of water and gold would thus be seen as a striking homology for the genesis of mortals and immortals from a common origin. By moving in the realm of light and gold, the actions of aristocratic heroes and Gods have evolved into exemplars of timeless virtues. While the physical body must 'yield to all-powerful Death', mind lights up the world, makes truth a brief possibility for human existence. The presence of reflexivity relates the world of men and the world of gods as spheres of one all-embracing Order of Being. In the Sixth *Nemean* ode, for example, the text articulates the commonality of Gods and mortals by explicitly repeating Hesiodic icons:

> There is one race of men,
> one race of gods.
> Yet from one mother
> we both take our breath.
> The difference
> is in the allotment
> of all power,
> for the one is nothing
> while the bronze sky exists forever,
> a sure abode.
> And yet, somehow,
> we resemble the immortals,
> whether in greatness of mind
> or nature, though we know not
> to what measure
> day by day and in the watches of the night
> fate has written that we should run.

In Pindar's world, self-knowledge is both the glory and tragedy of human praxis ('most men need interpreters' *Olympian* II, 'we have some resemblance in intelligence to the immortals' *Nemean* VI). An uncontrolled desire to possess divine intelligence can also lead mortals to their destruction. Unlike natural entities human beings must act in a chronically uncertain world. And in acting they perennially overstep their allotted place in the divine scheme of things. Mortals aspire to the estate of the Gods, failing to differentiate the appearances of divine reflexivity from the nature of divine existence (Pindar's warning comes from the same moral tradition as Alcman's 'Let none from mankind fly up to heaven' in Fragment 1.16, and the practical folk-wisdom of 'Nothing in excess', 'Know thyself', etc.). The root of the human comedy lies in the human proclivity to ignore this essential difference, confusing iconic participation with identity. The seeds of tragedy are thus sown when mortals take an intimation of divine *nous* for its substance. Mortals confuse sharing in the realm of divine attributes with *being* divine.

Isthmian V.14 admonishes its audience: *Seek not to become Zeus*: 'If a man fares well and hears his good name spoken ... You have everything, if a share of these beautiful things comes to you.' Simply: hold the model of the divine before you as an ideal. The Pindaric injunction is to live and suffer in the pursuit of glory. Human existence is stretched like a hyphen between the mindless cycles of nature and the significant actions of the Gods. Human existence as a life of praxis is delimited and defined by sharing and participating in a universe of divine qualities, but ultimately wisdom is only granted to those who can draw and respect the necessary limits between mortal and divine, finite and infinite, living and deathless orders. We are, as it were, already in the vicinity of the Platonic and Euripidean distinction between imitation and original, model and Form. 'Mortal ends befit mortal men' is Pindar's salutary message – each realized 'excellence' being shadowed by an awareness that every human achievement is framed in the 'clothes of Earth'. A man is a fragile, unstable existent, a 'creature of a day':'*What is man, what is he not? Man is the dream of a shadow*' (*Pythian* VIII.5):

> Ephemeral creatures are we not? Who shall say what each man is, and is not? For man is but the shadow of a dream. Yet if the Gods bestow upon him but a gleam (*aigle/aigla*) of their own radiance, bright flame surrounds him and his life (*aion*, 'age') is sweet'.
> (*Pythian* VIII.95–7; cf. *Od.* 18.136ff.; Euripides, *Bacchae* 395ff.; Heraclitus B 17)

Pindar introduces a theme which will echo throughout Western literature down to the European Renaissance and beyond. But the conclusion drawn from his diagnosis of the human condition is not nihilistic. We are not yet in the world of Macbeth's soliloquy:

> Tomorrow, and tomorrow, and tomorrow,
> Creeps in this petty pace from day to day,
> To the last syllable of recorded time;
> And all our yesterdays have lighted fools
> The way to dusty death. Out, out, brief candle!
> Life's but a waking shadow; a poor player,
> That struts and frets his hour upon the stage,
> And then is heard no more: it is a tale
> Told by an idiot, full of sound and fury,
> Signifying nothing.
> (Shakespeare, *Macbeth* V. v.18–27)

With Pindar we are still closer to the grandeur of Aeschylean drama and Sophocles' vision of human finitude: 'we living mortals, what are we but phantoms (*eidola*) all or unsubstantial shades?' (*Ajax* 125–6). Despite, or perhaps because of, this dark boundary to mortal existence, human action expressed in its extreme – and necessarily evanescent – achievements, for example, in sacrificing one's life for another (a theme celebrated by Pindar in *Pythian* VI) is existentially enhanced and aesthetically justified. Unlike Shakespeare's despairing soul, Pindar's hero sees beyond the empty sound and fury of futile death. This is still a universe glowing with the traces of divinity (*Pythian* VIII.97). The same light illuminates the truth of the dark earth. In

Pindar's poetic cosmology Truth is the daughter of the 'Lord of Light' (*Olympian* X.3–6: 'O Muse and Truth, daughter of Zeus'; cf. *Olympian* VIII.1–2: 'Mother of Games, gold-crowned, Olympia, Mistress of Truth'; *Paean* 6.6; Fr. 205 Snell, see Lattimore, trans., 1960: 60).

Far from signifying nothing, then, life-risking acts of excellence transfigure human beings in the radiance of divinity; heroic actions make mortals 'more than mortal', life 'more than life'. Pindar's universe is a world punctuated with the epiphanies of heroic transcendence. Each instance of *arete* participates in the memorable paradigms of excellence, archetypes that are ultimately of a divine provenance. While courage, glory, honour, noble sacrifice, and the rest of the virtues live beyond the lifespan of mortals, flesh returns to dust; yet in living briefly on an epic scale, in the midst of 'dusty death', the human body recreates the 'true image' of life and divinity. At such life-and-death moments the human frame is touched by divine light. No longer is a man 'similar' to 'the divine'; in heroic struggle and especially in the moment of victory he has become divine, transfigured in the truth of divinity. This is the relevance of Jean-Pierre Vernant's observation:

> It is also necessary to correct the commonly held view that the anthropomorphism of the Greek Gods means they were conceived in the image of the human body. It is rather the reverse: in all its active aspects, in all the components of its physical and psychological dynamism, the human body reflects the divine model as the inexhaustible source of a vital energy when, for an instant, the brilliance of divinity happens to fall upon a mortal creature, illuminating him, as in a fleeting reflection, with a little of that splendor that always clothes the body of a God.
> (in Feher, ed., 1989: 28)

It is a small step to move from this myth-saturated world of exemplary paradigms to the generic, philosophical idea of Forms immanent in every sphere of being. Glory – and the luminous splendour of celebrity in the here-and-now and in the shining memories of future generations – can only be won inside the horizon of action, a space lit by the Goddess Theia, mother of the Sun. A life without truth is a life lived by shadows and sleepwalkers: 'Mother of the Sun (Helios), the many-named Theia, for your sake men have made the great strength of gold to be a thing prized above other possessions' (*Isthmian* V.1ff.). Even the light of natural existence is a golden gift of the Gods and, as such, is ruled by Fate and Time, and experienced by men as chance and contingency. Pindar's theatre of praxis is ruled by Zeus ('Zeus disposes this and that, Zeus is the master of everything' *Isthmian* V.3; cf. *Olympian* 7.1–11), but Kronos remains one of the supreme divinities: '*treacherous Kronos hangs over men and twists awry the path of life*' (*Isthmian* VIII.2; 'Time's hand, throwing at you the unforeseen turns calculation upside down, and gives you one thing, but another not yet', *Pythian* XII). Zeus is increasingly connected to the remorseless work of time; not the homogeneous temporality of passing time, but a time of action and unforseen events that may create or destroy the fortunes of men and cities. Contingency – and the ensuing threat of failure, grief, and pain – prefaces each heroic ordeal and achievement with a reminder of human fragility: *today* you are happy.

To avoid the evil of *hubris* and the destruction it brings in its train, the *psyche* must learn to stay within the limits of divine legality and experience only what has been ordained (*Pythian* II.2.34). Pindar frequently adopts the mantle of the prophet enunciating a stern message: individuals must not overstep the boundaries of things, surrendering to the temptation to move beyond the Pillars of Hercules (*Isthmian* IV; *Olympian* III.3; *Olympian* V; *Nemean* III.1, the traditional formular symbol of the limits of the divinely ordained universe: 'Beyond no wise man can tread; no fool either. I will not venture; a fool were I', *Olympian* III, trans. Lattimore). In different contexts *hubris* assumes different senses; among these: defying the gods, forgetting divinity, ignoring the difference between mortal and immortal aspirations, immoderation, excessive desire, envy, deceit, and violence. To avoid *hubris* mortals must not seek to become gods (*Olympian* V), or venture beyond the 'impassable sea' (*Nemean* III). In the language of *Olympian* XII (written *c.* 470 BC), for even the best of men there can be no certainty:

> No man on earth has yet found from the Gods
> A certain token of success to come,
> But their sight is blinded to what is to be.
> Many things fall against men's reckoning.
> Contrary to delight, and others,
> After facing the enemy surges,
> Exchange in a brief moment
> Sorrow for deep joy.

2 THE HEROIC ETHIC IN REFLEXIVE MIMESIS

> But victory in the Games loves song most of all.
> Pindar, *Nemean* III.1)

Pindar's 'existential' world-view provided the cultural context for his poetic redefinition of the heroic ethic which, I will suggest, hinges on the idea of the lyrical 'imitation' of noble acts which are themselves projected as the reflexive 'imitation' of divine exemplars. In this sense Pindar's work can be considered as both an aesthetic and a political intervention in the age of the Greek tyrants – a period which coincides roughly with the second Persian War (480–479 BC).

Like many other forms of contemporary choral poetry, Pindar's epinician odes (*epinikia*) were intended to be sung, often by a guild-trained choir. They formed one part of a larger, orchestrated performance requiring extensive preparation and training on the part of its participants. On a biographical level we can assume that Pindar himself served a long and comprehensive apprenticeship in learning the skills necessary to practise as a professional musician-poet – he may even have been a member of a guild of poet-singers. His verses were typically performed at the court of royal patrons or in the wake of victory at the games, commissioned by powerful aristocratic families and 'tyrants' (some of his greatest works were commissioned by the powerful Deinomenid and Emmenid dynasties in Sicily). The Victory odes thus return again and again to the 'boundless glory' of Hieron and Theron – two of the most powerful dictators of the early fifth-century Greek world in the West.

Accepting the militarist warrior code of the Sicilian tyrants, itself woven from recycled images from the Homeric epic, Pindar articulated a conservative 'play form' of the martial way of life in his glorification of athleticism and physical dominion. The traditional hierarchy of the virtues is crystallized in the figure of the powerful athlete, victor at the pan-Hellenic Games who, in Pindar's mock epic *mimesis*, is used to embody the moral and physical excellences of 'the good and noble'. In historical fact the archetypal athlete was the charioteer, exemplified by the paid champions of the tyrants Hieron (autocrat of Syracuse from 478 to 467 BC) and Theron, tyrant of Acragas. Hieron is said to have personally won the chariot race at Delphi in 470 BC and at Olympia in 476 BC (*Olympian* I, written in 470, celebrates Hieron's triumph in the horse race, and *Olympian* II and III honour his victory in the chariot race; cf. *Pythian* I, *Pythian* II.81–8, II.94–6; *Olympian* II.41–7). For Pindar, Hieron can be called both 'king' (*basileus* at Olympian I.23) and 'tyrant' (*tyrannos* in *Olympian* I and *Pythian* V; cf. Archilochus, Fr. 19); in the elevated style of the elegiac ode, the words appear to be synonyms (Andrewes, 1956: 23–4). As Trypanis observed,

> He was a guest of the great families of Rhodes, Tenedos, Abdera, Sparta, Corinth, Argos and Aegina and even of Alexander of Macedon, but he devoted his greatest efforts above all to Arcesilas IV, king of Cyrene, for whom he wrote one of his masterpieces, an ode of almost epic scale.
> (1981: 109)

In this simulacral universe, human existence has not yet become a 'spectatorial life' – as this would be understood several generations later in the image of the life of reflective *theoria*; Pindar's heroic ideal is a life of competitive struggle in one of life's many spheres of honorific praxis (significantly, after Zeus, the patron gods of the games are Heracles, god of physical prowess, and the mobile, mediator god, Hermes). Heracles had special significance in Pindar's cosmology given the god's traditional epithet 'Theban-born' (cf. Hesiod, *Theogony* 530). Celebrating the god Heracles in this context would also have been interpreted as invoking the spirit of Spartan military culture. In one sense the courage and competitive ambitiousness of the *tyrannos* embodied the core values of the Pindaric code (*Pythian* I, VI, VII). As Kenneth Dover has reminded us, Pindar, 'like most Greeks' 'looked more to the good that a man accomplished than to the morality of his intentions' (1982: 30). The Pindaric self lives by an ethic of struggle and results not contemplation and intention. And only in the recognized theatres of action can individuals participate in the radiance of divine *arete* – the Gods give and take glory as they mete out life and death. This is one of the reasons why the pan-Hellenic Games (the Games at Olympus are traditionally dated to 776 BC) served as a powerful symbol of divine action and communality: spectators and athletes are gathered into the encircling structure of the stadium as the pantheon of gods and mortals are collected within the world horizon. Here decisive encounter and movement are taken to be the axial principles of existence. We recall that in the earliest appearances of the Games the events were located at important altars. For the duration of the *agon* (the Games were called *Olympiaki agones*, which might be more literally translated as 'Olympian struggles' or 'Olympian combats') universality and particularity are conflated in the heroic enactment of memorable *acts*.

If not the mouthpiece, Pindar was certainly a celebrant of the constitutive values associated with 'tyranny' (in its specifically Greek sense of an 'ethic of aristocratic success' (Murray, 1993: 206)). What the philosophers Plato and Aristotle later sublimated into 'logical' and dialectical conflict (the *elenchus dialektike*) appears in Pindar's poetry as the very medium of human life: 'Trial is the true measure of mortal men' (*Olympian* IV.15–20; *Pythian* VIII.81–97). It is somewhat ironic that the later philosophical ideal of the reflexive *psyche* reconstructed the key terms of this aphorism (*elenchos, logos, broton (anthropos)*) as an explicit inversion of Pindar's aristocratic ethic, giving the watchword of the dialectical form of life: *dialectic (theorizing) is the true measure of mortal men.*

Pindar's epinician odes celebrate values that are profoundly agonistic, patriarchal, and militaristic. Icons of wealth, 'good breeding', war, and athletic prowess define the hierarchy of 'excellences'; and these 'virtues' can only be realized through the conflicts of collective spectacles. Just as the 'heroes' of the Games are inscribed on the public roll of honour, so the poet's task is to recollect and immortalize the cosmos of noble acts, preserving their significance in language, giving a voice to the stuff of shadows. For the 'insubstantial' word lives longer than action (cf. *Nemean* VI.1). In fact, language is graced with the most remarkable powers of resurrection. The *logos* is the *anamnesic* organ of value in Archaic Greek culture. The poetic word memorializing the hero's *kleos* is time's only witness, celebrated by the holy Graces, *Aglaia* – (Glory), *Euphrosyna* (Music, Mirth) and *Thalia* (Health, 'lover of dancing') who 'dispose all that is done in Heaven' (*Olympian* XIV.1; cf. the opening stanza of *Pythian* I). Every order of human existence is a gift of divine provenance:

> Without the Graces, not the gods even marshal their dances, their festivals; mistresses of all heavenly action, they who have set their thrones

beside Pythian Apollo of the bow of gold keep eternal the great way of the father Olympians.

(*Olympian* XIV, trans. Lattimore)

It is thus wholly appropriate that Pindar's victory odes are named after the four great pan-Hellenic festivals: the *Olympian Odes* (from the Games at Olympia), the *Pythian Odes* (founded in 588 BC after the religious festival held at Delphi), the *Nemean* (founded in 573 BC at Nemea) and the *Isthmian Odes* (founded in 582 BC in the city-state of Corinth). With tragic drama, the pan-Hellenic games are 'aesthetic-religious' institutions unique to the ancient Greek world. Both tragedy and the games had their social roots in Archaic religious practices; and both were sponsored by the aristocratic ruling class (and frequently dynastic 'tyrants') as a showcase for their respective cities. The Greek athletic contests should therefore be approached as a complex configuration of religious, political, and cultural practices – an organized social matrix for the reflexive celebration of an emergent Greek 'cultural' identity. On a more prosaic level, the Games served direct political functions, facilitating both overt and covert political bargaining and alliance formation. In terms of their long-term effect, they helped articulate and reproduce an ideology of Hellenic selfhood and physical presence (given the patriarchal value system, no women or non-Greek competitors – 'barbarians' – were permitted to participate in these ceremonial occasions). As acts of ceremonial praxis, the epicinian ode, tragic drama, and athletic competitions served in their different ways to legitimate and codify the unique aristocratic 'tragic sense of life' so characteristic of late sixth and early fifth-century Greek civilization.[1]

In the terminology of logological inquiry, the pan-Hellenic Games functioned as a living medium and 'technology' of self-reflection, cultural self-definition, and self-understanding. In the four-year intervals they became the central 'social imaginary' system of Greek civilization, reflecting and, more importantly, physically crystallizing the discourses and value premises of an idealized way of life. On the face of it these periodic athletic contests were tests of individual athletic skill, prowess, and power; the most popular competitions after the four-horsed chariot race were uncompromisingly violent – the *pankration* (combining wrestling and boxing) and the physically exhausting races in heavy armour ('the naked foot-races and in the running of warriors in clanging armour', *Isthmian* I.2). But in terms if the society's dominant value system, they were conspicuous 'trials' of the foundational 'discourses' of the Greek *polis* system. Each victor at the games was regarded as a representative of his home city and its honour. And the image of a collective testing or 'trial' of the whole city in the person of the athlete is extremely apt. As in war where a city survived or was destroyed, so the contests were zero-sum games. Only one individual from the many competitors could triumph, and there were no 'runners up' or consolation prizes. The institution of the Games thus helped to disseminate the competitive ethos of Archaic culture on a pan-Hellenic scale.

PINDAR AND THE AGE OF LITERARY CONSCIOUSNESS

So central were the Games to Hellenic civilization that their periodic occurrence (usually on a two-year or four-year basis) served as a calendar throughout the Greek-speaking world. If Greek 'logological space' (as an 'elenctic' universe of rare, semi-divine 'excellences') could be modelled on the imagery of the festive stadium as a theatre of praxis and collective trial, so 'time' could be plotted by means of the various cycles of Games. The Greek ruling strata literally took their temporal bearings and ideological orientations from these belligerent festivals. After the temple, the sacred sanctuaries, and the public administration buildings, the most important capital outlay for any influential city-state lay in investment programmes for the amphitheatre and stadium. In a manner unique to the ancient Greek world, civic experience revolved around these mythosymbolic architectural references. The gymnasium and amphitheatre evolved into highly charged *social-symbolic texts*, microcosms of the imaginary macrocosm of Greek civilization. But more significantly, the 'world-as-imagined' by means of these material structures, the sacred spaces of Greek consciousness, were also reconstituted around the ritual icons of the competitive Games – it was here that all could witness the agonistic life concretely enacted and materially reproduced. Even forms of music – including flute-playing and recited choral and lyric verse – were subject to competitive norms. And after honour in war, to win at the Games or, in the fifth century, to have a drama performed at the festival to Dionysus was the greatest achievement for a citizen. As one student of the ancient Games has observed: 'at Sparta, the most powerful military state in Greece from the seventh to the fourth century, Olympic victors had the enormous privilege of being stationed in front of their king in battle' (Cartledge, in Easterling and Muir, eds, 1985: 115). Social space and time were thus symbolically tied into the discourse formation of 'holiness' – creating an auratic topology that could be extended as a model for the mind and cultural life more generally.

Pindar, of course, was not unique in ordering his poetic craft around the symbolic paradigm of athleticism and the Game 'model' of divinity. Like other poets of the day he simply borrowed terministic screens from a tradition of existing reflexive systems. Practices and institutions like tragedy, athletic competition, lyric poetry, public architecture, sacred precincts, gymnasia, public speaking, and so on were already vested with the symbolic authority and power of the state; they were not private arenas, activities, or 'recreations' in the modern sense of these terms – and even 'architecture' has a very different social function and significance in this context; each of these practices functioned as a public medium of self-reflection, an embodiment of the habitus of Hellenic identity and cultural continuity. To use the terminology of Volume 1, they constituted a powerful 'rhetoric' of societal reflexivity (cf. Raschke, ed., 1988).

To return to the Pindaric victory ode: in the context of the structures we have briefly described, lyric poetry as it circulated through the ruling *echelons* of the *polis* system of Pindar's day functioned as a primary ideological medium. The boundaries between 'the political' and 'the religious' cannot be clearly drawn for early Greek culture. Pindar's songs were explicitly crafted to glorify and memorialize the public achievements of the ruling class, written in a style that was intelligible only to literate members of this class, patronized and materially sustained by aristocratic families, and intended as a symbolic act of patrician legitimation. Not surprisingly, a concern for the internal cohesion of the *polis* and the integrity of its class structure pervade Pindar's language. This implicit value code is even evident in the formal pattern of the Pindaric ode and its four key elements: praise of the Gods; statements about the victor's person and family; a myth illustrating the occasion and suggesting genealogical links with the dynastic family; and 'grave general truths, presented in the form of maxims' (Trypanis, 1981: 110–11).

Pindar's chosen idiom was a complex, somewhat baroque, literary dialect, an ideolect never spoken by everyday Greek speakers; his works are not 'poetry' in the modern meaning given to this term; rather they elaborate the refined discourses of power codified into intricate lyrical formations – analogous to the specialized speech styles and narrative conventions of epic poetry. The elaborate plotting of the Pindaric stanza, with its irregular rhythm of strophe, counterstrophe, and epode was certainly a consciously evolved technique. The poet seems to have been acutely aware of the intricate craft of poetic textuality – particularly with respect to the increasingly esoteric references to mythology and family genealogy that are such characteristic features of the verse. In many of the odes 'complexity' gets the better of content and destroys the possibility of poetic communication (as though Pindar consciously designed his choral poems to be deciphered later as 'multilayered' textual objects). Lyric – like epic before it – achieves its effects by deviating from the rules of ordinary usage, particularly by means of its intertextual play of metaphoric and mythological allusion. Even the supreme symbols of the numinous that appear in these dense poetic texts are determined by rhetorical devices and verbal strategies.[2]

In Trypanis' useful summary, one source of unity in the Pindaric ode can be traced not only to the dominant theme of 'athletic success', but to the nexus of ethical and ideological values celebrated by the declining aristocratic order:

> These values colour Pindar's attitude towards the Gods, the heroic myths, human conduct and the position of the poet in society. He seems to have considered such values eternal and immutable. He believed in the innate and inherited qualities of a man and held that training can only develop such qualities, never impart them. Therefore a man who merely *acquires* ability (as distinct from displaying innate ability conferred by blood) 'never walks with a sure foot'. These views are fully illustrated in his use of the myths of the heroes, whose blood, he maintained, still ran in the veins of the noble families to which the noble victors belonged.
>
> (1981: 111)

Complex cultural threads connect the pan-Hellenic Games with myth, lyric poetry, music, politics, and even ancient medicine. To take the case of medical knowledge for illustrative purposes, it is well documented that the reflexive institution of recurrent public athletic festivals and gymnasia provided an ideal physical and ideological setting in which medical, dietary, and anatomical knowledge could be compared, criticized, and accumulated. Medical inquiry, like every other form of systematic reflection, does not appear in a social and cultural vacuum; it requires the continuous impulse of appropriate social practices and institutions. Since every large *polis* was proud of its gymnasia, staffed by professional trainers (the Athenian trainer, Melesias, is mentioned by name in *Nemean* VI.3 and *Olympian* VIII.3), directors, and doctors, so each city acted as a 'storehouse' of bodily regimes and 'professional' specialisms. A city like Sparta in the late sixth century effectively turned the whole of its social structure into one extended gymnasium or intensive training ground in the martial arts. We can also speculate that because of the dominance of aggressive athletic training, physical manipulation, the physiology of bone and muscle, and related forms of corporeal discipline were regarded as the 'paradigmatic' therapies (just as surgery and anatomy found a ready supply of 'cases' in the gladiatorial circus at the time of the Roman physician, Galen). The Games, then, formed one of the crucial preconditions and material infrastructures for the development of early Greek medicine. The traditional founder of empirical medicine – Hippocrates of Kos was a younger contemporary of Pindar.

In different media and corresponding to different criteria both lyric art and Hippocratic medicine helped to give concrete form to a previously amorphous videological culture. Medicine turned to the life-world of praxis, becoming the first experiential or phenomenological science (witness the endless compilations of case histories that now form the Hippocratic corpus). The instrument of the observational case study first appeared in the context of these 'histories': every disease (including the so-called 'sacred' disease of epilepsy) being regarded as a product of physical causes, manifested in observational symptoms and syndromes. Like Pindar's poetic craft, the art of medicine was also a practical hermeneutics – 'reading' symptoms back to underlying causes. Once established, empirical medicine would eventually displace magical, astrological, and other forms of speculative medicine. And by the time of Plato, medicine would be cited as a paradigmatic body of knowledge, prestigious enough to be continually referenced as an exemplar of genuine *episteme* (forming one term in an analogy with philosophy, as inquiries seeking knowledge of the body and soul respectively).

3 GODS AND MEN

Among many noble feats, gentlemen, for which it is right to remember Heracles, we ought to recall the fact that he was the first, in his affection for the Greeks, to convene this contest.

(Lysias, *Olympic Oration* XXXIII.1)

PINDAR AND THE AGE OF LITERARY CONSCIOUSNESS

In Pindar's poetry certain metaphors continually recur as symbols of human existence; among these the most insistent are the images of Light, War, Agonistic Struggle, the Journey, the Athletic Race, Old Age, the Bow and the Lyre, and the Bounded World of the Amphitheatre. The metaphorical machinery of his verse is governed by the attempt to turn the fact of death into the stuff of lyric celebration. Mortals are earth-born creatures who must shape their destinies by acting beneath the vault of heaven (human life is evanescent, but the bronze Sky stands forever). To exist is to 'wander' the face of the earth; man is *homo viator* following a path with an unknown origin, obstructed by imponderable forces and contingencies, leading to an unknowable end. Yet despite these fatal horizons men 'can in greatness of mind or of body be like the immortals' (*Nemean* VI.1). Once more, success in the Games provides a powerful image of the intersection of *arete* and divine good fortune (on the divine gift of prowess and skill, *Nemean* III.2; on the inborn gift of *arete*, *Olympian* X.1). By achieving perfection of bodily strength and performance an individual comes to resemble the god. Perfection transfigures mortal identity into an icon of divinity itself; the 'heroic' athlete shines with the golden light of 'the divine'. In Pindar the 'delimited cosmos' of the Games – the amphitheatre being a sacred place – stands as an icon for the intersecting space of Earth, Sky, and Kosmos:

> Best is water, and gold shines out like a blazing fire in the night beyond any proud wealth: and if you wish to sing of prizes, dear heart, seek no other bright star that is hotter in the day than the sun in the empty sky, nor shall we name a contest better than Olympia.
> (*Olympian* I.1–7)

And to say that 'life is a game' in this context is not to reduce human existence to ludic insignificance, but to frame it and give it its measure. Human life is fully human where it takes the sacred form of the Game (just as the Kosmos as a Whole becomes an aesthetic spectacle, a 'world-game' of the Gods and elemental Powers).

Because of the 'delimiting' auspices of the sacred there can be no human praxis that is not somehow touched by the light of divinity (this is reflected in the well-known paradox that the Greeks were not a 'religious' people because their gods – or 'the divine' – was present everywhere). Consciousness is not merely a sign of the divine since mind was itself of divine origin. Human intellect or *nous* manifests divinity (in the same way that the Homeric gods make themselves known in encouraging, restraining, or 'darkening' the *thumos* of men). A god does not delegate influence in the shape of a sign, but rather appears 'in person'. For instance, the supreme form of reflexive consciousness in an oral culture – Memory – appears and disappears from the human frame as a divine power (and with the absence of memory, the loss of self, the collapse of order, speech, human community, *aretai*). Memory and speech share a common origin in that which gathers, delimits, and frames the order of things.

To live without memory plunges existence into darkness and madness – appropriately symbolized by the abyss of Tartarus where even the Gods are forgotten ('the pit of Tartarus' in *Pythian* I).

One common bond of mortals and Gods lies in the logosphere, especially in the poetic word which preserves the heroic *agon* of the Games – and by implication the heroic actions of human beings. Poetry is memory raised to its most supreme form, a regathering of things human and divine. Thus every form of identity presupposes the memorial powers of the Word: 'And when I die, leave to my children a name of which no evil is spoken'; 'To utter fit praise of what has been done, and by songs a man takes the pain out of toil'; 'to his children ... he leaves the best of his treasures, a good and well-loved name'.[3]

Poiesis names the many-dimensional acts of 'making' (in song, poetry, memorializing language, city-building, and so on) which preserve things in their significance against dissolution, death, and oblivion. Poetry – like the marble structures of the city – outlasts the poet in possessing an ideality and objectivity that resists the tooth of time. Language belongs with the elemental forces in that it conserves the universe of mortals even when faced with the absolute certainty of death. It is still language which gives reflexive form to the nothingness of death:

> Let him remember: the limbs that he clothes are mortal
> And at the end of all he will put on a garment of clay.[4]

> Man's life is a day. What is he?
> What is he not? A shadow in a dream
> Is man.[5]

4 DEATH AND THE ELYSIAN FIELDS

> like the baseless fabric of this vision
> The cloud-capp'd towers, the gorgeous palaces,
> The solemn temples, the great globe itself,
> Yea, all which it inherit, shall dissolve,
> And, like this insubstantial pageant faded,
> Leave not a rack behind: We are such stuff
> As dreams are made on, and our little life
> Is rounded with a sleep.
> (Shakespeare, *The Tempest* IV. i)

> Let him remember: the limbs that he clothes are mortal
> And at the end of all he will put on a garment of clay.
> (*Nemean* XI.1)

The figure of death as an allegory of limits draws together many of these symbols of finite reflection and illumination. We have seen that Pindar's epinician odes lyricize death. While mortals are destined to oblivion, swallowed in the mute abyss of Tartarus, the Gods live a life of sustaining light in the Elysian Fields. Fragment 129 depicts this blissful state in the following lines:

> For them the sun shines at full strength – while we
> here walk in night.
> The plains around their city are red with roses
> and shaded by incense trees heavy with golden fruit.
> And some enjoy horses and wrestling, or table games and
> the lyre,
> and near them blossoms a flower of perfect joy.
> Perfumes always hover above the land
> from the frankincense strewn in deep-shining fire of
> the gods' altars.
> And across from them the sluggish rivers of black night
> vomit forth a boundless gloom'.[6]

Pindar's 'orphic' cartography of hell in *Pythian* I introduces the theme of horror in ancient Greek poetry; the Underworld is populated by the enemies of light and beauty; caverns of fire burn for ever in its depths: 'In the day-time its rivers pour forth a glowing stream of smoke: But in the darkness red flame rolls and into the deep level sea throws the rocks roaring' (Bowra, trans., 1969: 132). This volcanic, darkly sublime region becomes the place of punishment for wrongdoers and transgressors of Zeus' law. *Olympian* II.3 is even more suggestive of the impact of Orphic religion, suggesting that the souls of the dead will be judged by an 'unnameable' deity in Tartarus:

> The lawless souls at once pay penalty,
> And sins done in this kingdom of Zeus
> Are judged by one below earth
> With harsh inexorable doom.

The 'Zeus below the Earth' echoes the Zeus *Katachthonios* ('beneath the earth') in the *Iliad* and Hesiod's depiction of the 'terrible houses of gloomy Night' in the underworld (*Theogony* 744; recall that Hesiod has the dog Cerberus devouring those who attempt to leave the gates of the underworld (770–3); cf. Guthrie, 1977: 217). Although retribution for evil committed in this world does not seem to have been a primary Homeric theme (although cf. *Od.* 4.561–9, 11.568–71, 11.576–600; *Il.* 9.457; *Theogony* 558ff.), Pindar introduces a topic which would later have a wider impact on popular moral attitudes and ethics in fifth-century Greece. Plato, for example, has the aged Cephalus – father of the orator Lysias – anticipate with apprehension his coming death in the following Pindaric terms:

> when a man begins to realize that he is going to die, he is filled with
> apprehensions and concern about matters that before did not occur to

him. The tales that are told of the world below and how the men who have done wrong here must pay the penalty there, though he may have laughed them down hitherto, then begin to torture his soul with the doubt that there may be some truth in them ... he is filled with doubt, surmises, and alarms and begins to reckon up and consider whether he has ever wronged anyone.

(*Rep.* 330D–E)

We can assume that by the end of the fifth century the idea of hell – the murky realm of Hades and Rhadamanthys – as a palpable reality accompanied by the threat of eternal punishment was established (*Republic* 363A–366B). Indeed the Classical Greeks appear to have taken a morbid interest in the tales of Hades, the punishments inflicted on misbehaving mortals like Clytemestra, Aegisthus, and Orestes (Aeschylus, *Eum.* 94ff., 273–5, *Supplices* 228, 230–1; Sophocles, *Electra*; Euripides, *Electra*) and deviant heroes such as Tantalus and Prometheus (cf. Plato, *Cratylus* 395B–E; Aristophanes, *Frogs* 154–7). By the fifth century Hades has assumed the office of 'ruler of the dead' ('One of the commonest names of the lord of the dead is that which derives from *plutos*, wealth, and marks him as the treasurer of the earth's rich abundance no less than the king of souls', Guthrie, 1977: 219). Whereas the texts of Homer are relatively uninformative, Plato provides a graphic image system of late fifth-century discourse on hell:

I think people have many false notions about the power of this god [Pluto, king of the underworld], and are unduly afraid of him. They are afraid because when we are once dead we remain in his realm for ever, and they are also terrified because the soul goes to him without the covering of the body. But I think all these facts, and the office and the name of the god, point in the same direction.

(*Cratylus* 403B)

Unlike Hesiod, however, Plato attempted to 'civilize' these morbid fears of the 'yawning void' of death by suggesting that the fact that no soul returns from the Underworld can only be explained by the fact that they are held there by the most powerful bond – desire; and one desire in particular, the desire to know and to become virtuous in the Island of the Blest. In fact the king of the Underworld, Hades – ruler of the dead – turns out to be a philosopher, engaging the souls of the dead in sparkling conversation and endless dialectical contests. The realm of Hades is itself an 'Island of the Blest'. Plato's final 'proof' of this benign postmortem existence is ultimately clinched by an etymological subterfuge: 'the name 'Hades' [*Aides*] is not in the least derived from the invisible [*aeides*], but far more probably from knowing [*eidenai*] all noble things, and for that reason he was called Hades by the lawgiver' (*Cratylus* 404A–B).

The Hesiodic obsession with the terrors of death and the underworld is sublimated and reformulated as another scene of moral knowledge for the renascent soul.

5 DEATH AND THE POETIC *LOGOS*

There is no such thing as death in general.
(Martin Heidegger, 1992: §34)

Longer than action lives the word.
(*Nemean* IV.1)

Pindar is first and foremost the great lyric poet of light and death. The poetic act is itself but a concrete dialogue between the forces of death ('hated old age') and the light-preserving powers of the word. As truth-claiming discourse, the word places the speaker at risk. To speak truthfully, to re-present the world of mortals and immortals in speech, to find new ways of saying what is true and false, is to place oneself in danger (for the Gods jealously guard what is true and give only glimpses of the truth to mankind); the poet's quest for novelty also places tradition in danger ('To find new themes/And put them to the touchstone for proof/Is nothing but danger', *Nemean* VIII.2). Poets and prophets more than other mortals are especially indebted to the gods of light, beauty, and wisdom for their inspiration. They speak in the borrowed voices of the Muse or divine source of truth; and utter what was, is, and will be in signs and wonders.

Death and poetry are thus inextricably connected. The poetic word is primordially a 'naming' and domesticating of the elemental powers which delimit all things; and suffering and death are the first to inscribe themselves in human thought and awareness. Suffering and the ultimate threat of oblivion occasions reflexivity. Yet poetry's power to name even the 'event' of death promises a form of this-worldly transcendence. Like a shadow, death haunts Pindar's verse, and his vision of the human condition. The God-given, light-bringing power of the word appears in many of Pindar's meditations on 'black death':

> Do not against all comers let break the word that
> is not needed.
> There are times the way of silence is best;
> the word in its power can be the spur to battle.
>
> Mistress of high achievement, O lady Truth,
> do not let my understanding stumble
> across some jagged falsehood.[7]

Pindar's verse waxes lyrical over the word's memorial powers. His choral odes are quite literally communal discourses which gather noble names and deeds into the enlightened space of memory. Without the poetic word human beings become nameless. Poetry's wisdom stems the social death that accompanies forgetfulness: 'Great valour dwells in deep darkness for need of song. In one way only we know a mirror for noble deeds – if thanks to bright-clad Memory regard is found for labour in the famous songs of poetry' (Pindar, *Nemean* VII.11. Here *mimesis* (poetry), recognition (*kleos*), and the word (*logos*) are inseparably linked.

Self-reflexivity even extends to the narrative figure of Odysseus: 'I hold that Odysseus' story has become greater than his suffering because of the sweet poetry of Homer. There is something grand about his lies and winged devices'.[8]

Without the 'sweet-speaking' *logos* both individuals and communities fall back into the enveloping darkness – and darkness is the icon most associated with oblivion and death in the Greek language: 'the unpredictable mist of forgetfulness stalks us, it wrenches aside the right way of action far from our thoughts' (*Olympian* VII). Loss of memory, darkness, and death are variations on a common Pindaric theme. The phenomenological presence of darkness is the most concrete reminder of the ultimate darkness of wordless death. Here it is true to say that the word preserves the world. Even the Gods cannot stem the encroaching oblivion of time, and with the dissolution of memory comes moral and social death – the pathways of duty are erased and human beings wander from the way of truth.[9] Even more tragically, the loss of language prefigures the oblivion of Theia, the mother of the Sun, God of light and truth, and where the divine dispensation withdraws, so everything falls back into concealment (*lethe*). With the encroaching darkness all judgement and moral order dissolves – the god withdraws (one of the most evocative Pindaric epithets for Zeus is 'Lord of the Light'). Error and deception in human affairs bear an elective affinity with the powers of oblivion at work in the wider universe of Nature and Gods. For mortals only the *logos*, the poet's song, can preserve things from the boundless darkness and make them vividly manifest (*aletheia*).[10] Words are points of light in the enveloping night, grains of gold on the black earth.

Logos lives 'longer than deeds' and from the depths of the mind (*phrenos*) gathers and preserves the world of action.[11] Without the death-stemming work of living song guided by the holy Muses, great acts and noble discourse would be buried in forgetfulness. Life in its authentic and, for Pindar, transient sense can only be conserved in the rhythms of song, the gift of Memory.[12] While the time of mortals runs out like sand from a glass, the temporality of the logos endures. We can now see how Pindar expanded and extended Hesiod's discovery of the truth-enunciating powers of poetry. Poetry is a transformative force of truth in the fundamental sense of bringing to light and preserving what would otherwise drift into oblivion and death – it is thus not 'imitation' in the passive sense of verizimilitude; moreover, it is also a force of intelligibility that preserves 'disclosed things' in their unconcealment.[13] By appropriating, temporalizing, and shaping noble events, poetic discourse holds the key to immortality; *Logos* – the speaking of the beautiful word – is the only way mortals can transcend non-existence and death:

> For this goes forth undying in speech
> If a man says a thing well.
> Over the fruitful earth and across the sea
> The sunbeam of fine doings has gone
> Unquenchable for ever.
>
> (*Isthmian* IV)

Lattimore translates the lines: 'A thing said walks in immortality if it has been said well; and over the fruitful earth and across the sea fares the light that dies never of splendid deeds' (1959b: 137));

> But ancient beauty slumbers, and men forget
> Whatever has not been yoked to echoing streams of song
> To come to the topmost peak of art.
>
> (*Isthmian* VII)

In *Nemean* VI and VII and *Pythian* I and III poetry appears to be the only therapy mortals have against forgetfulness: 'reputation to come alone controls the way men speak of those that are gone, their life in song and story' (*Pythian* I; cf. the last lines of *Pythian* III). Individuals come into the world and pass away but words resist the gnawing tooth of time. Paradoxically what appears to be the most evanescent of realities – the breath which articulates names and songs – is the only reality which survives the decay of the human estate. By being re-collected and re-membered in song the 'objects' of poetry attain a quasi-divinity: ephemeral acts and events are transfigured into the 'immortal' ciphers of language. Poetic language is the only solace mortals have against the ruination facing all created being.[14] Even the physical and metaphysical terrors of death become bearable for one who is conscious of being regathered in the folds of language, leaving his soul as a 'good name' to his successors.[15] What moved and lived upon the dark earth will still be manifest (*phainetai*) in deathless language, in written symbols transcending place and time:

> Only the glory of fame which they leave behind them
> Proclaims men's way of life, when they die,
> In history and in song ...
> Good fortune is the best and first of prizes,
> Good name the second possession:
> The man who has found both and keeps them
> Has won the highest crown.
>
> (*Pythian* I.5)

Song, then, is that unique mode of *mimesis* in which what 'appears' can be redeemed beyond the space and time of the present: precisely in the mode of absence we experience as 'having-been-present'; like the written tables of laws inscribed in stone, the poet's song written in the hearts of the future will live forever. The poet of *Pythian* I, commanding word and writing, has the power to bestow immortality upon the noble and infamy upon the evil:

> The rich man and poor man together
> Come to death's boundary.
> But I hold that the name of Odysseus
> Is more than his sufferings
> Because of Homer's sweet singing;
> For on his untruths and winged cunning
> A majesty lies.[16]

The idea of a second life of poetic immortality appears to have been one of the recurrent themes of the lyric poets. We come across the same theme in Sappho's poem 'To a rival':

> You will die and be still, never shall be memory
> left of you
> after this, nor regret when you are gone. You have
> not touched the flowers of the Muses, and thus,
> shadowy still in the domain of Death,
> you must drift with a ghost's fluttering wings,
> one of the darkened dead.[17]

Pindar's image of the Shadow also resonates in the poetry of later Greek tragedy – in Sophocles 'Man is but a breath and a shadow' (*pneuma kai skia*, Fr. 13), in Mimnermus' lament for 'the generations of men dispersed like autumn leaves', and in Archilochus' melancholy vision of 'the ebb and flow of men'. Human existence is a dream:

> Not to be born is best
> Beyond all counting – or else, at least,
> Whence we were born, to be
> re-gathered speedily.[18]

This forms another subterranean connection between death, *psyche*, and poetry; for it is from the perspective of poetic reflexivity that a Sophocles or Pindar can enunciate the radical contingency and indeterminacy of human existence. The body which falls to 'all-powerful death' has been separated from the divine 'spark' of the soul. Yet even the inescapable necessity of contingent existence serves to frame the singular reality of human action and endow it with its vital sense and purpose. *Kleos*, so to speak, requires the dark horizon of oblivion. Human ventures are bordered by an irreducible opacity: 'From Zeus comes no clear sign to men' (*Nemean* XI.43). Each moment of happiness is won against the dark fate that only the gods comprehend, bounded by the silence of death. But death is also a facilitating horizon; only a self-conscious creature aware of death's horizonal structure can act in the full sense of this term: 'for our limbs are shackled to shameless hope, and the streams of forethought lie afar' (*Nemean* XI.43–6, trans. Lattimore). 'Transtemporal' notions of 'excellence', 'valour', 'fame', and so on only make sense to a creature that is already intuitively aware of its finite nature. Forethought (*promatheia*) is what makes the structure of human praxis possible: 'Forasmuch as we must die, why should one sit idly in the dark, nursing an old age unknown to fame, without part or lot in noble deeds?'.[19]

Reflexivity (*promatheia/boulais*) takes the predominant form of an active self-consciousness of human finitude; this 'existential' consciousness is precisely what delimits and defines the theatre of heroic praxis. A similar ethic resonates in that part of the Gilgamesh saga where the God-Man, Gilgamesh, describes human existence to the wild Enkidu:

> Who, my friend, can scale the heavens? Only the gods live forever under the sun. As for mankind, numbered are their days; Whatever they achieve is but wind! Even here thou art afraid of death. What of thy heroic might? Let me go before thee. Let thy mouth call to me, 'Advance, fear not'. Should I fall, I shall have made me a name: 'Gilgamesh' – they will say – 'against fierce Huwawa has fallen (long) after my offspring has been born in my house.
>
> Do we build a house forever? Do we seal contracts forever? Do brothers divide shares forever? Does hatred persist forever in the land? Does the river forever raise up and bring on floods? The dragon-fly leaves its husk that its face might but glance at the face of the sun. Since the days of yore there has been no permanence; the resting place of the dead, how alike they are. Do they not compose a picture of death, the commoner and the noble, once they are near to their fate? The Anunnaki, the great gods, foregather; Mammetum, maker of fate, with them the fate decrees; death and life they determine, but of death, its days are not revealed.[20]

In accepting the transition from wild Nature to civic Culture, human beings incur a terrible penalty: they become conscious of the boundary separating life and death. Pindar's theme has its parallel in the harlot's seduction of Enkidu, the 'natural man' in the Gilgamesh epic. Enkidu is literally seduced into culture by carnal knowledge; his fall from Nature is symbolized both by his alienation from nature (spreading fear in the animal kingdom) and by his acquisition of self-knowledge. And reflexive awareness sows the dangerous hope that mortals can inquire and learn the origins and ends of human life, a quest which frequently ends in *hubris* – human beings overstepping nature's limits and impiously aspiring to a state of absolute knowledge. The Theban aristocrat thus warns his audience of the dangers of overstepping the mean:

> Of what comes from Zeus
> We have no sure sign, and yet
> We set foot upon great endeavours
> And hanker for many things.
> Our bodies are chained to wanton hope.
> And the waters of foresight lie far away.
> We must hunt for the mean in our profits –
> Loves beyond reach sting too sharply to madness.
> (In C.M. Bowra's translation (1961); *Nemean* XI.3)

Sandy's renders the last lines: 'but far too keen are the pangs of madness that come from unattainable longings' (Pindar, 1919: 433); and Richmond Lattimore translates: 'too bitter are the pangs of madness after loves that are past attainment' (1959b: 129)).

In Pindar's lifetime the same moral would inform one of the stock themes of the tragic poets. Aesychylus deals with *hubris* in identical terms:

> Sand dunes of corpses will proclaim,
> even to the third generation,
> their silent message for the eyes of men:
> that never, being mortal, is it right
> for us to cast our thoughts too high.
> For *hubris*, in blossoming, has sown
> the sheaf of ruin
> from which a tearful harvest springs.
> Seeing such things deserved, remember, Athens.
> And Hellas, too. Let no man overlook
> the present good, lusting for more,
> and squander his great fortune.
> (Aeschylus, *Persians* 818–27)

Later in the fifth century, philosophy itself would be singled out as a dangerous practice conducive to *hubris*. For example in the advice given to Xerxes reported by Herodotus:

> Do you see how God with his lightning smites always the bigger animals, and will not suffer them to wax insolent, while those of a lesser bulk chafe him not? How likewise his bolts fall ever on the highest houses and the tallest trees? So plainly does he love to bring down everything that exalts itself ... For God allows no one to have high thoughts but himself.
> (*Histories* VII.10)

A similar moral informs the parable of the tyrant Polycrates who asks Amasis, a sage of Egypt, for his advice. Amasis responds:

> Your great successes do not please me, knowing as I do that the divine nature is jealous. I would prefer that I myself and those I care for should

be successful in some things and unsuccessful in others, experiencing through life alternate good and evil fortune, rather than that they should invariably succeed. For I have never yet heard of any one who was successful in everything, without perishing miserably, root and branch, at the last. Therefore hearken to me, and in view of the successes you have gained, act thus. Consider on what object you set the highest value, what it will grieve you most to lose, and take and throw it away, so that it shall never return among men.

(*Histories* III. 40–3)

Polycrates duly follows Amasis' advice, throwing his most valuable possession – a precious, jewelled ring – into the sea; unfortunately the return of the ring in the belly of a fish seals his fate.

6 CONCLUSION: PINDAR'S WORLD

To each thing belongs its measure.

(Olympian XIII)

Pindar's world is closer to the martial values of the *Iliad* than to Hesiod's *Works and Days* or the austere metaphysics of the tragic dramatist Aeschylus. His is a world of aristocratic pleasure, festive celebrations, and heroic actions played out under the gaze of the immortal gods. His art, however, already displays many of the tell-tale signs of 'mock epic' and moral didacticism (witness the censorious 'editing' of the Olympians' conduct in *Olympian* I.24ff. and *Pythian* III and ancient myth in *Nemean* V.16). We might even speak of the mock Olympian character of his poetic diction with its endless invocation of the theme of human finitude. The gods are frequently merely pretexts for a highly self-reflective poetry, overcoded in dense symbolic imagery. Even the high-god Zeus seems to be struggling to play his civilizing part and act in accord with the poet's ethical script. The terminal point of this evolution will be the appearance of god as a *deus ex machina* in fourth-century tragedy. Mythological heroism, in other words, is already well on the way to being 'theatricalized' into a high-minded, reflective moral habitus: *arete* assumes the role of edification, with a commensurate shift in the function of the 'carriers' of virtue, who now become paradigms of prescribed conduct (*Olympian* I.82).

But Pindar halts before embracing the full consequences of his own didactic heroism. The epinician ode is not yet fully allegorical. The Pindaric moment of 'mock epic' is still far from sliding into *legend* or – as in the early writings of Plato – *dialectical instruction*; Pindar's audience was too deeply enmeshed in the language-games of honour and noble breeding to see these lyrics as a dangerous venture in 'aestheticizing' tradition. In the final analysis Pindar was not an unconscious social critic, but an apologist for the way of life of a threatened aristocracy, and his first circle of listeners patronized the Theban poet as the voice of their own sense of divine legitimation and courageous action. But the very success of his experiment in poetic sublimation, and, more significantly, its acute self-reflexivity as 'poetic craft' spelled the end of this ethos as a living code.

We are in the presence of an ethic reflecting a form of life in decline. Of course it might be said that heroism is an unintelligible concept without the delimiting horizon of exaggerated, memorable death, and that this in turn requires a sober understanding of death as an absolute limit of existence. The latter notion, as we have briefly indicated, entails the existential possibility of choice, of the idea of a freely taken decision but also of irredeemable loss and nostalgia with their correlate emotions and moods. And decisiveness brings with it risk, the possibility of either choosing memorable acts or succumbing to the fate of temporal oblivion ('Those who make no trial win silences that know them not', *Isthmian* IV).

By the middle decades of the fifth century (*c.* 450–440 BC) Pindar's art was already the subject of imitations and parodies (cf. Aristophanes, *Birds* 926–30, 941–5). Toward the end of the century intellectuals were reading Pindar as a literary apologist of an anachronistic ideal of life and a source of verbal archaisms. The adjective 'Pindaric' had become a watchword for conservative values.

Once myth can be raided as a resource of edifying poetry we are in the sphere of didactic art:

> The story of the pious Pelops becomes the prototype for every victory in a chariot race; that of Tantalos, connected with it, provides a warning against the dangers inherent in success. The myth has acquired the significance of a paradigm. It constitutes the framework of reference that allows one to assess, understand, and judge the exploit that the poem is celebrating. It is only by being refracted through the legendary adventures of the heroes or gods that human actions, conceived as imitative, can reveal their meaning and fall into position on the scale of values.
>
> (Vernant, 1990: 213)

An example of this phenomenon is the fifth Olympian ode which was included in the Pindaric corpus by the Alexandrian philologist Didymos, but is now regarded as a Sicilian imitation 'in the manner of Pindar'. The anonymous writer of *Olympian* V (*c.* 448 BC) had successfully isolated the 'mock epic' elements of Pindar's involuted texts and used his knowledge of these formular themes to generate further edifying 'victory odes' to order. From myth as a matrix of the sacred we are confronted by a conception of poetry as a source of entertaining moral paradigms. In Frank Nisetich's translation, the last lines of the poem read:

and may you, Psaumis
... bring your life to completion in good cheer,
with your sons standing beside you.
If the wealth a man tends and cares for be sound,
his house ample, and his name renowned as well,
let him not envy the gods.

(1980: 102)

To pull the threads of this presentation together: Pindar attempted to continue the epic tradition within the formal structure of the choral ode; but despite his own literary intentions he unintentionally deepened the thematics of lyric reflexivity disclosed by his predecessors; the epic horizon was extended to incorporate named, individual athletes whose heroic feats form the theme of many of his most important verses; he 'ethicized' the finitude of human existence to a degree that the notion of the 'earth-born' for his successors possessed the indelible meaning of an existence within an undecidable sphere of fateful forces and radical choice: 'Even for men who struggle Fortune/stays undiscerned/Until they come to the lofty end/She gives of this and of that' (*Isthmian* IV). When Achilles steps onto the epic stage by *choosing* to withdraw from the campaign (and the 'community' of the assembled Greek warriors) he does not merely absent himself from the struggle against Troy; his absence stands forth as a freely chosen, wilful act of a Self, of an individual, idiosyncratic heroic choice; and *self-choosing* entails reflexivity in the minimal sense of requiring an individual to 'locate' himself in conflictual spheres of values.[21] Pindar recodes the god not as an embodiment of *arete*, but as a paradigm of values. In this transfiguration the incarnate realms of Archaic *arete* are literally visibilized in the ethical topography mapped by the epinician ode. Here Herman Fränkel has touched the heart of the matter:

> in Pindar's choral odes the idea of the good and great achieves self-awareness and triumphantly displays its own significance. Promise and performance here become one. It is for this reason that Pindar's art can so often and so explicitly speak about itself.
>
> (1975: 490)

Yet Pindar's world is still bound by a horizon of darkness which no amount of theory or speculative reflection can dispel; in stark contrast to the undifferentiated horizon from which a Heroic individual like Achilles steps forward, Pindar's heroes are collective agents, metonyms of a more solid world of 'political' identities and alliances. Pindaric heroism has become collectivized and the 'consciousness of freedom' is no longer an extreme clash of wills (Achilles and Agamemnon), but a 'dialogic' struggle of communal values against the powers that erode civic autonomy. At this point modern reflexivity with its problematics of liberation enters Western discourse.[22]

One major source of this change lies in the changed 'conditions of reception', the creation of new 'audiences' for Pindar's art. Pindar was primarily patronized by aristocratic families (Fragment 106 is an encomium for Alexander of Macedon) and local 'kings'- *Pythian* IV and V for Arcesilas IV, king of Cyrene, for example (or 'tyrants' such as Hieron of Syracuse and Theron of Acragas in Sicily – *Olympian* II and III for Theron), but these figures were themselves evolving into symbolic representatives – self-appointed paradigms, so to speak – of the power and wealth of their respective cities. One of the fundamental conditions of the dictator in antiquity was the ability to use force and civic culture to spread the tyrant's signature throughout social life. The tyrant had to 'stamp' his image upon every aspect of culture – from the coinage to the unconsidered realms of gossip, song, and dreams. Thus a Theron or Dionysius drew upon every instrument that might possibly extend their presence in the hearts and minds of the population. The poetic logos was simply another means of monumentalizing the tyrannical Self.

Pindar's unique fusion of aristocratic, quasi-philosophical heroism, and sublime mimetic visuality has thus been frequently compared with the formal ideals of Greek sculpture and architecture in the late Archaic and early Classical period. The

> perfect harmony of body and soul which those sculptured athletes represented lives and speaks to us again in Pindar's poetry, telling of a unique moment when the Greek world saw the height of divinity in the human body and soul... Pindar too writes about the victor not primarily as an individual but rather as the representative of an abstraction: the highest *arete*'.[23]

We should not forget that Pindar also wrote 'occasioned' choral works to be performed in the urban locations of Rhodes, Corinth, Thebes, and Athens. These compositions evoke an idealized, aristocratic community rather than the singular monarchies of an imaginary Greece or the political experiments carried out by the more democratic city-states. He was clearly opposed to every form of democracy and, toward the end of his life, became an outspoken enemy of Athenian imperialism – most poignantly, after Athens' defeat of Aigina and its hegemony over the poet's native Boeotia.[24] Yet, despite his own ideological commitments and ingrained traditionalism much of his verse anticipates the radical anthropomorphic and self-reflexive values of the Athenian century. The Boeotian aristocrat shared with the tragic dramatists and the great Athenian philosophers a fundamental impulse to 'aestheticize' and visually 'form' human experience by reworking the mythological legacy in a changed social environment. Perhaps most important of all, his intensely visual poetry prefigures some of the fundamental designs and metaphorical images of what we have called the videological form of life.

6
ORPHISM
Orphic discourse during the archaic period

Where do we come from? What are we? Where are we going?
(Paul Gauguin)

1 Introduction: the appearance of Orphism in Greek culture
2 Orphic cosmogony as an allegory of cosmic alienation
3 The Orphic body and the doctrine of cathartic reflexivity
4 The tropes of Dionysus
5 The Orphic background of the logos

1 INTRODUCTION: THE APPEARANCE OF ORPHISM IN GREEK CULTURE

Orphism

In the previous chapter we came across recurrent Orphic themes in the poetry of Pindar (particularly with regard to Fragment 131 which thematizes the spiritual imago of the soul as a gift of the Gods and the Orphic speculations about the postmortem soul in *Olympian* II). Pindaric texts like Fragments 129 and 131 are frequently cited as evidence of the influence of Orphism and the cult of Dionysus in Greek culture in the sixth century. But on first appearances Orphism is in many respects antithetical to Pindar's conservative aesthetic. The religion of Orpheus (after the mythical Orpheus – the singer of enchanting songs who journeyed to Hades to rescue his wife Eurydice only to lose her by turning back to gaze at her before leaving the Underworld) originated in popular religious cults and folk-customs, yet by the sixth century its influence was so pervasive that its concerns can be felt in even the most austere writers and poets. Like a popular mirror image of Hermes (the messenger of Zeus and God of thieves who led the souls of the dead down to the realm of Hades), Orpheus symbolized the return of life by conducting souls back from the dead. In Greek folk-culture, of course, Orpheus was primarily the patron of song and, in the generalized Greek sense of the word, *music*.

In this chapter I will deliberately focus on only one aspect of the complex phenomenon of Orphic discourse – the role of Orphic images of the self in redefining the idea of the soul and self-reflection during the sixth century. By situating 'the Orphic body' in the wider context of the genealogy of early Greek philosophical thought I hope to shed some light on the Orphic contribution to the Greek concepts of cognition and reflexivity. I will refrain from following the many paths which lead away from the topic of Orphism into the wider changes in belief and culture during the fifth century. As with other chapters we will concentrate on the principal theme of reflexivity. We will see that the tropes of rebirth and salvation in Orphic religiosity revitalized the problem of the *psyche* and placed the interrelated themes of personal individuality, the soul's immortality, and the conquest of death at the very centre of philosophical speculation.

It should be said immediately, however, that 'Orphism' has no clear doctrinal definition or ideological articulation. There is no Orphic equivalent of an Aristotle or Theophrastus compiling digests of the central ideas and doctrines. The tradition called 'Orphism' in fact was formed from a magma of arcane religious practices and vague ethicophilosophical myths fused into complex and sometimes confused cultic practices. Its poetic and institutional locus lay in the popular Orpheus cults and rites of purification in the latter half of the sixth century, themselves a product of the revival of salvational religions during the late Archaic period. The obsessive concern for the nature of the soul, pollution, and personal salvation is itself an important clue to changes in religious sensibilities during this period of Greek history. Like the Pythagorean sects, the devotees of Orpheus frequently prescribed vegetarianism and related ascetic practices as basic to their cathartic outlook and philosophy. Historians of Greek religion, for example, have typically viewed the spread of a belief in the immortality of the soul as a 'non-Greek intrusion' into the Greek world, usually tracing it to the societies encircling Greece to the north and east (in particular to Thrace – just as Euripides traces the origins of Dionysus to Lydia and Phrygia in the *Bacchae*; cf. 862). Orphism could then be 'explained' as an exotic product of 'barbarian' or 'oriental' provenance. Other scholars have argued, however, that the presence of primitive forms of Dionysian, Orphic, and Mystery religions represents a deep-rooted cultural phenomenon dating back to the beginnings of the Hellenic world in the Mycenaean age, suggesting that these forms maintained a vigourous existence down to the Macedonian period and beyond (e.g. Hammond, 1991; Webster, 1959: 38–9, 62, 70–1). Herman Fränkel describes the phenomenon in the following manner:

> The Dionysiac movement burst upon Greece in successive waves: many decades must have passed before it was established everywhere, and centuries before it reached its final developent, before the structure of the Greek mind was so reorganized as to harmonize new and old. This

movement too must have been non-literary: orgiastic worship must needs reject explanation in words and limitation through artistic forms.
(1975: 241)

Rose (1989: 149) also cites the evidence of the Phrygian form of the god's name, Diounsis – related to the sky god Dios. More recent scholarship has suggested that many of the traditional 'Thracian', 'Scythian', and 'Phrygian' aetiologies and etymologies may have been later rationalizations to account for a phenomenon which many Greek commentators found perplexing and not infrequently uncongenial to their classical tastes (cf. Euripides, *Bacchae* 155–60, 378–85; *Alcestis* 962–72).

In later Greek traditions Orpheus is presented as a divine musician, poet, and prophet risking everything in his descent into the dark realms of Hades (this is the portrait of Orpheus as he appears, for example, in the poetry of Ibycus of Rhegium and Pindar). His role as a mediator between music (culture) and the animal world (nature) is indicative of his ideological importance as a reconciler of binary oppositions in ancient Greek discourse (only Orpheus survives the journey across the Styx to rescue his wife Eurydice, since only this virtuoso of '*mousike*' can resolve the mysteries of the living and the dead – a feat that later became associated with *ta orphika*). In the myths of Dionysus it is Orpheus who is torn to pieces by the frenzied female worshippers of Dionysus.

While there is no gnostic literary canon (Walker, 1989: 20; Layton, 1987), the so-called 'Orphic texts' may well represent the earliest salvation literature in Western culture as well as the earliest cosmogonic literature to be used as an explicit source of religious authority (Burnet, 1930: 82; cf. Guthrie, 1977: ch. 11). Aristophanes and Plato refer to the commerce in Orphic tracts and 'mystery therapies' which were hawked from door to door by itinerant Orphic 'teachers' (the 'sibylline dust' in *Knights* 41–254; the 'Sibylline collection' in *Peace* 1084ff. (cf. *Frogs* 454–9; *Birds* 693ff.; cf. 685ff.); *Republic* 2.364B–E; *Laws* 908D–909B; cf. *Cratylus* 402B and *Philebus* 66C) and we also know Plato's sceptical views on the irrational frenzy of poetic 'inspiration' from the early dialogue *Ion* – for example at 533E–4E where poets are compared with the Corybants, attendants to Cybele – Goddess of fertility – and the Bacchic celebrants of the cult of Dionysus). Like the Corybants the poet must be 'inspired' and 'possessed' by the god – in the case of the rhapsode Ion, by the 'divine Homer' (534B–E; 536B–D). A later Neoplatonist like Iamblichus had no hesitation in tracing Pythagoras' theology to the 'inner mysteries of works of Orpheus' (*On the Pythagorean Life* 146–7). But the work he cites – *On the Gods* – is now known to have been spurious. An indication of the content of these 'oracular' books (*bibloi*) can be gleaned from O. Kern's collection *Orphicorum Fragmenta* (1963); also 'Orphic Literature', in *Oxford Classical Dictionary*, 758–9; Jaeger, 1965: 8, n. 14.

Scholars frequently explain the resurgence of the myth and cult of Orpheus (as with the receptivity toward the Phoenician cult of Adonis) as a 'protest' movement of the disaffected, the marginalized, and the lower strata of Archaic Greek society following the great waves of migrations in the seventh century. In essence, Orphism was a response to the social disorder and anomie of the middle decades of the sixth century. This is reflected in the appearance of similar cults in many different parts of the Greek world at this time. By virtue of its polycentric origins Orphic ideology appears to have had no consistent theological core (with the exception of elaborate initiation rites and strict prohibitions on the eating of animal flesh, practices common to many 'spiritual' movements in ancient Greece, cf. Plato, *Laws* 6.782C). Yet despite the absence of a definite ideological focus and lack of a consistent doctrinal system, Orphism helped to channel the new languages of visionary poetry, mythopoeic wisdom, and cosmogonic philosophy into a praxis of other-worldly salvation, a type of religious 'enthusiasm' which many historians have instinctively – and perhaps prejudicially – seen as untypical of Greek religiosity. As Guthrie explains, 'this was a religion which ran counter to the most typical and most cherished of Greek ideas' (1977: 326). Orphism began life as a fusion of popular cultural motifs and salvation discourses which could be appropriated and used by individuals from disparate social groups and classes. It 'asserted that all men had divinity within them, and that they should strive their hardest to throw off everything else and emerge as wholly divine and immortal' (1977: 326). The Orphic 'was an individualist. His attention was concentrated on the soul, with its long series of incarnations, and his object was to save it. The purifications and abstentions which he enjoined had this entirely self-centred end in view' (Guthrie, 1977: 327). In its inception it had little to do with the movement toward ascetic practices or the 'puritan' sensibilities of Hellenistic Greece (*contra* Dodds, 1951: 149).

Popularized by the impact of colonialism and increasing trade links crisscrossing the late sixth-century Aegean and Mediterranean world, however, Orphic practices exerted a pervasive and profound influence upon early fifth-century poetic and philosophical speculation about the soul's nature, divinity, and salvation. In more or less sublimated forms it would also have a major impact upon later ethical and philosophical discourse. Of course Orphism would not have spread so rapidly if its arcane idioms and unsettling imagery had not struck a resonant chord and fulfilled a spiritual need for its disparate audiences. In a period of social crisis Orphism provided the Greek equivalent of the salutary promise of Paradise found in many ancient cultures and civilizations. But from the perspective of the history of theoretical speculation and communities of reflexivity its importance lies in the fact, as Burnet was one of the first to emphasize, that the Orphic community 'suggested the idea that philosophy is above all a "way of life" (1930: 82–3), a quest for the One within the Many (cf. Guthrie, 1977: 318–26), an answer to something analogous to an original loss of Being (cf. Empedocles B 115). It was the spread of this amorphous 'religious consciousness' which encouraged further speculative reflection on the nature of the human condition in the transition from the sixth to the fifth century. Orphism, in other words, disseminated a distinctive conception of the spiritual nature of human being during the last century of the Archaic age.

Orphism itself presupposes a popular background of soteriological rites and initiation ceremonies, the most famous of which – the Eleusinian Mysteries – dates back to the emergence of the earliest forms of Hellenic culture (perhaps as early as the second millennium, c. 1800 BC). The appearance of Orphism also suggests that traditional religious practices and institutions had been weakened and subjected to various kinds of delegitimation throughout the late seventh and first half of the sixth century. As Gregory Nagy observed: 'Abstracted from their inherited tribal functions, religious institutions have a way of becoming mystical organizations' (1990: 230).

The Mysteries

The term 'Mysteries' derives from the Latin word *mysterium*, an esoteric doctrine or arcane teaching. In ancient Greece the Mysteries were dedicated to securing the regeneration of the harvest and, like many ancient agrarian fertility cults, were organized around the symbolic death of the old order and rebirth of the new. In Greece such fecundity rites were associated in particular with the Mysteries of Demeter (the Greek corn goddess and Mother god of fertility and agrarian life in general) and Persephone (goddess of the Underworld and the Dead). In Homer Demeter is an important protector of agrarian life (*Il.* 5.500). The earliest rites were most probably also connected with the cult of Artemis, the goddess of childbirth and protector of women and wild places (cf. Sophocles, *Electra* 1239–42). Artemis also brought death to women. Symbolisms of death and regeneration were fused and elaborated into a cycle of myths concerned with the abduction of Persephone by Hades, the Lord of the Underworld, and her eventual return and rebirth. Greek folk culture had for centuries before the fifth century identified corn as 'Demeter's grain' (cf. Hesiod, *Works and Days* 32, 393, 465–6; 'venerable Demeter', *Works* 300; 'pure Demeter', *Works* 466; 'Demeter's holy grain', *Works* 597, 805; cf. Bacchylides, Ode 3.1.1–4; *Hymn to Demeter*, 271ff.). Later traditions would connect the myth cycle with the Phrygian goddess Cybele or the Great Mother (*Meter*). The native Greek paradigm here was the figure of Gaia or 'mother earth' ('Earth, the mother of all' in Hesiod, *Works and Days* 563; cf. the 'all-nourishing Demeter' at *Theogony* 912; 'mother of Zeus, enthroned on the hills' in Sophocles' *Philoctetes* 391–4).

From the sophisticated standpoint of the older *élites* and aristocratic classes with their rigorous code of behaviour and bodily comportment such rites and cults were best left to the uneducated masses (the *laos* tied to the remorseless cycles of agrarian production). The ancient orgiastic cults belonged to a darker stage of matriarchal beliefs and practices which the 'civilizing' mythology of the Olympian religion and the epic sagas had sublimated if not entirely left behind. And this process of relinquishing the past also had immediate implications for the way the Classical Greeks developed styles of behaviour and expression. The world of cultic excess served as a useful foil against which an ideal of 'civilized' conduct could be developed for political and cultural ends. Thus Artemis was associated with the 'irrational' powers of nature, hunting, and wild places. Demeter was linked with the elemental powers of the earth, 'the giver of grain' (*Od.* 13.354), Demeter of the 'shining-harvest'. And Dionysus was represented as the protean and undisciplined god of wine, sexuality, and excess. All of these images constructed an antithetical picture of prerational disorder inimical to the *eunomia* of the well-ordered City. We hear hardly anything of the worship of Demeter or Dionysus in the works of epic and lyric poetry (the poem that is usually referred to as the *Homeric Hymn to Demeter* is a later, secondary 'epic' and Alcman's poem's in honour of Artemis in seventh-century Sparta remained an exception to the main course of Hellenic culture, cf. Bowra, 1961: 34– 9; Fränkel, 1975: 246–52). This may be an appropriate occasion to recall the idea that the construction of discourses is invariably accompanied by a measure of textual repression and revisionary occlusion – in this case the forms of identity and symbolisms of popular culture were systematically effaced by the patriarchal epic and early choral and lyric forms. Yet despite the powerful mechanisms of rationalization, the older Gods survived in the deepest layers of Hellenic popular culture (see Kerényi: 1967 and Hägg, *et al.,* 1988).

But it was not until the sixth century that the traditional fertility deities came to be amalgamated with new divinities, especially with Gods and demi-gods from northern Thrace – the orgiastic rites of Dionysus Zagreus, son of Zeus and Persephone and enemy of the Titans, ritual purification mysteries, and rites of death and rebirth, were among the more striking of these new practices. Finally, at the end of this evolutionary syncretism in the fifth century, the 'alien' Gods from the periphery of the Greek-speaking world would gain entry into the City's civic cults and festivals through the Trojan horse of Attic tragic drama. And by the time that something like Orphic 'wisdom' or 'mystery doctrine' is identifiable, the ancient cultic celebrations of cyclical fertility – centred on the phallic God Dionysus and the Demeter cult at Eleusis – had become important political property (especially during the age of the 'tyrants'), taking their place in the central religious festivals of the *polis*.[1]

Dionysus

Dionysus Zagreus represented a complex congery of symbolic images and functions: God of life and fire, of fertility, of the cyclical rhythms of the seasons, of wine, intoxicated excess, and uninhibited sexuality, but also of night, death, and destruction, of the endless absorption of finite things in the Chaos of the infinite (*Apeiron*) – symbolized most dramatically in the story of his own death by dismemberment. The history of the genesis and spread of this singular cult in the late sixth and fifth century would take us through the central religious and aesthetic institutions of the Greek world. Palaeographic evidence suggests the existence of a Dionysus cult prior to the Ionian colonization of Asia Minor (Vernant, 1990: 232; cf. Webster, 1959: 55–71). Hesiod in the seventh century was already singing of wine and fruit as the 'gifts of joyful Dionysus' (*Works and Days* 613–15), while in the classical period Dionysus became the divine patron of Attic tragedy and the tradition of tragic literature which followed in its wake. His symbol is the phallus, depicted and represented as the thyrsus or staff wreathed with ivy. A detailed reconstruction of the Dionysian phenomenon would also shed a great deal of light on the psychological motives and inhibition structures at work during the same period – processes that can be reconstructed only with great difficulty from the literary and artistic traces of these religious forms. This task is obviously not within the remit of the limited range of this essay. Here we will accept the findings of recent scholarship without further analysis or justification.

One of the most important features common to both the Mysteries and the Dionysian cult is the fact that women played a predominant part in the rites. On the assumption that women mediated between life and death – humane culture and wild nature – they were seen as central actors in the festivals of regeneration. The rapid diffusion of popular forms of the Eleusinian Mysteries (named after the small town of Eleusis fourteen miles outside of Athens), Dionysian rites, and Orphism reflected a rebirth of religious enthusiasm and a decline of the authority of the ruling, Olympian deities. But Orphism was never a disembodied ethical or metaphysical doctrine of 'mental' purification; rather it represented a popular religious movement which, at its height, swept through Greece with all the features of a frenzied mass movement. Dionysian rites served as vehicles for hitherto unarticulated popular desires. In undermining the aristocratic code of self-restraint they fulfilled a popular existential need for metamorphosis, transcendence, and redemption. Orphism's prescriptions were designed to bring absolute happiness in the here-and-now by the recovery of an era of perfect wholeness and virtue; its votaries were promised a paradisical state beyond the trammels of fallen matter and carnal embodiment. Here the idea of an ascending procession toward the Godhead became a powerful image of regeneration. As Max Weber noted in his essays on the sociology of religion, the salutary promises of religions of salvation

> at first remained tied to ritualist rather than to ethical preconditions. Thus, for instance, both the worldly and the other worldly advantages of the Eleusinian mysteries were tied to ritual purity and to attendance at the Eleusinian mass. When law gained in significance, these special deities played an increasing role, and the task of protecting the traditional

order, of punishing the unjust and rewarding the righteous, was transferred to them as guardians of juridical procedure.
(Gerth and Mills, eds, 1948: 273–4)

Forms of popular religion

At the turn of the sixth century the cult of Dionysus and Orphic religion might be denounced as archaic abominations by more aristocratic voices (for example, Heraclitus), cultivated by tyrants such as Periander of Corinth and the Peisistratids, or assimilated to the general heteroglossia of new expressive forms (as we have seen in the case of Pindar's art and, in more complex and sublimated forms, in the philosophical art of Plato); but its influence could not be ignored. In historical terms these religious currents represented a powerful force of cultural renewal, an outlet for repressed emotions, dissent, and sexuality. Orphism became one of the first popular forms of mystical consciousness, a 'discourse' speaking to the concerns of the forgotten groups of Greek history (we have seen that the voiceless strata of unpropertied artisans, peasants, and women played a significant initial role in spreading Orphic rites and doctrines). The cult of Dionysus may have provided something like a countercultural vehicle for hitherto repressed emotions and desires – its most typical vehicle being the uninhibited ecstatic dance and orgiastic 'possession' of individuals by the Gods (which our own language preserves in the expression 'enthusiasm') and the bacchic excesses of 'maenadism' with the female devotees of Dionysus running uncontrollably through the hills in search of identity with the godhead. The practice of 'divine possession' or 'mania' even penetrated the work of the great *literati* of the fifth and fourth centuries – witness, Plato's *Phaedrus* and *Symposium* as works touched by Orphic culture. It is hard not to interpret the spread of the cult of Dionysus in terms of the 'return of the repressed' – itself rooted in a widespread crisis of the institutionalized forms of patriarchal domination and social control during this period. The long-term effects of these cult practices on the position of women in Greek society were, however, largely negative:

> Even in Greek states where such a flight to the mountains was not practised, some form of ecstatic dancing by women in honour of Dionysus certainly took place. But if this was a liberation it was only a temporary one, and indeed in an important sense it tightened the chains, since it confirmed the belief that woman was a volatile and irrational being in need of close control. Maenadism could thus be readily accommodated within public religion.
> (Parker, in *OH*: 323–4; cf. Rose, 1989: 154–55)

Another important sociological feature of the Mystery cults is their implicit rejection of the honorific status hierarchies of the patriarchal aristocratic order. Recall that Dionysus was essentially an intrusion of an alien – or as the Greeks of the day would say, a 'barbarian' – deity into the Greek pantheon, a foreign God whose person and attributes concretely symbolized the transgression of the Apollonian pantheon. With Mikhail Bakhtin we may speak of the 'carnivalesque' spirit of the mystery religions and Dionysian cults of ancient Greece (Pausanias in the second century AD was still describing the ritual degradation ceremonies of initiates as they entered the cult's centre at Eleusis). Perhaps this also explains why Dionysus 'never develops into a God of social, moral or theological importance, in this respect contrasting sharply, not only with Apollo, but even with the Italian Mars, with whom he is identified in Graeco-Roman cult and legend' (Rose, 1989: 157; Burkert, 1985). In the presence of the mother goddess, Demeter and her daughter Kore (Persephone), all worshippers were of equal value. Each and every individual owed their continued existence to the bounty and fecundity of these ancient chthonic deities (materialists will read the Demeter myth as a trace of the empirical fact that Athens could not exist without a continuous supply of corn). They introduced, as it were, a temporary democracy of primordial dependency in the processional community of initiates. Whatever the status of individuals outside the sacred world of Eleusis, as 'participants' each was equal: 'What was common to all the mystery cults was that they catered for the individual, regardless of class or status; among the initiates of Eleusis were not only citizens of all classes, but also slaves' (Ehrenberg, 1964: 42). Moreover, as we have already noted, the nature festivities of Demeter and Persephone were overwhelmingly the concern of women (in the nocturnal rites of maenadism and the Bacchants this evolved into a strict rule, cf. Sophocles, *Trachiniae* 219ff.). The magical, utopian, and carnivalesque moments of Greek culture resurfaced in the exaggerated manifestations of corybantic religiosity (*'maenad'* literally means 'madwoman' and Persephone was also traditionally related to the loss of memory and madness; cf. Heraclitus DK 14, 15 and the evidence of painted pottery and reliefs where the theme of the collapse of self-constraint and breakdown of 'normal' comportment is quite common).

By the fifth century Orphism threatened to precipitate something like a pandemic cultural revolt against traditional religious forms (for example traditional Homeric religion and the more austere orthodox state cults had no place for the maenad or 'manic' possession) and even after its demise in Greece its cultural effects could still be felt centuries later in the Roman Mysteries (for example, in the Mithras – or sun god – cult associated with the Roman Army, the hellenized Egyptian Mysteries of Attis and Isis and the Phrygian Gods Atys and Cybele), in the second-century *Corpus Hermeticum*, in its impact upon the beliefs and practices of the Essenes as far as these can be reconstructed from Dead Sea scrolls, the Nag Hammadi texts (including the *Gospel of Truth*) and from such texts as the *Gospel of Thomas*, in early Christian Gnosticism, Neoplatonic and Neopythagorean wisdom-doctrines, and, finally, in the alchemical tradition and the teachings of the Jewish Kabbalah down into the late Middle Ages of the modern period). Gnosticism in the Middle Ages – for example in the teachings of Paracelsus, the ideology of the Cathars, and in Renaissance Neoplatonism – is essentially an attenuated species of Orphic theosophy. The utopian yearning for Gnostic wisdom and orgiastic release from the present sinful world into a realm of bliss and redemptive happiness were thus seeded within the Archaic social order and transmitted to medieval and modern Europe through this amalgam of arcane rites and mystical discourses. The theme is still alive in Rilke's *Duino Elegies* and his *Sonnets to Orpheus* in the twentieth century.

2 ORPHIC COSMOGONY AS AN ALLEGORY OF COSMIC ALIENATION

Orphic 'philosophy'

Is it reasonable to speak of the 'philosophical' content of Orphism? At its most explicit, Orphic cosmogony helped to articulate a dualistic account of the origins of the soul, a 'theory' of the *kosmos*, and a speculative view of material existence as an 'evil' process of alienation from a previously perfect – and hence 'divine' – state of unity. The popular theosophy of duality and alienation are well documented in the literature in this field: every order of existence, each form of life, has emerged into being through a process of differentiation or 'splitting', typically described as a 'fall' from a primordial Unity or as the result of a conflict of opposites within the One. The ubiquity of existential tensions and dualities in human life were interpreted as living evidence of the fall from the whole. To reverse this fallen state the initiate must 'return' to the source of blessedness, journeying back to the One source of true Being. Even the longing of the soul for cathartic purification and reunion with the One is evidence of the fall from the Godhead and the unconscious impulse of the soul's desire for atonement.

Far from being the consummation of bodily perfection, the *psyche* within the human frame is a continuous reminder that embodiment is a fallen state; the soul (or as this was sometimes expressed, 'the *daimonion*') has been abandoned in an alien vessel, wandering from the immortal *kosmos* of the Gods; but being originally united with the eternal One the spiritual core of the soul desires to be reunited with its source and lives on after the death of the body; indeed every spiritual striving of the soul is a trace or 'spark' of the ultimate *eros* which would return the soul to its divine status (in some versions the wandering soul may have to endure reincarnation in a number of bodies or animal forms before being restored to the divine source – a myth that is elaborated for philosophical purposes in Plato's *Phaedrus*). Unlike the traditionalism of Olympian religion, Orphism asserts that the only escape from this fallen state is through esoteric knowledge (the word *gnosis* came to be used for this arcane wisdom, beginning the tradition of Gnosticism).

Wisdom (*gnosis*, 'knowledge') is a recollective act which reverses this alienation process – a type of *anamnesis* where the soul escapes from its material abasement and sinful state and ascends to the state of bliss. One temporary form of *ecstasis* – literally 'standing out' from the body – was the prophetic knowledge granted in the dreaming state. Another was ecstatic possession. In both cases the soul was partially released from the grip of material existence. Dreaming might give the soul a glimpse of its state prior to incarnation. While lost in such extraordinary states of consciousness the soul might recall its earlier state of being.

These analogies led some of the Orphics to embrace the doctrine of reincarnation. By shedding its material existence through purification rites the soul could escape from the cycle of birth and death and return to the absolute source. Later traditions of Gnosticism, influenced by Platonism and Neopythagorean doctrines, did not hesitate in calling this source 'the One' or, in the Graeco-Roman period, the *Logos*.

In practice Orphic ritualism evolved a ceremonial symbolism, an arcane patois, and 'masonic' paraphernalia common to many such secret societies and sects. Its doctrines were also subject to rationalization and allegorical reinscription. How far these processes developed, of course, was subject to particular historical and regional conditions. As Weber reminds us, the majority of the population

> have everywhere remained engulfed in the massive and archaic growth of magic – unless a prophecy that holds out specific promises has swept them into a religious movement of an ethical character. For the rest, the specific nature of the great religious and ethical systems has been determined by social conditions of a far more particular nature than by the mere contrast of ruling and ruled strata.
> (Gerth and Mills, eds, 1948: 277)

Pherecydes of Syros

One influential formulation of Orphic cosmogony is associated with the speculative ideas of Pherecydes of Syros (*c.* 600–550 BC), ideas which appear to have had a considerable impact on the development of Hesiodic theogony, Ionian cosmology, and Pythagorean philosophy. In antiquity Pherecedyes was regarded as one of the first thinker-poets to publish his allegorical readings of myth and Homer in prose form. In Pherecydes' theogonic scheme, unity and the fall from grace are presented as a *kosmos*-generating 'intercourse' between 'seminal Zeus (*Zas*)' and 'receptive Chthonie' (*Ge* the earth goddess): the *kosmos* is created by the splitting of primal Night into *Kronos*, which then differentiates into Aither, Erebus, and Chaos, out of which emerges a cosmic egg to be fertilized by the father archetype (*Phanes* or *Phanes-Dionysos*), intellect (*Metia*), and power (*Erkepaios*). Time forms the matrix of all creation. All beings arise from this dialectical differentiation or profanization of the paradisical unity of Being. *Time, Earth*, and *Zeus* are, in Arisotelian terminology, originative principles and cosmic forces. For Pherecydes, the alienation process is dramatically visible in the ambivalent relation of the material body and immaterial soul.²

Beneath the fable-like imagery, Pherecydes' story contains an account of the genesis of Form from an inseminating, divine, patriarchal principle. As a work of prose it is indicative of the shift toward a concrete-universal principle of cosmic intelligibility. From the perspective of later Greek philosophy its allegorical structure could be understood as an early exploration of the fundamental duality of existence. As a distant antecedent of a Manichean view of the world it might be further rationalized to provide dualist symbolisms for a diverse range of creation stories. For example, in the Orphic literature Dionysus is created from the union of Zeus and Demeter; in Pythagorean metaphysics, Number is an originative principle 'in-forming' chthonic matter (or the void); it appears as the world-organizing 'principle' in the Ionian cosmologists; the formative qualities of Democritean atomism, Plato's theory of Forms – the *Demiourgos* in the *Timaeus* as a formative artificer of the *kosmos*, down to Aristotle's hylomorphism (Aristotle's *aita, telos, techne, genesis, kinesis, morphe, arche*, and so on). These are all recognizable family relatives of the basic Pherecydean logic. Such allegorical interpretations may have played a considerable role in the construction of quasi-ontological and philosophical categories in the last decades of the sixth century. We might even go further and see some of the formative influence of modern thought – particularly where radical forms of dualism are at issue – as continuous with Orphic mysticism and Pythagorean number theory: including the Neoplatonic and Gnostic elements in Christian metaphysics, medieval philosophy's obsession with pure form separated from fallen matter, and the modern consciousness of the structuring operations of pure forms ('structures') on the 'data' or 'materials' of sensibility. Despite obvious dissimilarities, the dualistic schema embedded in Pherecydes' narrative was still at work in the Copernican revolution initiated by the author of the *Critique of Pure Reason*.

3 THE ORPHIC BODY AND THE DOCTRINE OF CATHARTIC REFLEXIVITY

Immortality

It is hard to resist the impression that the fate of the individual soul is at the heart of Orphic religion in the fifth century. Orphism reformulated popular and Homeric images of the soul as a shade-like wraith into a symbol of theological alienation. Where the Homeric *psyche* is a vaporous shadow, the Orphic soul is the most valuable 'possession' of the person (in fact it is the 'soul' which expresses the spark of divinity in human reality and the core of the individual person). It is this *'daimon'* that survives the destruction of the body. Against the dominant themes of Homeric psychology, Orphism separated the essence of the soul from the existence of the material body. The different modes of existence of soul and body were, in fact, taken as living evidence of a primal profanation: mankind exists in a fallen state; the human frame is irrevocably divided into two antagonistic principles. Embodiment, far from being a celebratory condition (as we have seen in the Homeric epic), was interpreted as a sign of profanation and evil; 'possessing' a body or being rooted in the profane facts of physical existence now appears as an unwholesome and even vicious condition. Unlike the 'gleaming' embodiment of the Homeric warrior or the semi-divine body of the Pindaric athlete, the Orphic body has darkened into an obstacle of clay which must be rejected in the pursuit of salvation. In this radically dualist metaphysics, human embodiment is a condition that must be healed by 'purification' rituals. The soul's life within the physical body is a mark of alienation from a purer form of disembodied existence. This is the 'sweet hope' regarding both the end of life and eternity which inspires those who participate in the Mysteries (Isocrates, *Panegyricus* 4.28).

The body-tomb

What had been essentially a minor theme in Homer – the possibility of the soul's survival after death, had become an obsessive concern of Orphic culture. *Psyche* or 'soul' indicates the 'absent presence' of divinity animating the material body like a faint memory of an earlier divine condition. *Psyche* is the immaterial essence of the person, the 'ghost' that is led away to the Isles of the Blessed leaving the body's 'encasement' to death and corruption. For the Orphics the soul is the true principle of human existence while the human body (*soma*) is to be regarded as a tomb or prison, a temporary prison of the godly element. Life is no longer the heroic site of the Homeric will to power – the joyful wisdom of action and sensory enjoyment. It has now been cursed with materiality, guilt, and sin. In its unavoidable corporeal and mutable states life is a disease, a constant reminder of the *telos* of death. Rather than celebrating the human body – in the Classical Greek cult of sport and athleticism – we must flee from carnal life by means of the most uncompromising pursuit of individual salvation. While the body carries the burden of mortality, the soul is god-like in surviving the trials of death.

Paradoxically, this outright attack on the symbols of *individual* and *collective* embodiment led to a greater sense of the individuality of the body by accentuating the individual's sense of being 'thrown' into an alien vessel. The idea of individual salvation – a notion that is untypical of Greek religion and ideology – was thus seeded by the Orphic cults, and this belief in the immaterial essence of the soul would subsequently form the central teaching of the Neopythagoreans and Neoplatonists.

As Plato playfully reminds his reader, the word for body (*soma*) has its origin in the verb *sozesthai*, to keep safe or guard: the body (*soma*) is a prison or tomb (*sema*) of the soul; (*Cratylus* 400B–C: 'for some say it is the tomb (*sema*) of the soul, their notion being that the soul is buried in the present life; and again, because by its means the soul gives any signs which it gives, it is for this reason also properly called "sign" (*sema*). But I think it most likely that the Orphic poets gave this name, with the idea that the soul is undergoing punishment for something; they think it has the body as an enclosure to keep it safe, like a prison, and this is, as the name itself denotes, the safe (*sema*) of the soul, until the penalty is paid, and not even a letter needs to be changed'; cf. '*to soma estin hemin sema*': 'our body is a tomb', *Gorgias* 493A; *Phaedrus* 250–1; *Phaedo* 62B; cf. the Homeric usage of *sema* at *Il.* 23.45, 331–3 and *Od.* 11.75).

While the body is finite and temporal, the soul is immortal and atemporal: the body is the 'natural' site for sensory enjoyment and the cognitive processes linked to sensory consciousness, but the soul is the authentic site of the intelligible Forms or 'Ideas'. This is the origin of the dualist metaphysical idea that an enlightened soul might have knowledge of both the material world and the world beyond all corporeal existence. The fundamental promise of Orphism was to initiate the soul into this prenatal state of *knowledge*. And Plato would essentially continue the same line of thought in the more rarefied realm of transcendental philosophy stripped of the Orphic phantasmagoria. Plato's image of the human condition in the *Timaeus* and *Republic* pictures the spiritual soul as temporarily sojourning in the body as a result of an earlier transgression: the body is a cage or prison in which the spirit is incarcerated until it atones for its sins. As we have seen, the idea derives from an allusion between *soma* and *sema* (body/tomb): embodiment is the garment of immortal spirit; the flesh is the soul's outer husk or bark; and catharsis strips away the material casing to reveal the immortal element. The state of being human is itself a 'fall' (*kathodos*) from the realm of the Gods into an alien materiality:

> Whole were we who celebrated that festival, unspotted by all the evils which awaited us in time to come, and whole and unspotted and changeless and serene were the objects revealed to us in the light of that mystic vision. Pure was the light and pure were we from the pollution of the walking sepulchre which we call a body, to which we are bound like an oyster to its shell.
> (*Phaedrus* 250, Hamilton trans., 1973)

The values of physical embodiment are simply icons of their originals, just as the body is a sign (*sema*) of the soul.

It is extremely revealing to trace the shift of images and symbols for the soul from the Homeric epics to the poetry and art of the fifth century. A revealing indicator of this shift is the spread of bird and animal symbols for the soul. In Homer the *psyche* is pictured as a 'ghost' or 'homunculus' of the deceased and there are relatively few similes or analogies linking the soul to the animal world.

By the middle of the fifth century popular art and decoration portray the soul in a wide range of animal symbols – the image of the dove (associated with the priestesses of Dodona), kingfisher (*halcyon*), sparrow (in Sapphic verse), owl (associated with Pallas Athena), swan (Apollo), nightingale (the spirit of song), hawk, bee, and similar creatures. The bee and swan in particular were closely associated with the necessary purity demanded by the Orphic cults. The bee came to symbolize persistence and fecundity (for example *Works and Days* 303–6) while the swan, Apollo's sacred bird, symbolized knowledge and wisdom. The bee with its perpetual motion would later become a powerful image of the reincarnated self (cf. Germain, 1962: 96). Plato's well-known allegory of the caged birds in the *Theaetetus*, for example, undoubtedly derives from a popular association of thought and soul 'imprisoned' in the cage of the body.

Survival of the soul

In Western culture the idea of the immortal soul is almost certainly a product of Orphic ideology. Orphism required the soul to 'die to the world' in order to return to a higher and more divine sphere, reincarnated in the primal One. The sensible *kosmos* is simply a cipher for an eternal and immaterial *kosmos*. The well-known Platonic definition of philosophy in the *Phaedo* as a 'learning to die' draws its rhetorical force directly from this Orphic-Pythagorean tradition, as does the argument for immortality placed in the mouth of Socrates in the *Phaedo* ('I desire to prove to you that the real philosopher has reason to be of good cheer when he is about to die, and that after death he may hope to obtain the greatest good in the other world', *Phaedo* 63–4). A related Orphic image of the carnal body is contained in the metaphor of the body as the soul's tool or instrument; in the third Book of the *Republic* the soul is said to fly from the body leaving behind only the instrument (469D–E; cf. *Alcibiades* I, 129E; Aristotle, *De Anima* 407b20ff., 410b27; also *Phaedo* 72E–77A and *Phaedrus* 246–50). Platonic psychology would consistently imagine the soul as a kind of controlling 'intelligence' using the body as its material form (*nous* becomes a directive 'spiritual' force directing the material activities of the person). Here the metaphors of the soul's reflexivity are profoundly Orphic: the body and the material world at large is an obstacle to the transcendence thought to be essential to spiritual life; embodiment has to be 'abandoned' – through various regimes and forms of reflexive practice – in order to liberate the soul to a life of bliss and spiritual happiness; truth is the promise of divine knowledge. In this framework an exclusive concern for the well-being of the body would be understood as abandoning the true vocation of 'caring' for the soul – which is now thought to pre-exist the body. Of course, there are adumbrations of these ideas in the language of the poets and dramatists. The most 'Classical' of the dramatists, Sophocles, is already speaking of Hermes as the guide of souls, leading them into the realms of Persephone and Hades (*Electra* 110–11; the precedent is Homeric, e.g. *Od.* 24.1ff.).

We can also anticipate the studies of Volume 3 dealing with the genealogy of Classical philosophy by observing that Plato's account of the soul's pre-existence and its separation from the body in death (*Phaedo* 61E–62C, 70C–72E; 77C–D, *passim*), immortality (*Phaedo* 95D–106E, 115Cff.), metempsychosis (*Phaedo* 81D–82B; *Phaedrus* 248–50, 252; *Timaeus* 91D–92C; *Laws* 870D–E), the early theory of Forms (throughout the early Socratic dialogues), the associated idea of knowledge as *anamnesis*, the idea of 'participation', the doctrine of the *periagoge* or 'turn' toward the supersensible Forms, and the image of the Cave in Book VII of the *Republic* (514A-521B) are all articulated in Orphic language and icons (the descent and ascent in the Cave symbolism is closely related to the Eleusinian mysteries and would in later Roman and Christian sects be associated with the trials of death and resurrection). Plato employed the Orphic trope of a 'final reincarnation' that would return the *psyche* to its divine home – the true 'homecoming' of the soul (*psyche*) recognizing its prenatal patrimony in the One after its deliverance from material flesh – as a schema for philosophical wisdom (*theoria*). True *philosophia* is pictured as the soul's 'participation' in an eternal symposium after death (cf. DK 44b14; *Republic* 363C; *Phaedo* entire, but especially 62B, 66–8C, 69C, 82D–E; *Phaedrus* entire, but especially 249B–250, 251–53, 256; *Apology* 40D–41C; *Laws* 872D–E; *Timaeus* 41E–42B; and the *Symposium* entire). This extensive textual evidence supports the thesis that at both formal and thematic levels Orphism exerted a most profound influence in shaping the idiom and problematics of Pythagorean and, subsequently, Platonic frameworks of transcendent philosophy. But the links between Orphism and the ideological-utopian orientations of Western philosophy go even deeper, as we shall see in the following discussion.

The leading impulse behind the movement of Orphism is a variant of the later philosophical dream of *absolute* knowledge. But now 'pure' knowledge is separated from the continuum of practical wisdom, technical knowledge, and abstract understanding. 'Authentic' *gnosis* is a product of the soul's insight into the nature of life and death, achieved by a radical abstraction from corporeal existence. Orphism initiated the long process which separated 'practical' from 'contemplative' knowledge, endowing the latter with honorific spiritual attributes. Thus in the work of later thinkers like Plato and Aristotle, the pure medium of spiritual knowledge is intellectual *vision*, a 'seeing' into the essence of things by the noetic part of the soul. This division between the sensory and the noetic realms would become a dominant theme in later concepts of cognition and self-reflection.

The wheel of birth and death

The Orphic 'discovery' of the noetic self was originally rooted in religious rather than cognitive interests. Platonic and Aristotelian psychology represent both a sublimation and a cognitive redefinition of the Orphic *psyche*. We have seen that Orphic rituals had the express aim of purifying and liberating the soul from its 'prison', returning it to the 'other world' through cathartic rites designed to reverse the primal schism of body and soul. When the material body dies (or is liberated from its dependence upon corporeal needs and desires as the philosophers will later claim) the soul is released; but without the necessary 'instruction' it may wander aimlessly or be utterly lost amongst the unfortunate shades that throng Hades. Plato refers to such rites in the *Republic*, referring to the books of Musaeus and Orpheus used in purification rituals designed to make 'not only ordinary men but states believe that there really are remissions of sins and purifications for deeds of injustice, by means of sacrifice and pleasant sport' (II 364E–365A). The sacrifices prepare those who are about to die to ward off evils in the Underworld 'while terrible things await those who have neglected to sacrifice'. Further evidence of the existence of a popular awareness of the doctrines of reincarnation can be found in fifth-century Sicily and southern Italy. Thus Socrates might have been speaking literally when he refers to 'those who established the Mysteries' as arcane philosophers:

> It is likely that those who established the mystic rites for us were not inferior persons but were speaking in riddles long ago when they said that whoever arrives in the underworld unitiated and unsanctified will wallow in the mire, whereas he who arrives there purified and initiated will dwell with the Gods. There are indeed, as those concerned with the mysteries say, many who carry the thyrsus but the Bacchants are few.
> (*Phaedo* 69C–D)

Confirmation of the antiquity of these ideas is provided by a text found inscribed on gold leaf in a tomb in South Italy. In Richmond Lattimore's translation it reads:

> You will find to the left of the house of Hades a wellspring,
> and by the side of this standing a white cypress.
> You must not even go close to this wellspring; but also
> you will find another spring that comes from the lake of Memory
> cold water running, and there are those who stand guard before it.
> You shall say: 'I am a child of earth and the starry heavens,
> but my generation is of the sky. You yourselves know this.
> But I am dry with thirst and am dying. Give me then quickly
> the water that runs out of the lake of Memory.'
> And they themselves will give you to drink from the sacred water,
> and afterward you shall be lord among the rest of the heroes.
>   (Lattimore, trans., 1960: 32; see also Kern, 1963: 81ff. and
>   *passim*; 'Orphism', in *Oxford Classical Dictionary*: 759)

We might compare this text to Plato's vision of corporeality as 'heavy, oppressive, earthly and visible', making the *psyche* 'infected' by matter, weighed down and dragged back into the visible world (*Phaedo* 81D). Perhaps the tradition of Orphic literature provided something like an Hellenic equivalent to the Egyptian Book of the Dead (cf. the Tibetan *Bardo Thodol*): by means of prior instruction the soul is given prior knowledge of death and the afterlife, in anticipation of its resurrection. For the Orphics genuine 'spiritual' life began in a return to life beyond the grave.

In earlier chapters we have seen that Homer provided the first literary account of the soul after death, and that poets like Sappho and Pindar gave it poetic form and existential significance. Orphic cosmology absorbed many of these earlier ideas and adopted them to its own ends. From this eclectic magma the problems of the soul's divine appearance (*theophany*), its unity, purification (*katharsis*), and immortality would then pass into Pythagorean, Platonic, Aristotelian, and eventually Christian thought. Its essential elements are already implicit in Pindar's metaphysical poetry:

> And, while the body of all men is subject to over-mastering death, an image (*eidolon*) of life remains alive, for it alone comes from the Gods. But it sleeps, while the limbs are active; yet, to them that sleep, in many a dream it gives presage of a decision of things delightful or doleful'.[3]

By the disciplined application of purification rituals, arcane initiation rites, and a secret knowledge of cosmogony, the soul in this world could already secure 'knowledge' of the topography of the other world and, presumably, save itself from the house of Hades; this promise served as a soteriological 'faith' for individuals drawn from many different strata of society who found themselves lost in a violent and rapidly changing social world (for yet another stratum, reflective cosmology and philosophy would come to fulfil similar needs: the dual interest in ecstatic salvation and esoteric *gnosis*, for example, were combined in the Pythagorean brotherhood and in sects that pursued the worship of Dionysus or Demeter). By a strange irony, ancient cultic worship of fecund Nature provided one of the crucial ingredients for such apparently incongruous doctrines as Pindar's epinician odes, Ionian cosmology, Pythagorean mathematics, the erotic cult of Dionysus, and a century later, Platonic theophanic cosmology. Each of these ideological currents centred its vision of the different orders of existence around a theory of the fall of the divine (*to theion*) into material existence, each promulgated a salutary account of regeneration or rebirth (metempsychosis, whether through arcane rite, the bacchanalian frenzy of the *sparagmos*, a Gnostic knowledge of mathematics, a cosmological undestanding of *phusis*, or by the contemplation of the Good), and each gave full rein to anxiety concerning the imminent threat of death. Presupposing a radical dualism of fallen matter and divine form, salvation could only be secured through an 'awakening' or 'resurrection' in the One.

In the *Phaedo*, Plato may have been quoting directly from Orphic tracts and Mystery traditions in having Socrates speak of the 'testing' of the soul in Hades in the following manner:

> We are told that when each person dies, the guardian spirit who was allotted to him in life proceeds to lead him to a certain place, whence those who have been gathered together there must, after being judged, proceed to the underworld with the guide who has been appointed to lead them thither from here. Having there undergone what they must and stayed there the appointed time, they are led back here by another guide after long periods of time. The journey is not as Aeschylus' Telephus describes it. He says that only one single path leads to Hades, but I think it is neither one nor simple, for then there would be no need of guides; one could not make any mistake if there were but one path. As it is, it is likely to have many forms and crossroads; and I base this judgement on the sacred rites and customs here.
> (*Phaedo* 107D–108A, trans. Grube)

Purification teletai

By a dialectical process unique to classical culture, the baroque complexity and 'stage-managed' character of Orphic and Mystery religiosity actively created in its participants an acute awareness of symbolism and ritual discourse – granting them a powerful new sense of selfhood. Orphism in particular was a hot-house for symbolic manipulation and liturgical reflexivity – creating a kind of vulgar or *ersatz* metaphysics for its adherents, a pseudo-philosophy which, nevertheless, generated a desire for a more rigorous, intellectually satisfying, and authentic form of 'theorizing' (of course, the term '*theoria*' in its classical philosophical sense was not commonly available to the Orphic communities and cult societies). Speaking through their superficial differences and grotesque symbolisms lay a problem which fuelled all these reflexive projects: how to cope with an acute awareness of the inevitability of suffering and death. How, if the *kosmos* is 'full of Gods', can absolute death be possible? How, faced with the contingency of this singular event, can mortals resist annihilation? How can the soul be 'purified' of the desires and needs of the flesh? What can they do in this life to secure their eventual immortality? How can the soul be returned to the divine origin?

The same order of questions that had been at work for centuries as the spiritual matrix of Egyptian culture, propelling its elaborate thanatonic civilization, found expression in the Greek axial age in Mystery religions, Orphism, Number-magic, Orgiastic cults, early Mathematical and Gnostic Philosophy. The vivid consciousness of death in the Homeric epics and the increasing fear of absurd death exemplified in the Lyric age (and implicitly, in Pindar's extreme aestheticizing of 'noble' death) was never far from the surfaces of Greek cultural praxis. Orphism and the cult of Dionysus were, as it were, volcanic 'vents' through which the repressed thanatonic complex of Greek civilization exploded in the sixth century.

The late sixth- and fifth-century obsession with initiation, identification, purification, atonement, metempsychosis, and rebirth rituals (manifest across the continuum of Greek religion from the 'transvestite' cult of Dionysus and the flesh-devouring Maenads to the sublimated symbolism of transcendental philosophy, Stoic and Plotinian psychopathology) might also be connected with the long-term shift from a tribal 'shame' *ethos* to a culture whose moral sensibilities were increasingly based on private norms of civility and guilt – a revolutionary transition from the public and performative world of Homeric and Pindaric *arete* to the private world of internalized moral consciousness and the growing preponderance of individual reflexivity in moral conduct. The same revolution is evidenced in the displacement of the earlier *lex talionis* and aristocratic vengeance ethics by a more personalized, individualized, self-reflective, and 'objective' notion of justice, by an ethic of mutuality, rectification and moral consequentialism (culminating in Aristotle's philosophical vindication of the 'mean' in moral and ethical relations). But the most immediate factor behind these changes in belief lay in the disruption and uncertainty spread through the Greek world by the rapid social and political changes which brought the *polis* into existence and, in the early fifth century, by the threat posed by the invading Persian army and fleet. It is no accident that the military incursions of Persia and the burgeoning of new 'cathartic' cultic and religious practices coincided. Concern for the duality of body and soul, the soul's destiny in the afterlife, doubts about immortality, and so forth, may be regarded as perennial human concerns; but they are typically articulated in periods of sudden and violent changes, especially in an age where the threat of sudden death has been generalized across all strata and classes (it is interesting to note the ebbing away of interest in such speculations during the early Hellenistic period, and the exponential rise in spiritual and mystical 'utopias' in times of acute social crisis – for example, in the first century BC and the middle of the second to the third century AD, the early eleventh century AD, the late fifteenth century and high Renaissance period (cf. Bottomley, 1979; Brown, 1988)).

In sociological terms, Orphism and the Mysteries presented themselves as a 'rational' response to the increasing democratization of violent, unregulated death. Ideologically they index the failure of previous religious forms and symbols as a coherent 'answer' to the universal question of suffering and death. The traditional city cults and their sacrificial rituals no longer seemed to carry universal authority. New forms which either bypassed or literalized the ethos of sacrifice flourished around the traditional practices (this is the subterranean connection which links the most extreme manifestations of the new religiosity – the austere Pythagoreans and the abandoned wildness of the cult of Dionysus). It is also very important for the subsequent history of reflexivity, particularly of modes of theoretical reflection in the Athenian world, that while 'domesticating' the Eleusinian Mysteries as an official state festival, Athens rejected the incorporation of Orphism as a state ideology. Again, like many decisive historical events, this was in no way a product of 'Athenian rationalism', 'the classical ideal', or 'the triumph of the Apollonian', but at root a consequence of a singular confluence of material circumstances and conditions.[4]

4 THE TROPES OF DIONYSUS

Orphism represented one of the earliest appearances of an ideology of human alienation (*allotriosis*) and catharsis, an acute sense of the radical 'alterity' or 'otherness' of nature and material existence accompanied by a chronic experience of being separated from the divine order of existence. Pathological self-hatred expressed as revulsion or disgust toward one's embodied condition and embodiment in general is one expression of this extreme form of self-experience: a view of the body as an absolute hindrance to wisdom, an obscene heavy 'flesh', an evil enemy to be disciplined, mortified, or in even more extreme manifestations, destroyed in the interests of spiritual knowledge. With Orphism, and even more emphatically, with the cult of Dionysus-Zagreus, we find metaphors of embodiment as a theatre of violence and of selfhood as a never-ending struggle between centripetal materiality and centrifugal spirituality (a polarity which Nietzsche formulated as the Dionysian-Apollonian experience).

Orphism articulated a conception of human existence as a strife-torn 'dialectic' of opposites. The same dualist schema seems to have been independently evolved in the polymorphous figure of Dionysus; here human existence is experienced as a tension between God and beast: separated from the godhead in the primal differentiation process mankind still bears within itself the agonistic principles of divinity and savagery. Dionysian religion provided a forum in which this dramatic clash of opposites could be acted out. Orphism and Dionysiac religion may have functioned as a cultural conduit for the repressed self, distilling its dark dualistic message from the wisdom literatures of ancient Egypt, Phoenicia, Lydia, Persia, and Babylon.[5]

The ambivalence created by the dualistic Orphic body produced extreme responses to the problem of overcoming evil and returning to the sources of divine order. On the one hand, we find the classical equivalent of ascetic self-denial (vegetarian proscriptions against the killing and eating of animals in the Pythagorean brotherhoods) and self-punishment (itself an important form of corporeal reflexivity): the soul can only be 'saved' by being literally 'purified' of its attachments to the material world. If it is to regain its original home in the divine cosmos, it must first cut its links with the present carnal world. This ascetic and disciplinarian tendency also illustrates the way in which the Orphic sects introduced hitherto untypically Greek elements into Greek religiosity. On the other hand, we also have the Dionysian response to the problem of rebirth – unity and 'harmony of the opposites' created by the ecstatic worship of Dionysus, violent identification with the sacred godhead by an orgiastic, typically sexual, abandonment of the public self to the flesh and barabaric 'natural' values. In total absorption the maenad is literally filled with the god, transfigured by *mania* and experiences the complete loss of the civilized body. One of the great attractions of the Dionysus cult was its ability to reconcile both these forms of consciousness in practical action. The tangible figure of Dionysus Zagreus became a powerful 'mediator' of these two paths by symbolizing the reconciliation and atonement of opposites:

> The followers of Orpheus not only made Zagreus the God of universal destruction and renewal, a true demiourgos, recalling not only the Brahmin Siva, but also, in his capacity as the first-born of Zeus, a kind of Logos, before Philo wrote about him. He manifested himself under all manner of names – he is the thousand-form Pan, the universal overlord. On the other hand, if he is the Great Hunter who catches men in his nets, as God of death, he is also the one who guarantees their immortality in his capacity as God of life and rebirth. In this way he justifies his name of Dionysus the Deliverer, the Saviour'.[6]

5 THE ORPHIC BACKGROUND OF THE *LOGOS*

Eduard Zeller provides an interesting account of the manner in which the experience of cultural ambivalence formed the seed-ground for the culture and psychology of Greek society in the late sixth and early fifth century. We can draw together some of the themes of these chapters and adumbrate the discussion of philosophical reflexivity which forms the topic of Volume 3. Zeller writes that the

> Greek of the sixth century who was no longer satisfied with the traditional religion had two courses open to him: that of rational thought and investigation, which the Ionic physicists followed, and that of religious mysticism, to which Orphicism pointed the way. These different lines of development were however not completely separated, but crossed and re-crossed; for religion and philosophy have a common end when they deal with the ultimate questions. The whole development of Greek philosophy appears as a continual controversy, and, in important phases, a compromise between national Greek monistic and oriental dualistic thought, in a word between intellectualism and mysticism'.[7]

Epic poetry, Hesiodic theophany, Pindar's self-conscious lyrics, Orphic Myth, Dionysiac religion and Maenadism provided variant ways of articulating the theophanic question of origins and resolving the ambivalence of traditional forms of self: respectively, the universe of Olympian deities, the genealogy of the Gods and *kosmos*, the appearance of 'the divine' in the person of the Olympian victor, the aboriginal source of the *psyche* in the primal One, and the total possession by the godhead in what the Greeks called 'enthusiasm'. The idea of a return to origins, as I will try to demonstrate in Volume 3, was vitally important for the development of later rhetorics of reflection; each of these cultural experiences implicitly framed a different dimension of the problematic of origins: the cosmological, anthropological, theophantic, and 'orgiastic' auspices of existence.

At another level, however, each rhetoric of reflection codified a definite social and political experience:

> Homer's gods had reflected an aristocratic human society, so the *kosmos* of the philosophers mirrored the political human community. As Homer's gods were the models of anthropomorphic religion, thus the chthonian cults, the mysteries, the Orphic beliefs reflected a divine world beyond human standards.
>
> (Ehrenberg, 1964: 43)

In creating the theophanic presuppositions of mythopoeic reflexivity, these different discourses encouraged later thought to recollect the topic of first beginnings and in the time of beginnings, the primordial human involvement with divine firstness. Plato's philosophical vision and Aristotle's metaphysics would still theorize within the framework of this way of thinking. As carnivalesque modalities of reflexivity these transgressive moments of Greek culture simultaneously negated and affirmed the traditional languages of Greek religiosity. They instituted an immanent critique of the religious tradition carried out by means of instruments which prefigure another sense of tradition:

> Beyond sacrifice, on the side of vegetarianism, asceticism and inner purificiation, it is men who take the initiative and strive to develop their own spiritual resources in order to be able to rise to the level of the gods, to reach them by an internal effort to pass beyond the normal limitations of human nature. At all events, by taking up a position outside the framework imposed by the practice of sacrifice both these 'mystical' experiences shaped the religious world of the Greeks and had a decisive effect on the orientation of ancient thought.
>
> (Vernant, in Detienne, 1977: xxxi-xxxii)

As I have argued in earlier chapters, it is only against the rich confluence of poetic, religious, and intellectual currents that Presocratic inquiry could begin its work of critical self-reflection; the first thinkers 'begin' by troping and transmuting the mythological thematics of divine origination into a more austere and self-reflexive cosmology. The universe of Presocratic thought was dialogically wedded to the forms of reflexivity created during the Archaic period, an indebtedness which pervaded the critique of the earlier tradition. Without these speculations the first forms of speculative thought would have taken quite different directions. From the late sixth century, however, *theoriz-*

ing found its identity in the project of recollecting primary origins, a return to the *arche* of Being through the rigour of pure thought. As Fränkel reminds us: 'It is worth noting that among the Greeks it was not the soul but thought that was first constituted an independent power to stand in opposition to the material world (fully developed in Anaxagoras)' (1975: 78, n. 10).

The earliest forms of reflexivity are thus not 'theological' as Aristotle claimed in writing the first philosophical history of his predecessors, but *theophanic* and *ecstatic*: self-reflections on the radical 'firstness' of 'the divine'. And it is in this precise sense that philosophical reflexivity receives its original meaning as *self-reflection upon origins*, a 'thoughtful return' to the divine ground of Being:

> And when Socrates holds that the preservation of man's soul from harm is the thing most important in life, and that in comparison with this everything else must recede, his emphasis on the value of the soul, so incomprehensible to the Greece of an earlier age, would have been inexplicable if the Orphic religion had not turned its attention inward with that faith which the watchword of this *bios* expresses: 'I, too, am of godly race'.[8]

In conclusion: the theogonic structure of Archaic discourse created the basic metaphorical framework and 'grammar' of Greek philosophy. Thus the characteristic Presocratic quest for the *Logos* of the *kosmos* is already framed in the symbolic forms of these earlier discourses. To pursue wisdom (*sophia*) will become definitive of 'philosophy' as a self-inquiry into the divine Logos itself (which, as we will see in Volume 3 is traditionally attributed to Pythagoras and the Pythagorean way of life). The way of thinking which culminates in the great teaching of Heraclitus that the *arche* of all things is the *Logos* has its source in these earlier speculations. It is also for this reason that subsequent inquiry into origins necessarily took the form of *logological inquiries*, explorations of the work of Logos in human experience. From this point onward, philosophy would define its fundamental problematic by weaving reflexivity, self-knowledge, and *Logos* as interdependent aspects of the investigation of existence and Being.

NOTES

1 MYTHOPOIESIS: THE PRAXIS OF MYTH

1 Szilasi, in Kockelmans and Kisiel, eds, 1970: 232.
2 Gouldner, 1985: 283.
3 In Mircea Eliade's words, mythic semiosis provides a practically-oriented theory of the world, an Archaic ontology facilitating the ordering, explanation, and control of natural phenomena. Myths are both second-order semiotic systems and narrative paradigms of action:

> we may say that every responsible activity in pursuit of a definite end is, for the archaic world, a ritual. But since the majority of these activities have undergone a long process of desacralization and have, in modern societies, become profane, we have thought it proper to group them separately.
>
> (Eliade, 1989: 28)

Cf. Eliade 1959, 1960, 1974; Roland Barthes speaks of myths as second-order semiotic systems in his essay 'Myth today' in *Mythologies* (London: Paladin, 1973): 109–45. For Greek myth as a protosociology of morals and theodicy see Vickers, 1973, Part 2, esp. chs 4, 5.
Contemporary discussion of 'myth as a cultural system' (and, more generally, the social functions of other forms of symbolic narrative) begins with the seminal work of Emile Durkheim, Ferdinand de Saussure, Marcel Mauss, Georges Dumézil, Vladimir Propp, Claude Lévi-Strauss, Lucien Lévy-Bruhl, Arnold van Gennep, G. van der Leeuw, Marcel Granet, and their students – Roland Barthes, Georges Bataille, Emile Benveniste, René Girard, Edmund Leach, Clifford Geertz, Alan Dundes, Dan Sperber, Tzvetan Todorov, Victor Turner, Jean-Pierre Vernant, among the more prominent of these.
The Cambridge school of Jane Harrison, Gilbert Murray, Arthur B. Cook, and Francis M. Cornford also emphasizes the key difference between myth and other modes of storytelling by grounding the *legomenon*, – the thing-said, – of myth in the thing-performed, the *dromenon* of ritual praxis; myth's vocation and power is to animate world-shaping rituals; other genres of fiction are not necessarily incarnated in ritual performances:

> The myth and the ritual act both seek to explain the nature of reality, of the processes of the universe and of man's place among them; but they also have a magical element in that the repetition of the processes by means of word and act gives men a sort of power over them or stabilizes the human role in a dangerous world liable to slip out of control. By word and act men are

NOTES

securely in the cosmic process and yet are separated out with special powers of their own.

(Lindsay, in Harrison, 1978: viii-ix)

Cf. the similar conclusions of the Marxist aesthetician, Ernst Fischer (1978) and the American student of comparative mythology, Joseph Campbell, who writes: 'In ancient times every social occasion was ritually structured and the sense of depth was rendered through the maintenance of a religious tone' (1973: 44). Or in a formulation even closer in spirit to the Cambridge school: 'Myths are the mental supports of rites; rites, the physical enactment of myths' (1973: 45). The important texts here are Cornford, 1957; Harrison, 1912, 1962, 1978 and Murray, 1940.

The earliest, prestructuralist account of the logic of 'elementary forms' of oral discourse is still André Jolles' *Einfache Formen* (Tübingen, Niemeyer, 1968). Jolles analyzes the elementary genres of oral speech into *Legende, Sage, Mythe, Rätsel, Spruch, Kasus, Memorabile, Märchen*, and *Witz* (legend, saga, myth, riddle, proverb, the case, the memoir, the tale, and the joke). One of the most influential studies of the genre of folk-tale is Vladimir Propp's *Morphology of the Folk-Tale* (1968 see also 1984). Yet despite these auspicious beginnings we still lack a comprehensive sociological theory of the riddle, proverb, parable, and fairytale and their interrelations. While mythic narrative – as a sense-making, symbolic, and rhetorical enterprise – shares many generic features with other oral genres – such as name-magic, gossip, folk-storytelling, legend, romance, folk-tale, and fairytale – for analytical purposes it is important to draw distinctions between these forms of narrative or 'systems of representations'. The literature on myth thus discriminates between narrative genres in material (subject matter), formal (textual organization and structure), and functional (context, use, reception) terms. Traditional myth theory, however, tends to ignore the complex figurative mediations of the target texts, the social and pragmatic contexts of use, and the social dialectic of narrative texts (performance) with their cultural contexts (cotextual and contextual presuppositions). To add to the problem of social analysis the denotations of terms like 'myth' and 'mythic narrative' are ill-defined and without a uniquely defined set of criterial properties. J.-P. Vernant writes:

> To declare that the symbols myth deploys are constant and carry universal archetypal meaning is totally to neglect the cultural, sociological, and historical context... linguistic studies have shown that there are profound phonological, morphological, and syntactical differences between different groups of languages. So how, without a vestige of proof, is it possible to accept the idea of a single symbolical language conceived, not as a system operating on several levels, but as a universal vocabulary the meaning of whose components could be determined just by correlating them term for term.

(1990: 239)

The question of the polycriterial nature of myth further underlines the context-specific nature of symbolic forms, and, correlatively, the importance of historical, cultural, and sociological studies of the production, reproduction, and reception of texts. It does not advance critical discourse analysis to equate myth with the concept of ideology in the sense of the naturalization and mystification of contingent relationships (as Roland Barthes tends to do; Barthes also fails to grasp the reflexive determinations of mythic categories in his own theorizing). Here it is good advice not to ask for the formal meaning or the controlling intention behind a given text (or corpus of texts), but for the *use* and *differential social work of texts in everyday language*. There are thus diverse mythical speech acts performing various kinds of world-work but no *Myth*. The ideological functions of myth (as with other discourses) are not something innate to mythic discourse, but arise in their specific appropriation by groups of individuals and communities. Even the concept of 'myth' as traditional storytelling risks framing the problem solely in terms of the conservation of oral lore, and thereby elides the ways in which mythic storytelling may reshape, transform, and change social arrangements. Here the recommendation is to ask for *functions* not *essences*, *practices* not *substances*, *articulations* not *structures*. As Pierre Bourdieu, among other contemporary writers, reminds us, it is as naive to wonder what the true sense of words is, as it is to wonder, in Austin's terms, what the "real colour" of the chameleon is'; in fact 'there are as many meanings as there are different usages and markets' (Bourdieu, 1991: 74; the internal reference is from John L. Austin, *Sense and Sensibilia* (Oxford: Oxford University Press, 1962): 66).

Bourdieu's principle applies more generally to reflexive inquiries into the social processes of mythopoeisis. Here no form of essentialism or etymologizing can aid us in understanding the social dynamics of meaning and discourse (cf. 'The original meanings of words are always interesting. But what is often most interesting is the subsequent variation ... there can be no question, at the level either of practice or of theory, of accepting an original meaning as decisive ... The vitality of a language includes every kind of extension, variation and transfer', Williams, 1976: 20–1 and G. S. Kirk: 'there can be no common definition, no monolithic theory, no simple and radiant answer to all the problems and uncertainties concerning myths'; 'Myths are not uniform, logical and internally consistent; they are multiform, imaginative and loose in their details' (1974: 19, 29; also 1970: 8ff.).

What remains unquestioned in every generic theory of myth is a particular ontology (and perhaps politics) of language: an image of language as words clothing an independent world, language as a fixed set of signifiers correlated with a fixed set of signifieds or referents. Ernst Cassirer's theory of symbolic forms is a notable exception:

> the special symbolic forms are not imitations, but *organs* of reality, since it is solely by their agency that anything real becomes an object for us. The question as to what reality is apart from these forms, and what are its independent attributes, becomes irrelevant here. For the mind, only that can be visible which has some definite form; but every form of existence has its source in some peculiar way of seeing, some intellectual formulation and intuition of meaning. Once language, myth, art, and science are recognized as such forms, the basic philosophical question is ... that of their mutual limitations and supplementation.
>
> (1946: 8–9)

In his book *An Essay on Man* he is even more explicit about the constructive mediation of such 'symbolic forms':

> Language, myth, art, and religion are parts of this universe. They are the varied threads which weave the symbolic net, the tangled web of human experience. All human progress in thought and experience refines upon and strengthens this net. No longer can man confront reality immediately; he cannot see it, as it were, face to face. Physical reality seems to recede in proportion as man's symbolic activity advances. Instead of dealing with the things themselves man is in a sense constantly conversing with himself.
>
> (1944: 25)

Cassirer's investigation of mythic symbolism can be found as vol. 2 of Cassirer, 1953–7.

NOTES

A genre term like 'myth' should not be regarded as labelling a 'real essence', but as a very general term for the disparate ways in which communities try to code and control signification; the use of the term should initiate a social history of their social and cultural uses rather than a formal analysis of narrative themes and motifs. I am in full agreement with the perspective developed by Raymond Williams:

> The emphasis of my own analyses is deliberately social and historical. In the matters of reference and applicability, which analytically underlie any particular use, it is necessary to insist that the most active problems of meaning are always primarily embedded in actual relationships, and that both the meanings and the relationships are typically diverse and variable, within the structures of particular social orders and the processes of social and historical change.
>
> (1976: 21–2)

In the studies which follow we will have a chance to explore the rhetorical interface of word and world, dismantling its underlying ontology and examining its historical formation as the product of specific rhetorics of representation; here we simply wish to register the idea that such representational accounts of mythic narrative preclude an understanding of narrative praxis as a constitutive reality in its own right or, perhaps more circumspectly at this stage, of narrative practices as a powerful world-making process. Language and discourse are not reflections of a preformed reality, but constitutive moments of social existence and social consciousness (again Raymond Williams' gloss is worth bearing in mind: 'New kinds of relationship, but also new ways of seeing existing relationships, appear in language in a variety of ways: in the invention of new terms (*capitalism*); in the adaptation and alteration (indeed at times reversal) of older terms (*society* or *individual*); in extension (*interest*) or transfer (*exploitation*). But also, as these examples should remind us, such changes are not always either simple or final. Earlier and later senses coexist, or become actual alternatives in which problems of contemporary belief and affiliation are contested ... my emphasis here is on a vocabulary of meanings, in a deliberately selected area of argument and concern' 1976: 22). For the epistemological and philosophical justification for this approach I refer the reader back to the studies of Volume 1 of *Logological Investigations*, especially Chapter 1, Section 2, 'Four metarhetorical views of language'.

For research that is sensitive to the interfaces, blurred genre rules, and family resemblances between ceremonial rituals, folk-tales, fables, legends, literary fiction, myth, and other verbal media see: Bakhtin, 1981, 1984; Benjamin, 1977; Bruno Bettelheim, *The Uses of Enchantment* (New York: Vintage, 1977); Wayne C. Booth, *The Rhetoric of Fiction*, 2nd ed (Chicago: University of Chicago Press, 1961); Wayne C. Booth, *A Rhetoric of Irony* (Chicago: University of Chicago Press, 1974); Kenneth Burke, *The Philosophy of Literary Form: Studies in Symbolic Action* (Baton Rouge: Louisiana State University Press, 1941); Kenneth Burke, *Language as Symbolic Action: Essays on Life, Literature, and Method* (Berkeley: University of California Press, 1966); Carpenter, 1962; and Cassirer, 1953–7.

For more specialized studies of mythic narrative see Roland Barthes, 'Introduction to the structural analysis of narratives', in *Image-Music-Text* (London: Fontana, 1977); R. Barthes, 'Theory of the text', in R. Young, ed., *Untying the Text* (London: Routledge and Kegan Paul, 1981); Benjamin, 1992; Hans Blumenberg, *Work on Myth* (Cambridge, Mass.: MIT Press, 1985); Wayne C. Booth, *The Rhetoric of Fiction* (Chicago: University of Chicago Press, 1961); Kenneth Burke, *A Rhetoric of Motives* (Englewood Cliffs: Prentice-Hall, 1950); Campbell, 1989; Georges Dumézil, *The Three Orders: Feudal Society Imagined* (Chicago: University of Chicago Press, 1980); Alan Dundes, ed., *Readings in the Theory of Myth* (Berkeley:

University of California Press, 1984); Tzvetan Todorov, *The Poetics of Prose* (Oxford: Blackwell, 1977); Victor Turner, *The Ritual Process* (Chicago: Aldine, 1969): Victor Turner, *The Ritual Process: Structure and Antistructure* (New York: Aldine de Gruyter, 1969): Eliade, 1989; Eliade, in J. Campbell, ed., *Man and Time*, Eranos Yearbooks, vol. 3 (London: Routledge and Kegan Paul, 1958): 173–200; Lévy-Bruhl, 1923, 1926: Lévi-Strauss, 1963, 1966, 1973, 1981; Claude Lévi-Strauss, *The Raw and the Cooked* (*Introduction to the Science of Mythology*, vol. 1) (London: Jonathan Cape, 1970): Lévi-Strauss 1981; Propp, 1968; Ricoeur, 1984–8; S. Rimmon-Kenan, *Narrative Fiction: Contemporary Poetics* (London: Methuen, 1983); Sebeok, ed., 1958.

4 *Poiesis* (from *poiein*, 'to make', the process of crafting a made object – the *poema* – by a skilled 'maker' or *poietes*) is not merely a poetry-making process but a 'world-making' praxis or, perhaps, in an enriched sense of fiction, one of the constitutive aspects of most modalities of human imaginative, world-shaping activity. Poetry in its limited sense is simply one region of world-making symbolic praxis; however, we would, unlike the modern usage, stress that such 'making' is inseparable from its 'material' preconditions and rhetorical modes (in the broadest sense of its 'modes of production'). As an icon of imaginative figuration, poetry carries the same universal import as the category of rhetoric – every rhetorical text has, so to speak, a poetic infrastructure. From the logological perspective, social and historical realities are poetic in being shaped by world-creating rhetorical forms, material practices, and institutions. I refer the interested reader to the studies in Volume 1 where the interfaces of communication, technopoiesis, and power may be fruitfully reread from the perspective of *mythopoiesis* developed in this chapter. It should also be said that this generic sense of *poiesis* as world-disclosing, sense-making, self-making praxis, was a commonplace in the ancient world (forming the core of classical *paideia*) and still echoed in the work of the Latin poet Horace (65 BC– AD 8) condensed in his maxim *ut pictura poesis*. For example, in his *Ars Poetica*, 'The art of poetry' (c. 13 BC) where Horace invokes a primary poetic way of life prior to the earliest poets Homer and Tyrtaeus, in which the singers of songs were indeed legislators for mankind: 'In days of old, wisdom consisted in separating public property from private, the sacred from the secular, in checking promiscuity, in laying down rules for the married, in building cities, in inscribing laws on wooden tablets. And that is how honour and reknown came to divine poets and poetry. After them came the great Homer and Tyrtaeus ... ' (*Ars Poetica*, 390–400, in Russell and Winterbottom, eds, 1978: 290; for a verse translation see Horace, 'The art of poetry', trans. John B. Quinn, in *Horace: Odes, Episodes, and Art of Poetry* (St Louis: Blackwell Wielandy, 1936)).

In its more traditional sense, poetry is simply one sphere of world-making, one universe of discourse (to borrow Nelson Goodman's terminology, 1978). Later in Volume 2 we will see how this narrower definition of *poiesis* as 'poetry' was constructed in the world of fifth-century Greece and how the wider cultural, political, and affective meanings of *poiesis* were still part of the effective horizon of the poetic institution in ancient Greece. These interweaving horizons of politics, *ethos*, and *eros* are precisely what are lost in the modern meaning of the word 'poetry'. The vicissitudes of the language of 'the poetic' are fundamentally related to the wider history of classical rhetoric, science, and philosophy following the dissemination of classical learning during the Hellenistic Age (during the course of several centuries 'poetry' would go the way of 'fiction and fabulation', leaving the dominion of truth to the epistemic discourses of logic, science, and philosophy). The detailed history of these logological reversals and inversions has still to be written.

The ancient idea of the world-shaping powers of *poiesis* informed many subsequent

NOTES

defences of poetry and the life of the imagination and became particularly influential in the poetic theorizing of the Italian Renaissance – from Giovanni Boccaccio's *Genealogy of the Gentile Gods* (*c.* 1360–70), to J.C. Scaliger's *Poetice libri septem* ('Seven books of poetics', 1561), the meditations of Torquato Tasso (1544–95) on poetic creativity (e.g. his doctrine of the 'two creators, God and poet'), Sir Philip Sidney's 'Poetry is of all human learning the most ancient', in *An Apology for Poetry* (1596) down to Shelley's conclusion that poets are the 'unacknowledged legislators of the world' (in his *A Defence of Poetry* (1821)) and Romanticism's sublimation of *poiesis* as the world-expressing work of the creative Self which in remaking creation emulates – and perhaps participates in – the creative powers of the Godhead. In medieval and early modern culture it is God who appears as the first creator or 'maker' and Nature – the Book of God – as the product of his 'poesy': Nature as a work of divine poetry, the prose of the world as a sacred poem. In the seventeenth century John Donne could still describe poetry as a 'counterfeit Creation' (see Williams, 1976: 82). By the beginning of the nineteenth century, Romanticism has replaced the godhead with the divine legislation of the creative, expressive, imaginative poet. As an ideological current this was then embedded in the notion of *Bildung* as the self-development of the soul through creative – typically aesthetic – activities. The German ideal of *Bildung* is, in many senses, a secular variant of the ancient notion of *poiesis*; both preserve the core theme of world creation as the 'imaginative' expansion, education, and enrichment of the self (which the ancients called *paideia*). On this theme see W. H. Bruford, *The German Tradition of Self-cultivation* (Oxford: Oxford University Press, 1975).

To return to Horace's older and more secular usage, the term *poiesis* embraces a diverse range of creative practices: legislation, religious divination, the founding of cities, establishing of moral norms, instituting customs and codes of behaviour – all resolutely concerned with the constitution of civility, the 'making of civil society'. Horace, in other words, adumbrates a semiotic view of *poiesis* or 'symbolic making' that has little difficulty in incorporating 'civilizing' dance and music as well as the material structures of architecture (on the complex unity of 'singing-making-doing' in ancient 'pantomimic dance' see Harrison, 1978: chs 2, 3, and Langer, 1953: 189ff.). Note also the remark of Mircea Eliade that 'all dances were originally sacred; in other words, they had an extrahuman model', 1989: 28; the 'spacing' activity of dance or gestural imitation was formulated by Plato in the third book of the *Republic* (398C ff.) and followed almost word-for-word by Aristotle in his *Poetics* where he noted that 'even' dance is a form of *mimesis*, 'imitating' character, emotion, and action by means of rhythmical movement. Dance, rhythm, gestural signification, and *mimesis* belong together. The ancient Greek term 'mimesis' thus incorporated music and dance as two of the most powerful forms of symbolic 'imitation'; in fact there is an important sense in which the earliest types of rhythmic music constitute the most mimetic art form for Plato who – as a good Pythagorean – accepted the intimate relations between the structure of the *psyche* and the forms of musical 'harmony' (cf. *Rep.* 400A–401A; 402C–D on the elective affinity between the 'beautiful soul', the beautiful body, and aesthetic forms; 403, 424C–425A). This ethno-ontology of music (bearing in mind the wider content of *'mousike'* which is close to the modern concept of 'culture') and its work of shaping the souls of its hearers is compressed into the following sentence:

> a change to a new type [*eidos*, 'form'] of music is something to beware of as a hazard of all our fortunes. For the forms of music (*mousikes tropoi*) are

never disturbed without unsettling the most fundamental political and social conventions (*politikos nomos*), as Damon affirms and as I am convinced.
(*Rep.* 424C)

The English philosopher R. G. Collingwood returned to this ancient idea in his claim that 'dance is the mother of all languages' (*The Principles of Art* (Oxford: Clarendon Press, 1938): 243). Dance, in other words, is the matrix of culture and with culture, reflexivity. This is not the place to explore these connections further; only to note that the differences between the ancient ideal of *paideia* through '*poiesis*' and the modern ideal of individuation through '*culture*' constitutes an important field of logological topics.

These observations can also be treated as a reformulation of Giambattista Vico's (1668–1744) insight into the reality-disclosing constitutive ('creative', 'spacing', 'imaginative') powers of what he called poetry or poetic language – here the gestural, symbolic, metaphoric, and allegorical language of sacred ritual, narrative myth, cosmogony, and early cosmology (cf. Vico, 1970: Part 2, Ch. 5). Whether we speak of primordial metaphor, *symbolpoiesis*, symbolic praxis, *mythos*, *narrative*, *rhetoric*, or *text* is of secondary importance; what these expressions all articulate is the instituting capacities of metaphoric signification and, particularly, the metainstituting powers of gestural language as a privileged signifying practice. What is at issue is not merely an enlarged theory of poetry, but a renewed sense of the poetry of theory. If you like, theory as sociality has its creative matrix and orientation in the strategic imaginative interactions of narrativized culture, whose terms and imaginary networks serve to pattern and mediate action and interaction (as the intersection of *ethos*, *pathos*, and *logos*). From the logological perspective all social action – as language-mediated praxis in specific text-social context configurations – is an essentially symbolic and necessarily reflexive activity (cf. Roland Barthes: 'narrative is present in myth, legend, fable, tale, novella, epic, history, tragedy, drama, comedy, mime, painting, stained glass windows, cinema, comics, news items, conversation ... narrative is present in every age, in every place, in every society ... Caring nothing for the division between good and bad literature, narrative is international, transhistorical, transcultural: it is simply there, like life itself' (Barthes, in Barthes *Image-Music-Text* (London: Fontana:, 1977), 79); knowing that Barthes conscientiously studied the history of rhetoric with great intensity, we would not be betraying his intentions by replacing the term 'narrative' by the term 'rhetoric' in this formulation.

5 Gadamer, 1960. We are reminded of Marx's comments in the *Grundrisse* (1973) that Greek mythology

> is not only the arsenal of Greek art, but also its basis. Is the conception of nature and of social relations which underlies Greek imagination and therefore Greek art possible when there are self-acting mules, railways, locomotives and electric telegraphs?... All mythology subdues, controls and fashions the forces of nature in the imagination and through imagination; it disappears therefore when real control over these forces is established. What becomes of Fama side by side with Printing House Square?

Also cf. Henri Lefebvre, *The Sociology of Marx* (London: Allen Lane, 1969): 78–80, 81ff.

6 Cf. Paul Ricoeur's formulation of this dialectic of tradition and innovation: 'the living transmission of an innovation always capable of being reactivated by a return to the most creative moments of poetic activity... a tradition is constituted by the interplay of innovation and sedimentation. To sedimentation must be referred the paradigms that constitute the typology of emplotment. These paradigms have

NOTES

issued from a sedimented history whose genesis has been covered over' (1984–8: Vol. 1, 68); Ricoeur's phenomenological language is itself indebted to the Husserlian 'tradition' of explicating meaning formations by turning to the lived processes of meaning sedimentation and reactivation – most famously explored in Husserl's seminal work, 'The origins of geometry', 1970. For a related exposition of the same dialectic of sedimentation and creativity developed from Kuhn's earlier analysis in *The Structure of Scientific Revolutions* (1970) of the role of paradigms in the 'revolutionary changes' characterizing the history of the physical sciences, see Kuhn, 1977. The logological frames of cultural experience, belief, and thought are of, course, much wider than Kuhnian paradigms of inquiry, embracing as they do social practices, institutions, and reflexive technologies (see Martin, Gutman, and Hutton, eds, 1988). We should also bear in mind Pierre Bourdieu's notion of the *habitus* as a matrix of thought and inquiry:

> one sees that the thinker is less the subject than the object of his most fundamental rhetorical strategies, those which are activated when, led by the practical dispositions of his *habitus*, he becomes inhabited, like a medium, so to speak, with the requirements of the social spaces (which are simultaneously mental spaces) which enter into relation through him.
> (Bourdieu, 1991: 105)

7 On the mutual interweaving of *mythos* and *logos*, figuration and referentiality, identity and polysemy in the desire to return to a primordial origin see Derrida, 1976, 1978a, 1981a, 1982.
8   All word magic and name magic is based on the assumption that the world of things and the world of names form a single undifferentiated chain of causality and hence a single reality. The same form of substantiality and the same form of causality prevail in both, linking them into one self-enclosed whole.
(Cassirer, 1953–7: vol. 1, 118)

> Mythology is static, we find the same mythical elements combined over and over again, but they are in a closed system, let us say, in contradistinction with history, which is, of course, an open system.
> (Lévi-Strauss, 1978: 40)

> Myth aims at disposing of the difference of language, as if this difference were simply non-existent in the myth's own language.
> (Pucci, 1977: 114)

This suppression and forgetting of difference is one of the universal motives for the dream of totality, of bringing the Whole before the mind's eye and grasping the truth of the Whole in unmediated, absolute reflection – the beginnings of which can be found in the earliest forms of philosophical reflexivity; here my point is that the dream of absolute reflection is premised on the occlusion of archetypal difference, incarnated in the figural-symbolic discourse of myth, which, in turn, serves as an icon for the dialogic nature of language. In fact, of course, the repressed figures of difference and dialogue invariably return in the founding categories and discursive projects of absolute reflection.
9 Armstrong, in Finley, ed., 1984: 347. The collection of essays in Easterling and Muir, eds, 1985 is a good place to begin exploring the nature of Greek religiosity in its social and cultural contexts.
10 On the City Dionysia in Athens see A. W. Pickard-Cambridge, *The Theatre of Dionysus at Athens* (Oxford: Oxford University Press, 1946) and *Dramatic Festivals of Athens* (Oxford: Oxford University Press, 1953): 56ff. 'In the sphere of

religion there was, strictly speaking, no "church". That is to say, there was no body of men with a divine mission or sanction, as there was no revelation (oracles and other divine messages merely gave instructions about specific situations, as often as not secular ones). The Greek word *hiereus* that we translate "priest" normally referred either to an official, a layman, whose duties happened to be the management of public cult, or, as in the cult of Demeter at Eleusis in Attica, to a member of the family or families who by ancient tradition had a charge of the local shrine. Thus, in Athens the highest cult official was one of the annual archons, given, interestingly enough, the generally obsolete title of basileus ("king")' (Finley, ed., 1984: 6; cf. Finley, 1963: 46–53, esp. 47–8 and Finley, 'Foreword' to Easterling and Muir, eds, 1985: xiv: 'Greek religion had no sacred books ... no revelation, no creed. It also lacked any central ecclesiastical organization or the support of a central political organization'). Guthrie goes so far as saying that 'personal religion was something almost unknown in Greece' (1977: 334). See also: Burkert, 1985; Cornford, 1923; Dodds, 1951; Dover, 1974; Easterling and Muir, eds, 1985; Guthrie, 1977; Harrison, 1912,1962, 1978; Lloyd-Jones, 1971; Nilsson, 1948; and the older works of Farnell, 1896–1909, 1912.

11 As we have emphasized (note 10 above) *hiereis* has the primary sense of 'sacrificers' (see Gould, in Easterling and Muir, eds, 1985: 1–33, 7). The lack of the institution of an official priesthood was also reflected in the social uses of Greek temples: 'As a general rule the temple was never a place for congregational worship, like a Christian church; it was simply the house of the god, the place where the god's image resided' (Coldstream, in Easterling and Muir, eds, 1985: 68). As Vernant observes: 'Sacrifice is the corner stone of the religion of the city' (1977: xxix).

12 I. M. Finley writes that 'the sacrifice was the central act in worship, if one may be singled out. It is hard to think of a public action in which some god or gods were not sacrificed to as a preliminary step in seeking divine favour and support' (in Easterling and Muir, eds, 1985: xvii). Gould is emphatic: 'there is no system of relationships joining them [*manteis* or dream-interpreters] together and making them conscious of a common stance or a common ideology; there is no "training for the priesthood"'(in Easterling and Muir, eds, 1985: 7). On sacrifice as a powerful matrix of cultural metaphors and discourses rooted in earlier cultic and ritual practices see the work of those associated with the Durkheimian *Année Sociologique*, especially the classic essay by H. Hubert and M. Mauss, 'Essai sur la nature et la fonction du sacrifice', *Année Sociologique*, 2, 1899: 29–138, trans. W. D. Halls, as *Sacrifice: Its Nature and Function* (London: Routledge and Kegan Paul, 1964); also the seminal work of W. Robertson Smith, *Lectures on the Religion of the Semites*; for the 'total social fact' of sacrifice in the culture of Archaic Greece see: Burkert, 1985; Nilsson, 1972; M. P. Nilsson, *Greek Popular Religion* (New York: Columbia University Press, 1940). The tradition is continued in a revised and more structuralist form in the work of J.-P. Vernant (e.g. 1990) and P. Vidal-Naquet (e.g. Vidal-Naquet, 1986; Vernant and Vidal-Naquet, 1981).

13 The role of local deities and city heroes is of inestimable importance in explaining the pluralism of Greek religious discourse, its organic connection with the 'culture of festivals' (music, choral poetry, dance, and so on), and as one of the crucial background conditions for a relatively open-minded attitude toward 'the divine' – the operative polytheism of the Greeks constituted one of the fundamental cultural premises of Hellenic liberalism toward the polymorphic appearances of divinity, which in its later secularized forms is one of the basic logological conditions for a culture of critical discourse. This openness may be explicable in terms of the multiple streams of cultural and ideological influence prior to the Archaic period – a constellation of ecumenical religiosity which can be found as early as the Minoan-Mycenaean period. Here a magma of influences from the

NOTES

Indo-European world, Aegean and Near Eastern sources can be found. As Gould rightly notes:

> Greek religion remains fundamentally improvisatory... [it] is not theologically fixed and stable, and it has no tradition of exclusion or finality: it is an open, not a closed system. There are no true gods and false, merely powers known and acknowledged since time immemorial.
> (in Eaterling and Muir, eds, 1985: 8)

For the pervasive impact of Mycenaean and Homeric religious beliefs upon the architecture, art, and literature of Archaic Greece see Oliva, 1981: ch. 6, 151–84. On the Athena cult in fifth-century Athens see C. J. Herington, *Athena Parthenos and Athena Polias: A Study in the Religion of Periclean Athens* (Manchester, 1955); B. Bergquist, *The Archaic Greek Temenos* (Lund, 1967). On the heterogeneity of Greek myth see Kirk, 1974: 113–75. Chester G. Starr goes so far as seeing the origin of Greek public administration in the management and financing of the civic temple: 'The first beginnings of public administration seem without doubt to have been the product of the need to safeguard and to inventory temple treasures, to provide technically skilled personnel for cult ceremonies and the determination of divine will in critical issues, and to set down laws for the regulation of such matters' (Starr, 1986: 50; Starr refers his reader to A. Andreades, *A History of Greek Public Finance*, 1 (Cambridge, Mass., 1930: 230) (Starr, 1986: 115 n.21). Further essential historical background can be found in Sealey 1976.

Consider also the central role of hero myths in the genre of choral lyric which, again, evolved as a collective performance at public religious festivals:

> Performed by citizen choruses – men, boys, women, or girls – as well as by guilds of professionals, these poems were sung by a dancing chorus at public religious festivals or at important family events like weddings or funerals. Because the festivals in honour of the gods also celebrated the civic life of the polis, choral song played a major role in affirming the values and solidarity of the community (cf. Porphyry, *De abstimentia* 4.22). The connexion between music and ethical values, in fact, remains strong through the archaic and classical periods. Like much of early Greek poetry, choral lyric is public rather than personal in outlook, expression and orientation.
> (Segal, in *CHCL*: 'Early Greek poetry': 124)

See also Easterling, in Easterling and Muir, eds, 1985: 34–49; Cartledge, in Easterling and Muir, eds, 1985: 98–127; and Robertson, in Easterling and Muir, eds, 1985: 155–90. For Athens in particular see *WA*.

14 Cottrell, 1985: 133; the very name and civic identity of Athens as a city-state was, we should recall, derived from the goddess Pallas Athena; in the evolution of Greek Olympian religion from Bronze Age folklore, magical practices and polytheism to the aristocratic pantheon of the Athenian century we have an ideal-typical instance of religious rationalization or the disenchantment of the world in the sense given to these terms by Max Weber. Epic, as we shall see below, continued the same process of humanization: 'no Homeric hero possesses magic powers. It has been often and rightly stressed that one of the greatest achievements of Homeric poetry is its humanization of myth and legend' (Trypanis, 1977: 99–100). Also see Otto, 1947; 1954. As Gilbert Murray observed: 'The anthropomorphic gods of classical Greece represent not a primitive religion but a reformation against the savagery of such religion. Religion itself was humanized' (1946: 9). Gregory Nagy has explored the theme in great detail in his study of institutional transformations in the eighth century (1990: Parts I, II).

15 Mythical narration forms a particularly important part of these poems

[choral song/lyric], not only as ornament, but also as illustration of moral norms and precepts, often reinforced by a concluding ethical maxim. The poet could exploit a rich mythic tradition, confident that an audience brought up on Homer, Hesiod, the Cyclic epics would grasp and appreciate his allusions to or departures from earlier versions. Rapidity, selectivity of detail, elaborate compound adjectives, decorative richness, epithets borrowed or adapted from Homer are the most constant features of the style.

(Segal, in *CHCL*: 'Early Greek poetry', 126)

The Greek literary form known as the 'Homeric hymn' represents an interesting hybrid between epic and choral lyric, and deserves to be analyzed in greater detail than is possible given the aims of this present chapter; in lieu of this see: A. N. Athanassakis, trans., *The Homeric Hymns* (Baltimore: Johns Hopkins University Press, 1976) and N. J. Richardson, ed., *The Homeric Hymn To Demeter* (Oxford: Clarendon Press, 1974), especially ch. 5 of the 'Introduction' on the language of epic, 30–55. The polis-forming functions of civic mythologies in Greek antiquity might be compared with the mythological functions of 'nationalism' and 'nationhood' for modern states (see Anderson, 1983 and Greenfeld, 1992).

16 Aristotle, *Met.* 1.2.982b11–22.
17 Martin Heidegger has identified the historicist error of those historians of philosophy who interpret the origins of philosophical reflection in terms of the elimination of myth:

Myth means the telling word. For the Greeks, to tell is to lay bare and make appear – both the appearance and that which has its essence in the appearance, its epiphany. *Muthos* is what has its essence in its telling – what is apparent in the unconcealedness of its appeal. The *muthos* is that appeal of foremost and radical concern to all human beings which makes man think of what appears, what is being. *Logos* says the same; *muthos* and *logos* are not, as our current historians of philosophy claim, placed into opposition by philosophy as such; on the contrary, the early Greek thinkers (Parmenides, fragment 8) are precisely the ones to use *muthos* and *logos* in the same sense. *Muthos* and *logos* become separated only at the point where neither *muthos* nor *logos* can keep its original nature. In Plato's work, this separation has already taken place. Historians and philologists, by virtue of a prejudice which modern rationalism adopted from Platonism, imagine that *muthos* was destroyed by *logos*. But nothing religious is ever destroyed by Logic; it is destroyed only by the God's withdrawal.

(Heidegger, 1968: 10)

18 The languages of myth provided narrative matrices and rhetorical strategies for rendering existential problems into recognizable and intelligible dilemmas. The earliest narratives are thus understandably oriented toward such domains of ambivalent *human* experience as origination, birth, life, fecundity; transformations relating to disease, ageing, and death; the making and transgression of social bonds; desire and sexuality; dreams and their interpretation; the nature of the gods and the universe as a divine system; the origin and appearance of the gods; fate; power and conflict, etc. A sense of these concerns can be glimpsed in the earliest inscriptions of Greek antiquity (see Tod and *Dox. Gr.*).
19 Weber, 1968: vol. 1, Part I, ch. 3, esp. 231–41. See also Weber, 1967. In the ancient empires of the Middle East the sphere of religion, the patrimonial rule of the gods and their serving priesthoods formed a symbolic centre of the centralized state. The gods were divine guarantors of the political system: the king was thus related to the gods either directly as a descendant of heaven (Pharaonic Egypt) or, more

NOTES

indirectly, as the God's ambassador mediated through a bureaucratic priesthood. Religion was an integral part of the centralized apparatus of social control and governance. Hence there was no way of separating social life from political, legal, and religious structures (for example, the fusion of religious, juridical, and cultural practices exemplifed by the Hammurabic code during the late Amorite dynasty (c. 1728–1686 BC). Moral and legal practices are undifferentiated from sacred and political institutions – and the whole structure is oriented toward the maintenance and consolidation of an empire or dynastic house – the centralized, patrimonial gods of the Near East can thus be said to have evolved as direct products of *raison d'état*. In this way we may trace the *content* of myths and religious narratives from the decisive material conditions of specific forms of life – in Marxist language the decisive 'mode of production' shapes the social form of culture:

> In Mesopotamia, irrigation was the sole source of the absolute power of the monarch, who derived his income by compelling his conquered subjects to build canals and cities adjoining them, just as the regulation of the Nile was the source of the Egyptian monarch's strength. In the desert and semi-arid regions of the Near East this control of irrigation waters was probably one source of the conception of a god who created the earth out of nothing ... The monarch even created law by legislation and rational codification, a development the world experienced for the first time in Mesopotamia. It seems quite reasonable, therefore, that as a result of such experiences the ordering of the world should be conceived as the law of a freely acting, transcendental and personal god.
>
> (1968: vol. 1, 449)

20 Dvornik, 1966: Vol. 1, 151; on the Mycenaean origins of the supreme Kingship of Zeus, see 149–51. Cf. 'The monarchical State of the Gods goes counter to the republican ideas of the historical Greeks; it was an heritage of the old Mycenaean monarchical rule, impressed by the authority of Homer on the following ages'; 'the Homeric picture of the State of the Gods represents the ideas of the ruling classes of the Mycenaean age, not those of the republican Greeks of the classical period' (Nilsson in Thomas, ed., 1970: 64–71, 66). Cf. Aristotle:

> The rule of a father over his children is royal, for he rules by virtue both of love and of the respect due to age, exercising a kind of royal power. And therefore Homer has appropriately called Zeus 'father of Gods and men' [*Iliad* 1.544], because he is the king of them all. For a king is the natural superior of his subjects, but he should be of the same kin or kind with them, and such is the relation of elder and younger, of father and son.
>
> (*Politics* 1259b10–16)

On the polysemy and manifold functions of Zeus in Greek religion see Vernant, 1990: 101–19.

21 Background to this section can be found in Kirk, 1970, 1974; Kerényi, 1959; Lloyd-Jones, 1971 Otto, 1954; Vernant, 1990; Vidal-Naquet, 1986.

22   Among the tools of Greek thought was a polar opposition between force (or violence) and persuasion. There is no more insistent theme in the later Aeschylus. In the Danaid trilogy force and persuasion are contrasted modes of sexual approach and Aphrodite will have to persuade. The ministers of Zeus in *Prometheus Bound* are Mastery and Violence, evoking an answering stubbornness in the hero.

(Winnington-Ingram, in *CHCL*: 'Greek drama' 43)

On the bipolar division between Olympians and Chthonians see Guthrie, 1977:

313

ch. 9, 217–53, esp. 220–3. On the duality of harmony and conflict as a basic rule of tragic experience see Vernant, 1990: 101–19, esp. 116–19.

23 On the role of oppositional categories and the principle of polarity in oral modelling systems and symbolic classifications see the essays in Rodney Needham, ed., *Right and Left* (Chicago: Chicago University Press, 1974). For the structural logic of symbolic taxonomies: Lévi-Strauss, 1963, 1964, 1966. Edmund Leach's introduction to the topic is still useful: E. Leach, *Lévi-Strauss*, 2nd edn (London: Fontana, 1974). On the diverse cultural functions of the *schema of polarity* in early Greek thought, and by implication, for the social psychology of Greek consciousness – its 'love of opposition' or *agonphilia*, see Lloyd, 1971. Lloyd's original paper, 'Right and left in Greek philosophy' was originally published in *Journal of Hellenic Studies*, 82, 1962: 56–66. On binary oppositions as a universal feature of language and signification see Saussure, 1983; Hawkes, 1977; and Lévi-Strauss, 1966, 1978, and for Greek mythology in particular Detienne, 1977; Vickers, 1973; and Vernant, 1990; for criticism see Derrida, 1976, 1978a, Hawkes, 1977; and Kurzweil, 1980. Emile Durkheim and Marcel Mauss somewhat reductively derive such principles from primitive social forms and structures. For example the notion of the *whole* (unity, totality, the One) would be central to Archaic Greek thought for the same reason that makes it basic to totemic thought in general, i.e. it represents the gathering of all things into unity by abstractly codifying the gathering of social life in the circle of the tribe or clan group. Sociality becomes the singular paradigm from which all subsequent logical categories and conceptual representations are derived: 'logical hierarchy is only another aspect of social hierarchy, and the unity of knowledge is nothing else than the very unity of the collectivity, extended to the universe' (Durkheim and Mauss, 1963: 84); and

> The first logical categories were social categories; the first classes were classes of men, into which things were integrated. It was because men were grouped, and thought of themselves in the form of groups, that in their ideas they grasped other things, and in the beginning the two modes of groupings were merged to the point of being indistinct. Moieties were the first genera; clans the first species. Things were thought to be integral parts of society, and it was their place in society which determined their place in nature.
> (Durkheim and Mauss, 1963: 82–3)

For Durkheim's general sociological framework see Steven Lukes, *Emile Durkheim: His Life and Work* (London: Allen Lane, 1973).

24 When the tree is no longer approached merely as tree, but as evidence for an Other, as the location of *mana*, language expresses the contradiction that something is itself and at one and the same time something other than itself, identical and not identical. Through the deity, language is transformed from tautology to language.
(Adorno and Horkheimer, 1979: 15)

In terms of the homologous passage between *mythos* and *logos*, the pursuit of rational articulation had already been perfected in the reflective transparency of the Greek myths – as though they were already translating themselves into 'structural' terms; here theory simply completed a process that was underway within the mythological network. Cf. Marcel Detienne who speaks of 'the remarkable parallelism between the categories operative in the rational thought of the fifth and fourth centuries on the one hand and the principal concepts underlying the mythical material on the other'. The secular *logos* simply explicated

> in a decoded form the major types of opposition on which the myths hinge. It is a decoding that is, no doubt, much facilitated by the transparently

NOTES

obvious nature of the basic framework of most of the myths in this group [the mythology of Adonis and spices]: they are told in a style so sober and apparently unadorned as to express only what is essential ... the structural analysis applied from the outside turns out to be in agreement with the analysis which the Greeks who were contemporary with these myths elaborated from within.

(1977: 131)

25 On the fragility, precariousness, and instability of polarized terms expressed in situations where they 'drift' or 'merge' and in general fail to act out the narrative requirements of the Polarity principle see Pucci, 1977: ch. 5; for this feature in Hesiod's text, see Pucci, 1977: 132–3:

The collapse of the polarized structure uncovers a chiastic figure: we may schematize this figure as *ab, ba*. One pole (a), that of truth, straightness and sweetness, reveals under the surface of the text, the movement of crookedness, deceit, and violence (b); and accordingly the opposite pole, that of deceit, violence, oblivion (b) also reveals the movement of (a).

Albert Cook has constructed a four-stage model of the history of mythology – as a Weberian *Gedankentypen* – in which the Mother goddess of Paleolithic culture is ousted by the binary logics of the 'Neolithic revolution' which accompanied the birth of the myths of empire in Egypt, Mesopotamia, Persia, and Egypt, resolving itself in a third phase characterized by abstract thought, reflection, systematization, and rationalization; a fourth stage appears when the abstractions and allegories of mythic discourse are recycled for literary and ironic effect (culminating in a fifth stage when 'not only the myths themselves but the process of myth formation may come under examination'); indeed a sixth phase is implicit in this examination when it is applied reflexively: 'in which the paradigmatic activity of the fifth phase is itself subjected to reexamination and set to work reflexively so as to produce, even at random, new "mythic" combinations in language' (1980: 59 and 63); see Cook, 1980: esp. 37–66.

26 The 'anxiety of influence' theme derives from Harold Bloom's theory of poetic influence in his *The Anxiety of Influence* (New York: Oxford University Press, 1975). The crisis precipitated by myth's dream of totality and the undisciplined energy of narrativity provided a fruitful setting for linguistic reflexivity:

the whole of our culture has conceived language as a peculiar medium. Though we have long been aware that language constitutes a system of arbitrary signs relating to a referent ... it has been tacitly assumed that we recover the referent as it is. As though the signifier were only a screen that disappears as soon as it indicates the signified, language has been taken as a medium that takes us to the referent and recovers it *hic et nunc* ... The shattering and deconstruction of this metaphysical conception of language have occurred in various degrees in certain periods of our intellectual history.

(Pucci, 1977: 15)

The most radical and systematic examples of this 'shattering' in contemporary thought, for Pucci, arises from the philosophical deconstructions of Jacques Derrida (Pucci, 1977: 15). Derrida uses the evocative image of European metaphysics as a 'white mythology' which codes and reproduces the desire of totality already at work in Greek mythology, 'which reassembles and reflects the culture of the West'. This white mythology deletes its own origins (and scriptural medium): 'the white man takes his own mythology, Indo-European mythology, his own *logos*,

NOTES

that is, the *mythos* of his idiom, for the universal form of that he must still wish to call Reason' (1982: 213). In the terms of this chapter, the conditions of the possibility of Greek metaphysics in Archaic mythopoiesis are elided and repressed. Derrida speaks of this occlusion as the repression of *archi-écriture*: 'White mythology – metaphysics has erased within itself the fabulous scene that has produced it, the scene that nevertheless remains active and stirring, inscribed in white ink, an invisible design covered over in the palimpsest' (1982: 213).

27 In Charles H. Kahn's words (1960: 134).

28 For instance, the lyrical and perhaps unintentionally phallic tone of Eduard Zeller who glosses and then evades the central analytical problems raised by the couplet '*mythos-logos*': 'Beneath the surface of the heroic poetry and its myths the Logos begins to stir, soon to grow bold and raise its head' (Zeller, 1969: 10). Zeller's conceit of *logos* as the figure beneath the surface of myth, is reminiscent of Derrida's image of mythic 'writing' as a palimpsest upon which the categories of metaphysics were to be inscribed (Derrida, 1982: 212–13; and note 26 above). The image of myth as the 'Mother of Logos' inverts Derrida's notion of 'The Father of Logos' ('Plato's pharmacy', in 1981a). The logological implication is that the matrix of earlier thought continued its subterranean life, even after the rise of reason and the hegemony of phallocentric superstructures. In the particular sphere of philosophical reflection

> one can see how the philosophers, who criticized so severely the ideas of their poetic forerunners, nevertheless tried to assimilate and re-interpret these ideas in the light of their own assumptions. The process can be observed at work in other areas of Greek religion, as for example in the case of beliefs about the nature of the gods themselves. This perhaps explains why in the field of ideas about life and death, as elsewhere, earlier and more primitive notions survived alongside the more advanced and sophisticated views of the philosophers, and continued to exercise a powerful influence over men's minds throughout the whole course of later antiquity.
>
> (Richardson, in Easterling and Muir, eds, 1985: 50–66, 65–6)

2 HOMERIC EPIC REFLEXIVITY

1 One of the earliest appreciations of the culture-forming power of Homeric myth is contained in Karl Marx's observation that the language of mythology not only provided the 'arsenal' of Greek art (his choice of metaphors is doubly significant), but also 'the very ground from which it had sprung'. Subsequent Greek culture presupposed the 'unconscious' artistry and imaginative figuration of myth or 'the mythological relation to nature'. And this mythopoeic 'relation to nature' is shaped by the polemical logics of Self-Other relationships constituted by the epic figuration of War. The polemical figurality, artistry and, perhaps, humanism of Greek epic are crucial preconditions for the dynamism of early Greek civilization: 'Egyptian mythology could never be the soil or the womb which would give birth to Greek art.' The prior work of *mythos* was critically important: 'But in any event [there had to be] *a* mythology.' Marx goes further than the humanist idealization of German Neoclassicism, prefiguring the terms of logological analysis with its concern for the constitutive *praxis* of myth: 'There could be no social development which excludes all mythological relation to nature, all mythologizing relation to it, and which accordingly claims from the artist an imagination free of mythology.' Marx saw that the growth of Greek art, and in particular the Homeric epic, was bound up with definite forms of social relations and material development, but

NOTES

had no direct relationship with the general development of society, its material basis, or the 'skeleton structure of its organization'; in the rather limp language of theoretical Marxism, art and cultural forms are 'relatively autonomous' developments in relation to the economic infrastructure; but Marx did not resort to the language of 'relative autonomy'; rather he conceives the relation in dialectical terms: certain forms of culture are possible 'only at an undeveloped stage of art development'; there is a structure of 'uneven' relationship and even 'contradiction' between art forms and social development: 'It is well known that certain periods of highest development of art stand in no direct connection with the general development of society, nor with the material basis and the skelton structure of its organization'; the *epos* is one of those 'art forms' that 'are possible only at an undeveloped stage of art development'. An 'undeveloped' social order appears to be the constitutive precondition of art forms like the Greek epic tradition. But in the last analysis Marx fails to offer any sociological explanation of the formal complexity of the epic, why Homer could still 'afford us aesthetic enjoyment', and how 'in certain respects' the *Iliad* and *Odyssey* still 'prevail as the standard and model beyond attainment'. Instead he resorts to the Schillerian myth of 'naive' beginnings and 'childish' aesthetic origins (ironically, a literary myth takes the place of reflexive analysis and theorizing):

> A man cannot become a child again unless he becomes childish. But doesn't he enjoy the naive ways of the child, and musn't he himself strive to reproduce its truth again at a higher stage? Isn't the character of every epoch revived perfectly true to nature in child nature? Why should the historical childhood of humanity, where it had obtained its most beautiful development, not exert an eternal charm as an age that will never return? There are ill-bred children and precocious children. Many of the ancient peoples belong to these categories. But the Greeks were normal children. The charm their art has for us does not stand in contradiction with the undeveloped stage of the social order from which it had sprung. It is much more the result of the latter, and inseparably [*sic*] connected with the circumstance that the unripe social conditions under which the art arose and under which alone it could appear can never return.
> (in Baxandall and Morawski, 1974: 136–8)

By respecting the texture of mythic praxis we may grasp the constitutive role of narrative in Greek culture, especially its role in the evolution of the sculptural arts:

> What was it that made possible, indeed perhaps necessitated, this artistic enterprise? The answer is clear: narrative, and specifically, mythical narrative. The fact that the narrative art had by this time reached such heights in Greece – first in the medium of epic poetry, then more tentatively in some of the two-dimensional arts, and then with increasing confidence in lyric and choral ode, vase-painting and work in shallow relief – made it inevitable that, when placing a series of figures side by side in the triangular frame of a pediment, sculptors would try to relate them to each other by involvement in a story. So that their portrayal would be clearly intelligible to a spectator looking up from ground-level, actions and gestures had to be forthright and expressive ... By this fusion of the twin arts of narrative and sculpture in the round, the Greeks were simply carrying to a more spectacular level the process which had begun with the first tentative compositions of the Diplyon Monster and his associates in the vase-painting of the mid-eighth century.
> (Snodgrass, 1980: 183–4)

NOTES

> The innovatory sculptors of the sixth century were making a contribution to Western thought which stands comparison with that of their contemporaries the philosophers. Their advances required a similar exercise of individualism and a similar kind of intellectual, perhaps even moral courage.
>
> (Snodgrass, 1980: 186)

See also the references to works on Greek art, sculpture, and architecture in Wace and Stubbings, eds, 1962 and in the general bibliography on this period. In his essay 'Homer and his Influence', J. A. K. Thomson notes the impact of Homeric classicism upon the philosophical tradition:

> In philosophy Socrates encounters prophetism with an ironical, Democritus with a scientific, detachment; in both we find a spirit of *sophrosyne*, that eminently classical and Homeric virtue. That this change was entirely due to Homer is altogether improbable. But it is reasonable to believe that the steady indoctrination of the Greek mind with the Homeric spirit, which was the necessary consequence of Greek education, must have been by far the most potent of all the influences at work upon it ... It is the consciousness of this which inspires the polemic of Plato and other moralists against the tendency of Homeric ethics.
>
> (in Wace and Stubbings, ed., 1962:3)

2 Ancient Greek is, of course, an Indo-European language made up of a number of different dialectal forms: Ionian, Aeolian, Dorian, and Attic. 'Ionian' or 'Ionic' is named after the region of Ionia along the western coastal strip of Asia Minor and the Aegean islands. The original carriers of these dialects – belonging to the great waves of Indo-European peoples who spread east and west in the third and second millennia are unknown; it is thought, however, that the immediate ancestors of the Greeks invaded from the north about 2000–1900 BC. The dialect that would dominate Greek civilization from the eighth century to the Graeco-Roman period – Ionic Greek – was also the product of a large-scale invasion over the course of many centuries. Ionic Greek was thus the language of a colonial civilization that had been forced to move to this part of the ancient world after the Dorian invasions of central Greece (in the twelfth century BC and in a second wave around 1000 BC). The deep affinity between the languages of the Indo-European family of peoples (in India, Iran, and Europe) dates back to this period of vast population displacements. On the language of the inhabitants of the region prior to the the Dorian invasion and on other Aegean languages see A. J. Beattie, 'Aegean languages of the heroic age', in Wace and Stubbings, eds, 1962: 311–24. Beattie draws attention to the long-term impact of invasion and war in the ur-history of the Greek language between the nineteenth and twelfth centuries BC:

> At some time in this period the Achaeans passed over from the mainland to Crete and seized power in Knossos and the other centres of Minoan culture. Presumably linguistic pockets remained in their wake, on the mainland as well as in the islands; the last of these pockets, in Crete, survived till classical times. In the elimination of these non-Greek languages, the Dorian invasion must have been of decisive importance. By flooding the south Achaean lands with a new race of conquerors, not, perhaps, very numerous but destined to establish themselves permanently, the invasion confirmed Greek as the language of that region and ultimately set in motion a new wave of Greek-speaking colonists towards Asia Minor.
>
> (in Wace and Stubbings, eds, 1962: 324)

Ionic eventually became the literary dialect of Homeric verse, as it would later in the seventh and sixth centuries become the idiom of elegiac and iambic poetry (see Chapter 4), Ionian natural philosophy, and the chosen medium of the 'father of history', Herodotus. The language of Plato and Aristotle (as of Greek tragedy, classical rhetoric and oratory) – Attic (Athenian) – however, was a branch of Ionic Greek, achieving dominance during the 'Athenian' fifth century. In antiquity, dactylic hexameter (an artificial metre composed from lines of eighteen syllables divided into threes, the first syllable being accented and the last two unaccented) was regarded as the canonical form of Ionic epic verse. See Bowra, in Wace and Stubbings, eds, 1962: 19-25. Also Camps, 1980: 40-1, 88-9, n. 48, 98-9; Nagy, 1974.

The idea of dactylic hexameter with its dactyls and spondees as a pure Homeric verse form is, of course, a myth; like the various streams of discourse interwoven in the epic form, Homer's mixed Ionic dialect also contains many fossilized forms and strands of other archaic dialects – the most powerful being a form of Aeolic and a dialect described by classical linguists as Arcado-Cypriot (Arcadian and Cypriot relating directly to the language of the Mycenaen Greeks; see Oliva, 1981: 44; Fränkel, 1975: 27ff.). Classical scholarship and ancient Greek philology have been engaged for several generations in disentangling the phonological, semantic, and syntactical patterns of the 'interdialectal' space of the *Iliad* and *Odyssey* (see Palmer, in Wace and Stubbings, eds, 1962: 75-178, esp. 84-94): 'There remains no other choice than to accept dialect mixture as *a characteristic of the language in which the Homeric poems were actually composed*', 100). Cf.: 'we cannot yet rule out the possibility that Ionian poets sometimes introduced an Aeolic form or word because the two dialects, notably in Chios, were not entirely distinct' (Bowra in Wace and Stubbings, eds, 1962: 28); and 'the tradition was built up layer upon layer, with the remoter past submerged but not always discarded. In content, as in language, the Homeric poems form a complex amalgam of elements derived from different epochs, and artificially welded together by the craft of song that each singer inherited from his forerunners. It will be the task of the next chapter [ch. 3, 'The overlapping worlds of Homeric poetry', 49-70] to analyze out some of these elements, and to try to assign them to successive periods in the development of the Greek world from Mycenae to Homer' (Luce, 1975: 47; cf. Beattie, in Wace and Stubbings eds, 1962: 311-24, esp. 319-21 where borrowed elements in classical Greek are illustrated with place-names, divine names, personal names, general vocabulary, syntactical forms, and phonetic differences from earlier dialects; see also Palmer, in Wace and Stubbings, eds, 1962: 97-106; Palmer cites the ancient author Dio Chrysostom (Dio Chrys. *Orations* xi.13) for the description of Homeric language as 'mixed', 98). For a sample of the criticism of Dio Chrysostom see Russell and Winterbottom, 1978: 504-33. According to Wood (1985, 131)

> in all of Homer only one phrase looks to be certainly Mycenaean, namely the *phasganon arguroelon*, 'silver-studded sword', with its variant, *ksiphos arguroelon*. *Phasganon* and *ksiphos* ('sword') are Mycenaean words, as is *arguros* ('silver') and perhaps *alos* ('stud'). Such words have not so far been found between the later Mycenaean period and around 700 BC, which suggests that the epithet became attached to swords in the Bronze Age. But such a poor harvest suggests that direct verbal survivals coming down to the Ionian bards were very rare indeed.

See also Camps, 1980: 39-60; Knox, 1990: 12-3; Levi, 1985: 23.

For the ancient Greek language and its grammar see Friedrich Bechtel, *Die Griechischen Dialektik*, 3 vols (Berlin: Weidmannsche Verlagsbuchhandlung, 1963); Buck, 1933, 1955.

The most accessible English versions of the *Iliad* and *Odyssey* are still the transla-

NOTES

tions of Richmond Lattimore (1962 and 1967); his translation of the *Odyssey* in particular has been universally acclaimed as a major achievement of modern Greek translation. See also the verse translations of the *Odyssey* and *Iliad* by Robert Fitzgerald (1961, 1979), and E. V. Rieu's popular text in the Penguin Classics series (1950). The most recent verse translation is by Robert Fagles (1990). The 'epic' story of the history of the translation of Homer has not yet been fully told; among the more illustrious of Homer's English translators are Alexander Pope, George Chapman, Thomas Cowper, Andrew Lang, Samuel Butler, A. T. Murray, T. E. Lawrence, W. H. D. Rouse, Walter Leaf, E. V. Rieu, Richmond Lattimore, Robert Fitzgerald, and Martin Hammond. For a notable beginning see the long introduction to Robert Fagles' translation of the *Iliad* by Bernard Knox (1990: 1–67).

3 The 'introduction of the Greek alphabet cannot have been much earlier than 750 BC' (Bowra, 1972: 2);

> I believe that Homer composed the poems without the aid of writing, that he gained great kudos through their recitation, and that to ensure their preservation he either wrote or dictated the definitive version of them. This implies, of course, that writing was practised in the community in which he lived, and this in turn implies that he lived not earlier than c. 750 BC. I believe that his *floruit* falls in the second half of the eighth century, and that he was a native of Ionia.
>
> (Luce, 1975: 10)

The reference to Chios as the home city of Homer was already circulating by the time the 'Homeric Hymns' were written (sometime after 650 BC); see for example the line, 'the blind man from rocky Chios' in *To Delian Apollo* 170–4 and the reference to 'the man from Chios' in the late seventh-century poet, Semonides. The later work *Of the Origin of Homer and Hesiod, and of their Contest* (see *Homeric Hymns*) gives Chios, Smyrna, and Colophon as Homer's birthplace (line 313).

We should be careful not to overstress or unconsciously valorize the emergence of alphabetic literacy without further detailed argument and evidence, bearing in mind that other complex cultures and civilizations operated quite successfully without the aid of alphabetic script. The point has been eloquently made by Albertine Gaur:

> If all writing is information storage, then all writing is of equal value. Each society stores the information essential to its survival, the information which enables it to function effectively. There is no essential difference between prehistoric rock paintings, memory aids (mnemonic devices), wintercounts, tallies, knotted cords, pictographic, syllabic and consonantal scripts, or the alphabet. There are no primitive scripts, no forerunners of writing, no transitional scripts as such (terms frequently used in books dealing with the history of writing), but only societies at a particular level of economic and social development using certain forms of information storage. If a form of information storage fulfils its purpose as far as a particular society is concerned then it is (for this particular society) 'proper' writing.
>
> (Gaur, 1987)

Taken at face value, however, Gaur's reminder would close down one of the most important avenues of logological inquiry – concerning the larger social and cultural consequences of introducing different *types* of writing or techniques of literacy in a particular society, and how such innovative technologies of reflection reciprocally influence and change the practices and institutions of the larger social order. In principle we accept that the analysis of the sociology of different forms of

NOTES

writing should avoid *a priori* judgements (particularly of an unreflexive evolutionary nature), but that we should not ignore the highly differentiated effects, whether intended or unintended, of such structures on wider social configurations. We will later see that the impact of new literary modalities of reflexivity can have a revolutionary impact on the social and political direction of a society, but only in the context of specific material structures and preconditions. More typically the dialectic at work here is one of differentiated cultural innovation and conservation:

> nowhere do we find a case where a society first developed a systematic form of writing and then increased its level of social and economic efficiency. Scripts do not create civilizations or new forms of society, but societies can create a new form of information storage.
>
> (Gaur, 1987: 16)

No literary work testifies more eloquently to the interconnectedness of enlightenment and myth than Homer's which is the fundamental text of European civilization.

(Adorno and Horkheimer, 1979: 45–6)

Homer looks both backwards and forwards. He is in the direct line of descent from the court poets of Mycenaean Pylos. His idiom is still the idiom of Mycenaean court poetry, which has become the convenient mnemonic of post-Mycenaean oral poets but which for him again was a live style expressing a particular view of life in which the essential and typical was more important than the transitory and particular. This style could not survive the birth of individualism any more than its parallel in art, the figure style of geometric painting; and the ease of alphabetic writing and reading destroyed its mnemonic convenience. The audience of the *Iliad* and *Odyssey* was no longer the court or even the big house but the great festival attended by the well-to-do citizens of many cities... They were the hoplites who formed the fighting line of their cities, and here and there the traditional Mycenaean battles are related as if they were modern hoplite battles.

(Webster, 1959: 4)

On the Homeric poems as a source of evidence for the history of Bronze Age Greece and more particularly of Mycenaean culture see the archaeological evidence and related debate presented by J. V. Luce in his *Homer and the Heroic Age* (1975), C. G. Thomas, ed., *Homer's History: Mycenaean or Dark Age?* (1970), and the indispensable essays on the social and material culture of the Homeric World in Wace and Stubbings, eds, (1962): esp. Part 2, Sections C and D. For the excavation of the site of Troy see Blegen, in Wace and Stubbings, eds, 1962: 362–86; for Pylos, see Blegen, 422–9; for the archaeology of Mycenae, Wace, in Wace and Stubbings, eds, 1962: 386–98; and for Ithaca, Stubbings, 'Ithaca', in Wace and Stubbings, eds, 1962: 398–421. The Wace and Stubbings collection of essays should now be complemented by the comprehensive critical commentary of A. Heubeck, S. West, J. B. Hainsworth, A. Hoekstra, J. Russo, and M. F. Galiano, *A Commentary on Homer's Odyssey*, 3 vols (Oxford: Oxford University Press, 1988–90); Kirk, 1962; 1985.

Luce concludes his interesting study with an affirmation of the historical veracity of Homeric poetry:

> The songs of Homer are true to life. In their conception of the Heroic Age, the Homeric poems have distilled the truth of a nation's past. The tradition, inherited by Homer was inherently sound. At its heart lay the valid memory of a great period of Greek history, an age of wealth, refinement, and military

prowess, when the long-haired Achaeans travelled far and endured much suffering while the will of Zeus was accomplished.

(1975: 181)

For a popular account of the discovery and excavation of the ruins of Troy see Wood, 1985; ch. 2, 47–93 is devoted to the archaeological work of Heinrich Schliemann.

4 In his *Anatomy of Criticism*, Northrop Frye defines the epic as an encyclopaedic literary form; see 1957: 315–26. Homeric epic is an example of the genre of 'high mimetic epic' whose defining criteria Frye itemizes as: encyclopaedic range of its thematic; articulation of an 'enormous mass of traditional knowledge'; monumental scope and length; episodic character; epic action as 'a consistent order and balance running through the whole'; objectivity/disinterestedness – exemplified by the austere poetry of the *Iliad*; and a cyclical scheme of action and events. On the objectivity and 'realism' of the Homeric epic see the first chapter of Auerbach, 1951. From very different ideological premises the Marxist critic Georg Lukács also singled out Homer as the founding text of classical realism ('from Homer to Thomas Mann and Gorky'); Lukács contrasts the 'static and sensational' epic style of writing in Joyce's *Ulysses* with the more 'dynamic and developmental' narrative of Thomas Mann (see his 'The ideology of modernism', in *The Meaning of Contemporary Realism* (London: Merlin Press, 1962: 17–46). Joyce, of course, was attracted by the structural order of Homer's plot in developing his own epic novel which, in its reflexive artifice and dream of exhaustive depiction can be seen as a respectful parody of its precursor. The parodic element penetrates the basic structure of the novel:

Homer's *Odyssey*	Joyce's *Ulysses*
Odysseus	Leopold Bloom
Peripatetic Greek	Wandering Jew
Telemachus	Stephen Dedalus
Faithful Penelope	Unfaithful Molly Bloom
Suitors	'Blazes' Boylan

In his pre-Marxist study, *The Theory of the Novel*, Lukács speaks of the *Iliad* as a true epic form, without beginning or end, evoking 'the extensive totality of life'; according to Lukács we recognize the 'true' epic by means of the criteria 'spontaneous life' (antedating the modern separation of subject and object), 'objectivity of the empirical', 'immanence', and totality:

> Great epic writing gives form to the extensive totality of life, drama to the intensive totality of essence ... For the epic, the world at any given moment is an ultimate principle ... it can never, while remaining epic, transcend the breadth and depth, the rounded, sensual, richly ordered nature of life as historically given.

(1971: 46)

By uncritically adopting the categories of German idealist aesthetics, Lukács does not flinch from idealizing Archaic Greece as represented in the *epos*; agreeing with the German Neoclassicists Lukács claims that Homeric poetry is simply a formal reflection and codification of an organic social world where 'life and meaning were present with perfect immanence in every manifestation of life' (1971:80) (the same idealist and humanist standpoint is implicit in the contemporary criticism of Trypanis (cf. 'epic poetry creates a completely human world ... it succeeds in integrating with the present and creating a harmonious whole, which embraces nearly every aspect of life', 1977: 91) and 'This inclusiveness helps to create the conviction in the reader that justice is being done to reality, not just to specially selected areas of it, and this is important', Griffin, 1980a,: 12). Led by these premises, Lukács ignores the complexity and contradictory reflexivities of the epic form; there is no 'individuality' or 'personality' in the *epos*; Achilles and Odysseus are simply ciphers of an organic social order, connected by 'indissoluble threads to the community whose fate is crystallised in his own' (1971: 67). Lukács does not flinch from traducing Hegel by describing the novel as a bourgeois epic, a parodic form in an age where the integral 'immanence of life' has been shattered and totality has been rendered problematic 'yet which still thinks in terms of totality'; when necessary he also draws freely from Nietzsche in claiming that the novel is the epic of a 'world abandoned by God'; the modern novel is an *ersatz* epic, a distant echo of the Homeric prototype ('epic verse should sing of the blessedly existent totality of life'). In the novel, the task of integration is assumed by the central character, the problematic hero as a figure attempting to reconstitute meaning and order from within the heart of darkness ('transcendental homelessness', 'alienation' from the outside world, 1971: 66). The modern Odyssey of the novel form is an egocentric quest for self-certainty, of 'the problematic individual's journeying towards himself' typified in the *Bildungsroman* or *Erziehungsroman* genre: 'The novel hero's psychology is demonic; the objectivity of the novel is the mature man's knowledge that meaning can never quite penetrate reality, but that, without meaning, reality would disintegrate into the nothingness of inessentiality' (1971: 88).

With the flight of the Gods and the onset of modern nihilism, the novel provides the last semblance of coherence in a fragmented world; it becomes 'the representative art-form of our age', for the reason that the 'structural categories of the novel constitutively coincide with the world as it is today' (1971: 93). The post-Enlightenment world is, in Fichte's apocalyptic phrase, an epoch of absolute sinfulness (1971: 152). Another, and altogether more subtle, critic in the Marxist tradition, unburdened by either Hegelian historicism or Neoclassicist idealist aesthetics, glimpsed more of the epistemic and logological significance of the Homeric epics:

> The epic poem is in fact a history of signifying nature in its classical form, just as allegory is its baroque form. Given its relationship to both of these intellectual currents, romanticism was bound to bring epic and allegory closer together. And thus Schelling formulated the programme for the allegorical exegesis of epic poetry in the famous dictum: The *Odyssey* is the history of the human spirit, the *Iliad* is the history of nature.
> (Benjamin, 1977: 167)

5 The third-century Hellenistic epic narrative of Apollonius Rhodius, the *Argonautica*, has been described as one of the most important poems written in Alexandria and also as 'one of the finest failures in the whole of Greek literature' (Bulloch, in *CHCL:*, Vol. 1, Part 4, 46); J. A. K. Thomson speaks of it as 'a baroque or even a rococo poem' (in Wace and Stubbings, eds, 1962: 4). From our point of view the *Argonautica* is the paradigm of a secondary literary epic; it is also the only surviving long epic from the Hellenistic period – one of the missing links between Classical literature and the later Greek novel of the second and third century AD (Cf. Bulloch, in *CHCL*, vol. 1, Part 4, 58). Like Virgil's *Aeneid*, written in the first century AD., the *Argonautica* is a self-consciously literary attempt to reproduce its Homeric precursor. But of even greater significance for the evolution of Western literary consciousness is the impact of the *Iliad* (and the *Argonautica*) on the *Aeneid*. In Thomson's words: 'in the design and structure of his poem, in his management of the epic machinery, in his use of the epic conventions, in his

understanding of the heroic age, Virgil stands supreme among the ancient followers of Homer' in Wace and Stubbings, eds, 1962: 4–5).

6 'Rhapsode' in ancient Greek literally means one who stitches together songs (probably a spurious etymology from the verb *rhaptein*; hence *rhapsodein*), to sing of the wonderful deeds of men (*Il.* 9.189). In the seventh century the *rhapsode* evolved into the role of a professional reciter of poetry, and the most famous rhapsodes were members of Homeric 'schools' or guilds (the *Homeridai*) specializing in the recitation of Homeric verse (cf. Herodotus, 5.67.1; Plato, *Ion* 530A–B, 531B). In Greek art the rhapsode is usually pictured holding a lyre or a staff, symbolizing the gift of the Muses (see the Cycladic marble statuette of a harp player from Keros (c. 2500 BC) in Oliva, 1981: 50 (the original is in the National Museum, Athens), the bronze eighth-century BC statuette of a singer in the Iraklion Archaeological Museum that serves as the frontpiece to Thomas, ed., 1970, and the portrait of a fifth-century rhapsode on an Attic red-figured amphora found near Vulci, now in the British Museum, Plato 4, between pages 18–19 in Wace and Stubbings, eds, 1962). The image of the rhapsode is thus of great antiquity, dating back to the Mycenaean period – for example the fresco of the lyre player from Pylos, Figure 36 in Wace and Stubbings, eds, 1962: 426).

Tradition depicts Homer as a blind singer of songs (*aoidoi, aoidos*, a singer or bard; *aoide*, the art of singing and the song): 'The *Iliad* and the *Odyssey* ... mark the end of the long period of oral epic tradition. The *aoidoi* (bards) improvising to the accompaniment of the lyre are replaced by the *rhapsodes* (reciters) whose text is predetermined ... The heroic age as Homer described it in the *Iliad* and the *Odyssey* became the prime source of classical mythology. As long as classical Greek civilization endured, Homer was the most famous and most widely read author. This was especially so for the *Iliad*, the text most frequently found copied on Egyptian papyri' (Oliva, 1981: 61–2; Trypanis, 1977: 105: cf. Ehrenberg, 1964): esp. 1–22 ('After all, the word 'rhapsodes' itself contains the concept of song', Ehrenberg, 1964: 11)). On the question of the later role of teams of rhapsodes *reciting* the homeric poems, the *Homeridai* as fifth and fourth-century interpreters and critics in the creation and transmission of a Panathenaic text of Homer see J. A. Davison, 'The transmission of the text', in Wace and Stubbings, eds, 1962: 215–33, esp. 218–22; also *The Homeric Hymns and Homerica*, trans. Hugh G. Evelyn-White, 1936). The 'Homerids' or *Homeridai* were paradigmatic examples of specialists in the arts of literary reflexivity codifying oral performances into a literary canon ('They served a public need by their recitals, probably also by writing some verse, such as the additions to Hesiod or some of the Cyclic epics. There was a demand for more and more material, even without concern for artistic composition. At that moment, the personal union between poet and rhapsode had definitely come to an end', Ehrenberg, 1964: 12). Pindar introduces *Nemean* II with a reference to the *Homeridai*, 'singers of tales' (*Nemean* 1.1–3, also DL: 1.57; cf. Lattimore, 1959b, 99).

7 'In a purely oral tradition, songs, epics, and sayings do not hover above life. That life is a delicate, complex tissue steeped in epic recollections' (Illich and Sanders, 1988: 16). The long-durational sedimentation of oral song cycles into epic poetry may explain why most of the secondary literature on Homeric epic speaks of its 'monumentality', 'inclusiveness', 'comprehensive vision', 'seriousness', and 'noble and high moral tone': the *Iliad* is the monumental poem of the European tradition, of epic 'inclusivness' and 'encyclopaedic' vision, the 'universal Trojan song' as an epic 'totality'; indeed 'strict Critics' would regard the *Odyssey* as falling below the *Iliad* in these respects:

Of all poetical works, [the Epic is] the most dignified, and at the same time, the most difficult in execution. To contrive a story which shall please and interest all Readers, by being at once entertaining, important, and instructive; to fill it with suitable incidents; to enliven it with a variety of characters, and of descriptions; and throughout a long work, to maintain that propriety of sentiment, and that elevation of Style, which the Epic Character requires, is unquestionably the highest effort of Poetical Genius. Hence so very few have succeeded ... that strict Critics, will hardly allow any other Poems to bear the name of Epic, except the *Iliad* and the *Aenid*.

(H. Blair, 1825, 564–5)

Cf. Bowra, in Wace and Stubbings, eds, 1962: 19–25, and 26–37; one ancient precedent for this judgement is 'Longinus'' *Peri hypsous* (*On the Sublime*), c. AD 1, which ranks the *Iliad* as a masterpiece of 'sublime' language, and the *Odyssey* as merely an 'episode' of the *Iliad*: in the *Odyssey* Homer is a setting sun: the grandeur and intensity has disappeared, but there remains the greatness (*On the Sublime*, IX); the author of *Peri hypsous* is himself indebted to earlier Athenian and Alexandrian critics of the two epic works – the cynic philosopher and grammarian Zoilus (fourth century BC), 'the Scourge of Homer', is explicitly mentioned by Longinus in Section IX (Zoilus we should also note was notorious for his extreme critical views on Plato, Isocrates, and Homer; it is probable that he visited the Museum at Alexandria in its period of construction; see *Oxford Classical Dictionary*, 1147).

Cf. the evaluative criteria in the following statement of epic's qualities: 'the nobility and the depth of the emotions portrayed, by the effective contrast of the characters introduced, by the clarity and variety of the scenes described; by the musical flow of the hexameter and the wealth and brilliance of the epic diction; and not least by the recurrent descriptive epithets and the magnificent similes, always drawn from the poet's own world, as well as the moral sentences, which convey a light on the whole of life. Nor should the plainness of thought, the rapidity of the narrative and the blending of divine with human action be overlooked' (Trypanis, 1971: xxix); on the 'restrained use of metaphor' alongside 'brilliant simile' see Trypanis, 1977: 73, 74, 75–8, 101–2; on the use of *extended* similes, Griffin, 1980a: 11–12 and Edwards, 1987: 102–20; all these aesthetic epithets hark back to Matthew Arnold's observations contained in his famous Oxford lectures, *Essays on Translating Homer* where he condenses the Homeric 'grand style' into four distinctive qualities: plainness of thought, resulting in directness and simplicity; plainness of style, resulting in clearness; rapidity; and nobleness; also see Thomson, in Wace and Stubbings, eds, 1962: 1. Matthew Arnold's views are, in turn, indebted to Aristotle's praise of the 'serious style' of which Homer was 'preeminent among poets' (*Poetics* 4): 'the heroic of all measures is the stateliest and the most imposing; and hence it most readily admits rare words and metaphors; as indeed the narrative mode of imitation is in this respect singular' (*Poetics* 14); it is also most likely that Arnold was aware of 'Longinus'' celebration of 'the sublime' qualities of Homeric verse (though the critical precedent derives from Giambattista Vico's description of Homer in the *New Science* as the most sublime of all the sublime poets, 1970: ch. 4, §807).

For the *intertextual* organization of the Homeric logological space: the Homeric epic as a sedimentation of many different strata of ancient Greek history and culture, or 'cultural amalgam': Trypanis, 1977: 46–9; Edwards, 1987: Part I, 15–169; also cf. the archaeological evidence which supports the same intertextual and intercultural structure of the Homeric narratives; the Homeric text is a densely mediated matrix of earlier genres tracing more than a millennium of early Greek history, 'with some elements dating back to the period of the Trojan War and even

NOTES

further back into the Mycenaean Age, some elements originating in the so-called Dark Age between 1100 and 800, and finally some elements that reflect life in Homer's own day', a composite archive of the 'Greece before Greece',

> the rise and fall of different centres of power and schools of art, of changes in architecture and pottery styles, of evolution in burial customs and technology, of objects that became obsolete and skills that were lost and regained. More importantly, it is the history of the Greek-speaking tribes as they explored, expanded, conquered, traded, prospered, declined, migrated, and colonized'
>
> (Luce, 1975: 26, 11, 47, 49–70)

Epic or *epos* as a self-consciously aesthetic genre or reflexive verse form (in dactylic hexameter) is first explicitly noted in Aristotle's contrast between the merits of the iambic trimeter and dactylic hexameter: 'Once dialogue had come in [in Tragic Drama], Nature herself discovered the appropriate measure. For the iambic is, of all measures, the most colloquial: we see it in the fact that conversational speech runs into iambic form more frequently than into any other kind of verse; rarely into hexameters, and only when we drop the colloquial intonation' (*Poetics* 1449a22); but cf.: 'an artificial literary language that was never spoken in any part of the Greek world' (Trypanis, 1977:98; 'the language of Homer was one nobody, except epic bards, oracular priests or literary parodists would dream of using' (Knox, 1990: 11); cf. M. Bowra's 'Homer's language can never have been spoken by men. It contains too many alternative forms, too many synonyms, too many artificial forms for it to be in any sense a vernacular. It is a language created for poetry by the needs of composition', in Wace and Stubbings, eds, 1962: 26.

On epic as a complex linguistic technology of reflection:

> The language of Attic tragedy in both its subvarieties, sung and spoken, is a *Kunstsprache*, an artificial language never actually spoken by anybody but created or developed for poetic purposes ... we are not tolerably familiar with another such Greek language, the Homeric *Kunstsprache*, and we can see that it, though basically Ionic, is not identical with any actual Ionic dialect of any period. Indeed its most striking trait is its complexity; and this complexity includes a strong admixture of non-Ionic forms.
>
> (Else, 1965: 72; cf. Bowra, in Wace and Stubbings, eds,1962: 26–37; Edwards, 1987: Part 1; Bernard Knox, 'Introduction' to Robert Fagles' translation of the *Iliad* (1990: 11ff.))

For the Vician idea of the *epos* as the mother language and origin of European literature: 'At the sources of Western civilization, themselves its main source, stand two poems on the grand scale which for sustained beauty and splendour have found no superior, perhaps no equal, in all the poetry that has followed them. This is the most remarkable fact in the history of literature' (Thomson, in Wace and Stubbings, eds, 1962: 1); 'Western literature begins with Homer' (Griffin, 1980a: 1).

8 'If it is true that European history began with the Greeks, it is equally true that Greek history began with the world of Odysseus' (Finley, 1964: 25). Finley wrote an influential book with the title *The World of Odysseus*, 2nd edn (1978). This might be compared with the dialectical commentary of Theodor W. Adorno and Max Horkheimer, where they claim that the iconic figure of Odysseus, as represented in the *Odyssey*, is the founding prototype of Western European Individualism, indeed, a prefiguration of the fundamental ideology of the Bourgeois-Capitalist World (in their *Dialectic of Enlightenment*, 1979). On Homer as the pedagogic matrix of Greek culture: Herodotus: 'Homer first fixed for the

NOTES

Greeks the genealogy of the Gods, gave the gods their titles, divided among them their functions, and defined their images' (*Herodotus*, II, 53); Aristophanes: *Frogs* 1030–6; Plato: *Republic* 606E; Xenophon: *Symposium*, 3.5; 4.6–8 ('Homer, that learned man, dealt with almost every form of human activity in his poems. That is why, if any of you wishes to become capable of running his household or arousing the people or commanding an army, you ought to cultivate my society, since from my knowledge of the poems I am an expert in all these matters' (4.6); for Plato's satire on this attitude in the rhapsode Ion, see the dialogue *Ion*). Cf. the following selection of modern assertions on the same theme:

> In its pre-literary form epic poetry was a necessary part of the social life of a family or of a community. Whatever its functions may have been in its earliest pre-history and in its origins, we find it in historical times serving as tribal, family, or national history, panegyric, political propaganda, as a model for education, and finally as entertainment. It is sung at religious festivals, both pagan and Christian, at the courts of princes, at community gatherings, at solemn family feast days, and in the peasant hut. The audience for epic songs seems never to have been exclusive. Although sung in the courts of princes, it was also sung for the farmers, and was not restricted to any single group.
>
> (Lord, in Wace and Stubbings, eds, 1962: 181)

> Not a single educated generation of Greeks has grown up without having received some sort of instruction in Homer, and this surely constitutes the longest and perhaps most illustrious educational tradition in all the Western world.
>
> (Trypanis, 1977: 108)

> Indeed it was through the knowledge and practice of the Homeric poems that Greek culture first took shape.

> The *Iliad* and the *Odyssey*, without being regarded as in any way sacred works, were the Bible of the Greeks, pre-eminently 'the Book'. Not only second-rate poets such as Ion, the chief character in Plato's dialogue of that name, but also authentic philosophers have defended Homer against all attack, even against criticism, based on the three exegetical principles: physical, moral, and mystical allegory.
>
> (Flacelière, 1964: 63, 61; cf. Griffin, 1980a: 6)

For the concept of epic as a tribal encyclopaedia or conspectus of everyday tribal knowledge grounded in oral culture see the writings of Eric A. Havelock, particularly his *Preface to Plato* (1963) and *The Greek Concept of Justice* (1978). In this chapter I prefer to interpret epic narrative as a complex, heteroglossial discourse formation codifying an ideological matrix reflecting powerful value interests, social practices, and beliefs. The epic matrix, as a reflexive site of discourse, facilitates further practices of interpreting domains of experience that are central to the legitimation and reproduction of ruling, aristocratic groups. The Homeric rhapsode functioned as an organic intellectual within the power structure of Greek tribal society and poetry functioned as a powerful institutional armature of this ruling group by codifying its values, memorializing its world-view, and reproducing associated knowledge systems – views of life, notions of the heroic, the soul, warfare, morality, ethical conduct, customary behaviour, ways of correcting transgression, etc. Homeric poetry became the armature of Archaic ideology and when we reach the world of Classical Greece, the Homeric poet has achieved the status

NOTES

of a traditional intellectual, obstructing the development of radically new, literate forms of cultural praxis. I will return to these topics in later chapters.

9 To judge from the extant fragments of literary papyri, the *Iliad* was easily the most popular book in Hellenistic Egypt. The *Odyssey* came some way behind it, but was the first Greek work to be translated for use in Roman schools ... Cicero in his *Letters* quotes Homer forty-five times, far more than any other author.

(Luce, 1975: 180)

M. I. Finley presents the following rough breakdown of surviving Greek papyrus texts found in Egypt:

Of all the fragments of Greek literary works rediscovered and published through 1963, there are 1,596 books by or about authors whose names are identifiable. Something less than half the total were copies of the *Iliad* or *Odyssey* or commentaries upon them. The second best represented author is the orator Demosthenes with 83 (again including commentaries), followed by Euripides with 77 and Hesiod with 72. The classical Athenian orators together reach a total of 154, close to three times that of the philosophical books of the same period.

(1975: 201)

The grammatical discipline was originally, and would always remain, principally a thorough study of the great writers, and especially the poets. To be a cultivated Greek was, first and foremost, to be deeply versed in Homer. A legacy of the archaic period, knowledge of Homer would characterize Greek education throughout its history. For example, in the Byzantine period, Michael Psellus took pride in having learnt the whole of the *Iliad* by heart as a child just like a character in Xenophon fourteen centuries earlier. Similarly, the author of the most detailed Greek commentary on Homer, regularly consulted by philologists today, was Archbishop Eustathius of Thessalonica in the twelfth century.

(Marrou, in Finley, ed., 1984: 191)

10 Presumably this is what occasioned Schiller's famous misdescription of Homer as a genius of 'naive' poetry' in his influential essay *'Über Naive und Sentimentalische Dichtung'* (1796). See Friedrich von Schiller, *'Naive und Sentimental Poetry' and 'On the Sublime'*, trans. Julius A. Elias (New York: Frederick Ungar, 1966); also Schiller's *On the Aesthetic Education of Man: In a Series of Letters* (New York: Frederick Ungar, 1965). The reflexive concept of 'narrative tradition' presupposed by traditional narrativity has been recently developed by Jean-François Lyotard:

a narrative tradition is also the tradition of the criteria defining a threefold competence – 'knowing how' (*savoir-faire*), 'knowing how to speak' (*savoir-dire*), and 'knowing how to hear' (*savoir-entendre*) – through which the community's relationship to itself and its environment is played out. What is transmited through these narratives is the set of pragmatic rules that constitutes the social bond.

(Lyotard, 1984: 21)

See also J.-F. Lyotard, *Discours, figure* (Paris: Klincksieck, 1971), J.-F. Lyotard, *Instructions païennes* (Paris: Galilée, 1977), and J.-F. Lyotard, *Le Différend* (Paris: Minuit, 1983), trans. as *The Differend: Phrases in Dispute* (Manchester: Manchester University Press, 1989). Lyotard's formulation might be compared to the concept of tribal encyclopaedia or to our own notion of a *discourse matrix* in its central social function of crystallizing, transmitting, and sedimenting the social knowledge

NOTES

and social networks normative for a given community or *ethos*; in other words, the matrix of generative rules governing terms such as 'real', 'value', 'excellence', 'honour', 'shame', and so forth, distributed throughout a community's practical, moral, ethical, and political networks. The discourse matrix of a specific society articulates such knowledges into manageable chunks of causal motivational sequences and symbolic actions. Homer

> does not passively accept tradition: he does not relate a simple succession of events, *he presents a plot that develops by its own compulsion from stage to stage, governed by an unbreakable connection of cause and effect*... And the plot does not develop in a loose chronological sequence. It is ruled throughout by the principle of sufficient reason. Every action has its roots in character'
>
> (Jaeger, 1945: vol. 1, 51)

Character, moreover, is a discursive product of the heroic code of honour. The language of honour as we will see in the main text is one of the central vocabularies of the Homeric universe:

> Honour is of supreme importance because a man's sense of his own worth is affected naturally by his awareness of the judgement passed on it by others; and the confidence of a man's own worth is what, for a hero, gives his life itself its value. Honour is diminished by any infringement of a person's rights or denial of his legitimate expectations... Honour is enhanced by the possession and exercise of personal qualities that are exceptionally esteemed for their usefulness to their possessor and to the community: chief of these are courage and strength and military and athletic skills, also resourcefulness and persuasive speech, and, to a lesser extent, physical beauty.
>
> (Camps, 1980: 7)

11 For background on the structure and evolution of heroic poetry more generally see N. Austin, *Archery at the Dark of the Moon: Poetic Problems in Homer's 'Odyssey'* (Berkeley and Los Angeles: University of Califonia Press, 1975); Bowra, 1951, 1972; Burn, 1960; Carpenter, 1962) and Chadwick & Chadwick, 1932–40; Edwards, 1987; Finley, 1964; Grandsen, 1984; Griffin, 1980a, 1980b; J. B. Hainsworth, *Homer* (Oxford: Clarendon Press, 1969); Kirk, 1970, 1974; G. S. Kirk, *The Songs of Homer* (Cambridge: Cambridge University Press 1962): esp. Part 2; Kirk, 1970; G. S. Kirk, *Homer and the Oral Tradition* (Cambridge: W. Heffer, 1976); Kirk, ed., 1964; M. S. Jensen, *The Homeric Question and the Oral-Formulaic Theory* (Copenhagen: Museum Tusculanum Press, 1980); Lord, 1971; Luce, 1975; J. L. Myres, *Homer and his Critics* (London: Routledge 1958); Page, 1955, 1959, A. Parry, *The Making of Homeric Verse* (Oxford: Clarendon Press, 1971); Redfield, 1975; R. H. Simpson and J. F. Lazenby, *The Catalogue of the Ships in Homer's 'Iliad'* (Oxford: Clarendon Press, 1970); Trypanis, 1977; A. J. B. Wace and Stubbings, eds, 1962; Wade-Gery, 1952; Webster, 1958; C. H. Whitman, *Homer and the Homeric Tradition* (Cambridge, Mass: Harvard University Press, 1958); C. H. Whitman, *The Heroic Paradox: Essays on Homer, Sophocles, and Aristophanes* (Ithaca, N. Y., 1982).

12 This is in keeping with Aristotle's stricture that the epic should focus on one whole or complete action 'with a beginning, middle parts, and end' – organized with the harmony of a living being (*Poetics* 1459). As a syntax of *praxis*, Homeric epic takes a resolutely 'anthropocentric' turn in its conception of life and reality. The grammar of praxis has its first authentic vehicle in Greek epic poetry:

NOTES

Greek epic poetry looked at life from a standpoint infinitely higher and more objective than did mediaeval epic poetry, and it gave a first shape to the anthropocentric conception that was later to prevail in ancient Greek civilization; one may justly say, as has often been said, that Homeric poetry contains the seeds of all Greek philosophy which developed subsequently.

(Trypanis, 1977: 97)

This is also the reason why one of the most pervasive narrative strategies of epic verse is the praxial logic of personification: 'Homer, the father and prince of poets, is remarkable for the use of this figure. War, peace, darts, spears, towns, rivers, every thing, in short, is alive in his writings' (Blair, 1825: 206).

13 The seminal research on Homeric formulae is still that of Milman Parry, dating back to the 1930s ('Studies in the epic technique of oral verse-making: I: Homer and the Homeric style', *Harvard Studies in Classical Philology*, 41, 1930: 73–147 and 'Studies in the epic technique of oral verse-making: II: the Homeric language as the language of an oral poetry', *Harvard Studies in Classical Philology*, 43, 1932: 1–50. See Parry, ed., 1971). Walter J. Ong has recently explained the formulaic structure of epic as a product of the discursive constraints of primary oral, 'sound-dominated' communication (dependence on formula – 'Wine-dark Sea', Adjective-Noun aggregates, repetition or a high degree of semantic redundancy, a preference for holistic units, agglutinative grammar, paratactic syntax, 'dialectical' communication in terms of oppositions, polarities, etc., and a high use of situationally specific, embodied knowledge):

A sound-dominated verbal economy is consonant with aggregative (harmonizing) tendencies rather than with analytic, dissecting tendencies (which would come with the inscribed, visualized word: vision is a dissecting sense). It is consonant also with the conservative holism (the homeostatic present that must be kept intact, the formulatory expressions that must be kept intact), with situational-thinking (again, holistic, with human action at the center) rather than abstract thinking, with a certain humanistic organization of knowledge around the actions of human and anthropomorphic beings, interiorized persons, rather than around impersonal beings.

(Ong, 1982: 73–4)

Also Lord, in Wace and Stubbings, eds, 1962: 179–214; Duggan, 1973.

14 Some interpreters see the power of formular, mnemonic techniques as the key to the preliterate *pensée sauvage*, the fundamental medium of tribal memory and consciousness. However, rather than seeing the Homeric world as a universe of 'savage thought', it seems more economical to assume that their discrete, aggregative, additive, and iterative forms of experience arise from powerful oral techniques such as paratactic description, formulaic *Gestalten*, and symmetrical, polarized distribution of narrative qualities and action predicates. For an alternative, Whorfian view of 'the paratactic universe of the archaic Greeks':

the modes of representation used during the early archaic period in Greece are not just reflections of incompetence or of special artistic interests, they give a faithful account of what are felt, seen, thought to be fundamental features of the world of archaic man. This world is an open world. Its elements are not formed or held together by an 'underlying substance', they are not appearances from which this substance may be inferred with difficulty. They occasionally coalesce to form assemblages. The relation of a single element to the assembly to which it belongs is like the relation of a part to an aggregate of parts and not like the relation of a part to an overpowering whole. The particular aggregate called 'man' is visited, and

NOTES

occasionally inhabited by 'mental events'. Such events may reside in him, they may also enter from the outside. Like every other object man is an exchange station of influences rather than a unique source of action, an 'I' (Descartes' *cogito* has no point of attack in this world, and his argument cannot even start). There is a great similarity between this view and Mach's cosmology except that the elements of the archaic world are recognizable physical and mental shapes and events while the elements used by Mach are more abstract, they are as yet unknown *aims* of research, not its object. In sum, the representational units of the archaic world-view admit of a realistic interpretation, they express a coherent ontology, and Whorf's observations apply

(Feyerabend, 1975: 248–9; see also 1987: 90–103

15 The distinction has been drawn with admirable precision by Eric Gans:

All biblical narration is made to justify a sacred law, which is always ultimately an ethical law. Homeric narration has a very different orientation. Discursive – desiring – identification with the characters is prior to any relation to transcendental values. The primary mediation that binds the community of hearers to the Homeric text is that provided by the fictional discourse itself, and transcendental values are relevant only insofar as they are incarnated within this discourse ... Discourse is for the Greeks a self-contained phenomenon, an institution without explicit institutional constraints. Fictional discourse better exemplifies this institution than philosophy, because its audience requires no motivation extraneous to the discourse itself. 'Esthetic pleasure' is sufficient reason for joining this audience ... The biblical text is designed to inspire fear of God, that is respect for ethical constraints. The Homeric text contents itself with inspiring a love for the text itself, or more precisely, for the position of hearer subordinated to the reciting Subject.

(Gans, 1985: 7)

Also cf. the same typological contrast in Eric Auerbach's famous essay 'Odysseus' Scar', Auerbach, in 1957. As usual Aristotle had already touched upon the fundamental issue:

The heroic [or dactylic hexameter] in fact is the gravest and weightiest of metres – which is what makes it more tolerant than the rest of strange words and metaphors, that also being a point in which the narrative form of poetry goes beyond all others. The iambic and trochaic, on the other hand, are metres of movement, the one representing that of life and action, the other that of the dance. Still more unnatural would it appear, if one were to write an epic in a medley of metres, as Chaeremon did. Hence it is that no one has ever written a long story in any but heroic verse; nature herself, as we have said [1449a24], teaches us to select the metre appropriate to such a story.

(*Poetics* 24.1459b30–1460a5)

16 Epic heteroglossia may well have been one of the deeper reasons behind Aristotle's argument that tragedy is a superior art-form to epic narrative: tragic *mimesis* is more discrete, bounded, and concentrated within definite spatial and finite limits, more unified and centralized than the centripetal, proliferating plot structure and digressive mimesis of the epic ('if the more refined is the higher, and the more refined in every case is that which appeals to the better sort of audience', then tragedy fulfils its specific function better than does epic, *Poetics* 26). 'Knowledge' here must be interpreted generously – following the directives of Volume 1,

331

NOTES

Introduction, notes 1 and 2 – to cover all forms of significant practice and culturally relevant systems of meaning. The monopoly of epic syncretism became the unique vocation of the preliterate guilds of poets, and this 'cultural capital' would typically include: (i) the assembly and codification of cultural forms and representations (as befits a 'stitcher of songs'); (ii) the articulation of cultural lore, values, and belief systems, into a stock of operative knowledge; (iii) the transmission and reproduction of the 'tribal consensus' in oral performance; (iv) the periodic reactivation of the idealized value paradigms of the society; (v) the ritual involvement of the audience in this value system; (vi) the legitimation of everyday practices and common sense by embedding them in the heroic world of the epic genre; (vii) the redefinition of cultural self-images; (viii) the provision of exemplary instances of cultural identity; and (ix) the stabilization of cultural changes and innovations under the stabilizing influence of formulaic transmission.

The receptive, heteroglossial character of the epic genre might also be related to the 'structural and thematic unity' of its dominant, quantitative metre, the dactylic hexameter which was 'at once formal and flexible' and as such has been called 'the great achievement of classical prosody' (Gransden, 1984: 67). Cf.:

> the narrative form, unlike the developed forms of the discourse of knowledge, lends itself to a great variety of language games. Denotative statements concerning, for example, the state of the sky and the flora and fauna easily slip in; so do deontic statements prescribing what should be done with respect to these same referents, or with respect to kinship, the differences between the sexes, children, neighbors, foreigners, etc. Interrogative statements are implied, for example, in episodes involving challenges (respond to a question, choose one from a number of things); evaluative statements also enter in, etc. The areas of competence whose criteria the narrative supplies or applies are thus tightly woven together in the web it forms, ordered by the unified viewpoint characteristic of this kind of knowledge.
> (Lyotard, 1984: 20)

17 One way this 'standing now' or 'dramatic present' is maintained is by the omission of reference to the narratorial voice of 'Homer' (the events and action must appear fully formed in the moment of their narration as though they were presenting themselves:

> It is not in the manner of the epic for the poet to speak of himself; the Muse inspires him and speaks through him, and in the twenty-seven thousand lines of the Homeric poems we are not told a single fact about the poet... 'Homer' is in effect no more than a synonym for the epics themselves.
> (Griffin, 1980a: 5)

The non-authored voice also strives to eliminate all unnecessary detail, background information, and context in presenting set tableaus of action. This foregrounding of the present to the detriment of either the past or the future might also be a product of the narrative demands placed on an oral audience – a suggestion Maurice Bowra makes: 'Since he usually composes for people who have no clocks or calendars, he is not very interested in chronology. Just as the Homeric poems give no hint of a date for the Trojan War, so the poet is not much worried by problems raised by time in his story'; 'This concentration on the dramatic present impels the poet to place certain high occasions where they can stand out in their splendour and not be interfered with by other episodes', and 'the poet concentrates on the moment and gives everything to it', (in Wace and Stubbings, eds, 1962: 51, 48, and 49).

On the contemporaneous temporality of the traditional narrative perspective: 'The

NOTES

narrative's reference may seem to belong to the past, but in reality it is always contemporaneous with the act of recitation. It is the present act that on each of its occurrences marshals in the ephemeral temporality inhabiting the space between the 'I have heard' and the 'you will hear'. This mode of temporality can be said to be simultaneously evanescent and immemorial' (J.-F. Lyotard, *op. cit.*, 1984, 22).

18 Curtius, 1953: 64; Camps, 1980: 'about half of the total extent of the *Iliad* and *Odyssey* consists of direct speech of the participants. Seldom in either are there more than fifty continuous lines of uninterrupted narrative'; cf. the observation of Blair, writing in 1825: 'There is much more dialogue in Homer than in Virgil; or, indeed, than in any other Poet. What Virgil informs us of by two words of Narration, Homer brings about by a Speech. We may observe here, that this method of writing is more ancient than the narrative manner. Of this we have a clear proof in the books of the Old Testament' (Blair, 1825: 581); and 'It was precisely for his use of dialogue and monologue that Homer was named the first of the tragic poets (by Plato, *Republic* 394B)';

> The Homeric epics employ monologue as well as dialogue; there are some twenty examples of this. If the atmosphere is overcharged with emotions and a dialogue therefore becomes impossible, then the hero thinks aloud ... 'Homer' in fact makes more use of direct speech than any other epic poet of the Western world.
>
> (Trypanis, 1977: 60 and 62)

The importance of studying the evolution of dialogic forms for a history of generic reflexivity is implicit in the following text from Diogenes Laertius:

> Just as long ago in tragedy the chorus was the only actor, and afterwards, in order to give the chorus breathing space, Thespis devised a single actor, Aeschylus a second, Sophocles a third, and thus tragedy was completed, so too with philosophy: in early times it discoursed on one subject only, namely physics, then Socrates added the second subject, ethics, and Plato the third, dialectics, and so brought philosophy to perfection'.
>
> (DL: 3.56)

He is, of course, glossing Aristotle's well-known discussion in the *Poetics* (cf. *Poetics* 24.14).

19 Auerbach, 1957: 4.
20 '[F]ully externalized description, uniform illumination, uninterrupted connection, all events in the foreground, displaying unmistakable meanings, few elements of historical development and of psychological perspective' Auerbach, 1957: 5 and 23. See note 15 above.
21 [T]he Homeric poems conceal nothing, they contain no teaching, and no secret second meaning. Homer can be analyzed... but he cannot be interpreted', Auerbach, 1957: 11. As Northrop Frye also notes, Homer projects a vision of nature as an impersonal order.
22 The canon of epic mimesis includes as we observed in note 20, externalized description, uniform illumination of events, ininterrupted connection, all events foregrounded, little historical development and psychological depth (see note 20). Auerbach contrasts this style of narrative with that of the Bible (for analytic purposes treating both as 'finished products' rather than as complex diachronic structures, discursive formations or intertextual-logological spaces); Biblical narrative in the Old Testament is, not surprisingly, found to possess antithetical qualities:

> certain parts brought into high relief, others left obscure, abruptness,

333

NOTES

suggestive influence of the unexpressed 'background' quality, multiplicity of meanings and the need for interpretation, universal-historical claims, development of the concept of the historically becoming, and preoccupation with the problematic.

(*ibid.*, 19ff.)

Auerbach's typological method prevents him from grounding his contrast in further cultural or logological investigations of how such stylistic and generic characteristics originated, how they were materially transmitted and transformed by their variant audiences and interpretive communities; in lieu of such a logological study he resorts to the typical idealist move which makes a fixed form, idea or discourse an independent variable in the creation of culture, closing such possible lines of investigation with the following conclusion: 'a consideration of this question is not necessary; for it is in their full development, which they reached in early times, that the two styles exercised their determining influence upon the representation of reality in European literature'. Needless to say, a more radical sociological poetics only *begins* at the point where Auerbach's stylistic typology breaks off.

Like many other commentators the poet Cesare Pavese also regarded the epic as a work of passionate intelligence, indeed of a highly reflexive intellectuality, possessed by a handful of great poets – among these Dante, Shakespeare, and perhaps Milton and Goethe:

> these are not the men for the unexpected, irritating exclamation that breaks out at any experience, takes it as having a hidden meaning, works it up into a sensation; but clear-sighted observers meticulously describing what they see; calm, imperturbable instigators of variety, subtly skilled in exploiting experience, cutting it into facets and shapes as if in sport, ending by taking its place. Men of the utmost astuteness, with nothing in the least naive about them.
>
> (Pavese, 1980: 29–30)

23 Auerbach, 1957: 20; Auerbach also has interesting observations concerning the relation between the quotidian reality of everyday life and the sublime life of kings and warriors: epic narrative, constructed around transcendent myths and legends, projects a radical dualism between the world of heroes and the world of mundane life – the latter forming a relatively unexplicated and amorphous background (the most famous exception being the everyday events depicted in the phenomenological explication of the Shield of Achilles); the Old Testament stories, on the other hand, dissolved these two spheres; 'the sublime influence of God here reaches so deeply into the everyday that the two realms of the sublime and the everyday are not only actually unseparated but basically inseparable' (1957: 19). However, as far as I can determine, Auerbach does not theorize the category of the epic sublime, or offer detailed textual evidence for these contrasts; the question of the applicability of the modern notion of the sublime, sublime transcendence, divinity, and so forth to Homeric epic is taken for granted as an unjustified premise of his analysis.

24 On the absence of magic and lack of reference to magical intervention in the *Iliad* see Burn, 1966: 7; on the 'objective' attitude toward death and the dying see Vermeule, 1979: ch. 2. The resurgence of magic and mystical elements from Greek traditions of legends and fantastic tales in the *Odyssey* is frequently used as evidence for the later composition of this work; some commentators also see the prevalence of fairytale motifs in the *Odyssey* as evidence for separate authorship of the two works.

NOTES

25 For a phenomenological description of such a *chora* see the unpublished manuscript of Edmund Husserl on the *Ur-arche* of the Earth, titled 'Grundlegende Untersuchungen zum phänomenologischen Ursprung der Räumlichkeit der Natur', in Farber, ed., 1940: 307–25; the theme is taken further by Martin Heidegger in his notion of the earth as ground of human dwelling in 'The origin of the work of art', in Heidegger, *Poetry, Language, Thought* (New York: Harper, 1971); for further analysis of the 'aboriginal Earth' see Derrida, 1978b and Kisiel, in Kockelmans and Kisiel, eds, 1970: 5–44, esp. 37–40. While not linking Husserl's and Heidegger's phenomenological accounts of the aboriginal earth to the nascent videological perspective of the Homeric epic, Kisiel provides an apt formulation of what we have described as the Homeric *chora*:

> There is only one humanity and one earth as primordial home, and it is the *Ur-arche* world to which all planets, parts of planets broken off like icebergs from their parent, space ships, missiles, and even the Ptolemaic earth belong... The time has come to exhume this aboriginal nonobjectifiable earth buried beneath the sedimented deposits of our scientific culture. For though it never enters into the equations of the global earth, it is the starting point from which it is possible to speak of the Copernican earth.
> (in Kockelmans and Kisiel, eds, 1970: 40)

In logological terms, the dramaturgical world of the *chora* (as exemplified in the Homeric *kosmos* as a *theatre of praxis*) is a genealogical precondition and operative presupposition of all subsequent videological worlds and their logics. The realism of Homer excludes any generalized doubt about the structure of the world or the emergence of idealism in any shape or form. As Edward Hussey has observed, in the Homeric universe it is

> prudent to be sceptical about some particular claims to knowledge. But there is no scepticism about the general structure of the world. Homer and his characters take the structural and determining features of the world to be absolutely beyond doubt: in particular, the existence of the gods, their separate individualities and powers, and their general relationship to human beings.
> (Hussey, in Everson, ed., 1990: 12)

The later videological systems of European philosophy and science grounded in essentially idealist premises were socially constructed against an occluded and forgotten background of prescientific mythological and epic 'spaces'. The long-durational linguistic construction of the *kosmos* as a visual and visualizable universe will form an important part of the studies in Volume 3. Our preliminary analysis of Homeric narrative has uncovered one of the earliest layers of the rhetoric of European visual grammar.

26 The humanization of the epic world is 'perhaps the greatest Homeric achievement' (Trypanis, 1981: 49); 'No religion has ever been so consistently anthropomorphic as that of Greece' (Nilsson, 1948: 20); 'In the *Iliad* and Odyssey anthropomorphism has attained the furthest limit' (Cornford, 1923: xv); Homeric divinity 'is not superimposed as a sovereign power over natural events; it is revealed in the forms of the natural, as their very essence and being' (Otto, 1954: 7); Homer's Gods 'have all the human passions' (Blair, 1825: 584); the subsequent 'decline' of oral recitation with its central heroic focus can thus also be linked with the emergence of literate systems which could operate without a 'godhead' or 'hero-figure' at the centre of their texts – 'knowledge' itself might even take the place of the Homeric hero – as in the later discourse conventions of science and philosophy. Anthropomorphism helps to explain

NOTES

the comparative absence of mysticism in this religion and the strong bias toward hero-cult which can be traced from the pre-Homeric age onwards. It equally explains the iconic or idolatrous impulse which has left so deep an imprint upon pre-Christian Hellenism and on the Greek Christian Church.

(L. R. Farnell, *The Higher Aspects of Greek Religion* (London: Williams and Norgate, 1912: 2–3)

The heroic and marvellous had served a specific function in organizing knowledge in an oral world. With the control of information and memory brought about by writing and, more intensely, by print, you do not need a hero in the old sense to mobilize knowledge in story form. The situation has nothing to do with a putative 'loss of ideals'.

(Ong, 1982: 70–1)

Also Camps, 1980: 8–9.

27 In our analysis above we have seen that the *ethos* of Homeric society clusters around values and forms of conduct central to an idealized warrior society: to avoid shame and public disgrace, to fight bravely, and where necessary, to die a heroic death. Excellence (*arete*) within the Homeric *chora* is also rigidly predefined by the basic motivational prerequisites of the narrative: 'prowess in battle, courage in the face of adversity [are] the central elements in the personality of all the main Homeric heroes' (Trypanis, 1981: 50).

28 The natural comparison is with the 'characterless' agents of Aeschylean tragedy:

The word *drama* can be paraphrased *what is going on*; elaboration of character [for example, following Aristotle's fourth-century prescriptions] would only distract attention from what is really going on; therefore it is kept to the minimum ... Our own lively interest in individuals can mislead us.

(Kitto, 1966: 103)

The distinction between modern introspective reflection and classical reflexivity can be traced back at least to Madame de Stael:

et cette réflexion inquiète, qui nous dévore souvent comme le vautour de Prométhée, n'eut semblé que de la folie au milieu des rapports clairs et prononcés qui existaient dans l'état civil et social des anciens (that gnawing reflection that often devours us, like Prometheus' vulture, would merely have seemed a folly in the clear and precise framework of the social and political conditions of the ancients).

les modernes ont puisé, dans le repentir chrétien, l'habitude de se replier continuellement sur eux-memes (from Christian repentance the moderns have derived the habit of continual introspection).

(Madame de Stael, *De L'Allemagne* (1810))

29 Cf. 'My soul [*phrenos*] is racked and shivers with fear' (Sophocles, *Oedipus Tyrannos* 156–7).

30 Achilles, 'a speaker of words and a doer of deeds' (*Il.* 9.443). *Thumos*' unpredictable force as a source of anger and violence became a commonplace in the tradition of the Greek homily or apothogem – root of the saying *thumos kratein*, 'control anger' which Diogenes Laertius attributed to Chilon (DL: I.70). Cf.: 'A third of Homer is taken up with people talking to each other. Greeks placed a high premium on *peitho*, the ability to persuade by argument rather than force, and saw this as an essential ingredient of freedom and civilization' (*WA*: 357). The prestige

NOTES

of the suasive bard as a community's 'collective memory bank' is well known in Homeric research, but rarely linked to the wider sociocultural question of the 'civilizing process' (cf. Havelock, 1986: chs 8, 9).

31 The same formula appears in the description of the dying Hector (*Il.* 22. 361–6).
32 See Rohde, 1951. Jaeger comments on Rohde's central finding: 'Rohde himself says correctly enough that as soon as a Homeric man dies, his existence as an individual ceases; there is no soul in him which could live on after death. The shades of the dead which have entered Hades enjoy no conscious existence there' (1947: 74). On the representation of *psyche* as a bird see G. M. A. Hanfmann, 'Psyche', in *The Oxford Classical Dictionary*: 895.
33 The later lyric poet Sappho presents a similar shadowy picture of the soul after it has descended into Hades; as with Heraclitus' saying, it makes little sense to speak of personal immortality, beyond the recollective powers of those who preserve the memory of the departed in verse. The corporeal survival of the embodied soul is rejected:

> But when you die you will lie there, and afterwards there will never be any recollection of you or any longing for you since you have no share in the roses of Pieria [birthplace of the Muses]; unseen in the house of Hades also, flown from our midst, you will go to and fro among the shadowy corpses.
> (Sappho, cited in Stobaeus, *Anthology* 3.4.12;
> Campbell, trans., 1982: I.55)

Cf.:

> It is also made very explicit that the dead are wholly cut off, that they have no power, and that they cannot intervene in the world of the living. This is contrary to the virtually unanimous view held in early societies, and in fact Homer's contemporaries did bring offerings to the tombs of the mighty dead, which of course implies their continuing power; Homer's conception is again his own.
> (Griffin, 1980a: 34)

Mircea Eliade suggests an explanation of the fact that in the Presocratic Greek tradition only heroes preserve their personality (i.e. their memory) after death by locating this in the ideological structure of archaic ontology: 'having, in his life on earth, performed no actions which were not exemplary, the hero retains the memory of them, since, from a certain point of view, these acts were impersonal' (Eliade, 1989: 47).

34 Formulaically, the colour of grief, despair, and death in the Homeric code is black: 'a black cloud of grief enwrapped Hector' (*Il.* 17.591); 'When Achilles heard this he sank into the black depths of despair' (*Il.* 18.23), 'the fate of black death' seized Odysseus' dog Argos (*Od.* 17.326); in the symbolism of the epic 'melancholy' is thus related to Forgetfulness, Unconsciousness, Death, and the Underworld – the 'black pit of Tartarus' (the same images occur in Hesiod, for example, 'black death seized them, and they left the radiant light of the sun' (*Works and Days* 154–5)). The medicine which Helen sprinkles into the wine of Menelaus and his guests is also designed to free the mind from melancholy and 'black' despair (to 'bring forgetfulness of every sorrow'):

> for the day that he drank it would have no tear roll down his face, not if his mother died and his father died, not if men murdered a brother or a beloved son in his presence with the bronze, and he with his own eyes saw it. Such were the subtle medicines Zeus' daughter had in her posessions, good things, and given to her by the wife of Thon, Polydamna of Egypt, where the fertile

NOTES

earth produces the greatest number of medicines [*pharmaka*], many good in mixture, many malignant, and every man is a doctor there and more understanding than men elsewhere.

(*Od.* 4.220–32)

In a reflexive vein, the writing and narration of epic life itself is one instance of a talking therapy against the black despair of forgetfulness and death. Epic is the only secure *pharmakon* in a profoundly thanatonic culture. This is a point where the thanatonic experiences of the twentieth century intersect with the Homeric world. Is it possible that what we have described as coded melancholy is the most typical psychopathology of the Mycenaean world (or at least of the migrant descendants of the Bronze Age Greeks cut loose from their own cities and country), recast in the epic in the rhetoric of the idealized Homeric code?

35 On *muthos* as 'utterance', 'speech', or 'discourse' in the *Odyssey*: 'and to Alinous above all he declared his word [*muthos*], and said...' (*Od.* 13.37); 'long-robed Helen took the word [*muthos*] from him, and said...' (*Od.* 15.171); 'So he spoke, but her word [*muthos*] remained unwinged' (*Od.* 17.57); 'So he spoke, and they rose up and went, and hearkened to his word [*muthos*]' (*Od.* 17.177); 'So spoke Antinous, and his word [*muthos*] was pleasing to them' (*Od.* 18.50 ff.); also cf. *Odyssey* 1.124; 1.305; 1.356–9; 2. 137; 2.412; 3.23; 3.124–5; 4.774; 5.98; 5.388; 6.21; 6.148; 7.157; 7.226; 8.10; 8.141; 8.185; 10.561; 11.335; 11.367; 11.379; 12.450ff. If a rough count of linguistic contexts in which the word *'muthos'* appears can be trusted the prevalence of textual references to speech is even more emphatic in the *Iliad* (by linguistic contexts I refer to texts such as: 'So he spoke, and the old man was seized with fear and followed his word [*muthos*]' (*Il.* 1.33); 'they listened to what I said and followed my advice' (*Il.* 1.272); 'the words of godlike Odysseus' (*Il.* 2.335); 'Hector's speech was received in complete silence' (*Il.* 3.94); 'Dread son of Cronos, what a word you have spoken' (*Il.* 4.25); 'Be silent and listen to what I say' (*Il.* 4.412)). Among other analogous contexts in which the word *muthos* occurs see in particular: *Iliad* 1.552; 1.565; 2.17; 2.282; 5.420; 5.493; 7.46; 7.76; 7.95; 8.29; 8.209; 9.694; 14.91; 14.330; 16.440; 19.84; 19.185; 19.220; 19.242; 20.202; 20.246–8; 20.369; 20.433; 22.281.

36 On the spellbinding power of 'winged words', oral language and more especially poetic utterance: 'So he spoke, and they were all hushed in silence, and were spellbound throughout the shadowy halls' (*Od.* 13.1–4); 'among them the divine minstrel Demodocus, held in honour by the people, sang to the lyre' (*Od.* 13.25–28 (cf. *Od.* 17.359; 18.50)); 'To her, the swineherd Eumaeus answered, 'I would, O queen, that the Achaeans would keep silence, for he speaks such words as would charm your very soul' (*Od.* 17.512ff.; cf. *Od.* 17.1–395, esp. 7.319ff., 15.374ff.).

37 Odysseus, the peer of Zeus in wisdom (*Il.* 2.169; cf. 2.182ff.); 'the match of Zeus in counsel' (*Il.* 2.407; cf. 2.636); 'Odysseus ... beyond all mortals in wisdom [*noos/nous*]' (*Od.* 1.66); master of stratagems and cunning devices (*Il.* 3.202, 3.216ff.). The interplay of physical skills and practical wisdom (*noos*) is one of the unique features of Odysseus as a character. It is the predominance of *nous* – as the arts of strategy and cunning – which allows Odysseus to control and master the forces of impulse (*thumos*) and emotion (*phrenes*) (the crucial speech occurs at *Iliad* 11.401ff.). Odysseus is, as it were, well along the path of redefining his personality in the light of larger aims and objectives. He has 'taken the measure' of his own strengths and weaknesses and by virtue of this self-reflection distances himself from more one-dimensional warlords like Agamemnon, Ajax, and Diomedes. The three styles of declamation, identified with Odysseus, Menelaus, and Nestor in later rhetorical rheory were regarded as the three ideal forms of persuasive speech – the grand, dignified magniloquent style of Odysseus, the

elegant and restrained 'plain' style of Menelaus, and the 'middle' or moderate style of Nestor (for example in Aulus Gellius, *The Attic Nights* Book VI, xiv, 1–11).

38 The rhetorical virtuosity of Nestor is underlined in the first two books of the *Iliad*; it is Nestor who Agamemnon describes as one 'preeminent in speech above the sons of the Achaeans ... give me ten counsellors such as this' (*Il.* 2. 370ff.). For an analysis of the etymology of the name 'Nestor' see Frame, 1978: 81–115.

39 For the mimetic dream of pure reflection see *Logological Investigations*, Volume 1, Part I. The controlling power of reason and intellectual omniscience in the Archaic age were already stereotypical attributes of divinity; consider *Iliad* 2.484–7: 'Tell me now, Muses... who were the leaders and princes of the Greeks; for you are goddesses and you are present and know everything, but we only hear the report and do not know anything' (cited by Hussey, in Everson, ed., 1990: 12). In particular, Zeus is the God whose knowledge is certain (*sapha eidenai*); in Hesiod's *Works and Days* Zeus has become an all-knowing mind, concretized in the image of a panoptical knowledge: 'The eye of Zeus sees all, and understands, And when he wishes, marks and does not miss How just a city is, inside', (1985: 67); in Homer it is a standard frame for the 'all-knowing Zeus' (*Il.* 2.485; *Od.* 1.26–79; 4.379, 4.468; 5.3–42; 13.417; 20.75) or the Goddess Pallas Athena whose mind knows all things (*Od.* 13.418), who has no equal for cunning, cleverness and craft (as in the English word 'craftiness'; cf. the etymologically uncertain description of Hermes as 'keen-sighted Argeiphontes' in Book I of the *Odyssey*; *Od.* 1.38, 1.84). Later it becomes a stock epithet for the dramatists of the Classical period, where it is significantly illustrated with the self-reflexivity of absolute *seeing*, the Gods have witnessed all things (*eidenai/idein*):

> Down from their high-towered hopes
> He flings poor, wretched mortals,
> Donning no armour of might.
> For gods act without effort:
> High from their hallowed seats
> They somehow make their own thinking
> Come all at once to pass.
> (Aeschylus, cited in Jaeger, 1947: 45)

'All-seeing Zeus' (Sophocles, *Oedipus at Colonus*, 1083); 'All wise are Zeus and Apollo; and there is nothing that they don't see' (Sophocles, *Oedipus Tyrannos* 496ff.); 'For myself, I call/To witness Zeus, whose eyes are everywhere' (Sophocles, *Antigone* 183–4; cf. *Electra* 175; Aeschylus, *Agamemnon* 355–6; Hesiod, *Works and Days* 267–8). For further background on the deep generic and cultural links between Homeric verse and Greek tragedy see: Kitto, 1966; Bernard M. W. Knox, *The Heroic Temper: Studies in Sophoclean Tragedy* (Berkeley and Los Angeles: University of California Press, 1966); Albin Lesky, *Greek Tragedy*, 3rd edn (London: Barnes and Noble, 1978). These logological metaphors initiated a process of rationalization which would eventually culminate in the encomium to reason in the texts of Plato and Aristotle; for example, in Aristotle's *Nicomachean Ethics* where he praises the divinity of human understanding and reason:

> Now he who exercises his reason and cultivates it seems to be both in the best state of mind and most dear to the gods. For if the gods have any care for human affairs, as they are thought to have, it would be reasonable both that they should delight in that which was best and most akin to them (i.e. reason) and that they should reward those who love and honour this most, as caring for the things that are dear to them and acting both rightly and nobly. And that all these attributes belong most of all to the philosopher is

NOTES

manifest. He, therefore, is the dearest to the gods. And he who is that will presumably be also the happiest.

(*NE* 1179a22–33)

40 On physicians and surgeons: physicians first make their appearance in the Catalogue of Ships where we hear of the two sons of Asclepius, the doctors Podaleirius and Machaon, leading the fifty ships of Tricca (Trike), Ithome, and Eurytus (*Il.* 2.729ff.). In Book 4 Agamemnon has Machaon attend to the arrow wound of Menelaus; Machaon extracts the arrow, sucks out the blood and applies an ointment which had been given to his father by the legendary Cheiron (*Il.* 4.188ff.); later (at the end of Book 11), as both physicians are absent – one seriously injured (Machaon lies wounded in Nestor's camp at the beginning of Book 14, *Il.* 14.1ff.) and the other engaged in the fighting with the Trojans – Patroclus attends to the wounded Euryplus, removing the arrow head, washing the wound, and applying a 'root of a bitter herb' to deaden the pain, 'a sedative which banished all pain' (we can assume that this generic pharmacopoeia also contained a coagulant, as the text ends with 'the wound began to dry and the blood ceased to flow', *Il.* 11.825–48). In Book 10 of the *Odyssey* the witch Circe is described as 'skilled in medicines'; and Odysseus has to be protected by a *pharmakos* given to him by Hermes before entering Circe's house – presumably on the principle of good medicine driving out bad:

So spoke Argeiphontes [Hermes], and he gave me the medicine, which he picked out of the ground, and he explained the nature of it to me. It was black at the root, but with a milky flower. The gods call it moly. It is hard for mortal men to dig up, but the gods have power to do all things.

(*Od.* 10.302–6)

41 On the divine gift of prophecy and the reading of natural signs: 'Now, I will make you a prophecy, in the way the immortals put it into my mind, and as I think it will come out, though I am no prophet, nor do I know the ways of birds clearly' (*Od.* 1.200–3). The translator of the Loeb Classical Edition stays closer to the Greek phrasing: 'I am in no wise a soothsayer, nor one versed in the signs of birds.' In Sophocles' *Antigone*, the blind seer Teiresias deciphers the fate of Creon in the *sounds* of birds; he is also shown 'confirming' these signs and their meaning by means of divination by fire (*Antigone* 998–1032). For the history of Greek divination see A. Bouche-Leclerq, *Histoire de la divination dans l'antiquité*, 4 vols (Paris, 1879–82). On augury by means of inspecting the liver (or hepatoscopy) in the Near East and Greek world see Burkert, 1992: ch. 2, esp. 46–53.

42 Michael Ventris' decipherment of the Minoan-Mycenaean Linear B script in 1952 was an important step in showing that the Greeks controlled cities such as Pylos from at least 1200 BC and that something like an absolute kingship or rule by one lord (*wanax, basileus*) was accompanied by a well-organized political and economic system operated by a large, functional bureaucratic class: 'in the Mycenaean Age political organization was characterized by a vast and specialized bureaucracy interested in and capable of maintaining elaborate written records on all conceivable forms of human activity' (Alexander, ed., 1963: 52). The classic account is still that given in Ventris and Chadwick, 1956; see also Chadwick, 1967, 1976. According to Sterling Dow (in Kirk, ed., 1964: 140–73) their work suggested that the Greeks had controlled Knossos and Crete *c*. 1400 BC, confirming the speculations of the early Cretan archaeologists (among the most famous being the excavator of Cnossos, Sir Arthur Evans). It also suggests a direct historical link to the world described by the Homeric epics (see Luce, 1975). For further background and scholarly reading on the decipherment, translation, and transliteration of the Mycenaean Tablets and possible grammar of Mycenean Greek see: Palmer, 1963

NOTES

(which includes *The Find-Places of the Knossos Tablets* by L. R. Palmer, and *The Date of the Knossos Tablets* by John Boardman); Palmer and Chadwick, eds, 1966; Jean-Pierre Olivier, *The Mycenae Tablets IV: A Revised Transliteration* (Leiden: E. J. Brill, 1969); Melian Stawell, 1931; Vilborg, 1960: esp. 24–39; Cottrell, 1972: chs 12–16; Harris, 1986; Gelb, 1963.

On the Mycenaean origins of Greek mythology and epic poetry see Nilsson, 1927, 1963. Nilsson argued that epics 'do not originate in collective popular poetry' but are rather the creation of a heroic age, originating in

> an aristocratic or even feudal society, praising the deeds of living men ... Epic poetry is composed not by the people in general but by certain gifted individuals, who live as minstrels and often court minstrels in the *entourage* of some great man.
> (1963: 16–17)

See also: *Cambridge Ancient History*, vol. 2; Finley, 1963: chs 1–3, 1978, 1987; M. I. Finley, *Early Greece: The Bronze and Archaic Ages* (1981), J. T. Hooker, *Mycenaean Greece* (London, 1977); Nilsson, 1933; Page, 1959; Murray, 1993: 5–15, 35–54; Palmer, 1965; A. E. Samuel, *The Mycenaeans in History* (Englewood Cliffs: Prentice Hall, 1966); Thomson, 1954; Wace and Stubbings, eds, 1962; Wace, in Wace and Stubbings, eds, 1962: 331–61; Vermeule, 1964; Webster, 1958.

43 'The picture we get from the Linear B inscriptions is of a centralized government, dependent on a network of roads connecting with distant areas whose agricultural produce was essential to its survival'; thus the remaining Linear B tablets are 'preoccupied with the function of the palace in running the economy and in maintaining law and order' and 'the sole function of writing ... was palace record-keeping' (Cottrell, 1985: 104, 102, 116).

> There is endless counting and classifying, measuring and weighing, assessing and collecting and distributing. It is as if everything done by everybody was open to official inquiry and subject to official orders. We possess a part only of the archives for a single year at Pylos: they record thousands of transactions in hundreds of places.
> (Page, in Thomas, ed., 1970: 19)

44 The evidence for the existence of a literate class or guild of administrators does not mean, of course, that the society as a whole was literate. Literacy in the Mycenaean age was a highly restricted, instrumental skill. Thus the Mycenaean bureaucracy evolved an ideal-typical social form of official discourse: the quantitative state actuarial inventory or archival record; similar techniques of state-controlled reflexivity can be found in other palace-centred distribution economies in the Minoan world, in ancient Syria (at Ugarit and Alalakh in Syria) and in Anatolia (Hattusas). Mycenaea is different from such despotic systems in terms of its fundamental feudal system of service and conditional tenures (based on property relations of feudal land tenure). The Mycenaean system also differs from other bureaucratized empires in the ancient world in other important aspects:

> The agricultural and irrigation bureaucracies of Egypt and Mesopotamia, the foundation of which is thus economic, are the oldest officialdom in the world; it remains throughout its history an adjunct of the king's personal economic enterprise ... The tax administration of the king was based on payments in kind, which in Egypt were stored up in warehouses from which the king supported his officials and laborers. Such provision is the oldest form of official salary.
> (Weber, 1981: 57)

NOTES

We might think of the Mycenaean palace system as a special type of feudal-bureaucratic monarchy based on a system of centralized land tenure, differentiated and graded on the basis of a strict hierachy of property owners. The division of labour and specialization of social functions which this system presupposed is reflected in the scribal recording system invented by the Mycenean bureaucrats as an instrument of economic and social control. Like the bureaucratic-scriptural mind of the compilers of the Domesday Book after the invasion of England in the eleventh century, the intimate fusion of power, socioeconomic control and the new technology of actuarial writing in the hands of professional bureaucrats created a unique 'actuarial' state formation (Polanyi, Arensberg and Pearson, 1967; Palmer, 1961: 96–104);

> The comprehensive and centralized administrative system suggests an autocratic monarchical régime: we suppose that the *wanax* was the head of the state and supreme authority, for his palace officials seem to be all-powerful everywhere. I notice in passing one most significant omission in the Tablets: there is not a word about the administration of *justice*, no reference whatsoever to *law*.
> (Page, 1959: 97)

45 Page, 1959. Page speaks evocatively of 'the omniscience of the bureaucracy' and 'the insatiable thirst for intimate detail':

> They have the power to demand, and the duty to record, infinite detail about men and women and children, industrial manufactures and materials, agricultural produce and livestock, all kinds of holdings of all kinds of land, the administration of religious ritual, movements of troops and the manning of ships. There is endless counting and classifying, measuring and weighing, assessing and collecting and distributing. It is as if everything done by everybody was open to official inquiry and subject to official coders.
> (1959: 180)

Palmer, in his *Mycenaeans and Minoans* (1961) also describes Knossos and Pylos as complex 'bureaucratically controlled societies'(1961: 97), suggesting that the amount of detail in the Pylos fragments is evidence of a society 'organizing itself with meticulous bureaucratic detail for its final ordeal. Women and children are gathered together into two main concentration areas, and arrangements are recorded for their supervision and provisioning' (1961: 22–3). In the remaining sherds of a lost civilization we 'possess some of the last records inscribed in the Mycenaean age of Greece' (1961: 60), preserved as visible traces by being 'unintentionally baked in the fire that destroyed the palace' (1961: 143).

46 Bowra, in Kirk, ed., 1964: 25–6; Bowra suggests that the *lawagetas* ('leader of the *lawos*'), which he translates 'Leader of the People' suggests a social structure closer to the Hittites than to anything reported by Homer (for the social structure and culture of the Hittite empire see Lehmann, 1977: esp. Ch. 7. For reconstructions of the social structure, land tenure system, administration, economy, and religious beliefs evidenced by the Pylos fragments see Palmer, 1961: esp. chs 3 and 4, and Luce, 1975: 79–80: 'It has proved possible to elucidate the grain ration scales, and it has become clear that a scheme of allocations according to social grade and function was in operation' (Palmer, 1961: 21);

> the *wanax*, the king. He is credited with a *temenos*, literally a 'cut', measured as thirty units of seed corn. A *temenos* is registered in the next line against the *Lawagetas*, literally the 'Leader of the War Host', for the word *lawos*

NOTES

'folk' in Homer has the narrower meaning 'the body of warriors'... an entry relates to *telestai* ... 'service men'... an entry for the *damos* ... the 'commune'.

(Palmer, 1961: 99; cf. 96–104)

The relevant sections from Palmer's book are reprinted in Thomas, ed., 1970: 48–53. The description of the social structure of land tenure, the royal palace, and the Mycenaean polity occurs on 50–1.

47 As C. M. Bowra observed, its almost total absence from Homer's picture of the heroic world shows how inadequately he was informed about it (Bowra, in Kirk, ed., 1964: 25–6); Bowra faults Homer as a poor historian who misrepresents the wealth posssessed by these palace states:

> Odysseus and Alcinous each keep fifty women to work in their houses ... the Pylos tablets, which come from a single place and a very short period give the name of 645 slave women, together with some 370 girls and 210 boys.
>
> (Bowra, in Kirk, ed., 1964: 26)

Cf.: Homer

> knew where the Mycenaean civilization flourished, and his heroes lived in great Bronze Age palaces unknown in Homer's day. And that is virtually all he knew about Mycenaean times, for the catalogue of his errors is very long. His arms bear a resemblance to the armour of his time, quite unlike the Mycenaean ... His gods had temples, and the Mycenaeans built none, whereas the latter constructed great vaulted tombs in which to bury their chieftans, and the poet cremates his. A neat little touch is provided by the battle chariots. Homer had heard of them, but he did not really visualize what one did with chariots in a war.
>
> (Finley, 1978: 47–8)

> What the Homeric poems have lost is not primarily a number of words but *the whole elaborate structure of government, the whole complex system of society, depicted in the [Mycenaean] Tablets*. Time and again the *Iliad* and *Odyssey* show how they have no notion that their Heroic world was in truth a model bureaucracy, a society divided and subdivided and labelled and inspected and rationed and in general controlled in all its phases by a restless and pervasive army of officials.
>
> (Page, 1959: 187; also Page, 1955)

48 Cf. Joseph ben Matthias, or Josephus (c. 90 AD), in his polemic against the Greek writer Apion, *Contra Apionem* i.2.12 on the art of writing: 'writing could not have been known to the Greeks of the Trojan War; that even Homer did not leave his poetry in writing, but that it was transmitted by memory, and afterwards put together from the separate songs; hence the number of discrepancies' (cited in Sandys, 1908: 55); also Pfeiffer, 1976). The same text is cited by J. A. Davison in his essay 'The transmission of the text', in Wace and Stubbings, eds, 1962: 215–33, 216, n. 10. On the nature and extent of literacy and illiteracy in the Graeco-Roman world see Harris, 1989. See also Havelock, 1986. For an accessible introduction to the question of ancient Greek literacy see Thomas 1992.

49 The Linear B Tablets belong to a highly centralized military state, which relied on an efficient bureaucracy to exploit the wealth of the countryside. Without agricultural surpluses the palace could not exist, no matter how aggressive its soldiery might be, and therefore any drop in productivity was very serious. Too much shepherding in Crete, too much corn growing in Messenia; an overspecialized

NOTES

economy, too dependent on a central administration: these were the likely factors weakening the Mycenaeans at the close of the turbulent thirteenth century BC.
(Cottrell, 1985: 116)

'It was probably riven by internal disunities; and the belief that a new wave of Greek invaders or immigrants, the Dorians, played a major part in the destruction could well be correct' (Grant, 1991): 8). Cf. Carpenter, 1966 and Childe, 1942. Luce outlines three main possibilities for the collapse of Mycenaean civilization: internecine warfare and civil strife within the Mycenaean world; barbarian invasions from outside the Mycenaean world; and persistent drought deriving from climatic changes in the Argolid leading to famine and popular uprisings (Luce, 1975: 37; cf. Snodgrass, 1987: 46). The causation appears to be complex, multiple, and configurational, as emphasized by D. H. Trump:

> The likeliest solution lies in a combination of factors, of which overpopulation and rigid bureaucracy, as hinted at by the tablets, may have been the major ones. A serious crop failure in one area ... would have led to local famine; with too many people and too little food, there were no reserves; desperate survivors would rapidly become a threat to neighbouring towns, spreading disorder. The whole economic basis of the civilization would be progressively destroyed, and as trade withered, subsistence farming could support only a fraction of the population; the rest would pour out as refugees, spreading the chaos ever more widely... The Dorians did not burst in but were sucked in to the resulting vacuum.
> (1980: 192–3; also V. R. d'A. Desborough, *The Greek Dark Age* (London: Benn, 1972))

See also the concluding chapter of Wood, 1985: 242–57.

50 The eruption of Thera or Santorini (conventionally dated to between 1500 and 1450 BC) is often cited in this context (for example, by the archaeologist Spyridon Marinatos) as the major cause of the global catastrophe that swept away the early Minoan empire leading to the first Greek dynasty in the Agean in the thirteenth century; if the destruction of this Aegean island, however, is to be regarded as a primary explanatory factor, on purely logical grounds we might have to suggest an earlier date – perhaps around 1628 BC. Similar volcanic and/or earthquake activity may later have led to the catastrophe of 1450 BC and several centuries later to the destruction of Mycenaean power (with the devastation of Mycenae, Tiryns and Pylos):

> soon after 1400 BC their palace at Knossos was burnt down, never to be rebuilt. Opinions are divided as to the cause of this fresh disaster, but the most likely theory is that it was a rebellion by the native Cretans against their alien Mycenaean overlords.
> (Higgins, 1973: 17; cf. Finley, 1981: 43–4)

Some historians have come to similar conclusions about the abrupt termination of the Shang dynasty during the Bronze Age (c. 1100 BC), the fall of the Hittite Empire between 1200–1150 BC, and other Bronze Age settlements around 1190–1150 BC in the northern hemisphere (in Bronze Age Scotland, for example). The collapse of so many ancient power systems around 1150–1100 BC may not be coincidental – and strengthens the case of those scholars who have argued for the long-term effects of global climactic changes. Without precise radiocarbon evidence, however, all these dates and hypotheses must remain conjectural and subject to revision pending the outcome of future statigraphic and radiocarbon research. It is most probable that the historical origins of the Atlantis legend derive from the fate of

NOTES

Thera. On the ecological disaster following the eruption of Thera and its cataclysmic effects on Minoan Crete see Trump, 1980: 156–228, esp. 182–5; Oliva, 1981: 22; Doumos, 1983; Page, 1970; Phyllis Young Forsyth, *Atlantis: The Making of Myth* (London: Croom Helm, 1980): chs 7–9.

51   On the Greek mainland a vast destruction brought the Mycenaean world to an end, but tales of it survived in such places as Attica and Pylos and were taken with them by colonists who fled to found new cities in Asia Minor. These men looked back, with ample justification, to a time when the Achaeans had indeed been masters of Aegean lands, and preserved with tenacious loyalty the memory of a glorious past. The names of its heroes and the outline of their doings were passed on by a long succession of oral poets, of whom Homer was among the latest.

(Bowra, in Kirk, ed., 1964: 35–6)

Not even the great walls of Tiryns and Mycenae could protect the palaces from destruction by fire. Athens was the only major Mycenaean citadel to survive intact.

(Luce, 1975: 36)

On the 'terminal' nature of the Homeric achievement:

Though Greece entered a Dark Age of poverty and isolation, there was continuity in language and cult. Memories of the great past were enshrined and transmitted in legend.

(Luce, 1975: 26)

A whole civilization had risen and fallen to produce Homer. Without the splendours and the social disintegration of the Bronze Age, and without its fall, the individualist and humanist code of the Hero could not have come into being.

(Burn, 1960: 10)

A similar thesis linking the political ramifications of the Mycenaean catastrophe to the subsequent course of Greek history has been developed by Cottrell. Thus even while 'the immediate consequence of breakdown was a reversion to subsistence agriculture and the formation of small inward-looking communities', the long-term effects of the collapse of the bureaucratic monarchy cannot be underestimated: 'The palace, inhabited by a warrior-king and his privileged followers, had vanished from the Aegean scene, thus freeing the Greeks from the absolute monarchical rule common in the rest of the ancient world' (Cottrell, 1985: 116; cf. Murray, 1993: 8–9).

52   We know that about 1200 BC the palace at Pylos was burnt; that a little earlier considerable destruction took place at Mycenae, though the acropolis survived. Finally about 1100 it too succumbed, and with its fall the brilliant culture of the Mycenaean age undergoes an eclipse from which it emerged only in the archaic period ... Dorics ... raiding bands of marauders were probably attacking the fringes of the Mycenaean empire long before its final fall; only gradually would these raiders begin to found settlements in the new lands and to impose their rule on a population which no doubt survived the loss of their ruling class with little change. They may well have taken a hand in the overthrow of their masters.

(Chadwick, in Kirk, ed., 1964: 116)

Michael Wood refers to the way the Ionian princelings of Homer's day legitimized their rule by constructing genealogies linking their power to the states of the 'Heroic Age' (1985: 244).

NOTES

53 'The Homeric poems portray a moneyless economy, in which wealth consists of land and its products, houses, goods and chattels. The land is in the hands of a restricted number of large landowners, and passes by inheritance' (Adkins, 1972: 13). 'Mycenaean society had been decapitated and those who remained, proceeded together with the new invading element, to build a new kind of society' (Finley, 1981: 65–6).

54 The 'most powerful values of this society commend success and decry failure in securing the prosperity and stability of one's group, *oikos*... [the *agathos*] must ensure the success of his *oikos*'. In other words the intense competitive environment of agrarian survival and aggrandizement encourage this-worldly, action-oriented interests: 'Homeric *arete*, *time*, and *philotes* suit the *oikos*-based society' (Adkins, 1972: 21, 18).

55 'Odysseus put together the mighty bed which he shared with Penelope' (Hegel, cited by Plant, 1983: 31; the text Hegel has in mind is *Odyssey* 23.192ff.:

> round this [bed] I built the room with stones close-set, and I roofed it and added doors ... then I rough-hewed the trunk upwards from the root and smoothed it with the adze ... I made it beautiful with inlaid work of gold and silver and ivory.

Cf.:

> In the *Odyssey*, the daughter of King Alcinous does the washing, together with her female slaves; Prince Odysseus does not challenge his rival to a duel, but to a competition in mowing and ploughing, and on return to his homeland he finds his father working in the garden with a shovel. Besides, Odysseus and his son Telemachus are the object of the affectionate regard of their slave, the 'divine swineherd' Eumaeus.
> (Karl Kautsky, in Bottomore, ed., 1983: 68)

In the *Iliad* we catch glimpses of a similar craft-based, 'oikos mentality': Priam's sons work on the farm (24.247–80) and even Priam himself feeds his horses (5.271); see Griffin, 1980a: 8 and Murray, 1993: 35–54. Cf:

> Both Odysseus and Penelope are tricksters and master strategists. Life for him is a performance art. He brings down Troy by a ruse, where brute force has failed. He can make a boat from scratch or carve a bed from a living tree. He escapes Cyclops' cave by improvising a cruel log tool and mimicking the Trojan horse by riding out under a ram. Homeric mind is ingenuity, practical intelligence. There is no Rodin-like deep thinking, no mathematical or philosophical speculation. That comes much later in history. Odysseus thinks with his hands. He is athlete, gambler, engineer. Athena rules technological man, the Greek heir to Egyptian constructionism.
> (Paglia, 1990: 85)

56 *Oikos* not only included the immediate family, but 'all the people of the household and its goods; hence "economics" (from the Latinized form, *oecus*), the art of managing an *oikos*, meant running a farm, not managing to keep peace in the family' (Finley, 1978: 61).

> Historically there is an inverse relationship between the extension of the notion of crime as an act of public malfeasance and the authority of the kinship group. Many primitive societies are known in which it is not possible to find any 'public' responsibility to punish an offender. Either the victim and his relations take vengeance or there is none whatsoever. The

NOTES

growth of the idea of crime, and of criminal law, could almost be written as the history of the chipping away of that early state of family omnipotence.
(1978: 83)

The violation of kinship rules and the conduct of the vendetta is, we recall, the basic plot motivation of the *Iliad*: the 'theft' of Helen leading to a vendetta by her extended 'family' of Greek warlords and their allies; equally well, later Greek tragedies are all situated in the *oikos* of a noble house. The laws of abduction, murder, and personal injury are tied to kinship practices of 'rectification' or 'vengeance' legality: 'Homicide, as the most obvious example, remained largely a private affair' (1978: 83).

57 Bowra, 1966: 3–4.

58 All this [bureaucratic] activity presupposes a literate bureaucracy and a hierarchy of officialdom of which little or no trace appears in the Homeric poems ... The sudden and complete loss of the art of writing in the Dark Age suggests that it was more or less confined to a scribal class attached to the palaces.
(Luce, 1975: 75)

59 It goes without saying that the origins and dating of the Greek alphabet and alphabetic script is a subject that is still controversial:

It therefore seems to be most generally agreed that the epic tradition which produces the *Iliad* and the *Odyssey* was in living evolution down to the eighth century BC, and only then were the poems fixed, and, allowing for certain vagaries of spelling, were transmitted to us in the form they then received.
(Chadwick, in Kirk, ed., 1964: 119; cf. Luce, 1975: chs 1–3; Goody and Watt, in Goody, ed., 1968: 45)

After about 750 BC evidence of alphabetic writing with signs for vowel sounds becomes more and more common: 'Whether one calls it genius or common sense, someone made the suggestion that certain of the twenty-two Phoenician letters representing sounds missing from Greek, glottal stops, and the like, should be quite arbitrarily given new values as vowels, so *'aleph* became alpha and so on. The system worked perfectly, and the Greeks had a script as well adapted to their tongue as the Phoenician to theirs' (Trump, 1980: 256); 'There may then have been trained scribes in Ionia in the seventh century who could undertake the colossal task of writing out the *Iliad* and *Odyssey* on scrolls. At present, it can only be said that the ability to write was there, and the material; and it seems on the whole safest to regard the last third of the sixth century, the time of Polycrates and the Peisistratidae, as the latest possible, rather than the likeliest, date for the establishment of the poems in writing' (Jeffery, in Wace and Stubbings, eds, 1962, 545–9, 559); also Jeffery, 1990; the same idea occurs in Wade-Gery, 1952; Michael Wood (1985: 123–44) puts the transcription of the Homeric epic into the middle of the seventh century (c. 650 BC). And a late date of around 600–550 BC is by no means inconceivable. It is certainly one of the great achievements of this period to have applied alphabetic script to the monumental task of transcribing the Greek epics. Luce writes in a speculative vein that:

The Greeks at once realized the value of the innovation, and literacy spread rapidly. Hexameters appear scratched on an Attic vase dated c. 730, and there are examples of similar inscriptions on pottery from Ithaca and Ischia before the end of the eighth century. There is no reason why longer poems could not have been inscribed on papyrus or vellum at the same period. The

NOTES

existence of a manuscript of the Homeric poems by c. 700 BC is by no means out of the question. We may well owe the preservation of the text to an eighth-century copyist.

(Luce, 1975: 68; see also Jeffery, 1990: 1–40; Murray, 1993: chs 1, 2)

But compare the revisionary work of P. Kyle McCarter, Jr who puts the origin of alphabetic writing to the ninth century BC (in his *The Antiquity of the Greek Alphabet and the Early Phoenician Script*, (Harvard: Harvard Semitic Monographs/Scholars Press, No. 9, 1975)). Evidence for earlier forms of the Phoenician-Greek prototype (the 'Proto-Canaanite' script) have also been put forward (cf. Naveh, 1975: Section I, 3–4 on the Phoenician and Hebrew script), and Naveh, 1982). Naveh writes:

> The Canaanites developed the first alphabet in the middle of the 2nd millennium BC ; gradually other Semitic peoples and the ancient Greeks learned this way of writing. Each nation developed its own independent script, basing itself on the Canaanite prototype.
>
> (1975: 7)

For Naveh the crucial 'mediators' between the early Semitic scripts and the Greek (and through them, Western) alphabets are the 'lost' civilizations of northern Syria and Palestine – the Phoenicians, the Aramaeans, and the Nabataeans. Of more general interest see Coulmas, 1989; Diringer, 1968; Gelb, 1963; Goody, 1977; Harris, 1986; Kristeva, 1989; Lloyd, 1983; Sampson, 1985.

60 On Friedrich August Wolf, see Pfeiffer, 1976: ch. 14. Pfeiffer describes the influence of Wolf's *Prolegomena ad Homerum* on the subsequent development of classical scholarship as 'incomparable' in making the Homeric question the first question of the day and in providing the critical impulse 'for the employment of the analytic method by generations of scholars in the epic field' (1976: 175). See the modern translation of Wolf's work by A. Grafton, G. W. Most and E. G. Zetzel, F. A. Wolf, *Prolegomena to Homer, 1795* (Princeton: Princeton University Press, 1985). On the Homeric question in antiquity, see Davison, in Wace and Stubbings, eds, 1962: 234–65. Davison writes that 'every serious attempt to grapple with the Homeric problem since 1795 has been forced to accept Wolf's essential conception of the *Iliad* and *Odyssey* as the products of evolution' (in Wace and Stubbings, eds, 1962: 246). Ulrich von Wilamowitz-Möllendorff's views are contained in his *Homerische Untersuchungen* of 1884, where in Davison's words Wilamowitz argues the the *Odyssey* was cobbled together by 'a not very gifted patch-worker' (in Wace and Stubbings, eds, 1962: 251). Davison also notes that Wilamowitz

> later revised (and somewhat simplified) his views on the evolution of the *Odyssey* (*Die Heimkehr des Odysseus*, 1927), but he never departed from his fundamentally revisionist view of our *Odyssey* as an incompetent patchwork, further deformed by later interpolations; and most of the studies of the *Odyssey* which have been published in Germany since 1884 have followed more or less closely the pattern set by Wilamowitz.
>
> (in Wace and Stubbings, eds, 1962: 252)

See also Ulrich von Wilamowitz-Möllendorf, *Die Ilias und Homer* (Berlin: Weidmann, 1966).

61 For Vico's conception of the premodern 'gentile' world and his periodization of its history into the age of Gods, Heroes and Men see 1970: Sections 31–4. 5.

> Vico removed this veneer and saw Homer as the poetically splendid mirror of a magnificent barbarism. He did not look at him in personal terms but as

348

NOTES

> the reflection of a whole people, who were really the authors of this poetry insofar as it represented their history celebrated in song. All the thought and speech of primitive man was poetic and imaginative through and through. The myths represented ... nothing but poetical historical narrative presented through different categories of imaginative ideas arizing from the vast store of human fancy.
>
> (Meinecke, 1972: 44–5)

> [T]he Homeric writings were the holy writ of Lesser and Greater Greece, of the Romans and of all the civilizations that sprang directly from Greek or Roman influences on the world. For the work of Homer is at once a religion, a code of ethics, a map of chivalry, of health, domestic pursuits and of metaphysics. It embraced every subject that was necessary and desirable for primitive and undecadent Mediterranean mankind to know
>
> (Madox Ford, 1947: 107)

62 Lord, in Kirk, ed., 1964: 124–34, 126. Parry's published works are collected with previously unpublished materials in Parry, 1971, edited by his son Adam Parry; see the important reformulations of his father's theories in Parry, 1989. J. V. Luce summarizes Milman Parry's contributions as follows:

> he demonstrated that the *Iliad* and *Odyssey* were composed with the aid of what Kirk calls 'a traditional store of fixed phrases which covered most common ideas and situations'... Parry's second contribution to the Homeric problem was to study the techniques of oral composition as practised by 'singers' in Yugoslavia. He spent three years (1933–35) in field-work in the Serbo-Croat area, and collected over 12,000 texts, partly by direct recording and partly from dictation. As a result he was able to make illuminating comparisons between the technique of the Yugoslav singers and that of the bards described by Homer. He also gained valuable insights into how an oral tradition is conserved and transmitted.
>
> (Luce, 1975: 45–6)

Also cf. Bowra, 1951, 1972, G. S. Kirk, *Homer and the Epic* (Cambridge: Cambridge University Press, 1965); and Lord, in Wace and Stubbings, eds, 1962: 179–214; and more extensively in Lord, 1971.

63 Nagy has theorized that the traditional theme 'is the key to all the other levels of fixity in oral poetry – including both the formulaic and the metrical levels' (1990: 18–35, 25). Nagy's theoy can be condensed in the formula 'that formula generates meter' (1990: 31). For extensive documentation see Hainsworth, 1968: chs 3, 4; and Lord, 1971. For analogous verbal devices in non-Greek cultures see Finnegan, 1977.

64 The formulaic norms of oral epic are also found in other genres of oral discourse. For example the complex structural constants and constraints in mythological symbolism uncovered by Claude Lévi-Strauss; in the obligatory formulae that structure much of the central texts of the Old Testament – *Proverbs*, the repetitive verse of the *Songs of Solomon* and *Psalms*; and also in oral genres such as the saga, ballad, legend and folk-tale. Lord proposes that 'with Lévi-Strauss we might question whether we have something that is both *langue* and *parole* at the same time under different aspects, thus making a third form of communication, or of relationship, peculiar to oral verbal art' (1971: 279–80, n.7). The notion of myth and folklore as a dialectic of *langue* and *parole* is a standard theme in structural linguistics. Roman Jakobson and Petr Bogatyrev, in their early paper 'On the boundary between studies of folklore and literature' (1929) claimed that

NOTES

folklore is extraindividual and exists only potentially... it is a skeleton of actual traditions which the implementers embellish with the tracery of individual creation, in much the same way as the producers of a verbal message (*la parole* in the Saussurian sense) act with respect to the verbal code (*la langue*).

(in Matejka and Pomorska, eds, 1971: 91–3, 91)

65 'The oral poet ... at the moment of performance makes spontaneous, and therefore original realizations of inherited, traditional impulses' (Michael M. Nagler, *Spontaneity and Tradition. A Study in the Oral Art of Homer* (Berkeley: University of California, Press 1974): xxiii, xxi). Still one of the finest meditations on the dynamic relation between epic tradition and poetic innovation is Sir Maurice Bowra's essay on Homeric composition in Wace and Stubbings, eds, 1962: 38–74. Bowra concludes his essay:

> The rich, varied, resourceful language, the many ways in which a story can be made more dramatic or more human, the ability to combine convention and surprise, the sense of a heroic world and of the grandeur of brave exploits, the vision of the gods and the unique distinction which human life gains from being set against the darkness of death, all these we owe in large degree to the tradition, and it is conceivable that, if we had not the *Iliad* and the *Odyssey* but only the work of some uncreative bard who relied entirely on traditional material, we might well be impressed and delighted by it. Yet when we have made every allowance for this, we must still feel that there is something else, not easily defined and in the last resort beyond precise analysis, which reveals a great poet at work. It lies in his vision of humanity, seen almost always with affection, sometimes with compassion, sometimes with admiration, sometimes with humour. These men and women live for us because they are portrayed from the inside ... But these characters are set in surroundings as real as themselves. They are seen from without as well as from within, and play their parts in scenes which the poet loves hardly less than them and describes with affectionate care, from the constellations and the sea to birds and flowers and insects ... Despite all the arguments to the contrary, it is not unreasonable to believe that a single poet composed both the *Iliad* and the *Odyssey* and, since the Greeks said that his name was Homer, and there is no other name by which we may call him, we may perhaps be content with it.

(Bowra, in Wace and Stubbings, eds, 1962: 73–4)

66 Parry writes that the Homeric poems are what they are as 'the products of an oral technique with its abundant opportunities for freedom of creation, recorded by a method and under circumstances which bring to the fore the very best which an inspired poet can instill into them. Even as the moment of singing is the normal moment of creation of oral epic, so the moment of dictating is the moment of creation of our texts from the past' (M. Parry, in Kirk, ed., 77–8); cf. Bowra, in Wace and Stubbings, eds, 1962: 38–74; and the more extensive treatment given to similar issues in C. Macleod, *Iliad. Book XXIV* (Cambridge: Cambridge University Press, 1982). The paradoxical phrase 'premeditated spontaneity' is used by Robert P. Sonkowsky, in David W. Thompson, ed., *Performance of Literature in Historical Perspectives* (Lanham: University Press of America, 1983): 1–30, 2. Or in Lord's words, the oral poet is 'not a mere carrier of the tradition but a creative artist making the tradition ... we are not in the habit of thinking of a performer as a composer', yet the 'oral poet is composer. Our singer of tales is a composer of tales. Singer, performer, composer, and poet are one under different aspects *but at*

NOTES

the same time. Singing, performing, composing are facets of the same act'; the creation of tradition occurs in its revisionary transmission: 'the preservation of tradition by the constant re-creation of it' (Lord, 1971. 13, 29, also 3–29, 99–123); and

> the song is not in a fixed form in his mind; he remakes its form each time he tells it; each time the configuration of the themes may be somewhat different and their expression in formulae will fit the requirements of the moment, metrical, melodic, psychological ... This is the process which he goes through at every performance. This is oral composition.
> (Lord, in Wace and Stubbings, eds, 1962: 186)

On the unitary authorship of the *Iliad* and *Odyssey*:

> The whole conception [of the *Iliad*], in scale and originality, was so bold and individual that we can be confident that it as that of one man. The days when romantic scholars believed in 'folk poetry', producing the *Iliad* by collective action, are over.
> (Griffin, 1980a: 15)

See also Griffin, 1980b; D. M. Shive, *Naming Achilles* (Oxford: Oxford University Press, 1987); Burkert, 1992. Burkert writes of the *Iliad*: 'I, for one, am inclined to think that our text is a well-planned composition from beginning to end, to be dated in the first half of the seventh century, though relying on generations of earlier oral singers', 1992: 204, n. 32.

67 Similar displays of his authority occur at *Odyssey* 17.46 and 21.350ff. Authority over the household (*oikos*) is simply the most local form of patriarchal control, which extends as Telemachus' rebuke indicates to language, politics, and the conduct of war. In Greek, the word *logos* is, we recall, a masculine noun. By the eighth century, Homeric patriarchy is already an ancient value system; cf.: 'We cannot all be kings here; and mob rule is a bad thing. Let there be one commander only, one king [*basileus*], set over us by Zeus the son of Cronos of the Crooked Ways' (*Il.* 2.202–6); 'It is no bad thing to be a king [*basileus*]... I will be lord [(*w*)*anax*] over my own household and of the slaves that goodly Odysseus won for me' (Telemachus, at *Od.*. 1.392, 396–7). As we have noted in the text the term *wanax* is the ancient Mycenaean term for king, *basileus* referring to a prince or local warlord.

68 The American sociologist C. Wright Mills was thus unconsciously sketching a 'Homeric sociology' in drawing attention to the collective properties of 'vocabularies of motive':

> The motives actually used in justifying or criticizing an act definitely link it to situations, integrate one man's action with another's and line up conduct with norms. The societally sustained motive-surrogates of situations are both constraints and inducements. It is a hypothesis worthy and capable of test that typal vocabularies of motives for different situations are significant determinants of conduct. As lingual segments of social action, motives orient actions by enabling discrimination between their objects. Adjectives such as 'good', 'pleasant', and 'bad' promote action or deter it... such words often function as directives and incentives by virtue of their being the judgements of others as anticipated by the actor.
>
> Genetically, motives are imputed by others before they are avowed by self.
>
> The motives accompanying institutions of war, e.g. are not 'the causes' of war, but they do promote continued integrated participation, and they vary

NOTES

from one war to the next. Working vocabularies of motive have careers that are woven through changing institutional fabrics.

(Wright Mills, 'Situated Actions and Vocabularies of Motive', in 1963: 445)

A. W. H. Adkins' *Merit and Responsibility* (1960) and *Moral Values and Political Behaviour in Ancient Greece* (1972) constitute such an 'experimental validation' of Mills' sociological hypothesis for the agonistic-antagonistic culture of early Greek society. We might also claim independent validation for Mills' idea from our exploration of the motivational complex of epic narrative 'rhetorics of reflection':

> What is needed is to take all these *terminologies* of motive and locate them as *vocabularies* of motive in historic epochs and specified situations. Motives are of no value apart from the delimited societal situations for which they are the appropriate vocabularies. They must be situated. At best, socially unlocated *terminologies* of motives represent unfinished attempts to block out social areas of motive imputation and avowal. Motives vary in content and character with historical epochs and societal structures.
>
> (Wright Mills, 1963: 452)

Cf. Oliver Taplin's judicious comment on the way Homeric narrative engages in a questioning reflection on values:

> The 'Heroic Code' consists of precepts such as that you must strive to be first, you must kill and humiliate your enemies, and you must preserve your honour, which is measurable in material goods. But much of the *Iliad* is spent in disputing and debating about these very precepts, and many others. If the 'Heroic Code' were agreed and beyond dispute, there would be no real conflict. In fact the criteria for approval and disapproval are open for consideration; and much of the power of the *Iliad* comes from its lack of moral simplicity and consistency.
>
> (Taplin, in *OH*, 77)

69 See J. V. Luce's useful image of Homer as standing on the borderline of two overlapping worlds, the pre-literate oral culture of Greece and the literate universe of the Archaic age; Homer's marginality makes him a perfect emblem for the creative conflicts and contradictions which encourage cultural experimentation and innovation (Luce, 1975: 69 and the whole of ch. 3). The overlapping worlds can also be described socioculturally as the transition between the preliterate 'shame culture' and 'guilt culture' of ancient Greek civilization. For explorations of the change from traditional shame culture to guilt civilizations as a shift away from the tribal, public performance code of motivation in which reflection is under the dominion of an omniscient Generalized Other, to a more individualized, ethical, and internalized pattern of moral self-control, individuality, and articulable interests – exemplified by the social differentiation of conscience and self-consciousness as an interiorized motivational forum see: Adkins, 1969, 1972; A. W. H. Adkins, 'Homeric Values and Homeric Society', *Journal of Hellenic Studies*, 91, 1971: 1–14; Dodds, 1951: chapter 1; Havelock, 1963: Hirschmann, 1977. We should also cite the seminal paper by C. Wright Mills mentioned in note 68 above. Mills writes: 'the verbalized motive is not used as an index of something in the individual but *as a basis of inference for a typal vocabulary of motives of a situated action*' (emphasis in original text);

> In folk societies, the constellation of motives connected with various sectors of behavior would tend to be typically stable and remain associated only

with their sector. In typically primary, sacred, and rural societies, the motives of persons would be regularly compartmentalized. Vocabularies of motives ordered to different situations stabilize and guide behaviour and expectations of the reactions of others. In their appropriate situations, verbalized motives are not typically questioned. In secondary, secular, and urban structures, varying and competing vocabularies of motives operate co-terminally and the situations to which they are appropriate are not clearly demarcated. Motives once unquestioned for defined situations are now questioned.

(Wright Mills, 1963: 447, 449)

70 Maurice Bowra makes the interesting point that Homer's humanism and his ethical concern for the 'claims of ordinary people' led him to include a wide variety of identifiable individuals from the otherwise mute world of the *demos*: the mother who wards off flies from her child, the reapers in the barley, the boys who beat an ass which has broken into a cornfield, the woman working at her wool to save her children from poverty, the child who treads down his sand-castle, the traveller uncertain of his way, the inexperienced cowherd who cannot keep off a lion, the fisherman with his line and hook, the craftsmen who puts gold on silver, the woman whose husband is killed in war and who is herself dragged into slavery, the shipwright who bores a ship's timber, the smith who tempers an axe by dipping it in water, the man who watches a bard as he sings: 'The Homeric similes reveal a personal interest in human beings who lie outside the scope of the heroic tale, and in them the poet surely displays his own wide sympathy and understanding' (Bowra, in Wace and Stubbings, eds, 1962: 68; full references for these figures are provided on 67–8).

3 HESIOD AND THE BIRTH OF THE GODS

1   The extant remains of Egyptian and Babylonian medicine, mathematics, and astronomy can be combed in vain for a single example of a text where an individual author explicitly distances himself from, and criticizes, the received tradition in order to claim originality for himself; whereas our Greek sources repeatedly do just that. Even where we can *infer* innovations in Egyptian or Babylonian texts, that is to say, it is not the *style* of their cultures to publicize the fact or even to mention it.

(Lloyd, 1987: 57)

For the textual remains of these values, practices, and institutions see *ANET*; Breasted, 1912: ch. 1; Cameron, 1948; Brandon, chs 1–3; and Frankfort, *et al.*, 1949. In a related context G. B. Kerferd makes the following observation:

One element was new in the Presocratics and is found neither in their Hellenic predecessors nor in Babylonian or Egyptian speculations, and that is the basing of cosmological speculation on rational argument instead of putting it forward as dogma only. It is here that we must look for the true beginning of philosophy.

(in B. R. Rees, ed., *Classics* (London: Routledge and Kegan Paul, 1970): 41)

The full analysis of these institutional preconditions will form the substantive topic of Volume 3, Chapters 1 and 2, 'Presocratic thought and the origins of Western European reflection' and 'Thales and the origins of Ionian cosmology'.

2 The work of Pherecydes of Syros, Epimenides, and the Orphic poets is usually

NOTES

mentioned in this context (Vernant, 1990: 217–18; also KRS: 50–71; Murray, 1993: 92); the fourth-century AD Neoplatonist, Iamblichus links Pherecydes with Pythagoras as teacher and student (*On the Pythagorean Life*. 2.9)). Even Hittite and Hurrian cosmologies have been cited as the proximate source of Hesiodic mythogony (Kerferd, in B. R. Rees, ed., *Classics* (London: Routledge and Kegan Paul, 1970): 40; Murray, 1993: 87–92). For cosmogonic speculation in the choral poetry of the mid seventh-century Spartan poet Alcman, see Fränkel, 1975: 163–5, 252ff.; the whole of Fränkel's third chapter on Hesiod should be read in this context; cf. Fränkel 1960: 395–6; see also the relevant discussion in KRS, *CHCL* and Bowra, 1961: 26–7. Bowra makes the relevant connections: 'In his conception of an original *hyle* he is not far from Hesiod's Chaos, but when he sets Thetis to work he seems almost to anticipate Thales, who made water the *arche* of everything' (1961 26), 'In Alcman we see the first rays of the Ionian enlightenment, and watch how he moves forward from Hesiod to something more abstract and more scientific' (1961: 26). In addition: Segal, in *CHCL*: 'Early Greek poetry', 124–60, 138; Vernant, 1990: 203–79, esp. 216–18; M. L. West, 'The rise of the Greek epic', *Journal of Hellenic Studies*, 108, 1988: 151–72; Havelock, 1986: 75–6; Lesky, 1966; and Burn, 1960, 1966. For the links between these early fragments of poetic cosmogony and orphic discourse see Chapter 6 below on Orphic theogony and theology.

3 This would give a date from around 700–680 BC to the middle of the seventh century for Hesiod's poetic activity (cf. West, 1966: 40–8). The funeral games are historically recorded as a celebration inaugurated by the Chalcidians to honour the death of the naval leader, Amphidamas, killed in the Lelantine War (Plutarch, *Moralia* 153ff.; cf. *The Contest of Homer and Hesiod* 315–23; on Euboean society and the Lelantine war see Murray, 1993: 69–80). Note the important observation of Nietzsche on the underlying competitive ethic of Greek culture: 'The Greek artists, the tragedians for example, poetized in order to conquer; their whole art cannot be thought of apart from contest: Hesiod's good Eris, ambition, gave their genius its wings' (1984: §170). The same thought is found in his earlier work *Philosophy in the Tragic Age of the Greeks* where, speaking of Heraclitus' philosophy of becoming, he observes:

> it is Hesiod's good *Eris* transformed into the cosmic principle; it is the contest-idea of the Greek individual and the Greek state, taken from the gymnasium and the palaestra, from the artist's *agon*, from the contest between political parties and between cities – all transformed into universal application so that now the wheels of the cosmos turn on it.
>
> (1962: §5, 55)

The theme of the poetic *agon* is, of course, Platonic (cf. Plato, *Laws* 659A-B). The *institutionalization of combat* within the structure of religious festivals is one of the unique cultural forms of ancient Greece and deserves more detailed analysis as one of the formative preconditions for the development of cultural – especially literary – reflexivity (cf. Greenhalgh, 1973). The absence of competition in the plastic arts is also an important 'negative phenomenon' which requires social and cultural explanation (cf. 'There was ... one feature of a number of festivals that was peculiarly, perhaps uniquely, Greek. That was the practice of competition in athletics, music, dance and theatre (but never in the plastic arts)' (Finley, in Easterling and Muir, eds, 1985: xiii-xx, xviii). If space permitted we would look for an explanation of this absence in the specific institutional context of ancient Greek culture and society. Two crucial developments are relevant here; first the evolution of Greek city-state warfare and its associated political institutions (see Vernant, 1990: 29–53) and, second, the emergence of pan-Hellenic institutions and ideologies (see Nagy, 1990: 36–82, esp. 79–82). For later Athenian developments of this cultural agonism see Gouldner, 1966.

4   Only a society which can write, can sort out, preserve and transmit its knowledge on paper, is capable of systematic inquiry into its religious beliefs (or any other kind). The first step was a theogony. Here Herodotus is somewhat misleading: Homer shows the beginning only, and the first proper theogony must be assigned to Hesiod, who belongs to the fully historical world of the Greeks, while Homer stood on the threshold.

(Finley, 1963: 27–8)

Cf. West, 1978: 25–30, 30–2. For the view of primary oral/aural poetic traditions as dynamic, revisionary cultures see Baumann, ed., 1986; Finnegan, 1977; Ruth Finnegan, *Oral Literature in Africa* (Oxford: Clarendon Press, 1970); Havelock, 1982; Ong, 1982: esp. chs 1–3; see also Ong's extensive bibliography, 180–95; J. Vansina, *Oral Tradition: A Study in Historical Methodology* (Harmondsworth: Penguin, 1973), esp. 19–46; J. Vansina, *Oral Tradition as History* (London: James Currey, 1985). For the complex cultural interfaces and sociocultural processes linking oral and literate civilizations see Goody, 1986; Havelock, 1963, 1986: esp. chs 8–11; F. D. Harvey, 'Literacy in the Athenian democracy', *Revue des Etudes Grecques* 79, 1966: 585–635; Harris, 1989: Parts 2, 3; Ong, 1982: chs 4, 5.

Only *Works and Days* and the *Theogony* are regarded as genuine works of Hesiod; other writings attributed to him have included a short epic, the *Shield of Heracles*, narrative poems such as the *Marriage of Ceyx, Suitors of Helen, Epithalamium of Peleus and Thetis*, the *Descent of Theseus into Hades*, the *Circuit of the Earth, Catalogue of Women* or *Ehoiai* (a later continuation of the *Theogony*), and odd, almost unclassifiable, works such as the *Precepts of Chiron, Astronomy, Aegimius, Melampodia*, the *Marriage of Keyx, Descent of Pirithous, Idaean dactyls, Augury by Birds* and other fragmentary poems (see Trypanis, 1981: 67, 706–7 n. 40). We should observe that the innovative idea of a 'catalogue of the Gods' (*Theogony*), a 'catalogue of Women', and so on is a literary possibility created by the the spread of the alphabet during the late seventh and sixth centuries – inventories, catalogues, genealogical diagrams, maps, and so on are inextricably linked to alphabetic competences. On the particular alphabetical background of Hesiod's writing praxis see Jeffery, 1990. On the place of the *Ehoiai* in the Hesiodic corpus see Fränkel, 1975, 108–12. As with the earlier Homeric works, Hesiod's *Theogony* and *Works and Days* were written in dactylic hexameter, the metre of epic poetry. Trypanis writes that 'it is very probable that he wrote his poems down or dictated them' (1981: 61), citing as evidence for this claim that

> there is too much in Hesiod's poetry that is personal to the poet for us to accept the idea that his poems were ever in the repertoire of rhapsodes. Moreover, the laboured quality of much of the composition has rightly been said to suggest the painful task of writing rather than the unfettered ease of oral creation.
>
> (1981: 706 n. 27)

For the original texts see Rzach, 1913. Rzach's edition also contains the fragments of other works ascribed to Hesiod, *Fragmenta*, 129–230. For a readable English translation in blank verse (unrhymed iambic pentameter) consult Dorothea Wender's translation for the Penguin Classical Edition, *Hesiod and Theognis* (Harmondsworth: Penguin, 1985). The Greek text can also be found in M. L. West's carefully annotated work (1966), and an English/Greek parallel text is available in the Loeb Classical edition, translated by H. G. Evelyn-White (1936); this edition includes the Homeric Hymns and other writings attributed to Hesiod.

NOTES

I have also used A. W. Mair's translation, *Hesiod, The Poems and Fragments done into English Prose* (Oxford: Clarendon Press,1980). For the *Works and Days*, West's edition is recommended (West, ed., 1978), especially for its useful background material. An accessible translation of Hesiod can be found in *Hesiod, The Works and Days, Theogony and The Shield of Herakles*, trans. Richmond Lattimore (1959a); see also Norman O. Brown's Introduction to the Library of Liberal Arts edition of Hesiod's *Theogony* (Indianapolis: Bobbs-Merrill, 1953): 7–49. Biographical evidence suggests that Hesiod's poems were available as written texts in the lifetime of their author. Consider the following predeconstructionist account from B. M. W. Knox:

> Hesiod's solid presence in his work ... suggests that he expected the poems to be handed on in the form he had given them, securely identified as his work. The most reasonable explanation for such confidence seems to be that the poems were fixed in writing.
> (Knox, in *CHCL* vol. 1, Part 4, 156)

See also A. R. Burn, 1966. But note the qualification of W. V. Harris concerning Hesiod's *Works and Days*:

> it is to be seen not as a didactic poem for farmers but rather as an example of wisdom literature, and hence it no more presupposes a numerous readership than do its ancient Near Eastern predecessors in the same genre. The fact that Semonides and Alcaeus knew this poem is of interest, especially as they were not Boeotians; but this fact tells us nothing about general literacy. There was clearly an 'international' circuit for rhapsodes, and it had existed before any poetry was written down.
> (1989: 49)

Harris therefore concludes: 'There is thus no epigraphical or literary evidence to suggest that more than a very small percentage of Greeks were literate before 600' (1989: 49; his evidence and conclusions are contested by Murray, 1993: ch. 6, esp. 92–101).
While the genesis of more individual, subjective forms of cultural expression such as the theogonic genealogy and, later, lyric poem do not necessarily have to await the 'decline' of the epic and choral traditions, the spread and popularity of these individualized forms is certainly premised on the weakening and questioning of earlier collective song traditions; this tension between the communal ideology of the choral as against the individualized ideology of lyric poetry recurs in later historical periods; the creative interplay between the ballad form and courtly love poem in Renaissance and Baroque poetry is a case in point: 'The two forms – ballad and the Renaissance courtly poem – exemplify opposed kinds of discourse: one collective, popular, intersubjective, accepting the text as a poem to be performed; the other individualist, elistist, privatized, offering the text as representation of a voice speaking' (Easthope, 1983); and Trypanis: 'This new personal element opened the way which Archilochus and, after him, other iambic, elegiac and lyric poets were to follow' (1981: 61).

5 Zeller, 1969: 10. This is echoed by Gigon (1945), Fränkel (1960, 1975: ch. 3), and contemporary writers like J.-P. Vernant, who, following Zeller's lead, speak of Hesiod as 'the first Greek thinker to put forward an ordered, general vision of the divine and human universe' (1990: 216). Cf. Werner Jaeger who substantially repeats the same point:

> Here the new emergence of the subjective is already clearly expressed. But its appearance also implies a new responsibility. The Muses say to Hesiod:

NOTES

'We know how to tell many falsehoods that sound like the truth; But we also know how to utter the truth when we choose' [*Theogony*, 27].

(Jaeger, 1947: 11; see also Jaeger, 1945: vol. 1, 151–2)

Victor Ehrenberg follows in the footsteps of Jaeger in seeing Hesiod as a critic of Homeric verse: 'Hesiod accepted the task demanded by public opinion and turned away from the art of the Muses which, as he says, could tell beautiful lies – clearly an allusion to Homer. Hesiod aimed at teaching the truth' (Ehrenberg, 1964: 14). For an instructive analysis of Hesiod's poetry, stressing in particular the role of language and Hesiod's self-awareness as a poet, see Pucci, 1977 and Edwards, 1971: 199–206. Pucci reminds his reader that Hesiod's language 'for all its originality' is still indebted to an inherited poetic and mythic tradition: 'his dictum is heavily epic and is indebted to a historical tradition; his myths and his culture derive from a long past ... a relationship of difference with its linguistic and cultural tradition (1977: 33). Malcolm Nagy goes even further in seeing 'Hesiod' as a name for a collective tradition: 'the persona of the poet in any given archaic Greek poem is but a function of the traditions inherited by that poem ... Suffice it for now to observe that there are no analogues to the complementary characterizations of Hesiod and Perses even in Homeric poetry'; 'he represents a culmination of what must have been countless successive generations of singers interacting with their audiences throughout the Greek-speaking world' (1990: 71, 79). Nagy concludes: 'it would be better to speak in terms of *a tradition of performing a certain kind of poem*' (1990: 79). The complexity of Hesiod's generic situation straddling oral and written compositions led J.-P. Vernant to require of any analysis of the Hesiodic text that it reveal 'the semantic relationships, the interplay of corresponding symbols, the many layers of meaning in the text, and the hierarchy of the codes by which its message is conveyed' (1990: 216). He exemplifies this kind of hermeneutic decoding in the work of Peter Walcot and Hans Schwabl (P. Walcot, 'The composition of the *Works and Days*', *Revue des Etudes grecs*, 1961: 4–7 and H. Schwabl, *Hesiods Theogonie: Eine unitarische Analyse*, (Vienna, 1966)). See also Peter Walcot, *Hesiod and the Near East* (Cardiff, 1966), M. Detienne, *Crise agraire et attitude religieuse chez Hésiode* (Bruxelles, 1963), cited by Vernant, 1990: 276–7, nn. 13, 14, and Nagy, 1990: 36–82.

On the Indo-European origins of oral wisdom, poetry and folkloric traditions reaching back to the Neolithic period see Cottrell, 1985: 10–30 and Nagy, 1990: Part 2. On the larger logological conventions of narrative and literary self-mimesis:

> In early literature the first person is generally associated with such loose and personal forms as the epistle and the memoir, the forms of the amateur rather than the professional. We find occasionally a sense of self-awareness in the authors of works which are essentially neither first-person in form nor autobiographical in spirit, as when Hesiod opens the *Theogony* with a reminiscence of the time when a delegation of Muses visited Hesiod (referring to himself in the third person) and persuaded him to enlighten the world with the true histories of the deathless gods; but we find almost no first-person narrative in early Greek literature, with the important exception of the story of his travels told by Odysseus to the Phaeacians, which is embedded in the larger narrative structure of Homer.

(Scholes and Kellogg, 1966: 72–3)

The subsequent history of first-person narrative provides an important clue to the development of rhetorics of self-reflection:

> The ultimate development in Roman first-person narrative form, which had

NOTES

certainly been hinted at by both Lucian and Apuleis, was the achievement of St. Augustine, who first employed the form of the full-scale autobiography as confession ... anxious to demonstrate the way in which God works through man for his salvation ... Augustine was the first to probe deeply into the psyche, to substitute self-observation for observation of the world, and to feel that the story of the self alone was important enough to sustain a lengthy narrative ... It is the Christian and especially the Augustinian approach to man and the universe which leads the way to psychology. Without Augustine we would never have had a Freud.

(Scholes and Kellogg, 1966: 78–9)

6 Finley, 1963:, 27–8. Finley asks the crucial question of the cultural conditions of reflexivity:
And who gave Homer (and Hesiod after him) the authority to intervene in such matters? What they did, both in the action itself and in its substance, implies a human self-consciousness and self-confidence without precedent, and pregnant with limitless possibilities.

(1963: 27)

Some would see the name 'Hesiod' as indexing the first reflective cultural crisis of the whole mythological tradition, with Hesiod as both the preserver of the old and voice of the new mythology. Thus Vernant:

In the work of Hesiod... we have to recognize what may be described as a learned mythology richly and subtly elaborated that possesses all the finesse and rigor of a philosophical system while at the same time remaining totally committed to the language and mode of thought peculiar to myth.

(Vernant, 1990: 217)

See also Vernant, 1990: 183–201.
7 Trypanis, ed., 1971: xxix-xxx; see Trypanis' account of Hesiod's poetry and its impact in 1981: 60–7. Also see Baldry, 1968: 43; Evelyn-White, trans., 1936; Burn, 1966; F. Solmsen, *Hesiod and Aeschylus* (Ithaca; Cornell University Press, 1949).
8 Trypanis, 1981: 65–6; Cf. Finley, 1963: 30–1; Vernant, 1990: 183–201.
9 Barron and Easterling, in Easterling and Knox, eds, 1989: I, 52–3. *CHCL*: vol. 1 I, 93–4.
10 Finley, 1981: 129. Finley's point is directed toward the type of reconstruction we can find in histories of early Greek poetry and philosophy. Theodor Gomperz's Hesiodic romance is a case in point:

Legends clustered like weeds in a pathless and primeval forest ... The thinning axe was wanted, and a hand was presently found to wield it ... A peasant's vigour and a peasant's shrewdness accomplished the arduous task, and we reach in him the earliest didactic poet of the Occident. Hesiod of Ascra, in Boeotia, flourished in the eighth century BC.

(Gomperz, 1920: 38)

11 Martin West, in *OCD*: 511.
12 Bury and Meiggs, 1975: 81.
13 Compare the realistic appearance of poverty, physical hardship and distress, and an equally bleak view of human life in the poetry of the sixth-century poet, Hipponax of Ephesos; for instance, the highly concrete, individualized 'referents' (including *sphragis* or self-reference) in the following text:

Hermes, dear Hermes, Maia's son from Kyllene, I pray to you, I'm suffering from extreme shivers, so give an overcoat to Hipponax, give him a cape, and

NOTES

sandals, and felt overshoes, sixty pieces of gold to bury in his strong chamber.

(Lattimore, trans., 1960: 12–13)

F. M. Cornford compares Hesiod to the Old Testament prophet Amos; both responded to similar conditions:

the opening or re-opening of the Mediterranean lands to commercial enterprise and the consequent rise in the standard of living had occasioned simultaneously in Greece and Palestine those conditions which led to revolutions, dictatorships, and the cancellation of debts in seventh-century Greece. Hesiod and Amos alike bitterly condemn the violence, injustice, and corruption of the richer classes; both associate justice with the deity and are convinced that injustice will lead to disaster.

(Cornford, 1965: 88–106, 99)

On the social struggle of 'gift-devouring lords' and 'the people' see Finley, 1978; Ehrenberg, 1964: 15–16; Detienne, cited by Vernant, 1990: 217, n. 14.

14 Solon, Fr. 5 (see J. M. Edmonds, *Greek Elegy and Iambus*, I (London, William Heinemann, 1931). See Plutarch, *Solon* 8–9. Of course, after Hesiod, Solon is one of the first known writers to refer to his own work and activities in the first person; certainly the first major political figure to use written texts to objectify and examine the causes, nature, and consequences of his own efforts as a legislator and 'constitutional' reformer and, as far as we know, one of the first to utilize poetic means for explicitly political and, perhaps, propagandist ends. His is the first recognizable voice to project itself as the salutary, representative discourse of an identifiable city-state, the voice of moderation advocating the strategic middle path between the aristocratic and democratic factions. In this sense, a century prior to classical Athenian tragedy, Solon assumed the unenviable role of hero of his own discourse and its political concerns – saving the traditional Athenian constitution by reforming the socioeconomic system of Athenian land tenure and production. It is fully in keeping with this essentially self-reflexive stance that he should consciously refuse to assume the role of 'tyrant' when it was offered to him after 580 BC. Cf. Knox, 'Solon', in *CHCL*: 'Early Greek poetry', 105–12. Fränkel provides a detailed analysis of Solon's poetic activities in 1975: 217–37.

For Solon, as for Hesiod, the true guardian of the moral law is Zeus, and his elegy speaks in a really inspired manner of the vengeance of Zeus and of divine retribution falling upon sinful man with the sweeping power of a sudden gale. It combines insight into the limitations of human action and of 'empty' human hopes with a deep belief in the moral government of the universe. Its ultimate message is that wisdom lies in moderation with the Golden Mean.

(Trypanis, 1981: 89; cf. Fränkel, 1975: 232–7; Havelock, 1978: 249–62)

15 At *Theogony* 27 and 33ff. Compare the Homeric precedent of divine inspiration in Phemius' life-saving plea, framed in terms of the divine nature and authorization of his own poetic vocation at *Od.* 22.347ff.: 'Self-taught (*autodidaktos*) am I, and the god has planted in my heart all manner of songs, and worthy am I to sing to thee as to a god; wherefore be not eager to cut my throat.'

16 The Olympians have to be remembered of their existence as the presence of divine order, victorious over the disorder of the older gods from whom they stem and who still are alive. Remembrance, in the sense of the Hesiodian symbol, does not recollect a dead past but 'remembers' a presence that is a living presence only if it is fully conscious of its ordering victory over forces

that once were just as victoriously present ... Hesiod expresses his insight into Remembrance as the reflective distance to the existentially ordering event in the metaxy. The reflectively distancing Mnemosune is the dimension of consciousness in which the presence of the Beyond, experienced as the ordering force in the event, gains the reality of its Parousia in the language of the gods. The 'existence' of the gods is the presence of the divine Beyond in the language symbols that express its moving Parousia in the experience of the non-experientiable ordering force in the existential event. With Hesiod, we are touching the limits of symbolization in the language of the gods: there are no gods without a Beyond of the gods.
(Voeglin, 1987: 71–2)

17 Cornford, 1950: 100. See also Cornford, 1965: 187–201, esp. 198. For background see: Blumenberg, 1987; Fränkel, 1960; Gigon, 1945; Hölscher, 1968: 9–89; Rose, 1989: chs 2–4; Bruno Snell, *Die Ausdrücke für den Begriff des Wissens in der vorplatonischen Philosophie* (Philologische Untersuchungen, 29) (Berlin, 1924); 1953: esp. 138–40. Jean-Pierre Vernant summarizes this view of Hesiod as an innovatory marginal figure 'between' *mythos* and *logos* as follows:

In the work of Hesiod, then, we have to recognize what may be described as a learned mythology richly and subtly elaborated that possesses all the finesse and rigor of a philosophical system while at the same time remaining totally committed to the language and mode of thought peculiar to myth.
(1990: 217)

See note 5 above.

18 *Works and Days*, lines 50–100. See Pietro Pucci (1977) for an extended analysis of these figures. Pucci refers to the operation of Discord as a textual principle in the constitution of Hesiodic poetry, the 'force' that combines two polar opposites to generate a new mimetic figure of difference and detour 'forever removing the text from presence'. Discord 'sits in the middle of the polarities' (1977: 125) supplementing and deferring the very attempt to centre the event of events, the birth and presence of the gods; presumably, the dispersing, differentiating force of discord constitutes the 'blindness' – after Jacques Derrida's and Paul de Man's analysis – which constitutes the insightful potential of the poem. F. M. Cornford had come to substantially the same conclusion in an essay on Hesiod written in 1941:

This cosmogony... is not a myth, or rather it is *no longer* a myth. It has advanced so far along the road of rationalization that only a very thin partition divides it from those early Greek systems which historians still innocently treat as purely rational constructions. Comparison with those systems shows that, when once the cosmic order has been formed, the next chapter should be an account of the origin of life. In the philosophies, life arises from the interaction or intercourse of the separated elements: animal life is born of the action of the heavenly heat on the moist slime of earth. This is the rationalized equivalent of the marriage of Heaven and Hell. And surely enough this marriage follows immediately in Hesiod: Gaia lay with Ouranos and brought forth the Titans.
(in Cornford, 1950: 100)

Cf. the similar wording in his essay in 1965: 198. Cornford's Durkheimian point is that the 'blindness' of Hesiod (his unreflexive transmission of earlier narrative codes for example) which serves to found his insightful yet partially mythical cosmogony is precisely the cultural logic of *ritual praxis*: that 'the early philosophic cosmogony is not only a transcription of mythical cosmogony, but finally has its

NOTES

root in *ritual*' 1950: 115–16). For a comprehensive exploration of the role of polarity in early Greek thought see Lloyd, 1971.

19 On the dialectical figures of differentiation and self-differentiation in early Greek and Hebraic cosmogonies:

> – separation or differentiation out of a primitive confusion. And as measured by the absence of allegorical personification, Genesis is less mythical than Hesiod's *Theogony*, and even closer to the rationalized system of the Milesians ... the value of the parallel I have drawn with Hebrew cosmogony lies in the fact that the Old Testament has preserved elsewhere other traces of the original myth of Creation which the priestly authors of Genesis have largely obliterated. This myth has been restored by scholars, and, what is more, traced to its original in ritual. And behind the Palestinian myth and ritual lie the Babylonian Hymn of Creation.
>
> (Cornford, 1950: 100–2)

The yawning *Chaos* in Hesiod's account, like the old Nordic account of the *Ginunga-Gap* – a chasm stretching between the ice of Niflheim and the scorching heat of Muspilheim – implies the possibility that this *kosmos* might also have not come into existence, that there may have been Nothingness rather than Being. José Ortega Y Gasset has suggested that Archaic Greek culture resisted this dangerous thought of the abysmal and the infinite and by reaction obsessively sought the *metron* – the bounded, measured, finite mean – in everything. Thus domesticated, *Chaos* could play an important foundational role in reminding transgressors of the consequences of injustice (*adikia*), excess or immoderation (*hubris*), cruelty (*eris*), and so forth – that the 'enemy' of order and culture lies in violation of just measure (*nomos*). See Burnet 1930: 7, and note 1 page 7, where the comparison with the Scandinavian *Ginunga-Gap* is traced to Grimm; cf. Dodds, 1951; Onians, 1954.

20 Cornford, 1950: 103–4. Cornford explores the 'biography' of Zeus in more detail in 1965: 214–24.

21 Cf. *Theogony* 883.

> Zeus institutes the natural and social order. This royal function is allegorically expressed by the marriage of Zeus with Themis (social order) and the birth of their children, the Seasons (whose names are Good Government, Justice, and Peace) and the Moirai, who give men their portions of good and evil.
>
> (Cornford, 1950: 114–15)

Cf. Trypanis:

> In his conception of a just Zeus Hesiod goes far beyond the theology of the *Odyssey*; in fact, it is with the *Theogony* that the line of development starts which leads to Solon and culminates in the lofty Aeschylean conception of Zeus.
>
> (1981: 62)

22 Trans. Wender, 1985: 59; compare Richmond Lattimore's translation in 1959a: 'So the neighbour envies the neighbour who presses on toward wealth. Such Strife is a good friend to mortals.' According to Jaeger's reading Hesiod introduces the dual doctrine of Strife to 'correct' his own *Theogony*

> for he now gives the spiteful Eris of the *Theogony* a sister goddess, the good Eris, who presides over all the more wholesome competition in this world. The very existence of this later correction is striking evidence of the extent

NOTES

to which Hesiod's attitude towards mythology was affected by the new issues he raised.

(1947: 12–13)

See also Barron and Easterling, *CHCL*: vol. I, 97.

23 In the work of compilation which created the 'Old Testament' (by the so-called Redactor), the archaic cosmogonies narrating the battle between God and watery chaos (or between Yahweh and the representatives of the sea gods – including dragons) are displaced to an irrelevance (as in *Psalms* 74, 89 or *Isaiah* 51:9–10) or else excised completely – e.g. by the work of the 'Priest' (or Priestly Authors). See Rosenberg and Bloom, 1991: esp. 9–49. Bloom writes: 'The God of the Priestly Author is too transcendent, and too powerful, for anyone to imagine his stooping to a struggle with a sea serpent' (1991: 27). However, according to Bloom, the authoress of one of the oldest texts of the Hebrew Bible (who he calls 'J') included these Mesopotamian tales in the Creation story. For the cosmological stories of ancient Sumeria and Mesopotamia contrasted with those of ancient Greece see: Thompson, 1930; Brandon, 1963; S. Dalley, *Myths from Mesopotamia* (Oxford: Oxford University Press, 1989); Jacobsen, in Frankfort, *et al.* 1949: 137–234; Nilsson, 1962; *ANET*; R. A. Labat, M. Caquot, M. Sznycer, and M. Vieyra, *Les religions du Proche-Orient asiatique: Textes babyloniens, ougaritiques, hittites* (Paris, 1970). For ancient Egyptian myths and literature: Breasted, 1912; Frankfort *et al.*, 1949; Erman, 1966; R. T. Rundle Clark, *Myth and Symbol in Ancient Egypt* (London: Thames and Hudson, 1959); Simpson, ed., 1973. Ancient Persian cosmology is in some ways even closer to Hesiod's account, depicting a polarized conflict between infinite light above and darkness below, an eternal struggle personified by the conflict of Ahura Mazda and Ahriman (Angra Mainyu); the onset of their struggle brings an end to an earlier Golden Age; the 'space' of their conflict bears striking similarities to the Hesiodic account of *Chaos* (see Cameron, 1948; Hallock, 1969).

24 'Eros is the allegorical image of that intercourse of the separated opposites which will generate life. His physical equivalent is the rain, the seed of the Heaven-father which fertilizes the womb of mother Earth' (Cornford, 1950: 99). Cf.

> To Empedocles, Love (or, as he calls it *Philia*) is the efficient cause of every union of cosmic forces. This function has simply been taken over from the Eros of Hesiod. At the very beginning of his account of the world's origin, the poet introduces Eros as one of the oldest and mightiest of gods, coeval with Earth and Heaven, the first couple, who are joined in loving union by his power. The story of Earth and Heaven and their marriage was one of the traditional myths; and Hesiod reasons quite logically when he infers that Eros must have been as old a divinity as they, and so deserving of one of the first places. The union of Heaven and Earth begins the long series of procreations which provides the main content of the *Theogony* and occupies the centre of Hesiod's theological interest.
>
> (Jaeger, 1947: 15)

Paul Tillich, in his short work, *Love, Power and Justice* (1954) has traced the theme of *eros* as a dialectic of unity and strife from Hesiod to Empedocles, Parmenides, Plato, Aristotle, Neoplatonism, Augustine, down to Schelling and Hegel ('Hegel's dialectical scheme is an abstraction from his concrete intuition into the nature of love as separation and reunion', 1954: 22). He asks the basic question as to the nature of Eros and suggests that what is personified in these diverse traditions is a recognition of the fundamental drive toward the unity of the separated and differentiated. Not 'union of the strange', but the 'reunion of the estranged'. As estrangement or alienation presupposes an aboriginal unity or oneness, 'love manifests its greatest power where it overcomes the greatest separation. And the greatest separation is the separation of self from self' (1954: 25). In essence, we are returned to Hesiod's fundamental insight: Eros is a recollective passion, the state of being driven towards reunion (1954: 27). Jaeger comes to substantially the same conclusion:

> in the Hesiodic conception we already find the germ of the quest for a single natural principle which we meet in the later philosophers. Its influence will become particularly clear in the new forms which the Hesiodic Eros takes in the works of Parmenides and Empedocles. When Hesiod's thought at last gives way to truly philosophical thinking, the Divine is sought inside the world – not outside it, as in the Jewish-Christian theology that develops out of the book of Genesis.
>
> (1947: 17)

25 For the fable of the hawk and the nightingale, *Works and Days* 202–12, 276ff.; Trypanis, 1981: 65; also see Burn, 1966: esp. 31–81: P. Walcot, *Hesiod and the Near East* (Cardiff, 1966); cf. *CHCL*: vol. 1, 98–9: 'in this passage above all Hesiod turns his back on Homer and the heroic tradition.' Fränkel: 'The special concern of the *Works and Days* with the concrete details of workaday life remains without successor in Greek poetry; but the two-fold theme of justice and success is symptomatic of the age at whose threshold Hesiod stands' (1975: 113). See also Burn, 1960; and Ehrenberg, 1964:

> Hesiod was the first poet to conceive the idea of Zeus as the guardian of supreme justice, an idea which was to guide Greek religious and philosophical thought for all time to come. This idea colored the religion of the community as well, and it was the basis of the claim of the Polis to be the bearer of justice, the state under Dike and the Law, a claim which was to be supported by the written legislation of individual lawgivers.
>
> (1964: 17)

Also H. T. Wade-Gery, *Essays in Greek History* (Oxford: Basil Blackwell, 1958): 1–16; L. R. Palmer, 'The Indo-European origins of Greek justice', *Transactions of the Philological Society*, 1950: 149–68.

26 In Richmond Lattimore's translation from *Works and Days* 1959a, 286ff., the passage is rendered:

> Famine is the unworking man's most constant companion.
> Gods and men alike resent that man who, without work himself, lives the life of the stingless drones, who without working eat away the substance of the honeybees' hard work; your desire, then, should be to put your work in order so that your barns may be stocked with all livelihood in its season.
> It is from work that men grow rich and own flocks and herds;
> by work, too, they become much better friends of the immortals.

In A. W. Mair's free translation (Hesiod, 1908):

> work, noble Perses, that hunger may abhor thee, but worshipful Demeter of the fair crown love thee and fill thy barn with livelihood. For hunger is altogether meet companion of the man who will not work. At him are gods and men wroth, whoso liveth in idleness, like in temper to the stingless drones, which in idleness waste and devour the labour of the bees. Be it thy choice to order the works which are meet, that thy barns may be full of seasonable livelihood. By works do men wax rich in flocks and gear; yea,

NOTES

and by work shalt thou be far dearer to immortals and to mortals: for they utterly abhor the idle ... Wealth is not to be seized violently: god-given wealth is better far.'

27 Ovid, *Metamorphoses*, cited by Heinberg, 1982: 49. See also A. S. Hollis, ed., *Ovid: Metamorphoses Book VIII* (Oxford: Clarendon Press, 1970); Pfeiffer, 1976: 117ff. For ancient utopianism see Finley, 1975 178–92 and John Ferguson, *Utopias of the Classical World* (London: Thames and Hudson, 1975).

4 LYRIC REFLEXIVITIES

1 Of known individual poets during the Archaic period we have to mention not only the great exponents of the classical lyric form such as Sappho of Mytilene (*fl. c.* 600), Alcaeus, and Pindar, but a galaxy of other luminaries who all contributed in different ways to the formation and perfection of lyric poetry during this period: Archilochus of Paros (720–670), Alcman, the Spartan choral poet (seventh century), Tyrtaeus of Sparta (second half of the seventh century), Mimnermus of Colophon in Ionia (middle seventh to early sixth century), Terpander of Lesbos (*fl. c.* 676), Theognis of Megara (late sixth century), Anacreon of Teos (*c.* 560–490), Simonides of Ceos (*c.* 556–468), Bacchylides of Ceos (*c.* 520–430) and Stesichorus of Himera on the northern coast of Sicily (late seventh to middle of the sixth century). We should also include the less-well-known figures of Callinus, Praxilla, Hipponax, and Ibycus of Rhegium in south Italy in this list. Although lesser poets than an Archilochus or Sappho their work is important for any cultural archaeology of literary discourse and reflexive consciousness during the sixth century BC. We might also include the Athenian legislator Solon on the grounds that the critics of antiquity regarded the verse of the Athenian reformer as part of a unified lyric tradition.

Like the fragmentary textual remains of the early Greek philosophers much of the work of the lyric poets derives from two sources – citations in later commentaries, particularly by the Alexandrian commentators and reconstruction from papyri rediscovered from Egyptian sites. A large part of what we know of the writing of the first European poets can be credited to the climate and sands of Egypt. The purely fortuitous transmission of otherwise lost texts is best illustrated by an observation from the translators of some of the non-literary papyri:

> In the Ptolemaic period, discarded sheets of papyrus were often used in making painted cartonnage for the embellishment of mummies, and many valuable texts have been extracted from these. Sometimes too they were included in the wrappings of mummified sacred animals: a cemetery of crocodiles at the ancient Tebtunis provided material for a large volume.
> (A. S. Hunt and C. C. Edgar, trans., *Select Papyri: Volume 1: Non-literary Papyri and Private Affairs* (London: William Heinemann, 1932): x)

A select bibliography for this chapter includes the following works: Lattimore, trans., 1960; Barnstone trans. 1972; Trypanis, ed., 1971; Campbell, trans., 1982; Grant, ed., 1977; West, ed., 1971–72; M.L. West, ed., *Delectus et Iambis et Elegis Graecis*, (Oxford: Oxford University Press, 1980); E. Lobel and D.L. Page, eds, *Poetarum Lesbiorum Fragmenta* (Oxford: Oxford University Press, 1955); D.L. Page, ed., *Greek Literary Papyri* (London, Loeb Classical edition, 1942); D.L. Page, ed., *Poetae Melici Graeci* (Oxford: Oxford University Press, 1962); D.L. Page, ed. *Lyrica Graeca Selecta* (Oxford: Oxford University Press, 1968); D.L. Page, ed. *Epigrammata Graeca* (Oxford: Oxford University Press, 1975); Bowra,

1961; D. A. Campbell, ed., *Greek Lyric Poetry* (Bristol, 1981); D. A. Campbell, *The Golden Lyre: the Themes of the Greek Lyric Poets* (London, 1983); Gilbert Murray, et. al., *The Oxford Book of Greek Verse* (Oxford: Clarendon Press, 1930); Page, trans., 1941; D. L. Page, *Sappho and Alcaeus* (Oxford, 1955); and, finally, as indispensable background works: *CHCL* vol. 1, Part 1; Fränkel, 1975; Trypanis, 1981.

2 Here and throughout our discussion of lyric reflexivity we must emphasize that the availability of alphabetic script and the spread of literacy – following the changing economic and political patterns of colonialism and mercantile trade – formed the single most important precondition for the emergence of lyric expression and 'the literary institution'. Peripatetic figures like Archilochus and Hipponax may well have been able to read and write in both Greek and non-Greek scripts (Phoenician, Akkadian, and so on). From the point of view of our interest in institutions of reflexivity it is not so much the explosion of interest in personalized lyric song that is central, but the incarnation of this polymorphous lyricism in the objectified forms and practices of *written* poetry and its sustaining institution of *authored composition*: in essence the 'decline' of choral lyric was accelerated with the growth and popularization of a market for lyric writing; the Greek lyric poets were first and foremost inventors of the institution of reflexivity we know as 'writing poetry'. Historical, philological, and linguistic studies support the claim that we should extend the expansion of the institutions of literacy well back into the Archaic period – even though literacy was restricted to small circles and *élites* of the Archaic intelligentsia (for documentation see Harris, 1989). Of course if we accept a narrow definition of the sociological relevance of lyric poetry then we can glean nothing of historical relevance from these fragmentary texts; they will remain the preserve of the literary historian. This appears to have been M. I. Finley's judgement: 'For two centuries all the poetry was personal... it dealt with personal problems and with generalities, not with narration nor with politics or society in their concrete institutional expressions' (1975: 21). But we need not reduce such texts to the narrow optic of 'historical evidence' to grasp their cultural significance. For example, the very *existence* of 'two centuries' of 'un-heroic, un-Homeric' literary expression is a precious piece of historical information concerning the changing functions of early literacy and literate attitudes. Everything here hinges on the attitude we take toward these textual remains. As Finley rightly says (but fails to adopt in his own evaluations of the lyric corpus):

> Thucydides and his contemporaries knew the full corpus of lyric and elegiac poetry, but they made less use, and less skilful use, of this material for historical analysis than we make of the few scraps which have survived in our time. Again neither technique nor intelligence is a useful criterion; only interest will explain the difference.
>
> (1975: 22–3)

The underlying attitude which enables a later tradition to 'see' the fragments of the lyric poets *as documentary evidence* is absent from early Greek self-reflection (a phenomenon, of course, which deserves more detailed study). In this context C. M. Bowra's approach is more fruitful:

> These scattered lines and incomplete quotations are not only contemporary records, worth more than the traditions preserved in later historians; they are in themselves the relics of an art, which if it had survived complete, would be one of the wonders of the world ... [the poetic fragments] grew from the social circumstances of their time, and without some consideration of these they cannot be properly understood.

(1961: 15)

On the spread of literacy during the colonial period I accept the main conclusion of Knox's argument:

> When the Alexandrians came to edit and arrange in 'books', i.e. papyrus rolls, the poetry which had come down to them from the seventh and sixth centuries BC, they produced six books of the Spartan choral poet Alcman, two of the Ionian poet Mimnermus and seven of the Spartan Tyrtaeus, ten books of Alcaeus and nine of Sappho, seven books of Ibycus of Rhegium in south Italy, seven books of Anacreon of Teos, five thousand lines, elegiac and iambic, of Solon of Athens, and no less than twenty-six books of the Sicilian poet Stesichorus of Himera ... it suggests that there was a certain circulation of texts and multiplication of copies in the archaic period. For otherwise it is hard to undestand why more archaic and classical literature was not already lost without trace ... when the Alexandrian scholars began their work of collection, correction and interpretation.
> (Knox, in *CHCL*: vol. 1, Part 4, 158)

Harris also emphasizes that the *cultural* sensibility – we would say the logological orientations – displayed in the early Greek poets and thinkers *predated* the diffusion of writing:

> the mentality of the Greeks was particularly inclined towards certain kinds of intellectual development, and this inclination was not a consequence – not in any case a direct consequence – of literacy. The agonistic and the inquisitive aspects of this mentality are highly visible in the earliest period of Greek literature.
> (1989: 336)

3 Bowra, 1965: 58. For the Homeric Hymns see Evelyn-White, trans., 1914. See also Adorno, 1991: 37–54: 'The greatness of works of art... consists solely in the fact that they give voice to what ideology hides. Their very success moves beyond false consciousness, whether intentionally or not' (1991: 39). Lyric form distils the work of language in the education of the senses: 'the highest lyric works are those in which the subject, with no remaining trace of mere matter, sounds forth in language until language itself acquires a voice' (1991: 43). From diametrically opposed premises Gilbert Murray comes to substantially the same conclusion in his claim that 'the great poetry of the world, especially the poetry of the classical tradition, is ultimately about the human soul; and not about its mere fortunes, but its doings' (1927: 178–204, 185–6; also 241–62). The present study of the social rhetorics of ancient poetic forms is a contribution to the genealogy of the self and traditions of selfhood constituted by these literary devices. It is one small contribution to the comprehensive programme suggested by W. V. Harris at the end of his magisterial study of ancient literacy:

> To trace the possible influences of ancient patterns of literacy on the intellectual history of Greece and Rome would require a separate investigation, especially as that history has in some fundamental respects been strangely neglected. We would have to ask innumerable specific questions about the works of ancient authors, and general ones too about the development of language and logic, about verbal precision, about the invention of fiction, about scepticism and rationalism, about attitudes towards the past and towards the outside world, in other words questions about the entire intellectual style of the Greeks and Romans.
> (1989: 337)

NOTES

These self-involving questions are, in the idiom of the present text, logological investigations. For the origins and development of literary criticism in the ancient world see Kennedy, ed., 1989.

4 Barnstone trans., 1972: 2–7; see also Plato, *Laws* 700A–B, 701A, 764C–5B; *Rep.* 607A; *Symposium*. 177A; cf. Bowra, 1961: 1–15, esp. 7–9; Trypanis, 1981: 102–14. Following Bowra (1961: 6–7), Segal notes that the division between choral lyric and monody is 'convenient, but artificial, for many poets composed songs of both types' *CHCL*: vol. 1, 166. For a detailed mapping of this complex terrain see Nagy, in Kennedy, ed., 1989: 1–77. Also Bruno Gentili, *Poetry and Its Public in Ancient Greece: from Homer to the Fifth Century* (New York: Johns Hopkins University Press, 1989).

5 Segal, in *CHCL*: 'Early Greek poetry', 203. Cf. Oliva, 1981: 170–2. The fundamental importance of pan-Hellenism for the evolution of Greek poetry is explored by Gregory Nagy in his indispensable essay 'Early Greek views of poets and poetry', in Kennedy, ed., 1989: 1–77. Nagy suggests that

> the very evolution of what we know as the Classics – as both a concept and a reality – was but an extension of the organic pan-Hellenization of oral traditions. In line with this reasoning, the evolution of an ancient Greek canon in both *poetry* and *song* need not be attributed primarily to the factor of writing ... the key to the actual evolution of a canon must be sought in the social context of performance itself.
>
> (in Kennedy, ed., 1989: 44–5, 73–7)

For the evolution of musical forms in Greek life see the entry 'Music' in *the Oxford Classical Dictionary*: 705–13. The *Oxford Classical Dictionary* essay reminds us that the centrality of musical culture in ancient Greece, the 'respect for the power of music' found expression in an artistic conservatism: 'In Argos, for instance, the purity of music was regulated by law; and at Sparta venturesome innovators are said to have had their instruments destroyed' (*Oxford Classical Dictionary*: 706). By the sixth century choral lyric formed the centre of Greek *paideia*:

> Doubtless the main triumphs of Greek music in this period were in choral lyric, an indissoluble complex of poetry, melody, and dance, which culminated with Pindar, Simonides, and the early tragedians. To later – and moralizing – theorists this was the epoch of the 'educative' style, in contrast to the 'theatrical' or 'popular' style that developed in the fifth century.
>
> (*Oxford Classical Dictionary*: 711)

The author highlights the crucial feature of the overlap between ancient Greek rhythm in music and in the metres of poetry:

> The rhythms of Greek music were practically identical with the metres of Greek poetry; and, where the natural quantities of the syllables are distorted, such a distortion is also a concern of the metrist ... the Greek lyric metres themselves were elaborate partly because they were musical and choreographic as well as poetic rhythms.
>
> (*Oxford Classical Dictionary*: 712)

6 Davies, in Finley, ed., 1984: 97–8. For a brief review of the genre see Bowie, in Boardman, et. al., eds, 1991: 107–25. Trypanis (1981: 87–114) provides a useful overview of ancient Greek elegiac poetry. See also the concise account by Campbell, in *CHCL*: vol. 1, 202–21 and Bowra's reflections on the origins and coexistence of choral song and monody in 1961: 1–15. On the importance of the metrical pattern of choral and lyric composition see Bowra, 1961: 10–12.

7 Jebb, in Whibley, ed., 1968: 130. Elegiac lyric in effect intersperses the pentameter

NOTES

line between traditional dactylic hexameters – quite literally 'breaking up' or 'deconstructing' the rhythm of the homogeneous hexameter pattern; the performance of this ambivalent rhythm was accompanied with the flute or *aulos* rather than the resonant rhythm of the traditional lyre. This accompaniment may also have reinforced the element of difference within the unitary movement of dactylic hexameter. Cf. Bowie, in Boardman, *et al.*, eds, 1991: 109. Trypanis emphasizes the 'national' associations conected with the different Greek dialects and poetic forms: 'the flavour of Ionic had connotations of epic, Doric of choral poetry, and Aeolic of erotic verse. Such means of giving verse a special character were further developed by the Attic dramatists' (1981: 83).

8 Trypanis, 1981: 130.
9 Snodgrass, 1980: 174. On Terpander:

> Two facts, however, we do know about him. He founded a school of lyric poetry on his native Lesbos; and he was so famous as a *citharoedos*, or solo singer accompanying himself on the lyre, that he was invited to Sparta so that he might calm the passions of civil strife with his music.
> (Trypanis, 1981: 94)

'That Terpander was conceived as a solo-singer is clear from his being regularly designated as a *kitharoidos*' (Nagy, in Kennedy, ed., 1989: 42). Terpander, in fact, is often credited with inventing the seven-stringed lyre and setting Homer to music (cf. Evelyn-White, trans. 1914, 1936: xxxvii-xxxviii; Bowra, 1961: 9–10, 21–3).

10   Tyrtaios was composing martial elegies in which an older communal ethos still lived. The Spartans were the nearest approximation among the Greeks to the collectivist mentality. It is therefore fitting that their gift to the Lyric Age should have been the most collective of forms, the choral ode.
(McCulloh, 1972: 8)

Murray suggests that by the time of Tyrtaeus 'a new ethical principle had become established, the duty of the individual to the state' (1993: 135) and Bowra aptly refers to the martial elegiacs of Callinus and Tyrtaeus as 'the voices of regiments' (1961: 13).

> And perhaps most significantly, class consciousness and a set of class values emerged for the warriors: on the battlefield birth and wealth no longer mattered, compared with courage, in which all must be equal – should not these two principles of the battlefield, cooperation and equality, also determine the political life of the community?
> (Murray, 1993: 136)

> Tyrtaeus was certainly connected with the political reforms of his time, though he was not necessarily a prophet of the so-called Lycurgan constitution. He writes in an epic language, with many echoes of Homer, and at times he is unskilful in his adaptation of a Homeric motive to new uses ... His importance is more political than literary, though he seems to have influenced Solon. The Spartans are said to have sung his songs on the march.
> (Bowra, 'Tyrtaeus', *Oxford Classical Dictionary*, 1102)

Also Jaeger, 'Tyrtaeus on true arete', in *Five Essays* (Montreal: Casalini, 1966). Finley speaks of the 'sixth-century revolution' which produced the distinctive Spartan social system with its stratification of land allotments, helots and *perioeci* (the 'dwellers-about'), the military-governmental system, and the ritual system of *rites de passage*, *agoge*, age classes, *syssitia*, etc. (see Finley, 1975: 161–77, esp. 162–4).

11 'The Spartans about 600 BC are not yet stereotyped, but fresh and vigorous, in

NOTES

touch with foreigners; a people fond of poetry, musical contests, and art' (Hicks, in Whibley, ed., 1968: 87). See also Huxley, 1962: chs 1–4; G. L. Huxley, *Greek Epic Poetry* (London, 1969), Cartledge, 1979: Parts 1–2; Finley, 1981: 106–15; Segal, in *CHCL*: vol. 1, Part 1, 124–60, 181–203; W. G. Forrest, *A History of Sparta* (London: Hutchinson, 1968); Michell, 1964; E. Rawson, *The Spartan Tradition in European Thought* (Oxford: Oxford University Press, 1969): ch. 1; and Murray, 1993: 159–80. The chapter on Alcman in Bowra, 1961: 16–73 is still essential reading. On seventh-century Sparta as the social context of Alcman's creativity:

> the wealthy patronage of the Spartan state during its years of peaceful abundance, in the later seventh century, attracted talented poets and gave them the means to produce their choruses for the public festivals. Significantly, most of the earlier of these commissioned poets were from the East, the older and subtler culture. The Eastern influence and the years of peace are perhaps the explanation for the un-Spartan playfulness and charm of the first surviving choral poet, Alkman.
> (McCulloh, 1972: 9)

Cf.: 'Alcman's poems, often down-to-earth and hearty, often highly poetical and spirited, reflect a Spartan life otherwise almost unknown to us' (Ehrenberg, 1964: 34). The crucial event that destroyed this free-living culture was the Second Messenian War which 'started a social revolution which was to bring back their traditional militarism, as preached by Tyrtaeus. The so-called Lycurgan order slowly stifled most cultural activities and made of Sparta from the second half of the sixth century a military camp and an authoritarian state' (Ehrenberg, 1964: 35; cf. Bowra, 1961: 19–20: 'in the rich cycle of its festivals Spartan life offered full opportunities for a poet who could interpret the spirit of its rites and ceremonies' (20; cf. 72–3)).

12 Archilochus 'perhaps the first great personal poet of European literature' (Davies, in I. M. Finley, ed., 1984: 99), 'the first historical Western personality, and for us, the impoverished heirs, the inceptor of European lyric' (McCulloh, in Barnstone, trans., 1972: 2); 'He conveys a stronger and more intimate sense of personality than any other ancient Greek poet' (Levi, 1985: 67); 'he spoke unashamedly about himself. His frankness horrified, while it delighted, posterity, and his songs of hate struck Pindar as an awful example of the harm that a man's tongue can do to him' (Bowra, 1961: 13); 'an unpleasant character who started the fashion of writing about oneself'; Tarn, in Sir Ernest Barker, et. al., eds, *The European Inheritance* (Oxford: Clarendon Press, 1954): 163; cf. A. R. Burn, 1960: 159–70; Fränkel, 1975, 132–51. See also: Fränkel, 1975: 148–51; and Trypanis, 1981: 83–7.

13 First

> there had to be the discovery of an individual voice and of its ability to command attention. But, within perhaps a generation of the *Odyssey* and the *Works and Days*, we are confronted with the extraordinary figure of Archilochos of Paros.
> (Snodgrass, 1980: 169)

And one of the 'extraordinary' pursuits of this 'extraordinary' figure is his commitment to the institution of writing poetry:

> the variety of his metres, the intensely personal tone of many of his poems, the wide range of subject matter and above all the freedom from formula make it unlikely that his work could have survived the centuries by any other means than through written copies of the poet's own manuscripts.
> (Knox, *CHCL*: vol. 1, Part 4, 156–7)

NOTES

The commodification and circulation of Archilochus' poetry may explain the appearance of his name in the work of Heraclitus (DK B42) and others (cf. Pindar *Olympian* IX.1; *Pythian* II.55).

14 A practice that was later emulated by the Eleatic philosopher, Xenophanes. Archilochus is conventionally presented as the founder of the iambic lyric (Oliva, 1981: 172). He is mentioned by Herodotus in a related context: 'the iambic verses of Archilochus of Parus' (1.12), cf. Trypanis, 1981: 84–5.

> The origins of iambic poetry are to be found in the early fertility cults, a widespread feature of which was coarse, often violently obscene invective. This literary 'ugliness', corresponding to a deliberate 'ugliness' in some religious art, was supposed to have an apotropaic function; its purpose was to ward off evil. Such ritual obscenity came to be so closely associated with the iambus that 'to speak in iambs' came to mean the same as 'to abuse' or 'to revile.
> (Trypanis, 1981: 83)

15 Frs 1 and 2, trans. Lattimore.
16 Horace, in Dorsch, trans., 1965: 81–2. Compare the Archilochean lines of Aristophanes' *Peace* 1128ff. The Horatian reading is repeated by historians of ancient Greek poetry:

> [Archilochus'] greatest legacy to Greek poetry is the change of emphasis from the heroic and impersonal to the contemporary and personal, without which lyrical poetry could never have developed. For this reason he is much more than the creator of lyrical satire and the first realist in Western poetry; he is the ultimate parent of all personal literature in Western lands.
> (Trypanis, 1981: 85)

Burn, however, dampens the enthusiasm of those who take Archilochus to be the sole generic innovator of Archaic poetic forms: 'Archilochus' work as a sheer inventor of metres can be exaggerated; his greatness is in the fact that he used them superbly well' (1960: 169). Bowra adopts the same line: 'His influence was greater on the tone and language of monody than on its technique ... He put the self into poetry, but he himself preferred an art which was closer to speech than to song' (1961: 14). Gregory Nagy makes the direct link between iambic and Bakhtin's 'carnivalesque':

> This general notion of 'iambic', with its emphasis on fertility, is analogous to the concept of 'carnival' as applied by M. M. Bakhtin to the traditions inherited by François Rabelais in the sixteenth century... we see a striking analogy with the figure of Archilochus and the institution of Old Comedy as represented by Aristophanes.
> (in Kennedy, ed., 1989: 65)

17 This is why Peter Levi is undoubtedly right in his observation that 'Archilochos and his attitudes deserve a book of their own, few as his fragments are' (1985: 68–9). Trypanis:

> It has been pointed out that his attitude is rooted in the great age of colonization, which challenged the status and ideals of the aristocracy; for overseas expansion had opened the eyes of many Greeks to the possibilities of other social systems. But Archilochus' unashamed frankness in rejecting the heroic ethos horrified posterity.
> (Trypanis, 1981: 84)

Archilochus 'completed the transformation from the epic to the lyric age, and he

NOTES

formulated a revolutionary programme with Greek clarity' (Fränkel, 1975: 149). We might also note McCulloh's observation concerning the cultural role of Archilochus' formal innovations in the genre of iambic verse:

> The greatest offspring in Greek of iambic poetry was the dialog in Athenian drama. The drama is thus a hybrid of the chorodic and iambic traditions. But it has been further maintained [by Highet, in his *Classical Tradition*, 131] that even Shakespeare's blank verse originally came, by way of Italian Renaissance imitations, from ancient drama and thus originally from the iambic poets.
>
> (McCulloh, in Barnstone, trans., 1972: 6)

The logological or 'archaological' links between satire, iambic and blank verse, tragedy, and dramatic theatre to the folk-cultural, ceremonial-liturgical, and 'carnivalesque' forms antedating lyric poetry should also be noted at this juncture.

18 'Humanity steps forward as it is, in heroic nakedness; with virile resolution it strips itself of all restricting conventions and all meretricious adornment' (Fränkel, 1975: 150). 'Archilochus' revolution did not of course transform the whole of subsequent poetry. It seems to have been the regions of the Eastern Greeks, the Aiolians and Ionians of Asia Minor and the islands, which proved most receptive to the new spirit' (McCulloh, in Barnstone, trans., 1972: 8). For a recent translation of the so-called 'seduction poem' of Archilochus see Levi, 1985: 69.

19 See Trypanis, 1981: 95; Campbell, in *CHCL* 'Early Greek poetry', 168–73; D.L. Page, *Sappho and Alcaeus* (Oxford: Oxford University Press, 1955): 169ff. and Alcaeus' verses in the Lattimore, trans., 1960: 42–5.

20 Aeschylus, *Seven Against Thebes* 1ff., 794ff. cf. Plato, *Euthydemus* 291C–D; Sophocles, *Oedipus Tyrannos* 22–30, translation of F. Storr modified. The 'storm-tossed' ship of state would later become a stock figure for the Athenian orators (for example, Lysias, *Against Andocides* 6.48–9).

21 *Oedipus Tyrannos*, 100–1; cf. 103–4; Sophocles places the same figure in Creon's mouth in *Antigone* (163ff.). Cf. Praxagora's speech in Aristophanes' *The Assemblywomen*, where the fact that the Athenian 'ship of state' is adrift is given as grounds for her plan to place political power in the hands of the women of Athens (43–109).

22 Barnstone, trans., 1972: 60. Cf. Pindar's *Pythian* X, written in 498 BC to celebrate the dictator of Thessaly, Thorax and his brothers, Eurypylos and Thrasydaios; the last lines of *Pythian* X.4 read:

> I have praise yet
> For his excellent brothers, who bear on high
> The Thessalians' land
> And bring it to power
> In the hands of good men lies
> The noble piloting of cities
> Handed from father to son.
>
> (in Bowra, 1969: 24)

23 Alcaeus, trans. R. Lattimore, pp. 44–5; also in Loeb editions, *Greek Lyric*: vol. 1, 305–6. Also D. L. Page, *Sappho and Alcaeus* (Oxford: Oxford University Press, 1955). Trypanis observes: 'His success arises from the immediacy with which he conveys impressions of the world about him. Dionysius [Dionysius of Halicarnassus] was right when he gave as the characteristics of Alcaeus' poetry, brevity, sweetness and force' (1981: 96). For a full analysis of Alcaeus' poetry and its social context see Bowra, 1961: 130–75. On the political context of the Mytieine tyranny

NOTES

and its significance in Alcaeus' verse see Page, *Sappho and Alcaeus*, Oxford: Oxford University Press, 1955: Part 2.
24 Sappho, in Lattimore, trans., 1960: 42. While poets like Tyrtaeus and Semonides used the elegiac metre for ideological and mysogynous purposes, some of the finest lyric poems in the Greek elegiac form were created by the female voices of Sappho, Corinna, Myrtis, Telesilla, and Praxilla. The work of these poets only survives in fragments or as citations in other, later authors (see Segal, in *CHCL*: 'Early Greek poetry', 181–203, esp. 198–200. On the poetry of Corinna, Telesilla, and Praxilla see Trypanis, 1981: 100–2.)
25 (Voigt) Hephaestion, *Handbook on Metres* 11.5; in Campbell, trans., 1982: vol. 1, 168B. According to Trypanis the attribution of this poem to Sappho is now thought to be doubtful (1981: 98).
26 In Barnstone, trans., 1972: 95.
27 Julian, *Letter to Iamblichus*, 183; Campbell, trans., 1982: vol. 1, 48.
28 In Barnstone, trans., 1972: 72.
29 In Barnstone, trans., 1972: 74.
30 In Barnstone, trans., 1972: 74.
31 Trans. Lattimore; cf. Campbell, trans., 1982: vol. 1, 16: 'Some say a host of cavalry, others of infantry, and others of ships, is the most beautiful thing on the black earth, but I say it is whatsoever a person loves' (P. Oxy. 1231, Fr. 1). The fragmentary text from the papyrus is given by Bowra, 1961: 180, with translation.
32 In Lattimore, trans., 1960: 39–40; cf. the 'fire' of foreknowledge which consumes the prophetess Cassandra in Aeschylus' *Agamemnon* 1255–60. Cf. 'Longinus', *On the Sublime*. 10.1–3; Loeb Classical Library, 1. 31. Cf. Trypanis' observation: 'the fact remains that it is only the physical beauty of her companions that Sappho praises; there is never a word about any spiritual, moral or intellectual qualities they may have' (1981: 98).
33 In Lattimore, trans., 1960: 41–2.
34 In Lattimore, trans., 1960: 49. 'It will be noticed that it was in Lesbos, Boeotia and the Peloponnese that women were able to win a lasting reputation for poetry, certainly not in Athens' (Trypanis, 1981: 102).
35 In Barnstone, trans., 1972, 102–3. Cf. the aged Cephalus in his response to Socrates in *Republic* I: we old men meet and lament

> longing for the lost joys of youth and recalling to mind the pleasures of wine, women, and other things thereto appertaining, and they repine in the belief that the greatest things have been taken from them and that then they lived and now it is no life at all.
> (*Rep.* 329B; cf. Solon, Frs. 20, 22)

Trypanis: 'He [Mimnermus] is the first hedonist in Western literature, and his influence descends not only to all subsequent Greek love poetry, but also to Propertius, Tibullus and Ovid and, through them, to all later Western poets of love' (1981: 88).
36 In Lattimore, trans., 1960: 8–12. Also J. M. Edmonds, *Elegy and Iambus*, II (London: William Heinemann/Loeb Classical Library 1931). See H. Lloyd-Jones, *Females of the Species: Semonides on Women* (London, 1975). Hesiod continues the same tradition: 'Do not let a flaunting woman coax and deceive you; she is after your barn. The man who trusts womankind trusts deceivers' (*Works and Days*, 373–5; also 67, 68, 82–3, 586–7, 704).

> Behind these attacks no doubt lies the sexual antagonism which is an element of universal and age-old folk lore and which must have played its part in folk festivals. Semonides describes nine evil types of woman, seven of which

NOTES

are compared with animals – the swine, the fox, the dog, the ass, the weasel, the horse and the ape. At the end he acknowledges the existence of one good type, sprung, he says, from the bee.

(Trypanis, 1981: 86)

37 Fränkel provides a useful translation of Fr. 7 (1975: 202–4). Juvenal: 'There never was a case in court in which the quarrel was not started by a woman';

> There is nothing that a woman will not permit herself to do, nothing that she deems shameful, when she encircles her neck with green emeralds, and fastens huge pearls to her elongated ears: there is nothing more intolerable than a wealthy woman.
>
> (*Satires*, VI, 83–136; VI, 242–3, 457–60)

Misogyny and preaching on the evils of women are practices that reach back to the classics of early Greek poetry and into the preliterate world of folk-poetry. In Hesiod's *Works and Days*, the diligent farmer is instructed on marriage in the following terms:

> Bring a wife to your house when you are the right age, neither far short of thirty nor much older: this is the right age for marriage. The woman should be four years beyond maturity and marry in the fifth. Marry a virgin so that you can teach her proper conduct, and make a point of choosing someone who lives near, but take care not to make a marriage that will be a joke to your neighbours. For there is nothing a man can win that is better than a good wife, and nothing worse than a bad one – a parasite who scorches her husband without fire, however strong he is, and brings him to cruel old age'
> (695–705)

Earlier Hesiod offers Perses some advice on beginning an *oikos*: 'First of all, get a house, and a woman and an ox for the plough – a slave woman and not a wife, to follow the oxen as well' (*Works* 404–10; cf. *Theogony* 590ff.); cf. the didactic poetry of Phocylides of Miletus (Fr. 2).

Semonides' poem on the same topic in the late seventh century repeats Hesiod's sentiments almost word for word: 'No better thing befalls a man than a good wife, no worse thing than a bad one' (Fr. 6). Cf. the speech of the ghost of Agamemnon at *Od.* 11.405ff. (cf. 'There is no trusting in women', Iliad 11.456); Creon's speech against women in Sophocles' *Antigone* 640ff.: 'Son, be warned, And let no woman fool away thy wits'; or, finally, the encyclopaedic defamation of women in Book IV of Lucretius' *De Rerum Natura* (1141–1287). The tradition culminates in Arthur Schopenhauer's vitriolic essay 'On woman' (in 1974: vol. 2).

38 See Easterling, in *CHCL*: 'Early Greek poetry', 112–16. C. M. Bowra in his article 'Homer' in the *Oxford Classical Dictionary* assembles evidence of the early poets' knowledge and intertextual references to the *Iliad* and *Odyssey*: Tyrtaeus (Frs 6–7, 21–8 from *Il.* 22.71–6, fr. 8.29–34 from *Il.* 16.215–17); Semonides (fr. 29 from *Il.* 6.146); Alcman (Fr. 1. 48 from *Il.* 9.124, Fr. 73 from *Il.* 3.39); Archilochus (Fr. 65 from *Od.* 22.412, Fr. 41 from *Od.* 14.228, fr. 38 from *Il.* 18.309; Hesiod (*Works and Days* 159–60 from *Il.* 12.23 and *Theogony* 340ff. from *Il.* 12. 20ff.). See Bowra, *Oxford Classical Dictionary*: 524–6, esp. 524.

39 Easterling, in *CHCL*: 'Early Greek poetry', 116. Cf. Trypanis, 1977: 54–5, 103.

40 Stesichorus of Himera in Sicily (c. 640–555 BC) is the chief representative of the Dorian lyric in its earlier period. Heracles, Orestes, the Atreidae, Odysseus, Helen, and other persons of the epos, were taken by him as subjects for hymns, – a form of poem previously reserved for gods or demigods. He was, in fact, a lyric interpreter of epic tradition; his dialect was epic, with a Dorian tinge. It was he

who established the tripartite structure in *strophe, antistrophe* and *epode* as the norm for the choral lyric ... Further, he broke new ground by his lyric treatment of love-stories in his poems entitled *Daphnis, Rhadina* and *Calyca* – precursors of the Greek novel.

(Jebb, in Whibley, ed., 1968: 132)

Trypanis confirms Jebb's observation: 'A new fragment has confirmed what the *Suda* had previously maintained, namely, that it was Stesichorus who replaced Alcman's single strophe with the triple division of the epodic scheme. This enlargment of the choral framework suited his epic subjects, which called for a more massive structure; and this lead of Stesichorus' was followed by Pindar' (1981: 104); cf. 'His poetry combined grandeur with imaginative interpretations of old themes, and his "twist" to the Helen legend was later developed in Euripides' *Helen*' (Woodhead, 1962: 138).

A later commentator goes to the heart of Stesichorus' linguistic experiments by noting that he

> may well have shared his contemporaries' growing malaise about the epic as the norm for measuring human experience. His recasting not only of the form, but also of the substance of epic material is an indication of his awareness that the epic mould was not entirely satisfying.
>
> (Segal, in *CHCL*: 'Early Greek poetry', 149–50)

41 This is presumably an example of Hipponax's poetry which Fränkel omitted in silence: 'Such scraps do at least give an inkling of the subject and the style in which it was treated. Some are so filthy they cannot be reproduced' (1975: 216). Knox's analysis can be found in *CHCL*: 'Early Greek poetry', 121–2; see also Barnstone, trans., 1972: 119–20. The concluding mock-choral song of Aristophanes' *Peace* is an obscene celebration of marriage nuptials ('Sing hey for Hymen ...') and includes the line 'How sweet is her fig, how ripe is your cock'; trans. Alan H. Sommerstein in the Penguin edition, 1990: 146.

42 On the iambic *skazon* (*choliambus*) as the key to the genealogy of satire:

> *Satire* was more especially the purpose to which iambic verse was applied by its earlier masters, as Archilochus (c. 650 BC), Semonides of Amorgos (c. 640), and Hipponax of Ephesus (c. 540), the inventor of the 'scazon'. This side of the iambic tradition was contained in Attic comedy. The satirical vein was not, however, the only one in which these writers used iambic (and the kindred trochaic) metre. Solon's iambics ... have an energy and dignity which render them a worthy prelude to the iambic verse of Attic tragedy.
>
> (Jebb, in Whibley, ed., 1968: 131)

Knox concludes his account of Hipponax' work by observing that:

> Hipponax remains a mystery. We have lost the matrix of these fascinating but puzzling fragments; ripped from their frame they leave us in doubt whether to take them seriously as autobiographical material (unlikely, but it has been done), as complete fiction (but there is no doubt that Bupalus and Athenis were real people), as part of a literary adaptation of some ritual of abuse (a *komos* or something similar), or as dramatic scripts for some proto-comic performance. Whatever they were, they are a pungent reminder of the variety and vitality of archaic Greek literature and of how much we have lost.
>
> (*CHCL*: 'Early Greek poetry', 123)

43 Wender, trans., 1985: 111; cf. Barnstone, trans., 1972. But this kind of pessimism

did not prevent Theognis from expressing faith in the 'immortalizing' power of poetic language: 'And even after you pass to the gloom and the secret chambers of sorrow, Death's house hidden under the ground, even in death your memory shall not pass, and it shall not die, but always, a name and a song in the minds of men' (Theognis 237–54, in Lattimore, trans. 1960: 29). See Nagy, in T. J. Figueria and Gregory Nagy, eds, *Theognis of Megara: Poetry and the Polis* (Baltimore: Johns Hopkins University Press, 1985): 22–81.
44 Wender, trans., 1985: 119.
45 *Op. cit.*, 145, 142, 145 respectively. See also K. J. Dover, *Greek Homosexuality*, London: Duckworth, 1978.
46 Barnstone, trans., 1972: 114. Peter Levi comments: 'There existed no social convention in his world for any heterosexual kind of love-song. Marriage was linked to property and alliance, it was not subject to the free play of passion or of art' (1985: 88). On Ibycus' work see Bowra, 1961: 241–67; the Greek text of the poem cited in the text can be found in Bowra, 1961: 260.
47 Campbell, trans., 1982: vol. 2, 105. See Bowra, 1961: 268–307.
48 See Robert Fagles, *Bacchylides: Complete Poems* (New Haven: Yale University Press, 1961); A. P. Burnet, *The Art of Bacchylides* (Cambridge, Mass. and London: Harvard University Press, 1985); Lefkowitz, 1976. Peter Levi has a lucid chapter on Simonides and Bacchylides in his history of Greek literature, 1985: 133–49.
49 See Lattimore,trans., 1960; Bowra, 1961: esp. 373–97. Also Kennedy in Kennedy, ed., 1989: 78–91; Oswyn Murray, ed., *Sympotica* (Oxford University Press, 1990); and Murray, 1993: 201–19.

5 PINDAR AND THE AGE OF LITERARY CONSCIOUSNESS

1 The *ethos* of struggle and competition as a supreme value is unique to ancient Greek society. In the great pan-Hellenic Games it has been estimated that around forty to fifty thousand people attended, 'a figure larger than the total populations of all but ten or twelve city-states' (Finley, in Finley, ed., 1984: 7–8; cf. his 'Foreword' to Easterling and Muir, eds, 1985: xix). Finley writes: 'An estimated 40,000 men [*sic*] attended, many coming from considerable distance – the largest number of people assembled in one place on a particular occasion (other than a few major battles) in all Greek history' (in Easterling and Muir, eds, 1985: xix). Indirect evidence suggests that the numbers of visitors to the games led to the creation of 'tent cities' around the host city (the comic poet Aristophanes refers to the practice in relation to the Isthmian Games at *Peace* 865ff.).

> Some of the odes were composed to be recited at the scene of the festival, whereas others were sung when the victor returned to his home city. The ode would also be repeated on successive anniversaries at banquets, festivals or processions in honour of the victor. One at least was chanted by the poet himself as a monody in the halls of the victor's palace.
> (Trypanis, 1981: 110)

The largest amphitheatres designed for the tragic festivals were built to accommodate as many as 15,000 spectators (Taylor, 1986: xxiii). On the religious basis of the Games see Cartledge, in Easterling and Muir, eds, 1985: 98–127, esp. 103–15.
2 On the notion of poetry as 'craft' and 'craftiness' see *Isthmian* I.51 and *Pythian* I.92.

> In fact, one wonders if his poems can ever have been readily understood

when sung. In *Nemean* V the poet tells us how his sweet song will 'sail off from Aegina in the big ships and the little fishing boats' as they return from the festival. Yet one cannot easily imagine a Dorian fisherman who could seize at one hearing a song of such complexity.

(Trypanis, 1981: 113)

The main reason for this is, of course, that Pindaric odes were never intended for Dorian fishermen, but were transcribed by a fully literate mind, performed before a skilled literary audience, and probably read and examined in written forms after their first 'oral' performance. *Olympian* X opens with the line '*Read* me the name of the Olympian victor'. But the linguistic and contextual background for this 'reading' points toward a highly sophisticated and reflexive audience (on the intricacies of imagery and semantic complexity of the victory odes see Lefkowitz, 1976: ch. 1 on Pythian II, 'the most difficult of all Pindar's odes' and Ch. 4, a 'second reading'). As C. M. Bowra has also noted, Pindar's style 'like that of most Greek poetry, is a highly artificial creation with roots in a distant past', coming 'at the end of a long tradition' and condensing in himself 'the special outlook of the aristocratic age of Greece' (1969: xv-xvi). Bowra reinforces this point by noting that the epinician ode

> is extremely formal in structure and governed by strict rules. In its simpler form, as in *Pythian* VI or *Nemean* VIII, it consists of a series of strophes or stanzas, each of which is metrically identical with all the rest, and this identity extends even to small points of prosody. Alternatively, and more often, Pindar uses not a series of single, similar strophes, but a series of triads, or, as Ben Jonson called them, Turne, Counter-Turne, and Stand ... This is a very demanding structure, and its demands are seen more clearly when we find that no poem of Pindar is metrically the same as any other.
>
> (1969: xiii)

See: Pindar, 1919; Bowra, 'Pindar', in *Oxford Classical Dictionary*: 834; E. L. Bundy, *Studia Pindarica*, 2 vols (Berkeley: University of California Press, 1962); Lattimore, trans., 1959b; Bowra, trans., 1969; C. M. Bowra, *Pindar* (Oxford: Clarendon Press, 1964); C. Carey, *A Commentary on Five Odes of Pindar* (New York, 1981); J. H. Finley, *Pindar and Aeschylus* (Cambridge, Mass.: Harvard University Press, 1955); Nisetich, trans., 1980; Lefkowitz, 1976; R.W. Burton, *Pindar's Pythian Odes: Essays in Interpretation* (Oxford: Oxford University Press, 1962); U. von Wilamowitz-Moellendorff, *Pindaros* (Berlin: Weidmann, 1966).

3 *Nemean* VIII; *Pythian* XI; *Isthmian* VI.1. Cf. Fr. 21 (Bowra, trans., 1969).
4 *Nemean* XI.1. Cf. *Nemean* III.6ff., *Nemean* VIII. 39ff., and *Pythian* 9.103ff.,
5 *Pythian* VIII. Cf. 'We are such stuff/As dreams are made on/and our little life/Is rounded with a sleep', Shakespeare, *The Tempest* IV. i. The philosopheme of the 'democracy' of death was already a cliché by the end of the fifth century. The rhetor Isocrates repeats the theme: 'death is the sentence which fate has passed on all mankind, but to die nobly is the special honour which nature has reserved for the good' (*To Demonicus* I.43). The logographer Lysias writes:

> we know well that death is common to the basest and the noblest ... Death neither disdains the wicked nor admires the virtuous, but is even-handed with all ... Therefore it is fitting to consider those most happy who have closed their lives in risking them for the greatest and noblest ends ... their memory can never grow old, while their honour is every man's envy.
>
> (*Funeral Oration* 77–81, in Lysias, 1957)

Cf. Demosthenes, 1949: LX.37: 'of this pain we shall find the deity to be the cause,

NOTES

to whom mortal creatures must yield, but of the glory and honour the source is found in the choice of those who willed to die nobly.'
6 In Barnstone, trans., 1972: 160–1. Cf.

> What Pindar conveys in song is precisely the enhancement of consciousness which his athletes enjoy in the moment of triumph. This is the central inspiration of Pindar's work and accounts for his special quality. His vision is of a world in which both men and gods are active but all that really matters comes directly from the gods. For much of their time men lead a shadowy and unsubstantial existence, but when the gods send a divine brightness all is well with them. It is this brightness that Pindar seeks to convey ... What Pindar catches is the joy beyond ordinary emotions as it transcends and transforms them. It can be found in athletic success, convivial relaxation, song and music, friendship and love, in many natural sights and sounds, in prayer and hymns.
> (Bowra, 1969: xvi–xvii)

Cf. Bowra's essay 'Pindar', in *Oxford Classical Dictionary*: 833–4, where he suggests that Pindar

> seems to have made the rejoicing over victory a religious occasion on which he demonstrated the power of men to find, temporarily, a happiness like that of the gods by displaying their *arete*. This *arete* was itself partly inborn and due to men's having divine blood in their veins.
> (*Oxford Classical Dictionary*: 834)

7 Trans. Lattimore.
8 *Nemean* VII. 20–2; see Russell and Winterbottom, eds, 1978: 4 for these texts. Also the self-references in *Olympian* VI.5 to his own Boeotian ancestry, to his Spartan affiliations (*Pythian* V.3), to the poetic craft in *Olympian* I ('But if, my heart, you would speak', *Olympian* I.1, 'Like our joyful songs', *Olympian* I. 1, *Olympian* VI.5); the insistent poetic 'I' in *Isthmian* I, *Pythian* II, *Pythian* III, and *Pythian* IX: 'This song I am sending, like a Phoenician merchant, over the grey sea' (*Pythian* II.3); references to earlier epic and elegiac poets – Homer in *Nemean* VII.2, *Pythian* IV.13; Archilochus' Olympian ode in *Olympian* IX.1, Archilochus' slanderous verse in *Pythian* II.3.55; the reference to the constraining rules of the victory ode itself ('I am kept from telling the whole long tale by the rules of song and the hurrying hours', 'I cannot go through the whole tale of Aiakos' sons', *Nemean* IV.5 and *Nemean* IV.9; cf. *Pythian* VIII.2); the virtues of poetic brevity (*Pythian* I.5, *Isthmian* I.4: 'Truly what is kept in silence/brings even larger delight').
9 'Path' here translates Pindar's *odon, Olympian Odes* VII.46; cf. *Olympian* I.1: 'There are many wonders, and it may be/embroidered tales overpass the true account/and trick men's talk/with their enrichment of lies').
10 *Aletheia, Olympian Odes* XIII.95–9.
11 *Nemean* IV.1–10.
12 *Nemean* VII.10–20; cf. *Pythian* I.
13 Cf.:

> Truth does not always
> Gain if she displays
> Her face unflinchingly;
> And silence is often a man's wisest counsel.
> (*Nemean* V.1)

And here Martin Heidegger's translation of *aletheia* as 'un-concealment' aptly captures Pindar's notion of the 'truthfulness' of poetic utterance.

NOTES

14 Cf. *Pythian* III.100–15; cf. *Nemean* VI and VII.
15 *Pythian* XI.
16 *Nemean* VII, in Bowra, trans., 1969; cf. the Loeb Classical Edition, in the translation of Sir John Sandys (Pindar, 1915) and Richmond Lattimore's version, in 1959b.
17 In Lattimore, trans., 1960: 41. Pindar appears to have something similar in mind in the well-known text on the separate existence of body and soul:

> And all men's bodies follow the call
> Of overpowering death.
> And yet there still will linger behind
> A living image [*eidolon*] of life,
> For this alone has come from the gods.
> It sleeps while the members are active;
> But to those who sleep themselves
> It reveals in myriad visions
> The fateful approach
> Of adversities or delights.
>   (Fr. 131, cited by Jaeger, 1947: 75)

18 Sophocles, *Oedipus at Colonus* 1125. For tragedy see Vickers, 1973 and P. Walcot, *Greek Drama in its Theatrical and Social Context* (Cardiff: University of Wales Press, 1976).
19 *Olympian* I.83–4. Cf. the theme of 'undying *kleos*' in Sophocles (e.g. *Electra* 60). Later Nietzsche would evoke the same existential attitude by speaking of life as 'eternal recurrence', *amor fati*, the *'will to power'*, *'joyful wisdom'*, and so forth. Cf. the observation of P. Cartledge: 'death in Olympic competition was revealingly placed in the Greek scale of values on a par with the highest glory of all, death in battle on behalf of one's city' (in Easterling and Muir, eds, 1985: 112–13). Also S. G. Miller, *Arete: Greek Sports from Ancient Sources* (Berkeley: University of California Press, 1991).
20 *The Epic of Gilgamesh* in the translation of N. K. Sanders, 1960.
21 We recall the theme of Chapter 1, that many, if not all, of the mythic narratives of Archaic Greece are dramaturgies of 'value conflicts' – among which the 'dialectic' of nature and freedom is pre-eminent. See Chester Starr, *Individual and Community: The Rise of the Polis* (Oxford: Oxford University Press, 1986) and C. Segal, *The Theme of the Mutilation of the Corpse in the Iliad* (Leiden: E.J. Brill, 1971).
22 Homer celebrates individual heroes, whereas in the odes the victors are linked not only with their ancestry and kin but also with their communities in the honour that has come to them. In short, in the archaic *agon* there emerges that dialogue, and ultimately that tension, between individual and community which has been an element in western society ever since.
    (Finley, 1981: 133)
23 Trypanis, 1981: 112–13; cf. Finley, 1981: 139–41; Fränkel, 1975: ch. 9, 505–8. Pindar was the last great representative of the Archaic lyric. Unlike Archilochus he 'replaced the first person by the impersonal 'one' of society; the transitory and the unique were to him no more than illustrations of the universal and eternal' (Fränkel, 1975: 506). Trypanis also notes the 'unrepresentative' character of the Pindaric ode:

> Like most other forms of Greek literature, the lyric had been moving away from obscure force in the direction of lucidity – and in the writings of Simonides and Bacchylides it had already passed from one to the other. But Pindar set himself so firmly against this stream that we could find no greater

contrast to the free expression of personal feeling of Ionian and Aeolian poetry, from Archilochus to Sappho, than Pindar's subordination of his verse to a religious and aristocratic ideal.

(1981: 112)

24 Bowra concludes his *Oxford Classical Dictionary* article, 'Pindar' with the following thumbnail summary:

> Pindar was a true conservative in politics, morals, and religion, but the glory of his poetry lies largely in his sense of joy and honour. He was capable of deep emotion and, at times, of a sublimity to which there is no parallel.
> ('Pindar', *Oxford Classical Dictioary*: 834)

Also Fränkel, 1975: 425–508; R.W. Burton, *Pindar's Pythian Odes: Essays in Interpretation* (Oxford: Oxford University Press, 1962); L. R. Farrell, *The Works of Pindar: Volume 2: Critical Commentary* (London: Macmillan, 1932); Nisetich, trans., 1980: 1–77.

6 ORPHISM: ORPHIC DISCOURSE DURING THE ARCHAIC PERIOD

1 For the cultural background and influence of Orphism and the Eleusinian Mysteries, see L. J. Alderink, *Creation and Salvation in Ancient Orphism* (California, 1981); D'Alviella, 1981; Dodds, 1951; Farnell, 1896–1909; Guthrie, 1952, 1977; Harrison, 1962: esp. 478–571; Linforth, 1941; G. E. Mylonas, *Eleusis and the Eleusinian Mysteries* (Princeton: Princeton University Press, 1961); H. W. Parke, *Greek Oracles* (London: Hutchinson, 1967); Parke, 1977; N. J. Richardson, *The Homeric Hymn to Demeter* (Oxford: Oxford University Press, 1979); Rohde, 1925; G. Van Groningen, *First Century Gnosticism: Its Origins and Motifs* (Leiden, E. J. Brill, 1967); Parke and Wormell, 1956.

By the early decades of the fifth century the Eleusinian Mysteries had been incorporated into the Athenian state religion and 'a temple of the two Goddesses was built under the Acropolis and called the Eleusinion; and the Eleusinian Mysteries became one of the chief festivals of the Attic year, conducted by the King [*basileus*]' (Bury and Meiggs, 1975: 194); also Parker, in *OH*: 306–29, esp. 322–4; see also Parker, 1983: 15ff., 66–9, 130–43); Dodds, 1951: 28ff.; and Guthrie, 1977: 284–5, 287–94. The actual conduct of the Mysteries and arcane initiation ceremonies is still the subject of some controversy. In broad outlines it involved an imitation of the process of death, descent into the underworld (usually a cavern or deep cave) and rebirth (dramatized by ascent from the Cave). In many of these ceremonies the presiding God would be Hermes, the 'mediator' between Gods and men and the divinity responsible for conducting souls to the underworld (*psychopompos*):

> There was certainly a long series of initiation ceremonies and, in the course of a great feast held at night, the devotees re-enacted the drama centred on Demeter and Kore, reliving the changing moods of despair, anger, hope and liberating joy. They felt face to face with the powers of life and death, were reborn as the children of Demeter and became one with Kore. It was said that those who had partaken of the mysteries at Eleusis were thrice blessed; for them there would be life in the realm of the dead.
> (Erik Lund, Mogens Pihl, and Johannes Slok, *A History of European Ideas* (1962), trans. W. Glyn Jones (London: C. Hurst and Company, 1971): 94)

NOTES

Cf:

> The ensuing journey entailed a descent (*kathodos*) into a subterranean chamber echoing to harsh and threatening voices, then turnings and gropings through perilous labyrinthine passages which, according to Plutarch, 'create amazement, trembling and terror'. Origen, quoting an earlier account, speaks of a terrifying 'masque of phantoms', perhaps representing the denizens of the underworld.
> (Walker, 1989: 19–20; and Finley, in Finley, ed., 1984: 6)

For other ancient evidence see Xenophon, *Hellenica* 2.3.10 and his account of the Alcibiades affair relating to the profanation of the statues of Hermes dedicated to the Eleusinian Mysteries. See also Otto 1923; Hans Jonas, *The Gnostic Religion*, 2nd edn. (Boston: Beacon Press, 1963); A. D. Nock, *Conversion* (Oxford: Clarendon Press, 1933): ch. 11; K. Rudolf, *Gnosis: The Nature and History of Gnosticism* (San Francisco: Harper and Row, 1983); and the useful short survey of the Gnostic tradition in Walker, 1989. Translations of the Gnostic scripts are available in Layton, 1987.

The 'incorporation' and 'diffusion' of Orphic theogony, mystery cults, and the celeberation of Dionysus (at Athens in the Greater Dionysia) was not, however, a homogeneous process; it was subject to numerous local factors and variations; in historical fact it was connected with the struggle for economic and political power known as the 'age of the tyrants'. Orphism along with the new cult of Dionysus and the Mysteries provided useful channels – new semiotic media – for the manipulation and redirection of popular religious and political emotions, particularly in the struggles against the power of the traditional aristocracy and its Olympian ideology – and in this form these 'alternative religions' with their 'dangerous' conceptions of the self were one of a number of 'techniques of reflexivity' used by powerful figures and families in their attempt to consolidate their power and rule (other techniques being the physical imposition of rigorous bodily regimes, an increasing awareness of the importance of corporeal regulation, the fostering of public tragedy and comedy, patronage of the arts and civic architecture during the same period). Cf:

> Originally the orgiastic character of the Dionysian religion had been looked upon as something quite alien, an insult to all municipal order, as is clear from the myths of Pentheus and Lycurgus. But in the sixth century – often for political reasons – it came into favour with the tyrants, who were the representatives of the social stratum newly coming into power. We can see this change, for example, in the displacement of the old civic hero Adrastus of Sicyon by the Dionysiac cult under the rule of the tyrant Cleisthenes, and in the mighty rise of the Dionysiac festivals in Corinth under Periander and in Athens under the Peisistratidae, to which ceremonies the dithyramb and Attic tragedy and comedy owe their origin.
> (Jaeger, 1947: 57–8; see also under 'Dionysus', in Rose, 1989)

Moses Hadas writes of the political presuppositions of the 'Apollonian/Dionysian' duality:

> Apollo of Delphi was an old established Olympian who was concerned for religious conservatism and for the maintenance of ancestral usages in cults of heroic ancestors, loyalty to the traditions of the state, and the like. In its function as oracle the cult of the Delphian Apollo was in touch with the ruling classes in the cities, which it supported and by whom it was in turn supported. In the seventh century the peasant God Dionysus, a stranger to

NOTES

Olympus, makes his way into Greece, offering religious satisfactions to the common people which they were denied in the cult of Apollo. The rivalry of the two gods is reflected ... in different standards of approved conduct, the followers of Apollo (among whom almost all our writers are found) always counselling temperance, moderation, restraint – in a word, conservatism in all things – as against the fervour, emotional, innovating, tendencies of the followers of Dionysus. The religious rivalry was naturally an aspect of, an instrument in, political unrest. The 'tyrants' who rose to power by championing the cause of the common people against the aristocrats regularly patronized the religion of Dionysus. It was something in the nature of an eclipse for Apollo and a victory of Dionysus when under the Athenian 'tyrants' dramatic performances were made part of the Dionysian festivals. Though Apollo retained his antidemocratic character ... Dionysus became respectable in the Athenian democracy, and his votaries never felt bound as a sect.

(1950: 40–1)

2 DK: vol. 1, 43–51. For background information on Pherecydes of Syros see G. S. Kirk and J. E. Raven, *The Presocratic Philosophers*, 1971: 48–72; K. von Fritz, entry in Pauly-Wissowa, XIX, 2 (1938); Windelband, 1956: 27; Burnet, 1930: 7, who dates the earliest Orphic cosmogony back to the century of Hesiod; Jaeger, 1947: 55–72; Fränkel, 1975: 243–6; cf. Aristophanes, *Birds* 685ff. The accolade of being the first writer in prose is usually given to Anaximander rather than Pherecydes (see Harris, 1989: 50, n. 22; although cf. Fränkel, 1975: 243). However 'the fact that Pherecydes chose to write his cosmogony in prose, dispensing with the mnemonic assistance which verse would normally have offered to his hearers and readers, plainly marks an important step in the acceptance of written texts' (Harris, 1989: 50). In many ancient symbolisms we find world creation modelled on the birth of life from an egg; the *Upanishads* contains an archetypal instance: creation of the cosmos from chaos takes place through the self-manifestation of Brahman; the seed of this creation appears as an egg, which differentiates into the elements of the earth and the sky – 'What was the outer membrane is the mountains; that which was the inner membrane is the mist with the clouds. What were the veins were the rivers. What was the fluid within is the ocean' (*Chandogya Upanishad*, III, 19, 1–2, in Eliade, 1978: 113–14). For the religious and mythological background of Greek speculative cosmology and theology see: Burkert, 1985: chs 1–2; Burkert, *Structure and History in Greek Mythology and Ritual* (Berkeley: University of California Press, 1979); W. Burkert, *Homo Necans: The Anthropology of Ancient Greek Sacrificial Ritual and Myth* (Berkeley: University of California Press, 1983); W. Burkert, 'Craft versus sect: the problem of Orphics and Pythagoreans', in B. E. Meyer and E. P. Sanders, eds, *Jewish and Christian Self-Definition*, vol. 3 (London: SCM, 1982): 1–22; Cornford, 1957, 1965; Guthrie, 1952; Jaeger, 1947: esp. ch. 4; Onians, 1954; Kern, 1963; Lesky, 1966: 190–3; Nilsson, 1927.
Cf.

One must bear in mind that Orphism and its theologies were ranking intellectual phenomena in Greece at the time that Parmenides and Heraclitus began writing, and that *Pherecydes is a contemporary of Anaximander and belongs to the generation immediately preceding Pythagoras.*

(Ortega Y Gasset, 1967: 90)

Eduard Zeller ascribed an important role to the social and political changes from seventh to sixth-century Greece in stimulating speculative religious innovation and experiment:

381

NOTES

> The insecurity of property and life which the political revolutions brought with them could only intensify the deep innate feeling for the transience of all earthly things ... external insecurity ... a wide-spread internal uncertainty ... makes a striking contrast with the self-assured bearing of the Homeric heroes.
>
> (Zeller, 1969: 13)

Ironically, this impulse toward ecstatic practices, orgiastic cults, transcendent religious rites, and mystery religions represented a non-Hellenic current of culture; it stood full square against the ideology of the Homeric poems, Pindar's aristocratic lyric, and the pragmatism of Hesiod's world-view:

> This Orphic mystery religion is a complete reversal of the true Greek view of life, according to which the corporeal man is the real man and the soul merely a sort of strengthless shadowy image. In the Orphic philosophy on the other hand the eternal and indestructible is the soul, while the body is transient, unclean, and contemptible ... to the Orphic life here on earth is a sort of hell, an imprisonment, a punishment. It is only in the other world, after the liberation of the soul from the prison of the body, that the true divine existence awaits us ... this complete reversal of the original, pure Greek view of life, and the consequent change of values, especially the contempt and repudiation of the flesh, together with the practical asceticism arizing from this belief, is wholly foreign to the Greek nature.
>
> (Zeller, 1969: 15–16 and passim)

However, see Dodds, 1951; E. R. Dodds, ed., *Bacchae*, 2nd edn (Oxford: Oxford University Press, 1960): 97ff.; Burkert, 1992: ch. 3, esp. 124–7; Murray, 1912; Nilsson, 1940: ch. 3; 1957; Parke, 1967.

3 Pindar, Fr. 131 (96) (Pindar, 1919: 589; also see Pindar, *Olympian* II, *Nemean* VII.19–20, and Fr. 133. Cf:

> The Orphics had appropriated the belief in punishments in the Underworld. Though it was not peculiar to them it had a special note: whosoever had not undergone the purifications in this life was to lie in the mire in the Nether World; the initiated and righteous were to live in happiness. This belief appealed to the broad public and was important for Orphic practice. In the archaic age there was a tendency, opposed to general Greek ideas, to scorn this life and to attribute a higher value to the other life in which the soul is freed from the fetters of the body. This is consistent with Orphism.
>
> (Nilsson, in the Oxford Classical Dictionary: 759–60)

Cf. Dodds, 1951: 152; Jaeger, 1947: 73–89 and Bremmer, 1983. G. Reale comments that the Orphic interpretation of human existence

> was destined to revolutionize the ancient concept of life and death ... It postulates a new outline of the whole of existence, and in particular a mortification of the body and of all that which belongs to the body, and a life in relation to the soul and that which belongs to the soul.
>
> (1987: 292–304, 296–7)

4 The Apollonian-Dionysian polarity is, of course, a product of the speculative thought of Friedrich Nietzsche who not only saw the historical roots of tragedy in the cult of Dionysus, but theorized the worship of Dionysus as the metaphysical key to Greek civilization as a whole. Dionysus is the personification of the tragic 'will to live'. On the other-worldly attraction of the Mysteries and Orphic ritual during periods of acute social distress see Plato, *Phaedrus* 244D. Cf:

NOTES

> In such experiences of social and cosmic disorder, order is reduced to one's own person and is perhaps not to be found even there; these experiences produce certain extreme states of alienation in which death may appear as the release from a prison or as convalescence from the mortal disease of life. Practically nothing has changed in these fundamental symbolisms of alienation since the third millennium BC.
>
> (Voeglin, 1989: 75)

E. R. Dodds also writes that

> the post-mortem punishment did not explain why the Gods tolerated so much human sufferings, and in particular the unmerited suffering of the innocent. Reincarnation did. On that view no human soul is innocent: all were paying, in various degrees, for crimes of varying atrocity committed in former lives. And all that squalid mass of suffering, whether in this world or in another, was but a part of the soul's long education – an education that would culminate at last in its release from the cycle of birth and return to its divine origin. Only in this way, and on this cosmic time-scale, could justice in its full archaic sense – the justice of the law that 'the Doer shall suffer' – be completely realized for every soul.
>
> (1951: 150–1; cited in Reale, 1987: 300)

On the same theme but from a more historical and social psychological perspective see Norman Cohn's *The Pursuit of the Millennium*; cf.

> As Norman Cohn showed in *The Pursuit of the Millennium*, apocalyptic visions have tended to appear in profusion during historical periods of political and religious oppression, social upheaval, war, and pestilence. The Hebrew prophets lived in an age of defeat and captivity; Jesus lived at the height of the decadent and oppressive Roman Empire; and medieval millenarian movements seemed always to flourish in places and times of unusual hardship. We see the same association of apocalpytic vision with societal stress among tribal peoples: in North America, Africa, and the Pacific islands, new spiritual movements that have arisen during the last century in response to the onslaught of civilization have invariably been prophetic and millenarian in character.
>
> (Heinberg, 1982: 242)

Cf. Brown, 1988; A. D. Nock, *Essays on Religion and the Ancient World* (Oxford: Oxford University Press, 1972): 534–50: Nillson, 1957.
That Orphism did not – along with the Mysteries and Dionysian cults – become a dominant influence at Athens was the outcome of a fortuitious combination of circumstances – the strength of its unique city cults, the success of Athens as an imperial power, its radical democratic institutions, its urban outlook, the long-durational impact of 'native' pragmatism rooted in the realist ethos of mercantile trade and commerce, Ionian rationalism and the secularizing forces of the Athenian Enlightenment; for

> it is certain that, if it had gained the upper hand, it would have lent itself to the support of aristocracy and tyranny. The tyrants of Athens might have made an Orphic priesthood an useful instrument of terror; and the brotherhood of Pythagoras was an unmistakable lesson to Greece of what the predominance of a religious order was likely to mean.
>
> (Bury and Meiggs, 1975: 199)

As I will argue at length in Volume 4, it is possible to interpret the later writings

NOTES

of Plato (particularly the *Republic* and his unfinished *Laws*) as an abortive attempt to build a City upon Pythagorean-Orphic foundations, governed by a quasi-sacredotal Guardian class, initiated into the mysteries of the cosmos and supported by a terroristic Nocturnal Council.

For the social consequences of other culture-forming attempts to 'map' the soul's journey to another world after death see: R.T. Rundle Clark, *Myth and Symbol in Ancient Egypt* (London: Thames and Husdon, 1959); W.Y. Evans-Wentz, *The Tibetan Book of the Dead* (Oxford: Oxford University Press, 1927); E. A. Wallis Budge, *The Book of the Dead* (1899) (London: Arkana, 1989).

5 According to H. and H. A. Frankfort, such a stark cosmic duality is unknown to the cultures of the ancient Near East outside of Persia and its subject peoples (Frankfort *et al.*, 1949: 248–9). As a pan-Hellenic movement, Orphism may have created a site of dialogue between the western and eastern cultures of the seventh and sixth century (the period Jaspers speaks of as the 'axial' age); cf. Sinnige, 1971: 55:

> many elements of the so-called Orphic theology are akin to elements of eastern, and more especially Babylonian and Phoenician mythology. The most important are: the dark abyss of unbounded chaos, the egg as the first germ of vital power, the breath inhaled as a generating principle, and the part played by Eros in the development of the universe.

It may also have been the preparatory work of Orphism to 'initiate' fifth-century Greece to the worship of Dionysus and a vision of the world as based on an irreconcilable duality of death and resurrection, an ideology that contested the ruling classical ideals of the Greek polis:

> it must have been, as Rudolf Otto has suggested, a terrible awakening awareness of the contradictory and irreconcilable nature of our experience of life, in which pleasure and horror, life and death, light and darkness, are brought to us by the same ambiguous power – an awareness which had been firmly held in check by the aristocratic discipline of Homeric civilization, left to the countryside to be worked out in peasant rites, but which was moving now from silent acceptance to tormented consciousness.
> (Santillana, 1961: 56)

6 D'Alviella, 1981: 84. Cf. Vernant:

> The Dionysiac religion, in the savage form of possession, and Pythagoreanism, in the intellectual and ascetic form of spiritual purification, both – in opposite ways – bypass sacrifice in order to draw nearer to the gods. The aim they share explains how it is that, despite their mutual opposition, omophagy and vegetarianism are ... in certain instances practised within a single sect.
> (Vernant, in Detienne, 1977: xxxi)

Note the important observation of M. P. Nilsson:

> The Orphic view of man involved a mental attitude of self-denial and seriousness in religious matters; it required ethics of a high standard. But its high ideas were mixed up with crude myths and base priests and charlatans misused them in practice. In the classical age it was despised; only Pindar and Plato understood its great thoughts. It sank down to rise again with the recrudesence of mystic ideas in a later age.
> (*Oxford Classical Dictionary*: 759–60)

Also Dodds, 1951: 76–7; Ehrenberg, 1964: 41–3.

NOTES

7 Zeller, 1969: 17. Cf. Walcot, 1966; West, 1971; and Otto, 1955.
8 Jaeger, 1947: 88–9; the internal quote is cited as Orpheus B 19. Jaeger explores this theme in his major work, *Paideia*; see also Guthrie, 1952 for doubts about Orphism as a religion of the lower, unprivileged classes, esp. 326–32. A complementary perspective on the revolutionary impact of Orphism upon the philosophical culture of Presocratic and Socratic reflexivity can be found in Reale 1987: esp. 293–304.

BIBLIOGRAPHY

Ackrill, J.L., ed., *A New Aristotle Reader* (Oxford: Clarendon Press, 1987).
Adam, J., *The Religious Teachers of Greece* (Edinburgh: T. and T. Clark, 1908).
Adamson, R., *The Development of Greek Philosophy* (Edinburgh: William Blackwood, 1908).
Adkins, A.W.H., *Merit and Responsibility: A Study in Greek Values* (Oxford: Clarendon Press, 1960).
Adkins, A.W.H., *From the Many to the One: A Study of Personality and Views of Human Nature in the Context of Ancient Greek Society, Values and Beliefs* (Ithaca: Cornell University Press, 1970).
Adkins, A.W.H., *Moral Values and Political Behaviour in Ancient Greece: From Homer to the End of the Fifth Century* (London: Chatto and Windus, 1972).
Adorno, T.W., *Notes to Literature*, Volume 1 (New York: Columbia University Press, 1991).
Adorno, T.W. and Horkheimer, M., *Dialectic of Enlightenment* (London: Verso, 1979).
Aeschylus, *Agamemnon*, trans. Herbert Weir Smyth (London: William Heinemann/Loeb Classical Library, 1926).
Aeschylus, *Volume 1: Suppliant Maidens, Persians, Prometheus Bound, Seven Against Thebes*, trans. Herbert Weir Smyth (London: Heinemann/Loeb Classical Library, 1956).
Aeschylus, *Eumenides*, trans. Herbert Weir Smyth (London: William Heinemann/Loeb Classical Library, 1971).P. J. Alexander, ed., *The Ancient World: To 300 A. D.* (New York: Macmillan Company, 1963).
Alexander of Aphrodisias, *On Aristotle Metaphysics 1*, trans. William E. Dooley (London: Duckworth, 1989).
Alfarabi, *Alfarabi's Philosophy of Plato and Aristotle* (Ithaca Cornell University Press, 1969).
Alic, M., *Hypatia's Heritage: A History of Women in Science from Antiquity to the Late Nineteenth Century* (London: The Women's Press, 1986).
Allen, R.E. and Furley, D.J., eds, *Studies in Presocratic Philosophy: Volume 1: The Eleatics and Pluralists* (London: Routledge and Kegan Paul, 1975).
Anderson, B., *Imagined Communities: the Origin and Spread of Nationalism* (London: Verso, 1983).
Andrewes, A., *The Greek Tyrants* (London: Hutchinson's University Library, 1956).
Andrewes, A., *The Greeks* (New York: Knopf, 1971).
Archilochus, in *Greek Lyric Poetry*, trans. Willis Barnstone (New York: Schocken Books, 1972).
Archilochus, in *Greek Lyrics*, trans. Richmond Lattimore (Chicago: University of Chicago Press, 1960): 1–6.

BIBLIOGRAPHY

Aristophanes, *Lysistrata Thesmophoriazusae*, trans. B. Bickley (London: William Heinemann/Loeb Classical Library, 1963).
Aristophanes, *The Frogs and Other Plays*, trans. D. Barrett (Harmondsworth: Penguin, 1964).
Aristophanes, *The Clouds*, trans. B. Bickley (London: William Heinemann/Loeb Classical Library, 1967).
Aristophanes, *The Birds*, trans. B. Bickley (London: William Heinemann/Loeb Classical Library, 1968).
Aristophanes, *The Knights, Peace, Wealth, The Birds, The Assemblywomen* (Harmondsworth: Penguin, 1990).
Aristotle, *On the Art of Poetry*, trans. Ingram Bywater (Oxford: Oxford University Press, 1909).
Aristotle, *Rhetoric*, trans. John Henry Freese (London: Heinemann/Loeb Classical Library, 1926).
Aristotle, *De Poetica (Poetics), On Interpretation, Nicomachean Ethics*, in *The Basic Works of Aristotle*, ed. Richard KcKeon (New York: Random House, 1941).
Aristotle, *Problems*, Volume 2 trans. W. S. Hett and *Rhetorica ad Alexandrum*, trans. H. Rackham (London: Heinemann/Loeb Classical Library, 1957).
Aristotle, *De Anima*, trans. W.D. Ross (Oxford: Clarendon Press, 1961).
Aristotle, *Metaphysics*, trans. Hippocrates G. Apostle (Bloomington Indiana University Press, 1966).
Aristotle, *Politics*, trans. T. A. Sinclair, revised by Trevor J. Saunders (Harmondsworth: Penguin, 1981).
Aristotle, *De Anima*, trans. Hugh Lawson-Tancred (Harmondsworth: Penguin, 1986).
Aristotle, *On Rhetoric: A Theory of Civic Discourse*, trans. George A. Kennedy (New York and Oxford: Oxford University Press, 1991).
Aristotle, *Eudemian Ethics*, trans. M. Woods, 2nd edn (Oxford: Oxford University Press, 1992).
Aristotle, *The Politics*, ed. S. Everson (Cambridge University Press, 1994).
Aristotle, et al., *Classical Literary Criticism*, trans. T. S. Dorsch (Harmondsworth: Penguin, 1981).
Aristotle (Pseudo-Aristotle), *Magna Moralia*, trans. H. Tredennick (London: William Heinemann/Loeb Classical Library, 1935).
Armstrong, A.H., *An Introduction to Ancient Philosophy* (London: Methuen, 1972).
Armstrong, A.H., 'Greek philosophy and Christianity', in M. I. Finley, ed., *The Legacy of Greece* (Oxford: Oxford University Press, 1984): 347–75.
Auerbach, E., *Mimesis: The Representation of Reality in Western Literature* (1946) (Garden City: Doubleday Anchor Books, 1957).
Aulus Gellius, *Attic Nights*, trans. J.C. Rolfe, 3 vols (London: Heinemann/Loeb Classical Library, 1927).
Bacon, F., *The Essays* (Harmondsworth: Penguin, 1985).
Bakhtin, M.M., *Rabelais and his World* (Cambridge, Mass.: MIT Press, 1968).
Bakhtin, M.M., *The Dialogic Imagination: Four Essays by M. M. Bakhtin* (Austin: University of Texas Press, 1981).
Bakhtin, M.M., *Problems of Dostoevsky's Poetics* (Manchester: Manchester University Press, 1984).
Bakhtin, M.M., *Rabelais and His World* (Bloomington: Indiana University Press, 1984).
Bakhtin, M.M., *Speech Genres and Other Late Essays* (Austin: University of Texas Press, 1986).
Bakhtin, M.M., *Art and Answerability: Early Philosophical Essays by M. M. Bakhtin* (Austin: Texas University Press, 1990).
Bakhtin, M.M. and Medvedev, P.N., *The Formal Method in Literary Scholarship: A*

Critical Introduction to Sociological Poetics (Cambridge, Mass.: Harvard University Press, 1985).
Bakhtin, M.M./Volosinov, V., Marxism and the Philosophy of Language (London: Academic Press, 1973).
Bal, M., Narratology (Toronto: University of Toronto Press, 1980).
Baldry, H.C., The Unity of Mankind in Greek Thought (Cambridge: Cambridge University Press, 1965).
Baldry, H.C., Ancient Greek Literature in its Living Context (London: Thames and Hudson, 1968).
Barnstone, W., trans. Greek Lyric Poetry (New York: Schocken Books, 1972).
Barthes, R., Mythologies (London: Paladin/Granada, 1973).
Barthes, R., The Pleasure of the Text (New York: Hill and Wang, 1975).
Bataille, G., Visions of Excess: Selected Writings 1927–1939 (Minneapolis: University of Minnesota/Manchester: University of Manchester Press, 1985).
Bataille, G., 'The sorcerer's apprentice', in D. Hollier, ed., The College of Sociology (1937–39) (Minneapolis: University of Minnesota Press, 1988): 12–23.
Baumann, G., ed., The Written Word: Literacy in Transition, Wolfson College Lectures, 1985, (Oxford: Clarendon Press, 1986).
Baxandall, L. and Morawski, S., eds, Marx and Engels on Literature and Art (New York: International General, 1974).
Bell, D., The Winding Passage: Sociological Essays and Journeys (New Brunswick and London: Transaction Publishers, 1991).
Benjamin, W., The Origin of German Tragic Drama (London: New Left Books, 1977).
Benjamin, W., Illuminations: Essays and Reflections (London: Fontana, 1992).
Bernal, M., Black Athena: The Afroasiatic Roots of Classical Greek Civilization: Volume 1: The Fabrication of Ancient Greece (London: Free Association Books, 1987).
Bettelheim, B., Recollections and Reflections (London: Thames and Hudson, 1990).
Blacker, C. and Loewe, M., eds, Ancient Cosmologies (London: George Allen and Unwin, 1975).
Blair, H., Lectures on Rhetoric and Belles Lettres (London: T. Cadell, 1825).
Blegen, C.W. and Rawson, M., The Palace of Nestor at Pylos in Western Messenia (Princeton: Princeton University Press, 1966).
Bloom, H., The Anxiety of Influence: A Theory of Poetry (New York: Oxford University Press, 1973)
Blumenberg, H., Das Lachen der Thrakerin: eine Urgeschichte der Theorie (Frankfurt Suhrkamp, 1987).
Boardman, J., J. Griffin, and O. Murray, eds, The Oxford History of Greece and the Hellenistic World (Oxford: Oxford University Press, 1991).
Boas, G., The Limits of Reason (New York: Harper, 1961).
Borges, J.L., 'The immortal', Labyrinths: Selected Stories and Other Writings (Harmondsworth: Penguin, 1970): 135–49.
Bottomley, F., Attitudes to the Body in Western Christendom (London: Lepus Books, 1979).
Bottomore, T. and Goode, P. eds, Readings in Marxist Sociology (Oxford: Clarendon Press, 1983).
Bourdieu, P., The Political Ontology of Martin Heidegger (Cambridge: Polity Press, 1991).
Bowra, C.M., Tradition and Design in the Iliad (Oxford: Clarendon Press, 1930).
Bowra, C.M., 'The proem of Parmenides', Classical Philology, 32, 1937: 97–112.
Bowra, C.M., Heroic Poetry (London: Macmillan, 1951).
Bowra, C.M., Greek Lyric Poetry: From Alcman to Simonides, 2nd revised edn (Oxford: Clarendon Press, 1961).

BIBLIOGRAPHY

Bowra, C.M., *Classical Greece* (N.V., Netherlands, 1965).
Bowra, C.M., *Landmarks in Greek Literature* (London: Weidenfeld and Nicolson, 1966).
Bowra, C.M., *Ancient Greek Literature* (1933) (London and New York: Oxford University Press, 1967).
Bowra, C.M., trans., *The Odes of Pindar* (Harmondsworth: Penguin, 1969).
Bowra, C.M., *Homer* (London: Duckworth, 1972).
Bowra, C.M., ed., *Pindari Carmina* (Oxford: Clarendon Press, 1935).
Boyd White, J., *When Words Lose Their Meaning: Constitutions and Reconstitutions of Language, Character, and Community* (Chicago: University of Chicago Press, 1984)
Brandon, S.G.F., *Creation Legends of the Ancient Near East* (London: Hodder and Stoughton, 1963).
Braudel, F., *A History of Civilizations* (Harmondsworth: Penguin/Allen Lane, 1994).
Breasted, J.H., *Development of Religion and Thought in Ancient Egypt* (New York: Scribner's 1912).
Bréhier, E., *The Hellenic Age* (Chicago: University of Chicago Press, 1963).
Bremmer, J., *The Early Greek Concept of the Soul* (Princeton: Princeton University Press, 1983).
Brown, P., *The Body and Society: Men, Women and Sexual Renunciation in Early Christianity* (New York: Columbia University Press, 1988).
Buck, C.D., *Comparative Grammar of Greek and Latin* (Chicago: University of Chicago Press, 1933).
Buck, C.D., *The Greek Dialects: Grammar, Selected Inscriptions, Glossary* (Chicago: University of Chicago Press, 1955).
Burkert, W., *Greek Religion* (Oxford: Basil Blackwell, 1985).
Burkert, W., *The Orientalizing Revolution: Near Eastern Influence on Greek Culture in the Early Archaic Period* (Cambridge, Mass.: Harvard University Press, 1992).
Burn, A.R., *The Lyric Age of Greece* (London: Edward Arnold, 1960).
Burn, A.R., *The World of Hesiod: A Study of the Greek Middle Ages c. 900–700 BC* (London, 1936; New York: Benjamin Blom, 1966).
Burn, A.R., *The Warring States of Greece: From Their Rise to the Roman Conquest* (London: Thames and Hudson, 1968).
Burnet, J., 'Philosophy', in R. W. Livingstone, ed., *The Legacy of Greece* (Oxford: Clarendon Press, 1921): 57–95.
Burnet, J., *Early Greek Philosophy* 4th edn (London: Adam and Charles Black, 1930).
Burton, R.W., *Pindar's Pythian Odes*: Essays in Interpretation (Oxford: Oxford University Press, 1962).
Burtt, J.O., trans., *Minor Attic Orators*, 2 vols, trans. K.J. Maidment for Antiphon, Andocides, Lycurgus, Demades, Dinarchus, and Hyerides (London: William Heinemann/Loeb Classical Library, 1941 (vol. 1) and 1954 (vol. 2).
Bury, J.B. and Meiggs, R., *A History of Greece to the Death of Alexander the Great*, 4th edn (London: Macmillan, 1975).
Butler, S., *The Authoress of the Odyssey* (London: A. C. Fifield, 1897).
Cameron, G.G., *Persepolis Treasury Tablets* (Chicago: Chicago University Press, 1948).
Campbell, D.A., trans. *Greek Lyric*, 4 vos (London: William Heinemann/Loeb Classical Library, 1982).
Campbell, J., *Myths to Live By* (London: Souvenir Press, 1973)
Campbell, J., *The Business of the Gods...* (Caledon East, Ontario: Windrose Films, 1989)

BIBLIOGRAPHY

Campbell, J., ed., *Papers From the Eranos Yearbooks* (London: Routledge and Kegan Paul, 1955 (vol. 1) and 1958 (vol. 3).
Camps, W.A., *An Introduction to Homer* (Oxford: Clarendon Press, 1980).
Carpenter, R., 'The antiquity of the Greek alphabet', *American Journal of Anthropology*, 37, 1933: 9–29.
Carpenter, R., *Folk-tale, Fiction and Saga in the Homeric Epics* (Berkeley: University of California Press, 1962).
Carpenter, R., *Discontinuity in Greek Civilization* (Cambridge: Cambridge University Press, 1966).
Cartledge, P., *Sparta and Lakonia: A Regional History 1300–362 BC* (London: Routledge and Kegan Paul, 1979).
Cassirer, E., *Language and Myth* (New York: Dover, 1946).
Cassirer, E., *The Philosophy of Symbolic Forms*, 3 vols (New Haven and London: Yale University Press, 1953–7).
Cassirer, E., *The Myth of the State* (New York: Doubleday Anchor, 1955).
Cassirer, E., *The Logic of the Humanities* (New Haven: Yale University Press, 1961).
Cassirer, E., *An Essay on Man* (New Haven and London: Yale University Press, 1967).
Chadwick, J., *The Decipherment of Linear B* (Cambridge: Cambridge University Press, 1967).
Chadwick, J., *The Mycenaean World* (Cambridge: Cambridge University Press, 1976).
Chadwick, H.M. and Chadwick, N.K., *The Growth of Literature*, 3 vols (Cambridge: Cambridge University Press, 1932–40).
Childe, V.G., *The Dawn of European Civilization* (London: Kegan Paul, 1925).
Childe, V.G., *Man Makes Himself* (Oxford: Oxford University Press, 1936).
Childe, V.G., *What Happened in History* (Harmondsworth: Penguin, 1942).
Cicero, *The Verrine Orations* (Cambridge, Mass.: Harvard University Press/The Loeb Classical Library, 1960).
Clagett, M., *Ancient Egyptian Science: A Source Book*, Volume 1 (Philadelphia: American Philosophical Society, 1989).
Claus, D.B., *Toward the Soul: An Inquiry into the Meaning of Soul before Plato* (New Haven: Yale University Press, 1981).
Coldstream, N., *Geometric Greece* (London: Benn, 1977).
Conger, C.P., *Theories of Macrocosms and Microcosms in the History of Philosophy* (New York: Columbia University Press, 1922).
Conger, C.P., *The Horizons of Thought: A Study in the Dualities of Thinking* (Princeton: Princeton University Press, 1933).
Confucius, *The Analects*, trans. D. C. Lau (Harmondsworth: Penguin, 1979).
Cook, A., *Myth and Language* (Bloomington: Indiana University Press, 1980).
Cook, J.M., *The Greeks in Ionia and the East* (London: Thames and Hudson, 1962).
Cook, R.M., 'Origins of Greek sculpture', *Journal of Hellenic Studies*, 87, 1967: 24–32.
Copleston, F., *A History of Philosophy: Volume 1: Greece and Rome* (London: Burnes and Oates, 1961).
Copleston, F., *On the History of Philosophy and Other Essays* (London: Search Press, 1979).
Cornford, F.M., *Greek Religious Thought. From Homer to the Age of Alexander* (London: Dent, 1923).
Cornford, F.M., *The Unwritten Philosophy and Other Essays* (Cambridge: Cambridge University Press, 1950).
Cornford, F.M., *From Religion to Philosophy: A Study in the Origins of Western Speculation* (New York: Harper and Row, 1957).
Cornford, F.M., *Before and After Socrates* (Cambridge: Cambridge University Press, 1958).

Cornford, F.M., *Principium Sapientiae: the Origins of Greek Philosophical Thought* (New York: Harper and Row, 1965).
Cottrell, L., *The Bull of Minos* (London: Evans Brothers, 1953).
Cottrell, L., *Reading the Past: The Story of Deciphering Ancient Languages* (London: Dent, 1972).
Cottrell, L., *The Origins of European Civilization* (London: Rainbird, 1985).
Coulmas, F., *The Writing Systems of the World* (Oxford: Basil Blackwell, 1989).
Coulmas, F. and Ehlich, K., eds, *Writing in Focus* (Berlin: Mouton, 1983).
Coxon, A.H., *The Fragments of Parmenides: A Critical Text with Introduction, Translation, the Ancient Testimonia and a Commentary* (Assen/Maastricht: Van Gorcum, 1986).
Curtius, E.R., *European Literature and the Latin Middle Ages* (1948) (Princeton: Princeton University Press, 1953).
D'Alviella, G., *The Mysteries of Eleusis: The Secret Rites and Rituals of the Classical Greek Mystery Tradition* (Wellingborough: Aquarian Press, 1981).
Davenport, G., trans., *Carmina Archilochi: The Fragments of Archilochus* (Berkeley: University of California Press, 1964).
Davenport, G., *Archilochos, Sappho, Alkman* (Berkeley and Los Angeles: University of California Press, 1980).
Demosthenes, *Works* (London: Heinemann/Loeb Classical Library); vol. 3 trans. J. H. Vince, 1935: vol. 7, trans. N. J. DeWitt, 1949).
Derrida, J., *Speech and Phenomena. And Other Essays on Husserl's Theory of Signs* (Evanston: Northwestern University Press, 1973).
Derrida, J., 'White mythology: metaphor in the text of philosophy', *New Literary History*, 6 (1), 1974: 5–74.
Derrida, J., *Of Grammatology* (Baltimore: Johns Hopkins University Press, 1976).
Derrida, J., *Writing and Difference* (London: Routledge and Kegan Paul, 1978a).
Derrida, J., *Edmund Husserl's 'Origins of Geometry': An Introduction* (Boulder: Great Eastern Press, 1978b).
Derrida, J., *Spurs: Nietzsche's Styles/Eperons: Les Styles de Nietzsche* (Chicago: University of Chicago Press, 1979).
Derrida, J., *Dissemination* (London: Athlone Press, 1981a).
Derrida, J., *Positions* (Chicago: University of Chicago Press, 1981b).
Derrida, J., *Margins of Philosophy* (Chicago: University of Chicago Press, 1982).
de Saussure, F., *Course in General Linguistics*, trans. Roy Harris (London: Duckworth, 1983).
Detienne, M., *Les Jardins d'Adonis* (Paris: Gallimard, 1972).
Detienne, M., *The Gardens of Adonis: Spices in Greek Mythology* (Brighton: Harvester Press, 1977).
Detienne, M. and Vernant, J.-P., *Cunning Intelligence in Greek Culture and Society* (Chicago: University of Chicago Press, 1991).
Diringer, D., *The Alphabet: A Key to the History of Mankind*, 2nd edn (New York: Philosophical Library, 1968).
Dodds, E.R., *The Greeks and the Irrational* (Berkeley and Los Angeles: University of California Press, 1951).
Dodds, E.R., *Pagan and Christian in an Age of Anxiety* (Cambridge: Cambridge University Press, 1965).
Dorsch, T.S., ed., *Classical Literary Criticism* (Harmondsworth: Penguin, 1965).
Doumos, C.G., *Thera: Pompeii of the Ancient Aegean. Excavations at Akrotiri, 1967–1979* (London: Thames and Hudson, 1983).
Dio Chrysostom, *Discourses*, trans. J.W. Cohoon, 5 vols (London: William Heinemann/Loeb Classical Library, 1932).

BIBLIOGRAPHY

Diodorus of Sicily (Siculus), *Works*, trans. C.H. Oldfeather, 12 vols (London: William Heinemann/Loeb Classical Library, 1925).
Diogenes Laertius, *Lives of the Eminent Philosophers*, ed. and trans. R.D. Hicks (London: William Heinemann/Loeb Classical Library, 1925).
Dover, K.J., *Greek Popular Morality in the Time of Plato and Aristotle* (Oxford: Basil Blackwell, 1974).
Dover, K.J., *Greek Homosexuality* (London: Duckworth, 1976).
Dover, K.J., ed., *Ancient Greek Literature* (Oxford: Oxford University Press, 1980).
Dover, K.J., *The Greeks* (Oxford: Oxford University Press, 1982).
Duggan, J.J., *The Song of Roland: Formulaic Style and and Poetic Craft* (Berkeley: University of California Press, 1973).
Durkheim, E., *The Elementary Forms of the Religious Life* (London: George Allen and Unwin, 1915).
Durkheim, E., *The Division of Labour in Society* (New York: The Free Press, 1964).
Durkheim, E., *Pragmatism and Sociology* (Cambridge: Cambridge University Press, 1983).
Durkheim, E. and Mauss, M., *Primitive Classification* (1903) (London: Cohen and West, 1963).
Dvornik, F., *Early Christian and Byzantine Philosophy*, 2 vols (Washington: Dumbarton Oaks Centre for Byzantine Studies, 1966).
Easterling, P.E. and Knox, B.M.W., eds, *The Cambridge History of Classical Literature* (Cambridge: Cambridge University Press, 1989).
Easterling, P.E. and Muir, J.V., eds, *Greek Religion and Society* (Cambridge: Cambridge University Press, 1985).
Easthope, A., *Poetry as Discourse* (London: Methuen, 1983).
Eco, U., *Reflections on The Name of the Rose* (London: Secker and Warburg, 1985).
Edwards, G.P., *The Language of Hesiod in its Traditional Context* (Oxford: Basil Blackwell, 1971).
Edwards, M.W., *Homer: Poet of the Iliad* (Baltimore: Johns Hopkins University Press, 1987).
Ehnmark, E., *The Idea of God in Homer: Inaugural Dissertation* (Uppsala: Almqvist and Wiksells Boktryckeri, AB, 1935).
Ehrenberg, V., *Society and Civilization in Greece and Rome* (Cambridge, Mass.: Harvard University Press, 1964).
Ehrenberg, V., *The Greek State* (London: Methuen, 1969).
Ehrenberg, V., *From Solon to Socrates*, 2nd edn. (London: Methuen, 1973).
Eliade, M., Myths, *Dreams and Mysteries. The Encounter between Contemporary Faiths and Archaic Realities* (London: Harvill Press, 1960).
Eliade, M., *Myth and Reality* (London: George Allen and Unwin, 1964).
Eliade, M., *Rites and Symbols of Initiation: The Mysteries of Birth and Rebirth* (New York: Harper and Row, 1965).
Eliade, M., *Patterns of Comparative Religion* (New York: New American Library, 1974).
Eliade, M., *From Primitives to Zen* (New York: Harper and Row, 1978).
Eliade, M., *The Myth of the Eternal Return (or Cosmos and History)* (London: Arkana/Penguin, 1989).
Elias, N., *Time: An Essay* (Oxford: Basil Blackwell, 1992).
Eliot, T.S., 'Little Gidding', in T.S. Eliot, *Collected Poems 1909–1962* (London: Faber and Faber, 1983).
Else, G.F., *The Origin and Early Form of Greek Tragedy* (Cambridge, Mass.: Harvard University Press, 1965).
Emerson, R.W., *Nature, The Conduct of Life, and Other Essays* (London: Dent, 1963).

BIBLIOGRAPHY

Erikson, E.H., *The Life-Cycle Completed: A Review* (New York and London: W. W. Norton, 1985).
Erman, A., *The Ancient Egyptians: A Sourcebook of Their Writings* (New York: Harper Torchbooks, 1966).
Euripides, *Bacchae, Electra, Alcestis*, trans. A.S. May (London: William Heinemann/Loeb Classical Library, 1912).
Euripides, *Bacchae and Other Classics* (Harmondsworth: Penguin, 1954).
Euripides, *The Complete Greek Tragedies*, ed. D. Grene and R. Lattimore, Volume 4 (Chicago: University of Chicago Press, 1958).
Evans-Wentz, W.Y., *The Tibetan Book of the Dead* (Oxford: Oxford University Press, 1927).
Evelyn-White, H.G., trans. *The Homeric Hymns and Homerica* (Cambridge, Mass.: Harvard University Press, 1936).
Everson, S., ed., *Epistemology* (Cambridge: Cambridge University Press, 1990).
Fagles, R., 'Epilogue: Homer and the writers', in G. Steiner and R. Fagles, eds, *Homer: A Collection of Critical Essays* (Englewood Cliffs: Prentice-Hall 1962): 160–72.
Farber, M., ed., *Philosophical Essays in Memory of Edmund Husserl* (Cambridge, Mass.: Harvard University Press, 1940).
Farnell, L.R., *The Cults of the Greek States*, 5 vols (Oxford: Clarendon Press, 1896–1909).
Farnell, L.R., *The Higher Aspects of Greek Religion* (London: Williams and Norgate, 1912).
Farnell, L.R., *The Works of Pindar*, 3 vols (London: Macmillan, 1930–2).
Feher, M., ed., *Fragments for a History of the Human Body* (New York: Zone, 1989).
Fenik, B., *Typical Battle Scenes in the Iliad: Studies in the Narrative Techniques of Homeric Battle Description* (Wiesbaden, 1968).
Feyerabend, P., *Against Method: Outline of an Anarchistic Theory of Knowledge* (London: New Left Books, 1975).
Feyerabend, P., *Science in a Free Society* (London: New Left Books, 1978).
Feyerabend, P., *Farewell to Reason* (London: Verso, 1987).
Finnegan, R., *Oral Poetry: Its Nature, Significance and Social Context* (Cambridge: Cambridge University Press, 1977).
Finley, J.H., *Pindar and Aeschylus* (Cambridge, Mass: Harvard University Press, 1955).
Finley, M.I., *The Ancient Greeks* (Harmondsworth: Penguin, 1963).
Finley, M.I., 'Utopianism ancient and modern', in K.H. Wolff and Barrington Moore Jr, eds, *The Critical Spirit: Essays in Honor of Herbert Marcuse* (Boston: Beacon Press, 1967): 3–20.
Finley, M.I., *The Use and Abuse of History* (London: Chatto and Windus, 1975).
Finley, M.I., *The World of Odysseus* (Cambridge: Cambridge University Press, 1978).
Finley, M.I., *Ancient Sicily*, revised edn (London: Book Club Associates, 1979).
Finley, M.I., *Ancient Slavery and Modern Ideology* (London. Chatto and Windus, 1980).
Finley, M.I., *Early Greece: The Bronze and Archaic Ages*, revised edn (London: Chatto and Windus, 1981).
Finley, M.I., *Politics in the Ancient World* (Cambridge: Cambridge University Press, 1983a).
Finley, M.I., *Economy and Society in Ancient Greece* (Harmondsworth: Penguin, 1983b).
Finley, M.I., *Ancient History: Evidence and Models* (Harmondsworth: Penguin, 1987).
Finley, M.I., ed., *Slavery in Classical Antiquity* (Cambridge: Heffer, 1960).
Finley, M.I., ed., *Studies in Ancient Society* (London: Routledge and Kegan Paul, 1974).
Finley, M.I., ed., *The Legacy of Greece: A New Appraisal* (Oxford: Oxford University Press, 1984).

BIBLIOGRAPHY

Fischer, E., *The Necessity of Art: A Marxist Approach* (1959) (Harmondsworth: Penguin, 1978).
Flacelière, R., *A Literary History of Greece* (London: Elek Books, 1964).
Forrest, W.G., *A History of Sparta 950–192 BC* (London: Hutchinson, 1968).
Forsyth, P.Y., *Atlantis: The Making of Myth* (London: Croom Helm, 1980).
Foucault, M., 'The order of discourse' (Inaugural Lecture at the Collège de France, 2 December 1970), in R. Young, ed., *Untying the Text: A Post-Structuralist Reader* (London: Routledge and Kegan Paul, 1981): 48–78.
Foucault, M., *History of Sexuality: Volume 2: The Uses of Pleasure* (Harmondsworth: Penguin/Viking, 1986).
Foucault, M., *History of Sexuality: Volume 3: The Care of the Self* (London: Allen Lane, 1988a).
Fowler, H.W., *A Dictionary of Modern English Usage* (1926) (Oxford: Clarendon Press, 1950).
Frame, D., *The Myth of Return in Early Greek Epic* (New Haven and London: Yale University Press, 1978).
Fränkel, H., *Wege und Formen Frühgriechischen Denkens* (Munich: C. H. Beck, 1960).
Fränkel, H., *Early Greek Poetry and Philosophy* (Oxford and New York: Basil Blackwell, 1975).
Frankl, V.E., *Man's Search for Meaning: An Introduction to Logotherapy* (London: Hodder and Stoughton, 1959).
Frankfort, H., et. al., *Before Philosophy: The Intellectual Adventure of Ancient Man: An Essay on Speculative Thought in the Ancient Near East* (Harmondsworth: Penguin, 1949).
Frye, N., *Anatomy of Criticism* (Princeton: Princeton University Press, 1957).
Frye, N., *The Secular Scripture: A Study of the Structure of Romance* (Cambridge, Mass.: Harvard University Press, 1976).
Frye, N., *The Great Code: The Bible and Literature* (New York and London: Harcourt Brace Jovanovich, 1982).
Gadamer, H.-G., *Wahrheit und Methode* (Tübingen: Mohr, 1960).
Gadamer, H.-G., *Truth and Method* (1960), 2nd revised edn. (New York: Crossroad, 1989).
Gallop, D., *Parmenides of Elea: Fragments, A Text and Translation* (Toronto: University of Toronto Press, 1984).
Gans, E., *The End of Culture: Toward a Generative Anthropology* (Berkeley: University of California Press, 1985).
Gaur, A., *A History of Writing* (London: The British Library, 1987).
Gelb, I.J., *A Study Writing: The Foundations of Grammatology* (1952) (Chicago: University of Chicago Press, 1963).
Germain, G., 'The sirens and the temptation of knowledge', in G. Steiner and R. Fagles, eds, *Homer: A Collection of Critical Essays* (Englewood Cliffs: Prentice-Hall, 1962): 91–7.
Gerth, H. and Wright Mills, C., eds, *From Max Weber* (London: Routledge and Kegan Paul, 1948).
Goldmann, L., *The Hidden God* (London: Routledge and Kegan Paul, 1964).
Gigon, O., *Der Ursprung des Griechischen Philosophie von Hesiod bis Parmenides* (Basel: Benno Schwabe, 1945).
Glacken, G.C., *Traces on the Rhodian Shore: Nature and Culture in Western Thought from Ancient Times to the End of the Eighteenth Century* (Berkeley: University of California Press, 1967).
Gomperz, T., *Greek Thinkers: A History of Ancient Philosophy*, 4 vols, Volume 1 (London: John Murray, 1920).
Goodman, N., *Languages of Art* (Indianapolis: Bobbs-Merrill, 1968).

Goodman, N., *Ways of Worldmaking* (Indianapolis: Hackett, 1978).
Goodman, N., *Of Mind and Other Matters* (Cambridge, Mass.: Harvard University Press, 1984).
Goody, J., *The Domestication of the Savage Mind* (Cambridge: Cambridge University Press, 1977).
Goody, J., *The Interface Between the Written and the Oral* (Cambridge: Cambridge University Press, 1986).
Goody, J., ed., *Literacy in Traditional Societies* (Cambridge: Cambridge University Press, 1968).
Goody, J. and Watt, I., 'The consequences of literacy', *Comparative Studies in Society and History*, 5, 1962–3: 304–45.
Goody, J. and Watt, I., *Literacy in Traditional Societies* (Cambridge: Cambridge University Press, 1988).
Gouldner, A.W., *Enter Plato: Classical Greece and the Origins of Social Theory* (London: Routledge and Kegan Paul, 1966).
Gouldner, A.W., *Against Fragmentation: The Origins of Marxism and the Sociology of Intellectuals* (New York: Oxford University Press, 1985).
Grandsen, K.W., 'Homer and the epic', in M.I. Finley, ed., *The Legacy of Greece* (Oxford: Oxford University Press, 1984): 65–92.
Granet, M., *La Pensée Chinoise* (Paris, 1934).
Granet, M., *La Religion des Chinois* (Paris, 1922) trans. M. Freedman as *The Religion of the Chinese People* (Oxford: Basil Blackwell, 1975).
Grant, M., *The Classical Greeks* (London: Weidenfeld and Nicolson, 1989).
Grant, M., *A Short History of Classical Civilization* (London: Weidenfeld and Nicolson, 1991).
Grant, M., ed., *Greek Literature: An Anthology* (Harmondsworth: Penguin, 1977).
Graves, R., *Homer's Daughter* (New York: Doubleday, 1955).
Greenfeld, L., *Nationalism: Five Roads to Modernity* (Cambridge, Mass.: Harvard University Press, 1992).
Greenhalgh, P.A.L., *Early Greek Warfare* (Cambridge: Cambridge University Press, 1973).
Griffin, J., *Homer* (Oxford: Oxford University Press, 1980a).
Griffin, J., *Homer on Life and Death* (Oxford: Oxford University Press, 1980b).
Guthrie, W.K.C., *The Greek Philosophers from Thales to Aristotle* (London: Methuen, 1950).
Guthrie, W.K.C., *Orpheus and Greek Religion* (1935) (London: Methuen, 1952).
Guthrie, W.K.C., *A History of Greek Philosophy* (Cambridge: Cambridge University Press, 1962–81), esp. Volume 1 (1962).
Guthrie, W.K.C., *The Greeks and Their Gods* (1950) (London: Methuen, 1977).
Hadas, M., *A History of Greek Literature* (New York and London: Columbia University Press, 1950).
Hainsworth, J.B., *The Flexibility of the Homeric Formula* (Oxford: Clarendon Press, 1968).
Hägg, R., et al., *Early Greek Cult Practice: Proceedings of the International Symposium at the Swedish Institute of Athens, 26–29 June 1986* (Stockholm: Astrom, 1988).
Hallock, R.T., *Persepolis Fortification Tablets* (Chicago: University of Chicago Press, 1969).
Hamilton, W., trans., *Plato, Phaedrus* (Harmondsworth: Penguin, 1973).
Hammond, M., *The City in the Ancient World* (Cambridge, Mass.: Harvard University Press, 1972).
Hammond, N.G.L., *The Miracle that was Macedonia* (London: Sidgwick and Jackson, 1991).
Harris, R., *The Origin of Writing* (London: Duckworth, 1986).

BIBLIOGRAPHY

Harris, W.V., *Ancient Literacy* (Cambridge, Mass.: Harvard University Press, 1989).
Harrison, J., *Themis* (Cambridge: Cambridge University Press, 1912).
Harrison, J., *Prolegomena to a Study of Greek Religion* (1903 3rd edn (London: Merlin, 1962).
Harrison, J., *Ancient Art and Ritual* (1913) (Bradford-on-Avon: Moonraker Press, 1978).
Hartshorne, C., *Insights and Oversights of Great Thinkers: An Evaluation of Western Philosophy* (Albany: State University of New York Press, 1983).
Harvey, P., *The Oxford Companion to Classical Literature* (Oxford: Oxford University Press, 1984).
Havelock, E.A., 'Parmenides and Odysseus', *Harvard Studies in Classical Philology*, 63, 1958: 133–43.
Havelock, E.A., *Preface to Plato* (Cambridge, Mass.: Harvard University Press, 1963).
Havelock, E.A., *Origins of Western Literacy* (Toronto: The Ontario Institute for Studies in Education, Monograph Series 14, 1976).
Havelock, E.A., 'The preliteracy of the Greeks', *New Literary History*, 8 1977: 369–91.
Havelock, E.A., *The Greek Concept of Justice: From Its Shadow in Homer to Its Substance in Plato* (Cambridge, Mass.: Harvard University Press, 1978).
Havelock, E.A., 'The ancient art of oral poetry', *Philosophy and Rhetoric*, 12 (3), Summer 1979: 187–202.
Havelock, E.A., *The Literate Revolution in Greece and Its Cultural Consequences* (Princeton: Princeton University Press, 1982).
Havelock, E.A., *The Muse Learns to Write* (New Haven and London: Yale University Press, 1986).
Havelock, E.A. and Hershbell, J.P., eds, *Communication Arts in the Ancient World* (New York: Hastings House, 1978).
Hawkes, T., *Structuralism and Semiotics* (London: Methuen, 1977).
Heidegger, M., *Being and Time* (New York: Harper and Row, 1962).
Heidegger, M., *What is Called Thinking?* (New York: Harper and Row, 1968).
Heidegger, M., *History of the Concept of Time* (Bloomington: Indiana University Press, 1992).
Heinberg, R., *Memories and Visions of Paradise: Exploring the Universal Myth of a Lost Golden Age* (Los Angeles: The Aquarian Press, 1982).
Herodoti, *Historiae* (Oxford: Clarendon Press, 1991).
Herodotus, *History*, trans. A. D. Godley, 4 vols (London: William Heinemann/Loeb Classical Library, 1946).
Herodotus, *The Histories*, trans. A. de Selincourt (Harmondsworth: Penguin, 1954).
Hesiod, *The Poems and Fragments*, trans. A.W. Mair (Oxford: Clarendon Press, 1908).
Hesiod, *Hesiod, The Homeric Hymns and Homerica*, trans. H. G. Evelyn-White (London: Loeb Classical Library, 1914, 1936).
Hesiod, *Theogony* (Indianapolis: Bobbs-Merrill, 1953).
Hesiod, *Theogony*, trans. R. Lattimore (Ann Arbor: University of Michigan Press, 1959).
Hesiod and Theognis, *Theogony and Works and Days* (Harmondsworth: Penguin, 1985).
Higgins, R., *Minoan and Mycenaean Art* (London: Thames and Hudson, 1967).
Higgins, R., *The Greek Bronze Age* (London: British Museum, 1970).
Higgins, R., *The Archaeology of Minoan Crete* (London: Bodley Head, 1973).
Hipponax, in *Greek Lyrics*, trans. R. Lattimore (Chicago: University of Chicago Press, 1960): 12–13.
Hipponax, in *Greek Lyric Poetry*, trans. W. Barnstone (New York: Schocken Books, 1972): 117–20.

BIBLIOGRAPHY

Hirschmann, A.O., *The Passions and the Interests: Political Arguments for Capitalism before its Triumph* (Princeton: Princeton University Press, 1977).
Hollier, D., ed., *The College of Sociology (1937–39)* (Minneapolis: University of Minnesota Press, 1988).
Hölscher, U., *Anfängliches Fragen* (Göttingen, 1968).
Homer, *The Iliad*, trans. E.V. Rieu (Harmondsworth: Penguin, 1950).
Homer, *The Odyssey*, trans. E.V. Rieu (Harmondsworth: Penguin, 1959).
Homer, *The Odyssey*, trans. R. Fitzgerald (New York: Doubleday, 1961).
Hower, *The Illiad*, trans. R. Fitzgerald (New York: Doubleday, 1979).
Homer, *The Iliad*, trans. R. Lattimore (Chicago: University of Chicago Press, 1951, 1962)
Homer, *The Odyssey*, trans. R. Lattimore (New York: Harper and Row, 1967).
Homer, *The Iliad*, trans. A. T. Murray 2 vols (London: Heinemann, 1971).
Homer, *The Iliad*, trans. R. Fagles (Harmondsworth/London and New York: Penguin/Viking, 1990).
The Homeric Hymns and Homerica, in *Hesiod*, trans. H.G. Evelyn-White, revised edn (Cambridge, Mass.: Harvard University Press, 1936).
Hopper, R.J., *The Early Greeks* (London: Weidenfeld and Nicolson, 1976).
Hopper, R.J., *Trade and Industry in Classical Greece* (London: Thames and Hudson, 1979).
Horkheimer, M. and Adorno, T.W., *Dialectic of Enlightenment* (London: Verso, 1979).
Horton, J. and Finnegan, R., eds, *Modes of Thought: Essays on Thinking in Western and Non-Western Societies* (London: Faber and Faber, 1973).
Hunt, A.S. and Edgar, C.C., trans, *Select Papyri: Volumes 1 and 2: Non-Literary Papyri/Private Affairs* (1932); *Volume 3: Literary Papyri* (1941) (London: William Heinemann/Loeb Classical Library).
Husserl, E., 'The origins of geometry', in *The Crisis of European Sciences and Transcendental Phenomenology: An Introduction to Phenomenological Philosophy* (Evanston: Northwestern University Press, 1970): 353–78.
Huxley, G.L., *Early Sparta* (London: Faber and Faber, 1962).
Hyland, D.A., *The Origins of Philosophy: Its Rise in Myth and the Pre-Socratics: A Collection of Early Writings Selected, Edited, and with Explanatory Essays* (New York: Capricorn Books, 1973).
Iamblichus, *On the Pythagorean Life*, trans. G. Clark (Liverpool: Liverpool University Press, 1989).
Illich, I. and Sanders, B., *ABC: The Alphabetization of the Popular Mind* (London: Marion Boyars, 1988).
Isocrates, *To Demonicus, To Nicodes, Panegyricus, To Philip, Archidamus*, in Volume 1, trans. G. Norlin (London: William Heinemann/Loeb Classical Library, 1928).
Isocrates, in R.C. Jebb, ed., *Selections from the Attic Orators* (1888) (New York: St Martin's Press, 1966).
Isocrates, *On the Peace, Areopagiticus, Against the Sophists, Antidosis, Panathenaicus*, in Volume 2, trans. G. Norlin (London: William Heinemann/Loeb Classical Library, 1929).
Isocrates, *Orations, Letters*, trans. L. van Hook (London: William Heinemann/Loeb Classical Library, 1945).
Jaeger, W., *Paideia: The Ideals of Greek Culture*, 3 vols, 2nd edn, (New York: Oxford University Press, 1945).
Jaeger, W., *The Theology of the Early Greek Philosophers* (Oxford: Clarendon Press, 1947).
Jaeger, W., *Aristotle: Fundamentals of the History of His Development* (Oxford: Oxford University Press, 1948).

BIBLIOGRAPHY

Jaeger, W., *Early Christianity and Greek Paideia* (Cambridge, Mass.: Belknap/Harvard University Press, 1965).
Jaynes, J., *The Origin of Consciousness in the Breakdown of the Bicameral Mind* (Boston: Houghton-Mifflin, 1976).
Jean, G., *Writing: The Story of Alphabets and Scripts* (London: Thames and Hudson, 1992).
Jeffery, L.H., *Archaic Greece: The City-States c. 700–500 B. C.* (London: Methuen, 1976).
Jeffery, L.H., 'Greek alphabetic writing', in *Cambridge Ancient History*, 3rd ed., vol. 3 (Cambridge: Cambridge University Press, 1982): 819–33.
Jeffery, L.H., *The Local Scripts of Archaic Greece: A Study of the Origins of the Greek Alphabet and Its Development from the Eighth to the Fifth Centuries* BC (Oxford: Oxford University Press, 1990).
Jensen, H., *Sign, Symbol and Script: An Account of Man's Efforts to Write* (London: George Allen and Unwin, 1970).
Jolles, A., *Einfache Formen: Legende, Sage, Myth, Rätsel, Spruch, Kasus, Memorabile, Märchen, Witz* (Tübingen: Niemeyer, 1968), trans. into French as *Formes simples* (Paris, 1972).
Juvenal and Persius, *Satires*, trans. G.G. Ramsay (London: William Heinemann/Loeb Classical Library, 1940).
Kahn, C.H., *Anaximander and the Origin of Greek Cosmology* (New York and London: Columbia University Press, 1960).
Kant, I., *Logic* (New York: Bobbs-Merrill, 1974a).
Kant, I., *Anthropology from a Pragmatic Point of View* (The Hague: Martinus Nijhoff, 1974b).
Kant, I., *Anthropology from a Pragmatic Point of View* trans. Victor Lyle Dowdell and Hans H. Rudnick (Carbondale and Edwardsville: Southern Illinois University Press, 1978).
Kazantzakis, N., *The Odyssey: A Modern Sequel* (New York: Simon and Schuster, 1958).
Kelsen, H., *Society and Nature: A Sociological Inquiry* (London: Routledge and Kegan Paul, 1946.
Kelsen, H., *Essays in Legal and Moral Philosophy* (Dordrecht: D. Reidel, 1973).
Kennedy, G.A., ed., *The Cambridge History of Literary Criticism* (Cambridge: Cambridge University Press, 1989).
Kerényi, K., *The Heroes of the Greeks* (London: Thames and Hudson, 1959).
Kerényi, K., *Eleusis: Archetypal Image of Mother and Daughter* (London: Routledge and Kegan Paul, 1967).
Kern, O., *Orphicorum Fragmenta* (1922) (Berlin: Weidmann, 1963).
Kirk, G.S., *Heraclitus, The Cosmic Fragments* (Cambridge: Cambridge University Press, 1962).
Kirk, G.S., *Myth, Its Nature and Function in Ancient and Other Cultures* (Cambridge: Cambridge University Press, 1970).
Kirk, G.S., *The Nature of Greek Myths* (Harmondsworth: Penguin, 1974).
Kirk, G.S., *The Iliad: A Commentary: Volume 1: Books 1–4* (Cambridge: Cambridge University Press, 1985).
Kirk, G.S., ed., *The Language and Background of Homer: Some Recent Studies and Controversies* (Cambridge: Heffer, 1964).
Kirk, G.S. and Raven, J.E., *The Presocratic Philosophers*, 2nd edn (Cambridge: Cambridge University Press, 1971).
Kirk, G.S., J. E. Raven and M. Schofield, *The Presocratic Philosophers*, 2nd edn (Cambridge: Cambridge University Press, 1983).
Kitto, H.D.F., *Greek Tragedy: A Literary Study*, 3rd edn (London: Methuen, 1966).

BIBLIOGRAPHY

Kitto, H.D.F., *The Greeks* (Harmondsworth: Pelican/Penguin, 1991).
Knox, B., 'Introduction', to Homer, *The Iliad*, trans. Robert Fagles (London and New York: Viking/Penguin, 1990): 1–67.
Kockelmans, J.J. and Kisiel, T.J., eds, *Phenomenology and the Natural Sciences: Essays and Translations* (Evanston: Northwestern University Press, 1970).
Kristeva, J., *Language: The Unknown* (Brighton: Harvester Wheatsheaf, 1989).
Kroeber, K., ed., *Traditional Literatures of the American Indians: Texts and Interpretations* (Lincoln: University of Nebraska Press, 1981).
Kuhn, T., *The Structure of Scientific Revolutions*, 2nd edn (Chicago: University of Chicago Press, 1970).
Kuhn, T., *The Essential Tension: Selected Studies in Scientific Tradition and Change* (Chicago: University of Chicago Press, 1977).
Kundera, M., *The Art of the Novel* (London: Faber and Faber, 1988).
Kurzweil, E., *The Age of Structuralism: Lévi-Strauss to Foucault* (New York: Columbia University Press, 1980).
Langer, S.K., *Feeling and Form* (London: Routledge and Kegan Paul, 1953).
Lattimore, R., trans., *Hesiod, Works and Days* (Michigan: University of Michigan Press, 1959a).
Lattimore, R., trans., *The Odes of Pindar* (Chicago: University of Chicago Press, 1959b).
Lattimore, R., trans., *Greek Lyrics* (Chicago: University of Chicago Press, 1960).
Lattimore, R., trans., *The Iliad of Homer* (Chicago: University of Chicago Press, 1962).
Lattimore, R., trans., *The Odyssey of Homer* (New York: Harper and Row, 1967).
Laurie, J., ed., *Cosmology Now* (London: British Broadcasting Corporation, 1973).
Layton, B., *The Gnostic Scriptures: A New Translation with Annotations and Introductions* (Garden City: Doubleday, 1987).
Lefkowitz, M.R., *The Victory Ode. An Introduction* (Park Ridge: Noyes Press, 1976).
Lehmann, J., *The Hittites: People of a Thousand Gods* (London: Collins, 1977).
Lemon, L.T. and Reis, M.J., eds, *Readings in Russian Poetics: Formalist and Structuralist Views* (Lincoln and London: University of Nebraska Press, 1965).
Lesky, A., *History of Greek Literature* (London: Methuen, 1966).
Levi, P., *The Pelican History of Greek Literature* (Harmondsworth: Penguin, 1985).
Lévi-Strauss, C., *Tristes Tropiques* (Paris: Plon, 1955).
Lévi-Strauss, C., *Structural Anthropology* (New York: Basic Books, 1963).
Lévi-Strauss, C., *Totemism* (London: St Martin's Press, 1964).
Lévi-Strauss, C., *The Savage Mind* (London: Weidenfeld, 1966).
Lévi-Strauss, C., *The Scope of Anthropology* (London: Jonathan Cape, 1967).
Lévi-Strauss, C., *From Honey to Ashes* (London: Jonathan Cape, 1973).
Lévi-Strauss, C., *Myth and Meaning* (London: Routledge and Kegan Paul, 1978).
Lévi-Strauss, C., *The Naked Man: Introduction to a Science of Mythology – IV* (London: Jonathan Cape, 1981).
Lévi-Strauss, C., *The View From Afar* (Oxford: Basil Blackwell, 1985).
Lévy-Bruhl, L., *Les Fonctions mentales dans les sociétés inférieures* (Paris: Alcan, 1910).
Lévy-Bruhl, L., *Primitive Mentality* (New York: Macmillan, 1923).
Lévy-Bruhl, L., *How Natives Think* (London: George Allen and Unwin, 1926).
Liddell, H.G., R. Scott, and H. S. Jones, *A Greek-English Lexicon* (Oxford: Oxford University Press, 1925–40).
Linforth, I.M., *The Arts of Orpheus* (Berkeley and Los Angeles: University of California Press, 1941).
Lintott, A., *Violence, Civil Strife and Revolution in the Classical City 750–330 BC* (London: Croom Helm, 1982).
Livingstone, R.W., ed., *The Legacy of Greece* (Oxford: Clarendon Press, 1921).

BIBLIOGRAPHY

Lloyd, G.E.R., *Early Greek Science: Thales to Aristotle* (London: Chatto and Windus, 1970).
Lloyd, G.E.R., *Polarity and Analogy: Two Types of Argumentation in Early Greek Thought* (Cambridge: Cambridge University Press, 1971).
Lloyd, G.E.R., *Magic, Reason and Experience: Studies in the Origin and Development of Greek Science* (Cambridge: Cambridge University Press, 1979).
Lloyd, G.E.R., *Science, Folklore, Ideology: Studies in the Life Sciences in Ancient Greece* (Cambridge: Cambridge University Press, 1983).
Lloyd, G.E.R., *The Revolutions of Wisdom: Studies in the Claims and Practices of Ancient Greek Science* (Berkeley: University of California Press, 1987).
Lloyd-Jones, P.H.J., *The Justice of Zeus* (Berkeley: University of California Press, 1971).
Lobkowicz, N., *Theory and Practice: History of a Concept from Aristotle to Marx* (Notre Dame: University of Notre Dame Press, 1967).
'Longinus', *On the Sublime*, in D.A. Russell and M. Winterbottom, eds, *Ancient Literary Criticism: The Principal Texts in New Translations* (Oxford: Clarendon Press, 1978): 460–503.
Lord, A.B., 'Homer', in G. Steiner and R. Fagles, eds, *Homer: A Collection of Critical Essays* (Englewood Cliffs: Prentice-Hall, 1962): 62–78.
Lord, A.B., *The Singer of Tales* (Cambridge, Mass.: Harvard University Press, 1971).
Luce, J.V., *Homer and the Heroic Age* (London: Thames and Hudson, 1975).
Luce, J.V., *An Introduction to Greek Philosophy* (London: Thames and Hudson, 1992).
Lucian, *Dialogues* (with the *Vera Historia* or *True History*), trans. Francis Hicker (1634), reprinted from the 1902 imprint (London: The Watergate Library, no date).
Lukács, G., *The Theory of the Novel: A Historico-philosophical Essay on the Form of the Great Epic Literature* (1920) (Cambridge, Mass.: MIT Press, 1971).
Lycurgus, 'Against Leocrates', in *Minor Attic Orators*, Volume 2, trans. J.O. Burtt (London: William Heinemann/Loeb Classical Library, 1954).
Lyotard, J.-F., *The Postmodern Condition: A Report on Knowledge* (Manchester: Manchester University Press, 1984).
Lysias, *Works*, trans. W.R.M. Lamb (London: William Heinemann/Loeb Classical Library, 1957).
Mackail, J.W., *Lectures on Greek Poetry* (London: Longman, Green, and Co., 1926).
McKeon, R., ed., *The Basic Works of Aristotle* (New York: Random House, 1941).
McNeill, W.H., *A World History* (Oxford: Oxford University Press, 1979).
McCulloh, W.E., 'Introduction', to Willis Barnstone, trans. *Greek Lyric Poetry* (New York: Schocken Books, 1972): 1–13.
Madox Ford, F., *The March of Literature: From Confucius to Modern Times* (London: George Allen and Unwin, 1947).
Malinowski, B., *Argonauts of the Western Pacific* (New York and London: Routledge and Kegan Paul, 1922).
Malinowski, B., *Myth in Primitive Psychology* (New York and London: W.W. Norton, 1926).
Malinowski, B., *Magic, Science and Religion and Other Essays* (New York: Anchor-Doubleday, 1954).
Malkin, I., *Religion and Colonization in Ancient Greece* (Leyden: E.J. Brill, 1987).
Mann, T., *Mythology and Humanism: The Correspondence of Thomas Mann and Karl Kerényi* (Ithaca and London: Cornell University Press, 1975).
Mansfeld, J. and de Rijk, L.M., eds, *Kephalaion: Studies in Greek Philosophy and its Continuation Offered to Professor C. J. de Vogel* (Assen: Van Gorcum, 1975).
Maranda, P., ed., *Mythology* (Harmondsworth: Penguin, 1972).
Martin, L., H. Gutman, and P. Hutton, eds, *Technologies of the Self: A Seminar with Michel Foucault* (Amherst: University of Massachusetts Press, 1988).

BIBLIOGRAPHY

Martindale, D.A., *Social Life and Cultural Change* (Princeton: Van Nostrand Publishing Company, 1962).
Marx, K., *Pre-Capitalist Economic Formations* (London: Lawrence and Wishart, 1964).
Marx, K., *Economic and Philosophic Manuscripts of 1844* (Moscow: Progress Publishers, 1967).
Marx, K., *Selected Works* (London: Lawrence and Wishart, 1968).
Marx, K., *Grundrisse* (Harmondsworth: Penguin, 1973).
Marx, K., *Selected Writings* (Oxford: Oxford University Press, 1977).
Marx, K. and Engels, F., *The German Ideology* (London: Lawrence and Wishart, 1970).
Matejka, L. and Pomorska, K., eds, *Readings in Russian Poetics: Formalist and Structuralist Views* (Ann Arbor: Michigan Slavic Publications, 1978).
Mauss, M., *Essai sur le don dans Sociologie et Anthropologie* (Paris: Presses Universitaires de France, 1950).
Mauss, M., *The Gift* (Glencoe: Free Press, 1954).
Mauss, M., *General Theory of Magic* (London: Routledge and Kegan Paul, 1972).
Mauss, M., *Sociology and Psychology*, trans. Ben Brewster (London: Routledge and Kegan Paul, 1979).
Meiggs, R. and Lewis, D.M., *A Selection of Greek Historical Inscriptions* (Oxford: Oxford University Press, 1969).
Melian Stawell, F., *A Clue to the Cretan Scripts* (London: G. Bell and Sons Ltd., 1931).F.
Meinecke, *Historicism* (London: Routledge and Kegan Paul, 1972).
Michell, H., *Sparta* (Cambridge: Cambridge University Press, 1964).
Mimnermus, in *Greek Lyrics*, trans. R. Lattimore (Chicago: University of Chicago Press, 1960): 16–17.
Murray, G., A History of Ancient Greek Literature (London: William Heinemann, 1907).
Murray, G. *Four Stages of Greek Religion* (New York: Columbia University Press, 1912).
Murray, G., *The Classical Tradition in Poetry: The Charles Eliot Norton Lectures* (London: Humphrey Milford/Oxford University Press, 1927).
Murray, G., *Aeschylus: The Creator of Tragedy* (Oxford: Clarendon Press, 1940).
Murray, G., *Five Stages of Greek Religion* (London: Watts, 1946).
Murray, O., *Early Greece*, 2nd edn (London: Fontana, 1993).
Mylonas, G.E., *Eleusis and the Elusinian Mysteries* (Princeton: Princeton University Press, 1961).
Myers, J.L., *Homer and his Critics* (London: Routledge and Kegan Paul, 1958).
Nagy, G., *Comparative Studies in Greek and Indic Meter* (Cambridge, Mass.: Harvard University Press, 1974).
Nagy, G., 'Early Greek views of poets and poetry', in George A. Kennedy, ed., *The Cambridge History of Literary Criticism* (Cambridge: Cambridge University Press, 1989): 1–77.
Nagy, G., *Greek Mythology and Poetics* (Ithaca and London: Cornell University Press, 1990).
Naveh, J., *Origins of the Alphabet* (London: Cassell, 1975).
Naveh, J., *Early History of the Alphabet: An Introduction to West Semitic Epigraphy and Palaeography* (Jerusalem: Hebrew University, 1982).
Neumann, E., *The Origins and History of Consciousness* (New York: Harper, 1962).
Nietzsche, F., *Thus Spoke Zarathustra* (New York: Viking Press, 1954).
Nietzsche, F., *The Use and Abuse of History* (New York: Library of Liberal Arts Press, 1957).
Nietzsche, F., *Die Geburt der Tragödie aus dem Geiste der Musik (Griechentum und Pessimismus)* (München: Wilhelm Goldmann Verlag, 1959).

BIBLIOGRAPHY

Nietzsche, F., *Philosophy in the Tragic Age of the Greeks* (Chicago: Henry Regnery, 1962).
Nietzsche, F., *The Birth of Tragedy and the Case of Wagner* (New York: Vintage Press, 1967).
Nietzsche, F., *The Will to Power* (New York: Vintage Books, 1968).
Nietzsche, F., *On the Genealogy of Morals and Ecce Homo* (New York: Vintage Books, 1969).
Nietzsche, F., *The Gay Science* (New York: Random House, 1974).
Nietzsche, F., *Ecce Homo* (Harmondsworth: Penguin, 1979).
Nietzsche, F., *On the Advantage and Disadvantage of History for Life* (Indianapolis: Hackett Publishing, 1980).
Nietzsche, F., *Daybreak: Thoughts on the Prejudices of Morality* (Cambridge: Cambridge University Press, 1982).
Nietzsche, F., *Human, All Too Human* (Lincoln and London: University of Nebraska Press, 1984).
Nilsson, M.P., *The Minoan–Mycenaean Religion and its Survival in Greek Religion* (Lund: C.W.K. Gleerup, 1927).
Nilsson, M.P., *Homer and Mycenae* (London: Methuen, 1933).
Nilsson, M.P., *Greek Popular Religion* (New York: Columbia University Press, 1940).
Nilsson, M.P., *Greek Piety* (Oxford: Clarendon Press, 1948.)
Nilsson, M.P., *The Dionysian Mysteries of the Hellenistic and Roman Age* (Lund: C.W.K. Gleerup, 1957).
Nilsson, M.P., *A History of Greek Religion* (New York: W.W. Norton, 1962).
Nilsson, M.P., *The Mycenaean Origin of Greek Mythology* (1932) (New York: W. W. Norton, 1963).
Nisetich, F.J., trans., *Pindar's Victory Songs* (Baltimore and London: Johns Hopkins University Press, 1980).
Noiré, L., *Max Müller and the Philosophy of Language* (London: Longmans, Green, and Company, 1879).
O'Keefe, D.L., *Stolen Lightning: The Social Theory of Magic* (Oxford: Martin Robertson, 1982).
Oliva, P., *The Birth of Greek Civilization* (London: Orbis Publishing, 1981).
Ong, W.J., *Interfaces of the Word: Studies in the Evolution of Consciousness and Culture* (Ithaca: Cornell University Press, 1977).
Ong, W.J., *Orality and Literature: The Technologizing of the Word* (London: Methuen, 1982).
Onians, R.B., *The Origins of European Thought about the Body, the Mind, the Soul, the World, Time, and Fate*, 2nd edn (Cambridge: Cambridge University Press, 1954).
Ortega Y Gasset, J., *The Origin of Philosophy* (New York: W.W. Norton, 1967).
Ortega Y Gasset, J., *Some Lessons in Metaphysics* (New York: W.W. Norton, 1969).
Otto, R., *The Idea of the Holy: An Inquiry into the Non-rational Factor in the Idea of the Divine and Its Relation to the Rational* (Oxford: Oxford University Press, 1923).
Otto, W.F., *Die Götter Griechenlands. Das Bild des Göttlichen im Spiegel des griechischen Geistes* (Frankfurt, 1947).
Otto, W.F., *The Homeric Gods: The Spiritual Significance of Greek Religion* (New York and London: Thames and Hudson, 1955).
Ovid, *Metamorphoses*, trans. Frank Justus Miller, 2 vols, 3rd edn (London: Heinemann, 1977).
Oxford Classical Dictionary, ed. N. G. L. Hammond and H. H. Scullard, 2nd edn (Oxford: Oxford University Press, 1970).
Oxford History of the Classical World, edited by John Boardman, Jasper Griffin and Oswyn Murray (Oxford: Oxford University Press 1986).

BIBLIOGRAPHY

Oxford History of Greece and the Hellenistic World, ed. by John Boardman, Jasper Griffin, and Oswyn Murray (Oxford: Oxford University Press, 1991).
Owen, G.E.L., *Logic, Science, and Dialectic* (London: Duckworth, 1986).
Owens, J., *A History of Ancient Western Philosophy* (New York: Appleton-Century-Crofts, 1959).
Paci, E., *The Function of the Sciences and the Meaning of Man* (Evanston: Northwestern University Press, 1972).
Page, D.L., *The Homeric Odyssey* (Oxford: Clarendon Press, 1955).
Page, D.L., *History and the Homeric Iliad* (Berkeley: University of California Press, 1959).
Page, D.L., *The Santorini Volcano and the Destruction of Minoan Crete* (London: The Society for the Promotion of Hellenic Studies, 1970).
Page, D.L., trans., *Select Papyri: Volume 3: Literary Papyri/Poetry* (London: Heinemann, 1941).
Paglia, C., *Sexual Personae: Art and Decadence from Nefertiti to Emily Dickinson* (New Haven: Yale University Press, 1990).
Palmer, L.R., *On the Knossos Tablets* (Oxford: Clarendon Press, 1963).
Palmer, L.R., *Mycenaeans and Minoans: Aegean Prehistory in the Light of the Linear B Tablets*, (London: Faber and Faber, 1961; 2nd revised edn 1961).
Palmer, L.R. and Chadwick, J., eds, *Proceedings of the Cambridge Colloquium on Mycenaean Studies* (Cambridge: Cambridge University Press, 1966).
Parain, B., *A Metaphysics of Language* (Garden City: Doubleday/Anchor, 1971).
Parry, A., *The Language of Achilles and Other Papers* (Oxford: Oxford University Press, 1989).
Parke, H.W., *Greek Oracles* (London: Hutchinson, 1967).
Parke, H.W., *The Oracles of Zeus* (Oxford: Basil Blackwell 1967b).
Parke, H.W., *Festivals of the Athenians* (London: Thames and Hudson, 1977).
Parke, H.W. and Wormell, D.E.W., *The Delphic Oracle*, 2 vols (Oxford: Oxford University Press, 1956).
Parker, R., *Miasma: Pollution and Purification in Early Greek Religion* (Oxford: Oxford University Press, 1983).
Parry, A., ed., *The Making of Homeric Verse: The Collected Papers of Milman Parry* (Oxford: Clarendon Press, 1971).
Parry, A., ed., *Studies in Fifth-century Thought and Literature*, vol. 22, Yale Classical Studies (Cambridge: Cambridge University Press, 1972).
Parry, M., *L'Epithète traditionelle dans Homère* (Paris, 1928).
Parry, M. and Lord, A., *Serbocroatian Heroic Songs*, Volume 1 (Cambridge, Mass.: Harvard University Press, 1954).
Pausanias, *Guide to Greece*, trans. P. Levi, 2 vols (Harmondsworth: Penguin, 1971).
Pavese, C., *This Business of Living: Diaries 1935–1950* (London: Quartet Books, 1980).
Peters, F.E., *Greek Philosophical Terms: A Historical Lexicon* (New York: New York University Press, 1967).
Pfeiffer, R., *History of Classical Scholarship: From 1300 to 1850* (Oxford: Oxford University Press, 1976).
Pfeiffer, R., ed., *Callimachus*, Volume 1 (Oxford: Clarendon Press, 1949).
Philip, J.A., *Pythagoras and Early Pythagoreanism* (Toronto: University of Toronto Press, 1966).
Pindar, *Works*, ed. and trans. J.E. Sandys, 2nd edn (London: William Heinemann/Loeb Classical Library, 1919).
Pindar, *The Odes of Pindar*, trans. C. M. Bowra (Harmondsworth: Penguin, 1969).
Pindar, *Victory Songs*, trans. F.J. Nisetich (Baltimore and London: Johns Hopkins University Press, 1980).
Plant, R., *Hegel: An Introduction* (Oxford: Oxford University Press, 1983).

Plato, *The Symposium*, trans. W. Hamilton (Harmondsworth: Penguin, 1951).
Plato, *Protagoras and Meno*, trans. W.K.C. Guthrie (Harmondsworth: Penguin, 1956).
Plato, *The Dialogues of Plato* (Oxford: Clarendon Press, 1969).
Plato, *Timaeus* and *Critias*, trans. H.D.P. Lee (Harmondsworth: Penguin, 1971).
Plato, *Phaedrus* and *The Seventh and Eighth Letters*, trans. W. Hamilton (Harmondsworth: Penguin, 1973).
Plato, *Phaedo*, trans. G.M.A. Grube (Indianapolis: Hackett Publishing Company, 1977).
Plato, *Philebus*, trans. Robin A.H. Waterfield (Harmondsworth: Penguin, 1982).
Plato, *Early Socratic Dialogues* (Harmondsworth: Penguin, 1987).
Plato, *The Republic*, trans. Robin Waterfield (Oxford and New York: Oxford University Press, 1994).
Plotinus, *The Enneads*, trans. Stephen MacKenna (London: Faber and Faber, 1969).
Plutarch, *Moralia*, trans. F.C. Babbitt, *et al.* (London: William Heinemann/Loeb Classical Library, 1927).
Plutarch, *Moralia XIII, Parts 1-2*, trans. Harold Cherniss, 2 vols (Cambridge Mass.: Harvard University Press/Loeb Classical Library, 1976).
Plutarch, *The Rise and Fall of Athens* (Harmondsworth: Penguin, 1960).
Polanyi, K., *Origins of Our Time: The Great Transformation* (London: Victor Gollancz, 1946), published in America as *The Great Transformation* (Boston: Beacon Press, 1944).
Polanyi, K., C.M. Arensberg, and H.W. Pearson *Trade and Market in Early Empires* (New York: Free Press, 1967).
Propp, V., *The Morphology of the Folktale* (Austin: University of Texas Press, 1968).
Propp, V., *Theory and History of Folklore* (Manchester: Manchester University Press, 1984).
Pucci, P., *Hesiod and the Language of Poetry* (Baltimore and London: Johns Hopkins University Press, 1977).
Raschke, W.J., ed., *The Archaeology of the Olympics* (Wisconsin: Wisconsin University Press, 1988).
Reale, G., *A History of Ancient Philosophy: Volume 1: From the Origins to Socrates* (New York: State University of New York Press, 1987).
Redfield, J.M., *Nature and Culture in the Iliad: The Tragedy of Hector* (Chicago and London: Chicago University Press, 1975).
Ricoeur, P., *Interpretation Theory: Discourse and the Surplus of Meaning* (Fort Worth: Texas Christian University Press, 1976).
Ricoeur, P., *The Rule of Metaphor: Multi-disciplinary Studies of the Creation of Meaning in Language* (London: Routledge and Kegan Paul, 1978).
Ricoeur, P., *Hermeneutics and the Human Sciences* (Cambridge: Cambridge University Press, 1981).
Ricoeur, P., 'Dialogue with Paul Ricoeur', in R. Kearney, ed., *Dialogues with Contemporary Thinkers: The Phenomenological Heritage* (Manchester: Manchester University Press, 1984): 15–46.
Ricoeur, P., *Time and Narrative* (Chicago: University of Chicago Press, 1984–8).
Ricoeur, P., *Lectures on Ideology and Utopia* (New York: Columbia University Press, 1986).
Riedel, M., 'ARXH und APEIRON: Über das Grundwort des Anaximander', *Archiv für Geschichte der Philosophie*, 69, (1987): 1–17.
Rilke, R.M., *Duino Elegies*, trans. J.B. Leishman and S. Spender (London: Chatto and Windus, 1978).
Robertson, M., *A History of Greek Art*, 2 vols (Cambridge: Cambridge University Press, 1975).

BIBLIOGRAPHY

Robinson, T.M., *Heraclitus: Fragments, A Text and Translation with a Commentary* (Toronto: University of Toronto Press, 1987).
Rohde, E., *Psyche: the Cult of Souls and Belief in Immortality among the Greeks* (London: Kegan Paul, Trench, Trubner, 1925).
J. H. Rose, *A Handbook of Greek Mythology: Including its Extension to Rome* (1928) (London: Routledge, 1989).
Rosenberg, D. and Bloom, H., *The Book of J*, trans. David Rosenberg, interpreted Harold Bloom (London: Faber and Faber, 1991).
Rosenzweig, F., *The Star of Redemption* (1921) (London: Routledge and Kegan Paul, 1970).
Russell, B., *History of Western Philosophy* (1946) (London: Routledge, 1992).
Russell, D.A. and Winterbottom, M., eds, *Ancient Literary Criticism: The Principal Texts in New Translations* (Oxford: Clarendon Press, 1978).
Rzach, A., ed., *Hesiodi Carmina: Recensuit* (Leipzig, B. G. Teubner, 1913).
Said, E., *Orientalism* (London: Routledge, 1978).
Sampson, G., *Writing Systems* (London: Hutchinson, 1985).
Sandars, N.K., *The Sea Peoples: Warriors of the Ancient Mediterranean 1250–1150 BC* (London: Thames and Hudson, 1978).
Sanders, N.K., trans. *The Epic of Gilgamesh* (Harmondsworth: Penguin, 1960).
Sandys, J.E., *A History of Classical Scholarship* (Cambridge: Cambridge University Press, 1908).
Santillana, G., *The Origins of Scientific Thought* (London: Weidenfeld and Nicolson, 1961).
Saunders, T.J., ed., Plato: Early Socratic Dialogues (Harmondsworth: Penguin, 1987).
Schelling, F.W.J., *Of Human Freedom* (1809) (Chicago: Open Court Publishing Company, 1936).
Schelling, F.W.J., *On University Studies* (Athens: Ohio University Press, 1966).
Schelling, F.W.J., *The Ages of the World* (New York: AMS Press, 1967).
Schelling, F.W.J., *System of Transcendental Idealism* (1800) (Charlottesville: University Press of Virginia, 1978).
Schelling, F.W.J., *The Unconditional in Human Knowledge: Four Early Essays (1794–1796)* (Lewisburg: Bucknell University Press, 1980).
Schlegel, F., *Dialogue on Poetry and Literary Aphorisms* (University Park and London: Pennsylvania State University Press, 1968).
Scholes, R. and Kellogg, R., *The Nature of Narrative* (New York: Oxford University Press, 1966).
Schopenhauer, A., *Parerga and Paralipomena: Short Philosophical Essays* (Oxford: Clarendon Press, 1974).
Sealey, R., *A History of the Greek City States ca. 700–338 BC* (Berkeley: University of California Press, 1976).
Sebeok, T.A., ed., *Myth: A Symposium* (Bloomington and London: Indiana University Press, 1972).
Segal, C., *The Theme of the Mutilation of the Corpse in the Iliad* (Leiden: E.J. Brill, 1971).
Select Papyri, 3 vols (London: William Heinemann/Loeb Classical Library, 1932, 1941).
Sextus Empiricus, *Outlines of Pyrrhonism*, trans. R.G. Bury (London: William Heinemann/Loeb Classical Library, 1933).
Sextus Empiricus, *Against the Logicians*, trans. R.G. Bury (London: William Heinemann/Loeb Classical Library, 1935).
Sextus Empiricus, *Against the Physicists and Against the Ethicists*, trans. R.G. Bury (London: William Heinemann/Loeb Classical Library, 1936).

BIBLIOGRAPHY

Sextus Empiricus, *Against the Professors*, trans. R.G. Bury (London: William Heinemann/Loeb Classical Library, 1940).
Simonides, in *Greek Lyric Poetry*, trans. Willis Barnstore (New York: Schocken Books, 1972): 133–140.
Simplicius, *On Aristotle Physics 6*, trans. David Konstan (London: Duckworth, 1989).
Simpson, W.K., ed., *The Literature of Ancient Egypt: An Anthology of Stories, Instructions, and Poetry* (New Haven and London: Yale University Press, 1973).
Sinnige, T.G., *Matter and Infinity in the Presocratic Schools and Plato* (Assen: Van Gorcum, 1971).
Snell, B., *The Discovery of the Mind: The Greek Origins of European Thought* (Oxford: Basil Blackwell/New York: Harper, 1953).
Snodgrass, A.M., *Early Greek Armour and Weapons* (Edinburgh: Edinburgh University Press, 1964).
Snodgrass, A.M., *Arms and Armour of the Greeks* (London: Thames and Hudson, 1967).
Snodgrass, A.M., *The Dark Age of Greece: An Archaeological Survey of the Eleventh to the Eighth Centuries* BC (Edinburgh: Edinburgh University Press, 1971).
Snodgrass, A.M., *Archaic Greece: The Age of Experiment* (London: Dent, 1980).
Snodgrass, A.M., *An Archaeology of Greece* (Berkeley: University of California Press, 1987).
Snodgrass, A.M., 'Archaeology and the study of the Greek city', in J. Rich and A. Wallace-Hadrill, eds, *City and Country in the Ancient World* (London: Routledge, 1991): 1–23.
Solon, in *Greek Lyrics*, trans. R. Lattimore (Chicago: University of Chicago Press, 1960): 18–23.
Solmsen, F., *Intellectual Experiments of the Greek Enlightenment* (Princeton: Princeton University Press, 1975).
Sophocles, *Volume II: Ajax, Electra, Trachiniae, Philoctetes*, trans. F. Storr (London: Heinemann/Loeb Classical Library, 1967).
Sophocles, *Volume 1: Oedipus the King, Oedipus at Colonus, Antigone*, trans. F. Storr (London: Heinemann/Loeb Classical Library, 1968).
Sophocles, *The Theban Plays* (Harmondsworth: Penguin 1983).
Sörbom, G., *Mimesis and Art: Studies in the Origin and Early Development of an Aesthetic Vocabulary* (Bonniers: Svenska Bokfoerlaget, 1966).
Starr, C.G., *The Origins of Greek Civilization, 1100–650* BC (New York: Knopf, 1961).
Starr, C.G., *Individual and Community: The Rise of the Polis 800–500 B.C.* (Oxford: Oxford University Press, 1986).
Steiner, G. and Fagles, R., eds, *Homer: A Collection of Critical Essays* (Englewood Cliffs: Prentice-Hall, 1962).
Strabo, *Geography*, trans. H.L. Jones, (London: Heinmann/Loeb Classical Library, 1917).
Suetonius, trans. J.C. Rolfe, 2 vols (London: William Heinemann/Loeb Classical Library, 1913, 1914).
Taylor, D., 'Introduction' to Sophocles, *The Theban Plays*, trans. Don Taylor (London: Methuen, 1986): vii–lii.
Thomas, *The Gospel According to Thomas*, Coptic texts established and trans. A. Guillaumont, H.-Ch. Puech, G. Quispel, W. Till, and Yassah 'Abd Al Masih (Leiden: E.J. Brill, 1959).
Thomas, C.G., ed., *Homer's History: Mycenaean or Dark Age?* (New York: Holt, Rinehart and Winston, 1970).
Thomas, R., *Literacy and Orality in Ancient Greece* (Cambridge: Cambridge University Press, 1992).

BIBLIOGRAPHY

Thompson, R.C., *The Epic of Gilgamesh: Text, Transliteration and Notes* (Oxford: Oxford University Press, 1930).
Thomson, G., *Studies in Ancient Greek Society: Volume 1: The Prehistoric Aegean* (London: Lawrence and Wishart, 1954).
Thomson, G., *Studies in Ancient Greeek Society: Volume 2: The First Philosophers* (London: Lawrence and Wishart, 1955).
Thomson, J.O., *History of Ancient Geography* (London: Cambridge University Press, 1948).
Thucydides, *History of the Peloponnesian War* (Harmondsworth: Penguin, 1954).
Tillich, P., *Love, Power, and Justice: Ontological Analyses and Ethical Applications* (London: Oxford University Press, 1954).
Tilly, C., *Big Structures, Large Processes, Huge Comparisons* (New York: Russell Sage Foundation, 1984).
Toynbee, A.J., *Greek Civilization: The Self-Revelation of Ancient Greek Society* (1924) (New York: New American Library, 1953).
Tredennick, H., trans. *Aristotle, Metaphysics Books I-IX* (Cambridge, Mass.: Harvard University Press, 1978).
Tripp, E., *The Handbook of Classical Mythology* (London: Arthur Barker, 1970).
Trump, D.H., *The Prehistory of the Mediterranean* (London: Allen Lane, 1980).
Trypanis, C.A., *The Homeric Epics* (Warminster, Wiltshire: Aris and Phillips, 1977)
Trypanis, C.A., *Greek Poetry: From Homer to Seferis* (London and Boston: Faber and Faber, 1981)
Trypanis, C.A., ed., *Penguin Book of Greek Verse* (Harmondsworth: Penguin, 1971).
Varro, *De Lingua Latina (On the Latin Language)*, trans. R.G. Kent, 2 vols (London: William Heinemann/Loeb Classical Library, 1938).
Vermeule, E., *Greece in the Bronze Age* (Chicago: University of Chicago Press, 1964).
Vermeule, E., *The Art of the Shaft Graves of Mycenae* (Norman: University of Oklahoma Press, 1975).
Vermeule, E., *Aspects of Death in Early Greek Art and Poetry* (Berkeley: University of California Press, 1979).
Ventris, M. and Chadwick, J., *Documents in Mycenaean Greek: Three Hundred Selected Tablets from Knossos, Pylos and Mycenae with Commentary and Vocabulary* (Cambridge: Cambridge University Press, 1956).
Vernant, J.-P., *Mythe et pensée chez les grecs* (Paris: Editions Maspero, 1966).
Vernant, J.-P., 'Introduction' to Marcel Detienne, *The Gardens of Adonis* (Brighton: Harvester Press, 1977): i-xxxv.
Vernant, J.-P., *Mythe en société en Grece ancienne* (Paris: Editions Maspero, 1980).
Vernant, J.-P., *Myth and Society in Ancient Greece* (New York: Zone Books, 1990).
Vernant, J.-P. and Vidal-Naquet, P., *Tragedy and Myth in Ancient Greece* (Brighton: Harvester Press, 1981).
Vickers, B., *Towards Greek Tragedy: Drama, Myth, Society* (London: Longman, 1973).
Vico, G., *The Autobiography of Giambattista Vico* (Ithaca and London: Cornell University Press, 1963)
Vico, G., *The New Science of Giambattista Vico*, (Ithaca and London: Cornell University Press, 1970).
Vico, G., *Selected Writings*, trans. Leon Pompa (Cambridge: Cambridge University Press, 1982).
Vidal-Naquet, P., *The Black Hunter. Forms of Thought and Forms of Society in the Greek World* (Baltimore: Johns Hopkins University Press, 1986).
Vilborg, E., *A Tentative Grammar of Mycenaean Greek* (Göteborg: Almqvist and Wiksell, 1960).
Virgil, *The Pastoral Poems (Eclogues)* (Harmondsworth: Penguin, 1967).

Voeglin, E., *Order and History: Volume 5: In Search of Order* (Baton Rouge and London: Louisiana State University Press, 1987).
Voeglin, E., *Autobiographical Reflections* (Baton Rouge and London: Louisiana State University Press, 1989).
von Eschenbach, W., *Willehalm* (Harmondsworth: Penguin, 1984).
von Weizsäcker, C.F., *The Relevance of Science: Creation and Cosmogony (The Gifford Lectures 1959–1960)* (London: Collins, 1964)
von Wilamowitz-Moellendorff, U., *Pindaros* (Berlin: Weidmann, 1966).
Wace, A.J.B. and Stubbings, F.H., eds, *A Companion to Homer* (London: Macmillan, 1962).
Wade-Gery, H.T., *The Poet of the Iliad* (Cambridge: Cambridge University Press, 1952).
Walcot, P., *Hesiod and the Near East* (Cardiff: University of Wales Press, 1966).
Walker, B., *Gnosticism: Its History and Influence* (Chatham: Crucible, 1989).
Weber, M., *The Methodology of the Social Sciences* (New York: Free Press, 1949).
Weber, M., *The Religion of China: Confucianism and Taoism* (Glencoe: Free Press, 1951).
Weber, M., *The Rational and Social Foundations of Music* (Carbondale: Southern Illinois University Press, 1958).
Weber, M., *The Sociology of Religion* (London: Methuen, 1966).
Weber, M., *Ancient Judaism* (New York: Free Press, 1967).
Weber, M., *Economy and Society: An Outline of Interpretive Sociology* (New York: Bedminster Press, 1968).
Weber, M., General Economic History (New Brunswick: Transaction Books, 1981).
Webster, T.B.L., *From Mycenae to Homer* (London: Methuen, 1958).
Webster, T.B.L., *Greek Art and Literature 700–530 BC: The Beginnings of Modern Civilization* (London: Methuen, 1959).
Wellek, R. and Warren, A., *Theory of Literature* (1949) (Harmondsworth: Penguin, 1963).
Wender, D., trans., *Theogony and Works and Days* (with Theognis' *Elegies*) (Harmondsworth: Penguin, 1985).
West, M.L., *Hesiod: The Theogony* (Oxford: Clarendon Press, 1966).
West, M.L., *Early Greek Philosophy and the Orient* (Oxford: Clarendon Press, 1971).
West, M.L., *The Orphic Poems* (Oxford: Clarendon Press, 1983).
West, M.L., 'The rise of the Greek epic', *Journal of Hellenic Studies*, 108, 1988, 151–72.
West, M.L., ed., *Iambi et Elegi* (Oxford: Oxford University Press, 1971–72).
West, M.L., ed., *Hesiod: Works and Days* (Oxford: Oxford University Press, 1978)
Whibley, L., ed., *A Companion to Greek Studies*, 4th revised edn (New York: Hafner Publishing Co., 1968).
Whitman, C.M., *Homer and the Homeric Tradition* (Cambridge, Mass.: Harvard University Press, 1958).
Westen, D., *Self and Society: Narcissism, Collectivism, and the Development of Morals* (Cambridge: Cambridge University Press, 1985).
Williams, R., *Keywords* (London: Fontana, 1976).
Windelband, W., *History of Ancient Philosophy* (1899) (New York: Dover Publications, 1956).
Windelband, W., *A History of Philosophy: With Especial reference to the Formation and Development of its Problems and Conceptions* (1893) (New York: Macmillan, 1901).
Wittgenstein, L., *Philosophical Investigations* (Oxford: Basil Blackwell, 1968).
Wolff, F.A., *Prolegomena to Homer* (Princeton: Princeton University Press, 1985).
Wood, E.M. and Wood, N., *Class Ideology and Ancient Political Theory: Socrates, Plato, and Aristotle in Social Context* (Oxford: Basil Blackwell, 1978).

BIBLIOGRAPHY

Wood, M., *In Search of the Trojan War* (London: BBC Books, 1985).
Wood, R., *An Essay on the Original Genius and Writings of Homer* (1769) (Philadelphia, 1976).
Woodhead, A.G., *The Greeks in the West* (London: Thames and Hudson, 1962).
Wolf, F.A., *Prolegomena ad Homerum* 3rd edn Halle, 1884).
Wright Mills, C., *Power, Politics, and People: The Collected Essays of C. Wright Mills* (New York: Oxford University Press, 1963).
Xenophon, *A History of My Times (Hellenica)*, trans. R. Warner (Harmondsworth: Penguin, 1966).
Zeller, E., *Aristotle and the Earlier Peripatetics*, 2 vols (London, 1897).
Zeller, E., *Outlines of the History of Greek Philosophy* (1892) 13th edn ed. W. Nestle (London: Routledge and Kegan Paul, 1969).

NAME INDEX

Adkins, A.W.H. 84, 101, 113, 136
Adorno, Theodor W. 99, 206, 213, 314n24
Aelius Aristides 57
Aeschylus xv, 9, 49, 105, 124, 152, 176–8, 189, 193, 202–3, 204, 232, 255, 267, 273, 274, 336n28
Aesop 166
Alcaeus of Lesbos 65, 209, 210, 215, 226, 231–3, 233, 237, 364n1
Alcman 65, 209, 210, 224–5, 247, 252, 254, 283, 354n2, 364n1
Anacreon of Teos 209, 210, 244–6, 364n1
Anaxagoras (of Clazomenae) 301
Anaximander 41, 45, 185, 198, 381n2
Anaximenes 198
Andrewes, A. 223, 258
Apollodorus 11
Apollonius Rhodius 52
Archilochus 158, 159, 170, 209, 213, 214, 215, 219, 220, 222, 226–231, 238, 239, 242, 247, 258, 271, 364n1
Aristarchus of Samothrace 57
Aristophanes 159, 161, 229–30, 241, 267, 275, 280, 374n41, 375–6n1
Aristotle xv, xvi, 1, 4, 7, 18, 26, 34, 35, 36, 40, 41, 46, 59, 60, 63, 75–6, 77–8, 83, 86, 91, 92, 101, 113, 186–7, 189, 190, 205, 213, 223, 227, 252, 259, 279, 293, 297, 300, 301, 330, 331
Arnold, Matthew 325n7
Athene, Athena, Pallas Athena 96, 103, 125, 127 and throughout chapter 2
d'Aubignac, François Hédelin 143
Auerbach, Erich 58, 91–2, 93, 333n19, 333n20, 333–4n22
Aulus Gellius 52, 56, 57, 338–9n37

Bacchylides 40, 209, 210, 246, 247, 282, 364n1
Bakhtin, Mikhail M. 211, 286, 370n16
Barnstone, Willis 224, 225
Barthes, Roland 9,
Bataille, Georges 18, 23
Baudelaire, Charles 242
Benjamin, Walter 12, 14, 100, 163, 323n4
Bernal, M. 7
Bettelheim, Bruno 4, 50,
Blegen, Carl W. 53, 136
Bloch, Ernst 132
Bloom, Harold 147–8
Boas, George 2
Boccaccio 52
Böhme, Jakob 185
Bowra, C.M. 6, 145–6, 210, 211–12, 224, 365–6n2
Braudel, Fernand xiv
Bremmer, Jan 100
Broch, Hermann 52–3
Burke, Kenneth 25
Burkert, W. 7
Burnet, John xv, 162, 194–5

Callimachus 205
Callinus of Ephesus 209, 220, 222, 231, 234, 364n1
Campbell, Joseph 19, 24, 30
Carpenter, Rhys 74
Cassirer, Ernst 303n3
Chadwick, John 136, 340–1n42
Chaucer, Geoffrey 52
Claus, D.B. 101
Collingwood, R.G.
Corax (Sicilian originator of rhetoric) 127
Cornford, Francis M. 18, 25, 195–6

NAME INDEX

Curtius, Ernst Robert 74

Dante Alighieri 52
Demosthenes (orator) xvi, 41, 377n5
Derrida, Jacques 185, 186, 309n7, 315–16n26
Detienne, Marcel 209, 314n24
Diodorus Siculus 11
Diogenes Laertius 333n18, 336n30
Diogenes (the Cynic) 159
Dionysius I of Syracuse 277
Dodds, E.R. 196
Dover, Kenneth 258
Durkheim, Émile, 7–8, 36, 42, 123

Easterling, P.E. 9
Eckhart, Meister 185
Eco, Umberto 23, 207
Ehrenberg, Victor 51, 54, 286
Eliade, Mircea 19, 21, 23, 24, 25, 27–8
Elias, Norbert 19–20
Eliot, T.S. 48
Empedocles 127, 189–90, 208, 281
Epimenides 354n2
Euripides 7, 9, 46, 255, 267, 279–80

Fagles, Robert 5, 49, 80, 95, 96, 100
Feyerabend, Paul 10, 195–6
Fielding, Henry 52
Finley, Moses xv, 5, 9, 25, 32, 83, 141–2, 157, 310n10, 310n12, 365n2
Foucault, Michel 100
Fowler, H.W. 6
Frame, Douglas, 15, 30, 95, 102, 339n38
Fränkel, Hermann 4, 6, 48, 50, 58, 60, 95, 102, 103, 113, 212, 276, 279, 283, 300–1
Frankfort, H. 18
Frye, Northrop 10, 219

Gadamer, Hans-Georg 28, 29
Galen 263
Goethe, Johann Wolfgang von 143
Gorgias of Leontini xv, 127
Gouldner, Alvin W., 1, 354–5n3
Griffin, Jasper 60
Guthrie, W.K.C. 267, 281

Harris, W.V. 365–6n2, 366–7n3
Harrison, Jane 8–9, 30
Havelock Eric A. 10, 48, 49, 50, 51, 58, 59, 148–9
Heidegger, Martin 21, 185, 268, 378n13

Heinberg, R. 201
Heraclitus 28, 40, 45, 46, 116–17, 219, 224, 255, 285, 286, 301, 370n13
Herder, Johann Gottfried 143
Herodotus xv, xvi, 135–6, 160, 161, 177, 229, 273, 318–20n2, 370n14
Hesiod xv, 33, 36, 37, 40, 41, 44, 65, 87, 103, 105, 107, 141, 160, 161, 164, 167, 168, 177, 178, 180, 185, 186, 187, 188, 190–3, 195–204, 220, 226, 232, 238, 240, 251, 252–3, 254, 258, 266, 267, 268, 269, 282, 284, 288, 337n34, and throughout chapter 3
Hieron (Sicilian tyrant) 258, 277
Hippocrates of Cos 263
Hipponax 159, 209, 214, 220, 239–42, 242, 247, 358–9n13, 364n1
Hölderlin, Friedrich 185
Horace 230
Horkheimer, Max 99, 314n24
Huxley, G.L. 223, 369n11
Hyperides (orator) xvi

Iamblichus 280
Ibycus of Rhegium 209, 210, 244, 280, 364n1
Isocrates xv, xvi, 7, 31–2, 53, 58, 290, 377n5

Jaeger, Werner 27, 49, 103, 181, 197, 362n24
Joyce, James 52
Juvenal 238

Kant, Immanuel 211, 289
Kazantzakis, Nicos 53
Kelsen, Hans 86
Knox, B.M.W. 147, 148, 241, 365–6n2, 369–70n13
Kurosawa, Akira 73

Lattimore, Richmond 80, 89, 108, 175, 176, 180, 223, 224, 228, 259–60, 272, 294
Lessing, Gotthold Ephraim 143
Levi, Peter 50, 66, 210, 246, 370n17
Lévi-Strauss, Claude 15, 23, 43
Lévy-Bruhl, Lucien 21
Longinus 89
Lord, Albert 52, 53, 144–5, 147, 148, 149–50, 151
Luce, J.V. 78, 150, 152
Lucian 58

412

NAME INDEX

Lucius Livius 52
Lycurgus (orator) xvi, 32, 56, 222–3
Lysias xv, 7, 264, 371n20, 377n5

Mallarmé, Stephan 219
Malinowski, Bronislaw 9, 17
Malory, Sir Thomas 52
Mann, Thomas 52
Marx, Karl 308n5
Mauss, Marcel 17, 42, 120
Menander 229
Mills, C. Wright 351–2n68
Mimnermus 209, 215, 220, 237–8, 271, 364n1
Muir, J.V. 9
Murray A.T. 130–1
Murray, Gilbert xv, 6, 7
Murray, Oswyn 102, 210, 211, 223, 259, 368–9n10

Nagy, Gregory 9, 219, 221–2, 282, 367n5
Neumann, Erich 26
Nietzsche, Friedrich 210, 354n3, 383–4n4
Nilsson, M.P. 89
Nisetich, Frank J. 275–6

Oliva, Pavel 223
Ong, Walter J. 330n13
Ovid 201, 205

Page, D.L. 136–8
Palmer L.R. 78, 82
Parain, Bryce 12
Parmenides 40, 176, 185, 188, 189
Parry, Adam 150, 349n62
Parry, Milman 52, 53, 149, 144–50, 330n13, 349n62
Pausanias xvi, 205, 222, 286
Pavese, Cesare 334n22
Pericles 16
Petronius 241
Pherecydes of Syros 288–9, 354n2, 381–2n3
Phocylides of Miletus 220
Pindar 7, 40, 82, 175, 178, 209, 210, 216, 239, 247, 249, 250, 252, 253, 253–7, 258, 259, 261, 262, 264, 265–74, 275, 276, 277, 278, 280, 285, 295, 296, 299, 324n6, 364n1, and throughout chapter 5
Plato xiv, 7, 18, 22, 27, 36, 40, 46, 53, 55, 75, 90, 101, 110–11, 113, 115, 160, 185, 188, 189, 200, 202, 205, 223, 244–5, 255, 259, 263, 266, 267, 274, 280, 285, 287, 290–1, 292–3, 294, 300, 370n13
Plotinus 185, 205
Plutarch xvi
Polycrates 244, 273
Porphyry 205
Praxilla 209, 236–7, 364n1
Protagoras 7
Pseudo-Plato 55

Rabelais, François 241, 242
Reale, Giovanni 385n8
Redfield, J.M. 60
Ricoeur, Paul 16
Rilke, Rainer Maria 208, 287
Rimbaud, Arthur 219
Rosenzweig, Franz 16

Said, Edward 7
Sappho of Lesbos 65, 209, 210, 214–5, 215, 216, 220, 226, 231, 233–6, 237, 252, 271, 295, 337n33, 364n1
Schelling, F.W.J. 27, 185–6
Schliemann, Heinrich 53
Semonides 209, 213, 238–9, 320n3
Seneca 205
Sextus Empiricus 188
Shakespeare, William 117, 255
Shklovsky, Victor 13
Simonides of Ceos 206, 209, 210, 239, 246–7, 252, 364n1
Snell, Bruno 99, 211
Socrates 36, 101, 117, 159, 189, 203, 246, 294
Solon of Athens 173–4, 220, 359n14, 364n1
Sophocles xv, xvi, 43, 75, 117, 123, 131, 135, 152, 158, 176, 177, 189, 203, 232, 255, 267, 271, 282, 286, 292, 336n29
Steiner, George 5, 49, 95, 96, 100
Stesichorus of Himera 209, 210, 213, 239, 252, 364n1
Strabo 222, 237
Suetonius 57
Szilasi, Wilhelm 1

Taplin, Oliver 82
Terpander 222, 224, 364n1
Thales 33, 117, 198
Theocritus 225
Theognis 209, 219, 220, 242–4, 364n1

NAME INDEX

Theophrastus 279
Theron (Sicilian tyrant) 258, 277
Thersites (in the *Iliad*) 90, 157–9
Thucydides xv, xvi, 7, 48, 135, 161
Tillich, Paul 10, 362–3n24
Trypanis, C.A. 48, 66, 88, 96, 221, 258
Tyrtaeus 122, 209, 220, 222–4, 226, 234, 364n1

Varro, Marcus Tullius 194, 238
Ventris, Michael 53, 136, 340–1n42
Verlaine, Paul 219
Vernant, Jean-Pierre 9, 25, 40, 41, 209, 214, 256, 275, 284, 300
Vickers, Brian 5, 9, 16–17, 39
Vico, Giambattista 143–4
Vidal-Naquet, Pierre 9
Villon, François 219, 240, 242
Virgil 52, 205, 225
Voeglin, Eric 360n16

Weber, Max xiv, 23, 24, 37, 54–5, 284, 288
Webster, T.B.L. xv, 5, 50, 284
Weil, Simone 87
West, M.L. 51
White, James Boyd 90
Wilamowitz-Moellendorf, Ulrich von 143–4
Winckelmann, Johan Joachim 143
Wittgenstein, Ludwig 1, 11
Wolff, Friedrich August 143–4
Wood, Robert 143

Xenophanes of Colophon 7, 45, 161, 220, 237, 370n14
Xenophon xv, xvi, 379–80n1
Xerxes 273

Zeller, Eduard 171, 299
Zeno of Elea 46

SUBJECT INDEX

Achaean(s) xv, 60, 61, 72, 73, 75, 76, 111 and throughout chapter 2; army/confederacy 76, 81, 84–5
Achilles 39, 40, 60, 62, 63, 68, 75, 77, 81, 94; anger 105–6, 109–10, 118, 122–3, 155, 252; loss of self 60–2, 78, 79, 84, 110–12, 276; and melancholy 117–18; multiple self 110–11; as orator 74, 110–11, 123–4, 158, 336–7n30; reconciliation with Priam 90; as reflexive agent 78
Achilles' shield 64, 71–2, 92–3, 213
Acragas (Akragas) 258
action: in the Homeric epic 59–77
Aegean: Cretan-Minoan hegemony 136–9; Mycenaean domination 136–40
aesthetic (*aisthesis*): analysis; differentiation 14–15
aesthetics: social differentiation of aesthetic forms 12–26; lyric origins of the 'aesthetic object' 212–17, 252
affectivity: in lyric poetry 215, 220–1, 233 and *passim*; phenomenology of 220; in Sappho 233–6; *see* everyday life
Agamemnon 39, 60, 62, 63, 66–7, 75, 77, 78, 79, 81, 84, 94, 109, 111, 122, 127, 136, 155, 157, 176, 239; mental conflict 130; lack of persuasive speech 125
agon 30; agonism in cultural change 165; agonism in the epic 60–77, 100–23; agonism in games 120–1, 257–63; agonism in Hesiod's *Theogony* 44, 181–2, 182–94; agonistic nature of early Greek culture 43–6, 79–94, 165–6, 180–94, 354–5n3, 366n2, 375–6n1; in Pindar 253–63; poetry

competitions 168, 212–13; theme of themes of the *Iliad* 64, 83–4
agora 85
Aither 198
Ajax 61, 69, 81, 84, 111, 123–4
aletheia, alethic (truth, truthlike) 7, 175, 176–8, 183, 269–70, 270–4, 378n13; *see also* truth
alethic dialectic 181–2, 259
Alexander the Great 56
Alexandria 57
Alexandrian Museum/Library 57; destruction of 57
alienation: *see* Orphism
allegory 4–6, 11–12, 24, 43, 64, 92, 99, 182, 190, 207; and interpretation in Biblical narrative 92–3, 333n22; in Mimnermus 237–8; and philosophical speculation 184–5, 288–9; in Pherecydes 289; in Pindar, 266–8, 268–74, 274–5; in Plato 292; in Sappho 235–6
alphabetization 43, 48–9, 51, 55–6, 148–50, 168, 320–2n3, 355–6n4, 365–6n2
alphabets: Canaanite 347–8n59; Greek xv, 43, 48, 51, 53, 56, 136–9, 142–3, 167–8, 320–2n3, 340–1n42, 365–6n2; Phoenician 142, 365n2
analogy: in ancient mythology 42
ananke 35
Andromache 68, 73, 117
anthropomorphism: of archaic narrative 42–3; of Greek myth 4–6, 42, 85, 94, 164–9
Antigone 152–4, 203
aoidoi (singers or bards) 53, 54, 125–6, 162, 324n6; the *aoidos* as charismatic

415

SUBJECT INDEX

singer 125–6, 151–2, 177–8; *see* rhapsode
aorist (verbal form) 78–9, 79ff.; panoramic-visual tense 79–80; *see* videology
Aphrodite 209, 252
Apollo: 62, 70, 130–1, 162, 217, 252, 286, 291–2; festival of Apollo at Delphi xv
Apollonian 44–5
Apollonian/Dionysian 22, 44–5, 285–7, 298–9, 381n1, 383–4n4
appearance and reality: in Hesiod, 175–6; in tragedy 176–8
archaeology: of discursive practices xiii; *see* logology
Archaic Age, the xiv, 20, 43–6, 47, 50; selfhood 98–100, 100–23; social contradictions xiv, 172–4
Archaic Greece xii-xvii, 5–6, 18–20, 43, 45–6, 151–7, and throughout volume 2; homerization of 54, *passim*; late Archaic period (c. 750–500 BC) 47–8, 208–9; world-view 119–23, 330–1n14
arche: in Aristotle 190; in Hesiod 194–5; as divine (*to theion*) 163, 190; as source of motion 190
arete (excellence, virtue, goodness) 35, 43, 63, 78–9, 81, 82, 83, 94, 151–2, 156–7, 223–4, 242–4, 253–4, 259–63, 264, 276–7, 297–8, 336n27
Argos 217
aristocracy: Boeotian 168, 172–3, 202–4, 250ff., *passim*; declining 151–2, 165, 211, 242–4, 247–8, 250–1, 274–5; in the Greek world 36, 54–8, 80–94, 151–7, 157–9
art and arts (*technai*): creation of the sphere of art 8–10
Artemis 282, 283
Asia: as threat to Hellenic culture xv-xvii
Asia Minor 51, 140, 165, 211, 220
Athena 39, 109–10
Athenian: culture 248; democracy 243; tragedy 16, 20, 41, 313n22
Athens 217, 277; democratic 218, 243, 244, 246
athletes: celebrated by Pindar 253
aura (Walter Benjamin's concept of) 12–13, 14–15; death of 12; and storytelling 12–13
auratic circulation 9–10, 10–16
author(s): Hesiod as the first European 'author' 168, 169–74; lyric poets as authors 209–10, 212–15, 365–6n2
authorship/authored discourse 220 and throughout chapter 4
autobiography 219
axiological formations/rules 4, 6
axiology (axiological principles) xiii-xiv, 4

Babylon 165
Babylonian religion 165, 196, 298, 353–4n1, 361n19; script 165
beauty, *kallos*: in Pindar 251–2
Bible, the 17–18
bifurcation: in Classical thought; in Greek mythology 19–20, 38–43
binary oppositions 19–20, 40–1, 42–3; *see* polarity
bird: divination by birds in the *Iliad* 134–5, 340n41; as image of the soul 113, 291–2, 337n32
birth: cosmogonic imagery 160, 164–9; cosmology 301, 381–2n2
Boeotia (birth place of Hesiod) 167–8, 206–9, 232, 277
bow and lyre 127, 224, 264

Calchas 133, 134–5, 178
Calypso 63, 89–90, 96–7, 98, 104, 105, 119
Calypso's island 97, 119, 125, 141, 213
Cassandra 62, 105
chaos: in ancient Middle Eastern religion; in Greek mythology 39; as dialectical image 184, 194–5; in Hesiod 183–4, 185–6, 186–8, 195–6; as unnameable (in)difference 186–7, 195, 199–201
child, children: education of children 58
Chios 51, 320n3
chora in Greek mythology 36, 216; in Homer 81–2, 85, 87–8, 92–4, 186–7; in Plato's *Timaeus* 186
choral poetry: 6, 14, 25–6, 167, 211–15, 215–17; characteristics 14–15, 215; as collective genre 210–11; lyric 36, 217–22, 311n13; performance 26; and religion 215; sub-genres 217–18; traditional social functions 14, 24–6, 165–6, 215
Circe 63, 96–7, 131
city-state; *see* polis
civic autonomy: as Greek ethical ideal

xv-xvii, 32–4
civilizing process xiv
classical age (of Greece) xv, 47, 56, 143
classification(s): in archaic narrative 41–3; primitive 42
Claudius (Emperor) 57
Clytemnestra 62, 127, 131, 177, 267
colonization 36, 167
comedy: Aristophanic 159; in the Homeric epic 88; and lyric poetry 217, 229–30, 239
competition: *see agon*
concrete 234–6; ethic of the 235
conscience: origins in Archaic Greece 157, 352–3n69
contestation 3
conversation: in Homeric epic 73–5
Corinth 243, 260
cosmogonic: poem 65, 179–80; speculation 164–5
cosmological argument 353–4n1
cosmological theorizing 35, 164, 353–4n1
cosmology 35, 65, 179, 381–2n2
cosmos *see kosmos*
creatio ex nihilo: proscribed in Greek thought 188, 361n19
creation: of the world, throughout chapter 3, 361n19
critical activity 221–2; discourse 221–2; self-reflection 221; spirit: Greek origins of xiii, 221; *see* reflexivity
culture: as reflexive conversation 5–6, 11–12; collective common 163; founded upon *poiesis* 180; matrix of identity and community 162–3;
Cynic, Cynics, cynical, cynicism: 159

dactylic hexameter 51, 145–50, 155–6, 165, 166–7, 318–20n2, 325–6n7, 331n15, 331–2n16; lyric's critique pr deconstruction of hexameter verse 215–17, 220–2, 227–8, 240, 247–9, 368n7; *see* epic, lyric
daimones: in Hesiod 202; in Orphism 289ff.; Socrates' understanding of 203, 295–6
dark age (Greek, c. 1100–800 BC) xv, 48–50, 51, 139–40, 167
day and night: in Heraclitus 40; in Hesiod 41
death: ancient cultural responses to 21–6; as constitutive horizon 271–2; in the epic 66–77, 87–94, 95–9; fear of 88–9, 268; myths of 23–6; and poetry 268–74, and throughout chapter 5; in Pindar 265–74, and throughout chapter 5; return from the dead in prehistoric Greece 25; role in the symbolic economy of culture 25–6; *see* finitude
death and the Elysian fields 265–8
death and rebirth (in mythology and Greek religion) 22–6, 278, 282–3, 296–7, 379–80n1; *see* Orpheus
debt-slavery: in the ancient world 172–3
deconstruction 185, 315–16n26; autodeconstruction of the epic text 90–4; Hesiodic 'deconstruction' 180–94; in lyric metre 240, 368n7, 374n40 and throughout chapter 4
defamiliarization: of mythic discourse 13–16
Delos 33
Delphi 33, 70
Delphic oracle 165
democracy 243–4
Demodocus 82, 108, 126, 133, 338n36
demos 79, 81, 127, 242, 353n70; voice of the 157–9, 204
Demeter 209, 282, 283, 286, 295; *see* mysteries
description in the Homeric epic 65–77
desire: in Alcman 224–5; in Hesiod 198–9; in mythology 3–26, 187–8; *see also* eros
dialectic(s): Aristotle on 259; Platonic 259; of text and context 29–30; of tradition and innovation 3ff., 41, 308–9n6
dialectical: image 182, 183–94, 195–6; thinking 274; form of life: 259, 274; rationality 274
dialects (Aeolic, Attic, Doric, Ionic): 51, 318–20n2
dialogical agonism 45; *see agon*
dialogical reflexivity 159, 228–31, 276–7; *see* dialogue
dialogue 14, 158–9; in the epic 73–5, 211, 333n18; form of ancient epic 14; forms 333n18; institutionalized 158–9; in the lyric 218–22 and throughout chapter 4
difference: in Aristotle; and eros 189–90; in Empedocles 189–90; in Hesiod 181–2, 182–94; in the lyric poets

SUBJECT INDEX

210ff.; in Parmenides 189–90
différence (Derrida) 360n18
differentiation: in Hesiodic cosmogony 180–2, 182–94, 199–200, 361n19; in Hesiod's text 180–2; as a mythical phenomenology 182–3, 202–3; violence of 182, 183, 199–204; *see also agon, eris*, polemic
Dike (Justice) 35, 37, 43, 90–1, 142, 158, 202–4; *see* justice
Diomedes 62
Dionysus/Dionysian 22, 209, 217, 279, 283–5; cult 278, 279–80, 283–5, 295, 296, 298–9; the Great Dionysia (Athenian festival) 31, 261, 310n10, 379–81n1
discourse: formation 28–30, 32–4, 45–6; argumentative 158–9; critical-reflective 221–2; liturgical 215–17, 221, 240, 296; matrix: 150–7, 328–9n10; universe of 12; *see Logological Investigations*, volume 1
discursive struggles 216–17
dithyramb 219
divine: beginnings 160, 163; in Pindar 254–6, and throughout chapter 5; in Sophocles *Antigone* 152–4
Dorian Greeks ('Dorians') 53; invasion of 53, 140–1, 167
Doric order 219, 225, 374n40
Draco 173
drama: in Greek mythology 4–6, 8–10, 37–8; Greek origins of the term 21–22; dramatic art as instrument of societal reflexivity 14–16, 23–4
dramaturgy: in Greek tragedy 4–6, 16, 41; in myth 19–26
dreams: interpretation 133–4
dualism: ancient 38–43, and chapter 6

earth, *Gaia* : as *arche* 89–90; in Hesiod 186–8; in Homer 89, 92–3; in Husserl 335n25; matrix of all being 282; unchanging 93; unlimited 89, 92; *Ur-erde* or immobile earth 92–4
earth and heaven: separation in Hesiod 184–6
Eddas 52
education: aims of Greek 55; rhetorical and grammatical 58; schooling practices 58; traditional patterns 55–6, 58
Egyptian: civilization 165, 353–4n1;

cosmology 186, 298; *eidola*: 113–14, 295, *passim*; *see* psyche
Elea 46
Eleatics (Eleatic philosophers) 46
elegiac lyric 214, 215–16, 218–22, 224–5, 226–30 372n24; *see* lyric
Eleusis 282–3, 284, 286
Eleusinian: festival 379–80n1; mysteries: 279, 282–3, 284; *see* mysteries
embedding/disembedding techniques (in epic narrative) 59ff.
Enlightenment, the Greek xvii, 246–7, 277
epic: ancient Greek 5–6, 46, 51–3, 53–8, 58–62; anthropomorphic nature 6; didactic 169, 204–5, 274–5; form 5–6, 46, *passim*; as epistemic matrix 65–77; as generative cultural system 49; life-world 60, 77–94; as matrix of videological praxis 48–9; as mnemonic technology 64–77; mock 274–5; and myth 14; as oral encyclopaedia 48–9; as palimpsests 53; political role 49; primary and secondary 51–8; as reflexive verse form 325–6n7; and theory 54, 229–330n12; transcription of 145–50, 167; tribal memory 53–4
Epic of Gilgamesh 21, 52, 95, 179, 196, 199, 272
epinician odes 247, 257; *see* Pindar, victory odes
Erinyes ('Furies') 122, 189
Eris (Strife) 43, 105, 182, 190–4, 354–5n3; double eris 193–4, 198–9
Eros/eros 35, 44, 244–5; in Hesiod 184, 186, 187–8, 189, 198–9, 208–9, 362–3n24; in Anacreon 244–6; in Orphism 187; in Sappho 233–6
eroticism/eroticization of nature 27–30, 198–9, 206–9, 225
Europe: as an imaginary ideal xiii; the ideological construction of xiii-xvii
European culture/civilization: xii-xvii; eye 27–30
European thought 27–46; and throughout Volume 2
eusebeia (piety) 31–2
everyday life 68, 215; in the lyric, 206–10, 214, 239–42; objects in the epic 68–71; objects in the lyric 215–16, 225–6, 233
everydayness 215, 220, 231–2, 233–6,

418

SUBJECT INDEX

240
excellence (*arete*): in Homer 78–94; *see also* arete
eye: Odyssean 72–3

fable: Aesops' fables in classical culture 92, 166
fiction: in the *Odyssey* 96–9; *see* metacommentary
figure/figuration: in the Homeric epic 58–77; defined 75–6, 77, 161; *see* metaphor
figure and ground (in epic) 60
finite understanding 3, 254
finitude: in Pindar 253–6, 265–6, 266, 267–74
free speech xvi–xvii, 34–5
freedom: and civil morality xvi; in early Greek thought xiii, xiv, 276–7 and throughout chapters 4 and 5; in modern culture xiv–xv
friendship: Homeric 119–23; martial 121–2; *philia* 120–22

games: ancient Greek 165, 257–63; religious and political functions 260–1; size 375–6n1
genealogy: of classical philosophy 292–3; of discourses 45–6; of the European eye and voice xiii, 27–30, 35–8; of Western consciousness 48, 366–7n3
genesis of the Gods 180–94
Genesis 196–7, 362n23
genre of genres 65–6, 157; *see* epic, narrative
gnosis 287–8, 293, 294–5
gnostic canon 280
gnosticism 280, 286–7; *see* Orphism
gnostics 286–7
gods: Babylonian 165; Chthonian 41; Greek pantheon of 165, and throughout chapters 2 and 3; Homeric 94; Olympian 41, 89–94, 165, 179–80, 180–94, 299
Greek: alphabet xv; dialects 56, 318–20n2; grammar 77–94; ideology 44–6, 55–8; language; *see* alphabet
grammar: surface and depth grammar 11
grammar schools 58
grammatical: education 58; form of life 58
Greece/Greek: bronze age 53, 136, 137–9. 140, 167, 320–1n3; alphabet 51; culture/civilization: archaic xii–xvii, 6; dialects 51, 318–20n2; poetry: xii–xiii; *see* Mycenae
Greek religion 30–4; archaic 30ff. *passim*; classical 32; Mycenaean 37, 310–11n13, 313n20; polytheistic 165; pre-classical 165
guilds of Singers (*Homeridai*) 324n6

Hades (god of the death and the underworld) 88, 246, 267, 282; and Rhadamanthys 267; reformulated by Plato 267
Hades (hell or 'the house of Hades'): in Greek poetry and myth 31, 63, 112, 113–14, 115, 116, 280, 292, 294, 295; revised by Plato 267–8; and Tartarus 92–3, 116, 187, 198, 246, 265, 266, 337–8n34
heaven 92–3
Hector 39, 61, 63, 68, 69, 73, 81, 84, 85, 90, 94, 98, 117, 130, 131, 135, 155, 252
Hegias 50
Helen 61, 62, 72, 239; as reflexive narrator 98–9
Hellenic xv, 47–9, 165–6; canon 216–17; culture 282; identity 260–3; way of life 167–9, 260, 261–2
Hellenism/Hellenistic age 49, 297
Hephaestus 88
Hera 39, 162, 190
Heracles 162, 189, 239, 252, 258, 264
hermeneutic experience: origins in ancient Greece 174–7, 178–9
Hermes 113, 119, 178, 240, 258, 278, 292
heroes: in myth 2–3, 4–6; in epic 58–9, *passim*

heroic: code 60, 329n10; paradigms (of action) 4–6, 310–11n13; heroization of the self 6, 32–4
heteroglossia: in the epic 65–77, 74–5, 75–6, 157–9, 331–2n16; of Ionian civilization 165; in lyric poetry 211, 216–17 and throughout chapter 4; *see* lyric
hierarchy: in Aristotelian philosophy; in Greek mythology 37–43
Hipparchus 55–6, 244–5, 246
Hittites: 139; sudden demise of Hittite empire 344–5n50
Homer 33, 45, 49, 91, 155, 160, 161,

419

SUBJECT INDEX

238–9, 240, 267, 280, 282, 290, 295, 324n6
homeric: bard (singer of tales) 14, 53, 97; code 49, 78–94; culture 45–6 and throughout chapter 2; epic: 47ff., 51; composition of 48ff.51–8; formulaic techniques 14, 65–77, 144–50, 155–6, 330n13; kingship 78–94; psychology 100–23; selfhood 47, 49, 98, 99ff. and throughout chapter 2; ethic xiv, 317–18n1;
Homeric Hymns 55, 163, 167, 212, 214, 216, 252, 283, 312n15, 320n3
'Homeric Question' 51–2
Homeric Studies 53ff., 143–4, 144–50
Homeridai 75, 252, 324n6
homo significans 17
homosexuality: absent from Homer 120–1; in Theognis 243–4
honour: fundamental theme of the *Iliad* 61; in the heroic code 60–1, 78–94, 329n10; and political status 79–81, 81–94; *see* shame culture
hoplite phallanx 122, 223–4
hubris 89, 108, 179, 194, 202–3, 254–5, 256–7, 272–3
humanism: classical; Homeric 75, 87–91, 335–6n26; modern

iambic lyric 226–7, 227–31, 370n14, 370–1n17; *choliambic* or 'lame' iambic 240–2, 374–5n42; and dialogue in tragedy 370–1n17; *see* Archilochus, lyric, satire
Icelandic sagas 52
iconic symbols: in Pindar 253ff.; in Plato 291–2, 292–3; in the Presocratics 253
ideas: Platonic doctrine of 28
identity, identities; ancient Greek 49–50 and throughout chapter 2, *passim*; collective 162–3; and moral order 160–3, reflexive, social process 162–3;
ideology: ancient Greek 44–6; Homeric 49ff., 54, and throughout chapter 2
Iliad (Homer) xv, 35, 36, 46, 47, 48, 49, 51, 52, 53, 56, 58, 59, 60, 61, 63, 66, 68, 69, 70, 72, 73, 75, 76, 77, 79, 80, 83, 85, 87, 88, 93, 94, 95, 96, 97, 98, 100, 103, 104–23, 125, 126, 130, 131, 133–6, 139, 142, 143, 144–50, 157–8, 166, 167, 175, 176, 194, 198, 199, 213, 215, 221, 224, 226, 238, 240, 266, 274,

282, 291
immortality of the soul: in archaic myths 24; in Orphism 279, and throughout chapter 6
individual(s): in lyric poetry 169, 209–10, and throughout chapter 4
individualism: ancient 168–9, 210–12, 226–31
individuality: in Hesiod 169–74; of lyric voices 169, 206–11, 226–31, and throughout chapter 4
individuation (and predicates of): 169, and throughout chapters 3 and 4
Indo-European, language roots 318–20n2; myth 9–10, 26; people(s) 318n2
injustice (*adikia*): in Hesiod's cosmogony 184–6, 193–4, 202–4
inner conversation/voice 73–5, 107, 221
institutions of reflexivity 34–5, 54–8, 165–6, 218–22, 260–3; *see also* alphabetization, logological investigations, reflexivity
interior monologue 73–4, 333n18
intertextuality: of Homeric epic 51–8, 58–65, 96–9, 145–50, 158–9, 325–6n7; of the Pindaric ode 262–3
Ionia 51, 53, 139, 230–1
Ionian: cosmology 36, 65, 288, 295; mercantile economy 165; philosophy 36, 65; public culture 165–6
Ionians 55
Iphigenia 62, 176
irony: in epic narrative 73, 135; in lyric 219–22, 245–6; as narrative transformation 40
Isthmian games/odes 260; *see* games, Olympian, Pindar
Ithaca 63, 66, 71, 73, 94, 95, 100, 104, 119, 125, 131, 139, 141

Jason 252
jealousy (*phthonos*): of the gods 273–4
judicial metaphors (of *Dike*, *ananke*, etc.): *see* justice
justice (*Dike*) 35, 90–1, 153–4, 156, 158; in Hesiod 184, 193–4, 202–4, 251

Kalevala 52
kleos (glory) 82, 83, 254–5, 255–7, 259–63, 269, 270, 271–2, 378n19
kleros 169
Knossos 137–8, 139

SUBJECT INDEX

knowledge 179, and throughout Volume 2

kosmos: archaic conceptions of 28–46, 35, 39–40, 43, 88; in Aristotle; in the *Iliad* 86, 198; in Ionian philosophy 36, 94; in Hesiod 170, 180–3, 184, 184–94, 198–9, 199–201, 251; Homeric 28, 65, 86, 89–90, 251; in the *Odyssey* 88; in Orphism 287–98; in Pindar 251–2, 263–5, 274–7; in Plato 200, 290–1

Kronos 191, 192–3, 200–1, 209, 252, 256

language: and being 268–9, 270ff.; as constitutive 20–6; as gift of the Muses 179–80 and throughout chapter 3; and memory 269–70; as source of myth 3–16; and truth 269–74; and world-construction xiii–xvii, 268–74

Lebenswelt 29, 35; *see* life-world

Lesbos 231–3

liberty: dialectics of xivff., 276–7; ethic of xiv–xv; in Western culture xiv; *see* freedom

library: Alexandrian 57; first Greek libraries (under Pisistratus) 56–7; as political instruments 57; private libraries 57; as reflexive institution/technology 56–8

life-world 29, 35–8

Linear scripts (Cretan) 136

Linear B, tablets from Knossos and Pylos 136, 340–1n42; contents of; decipherment of 136, 340–1n42; language of 340–1n42

literary poiesis: as original matrix of the Western self xiii–xvii, throughout chapter 1; in codified mythologies 12–16, 160–3 and throughout chapters 2 and 3

literary reflexivity: in the lyric genre 218–22 and throughout chapter 4; in the *Odyssey* 95–9

literary: theory/criticism: 213–7, 366–7n3; self-consciousness 250–1, 252, and throughout chapter 5

literate revolution (in Greece) 48, 50–1, 145–50, 165, 248–9, and throughout chapters 2, 3 and 4

literature: as historical category 13–16; and the lyric genre 212–7; origins in epic myth 9, 49–51, 98; social construction of 8–10, 14, 51ff., 98–9,

and throughout chapters 2 and 4

logic: Aristotelian 41; Aristotle's creation; dialectical; formal 41; as *logos*; modern; origin of; of polarity 40; of the ambiguous 40

logocentrism: in the epic universe 158–9; and patriarchy 151–4

logological inquiry: summarized xiii, 11–12, 19–20; studies techniques of self-reflection 221–2, 379–81n1; 320–2n3; studies reflexive representations 50; studies 'discourses on discourse' 50; studies verbal culture 53, 260; studies the work of *logos* in human experience 301

Logological Investigations: Volume 1 xiii, 2, 3, 5, 15, 50, 54, 116, 157, 162, 261, 301, 305n3, 306–8n4, 331–2n16, 339n39, 366–7n3; Volumes 3 and 4 xvii, 65, 159, 162, 178, 253, 292–3, 335n25, 353–4n1

logological matrix xiii, 29, 50, 53, 150–7, 162–3, 213; *see also* discourse matrix

logological methods (strategies): *see Logological Investigations*, Volume 1

logological operator 40–1, 41–3; *see also* narrative

logos: constitutive 3, 24, 123ff.; of the cosmos 301; diacritical nature 43–4; epic 123–36; *logopoiesis* 5; and *mythos* 7, 23–6, 29–30, 35–8, 160ff.; patriarchal 153–4, 157–9; poetic 82–3, 175–8, 268–74; and truth 177–8

Logos, the (as in Judaic-Christian theology) 186, 197

logosphere 162–3, 265

love: in Empedocles 189–90; in Hesiod 189; in Parmenides 189; in Plato 189–90; *see* eros

Lydia 165, 237, 298

lyre: 155–6, 215, 219, 224; *see aoidoi*, choral

lyric poetry 49, 65, 159, 170, 206 and throughout chapter 4; characteristics 215–17; constituting the self 209; and the ephemeral 210; and crisis of Archaic Greece 213–15, *passim*; first-person voice 206, 215, 226–31; as form of theorizing 206; genre 209–11 and throughout chapter 4; ontology of the particular 207, 208, 210; polyvocality of 210, 216, 219;

SUBJECT INDEX

metacritique of epic tradition 206–10, 214–17, *passim*; as organon of experience 216; personal expression 206–7, 210, 215–17, 220–2; realism 207, 227–8; selfhood 210, 215–16; and subjectivity 209, 210–11, 215–16, 218–22, 226–31; voice 210–11, 226–7; *see also* heteroglossia

lyrical epic 252, 258

lyrical reflexivity: 210–11, 218–19, 220–2, 226ff., 247–9, 276–7, and throughout chapters 4 and 5

magic: 17, 96; absence of magic in Homeric culture 93–4, 166, 311n14, 334n24; in the *Odyssey* 95–99; as sociologic 3, 17–18; and speech 125–6

Mahabharata 21, 51, 52

male/female 40–1

master/slave dialectic 157–9

medicine/medical inquiry 263

melancholy: of Achilles 117–18; as mode of being-in-the-world 118; of Odysseus 98–9, 107–8, 108–9, 117–19; psychopathology of the Mycenaean world 338n34; symbolized by the colour black 337–8n34

memory: as epic faculty 47; oral 59–60, 162, 268–74

memory and recollection: 162–3, 264–5, 268–74; *see also* narrative, storytelling

Menelaus 39, 62, 70, 80, 98, 117, 120, 121, 136; style of speech 127–8, 338–9n37

metacommentary: in the epic 75, 96–7, 98, 100, 111; as metafiction 97; reflexive paradoxes 97–8

metalanguage: myth as 15–16

metanarrative(s): in the *Iliad* and *Odyssey* 61, 62–3, 96–9

metaphor(s): in Homeric epic 71; and myth 2, *passim*; subversive character 15–16

metonymy in the epic 76

Miletus: 230–1; and individualism 230–1; city of philosophy 231

mimesis: as copying; as creative poiesis 2–46, 160–3; as imitation 4; lyric 215 and throughout chapter 4; as performance 253, and throughout chapter 5; as representation 257–63; in Aristotle; as re-enactment 222; and representationalism; tragic 4, 16, 253;

in *Logological Investigations*, Volume 1 xii; *see also* poiesis

mimetic desire 3ff., 161, 162–3, 164; faculty (Aristotle) 18, 25–6; faculty (Benjamin) 14; space 216

Minoan civilization 139

Mnemosune (Memory, mother of the Muses) 163, 175, 178–9, 179–80, 187, 189–90, 269–70

moira 87

monologue: in the epic 74, 123, 128–34, 333n18; silent 74, 107, 128–9, 123–4, 128

Muses, the 126, 199; Muses of Helicon 168, 175, 176–8, 179–80, 251–2, 259–60

music/musical instruments: 218–19, 261, 278, 367n5

muthos: as act of saying 3, 35; epic 123–4, 338n35

Mycenae: 71, 85, 139–40; Mycenaean body shield (Dipylon type) 69; bureaucracy 136–9; Mycenaean burial ritual 89; Mycenaean civilization 53, 68, 86, 136–41, 311n13, 324n6; destruction of 53, 86, 139–41, 344n49; idealized by the Homeric texts 139

Myron 50

m1sogyny 194, 238–9, 372–3n36, 373n37

mysteries: of Eleusis 279, 282–3, 284, 290, 294; religions 279; *see* Orphism

mythic: aestheticization 13–16, 252–4, 274–7; envisioning 16; heteroglossia 12–13, 13–26, 74–5; mimesis 2, 161–3; order 16; rationalization 5–6, 12–13; symbols as icons 25–6; world-view 1–2, 12, 16–17, *passim*

mythology: continuous with the work of language 12ff.; as culture-forming process 5–6; as discourse 14–16 and throughout chapter 1; as a form of knowledge 1ff., 4–5, 7–10; as mode of reflexive communication 3–4; ethical functions of 2, 4–6, 7–8, 17–20; in language 1; in Pindar 252; pre-Homeric 2; universality 25–6

mythopoiesis (myth-making logos) 1–46; as auratic discourse 9, 10–16; as ceremonial praxis 25, *passim*; as collective memory 162–3, 265; as constitutive ontology 9–10, 48, 162–3; as cultural habitus 12–16, 163; defined 23–4, 35; as dialogical process

SUBJECT INDEX

12–13; as the matrix of Western culture 2; as matrix of early Greek philosophy 27–30, 34–5, *passim*; manifest and deep structure 11–12; as metalanguage 15, 17–26, 27–30, 302n3; as *organon* of ideality 5–6, 17–18; polysemy 38–43 and throughout chapter 1; as a reflexive archive 10–12, 24–6, 35, 160–3; as a sociology of morals 5–6, 8–10, 36–8; and truth 175–8

myth(s): as cartographies of the self 4–6; concept of 2–6, 302–6n3; as collective narrative 8–12, 13–26; and concern 10–11; and culture 3–6, 165–6; cycles 14, 25–6; and throughout chapter 1; defined 166; in Durkheimian sociology 7–10; and early Greek philosophy 2; as false representations and stories 6–7; Hellenic xvii; and ideology 303–6n3; of identity 4–6, and throughout chapter 1; literature on 302n3; as maps of the sacred 4, 12–13, 17–20, 21–6; as matrix of beliefs, 3–6, 11–13, 35–8; memorial functions 8–10; as mode of theorizing 8–10, 38–43; in Pindar 252ff.; and power 182–3; primary myth and mythology 12–13; as reality construction 2–46; and self-reflection 3–26, 43–6; social functions 6–16; world-making 17–26, 35–8

mythic tradition: aestheticization 252–4, *passim*; rationalization 166, 184–5, 360n18

mythos 160–3: *see* myth

name and naming: in Hesiod 206–8; in Homer 124–5; in myth 3–16, 18–20; 'naming of the world' 208; poetic 161–2, 207–8, 268–74; in Pindar 268–9, *passim*, and throughout chapter 5; *see also* mythopoiesis, poetry, poiesis

narrated dialogue 73–5; *see* reported speech

narrative: anthropomorphic 4; characterization 75; constitutive function 303–6n3; first-person 169–74; generative 62–3 and throughout chapter 2; grammar of action 59; memory 10–26, 162–3, 265; mobile 72–3, 157; organization 2, 3–26; performance 11–12; perspective 73; polysemy 44–6; positioning, 11; practices 3–26; reflexivity 96–9; schemata 162–3; structure 38–43, 49; strategies in Greek myth 38–43; tradition 328–9n10; transformations 40–1, 41–3; *see* symbolpoiesis

nature (*phusis*): in Hesiod 171–2, 206–7, 107–9; descriptions in Homer 71–2, 83–4; in lyric poetry 225, 232–3, 236–7; Presocratic doctrines of 65

Nausicaa 63, 96–7, 104, 142, 156

Nemean games/odes 260; *see* games, Olympian, Pindar

Nestor 73, 75, 81, 103, 133; as memory bank of the Achaeans 75; style of speaking 128, 338–9n37, 339n38; wisdom of 84, 85, 130, 131

Nibelungenlied 52, 74

Nike 43

noema 107

nomos 37; and *Dike* 152–4, 202–4

non-being 185

nothing/nothingness: in Hesiod 188; *see* chaos

nous: in Homer 84, 94, 95, 101, 107, 127; in Pindar 264–5

novel: Greek 65, 239; the *Odyssey* as proto-novel 97–9

objectivity: of epic narration 73, 91–4, 332–3n17 and throughout chapter 2; *see also* videology

ocularcentrism 35

Odysseus 39, 60, 62, 63, 66, 69, 70, 73, 76, 81, 82, 88, 92, 94, 116, 119, 126, 128–30, 139, 156; cunning 84, 94, 100, 127–8; curiosity 131–4; identity of 95ff.; manysided 98–9, 100–1; as orator 74, 99, 107, 123–4, 125, 126–9, 158, 338–9n37; as self-centred reflexive agent 100–23, 128–30, 131–4; speech-style 127–8; storyteller, 95–6, 97; voice of 95–9, 127, 128–9

Odyssey (Homer) xv, 35, 36, 37, 46, 47, 48, 49, 51, 52, 53, 56, 59, 64, 66, 70, 73, 74, 75, 76, 78, 79, 80, 82, 87, 88, 90, 92, 93, 94, 95, 96, 97, 98, 99, 102, 104, 105–23, 125, 126, 130–4, 135, 136, 139, 141, 143, 144–50, 152, 159, 167, 176, 177, 202, 213, 215, 220, 255, 266, 283, 291; first-person narration

423

SUBJECT INDEX

in 96–7, 98–9, 212, 292; later composition 48–9, 94–5, 166; magic in 334–5n24; and the modern novel 96; as poem of selfhood 102, and *passim*; as sub-plot of the *Iliad* 63, 96, 166; as self-reflexive literature 95–6
Oedipus 117, 124, 132–3, 154, 177
Oedipus Tyrannos (Sophocles) 124, 132, 232
oikos: 140; economy 141–2, 150
Okeanos 92–3; in Hesiod 198–9
Olympia 33, 260
Olympian: games (the Olympian, Pythian, Nemean, and Isthmian games) xv; gods 41, 99, 156, 181–94, 260; mythology 36–8, 156, 259–60; odes 260; panhellenic 165, 257–63; perspective 72–5; religion 32, 33, 37–8, 165, 282–3, 287–8, 299
Olympus 37, 156, 179
One-and-the-Many 159, 163; in Hesiod 180–2, 184–6; in Orphism 281–2, 292–8
One, the: 186; in Hesiod 195; in Orphic religion 281, 292, 287–98
ontological difference: in Hesiod 181–2, 182–94
operator (logological) 40–1, 64
opposites: asymmetrical 41–2; binary 38–43; Pythagorean table of 41–2; unequal 42–3
oracle(s): xv, 134–6, 165
oral culture 47, 124, 145–50; poetry 48, 82, 147–50, *passim*; 'literature' 50; tradition 3–4, 150–7; decay of oral wisdom 12
origin(s): polysemic term 29–30
Orpheus 278, 280, 294; *see* Orphism
Orphic: body 279, 289–98; cosmogony 287–9; doctrine 117, 187; and Greek philosophy 281; literature 280; mysteries 117, 252, 284–5, 290, 294; poets 354n2; religion 266, 279, 280; self 279; and throughout chapter 6
Orphism 187, 252, 266, 278; literature on 379–80n1; and later philosophy 291–8, 299–301; reincarnation in 287–9, 289–98; sociology of 296–8, 298, 299–301; as a way of life 281; women in 284–5; and throughout chapter 6
Other, the 156–7; Thersites as archetypal Other 158

paideia 49, 50, 367n5
pain and pleasure 224, 234
Panathenaic festivals 55, 217
Panhellenism xv–xvii, 55–8, 165, 166, 219
Panhellenic games xv, 57–8, 165, 258–63
Panhellenic ideals xv–xvi, 165, 259, 260–1, 262–3
parataxis in Homeric epic 64–77
Paris 61, 92, 98
particular(s) 206, 213, 245–6
particularity 207, 208, 215–17, 234–6
patriarchy: in ancient Greece 37, 82–94, 152, 351n67; in Homeric religion 37–8, 181–2, 182–94; in the *oikos* system 140–2, 152–4, 173–4; 351n67; the Mycenaean institution of kingship 37–8; questioned by lyric poetry 209; questioned by Orphism 283–7; in tragedy 62–3; *see* phallogocentrism
Patroclus 39, 61, 70, 84, 94, 113; death of 61, 63, 67–8, 112, 118, 122–3; ghost of 113–14
Peisistratean recension 55
Peisistratidai 55, 56, 57, 142–3, 285
Peisistratus 55, 56, 244
Peloponnesian War, History of the (Thucydides)
Penelope 63, 89, 99, 105, 108, 113, 119, 125–6, 128, 133–4, 141, 152
Persephone 282, 283, 286, 292; *see* mysteries
Persian empire xvi, 165, 298; threat xvi–xvii; wars xv–xvii, 248–9, 257, 297–8
person/personal experience 224–5; *see* lyric
personification 76–7
perspective: multiple 72–3; Odyssean 72–3; Olympian perspective of epic description 71–2, *passim*; *see* Rashomon effect, videology
persuasion: in epic speech 124–36
phallocentrism 41–2, 85–6, 86–94, 173, 234–5; critique by Sappho 233–6
phallogocentrism: of ancient Greek culture 44
phantasmal body 5
Phemius 82, 125–6, 359n15
Phidias 50, 56
philosophia 2, 29, 293
philosophy: early Greek 171, 177, 279; Ionian 28; Presocratic 159, 163, 185,

SUBJECT INDEX

300–1; Pythagorean 41–2
Phoenician: alphabet 142–3, 347–8n59; mercantile commerce 142
Phoenix 123
phrenos/phrena 101, 105, 127; *see thumos*
phronesis 84, 107, 132, 178
phusis (as growth, development, bringing-forth): 65
phusis: in pre-classical mythology 2; in Presocratic thought 163, 185, 301
Platonic metaphysics 50
plot 26; of archaic myths 39–43; of epic 59ff.; motifs 39–43, 61–2, 62–4; nesting 59–60; primacy of the plot in tragedy (Aristotle) 26, 64, 331–2n16; *see also* epic, narrative
poetic language 161, 268–74; and the sacred 174–80; as media of cultural self-reflection 165–6, 215–17, 219–22; and truth 174–80; *see poiesis*
poetry 5–6; as crafted object 262, 376–7n2, 377–8n8; and danger 268; and death 268–74; love 233–9, 244–6; as ideology 260–1, 262–3; as memory 264–5; as public discourse 183, 260–3; as transformative force 269–74; as vehicle of truth 170–1, 251–2, 268–9
poets: epic; central place in Homeric culture 82ff.; lyric 206–10 and throughout chapter 4
poiesis xii, 4–5, 6; as general term for *mimesis* 214, 222, 265; and self-definition 212–15; as world-making activity 161–2, 175–80, *passim*, 265, 306–8n4; *see also* mimesis, mythopoiesis, technopoiesis
polarity in Greek culture 36–8, 38–43, 106; logic of 40–3; literature on 314n23
polemic: as source of cultural creation 3–26, 28–30, 44–6, 134–5, 165–9, 351–2n68; institutionalized 354–5n3; polemical compared to dialectical logic 30; polemical logic of the epic 49, 58–9, 316n1;
polemos 46, 49, 120
political existence xvi-xvii
polis (city-state) xiv-xv, xvi-xvii, 31, 33, 32–4, 84, 167, 211–12, 214; as institutionalized dialogue 159, 260–1; and the literary revolution 48, 55–8, 149–50, 155, 217; and military values 223–4; and *psyche* 117; and *stasis* 242–3; state cults of 30–4; and urban culture 34–5, 44–6, 54–6, 153, 204; as videological model 85–6; *see* videology
Polygnotus 56
polytheism: ancient Greek 32–3, 310–11n13; and the institutionalization of reflexivity 34–5
Poseidon 39, 63, 73, 88, 252; Odysseus' antagonist 131–2
power: in Homeric society 78–94
practical reflexivity 11–12,
practical wisdom (*phronesis*) 84, 107, 131–3
praxis: as the content of the epic 59–77; 229–330n12 *see semiopraxis*)
prayer(s): as inner dialogue 130; in Homer 130–1; as public speech act 130–1
Presocratics 44, 159, 198, 253
Presocratic philosophy 28, 143, 185, 300; reflexivity 253; thought/thinking 163, 185, 301
Priam (King of Troy) 61, 63, 72, 77, 78, 84, 90, 115; monologue of 123; persuasion 125; palace of 80
priesthood: absence in ancient Greece 164–5
Prometheus 124, 194, 267
Prometheus Bound (by Aeschylus) 124
psyche 35, 112: as animating principle 112; as breath-soul 112–13; at death 112, 113–4; after death 116–17; as *eidola* 113–14, 295; as material substance 113; as personal double 113; Homeric *psuche* 100–23; as inner dialogue 109–10, 221–2; in Orphism 279–80, 287–98, 382n2; Plato on 110–11, 290–1, 292–3; in Pindar 251–2, 256–7; *see also thumos*

psychoanalysis 154
pure reason 161
pure reflection 1, 132–3, 293–4, 339–40n39
Pylos 71, 137–8, 140–1
Pythagorean: communities 279; doctrine 279, 288, 289; form of life 279–80, 295, 301; ideology 42, 279; initiation ceremonies 295
Pythian games/odes 260; *see* games, Olympian, Pindar

SUBJECT INDEX

Ramayana 52
Rashomon effect 72–3, 210, 211
realism in the epic 66, *passim*
reality: as congealed narratives and metaphors 4, 303n3
Reality, absolute (Being) 176, 293, *passim*
reason and belief 161–2
reason and unreason 161
reflection: institutions of xiv, 261; theoretical 161–2
reflexive: archive 11–12, *passim*; imagination 164; technologies 54
reflexivity: early Greek xv, 157–9; Greek origins of xiv–xv; in Hesiod 169–74; institutions of 34–5, 261–3; lyric 210–5, 247–9, and throughout chapter 4; in the *Odyssey* 94–9, and throughout chapter 2; in Pindar 251–2; praxical 12; verbal 212
reincarnation: in Empedocles; in Indian religion 24; in Orphism 293–6; in Pythagoras and Pythagorean culture 293–6, 295
religion: and the decay of living myth 12–13
reported speech 74–5; as characterization device 75
representation: as divine gift 18; mimetic 160–3 and throughout chapter 3
rhapsode (reciters) 56–7, 145–50, 151–2, 155–6, 165–6, 172, 221–2, 324–5n6
rhetoric(s): of Achilles 74; Aristotle on; generalized conception 306–8n4; invention 127; of reflection xiii, 299–301; of Odysseus 74, 126–8; rhetorics of selfhood (in Homer), 60–77, 94–123 and throughout chapter 2; of self-reflexivity 99–123, 169–74, 357–8n5; of speech and language 123–36; of vision 47 and *passim*; *see* narrative
rhetorical praxis 123–36
rhetoric and argument 127–8
ritual(s) 3, 7–10, 13; in ancient Greek religion 30–4; as paralanguage 15; role in the Cambridge School of myth analysis 9–10
ritual and myth, 3–4, 7–10, 13–14

sacred/profane 19–20, 36–8, 38–43, 160–3
sacrifice in Greek religion 31–4; in pre-Homeric religion 32
satire 219, 228–9, 230, 238–9, 245, 370n16; and the carnivalesque 240–2, 286–7, 370n16, 370–1n17, 374–5n42; reflexivity 230; *see* Archilochus, Hipponax, iambic lyric
scepticism (skepticism): ancient 134; origins in lyric 217
scribal caste(s) 137–9, 142–3, 347n58
scribal literacy 139, 148–50, 347n58
Scribes: Egyptian/Minoan/Sumerian 139
scripts 347–8n59
seeing: and knowledge 82–3, 293–8
self/other 156
self-experience 216
self-expression 14
self-knowledge 84, 96, 124, 254, 272–3
self-reference 220–2
self-reflection: in the Archaic age xii–xvii; in Hesiod 161–2, 215–17; in Homer 94–136, 106–9, 150–7; in the lyric 215–17, 220–2; Western 161
self-reflexivity: in Hesiod 169–74; origins xii–xvii, 94–136, 219–22; in Pindar 251–2
self-understanding 84
selfhood: in Homer 60–1, 94–123, 155–7; in lyric, 215–17 and throughout chapter 4; in the *Odyssey* 94–9
semiopraxis: and myth 7–26; and world-construction xiii, 214–15
shame/shame culture 83–4, 110, 118, 120–3, 124, 156–7; from a shame-culture to a guilt culture 157, 297, 352–3n69
shield of Achilles 64, 71–2, 92–3, 213
Sicilian origins of rhetoric 127
Sirens 131
slavery: ancient slavery 172–4
social criticism 219
sociological poetics xii–xvii, *passim*, 53, 164–5, 206–7, 333–4n22
sociology of ancient Greek civilization xvii, 45–6
song(s): pre-Homeric song cycles 3, 26, 59; epic song cycles 14, 51–8; homeric 14, 27, 324n6, 324n7; Theban 59, 166
The Song of Roland 52, 74
sophia 43, 84; in Pindar 252; in Presocratics 301
sophist(s) 46, 217
Sophists: ancient Greek 159, 180

SUBJECT INDEX

soul/body dualism: *see* Orphism
space: in the epic 92–4; mythic 19–20; *see* chora
space-time: socially constructed 19–20
spacing 182–3; *see aletheia*
Sparta 55, 217, 222–4, 225, 246, 263, 369n11
Spartan: constitution 368–9n10; culture, in the seventh and sixth centuries BC 55, 167, 222–4, 225, 258, 369n11; military 223–4, 225, 258, 261
speculation: 164–5, 167, 281–2, 300–1
speculative inquiry 165, 185, 300; *also see* theoria, theoretical knowledge, videology
speech: collective 150–7; genres 208; as magic 124, 125–6; *muthos* 123–4; as power 124; as praxis (in Homer) 73–4, 123–36, 150–7; thoughtful 107–8
sphragis 170, 219–20, 243, 358–9n13
Stoic cosmology 28
storytelling 5–6, 10–16; constitutive function 11–12, 161–2, 162–3, 182–3; *see* narrative, mythopoiesis
subjectivity: in Hesiod 169–74, 357–8n5; in lyric *see* lyric
subjectivity: history of 219; in myth 4–6 and throughout chapter 1; in lyric poiesis 206ff, 214–7, and throughout chapter 4
suffering 22–6, and chapter 6; *see* death, Orphism
symbolpoiesis (sense-making): 18–20, 160–3, 182–3; *see* myth, storytelling
symbolisms: of myth 5–7

technique of reflection 379–81n1
technology: of writing 48 and throughout chapter 2
technopoiesis 19, 214
technopoiesis hypothesis, the 19–20, 54
Teiresias 115
Telemachus 71, 80, 103, 119, 120, 125, 128, 134, 135–6, 152, 154
telos: as limit, necessary end, and horizon 87
textual production 48; productivity 48; sedimentation in the Homeric epic as 51–8; self-reference 214–5
textuality of lyric production 212–7, throughout chapter 4
Thebes (in Boeotia) 152–4, 217

themis 37, 87, 189, 242
theogonies 160, 162; as discourse and prototheorizing 163–9; first written theogony 168
Theogony (Hesiod's *Birth of the Gods*) 160, 162, 164, 167, 168, 175, 176, 180, 184–5, 187, 188, 189, 196, 198, 199, 202, 221, 258, 266, 282, 355–6n4
theology: Hesiodic 164–9
theomorphism: in Pindar 253–7
theophany 164, 181–2; in early Greek philosophy 300–1; in Hesiodic 'phenomenology' 181–94; in Orphism 293–8; in Plato 295
theoretical knowledge; *see theoria*
theoretical discourse 171
theoria 18–19, 35, 162, 258, 293, 296, 300–1
theory and practice 131–3, 293–8
Thersitean moment 90
Thersites 90, 157–9
Thetis (mother of Achilles) 40, 60, 62, 252
thinking and inner speech/conversation 73–4, 107, 128–31, 221–2, 352–3n69
thinking and *logos* 128–9
Thrace 73
thumos: 85, 90, 101, 103; as 'aggressive spirit' 103–4; as 'life' 102–3; location of the emotions 104–6; in Plato 115–16; as 'thinking heart' 106–8, 127, 128–30
time: socially constructed 19–20
time-space: constructed by mythopoiesis 19–20
tragedy: ancient Greek 16, 36, 41, 49, 50, 62, 117, 176, 232, 273, 284, 313n22, 339–40n39; defined by Aristotle 4; family conflicts in Greek epic and tragedy 17, 62–3, 152–4, 181, 182–94, 346–7n56; as synthesis of choral and lyric genres 215, 217, 239, 370–1n17
tragic irony: dramatic irony prefigured in the epic 73, 75; and misrecognition 135, 176–8
tragic sense of life 260, 283–5, 296–8; *see* Orphism
tribal culture: of pre-classical Greece 4–6, 37–8
tribe(s): tribal structures 37
Trojan: army 61, 62, 64, 72, 77, 158; horse 97–8; society 63; war 60 and throughout chapter 2

Troy 53, 61, 64, 71, 72, 79, 85, and throughout chapter 2; fall of 97–8
truth claims 170–1, 175, 177–8; of poetry 210–11
truth: absolute 44, 161, 293; as *Aletheia* 175, 176–8, 183ff. and *passim*; existential; pragmatic; and poetry 210 the Whole Truth 44, 161; *see* will-to-totality
Tyche 43
tyrant: Greek tyrants 55–8, 159, 217, 244, 246; age of the Greek 252, 257–9, 276–7, 379–81n1
tyranny 55, 244, 247–8; and Pindar 258–63

universalism: of truth 177–8
universality: of rational consciousness 7
universals and particulars 7, 207, 213, 215, 259
utopia 157; in Hesiod 201, 204–5
utopianism 157–9, 204, 235–6, 293, 297

value(s): competitive 194; conflicts 276–7, 378–9n21; as generative principles xiii–xiv, 12–13; public/performative nature in ancient Greece 156–7, 351–2n68; in the epic 156–7; and recollection 162–3; spheres 276–7; *see also arete*
victory ode (epinician ode) 6, 247, 251, 253, 257, 261–3, 376–7n2, and throughout chapter 5
videology/videological culture 27–30, 35, 82–3, 91–2; in the classical age 43, 58–77, 77–94, 293; prefiguring Western concepts of space and time 335n25; primacy of spatial over temporal relations 92–3, 277
violence as paradigmatic form of Western discourse 46, 49; seminal form and content of Hesiod's *Theogony* 181–2, 194–200; *see agon, eris,* polemic
virtue: *see arete*
vision 293
visual: art 5; culture (classical Greek) 58–9; depictions of death 66–77, 78–9; experience 41–3, 91–4; pleasure 70–1, 75, 75–7; grammar, throughout chapter 2, 335n25; metaphors 42, 75–7; *tableaux* in Homer 59ff., 66–77, 78–94; thematics of the Greek epic 49–50, 58–77; universe 93–4 *see videology*
vocabulary of motives 351–2n68

war/warfare 46; in the ancient world 81–94; in the Greek epic 49, 72, 78–94; paradoxes of 61, 82; *see* Trojan war on poetry (in Plato) xiv, 18, 22, 115–16, 193
war-lords 78–94, 158–9
Way of Truth/Way of Seeming 176
weapons in the epic 68–71
Western reason 161
will-to-knowledge: in pre-Homeric Greece 5; in Homer and classical Greece 132–3
will-to-totality 35; in early Greek philosophy 36–8, 44–5; in Greek mythology 35–6; in Hesiod 162
will-to-truth 132–3, 175
wisdom (*sophia*) 29, 84
wisdom and the *bios theoretikos* 29; *see theoria*
women: in the epic 96–7
wonder (*thaumazein*): and anxiety 16; and human nature 16; and the lover of myths v, 16, 34; origins of philosophy 16, 34; source of speculation 16, 160, 164–5; *see* poetry, philosophy, speculation
Works and Days (Hesiod) 167, 168, 169, 172, 173, 179, 184–5, 193, 194, 198, 201–2, 203, 204, 206, 207, 208, 209, 251, 253, 274, 282, 284, 292, 355–6n4
work: in Hesiod 203–4
world construction 5–6, 157
writing: absent in Homeric texts 138; alphabetic 48, 49, 51, 53, 148, 167, 320–2n3; as *archi-écriture* (Derrida) 186; as art/technique 48, 148–50, 167–7, 248–9, 365–6n2; bureaucratic scripts 138–9; early Greek 51, 136–9, and throughout chapter 2; Linear A and Linear B syllabaries 136–9, 142–3; Mycenaean use of 137–9, 214–5; Phoenician origins of the alphabet 142–3, 347–8n59, 365–6n2; subject 212–5, 215–7, 226–31, and *passim*; subversive 219, 226–31; as technology 48–9, 355–6n4; *see technopoiesis*

Zeus 28, 35, 61, 99, 105, 162, 184, 188–9,

252, 278, 361n20; all-knowing 87ff., 339n39; birth of 188; hegemony of 190–3; justice of 87–8, 193, 202–4, 251, 361n21; and oratory 125; as patriarchal symbol of kinship 37, 79, 85, 188–9, 191, 251, 351n67; as source of visual predicates (all-seeing) 37–8, 73, 79, 87, 204–5, 251, 269, 339n39; supreme authority and judge 204–5, 256–7, 266; and the Titans 182, 190–1, 192–3; will of 79–80, 83, 156, 251

zone/zoning 187

For Product Safety Concerns and Information please contact our EU representative GPSR@taylorandfrancis.com
Taylor & Francis Verlag GmbH, Kaufingerstraße 24, 80331 München, Germany